A Dictionary and Business

This book has been prepared for Pan Books Ltd by
Market House Books Ltd, Aylesbury
Series Editor: Dr Alan Isaacs
Book Editor: S. E. Stiegeler B.Sc.

Contributors
Ray Barrell B.Sc., M.Sc. (Econ.)
John Boyle B.Sc., M.Sc. (Econ.)
W. G. Hanks Cert. A.I.B.
Brian Hayes B.A., M.Sc. (Econ.)
David Holland B.A., M.Sc. (Econ.)
Michael Jenkins M.A., Solicitor
Anthony Lee B. Comm., M.A. (Econ.)
John Quarrell Ll.B., Solicitor
David Ryder B.A.
Michael Scherk B.A.
David Smart B.A. (Econ.), Chartered Accountant
Stephen Tipping, Systems Consultant
Leslie Chadwick M.B.A., F.C.C.A.
Christopher L. Pass B.Sc. (Econ.), M. Phil, Ph.D.

S. E. Stiegeler (Editor)

A Dictionary of Economics and Business

New and revised edition

Pan Books London and Sydney

First published 1976 by Pan Books Ltd,
Cavaye Place, London SW10 9PG
This new and revised edition published 1986
by Pan Books Ltd
9 8 7 6 5 4 3 2 1

ISBN 0 330 28819 9
Printed and bound in Great Britain by
Cox & Wyman Ltd, Reading

Preface to the Second Edition

This dictionary was first published in 1976 as the *Pan Dictionary of Economics and Commerce.* Its success over the last decade has provided the stimulus to update it for a new edition.

In this edition we have added some new pages containing up-to-date information relevant to the economist and the businessman. The legal and taxation entries, particularly, have needed to be updated throughout, as have the various organizations with which businessmen have to deal. In order to accommodate the wealth of new information within a reasonably expanded book, we have had to omit the biographical entries that appeared in the first edition.

The publishers and editors hope that this new edition will meet the needs of its users as satisfactorily as the first edition evidently did.

Preface to the First Edition

Theoretical economics and practical commerce now overlap to such an extent that it is not easy to be a practitioner or student of either without some understanding of the other. The businessman and the economist must understand each other's languages if they are to communicate – and the layman, the tax-paying citizen who is neither businessman nor economist, must have some grasp of the jargon of both if he is to be aware of what is going on around him.

The vocabularies of economics and commerce have different origins. The language of commerce has evolved slowly: conceived in the primitive market place, it blossomed in the age of the merchant adventurer, and reached maturity in the post-war era of the multinationals. What is slow to evolve is slow to change – in the City of London, cargo ships are still called *steamers* to distinguish them from *sailers*. Economics, on the other hand is a relatively new discipline with its own rapidly expanding terminology, only part of which derives from the language of commerce. Part of it derives from the hard sciences, part from sociology, and part is self-generated.

In this dictionary, we have attempted to provide an alphabetical list of all the useful words that are used in both economics and commerce. Each word is given a brief formal definition followed by a more discursive explanation of the concepts underlying it. If the term has a quantifiable aspect, the mathematics of the quantification is sketched. We have attempted to cover as completely as possible the fields of both microeconomics and macroeconomics, paying special attention to the newer, rapidly expanding subjects of cost-benefit analysis and welfare economics. In the field of commerce, we have included the principal words from the vocabularies of banking, accounting, insurance, the stock exchange, commodity dealing, shipping and transport, as well as commercial law. A selection of the terms used in the related fields of statistics, computing, government, and industrial relations will also be found in the alphabetic list. The dictionary includes biographical notes on the most prominent economists as well as the main organizations connected with economics and commerce.

Abbreviations are listed as they occur alphabetically, full stops being used between letters when they are spelled out in speech (e.g. U.S.A., E.E.C.) but not between letters that form acronoyms (e.g. EFTA, GATT). Cross-references in the text are denoted by asterisks. Words are not given an asterisk simply because they occur as separate entries in the dictionary – the asterisk is used to direct the reader to a source of further useful information. Words in italic type in a definition text are not defined separately but cross-reference has been made to them from elsewhere in the dictionary.

It is hoped that this dictionary will prove useful not only to students of economics and commerce (both at school and university and in business-study courses) but also to businessmen and their professional advisers, to civil servants, and to secretaries. The layman, too, will find much of this dictionary will be helpful to him – both in understanding what he reads in the papers and hears on TV and in coping with the problems of house buying, domestic budgeting, taxation, and a host of the other inescapable economic and commercial aspects of our complex daily lives.

A

abandonment. The act of relinquishing ownership of property. Property that has been insured may be abandoned in certain cases if its loss cannot be avoided or if the cost of repairs would exceed its value. In marine insurance, a ship may be abandoned as dangerous or unseaworthy in certain circumstances. For example, if a ship is stranded on rocks and cannot be salvaged she cannot become an *actual total loss until she breaks up. However, the right of abandonment enables the insured to make a claim immediately if he declares the vessel a *constructive total loss, by giving the insurer notice of abandonment. The vessel then becomes the property of the insurer.

The right of abandonment is not legally restricted to marine insurance. In non-marine insurance, however, a policy condition often specifically prohibits the insured from abandoning the property to the insurer and claiming as for a total loss.

ABC Code. *See* commercial codes.

ability-to-pay taxation. A method of taxation in which the amount of tax payable is assessed according to some criterion of the taxpayer's means to pay. The most frequent criteria are income and wealth. A value judgment is made that those with more should be expected to pay more, either because as income rises luxuries rather than necessities tend to be bought, or because the *marginal utility of money is thought to decrease as income, or wealth, rises. This form of taxation, together with *transfer payments, is the primary means towards *income redistribution. *See also* benefit taxation, progressive tax.

above par. Denoting a share that has a market value above its *par value.

above-the-line advertising. *See* advertising.

absenteeism. Nonattendance at work for no valid reason, e.g. not as a result of a public holiday, sickness, an industrial dispute, etc. In the U.K. more days are lost through absenteeism than through strikes. One of the most compelling reasons for the creation of a public holiday on New Year's Day was the high degree of absenteeism.

absolute advantage. A doctrine of international trade propounded by Adam Smith (1723–90). It is a limited version of the *comparative cost principle. If country I is more efficient at producing good A and country II more efficient at producing good B, then they will both profit if each produces what it is most efficient in producing and then exchanging. This was an extension of the idea of division of labour to international trade. Later under the doctrine of comparative cost a case was made for international trade even when one country had an absolute advantage over the other in the production of all goods.

absolute bill of sale. A *bill of sale in which title to the goods referred to passes absolutely. It has to be witnessed by a solicitor.

ACAS (Advisory Conciliation and Arbitration Service). *See* Employment Protection Acts.

accelerated depreciation. The writing off of *depreciation at a faster rate than is justified by the life of the asset concerned. In the U.K. the Inland Revenue has a system of *capital allowances, which are given in lieu of depreciation.

accelerator principle. The hypothesis that there is a direct relationship between the level of investment and the growth rate of output. It is supposed that a change in the rate of change in output (an acceleration in the rate of change in output) produces a proportionally much larger change in the output of investment goods. This dependency of the level of investment on the growth rate of output occurs because in equilibrium the rate of change in output is sustained by the same rate of change in the capital stock. A rise in the rate of change in output requires an equal rise in the rate of change in the capital stock to maintain the new growth rate. This implies that net investment will rise by a proportionally larger amount to accommodate the larger output. If a firm cannot meet an increase in demand from spare capacity it may invest in more machinery. Thus in addition to replacing worn-out (depreciated) machinery it will increase its net investment by buying extra new machinery.

For instance, imagine a firm with five machines of which one is replaced each year. If the firm suddenly faces an increase in demand for its products of 20% it must buy an extra machine to take advantage of this upsurge. An order for two machines represents an increase of 100% in business for the machine-makers, i.e. an acceleration of 20% in output has produced an acceleration of 100% in the output of investment goods.

The accelerator coefficient shows the amount by which investment changes in response to changes in output, and it is given by the change in the capital stock (net investment) divided by the change in output. However in any actual situation it is likely that the accelerator coefficient will be affected by other variables, such as changes in the rate of interest, the wage rate, or changes in the technology of production. It will also depend on whether entrepreneurs expect the change in growth rate to be a permanent or a transitory phenomenon. The accelerator principle is very important in post-Keynesian theories of the trade cycle and in growth models such as the Harrod–Domar model. Combined with the *multiplier, the accelerator has been effectively used by Paul Samuelson (*b.* 1915) and Sir John Hicks (*b.* 1904) in constructing models of the trade cycle. In the upswing of the cycle the accelerator is the mechanism whereby the expansion in output feeds itself by generating proportionally larger increases in investment, and so by the multiplier increases income further. In the downswing the accelerator works in reverse: a fall in output, a negative growth rate, results in a sharp decline in investment and so through the multiplier results in a decline in the level of output.

acceptance. 1. The writing on a bill of exchange by which the person on whom it is drawn agrees (i.e. accepts) the order of the drawer, thereby becoming the acceptor. It is sufficient for the drawee merely to write his name across the bill, but the commonest form of general acceptance is: "Accepted, payable at .... (name and address of bank): A.N. Smith".

2. A bill of exchange that has been accepted by the drawee.

3. Notice given by an insurance company agreeing to provide a specified insurance cover.

acceptance credit. A means of financing a transaction involving the sale of goods, most frequently found in international trade. A bank in the exporting country, usually a *merchant bank (*see also* accepting house), will open an acceptance credit on behalf of a foreign importer that it considers to be creditworthy. The exporter's goods will then be paid for by a bill of exchange drawn on the merchant bank (or accepting house). The bill can then be run to maturity or discounted in the money market.

acceptance supra protest (acceptance for honour). The acceptance or payment of a bill of exchange, after it has been protested for dishonour by nonacceptance or nonpayment, by any person to save the honour of the drawer or of an endorser of the bill.

accepting house. An institution, usually a *merchant bank, that specializes in accepting bills of exchange drawn on it by approved customers, who pay a service fee, thus facilitating negotiation of the bills by reason of its good name. With the decline of the bill of exchange as a means of payment other banking activities have been developed by these houses.

Accepting Houses Committee. A committee representing a number of the bigger *merchant banks. The main qualifications for membership are that a substantial part of the bank's business shall be the accepting of bills of exchange to finance trade, that such acceptances are freely taken by the Bank of England, and that they command the finest rates in the discount market. There were 16 member banks in 1982.

access time. The time required to obtain a particular piece of information from a computer *storage device.

accident insurance. A category of insurance that embraces a collection of loosely related classes of business. It includes *fidelity guarantee insurance, *personal accident and sickness insurance, *employers' liability insurance, *public liability insurance, *motor insurance, *livestock and bloodstock insurance, burglary, and miscellaneous business (e.g. rainfall, credit, and licence insurance).

accommodation bill. A bill of exchange to which a person (known as an *accomodation party*) puts his name as a guarantor. He does not expect to be called upon to pay the bill when it is due, but is liable to a *holder for the value. Such bills are known as *windbills*, windmills, or *kites*.

accord and satisfaction. An agreement by one party to a contract to release the other from his obligations under the contract. It was decided as early as 1602 in "Pinnel's Case" that such an agreement was not binding unless it was made under seal, or unless the party being released had, instead of performing his obligations under the contract, performed some equivalent act of benefit to the releasing party. In Pinnel's Case, Pinnel sued Cole for a debt of £8 10s, which was due on 11 November 1600. Cole's defence was that on 1 October 1600 he had paid Pinnel £5 2s 6d, which Pinnel had accepted as fully discharging the original debt. The court decided that, had Cole paid Pinnel the £5 2s 6d on 11 November, Cole could not have been validly discharged from the debt as although there would have been "accord" (agreement) there would have been no "satisfaction" (discharge of the whole debt). However, the payment by Cole of the money six weeks earlier than it was due was of considerable benefit to Pinnel, and was sufficient "satisfaction" to allow Cole to be validly released from the debt. This doctrine has been applied in English cases ever since.

account. 1. A period during which dealings on the London Stock Exchange are made without immediate cash settlement. The calendar year is divided into 24 accounts, most of which are of a fortnight's duration, the remainder being of three weeks' duration to cover statutory holidays.

*Settlement is made for transactions completed during an account on *account day. Thus the account period provides an efficient mechanism for dealing on the Stock Exchange in advance of payment (or receipt) of monies due. It is of particular importance for speculation (since it is possible to buy and sell the same shares within an account without paying for them).

2. *See* bank account.

accountant. A qualified person who specializes in book-keeping and the preparation and auditing of annual accounts. Accountants also advise on tax law and the financial organization of businesses. In the U.K. there are four main types of professional accountant: chartered, certified, cost and management, and public finance. *Chartered accountants* have qualified as associates (A.C.A.) or fellows (F.C.A.) of the Institute of Chartered Accountants in England and Wales or the Institute of Chartered Accountants in Ireland. In Scotland, chartered accountants use the initials C.A. and are members of the Institute of Chartered Accountants in Scotland. *Certified accountants* are professional accountants who have passed the exams of the Association of Certified Accountants and are either fellows (F.C.C.A.) or associates (A.C.A.A.) of that Association. They have the same duties and functions as chartered accountants, but their study course does not include a training contract with a firm of accountants. In addition certain accountancy bodies offer qualifications at technician level.

Specialist accountancy firms act as auditors and tax consultants for other firms, but many large companies employ their own qualified accountants. *See also* cost accountant, financial accountant, management accountant, public finance accountant.

account day. The day on which *settlement is completed by the transfer of monies due for all London Stock Exchange dealings that took place during the previous *account. Account day occurs on the Monday 10 days after the end of the account to which it relates; it is sometimes called *settlement day* or, more loosely, *pay day*.

accounting concepts. The fundamental assumptions that should underline the makeup of all sets of accounts. Four of the more basic concepts have been singled out for special mention by the Institute of Chartered Accountants in England and Wales in its Statement of Standard Accounting Practice on "Disclosure of Accounting Policies". These are described as the *going concern concept, the *accruals concept, the *consistency concept, and the *prudence concept. These are generally accepted and it is normally assumed that accounts embody these concepts unless specifically stated.

accounting cost. *See* economic cost.

accounting period. The period for which a company, partnership, or sole trader makes up its accounts. Normally this period will be for a calendar year, beginning and ending at any time as chosen by the concern. Obviously at the commencement and termination of a business the accounting period will not necessarily be of this length. It is on the profits of the accounting period that tax becomes payable, although with the rules of timing tax payments the time lag between the end of this accounting period and the payment of the tax liability will vary.

account payee. Words added to the crossing on a cheque (*see* crossed cheque) with the intention of ensuring that the cheque is paid into the bank account of the payee only. They do not affect the negotiability of the cheque, but do warn the collecting banker that he will be open to a claim for damages for *conversion by the payee if he collects it for anyone other than the payee.

accounts. 1. A statement of a company's financial affairs, normally produced at the end of the accounting period to which they refer. The accounts are split into two parts, the *balance sheet and the *profit and loss account, and together these list the value of the various assets and liabilities, the amount owned by the shareholders, and the profit or loss that the company has made during that accounting period. The accounts of a limited company are required by law to disclose a certain minimum of information and have to be certified by a qualified person, such as a chartered or certified accountant, as giving a *true and fair view of the company's affairs.

2. Records of financial transactions kept by any organization, either profit- or non-profit-making, including sole traders, partnerships, charities, and local authorities, which are used to prepare an income statement and balance sheet for submission to the tax authorities. *See also* books of account, published accounts.

accounts receivable. Accounts on which money is owing. They can be sold to a *factor or can be used as collateral in raising a loan.

accruals concept. A fundamental *accounting concept in which revenue and costs are accrued, i.e. taken account of when they occur, matched up where possible (receipts and the costs incurred in producing these receipts should be accounted for at the same time), and considered to be part of the profit and loss account of the period to which they relate. The only time the accruals concept should not be applied is when it comes into conflict with the *prudence concept, and in this case the latter should prevail. The need for the accruals concept stems from the fact that time lags exist between the earning of receipts and the occurrence of liabilities and the actual receipt or payment of money. *Materiality may also affect the application of this concept.

accrued charges. Known charges for goods and services received in the current accounting period which, at the end of that period, have still not been paid for, e.g. accountancy fees or vehicle repairs owing.

accumulative society. *See* friendly society.

acid-test ratio. *See* liquid ratio.

Acme Commodity and Phrase Code. *See* commercial code.

A.C.T. *See* advance corporation tax.

Act for International Development (1961). A U.S. act that set out the way in which overseas economic aid and development should be administered. It set up the *Agency for International Development (AID)*, bringing together the work of the Development Loan Fund and the International Cooperation Administration.

active market. A market for a particular share or sector of shares (e.g. gold-mining shares) in which there are regular and frequent transactions.

active partner. *See* partner.

active stocks. A table compiled both daily and weekly in the Financial Times from the dealings recorded in the London Stock Exchange Official List. It shows those shares in which there have been the most active markets.

act of God. An occurrence in the course of nature that is beyond human foresight and against which human prudence cannot be expected to provide. It is so unexpected that the damage caused must be regarded as too remote to form a basis for legal liability. An example is the damage caused by a motor car that crashes after a driver suffers a sudden heart attack. This has been held to be damage caused by an act of God for which the driver was not to blame.

act of war. Any act by the citizens or agents of one nation that damages the persons or property of another nation with whom they are at war. War risks for ocean voyages are covered by the Institute War Clauses (*see* cargo insurance). War risk insurance covers goods until they have been discharged at the port of destination but does not apply to transport by river craft or on land. Insurance covers risks caused by mines and derelict torpedoes even in peacetime.

actuals. Actual physical commodities (*see also* spot goods) that can be purchased for prompt delivery on commodity exchanges, as opposed to futures (*see* futures market).

actual total loss (in marine insurance). A total loss of a ship (as by sinking, fire, etc.) or a loss of a cargo that is either totally destroyed or so damaged that it is useless for the purpose for which it was purchased. In the case of an actual total loss no notice of *abandonment is required. *Compare* constructive total loss.

actuary. A person who is trained to assess insurance risks and premiums, using statistical probability techniques. Most actuaries are employed by insurance companies to draw up mortality and morbidity tables, assess the probability of risks to property, lay down underwriting procedures, calculate premiums, advise on the benefits likely to be claimed during the year, etc. Some actuaries are employed by government (*see* government actuary) or industrial firms to advise on insurance matters or pension funds. In the U.K. an actuary has to pass the examinations of the Institute of Actuaries in order to qualify.

Actuaries of insurance companies are required by the Department of Trade to certify reports of the liabilities of the company and submit these reports at regular intervals to the Department. Since the Insurance Company Amendment Act (1973), the Department of Trade has the right to inquire into the reasons for a company changing its actuary, which strengthens the actuary's position with respect to his employer.

Ada. A programming language named after Ada, Countess of Lovelace (daughter of Lord Byron), who was involved with the developing of the analytical engine, the forerunner of modern computers. It is used by the U.S. Department of Defense.

adaptive expectations. A behavioural assumption concerning the method by which economic agents review past expectations of the future in the light of present experience, to derive an estimate of future uncertain events. Future expectations depend upon the perceived error in past expectations relative to actual events. The usual model is of the form:

$$E_K = E_{K-1} + \lambda(A_{K-1} - E_{K-1}),$$

where E_K is the expected event in the Kth time period, A_{K-1} is what actually occurred, E_{K-1} is what was expected to occur; and λ is a positive constant interpreted as the speed of adjustment. The particular form of the model simply states that new expectations are generated from old expectations by revising the old estimate by a given fraction, λ, of the previous period's error in estimation.

additive utility function. A function based on the assumption that the utility provided by goods and services can be added to each other. Supposing x_1, x_2, . . . , x_n are the goods being consumed, the utility function may be written as the sum of the various utilities, i.e. $u(x_1, x_2, \ldots, x_n) = u_1(x_1) + u_2(x_2 + \ldots + u_n(x_n)$, so that goods consumed separately yield the same satisfaction as goods consumed together. This is clearly an untenable assumption and consequently it has been dispensed with in modern economic analysis. *See* separable utility function.

address. An identification number given to some part of the data in a computer memory.

adjuster. *See* loss adjuster.

administered price. A price set without close regard to costs. Obviously it must be above the break-even price. It generally occurs in oligopoly models and it tends to remain steady across variations in input prices.

administrator. *See* letters of administration.

ad valorem. (Latin for: according to value.) An ad valorem tax, duty, commission, charge, etc. is calculated as a percentage of the total value of the goods involved, rather than according to their quantity.

advance corporation tax (A.C.T.). A tax payable to the Inland Revenue in the U.K. under the *imputation system of taxation, when a company makes a distribution of dividends. This tax can, within limits, be offset against the corporation tax liability payable on profits arising in the same *accounting period as that in which the distribution was made. The amount of A.C.T. payable is a proportion of the dividend paid by the company equal to the basic rate of income tax on the net income receivable. Thus if the basic rate of income tax is 30% (as in 1984), the A.C.T. payable would be 30/70 of the dividend paid.

adverse balance. A deficit in the *balance of payments or in any of its constituent accounts, such as the current account, capital visibles, or invisibles. An adverse balance in the capital account must be offset by surplus from the current account if the balance of payments as a whole is to be in equilibrium.

advertising. The practice of informing the public or a section of the public of the benefits of a particular product, service, or activity in order to stimulate sales. *Consumer advertising* attempts to publicize the qualities, price, or other aspects of a product or service in order to increase sales. In a competitive market in which an increase in one company's sales is at the expense of another company, advertising usually attempts to persuade potential consumers to purchase a product that is identified by a *brand name. To this end, special qualities are emphasized when they exist. In some cases, such as common table salt, there are no distinguishing qualities and the advertising is then aimed at keeping the manufacturer's name before the public. However, not all products or services are identified in advertisements by a brand name; sometimes advertising is devoted to a type or category of product, such as milk or wool. *Trade advertising* is not directed at the public in general but to a specific section of it. For example, drug companies restrict to doctors their advertising of products that can only be purchased on prescription. Similarly, laboratory equipment would only be advertised in a medium likely to be seen by experimental scientists.

A distinction can be made between *informative advertising*, which assists consumers to choose between alternatives on offer and thus reduces market imperfections (as well as informing the public of the existence of a product), and *persuasive advertising*, which emphasizes and sometimes exaggerates the distinctive characteristics of a product – perhaps to the extent of increasing market imperfections by introducing monopolistic competition. Informative advertising is largely restricted to technical magazines.

Above-the-line advertising uses the traditional media of press, television, radio, the cinema, outdoor posters, etc. *Below-the-line* refers to all other kinds of advertising, e.g. direct mail, merchandising, etc. *Aerial advertising* has been tried in many different forms, e.g. smoke-writing in the sky, the trailing of banners from small aircraft, writing on airships, hot-air balloons, etc. In the U.K. aerial advertising is restricted by legislation to particular displays.

Although considerable sums are spent on advertising (about 2% of the GNP in the U.K. and 3% in the U.S.), there are strong arguments both for and against it. Apart from providing useful information about a product, it is claimed that advertising can lower production costs and therefore price by helping to stimulate a continuous demand. It can also assist in maintaining the quality of a product, since advertised productsmust meet the advertised specifications. Nevertheless, advertising often does not specify the composition of a product and it may emphasize false differentials or appeal to emotion rather than reason (sexual stimuli are extensively used in an attempt to sell a wide range of products, from toothpaste to cars). All too often advertising makes spurious appeals to the aspirations and fantasies of the consumer rather than restricting itself to the real benefits that a purchaser might expect to derive from a product. However, studies so far made have failed to confirm the belief that advertising can persuade people to buy things they do not want.

It is also argued that advertising cannot increase the total sales of an industry, although it can increase the share of the market of a particular firm, especially if its competitors do not advertise. If this hypothesis is true, advertising represents a waste of resources as all producers are forced to advertise in order to maintain their market shares, whereas if they all reduced their expenditure on advertising none would be worse off.

advice note. A document sent by a vendor to a customer advising him that an order has been fulfilled by the dispatch of goods. It will usually inform him of the quantity, marks and numbers (if applicable), quality, date of dispatch, and method of delivery. It may precede the goods themselves or accompany them. *Compare* delivery note.

advise fate. When a collecting banker wishes to know as soon as possible whether a cheque will be paid on its receipt by the paying banker he may send it direct, and not through the *Bankers' Clearing House, asking that its fate should be advised to him either on an enclosed stamped telegram form or by telephone. The paying banker cannot give a positive answer until he actually receives the cheque as the balance on his customer's account can alter or the customer may stop payment.

Advisory Conciliation and Arbitration Service (ACAS). *See* Employment Protection Acts.

affidavit. A sworn statement or declaration in writing that is made voluntarily and witnessed by a person who is acceptable to a court of law, such as a notary. Affidavits are usually made for use in legal proceedings.

affiliated society. *See* friendly society.

after date. The form of words used in a bill of exchange to indicate that the specified period for which the bill is drawn is to be calculated from the date inserted on the bill; for example, "30 days after date, we promise to pay . . . ". *Compare* after sight.

after-hours dealings (early bargains). Dealings made between the offices of Stock Exchange members (i.e. stockbrokers and stockjobbers) after the official close of business at 1530 hours. These are regarded as the first deals of the following trading day.

after-sales service. The service sometimes available to a customer after he has purchased a product. This may include an adequate supply of replacement parts and an adequate number of servicing and maintenance organizations. It may also include free replacement of faulty products or parts under guarantee, the availability of advice on the best use of the product, and a facility for maintenance and servicing contracts. Good after-sales service is an essential component of modern marketing methods.

after sight. The form of words used in a bill of exchange to indicate that the period for which the bill is drawn is to be calculated from the date on which the drawee is presented with it for acceptance. He usually inserts the date on which he accepts the drawer's order, but should he omit to do so the holder may insert the date he considers the bill to have been sighted by the drawee. *Compare* after date, at sight.

Agency for International Development (AID). *See* Act for International Development (1961).

agenda. A list of the items that are to be discussed at a meeting. It will usually be circulated to those who are to attend well in advance. Typically it will allot time for the reading of the minutes of the previous meeting, for any matters arising from this, for the discussion of items included on the agenda, and for the discussion of any other business (matters not specifically itemized on the agenda).

agent. A person who is given authority by another person (the *principal*) to act on that person's behalf. The extent of an agent's powers to bind his principal is limited to the terms of such authority. In order to avoid any personal liability when signing documents an agent must indicate that he signs on behalf of his principal. Bankers require to be supplied with an authority in precise terms before allowing an agent to sign cheques, etc., on his principal's account, and in the case of a limited company the authority must state which officials are authorized to act on behalf of the company.

aggregate demand. The total demand for goods and services in an economy at any one time, consisting of the total demand of households for consumption (C), demand for investment goods (I) both of firms and government, government demand for goods and services (G), and export demand less imports ($X-M$), given as

$$Y = C + I + G + (X-M),$$

where Y = national income. Aggregate demand determines the level of production and employment. *See also* income-expenditure model.

aggregated rebate scheme. A method of marketing in which a proportionately higher discount is offered as purchases increase. The size of the rebate that any buyer is entitled to is calculated from his total volume of purchases in a given period. A sliding scale of rebates that rises with the amount purchased is usual, with the highest rebate that the purchaser achieves applicable to all his purchases. These schemes have been condemned by the Monopolies and Mergers Commission on the grounds that they "impede competition from independent producers, because of their strong economic incentive to buyers to confine their purchases to members of the group (who operate the aggregated rebate scheme)". A purchaser might continue to buy some of his goods from the firm using the scheme rather than from an independent producer, because he might lose more in loss of rebate than he would gain in lower prices, so effectively tying himself to the larger firm. Aggregated rebate schemes must be registered with the Restrictive Practices Court, which has the power to ban them if it considers them to be against the public interest.

aggregate supply. The total supply of goods and services in an economy at any one time, consisting of total domestic output plus imports. When aggregate supply equals *aggregate demand, an equilibrium level of national income is reached.

aggregative model. An econometric model characterized by aggregated variables, i.e. variables that are constructed by aggregating groups of individual variables. The most frequently encountered aggregated variables are index numbers.

A.G.M. *See* annual general meeting.

agricultural bank (land bank). A credit bank specially established to assist agricultural development by granting loans for a longer period than is usual with mercantile banks. The system has not been successful in the U.K., but in many parts of the world such banks are strongly established, especially in West Germany.

Agricultural Credit Corporation Ltd. A corporation established in 1964 to provide medium-term loans to farmers for working capital for buildings, machinery, livestock, etc. The A.C.C. acts as guarantor for the loans to the farmer's bank.

Agricultural Mortgage Corporation Ltd. A corporation established under the Agricultural Credits Act (1928) to grant loans to the agricultural industry for periods of up to thirty years, mainly for the purchase of land. Government grants have been made to the Corporation and its share capital is provided by the Bank of England, the joint stock banks, and by the issue of marketable debentures. Applications for loans must be made through the commercial banks acting as agents of the Corporation, or directly to the Corporation, and are secured by mortgages or rent charges.

AID. Agency for International Development. *See* Act for International Development (1961).

aids to trade. The formal study of commerce usually recognizes four aids to trade: banking, insurance, transport, and advertising.

air consignment note. *See* air waybill.

air freight. 1. The transportation of goods by air. This method of transport is used if it is cheaper than other forms, which occurs if the value of the goods is high compared to their weight, of if an extra cost is justified for speed of delivery. In the latter case it is important not to overlook transit time to and from airports or the time that goods may lie in airport freight sheds awaiting customs clearance.

2. The cost of transporting goods by air. Air freight is usually based on a price per kilogram or per 7000 cubic centimetres (427 cu.in.), whichever is the greater. If the volume exceeds the weight, each unit of 7000 cubic cm is charged as 1 kilogram, so ultimately air freight, unlike marine freight, is based on weight.

air waybill. A numbered document (sometimes called an *air consignment note*) made out by, or on behalf of, the consignor of goods to be transported by *air freight. It shows the names of consignor and consignee; the airports of loading and destination; the nature, weight, and value of the goods; the marks, numbers, and dimensions of the packages; the route; and the freight charge. It is usually prepared at the same time as the *bill of lading.

ALGOL. A high-level *programming language used mainly for scientific and mathematical applications. The most widely used version is *Algol-60.* The name comes from *algo*rithmic *l*anguage.

allonge. An attachment to a bill of exchange to provide space for further endorsements when the back of the bill itself has been completely covered. It was sometimes necessary when bills of exchange passed freely from person to person by endorsement, but is now rarely needed.

allotment. *See* application and allotment.

allowances. *See* personal allowances.

all risks policies. A type of insurance relating to personal possessions and (for U.K. policies) usually covering the insured property anywhere in the British Isles, possibly Europe, and sometimes the rest of the world. This type of cover is particularly applicable to the insurance of jewellery, furs, photographic equipment, and other small valuable articles.

amalgamation. Unification of two or more organizations. *See* merger.

American account. One of the three groups of countries in which sterling was freely convertible when convertability of sterling was being restored after being suspended in 1947. The other groups were the *sterling area and the *transferable account. The members of the American account were the U.S., Canada, and certain Central American countries.

American National Standards Institute Inc. The U.S. organization concerned with establishing standards for industry, commerce, and science. It was founded in 1918 and is situated in New York. It represents the U.S. in the *International Standards Organization.

American Plan (White Plan). A plan to aid the development of international trade by creating stable fixed exchange rates and freely convertible currencies. It was proposed by the U.S. Treasury at the Bretton Woods Conference (1944) and was accepted in preference to the *Keynes Plan after some modification. It is also known as the Bretton Woods Agreement.

amortization. 1. *See* depreciation.

2. The payment of a debt in instalments, usually by means of a *sinking fund.

amounts differ. The form of words stamped or written on a cheque or bill of exchange by a banker returning it unpaid because the amount in words differs from that in figures. The Bills of Exchange Act (1882) states that the sum denoted by the words shall be the amount payable where there is a discrepancy between words and figures, but in practice a banker rarely pays the amount in words if it is the larger amount unless authorized to do so by his customer.

analog computer. A device for performing calculations and solving problems by use of electrical or mechanical analogy. For example, an electrical circuit can be constructed in which the output voltage bears some predecided relationship to the input voltage. Thus mathematical operations, such as multiplication, division, and integration, can be performed by representing known and unknown quantities by the size of the input and output voltages. The data has the form of a continuously variable physical quantity (the voltage): it is this that distinguishes the analog computer from the digital *computer, in which data is handled in discrete units. Analog computers are less common than digital computers but special-purpose analog devices do have some applications in simulating complex systems. For example, an economic model involves relationships between various parameters: investment, consumption, world trade, etc. The basis of the analog method is to represent these by physical quantities (voltage, resistance, etc.), and to form a circuit in which the relationships between these quantities obey the same rules as those governing the relationships between parameters of the model. Thus, an analogy exists between the economic model and the electrical circuit: unknown parameters can be obtained from known ones and the behaviour of the model can be investigated under a variety of conditions.

analysis of variance. The analysis of the total variation of a set of observations, as measured by the variance of the observations multiplied by their number (in other words, the sums of squares of deviations from the mean). It is often possible to separate such total variation into components representing different sources of variation that correspond to classification criteria for the observations. For instance, in the single-equation econometric model:

$$Y = a + bX + e,$$

Y is the dependent variable, X is the independent variable, a and b are coefficients, and e is a stochastic disturbance. The equation reduces to:

$$Y - \bar{Y} = b(X - \bar{X}) + e,$$

where $\bar{Y}$ and $\bar{X}$ are the means of Y and X respectively and e is assumed to have zero mean. From this latter equation it is possible to separate that part of the variation in Y which is explained, or represented by the variation in X, from that part which is unexplained, or represented by e.

Thus, from:

$$Y - \bar{Y} = b(X - \bar{X}) + e$$

it follows that for n observations:

$$\Sigma_n(Y - \bar{Y})^2 = b\Sigma_n(X - \bar{X})^2 + \Sigma_n e^2,$$

where $b\Sigma_n(X - \bar{X})^2$ is the explained variation and $\Sigma_n e^2$ the unexplained variation.

Annual Abstract of Statistics. An annual publication of the Central Statistical Office. It includes the United Kingdom's vital statistics, national income aggregates, major sectoral and industrial statistics, and social, legal, educational, health, and housing statistics. *See also Monthly Digest of Statistics.*

annual general meeting (A.G.M.). A meeting of the members of a company which every company is required to hold annually and at which the accounts of the period must be approved. Not more than 15 months must elapse between the date of one annual general meeting and the next. The annual general meeting has historic significance in that it provided an occasion for the members of the company to meet and judge the acts of the directors of their company. Now, however, the directors normally have full control over the voting at the annual general meeting.

annual report. A report that is sent by a company to its shareholders each year. It usually contains a report by the chairman of the year's trading and will often, in the case of large multinational companies, give an illustrated description of its operations worldwide. It also contains the company's *published accounts.

annual return. A document that every company with share capital must submit to the Register of Companies each year. It must contain those details specified by the Companies Acts (1948–81), such as the address of its registered office, the address of the register of members, charges and mortgages on the company, a list of the current members, and other sundry information. Attached to the annual return must also be a copy of the latest certified accounts. *See also* published accounts.

annuity. A form of pension in which an insurance company, in return for a certain sum of money (paid in a lump sum or by instalments), agrees to repay this money plus the investment income that it is able to earn over the expected lifetime of the investor, in the form of a guaranteed income. This means that the insurance company takes the mortality risk and therefore the individual investor gains substantially if he lives beyond the normal life expectancy for a man of his age and loses if he dies at an earlier age. Annuities can be paid in yearly, half yearly, quarterly, or monthly instalments that are in arrear or in advance. *See also* immediate annuity, deferred annuity, contingent annuity, self-employed annuity, annuity certain, purchased life annuity, joint life and last survivor annuities, retirement annuity.

annuity certain. An *annuity that is payable for a fixed period of, for example, 5 or 10 years, as opposed to an annuity that is payable for life.

ante-date. To enter on a deed or document a date earlier than that on which it was actually executed, signed, or issued. This practice may in certain cases be illegal, for instance where the ante-dating affects the amount of stamp duty that would otherwise have been payable on a deed.

anti-trust laws. The system of U.S. laws concerned with the prevention of a *monopoly and the preservation of a free competitive market. The first anti-trust law was the Sherman Antitrust Act (1890); subsequent legislation includes the Clayton Act (1914) and the Anti-merger Act (1950). These laws prevent the creation of any monopoly that harms the interests of the consumer. They are generally more stringent than the U.K. legislation. *See* Fair Trading Act (1973).

APL. A high-level *programming language originally designed for mathematical applications but subsequently used more generally. The initials stand for *A Programming Language*.

application and allotment. The two stages normally involved in the offer of shares to the public by a company. First (the application), the public are invited to make an offer for the shares on specified terms. Often the terms specify the price of the shares, the minimum and maximum numbers for which an individual may apply, and that the *application form* (*see also* pink form) should be accompanied by a cheque for the full amount of the shares applied for.

On receipt of the application forms the company, or its advisers, decide how these applications should be apportioned (if, as is usual in recent years, the application is oversubscribed). The apportionment may be carried out in a variety of ways: by ballot, by giving preference to employees or to small investors, or in relation to the size of the application. Successful applicants receive a letter of allotment telling them how many shares they have been allotted. If they have only been allotted a part of their application, a cheque is returned for the unallotted balance. Unsuccessful applicants have their money returned in full. *See also* stag.

applications program. *See* program.

applied statistics. One of the two main branches of statistical study. *See* statistics.

apprentice. A young person who has contracted to work for an employer for a fixed number of years in order to learn a skill and gain practical experience. During his apprenticeship he will normally earn a low wage, but this will be compensated for by his earnings after qualification. Characteristically an apprentice is training to become a skilled artisan; a trainee barrister or doctor is not thought of as an apprentice.

appropriation. 1. In a company, the allocation of the net profit before taxation between corporation tax, transfers to reserves, and dividends paid and proposed for the year in question. In a partnership, profits are appropriated between the partners according to their agreement on matters such as partners' salaries, interest on capital, and profit-sharing ratios.

2. In some produce contracts for goods for forward shipment, the exact parcel of goods cannot be identified (as they may not have been produced). At some stage before shipment, however, the exact parcel must be identified (by its marks and numbers) by the seller to the buyer. The document on which this identification is made is called an appropriation.

3. The allocation by a creditor to specific accounts of specific sums paid to him by a debtor. If the debtor does not state which sum is in settlement of which account, the creditor may choose to which debts the sum will be appropriated.

arbitrage. The practice of switching funds from one market or type of investment to another in order to exploit differences in price, *yield, interest rates, or exchange rates. Thus if bank lending rates are controlled, blue-chip companies (i.e. those with top credit ratings) may be able to utilize overdraft facilities in order to relend to the wholesale money markets, where rates will not be controlled. Arbitrage is of course only feasible when switching gains are of sufficient magnitude to outweigh any costs; thus any discrepancy between grain prices in London and Chicago will only attract arbitrageurs if it is large enough to offset the cost of shipping grain from one market to the other. Arbitrage is essentially an operation involving returns or prices that are definite, fixed, and known; a switch of ordinary shares on the Stock Exchange is therefore not arbitrage. Arbitrage serves the function of smoothing price and yield discrepancies in wholesale markets. *Compare* speculation.

arbitration. The settlement of a dispute between the parties to a contract by the decision of an independent person or body of persons (*arbitrator*) without recourse to legal action. The arbitrators act as judges and make their decision after hearing representations from both sides to the dispute. The exact procedure to be followed, if not laid down in the particular contract under which the dispute arises, is usually governed by the Arbitration Act (1950). It is often a quicker and cheaper method than taking legal action and is widely used in settling disputes that arise from commercial transactions.

arc elasticity. *See* point elasticity.

Ariel. A computerized share-dealing system under which subscribers can deal directly with each other rather than through the London Stock Exchange. Each subscriber receives a terminal (a screen plus a keyboard) through which broadcasts to other subscribers can be made. These broadcasts are anonymous and are in the nature of an invitation to treat rather than a definite offer. When broadcasting, there is no need for a subscriber to indicate the size (i.e. the number of shares) in which he wishes to deal although he must of course name the stock, indicate whether he is a buyer or seller, and name his price. The system of *settlement is the same as when dealing through the Stock Exchange. A subscriber can deal through Ariel in any of the following securities: U.K.-quoted equities, investment trusts, debentures, convertibles, certain local authority stocks, and Eurobonds. U.S. equities, European equities, unquoted securities, and gilt-edged securities cannot be dealt in through Ariel, although there are plans to introduce the first three of these to the system. Ariel is modelled on *Instinct, a similar U.S. system, and in fact the terminal equipment involved in Ariel has been imported from the U.S. Ariel, which is owned by a syndicate of 17 merchant banks, came into operation in the U.K. in February 1974 with the intention of winning some 5% of the share-dealing market (at the expense of stockbrokers and stockjobbers). Ariel's subscribers are all *institutional investors. The minimum size in which a subscriber can deal in Ariel is £10,000 and commissions run at the rate of 0.3% for equities and 0.2% for debentures (chargeable to both buyer and seller) subject to a maximum of £2000. These commission rates are substantially lower than those charged by stockbrokers. Ariel is a partial acronym for *A*utomated **R*eal-time *I*nvestments *E*xchange.

arithmetic mean. An average calculated by adding all the numbers concerned and dividing the sum total thus obtained by the number of numbers, e.g. the arithmetic mean of 6, 11, 9, 7, 12, is given by:

(6 + 11 + 9 + 7 + 12)/5 = 9.

The arithmetic mean is easily the most frequently encountered of all averages and is often abbreviated to *mean*. The main disadvantage of the arithmetic mean is the distortion caused to it by the presence of extremes among the numbers being averaged. A related problem arises when comparing two sets of numbers by use of the arithmetic mean. For example, the sets 16, 21, 23, 18, 22 and 71, -50, -1, 101, -21 both have a mean 20 but the two sets are quite dissimilar and any comparison based solely on the arithmetic mean could be misleading. These two disadvantages illustrate the importance of using a measure of *dispersion, such as the standard deviation, in addition to the arithmetic mean. The mean of any group of numbers is more useful when the dispersion is low. *Compare* geometric mean, harmonic mean, median, mode, quadratic mean. *See also* moment.

arithmetic progression. A mathematical series in which the difference between each consecutive value is constant, e.g. 2, 5, 8, 11, 14. *Compare* geometric progression.

arrangement. A plan submitted by a debtor to his creditors setting out his proposals for repayment.

articled clerk. A person who is apprenticed to a solicitor or to an accountant as part of his period of training, which will eventually lead to his becoming a fully qualified solicitor or accountant. During this period he may receive only a minimal salary and formerly a premium was often required from the trainee. The name derived from the document drawn up between the articled clerk and the person to whom he is apprenticed (his *principal*), called the *Articles of Clerkship*. This contains the rules with which the articled clerk must comply during his period of apprenticeship.

Articles of Association. The Companies Acts require that a newly formed limited company shall draw up a *Memorandum of Association and Articles of Association. The Articles prescribe the rules and regulations governing the internal working of the company and, among other things, set out the powers of the directors, which are especially important to bankers or others proposing to lend money to the company.

artificial intelligence. Computer software that makes machines respond in an "intelligent" manner, e.g. obeying simple commands given in English.

A shares. *See* nonvoting shares.

assembler. *See* programming language.

assented. 1. Denoting stocks or shares whose owners have agreed to accept the terms of a *takeover bid. During the course of a takeover there are often separate markets in assented and *nonassented stock*.

2. Denoting shares whose owners have agreed to a change in their terms or conditions of issue. It is especially applied to the stocks and shares of foreign governments that cannot meet their original obligations. Owners will generally assent to any new terms offered if the alternative is to receive nothing.

assessor. A person who estimates the value of damage for insurance claims on behalf of the policy holder.

asset. Anything owned by a company or individual that has a money value. Assets may be physical items, such as land, buildings, machinery, etc., or they may represent liabilities of others, such as cash and bonds, which are government liabilities, or equities, which are company liabilities. Assets are often classified by the ease with which they can be converted into money: the most liquid asset of all is obviously money. Assets are listed in the *balance sheet of a company and their total value is equal to the total value of liabilities. *See* current assets, fixed assets, intangible assets, deferred assets.

asset stripping. An entrepreneurial activity in which companies with share valuations below their asset value are taken over. Those assets that do not yield a profit are then sold off and what remains is revitalized, usually by the installation of new management. Some economists argue that the process is damaging to the economy as investment is drained away from industrial production; others argue that it is ultimately beneficial as it creates efficient enterprises.

asset value (per share). The value of a company (per share in issue), as calculated by deducting from the book value of the total assets all short-term and long-term liabilities, including deferred taxation reserves and any premium payable on redemption of debenture stock, intangible assets such as goodwill, and preference share capital, and dividing the resulting sum by the number of ordinary shares in issue. The asset value per share is frequently compared to the share price as a crude index of whether or not the latter is standing at a discount or a premium to the company's net assets. However, as a statistic, asset value per share is not very useful; first of all it is based on the book values of the assets and these may differ substantially from their market values, and secondly its relation to the share price will differ greatly as between capital-intensive manufacturing companies, labour-intensive manufacturing companies, service companies, companies with freehold properties versus those with leasehold properties, and companies with recently updated property values versus those with outdated values. Asset value is sometimes called *break-up value*.

assignment of insurable interest. The assignment of either the proceeds of an insurance policy or the policy itself to another person.

Assignment of the proceeds occurs when the policy-holder (the insured, the assured, or a subsequent assignee) gives instructions to the insurer to pay any monies due under the insurance to another person. In this sense, unless the contract specifically provides to the contrary, all policies are freely assignable.

Assignment of the policy involves the substitution of another person for the original insured in the contract, which remains in force. Normally the insurer's prior consent to such an assignment is essential.

assignment of life policies. Life assurance policies are treated in law as reversionary interests, which can be freely assigned. With an assignment of a life policy special procedures should be observed but life assurance is unique in that the assignee need not possess insurable interest.

Certain types of life assurance policies are affected by *nominations*, which are assignments of the proceeds of the policy as distinct from assignment of the policy itself. Nominations occur under policies written under the Married Women's Property Act (1882) and the Friendly Societies Act (1955). The object is to arrange that when policy monies become payable the amount is considered separate from the life assured's estate. The monies are then available for the dependants (named or otherwise) and not for any creditors; in addition certain tax or estate duty liability may be avoided in respect of the proceeds.

associated company. A company over which an investing company or group has a significant influence and in which the investor is either a partner in a joint venture or consortium or has a long-term and substantial interest.

associated states. States that are not members of the E.E.C. but are associated with the E.E.C. countries in trade. They usually have preferential trade agreements (*association agreements*) with the Common Market.

associate member. A member of the London Stock Exchange who is not a partner or director of the stockbroking or stockjobbing firm with which he is associated.

assurance. Another word for *insurance, though it has become customary in the insurance industry to refer to insurance with regard to eventualities that may or may not occur, e.g. fire, and to assurance for eventualities that must occur some time, particularly death. Premiums are paid at regular intervals and a fixed sum received in return at a specified time. Premiums make up the *common fund* of the assurance company and this is invested in long- and short-term investments, keeping it sufficiently liquid to ensure the availability of cash to pay policy-holders when it is due. *See* life assurance.

assured. The legal owner of a policy of *life assurance. When the policy matures or when a claim is payable the owner has control (subject to certain exceptions) of the payment of the sum assured. In general he is entitled to receive the amount payable.

When the assurance is effected the assured, if a person other than the life assured, must have an *insurable interest in the life assured, e.g. an employer may effect a life assurance policy on an employee.

at best. A qualifying instruction to buy or sell shares or commodities, given to a broker. It specifies either that a purchase must be made at the lowest possible price or that a sale must be made at the highest possible price at the time. Unlike an order *at limit, which may be good for the day, for the week, or until cancelled, an order at best must be executed immediately, irrespective of market fluctuations.

at limit. A qualifying instruction to buy or sell shares or commodities, given to a broker. It specifies either a top price at which a purchase may be made or a bottom price at which a selling order may be executed. *Compare* at best.

at sight. The form of words used in a bill of exchange to indicate that payment is due on presentation. *Compare* after sight.

attachment. The recovery by court order direct from a debtor of money owed to a creditor who in turn owes the money to the court. It usually applies to earnings, in which case the court will recover money owed by an employee direct from his employer out of wages due to the employee.

attribute. A characteristic for which numerical measurement cannot be made. Examples of attributes are educational achievement, occupation, sex, and marital status. Attributes can thus not be treated as variables in quantitative analysis, although they are often important. One device by which they can be introduced into an analysis is the dummy variable.

at warehouse. *See* spot goods.

auction. A method of sale in which goods are offered by an auctioneer in public, prospective buyers making competitive bids and the sale being made to the highest bidder (*compare* private treaty). Auctions are used for selling unique or rare goods or property when there are likely to be a number of competing prospective buyers. Works of art, furniture, and houses are frequently sold by auction as are certain commodities, such as tea, furs, bristles, wool, etc., that cannot be satisfactorily graded or sold on representative samples. In commodity auctions, the seller (or more usually a broker representing the seller) makes the goods available for inspection before the sale, just as works of art and houses are viewed by buyers before the sale.

The conduct of an auction and the rules under which it is conducted vary from one trade to another, but usually the auctioneer acts as the seller's agent and charges the seller a commission based on the prices realized at the sale. It is also usual for the seller to put a reserve price on an object for sale, below which the auctioneer is not permitted to sell. This reserve price may or may not be known to the public before the sale, but it will be declared by the auctioneer if it is not reached at the sale.

In a Dutch auction the goods are offered first at a high price and if no bid is received the auctioneer offers the goods at successively lower prices until a bid is made.

audit. An examination of the financial books and accounts of an enterprise and a scrutiny of the set of accounts, the balance sheet, and profit and loss account made up from these financial books and accounts. Every company in the U.K. is required by the Companies Acts (1948–81) to keep a proper set of books and to ensure that the periodic sets of accounts are the subject of an audit by an independent person with the requisite qualifications. A certificate of such an audit must be annexed to each set of accounts so produced.

The Institute of Chartered Accountants in England and Wales has split the audit into four essential stages. Firstly, the auditor should make a critical review of the system of bookkeeping, accounting, and *internal control. Secondly, he should make such tests as he considers necessary to form an opinion as to the reliability of the records as a basis of accounts.

Thirdly, he should compare the profit and loss account and balance sheet with the underlying records to ensure that these are in agreement. Fourthly, he should consider whether the profit and loss account presents a *true and fair view of the state of the company's affairs and complies with the various legal requirements.

auditor's report. A statement on the accounts of a company, made by an independent person with an approved qualification, who has conducted an *audit on the company and the accounts it has prepared. This person must state that the accounts under consideration give a *true and fair view of the company's affairs. If they do not, he must state why, without ambiguity, and if possible quantify the difference. Such a report must legally be attached to the company accounts when they are laid before its members at a general meeting.

Austrian School. A school of economic thought that developed after 1871 in Austria following the publication of *Grundsatze der Volkswirtschaftslehre* by Carl Menger (1840–1921); the ideas of this school were further developed by Eugen von Böhm-Bawerk (1851–1914) and Ludwig Edler von Mises (1881–1973). The original major element in the analysis was the formation of a theory of value based upon the subjective evaluation of a good in terms of its marginal utility. Böhm-Bawerk, in particular, developed its theory of interest and capital. The use of capital was seen as a more roundabout method of production as it requiredwaiting for the capital equipment to be manufactured, although it yielded a reward in that productivity was increased. On the other hand the preference of individuals for present consumption rather than saving (time preference) was such that a positive interest rate was required to induce savings in the form of deferred income.

autarky (autarchy). An economic system in which a country produces and consumes in isolation, i.e. it is economically self-sufficient. It is studied principally for the purpose of comparisons with trade models so as to evaluate better the effects of international trade on the countries involved under different sets of assumptions.

authority. An authorization from a client to a banker empowering him to act for the client in certain specified matters. Bankers receive authorities from customers to deal with many different matters, but in all cases they should be in writing. The majority are in connection with the signatures to be accepted on joint, partnerships', societies', or company accounts and must be strictly adhered to. An authority in connection with one matter must not be assumed to cover another.

authorized capital. The maximum aggregate nominal value of shares that the directors of a company may legally issue. The directors of a company with an authorized capital of £500,000 may, if the nominal value of each of its shares is £1, not issue more than 500,000 shares. If the nominal value of each share is 25p, they may issue up to 2 000 000. The amount of stamp duty payable to the Inland Revenue on the formation of a company is assessed according to a company's authorized capital. The company may subsequently resolve in a general meeting to increase or decrease its authorized capital, but in the case of an increase, additional stamp duty will be incurred.

authorized clerk. A stockbroker's clerk who under Stock Exchange regulations is entitled to make deals on behalf of his employer without being a member of the Stock Exchange himself.

autocorrelation. *Correlation between variables of the same series. In econometrics autocorrelation of the stochastic disturbances will occur when one of the assumptions underlying the *Gauss–Markov theorem, namely, that of zero covariance between different stochastic residuals, does not hold. This is likely to be the case if, for instance, a relevant variable has been omitted from the regression equation so that the stochastic term will include the (nonrandom) influence of this variable as well as the random disturbances that the stochastic term essentially represents. Least squares estimators derived from a model including autocorrelated stochastic residuals will still be unbiased but they will no longer be efficient and they will produce serious underestimates of the variances of the regression coefficients. Since autocorrelation largely vitiates the value of least squares estimation, it is desirable to remove it whenever it is discovered. This will be possible if the autoregressive structure to which the autocorrelated terms approximate is known. In this case a transformation of the original variables according to this autoregressive structure can be made and least squares estimation as applied to the transformed variables will then be valid. Autocorrelation can be detected by the *Durbin–Watson d statistic. *See also* autoregression, unbiasedness, efficiency.

automatic stabilizers. *See* built-in stabilizers.

autonomous investment. The part of total investment not determined by themacroeconomic variables (such as interest, sales changes, profits, or income) but by variables exogenous to the system. These variables may be the rate of population growth or the rate of innovation in the economy. Many economists claim that these variables are also determined, in the long run, by the rational choice of individuals, choosing family size, or investing in scientific effort. This view would leave no autonomous investment in the long run, but within the short-run horizon of macroeconomics it is a useful category. It is often used in *trade-cycle models to put a floor to the level of investment and thus to income and employment.

autoregression. *Regression involving autocorrelated variables. Such variables will commonly be the stochastic disturbances of a regression model, especially in the case of a time series when the stochastic residual of one time period is correlated with that of another, so that there is autocorrelation with a lag. If the form of an autoregression equation is known and it can be written so that its own stochastic term is not autocorrelated, then it will be possible to modify the procedure of least squares estimation in order to eliminate the effect of autocorrelation on the original regression model. *See also* autocorrelation.

available earnings. A company's annual profit after deduction of all trading costs, depreciation, taxation, and preference dividend. The resulting figure, sometimes referred to as "earned for ordinary", gives a measure of earnings available, i.e. available for distribution as dividend to ordinary shareholders in respect of the year in question. The division of available earnings by the number of ordinary shares in issue gives *earnings per share*, the denominator of the *P/E ratio and one of the statistics widely used in investment analysis.

average. 1. A single value calculated from a set of numbers the purpose of which is to represent such numbers by showing a measure of their central tendency. It should be noted that an average is not necessarily identical with any of the numbers it represents; for instance, the average number of individuals per household in a town may be 4.5. There are several different types of average that can be computed from any set of numbers but the most frequently encountered are the *arithmetic mean, the *median, and the *mode, which will not usually be the same (except in the case of a set of numbers following the normal distribution). *See also* weighted average, moving average, geometric mean, harmonic mean, quadratic mean.

2. Loss or damage. In *marine insurance, average is a partial loss. *Particular average* refers to a partial loss affecting one particular interest involved with the marine venture. Therefore, it can refer to loss or damage to the ship itself, i.e. average that is particular to the *hull insurance, or to partial loss or damage to cargo, i.e. particular to *cargo insurance. *General average* is independent of insurance and arises out of the contract between the cargo owner and the shipowner. While a particular-average loss falls on an individual, general average is shared amongst all concerned. If a vessel is in such peril that her safety depends on sacrificing part of the ship or the cargo, the loss or expense will be recovered by a *general average deposit* levied on all the interested parties. The *general average statement* shows how much each party must contribute. It is a compulsory *ad valorem charge on shipowner and cargo owners. Before a general average can arise the following conditions must be fulfilled.

(i) The loss must have been sustained voluntarily. For example, deck cargo may have to be thrown overboard during a heavy storm for the safety of the ship.

(ii) The sacrifice must save the whole venture. In the above example, general average will not be declared if the ship sinks despite the measures taken.

In *fire insurance, average is used to combat under-insurance. Where there is under-insurance the whole principle of insurance is being undermined, in the sense that the insured is not paying a fair premium into the common fund for the risk presented. Therefore, it would be inequitable to other policy-holders for full compensation to be paid in the event of a loss.

In fire insurance there are three main types of average.

(i) The pro rata condition of average means that an insured is penalized exactly proportionately to the degree of under-insurance that exists. If, for example, he insures for only 75% of the value of the goods insured, when he should have insured for the full value, he will receive payment of only 75% of any loss sustained.

(ii) The special condition of average means that under-insurance is not penalized unless the sum insured represents less than 75% of the value atrisk. Therefore, a certain degree of under-insurance is permitted: this concession may be found with policies insuring agricultural produce.

(iii) The type of average used sometimes with warehouse insurances comprises either the normal pro rata condition of average, as in (i) above, or an exclusion of property more specifically insured (except to the extent that the other insurance may be inadequate), as in (ii) above.

In *accident insurance, average signifies the same as for fire insurance. The application is also similar, except that the special condition of average is rarely, if ever, found and the two conditions of average are unknown.

average clause. A clause in an insurance policy stating that when goods or property are insured for less than their full value, claims will be settled on the basis of the ratio of the amount insured to the full value. If, for example, an article worth £100 is insured for £75 a claim for total loss will be settled for £75. However, if the article is damaged to such an extent that its value is reduced to £60, the claim will be settled on the basis of 75% of £40, i.e. £30.

average collection period. The average time taken to obtain payment for debts.

average (unit) cost. The total cost of producing a number of units of a product divided by the number of units. The difference between the average cost at a certain output and the sale price represents the *unit profit* or *loss* at that output.

Average cost may be broken down into two subdivisions: *average fixed cost* and *average variable cost*. The former is the total fixed cost divided by the number of units, the latter is the total variable cost divided by the number of units. The average fixed costs decline as output increases, since the fixed costs, e.g. interest payments, rent, cost of plant, etc., can be spread over an increasingly large output. On the other hand, the average variable costs rise as output increases, since total variable costs will increase disproportionately, as a result of overtime payments, costs of installation of new machinery, the new machinery itself, etc. Graphically, as the average cost curve plotted against output must remain above the curves for average fixed cost and average variable cost at all times, it will be approximately U-shaped.

average cost curve. The average cost of producing a number of units of a good as represented by a curve on a graph. This curve can demonstrate that when the selling price of a certain number of units is higher than their average cost, the firm will make a profit equal to the number of units sold multiplied by the difference between the two figures. Similarly when the selling price is lower than the average cost it makes a loss.

The average cost curve reaches its minimum value where it intersects the *marginal cost curve. Average cost curves can be drawn for *indirect costs and *direct costs as well as for total cost.

average cost pricing. A pricing policy in which a firm sets its selling price equal to its average cost. This means that the unit cost equals the unit revenue and the firm will always break even. However, to increase profits, price should be set equal to the *marginal cost, although in a perfectly competitive situation or a dynamic one in which the firms sales vary unpredictably, average cost pricing serves as an acceptable rule of thumb since average cost will equal marginal cost under perfect competition.

average deviation. *See* mean deviation.

average fixed cost. *See* average (unit) cost.

average revenue. Total revenue divided by the number of units of a good that is sold. Since total revenue is price multiplied by the quantity sold, average revenue and price are identical.

average variable cost. *See* average (unit) cost.

averaging. The practice of adding to one's holdings of a share or commodity when its price falls, in order to reduce the average purchase price. Occasionally the term is used to denote the converse process of selling shares or commodities from a holding that has already been reduced, in order to increase the average sale price.

avoirdupois. Units of weight that are used mainly in the U.S., U.K., and Commonwealth. 16 ounces (oz.) or 7000 grains equal one pound (lb.); 100 pounds equal one hundredweight (cwt.) in the U.S. while 112 pounds equal one hundredweight in the U.K.; 20 hundredweights equal one ton. An avoirdupois pound equals 453.6 grams or 1.22 troy pounds. The avoirdupois system is gradually being replaced by the metric system.

B

back door. The method by which the Bank of England injects cash into the money market through purchasing Treasury bills at the market rate, as opposed to lending money directly to the discount houses (*front door*), acting as *lender of last resort. When the discount houses are short of funds this method of assistance is often used instead of the front door method.

backing store. *See* storage device.

back-to-back (countervailing) credit. A credit given by a U.K. finance house to a foreign buyer, who has bought goods from a seller in another country (it may or may not be the same country as the buyer's). The seller sends his documents to the finance house, which substitutes documents made out in its own name for presentation to the buyer. This procedure conceals the identity of the seller from the buyer.

backwardation. 1. A rate of interest paid by a *bear speculator on the London Stock Exchange for deferring from one account day to the next final settlement of shares sold during the account. Backwardation is thus the price paid by a bear to give a transaction the nature of an *inter-account deal when it really straddles more than one account. Backwardation may not be payable on a certain stock if sufficient bull operators have *contangoed the same stock in the same account. The expectation of a bear who pays backwardation is that the price of the stock concerned will fall in the near future.

2. The extent to which the spot price of a commodity, plus the cost of rent and interest, exceeds the forward price.

backward-bending supply curve. *See* regressive supply curve.

backward integration. *Vertical integration of one firm with another that is nearer the beginning of the manufacturing process; for example, the integration of a machine manufacturer with a steel-refiner or a retailer with a wholesaler. This form of integration can ensure a more certain supply of materials but cannot increase the firm's monopoly power.

bad debts. Amounts owing to a business which it is estimated will not be recoverable. Most businesses incur such losses, in spite of taking every precaution, e.g. where a customer becomes insolvent and has insufficient assets with which to pay the debt. Actual bad debts written off are charged along with other business expenses in the profit and loss account. In addition it is possible to create a *provision for bad debts* in the profit and loss account, which will be subtracted from the closing debtors figure in the balance sheet. This provision may be general (e.g. a percentage of debtors) or specific (based on an analysis of debtors). A general provision for bad debts is not allowable for tax purposes but a specific one is allowed as a deduction in computing taxable profits.

bailment. The placing of goods into the possession (but not the ownership) of another person. The person placing the goods (*bailor*) must either be the rightful owner or one with a right to possess the goods. The person with whom they are placed (*bailee*) must be willing to take possession of them. The intention for the bailee to have full control of the goods to the exclusion of other people must be present. Thus a servant entrusted with goods by his master and ordered to take them to a third person merely has custody of the goods, possession remaining with his master until the goods are delivered to the third person, and no bailment exists. If the bailor receives no money from the bailee, the bailment is said to be gratuitous and the bailor's only obligation is to inform the bailee of any defects in the goods of which the bailor is aware. If the bailor receives money, the bailment is said to be for reward and the bailor must also compensate the bailee for any disturbance with the bailee's possession of the goods during the bailment. The bailee's obligation is to take reasonable care of the goods in all the circumstances of the case.

balanced budget. The budget is balanced when current government expenditure equals current government revenue. This was believed to be necessary by governments of the nineteenth and early twentieth centuries by analogy with the situation facing an individual. If he spends more than he earns he steadily increases his debt. However, an increase in the *National Debt is now considered to be of relatively minor consequence to a government provided interest repayments remain at a relatively low level. Although the effects of a balanced budget need not be completely neutral (an increase in the size of a balanced budget will raise government expenditure by a greater amount than it lowers private expenditure), in general it merely accentuates the trend in the economy. For example, with a balanced budget government expenditure will have to fall with revenue in a *depression so creating unemployment. Since the 1930s most governments have adopted unbalanced budgets in an attempt to stabilize the economy (*see also* built-in stabilizers), running *budget deficits* by increasing expenditure over revenue in a depression and running *budget surpluses*, which collect more revenue than is spent, in a boom.

balanced budget multiplier theorem. A theorem stating that an increase (or decrease) in government spending exactly matched by an increase (or decrease) in taxation will raise (or lower) income by the amount of the change in spending. This is because the initial spending generates income of an equivalent size; some proportion, say b, of this is spent and $(1 - b)$ is saved. The spending again generates equivalent income; a proportion of which is spent (b times b of the original) and $(1 - b)$ saved. These effects continue through a multiplier process to raise income. The matching rise in taxation lowers spending by a proportion of the total, b, and saving by $(1 - b)$. The fall in spending lowers income receipts and this in turn lowers spending and saving in a multiplier process. Tax changes cancel only the effects of the second and subsequent rounds, leaving income changed by the amount of the expenditure change. This theorem holds for any tax regime and economy with a foreign sector but in order to be valid the increase in income must not raise the interest rate through the money market as this will curb investment in the goods market.

balanced growth path. *See* steady-state growth path.

balance of payments. A record of all transactions between residents of a country (both the private and public sectors) and the rest of the world. It is divided into current and capital accounts. The *current account* represents national income and national expenditure. It is composed of visible trade (i.e. trade in tangible goods and merchandise including re-exports) and invisible trade (e.g. transportation, insurance and other services, interest payments, expenditure by tourists, and certain classes of government expenditure). Unrequited receipts, i.e. those receipts for which no consideration is given, may be included under *invisibles or kept separate. These include payments made by migrant workers to their families at home and other gifts. The *capital account* consists of capital inflows and outflows, both long term and short term, and includes intergovernmental loans. If current and capital accounts together are in deficit, there will be an outflow from the foreign exchange reserves.

If there is a persistent inflow or outflow of foreign exchange, there will be strong pressures on the exchange rate of the currency. It is possible that deficits and surpluses in the balance of payments may be cyclical or of a short-term nature. For example, a primarily agricultural country may export its crops after one harvest and be importing throughout the rest of the year; if its capital and exchange markets do not adequately smooth out the fluctuations it will have recurrent short-term deficits. The ultimate result of a chronic deficit or surplus in the balance of payments, which indicates a *fundamental disequilibrium* in the foreign exchange market, must be either a *devaluation or *revaluation of the currency.

balance of trade (visible balance). The difference between the total value of a country's exports and imports of visible items (*see* visibles). The balance of trade is an important part of the *balance of payments, which also takes account of invisible items and of capital transfers. The nature of the U.K.'s trading pattern usually results in an unfavourable balance of trade (i.e. the value of imports exceeds that of exports) and a favourable invisible balance (i.e. receipts for services exceed payments) and thus it has been possible to run at a deficit on the balance of trade when this was offset by the invisible balance. Since the terms favourable and unfavourable (or adverse) do not necessarily mean desirable and undesirable the terms *trade surplus* and *deficit* are now commonly used.

balance sheet. A statement of the assets and liabilities of a company at a particular time. Assets and liabilities are, usually, split into fixed assets, deferred assets, current assets, current liabilities, deferred liabilities, and other provisions. The net balance of assets and liabilities will be represented by share capital, various revenue and capital reserves, and a positive or negative balance on the *profit and loss account. The *balance sheet identity* (or *equation*) is: capital (i.e. shareholders' funds) = total assets less liabilities, or $C = A - L$.

Baltic Mercantile and Shipping Exchange. A market located in London and dealing in both commodities and freight. As a *commodity exchange, it is concerned with dealings in grains at the retail arm of the *Corn Exchange. This part of the Baltic contains a well-established futures market. In respect of shipping, the Baltic handles business connected with cargoes and shipping space and also with the arrangement of air freight. The *Baltic Exchange* is the largest shipping market in the world.

bank. A commercial institution with various financial activities, chiefly the handling of the money of its depositors. While there is no statutory definition of a bank, it has been considered that the test of a banking business should be that of accepting deposits and current accounts and the collection and payment of cheques. Although moneylenders are prohibited from registration under any name that includes the word *bank*, the commercial banks lend money as part of their business. In the U.K. the banking system comprises the *Bank of England (central bank), the *commercial joint-stock banks, *merchant banks, head offices of British Overseas and Commonwealth banks, London branches of other overseas banks, the *Trustee Savings Banks, and the *National Savings Bank. *See also* building society.

bank account. Bankers usually offer their clients three types of account.

A *current account* is an active account on which cheques are drawn and into which credits are paid. Interest is not usually allowed on a credit balance but interest is charged if the account is overdrawn. Some banks make charges for the running of the account, although modern practice is for current accounts to bear no charges if they are kept in credit over a certain level. A *deposit account* is one in which money can be deposited to earn interest. Withdrawal is subject to notice, usually seven days, so that the depositor cannot issue cheques on his account and normally withdrawals are by transfer to a current account. The rate of interest varies with the *base rate and may be higher for large amounts subject to a longer period of notice. A *savings account* is one into which small regular payments are made as a means of accumulating savings. Favourable rates of interest are usually offered and they were introduced to persuade those with limited income to save by small instalments.

A banker is required by law to inform the Inland Revenue authorities of amounts of interest exceeding £15 credited to deposit or savings bank accounts. *See also* budget account.

bank advance. An advance from a bank is either by way of *overdraft or by a *loan account. If it is arranged as an overdraft a limit is set to which the customer can overdraw his current account, the balance varying from day to day transactions. But if a loan account is opened the agreed advance is immediately debited to it and transferred to current account. In both cases interest is charged but with an overdraft the borrower only pays interest on the sum overdrawn, whereas if he takes a loan he pays interest on the full amount borrowed. Banks usually require advances to be secured. Most bank advances are made to provide industry with working capital, it being unusual for them to provide fixed capital. In times of inflation in the U.K. the monetary authorities have attempted to restrict bank lending by instructing them to make *special deposits with the Bank of England as bank advances create credit.

bank bill. A bill of exchange that has been drawn or accepted by a commercial bank or an *accepting house. It can be discounted at a preferential rate compared with trade bills.

bank charges. The amount of debit interest and commission charged to a customer's account by a bank, usually half-yearly. Depending upon the purpose of a loan, a rebate of income tax may be claimed for interest paid to a bank but not for commission, which is a charge for the work done by the bank on the customer's behalf. In times of low interest rates a handling charge may be made on an account with a credit balance.

bank draft. A cheque drawn on a bank by itself or its agent. It is used by a debtor when his creditor is unwilling to accept a personal cheque. The debtor pays the bank for it at the time of issue.

banker and customer. The relationship in law between a banker and his customer is that of debtor and creditor; the banker is the debtor when the customer has a credit account, but the positions are reversed when the banker makes a loan to a customer. The customer has the right to demand back any money that the banker is holding on his behalf, but during the time he holds it the banker has it at his free disposal to keep, invest, or lend. The banker is obliged to pay his customer's cheques to the extent of the customer's credit balance, but the customer only has the right to overdraw his account by special agreement. A banker is bound to secrecy regarding the accounts of his customers, but may be compelled by law to give information in certain cases, i.e. where a court orders him to do so, where there is a public duty of disclosure, or where it is necessary for the protection of the banker's own interests.

Bankers' Clearing House. An institution established by member banks to simplify exchanging, and obtaining payment for, the many thousands of cheques that are paid in to branch banks throughout the country. Indebtedness between banks is a result of the differences between the daily totals of cheques exchanged and as far as possible differences are set off against each other: final settlement is made by drawing on the Bank of England, where each of the clearing banks maintains an account.

bankers' indemnity. A guarantee required by a shipowner when goods are released without production of the *bill of lading. It must be countersigned by the consignee's bankers.

banker's order (standing order). A written order by a customer to his bank to make a payment or series of payments on his behalf. It is usually used to pay subscriptions, hire-purchase instalments, insurance premiums, etc., which fall due at regular intervals. *See also* credit transfer.

banker's reference. Bankers are frequently asked for opinions on their customers' trustworthiness for trade credit. The opening of an account is considered to be the customer's implied consent to such a reference being given, but a bank will only give one to another bank so it is necessary for the enquirer to act through his own bank. The report will only be in very general terms and is usually worded so that all responsibility is disclaimed.

Bank for International Settlements (B.I.S.). An international financial institution situated in Basle and founded in 1930 as a result of the Hague conference and other German reparations negotiations in that year. The founding members were Belgium, France, Germany, Italy, and the U.K., but membership has since expanded to include all West European central banks as well as Japan and Canada. The U.S. is also active in its operation. Its original purposes included the coordination of reparations payments between central banks, acting as a central bank for all other European central banks, and serving as a trustee and agent for various international agreements. Although the *I.M.F. has now taken over most of the functions of the B.I.S., it is still important in its capacity as a trustee and a medium for surveillance of international banking activities. In particular it is an agent for the O.E.C.D. and is a centre for the informal exchange of ideas and information for the central banks. In its transactions the B.I.S. takes up no speculative positions but always hedges its transactions on the forward market.

bank holidays. Public (though not statutory) holidays, when banks are closed. Bank holidays were established by the Bank Holidays Act (1871), which appointed four days to be bank holidays in England, five in Scotland, and five in Ireland. They are Easter Monday, Whit Monday (now Spring Bank Holiday), August Bank Holiday (now Summer Bank Holiday), and Boxing Day for England and Wales, including St. Patrick's Day for Northern Ireland. Scotland has New Year's Day, Christmas Day, Good Friday, the first Monday of May, and the first Monday of August. England and Wales now have New Year's Day and May Day. Any alterations in these days must be by Order in Council. Bills of Exchange that fall due on these days are payable on the next working day. Good Friday and Christmas day are also nonbusiness days, but if a bill falls due on one of them or on a Sunday, then it is payable on the preceding business day.

bank loan. *See* bank advance.

bank notes. Slips of paper issued by a bank promising to pay the bearer on demand a specified sum of money. They differ from promissory notes in that they may be reissued after payment. They originated in the receipts that goldsmiths gave for money left with them for safe keeping. In England the Bank of England is now the only bank with the right to issue bank notes; the last private bank to do so was Fox Fowler & Co., before amalgamation with Lloyds Bank Limited in 1921. Certain Scottish and Northern Irish banks still have a limited right to issue notes. Before 1931 English bank notes could be exchanged on demand for gold coins, but are now inconvertible. Government monetary policy controls the number of bank notes in circulation.

Bank of England. The central bank of the U.K. Incorporated in 1694 by London merchants in order to lend money to William III, it continued to be banker to the government although in its early years its business did not differ from other banks. With the failure of many of the smaller banks in the crises of 1825 and 1837, the Bank Charter Act (1844) aimed to restrict the issue of *bank notes and eventually the Bank of England became the only bank in England and Wales with the right to issue them. It also stores the country's gold reserves. In collaboration with the Treasury, its minimum lending rate has been used as an instrument of monetary policy. Since 1960, by calling on the commercial banks for *special deposits it has controlled credit policy. The Bank of England was nationalized in 1946. As a bank it retains some private accounts, e.g. for certain long-established institutions, but its main customers are the government, foreign central banks, international organizations, and the commercial banks (to which it does not lend), accepting houses, and discount houses (for which it acts as *lender of last resort). The Bank manages the National Debt, acting as registrar of stocks issued by the government, by nationalized industries, some Commonwealth governments, and some other public bodies such as local authorities. It administers exchange controls (when in force) and the *Exchange Equalization Account.

It is thus responsible for carrying out the country's monetary policy and its monetary relations with other countries.

bank rate. The former name (until October 1972) for the *minimum lending rate. *See also* base rate.

bank reconciliation statement. An account that reconciles the figures shown in a firm's bank statement with those shown in its *cash book. The two records usually differ since some cheques that have been issued or received might not have been banked and hence cannot be recorded on the bank statement. The reconciliation statement explains these discrepancies, so proving that a proper record of all transactions has been kept.

bankruptcy. The state of being adjudged by a court to be insolvent, i.e. unable to pay one's debts. This applies to individuals rather than companies, which are put into *liquidation when they become insolvent. A person becomes bankrupt initially by committing what is known as an *act of bankruptcy*, e.g. giving away his property with intent to defraud creditors, leaving the country in order to escape from creditors, or not complying with a bankruptcy notice filed against him by a creditor who has obtained a court judgment that money is owed to him by the debtor.

The next stage is for a creditor who is owed more than £50 to present a petition to a bankruptcy court. If he proves that an act of bankruptcy was committed during the preceding three months, and that the debt he is owed was in existence at the time, then the court will issue a *receiving order. The *Official Receiver will then take possession of all the debtor's property. The debtor must then submit a statement of his affairs to the Official Receiver. This must show particulars of the debtor's assets and liabilities, and the names and addresses of all his creditors, who are then invited to attend an examination of the debtor on oath (usually held in public).

The creditors then meet to decide whether or not to enter into a *deed of arrangement with the debtor. If they decide not to do this, the court must adjudicate the debtor to be bankrupt and appoint a trustee to whom all the bankrupt's property will be transferred for the benefit of the creditors. The creditors must prove their debts by sending affidavits to the bankrupt's trustee, giving evidence of the debts. Unsecured creditors, whose debts have been proved in this way, are then all paid the same ratio or dividend of their debts within four months of their first meeting.

Creditors who can prove that their loans were secured on an item of the debtor's property are repaid the amount which that item of property realizes, up to the full amount of their loan, with any excess being used to repay the unsecured creditors. Further dividends are paid to unsecured creditors at six-monthly intervals.

At any time after being adjudicated bankrupt, the debtor may apply to the court for a discharge. This is important to him because, with certain limited exceptions (e.g. state benefits and the tools of his trade), an undischarged bankrupt has no property that he can call his own. He is also barred from being a director of, or taking any part in the management of, any company and he is barred from a large variety of public offices. The court hears evidence from the trustee, from the Official Receiver, and from any creditor who wishes to speak and may grant a discharge to the bankrupt if satisfied that all reasonable efforts have been made to pay off his debts. Once he is discharged, most of the bankrupt's debts are cancelled. *See also* undischarged bankrupt.

bank statement. A loose-leaf sheet supplied to customers by banks listing all amounts withdrawn and all deposits credited on a customer's account and showing the balance as at the date of the statement.

banques d'affaires. *See* investment bank.

bargain. A transaction on the London Stock Exchange. Bargains made up to 1415 hours on each day are available for inclusion in the Stock Exchange Daily Official List for that day.

bargaining theory. The theory of wage determination that sees wage levels as the result of negotiation between management and trade unions, rather than the result of supply and demand in the labour market. The bargaining process is the focus of analysis, although this can also be seen as the means by which an equilibrium wage is reached in the overall context of supply and demand for labour.

barratry. 1. The misdemeanour of habitually starting quarrels or vexatious litigation.

2. Any act committed by the captain of a ship or his crew that is contrary to the interests of the shipowners, e.g. setting fire to the ship or stealing the cargo. It is one of the perils of the sea covered by *marine insurance policies.

barrier to entry. A market condition that impedes or prevents the entrance of new firms into an industry. In all cases it reduces competitiveness inside the industry so allowing established companies to charge higher prices than would otherwise prevail. There are several types of barrier to entry, both economic and institutional. They can be divided into six main groups:

I. Governmental prohibition. This occurs when the government controls entry into an industry either to safeguard the public's interests, as in medicine and pharmaceuticals, to ration some scarce public resources in those same interests as with radio and television licensing, to protect a government monopoly operating for the public good, as in public utilities and electricity, or for reasons of national security, as in the armaments industry and the armed forces.

II. Economic restrictions, caused by economies of scale, which make the optimal plant size large relative to the demand in the economy (*see* natural monopoly), or because the industry depends on some scarce resource, which is controlled by those already in the industry .

III. Set-up costs. Highly capital-intensive industries require a large initial capital expenditure, and entrants risk not being able to capture enough of the market to remain viable.

IV. Resistance of those in the industry which may take the form of price cutting, tying contracts with consumers, control over raw materials, or influence with essential related industries.

V. Patent or royalty restrictions (*see* patent monopoly).

VI. Product differentiation and consumer preferences for established products.

If these barriers are not prohibitive they can be overcome at a cost, reckoned per unit of output. This cost then represents the height of the barrier, and firms in an industry may price above their marginal cost up to the height of the barrier without attracting new firms. It is also argued that where barriers are present, existing firms will not exceed them in their pricing for fear of attracting competitors and reducing future profits, so that the reduction of barriers to entry should reduce prices in an industry, regardless of whether or not new firms actually do enter.

barter. A form of trading in which goods are exchanged directly for other goods without the use of money as an intermediary. Thus if someone has eggs and wants cheese he must find someone with cheese who wants eggs. In less pure forms of barter he will be allowed to exchange eggs for wheat so that he may trade with someone who has cheese and wants wheat. This is obviously a most inefficient type of economy and not surprisingly is not known to exist in its pure form in any society. It is surprising, however, that almost all microeconomic theory and general equilibrium analysis can be applied directly to a barter economy.

base metal. Copper, lead, zinc, and tin, as distinguished from the precious metals. *See* London Metal Exchange.

base period. The time period from which an index number or growth rate is based. Thus if the Wholesale Price Index is quoted as 130 (1970 = 100), then 1970 is the base period. The base period selected should be a typical period with respect to the variables being measured.

base rate. The rate of interest advertised by a commercial bank as the rate upon which it bases the rate it will charge on advances. Rates charged will be somewhat higher than the base rate and will depend upon the type of advance and the credit rating of the customer. The banks fix their rates independently but in practice they must be close together to retain their shares of customers.

base stock method. An accounting system for valuing stock. The stock is valued at the price at which it was originally bought, it being assumed that the last stock purchased will be the first to be used. If, therefore, the volume of stock at the beginning and end of the accounting period is identical, no inventory profits will be recorded for the year. This avoids any *paper profit that arises because of inflation.

base year. The initial year in an index number series. It is usually given the index number 100 so that the percentage change in subsequent years can be easily calculated. *See* index of industrial production, general index of retail prices, Paasche index, Laspeyres index.

BASIC. A high-level *programming language much used on *microcomputers. The initials stand for *B*eginner's *A*ll-purpose *S*ymbolic *I*nstruction *C*ode. As the name suggests it is one of the easiest programming languages to learn and use initially, and is consequently widely taught in schools and colleges.

bear. 1. A person who expects prices, especially of shares or commodities, to fall. **2.** An operator on a stock exchange or commodity market who expects prices to fall and therefore sells. A *covered bear* or *protected bear* is one who sells shares or commodities that he owns. The selling of shares or commodities that are not owned, in the hope of buying them later at a lower price, is called *short selling (this was the original meaning of the term). A *bear raid* is active selling of a particular share or commodity in order to force its price down so that it can be bought back later at a lower price. *Compare* bull.

bear closing. The activity in which *bears buy back shares that they have sold short. Bear closing is commonly encountered in a bear market and is noticeable towards the end of an *account for its effect of forcing up the price of certain shares. *See also* short selling.

bearer. As used in the Bills of Exchange Act (1882), the person in possession of a bill or cheque that is marked to be payable to bearer or on which the last endorsement is an endorsement in blank. Such a cheque, provided it is not crossed, can be cashed over the counter at the bank to which it is addressed without the presenter having to endorse it, and the banker incurs no liability even if the cheque has been stolen.

bearer bonds. Bonds in which possession is regarded as proof of ownership. They are transferred, without change of registration, simply by handing them over. This being the case, they are usually kept in a bank for security. Each bond has a sheet of coupons attached to it to enable interest to be collected on presentation of a coupon.

bear market. A market in which prices are falling, enabling bears to cover their short sales profitably.

bear position. *See* position.

bear squeeze. A situation in which *bears who have engaged in *short selling are faced with an increase (or a least no reduction) in the price of the share or commodity they have sold short. They therefore have to cover the sales before the end of the delivery period while the price is forced up against them.

bed and breakfast (on the London Stock Exchange). An operation designed to save capital gains tax by making a loss on a holding, without losing the holding. The shareholder sells his holding one evening (after hours) and thus establishes a loss, which can be set against other profits and so save capital gains tax. He makes an unofficial agreement with a jobber (through his broker) to buy the same holding back again when the market opens the following morning at an agreed price. Until April 1975 the Inland Revenue agreed to treat the transaction as two separate deals, as the market price could change overnight. However, from May 1975 it was ruled that companies establishing a loss on shareholdings for capital gains tax purposes through bed and breakfast deals had to wait one month between disposal and acquisition. If the transaction is effected through any medium other than the Stock Exchange or *Ariel, the prescribed gap is six months. For individuals, rather than companies, this restriction does not apply.

beggar-my-neighbour policy. Any economic policy intended to boost the level of economic activity within a country at the expense of its trading partners. It can take the form of tariff barriers or of other policies designed to switch demand from imports to the domestic sector. Currency devaluation is intended to accomplish these ends and also to stimulate exports, although its effectiveness in both respects is still undecided.

Beggar-my-neighbour policies were pursued by several nations in the *Depression of the 1930s. Their inherent danger is that they invite retaliation from trading partners, which can in the end lead to a reduction in the welfare of all concerned.

below-the-line. *See* advertising.

beneficial interest. The right to use and to benefit from an item of property and to take any income produced by it. This right usually belongs to the legal owner of the property but may be vested in some other person; for instance, when the legal owner is merely the trustee or nominee for that other person.

A beneficial interest is also known as an *equitable interest* because it was first recognized in the Courts of Equity (administered by the Chancellor) rather than in the Court of Common Law (administered by the Crown), which would only recognize the rights of the legal owner. When both systems of justice were merged in the 1870s, the rules of equity prevailed over the rules of common law in all courts, and beneficial interests were universally recognized.

beneficial owner. *See* nominee shareholding.

benefit taxation. A theory of taxation in which those who use services are expected to pay for them, regardless of financial circumstances. Examples of such taxes are the tax on petrol, for the finance of road construction and maintenance, and property taxes or rates for the finance of local services. *See also* user charge, ability-to-pay taxation.

Benelux. The association of countries consisting of Belgium, Luxembourg, and the Netherlands. It was agreed in principle in the Treaty of Ouchy (1932) and was formed in 1947 when a customs union was created by the abolition of internal tariffs. The imposition of a common external tariff followed in 1948. Integration continued with agreement on a common trade and payments policy in 1954 and the establishment (between 1958 and 1960) of the free movement of labour and capital between member states. In 1958 Benelux entered the E.E.C. It is the ultimate aim of the union, as stated in the 1960 treaty, to merge completely the fiscal and monetary systems of the three nations.

Bernoulli's hypothesis. A hypothesis put forward in 1730 by Daniel Bernoulli (1700–82) stating that the marginal utility of money income is inversely proportional to the level of income. (*See also* Weber–Fechner Law.) Bernoulli's restrictive assumption concerning the shape of the utility function is less important than the use to which he put it. He observed that choice under conditions of uncertainty (for example, how much of a premium to pay for insurance) was determined not only by the given (or estimated) probabilities, but also by the gain or loss associated with each probability state. Finally he observed in the discussion of the St. Petersburg paradox that individuals derive satisfaction from the use of money and the utility of money is liable to be subject to diminishing returns. Applying this to the principle of *expected utility maximization, Bernoulli was able to explain the paradox of people accepting a finite payoff from a lottery that had an infinite expected income loss by observing that the total potential utility loss could be finite if the marginal utility of money acted according to his hypothesis. In this approach he in part anticipated the work of von Neumann and Morgenstern by two centuries.

Bertrand duopoly. A model of duopolistic competition in which each producer assumes that the other will hold his previous price fixed and that by lowering his own price slightly he can capture the entire market. This will cause a series of price cuts that will stop only at the break-even point of each producer. Unlike the *Cournot duopoly model, this model assumes that firms determine prices, not quantities. *Compare* Edgeworth duopoly. *See* duopoly.

beta. A measure of the sensitivity of a company's share price to market fluctuations, i.e. a measure of market risk.

beta distribution. A statistical *distribution tribution involving a continuous variable. There are two types of beta distribution which, though mathematically related, have different ranges and are appropriate for application in different situations. Either kind can be analysed into a function of two *gamma distributions. The graph of a beta density function can be negatively skewed, unskewed, or positively skewed.

bias. A statistical inaccuracy caused by cumulative errors, i.e. errors that tend to be much more in one direction than the other. For instance, a political opinion poll carried out by interviewing commuters at a railway station would be biased because such a sample would be unrepresentative of the electorate as a whole. If, on the other hand, large amounts of money are rounded to the nearest million pounds, then the errors will not be biased because they will vary randomly between –£500,000 and +£500,000. The concept of bias relates only to the purpose in hand; a sample that is biased for one purpose may be unbiased for another. Results based on a sample that is biased in respect of the purpose for which the sample was taken are always of questionable validity. A random sample by definition is not biased; any errors it contains will be compensating rather than cumulative errors.

bid. 1. The price or terms at which a person is willing to buy. It may be made in response to a seller's *offer, in which case it will be at a lower price than the offer or will demand more favourable terms. The seller may accept the bid, make a *counter-offer, or withdraw. Once a bid has been made against an offer, the offer ceases to be valid.

2. On the London Stock Exchange, the bid price is the lower of two prices quoted by a stockjobber when approached by a stockbroker. *See also* offers, bids, and quotations.

3. An attempt by one company to buy another company's entire shares.

big four. The four major British commercial banks: Barclays, Lloyds, National Westminster, and Midland.

bilateral flow. A movement of money from one sector of the economy to another to match an opposite flow of goods and services. For instance, wages will be paid in return for work and prices will be paid in return for products. *Transfer payments, such as retirement pensions or children's pocket-money, are not bilateral flows since they are not paid in return for services. Government expenditure is a mixture of bilateral and *unilateral flows.

bilateral monopoly. An industry with a single producer and a single buyer, such as producers at intermediate stages of production. Since they cannot both act as price or quantity setters in the market, the models of monopsony or monopoly will not apply unless one agent for some reason manages to dominate the other.

A second possibility is that the two collude in order to maximize joint profits, then bargain together to divide the profits. Other approaches use dynamic or game theory models.

bilateral trade agreements. Trade agreements between two countries. A number of such agreements were made in the 1930s, but they are regarded as disruptive of world trade as a whole: under GATT attempts have been made to replace them with multilateral agreements. Trade between the West and the Communist bloc is still largely conducted on the basis of bilateral agreements.

bill broker. A dealer whose special business is to buy and sell bills of exchange. Bill brokers make their profit by the difference in the rates at which they buy from traders and sell to bankers. Since the decline in the use of the commercial bill, bill brokers now deal largely in Treasury Bills for which they are now the sole tenderers.

Sometimes bill brokers only act as intermediaries between buyers and sellers of bills of exchange.

bill in a set. *See* bill of exchange.

bill of entry. A form on which is entered detailed information about imports. This must be presented to H.M. Customs at the port of arrival before the goods are allowed to enter the country.

bill of exchange. As defined by the Bills of Exchange Act (1882), an unconditional order in writing addressed by one person to another and signed by the person giving it, requiring the person to whom it is addressed to pay on demand or at a fixed or determinable future time a sum certain in money to or to the order of a specified person or to the bearer. Bills were at one time commonly used to finance inland trade, but cheques (which are bills payable on demand drawn on a banker) have superseded them. A foreign bill is drawn up in triplicate, known as a *bill in a set*, each part being sent by separate mail to reduce the risk of loss in transit.

bill of lading. A document that gives the holder the right to acquire possession of goods that have been shipped. It is drawn by the shipowner usually in sets of three, with two copies. The original and one other are sent by separate mails to the consignee; the shipper retains one as evidence that the goods were loaded onto the ship; one copy is handed to the master of the ship, the other being kept by the loading brokers (forwarding agents). The bill of lading states the name of the vessel, the port of embarkation, the port of destination, and the rate of freight and any surcharges. It also gives full particulars of the goods, specifying the marks and numbers on the packages. A clean bill of lading will state that the goods have been loaded in good order, but if the packages are damaged in any way this will be marked on the bill. *See also* clean bill of lading, dirty bill of lading.

bill of sale. A document used to transfer the title to goods to another person. It is often used as a means of borrowing, using one's possessions as security. A *conditional bill of sale* transfers legal ownership of the goods to the lender, but the borrower retakes the title when he repays the debt. The bill of sale must show the rate of interest, the date of repayment, and any other conditions agreed between borrower and lender. The borrower is permitted to retain the goods, but he must not attempt to sell them or allow them to become distrained for rent, rates, or taxes. In these circumstances, or if he becomes bankrupt, the lender may take possession of the goods. A conditional bill of sale may not be for less than £30 and the signatures of both parties must be witnessed, though not necessarily by a solicitor.

An *absolute bill of sale* transfers title to the goods absolutely; the borrower cannot retake possession of them. The bill states when the lender may take possession. An absolute bill of sale has to be witnessed by a solicitor. All bills of sale must be registered and must comply with the requirements of the Bills of Sale Acts.

bill of sight. A document submitted to a customs officer by an importer if he is unable to give a full description of the goods he is importing. This document enables the goods to be landed and authorizes their inspection by the customs officer. Once landed, the importer must supply the full details, a process known as *perfecting the sight*.

bill rate. The rate at which *bills of exchange will be discounted. The quality of the bill determines the rate, being lower on first-class bills.

bills in a set. A set of two or three *bills of exchange all bearing the same reference number. Only one must be accepted, the duplicates being issued to reduce the risk of loss in the post. They are know as the First, Second, and Third of Exchange, respectively.

binary digit. *See* bit.

binary notation. A positional notation for numbers using the base two. The common method of writing numbers, *decimal notation,* employs the base ten: i.e. it has ten symbols 0–9 and numbers higher than 9 are written by placing these symbols in different positions. For example, one hundred and twenty three in decimal notation is written 123, which is equivalent to $1 \times 10^2 + 2 \times 10 + 3$. Binary notation, with base two, requires only two symbols, 0 and 1, and the positions represent powers of two, not ten. Thus 123 in binary would be written 1111011, i.e. $1 \times 2^6 + 1 \times 2^5 + 1 \times 2^4 + 1 \times 2^3 + 0 \times 2^2 + 1 \times 2 + 1$. The notation is extensively used in computer systems, in which the two digits (*bits) can be represented by alternative states of a component. Two other notations are also of use in computer applications: *octal notation*, which has the base 8, and *hexadecimal notation*, which has the base 16.

binomial distribution. A statistical *distribution of a discrete variable that can be characterized as the number of successes (or desired results) in a number of independent trials of an experiment for which there is a fixed probability of success in any single trial. For instance, the number of sixes obtained in four throws of an unbiased die follows a binomial distribution where the number of independent trials is four and the probability of success (obtaining a six) is 1/6. These are the only two independent *parameters required to find the probability of obtaining zero, one, two, three, or four sixes. The probability of failure, equal to 5/6 in the above example, is also required and this can be found by deducting from one the probability of success. The mean of a binomially distributed variable is given by np, where n is the number of trials and p is the probability of success; the variance is given by npq, where q is the probability of failure. A binomial distribution is skewed positively or negatively according to whether p is less than or greater than ½. If p (and q) equals ½ there is no skew. When the number of trials is very large and the probability of success is close to ½, the binomial distribution can be approximated by the normal distribution. The binomial distribution is the most important of the discrete distributions.

birth rate. The *crude birth rate* for any given year is the number of live births per 1000 of the average population for that year. The crude birth rate is obviously dependent on the age distribution of the population and for this reason it is often replaced by the *fertility rate or, in the case of a subpopulation, standardized. The *standardized birth rate* is obtained by dividing the subpopulation into age categories, calculating the crude birth rate for each category, and taking the weighted average of these crude rates. The weights are provided by the percentage subdivisions of a global standard population, often the population of a country as a whole. The birth rate for an entire country is a major demographic statistic, although it should be considered in conjunction with the *infant mortality rate. In industrial countries the birth rate has shown a secular decline, as has the infant mortality rate, since the commencement of industrialization, although there have been cyclical swings such as the postwar "bulge" in 1946-47. In developing nations this has not been the case, but there is a growing awareness in countries such as India that the population must be controlled if the Malthusian poverty cycle is to be avoided.

B.I.S. *See* Bank for International Settlements.

bit. A unit of information used in computer technology. The name, which is a contraction of *binary digit*, is applied to the digits 0 and 1 in *binary notation. In a *computer these can be represented by alternative states of the system. *See also* byte.

bivariate distribution (in statistics). A *distribution involving two random variables. Thus if a card is drawn from an ordinary pack of 52, it can be represented both by its suit and by its denomination. This can be translated into two random variables x and y, where x = 1, 2, 3, or 4 according to the four suits and y = 1, 2, ... 13 according to the 13 denominations, and a bivariate distribution can then be formulated by determining what the probabilities are that any particular card will be randomly selected from the pack. Clearly this probability is 1/52 for any particular card and this is the *joint density function for this particular bivariate distribution. Note that since there are 52 cards in a pack, the sum of the probabilities of the selection of all the individual cards is one. Generally, any bivariate distribution can be defined by a joint density function, although the latter will usually be an algebraic expression involving the random variables *x* and *y* rather than a simple arithmetic constant, as in the example above. *See also* density function.

black economy. Economic activity that goes unrecorded in the national income statistics because payment is made in cash and not declared for income tax, or by barter. In times of high unemployment and economic hardship especially, the black economy is believed to be of huge proportions, amounting to as much as a tenth of the gross national product, thus invalidating the official figures to a considerable degree.

blank cheque. A cheque that is signed by the drawer without the amount having been filled in, usually with the intention that the payee should complete it. Sometimees "Under £ . . . " is added as a safeguard.

blanket policy. An insurance policy that covers all the property insured against fire under one sum, in order to avoid the administrative work of itemizing separate values for each individual fire risk. This requires the insurance to be subject to *average.

blank transfer. The transfer of shares to an unspecified person. The name arises because the space provided for the insertion of the recipient's name on the transfer form is left blank. *See also* transfer form.

bliss point. A point at which a consumer reaches his highest level of satisfaction so that any variation in the combination of goods bought will cause a loss of utility. A bliss point can only exist when the *indifference curves are circular, forming a series of concentric rings around it. This implies that after a certain amount of a good has been consumed any added consumption yields disutility; more of the other good must be provided to compensate for the displeasure created in taking more of the first good. Therefore, a consumer will maximize his utility by consuming the amount of each good at which the marginal utility of each good becomes negative. This is the location of the bliss point.

blocked accounts. Bank accounts that are subject to restrictions imposed by the government of the country in which they are held. This usually happens in wartime when a country is unable to earn much foreign currency and has difficulty in paying for its imports. In such circumstances bank accounts are opened for the foreign exporters in the importing country but are blocked, i.e. any credit balances can only be used for internal transactions, their transfer abroad being forbidden.

blocked currency. Currency that cannot be removed from a country for any reason, especially because of *exchange control regulations or for political reasons.

Blue Book. The informal name given to the Central Statistical Office's annual publication *National Income and Expenditure*. The Blue Book contains all the main aggregates of national income accounting for the previous year and for ten years before that. Social accounting figures and such information as the distribution of trading profits by industry are also included.

blue button. An employee of a firm of stockbrokers who is not authorized to deal on behalf of his firm, but who nevertheless is allowed to enter onto the floor of the London Stock Exchange. (The badge required to be worn by such a person is blue.)

blue chip. An *ordinary share considered to be of the highest quality in the sense that it carries a lower risk than other shares of earnings failure, dividend failure, or bankruptcy. Blue chip status is thus normally assigned to the shares of large and well-established companies. There is no official list of blue chips, although they are sometimes regarded as the 30 companies constituting the *Financial Times Industrial Ordinary Index. The term comes from the game of poker, blue being the chip of highest value.

blue-collar worker. A manual worker, especially one working on the shop floor.

B.N.E.C. *See* British National Export Council.

Board of Trade. The former U.K. government department that was concerned with trade and commerce. It was founded in 1786. Its functions have been taken over by the Department of Trade and Industry.

bond. A security issued by a government, government agency, or private company as a means of raising money. Most are redeemable and carry a fixed rate of interest. Examples of bonds issued by the British government are Defence Bonds and Savings bonds. Bonds are issued in series of like amounts and conditions of repayment.

bonded warehouse. A warehouse, usually at a port, in which imported goods can be stored pending payment of customs duties or re-export. If, for any reason, customs duties on dutiable imported goods are not paid immediately at the port of entry, they are transferred from the ship or aircraft to a bonded warehouse, being released from bond only after the duty has been paid or permission has been granted to ship them out of the country. The owners of bonded warehouses guarantee that the goods will not be released unless the duty has been paid, except in the presence of a customs officer.

bond washing. The purchase of bonds by an investor as soon as they have gone *ex-dividend and their subsequent sale before the next dividend is due, thus minimizing the tax liability, since the profit will be in the form of capital gains (taxed at a flat rate) rather than progressive income tax. This type of investment is attractive to those paying a high rate of income tax.

bonus issue. The issue of shares by a company to its shareholders by way of *capitalization of reserves and for which no cash consideration by shareholders is required. A bonus issue is made in proportion to existing shareholdings so that, for instance, a *1 for 2* bonus issue means that for every two shares held by each shareholder, an extra one will be issued. In this case the company's issued capital would be increased by 50% and their denomination, i.e. their par value, would be reduced by one third. Bonus issues are purely book-keeping transactions since they involve no conveyance of money. They are made in order to increase the marketability of the shares by reducing their average quotation and to satisfy the well-known preference of investors for shares of fairly low denomination (and market price). The effect of a bonus issue on the market price of a share is to reduce it automatically in the same proportion as its par value is reduced. Thus if, prior to a *1 for 2* bonus issue, the shares of a company were quoted at 300p each, their *ex bonus quotation would be 200p. Bonus issues are made quite frequently on the London Stock Exchange. Terms such as *scrip issue*, *capitalization issue*, *share splitting*, and (in the U.S.) *stock split* are virtually synonymous with bonus issue.

books of account. A record of a company's financial affairs on a day-to-day basis. Accounts will be maintained of all assets and liabilities that appear on the balance sheet, subdivided as the company sees fit. The books also contain the various expense and revenue accounts that go to make up the profit and loss account. Further, these books contain whatever *control accounts are considered necessary by the company. In general, the books of account consist of the *nominal ledger and cash book, with back-up information obtainable from the sales and purchase ledgers and their respective day books. Magnetic tapes or discs are now widely used for recording these figures.

book value. The *written-down value* of an asset as shown in the books of a company. It is usually the cost less the total depreciation. This may or may not be the same as the market value.

boom. The phase in the standard *trade cycle following *recovery, in which the economy is working at full capacity, resources are fully utilized, and prices are rising rapidly. An upper limit to economic expansion is reached when all resources are fully utilized, although this state will not be achieved by all firms and some will continue with unwarranted investment. This is the upper turning point of the cycle and may ultimately be followed by a *recession.

Boston matrix. A matrix used in marketing and developed by the Boston Consulting Group to classify products according to their cash usage and cash generation. A "cash cow" is an established product requiring little advertising; it may have 50% of the market share but the market is stagnant. A "star" is a product that is selling well in a growing market. A "problem child" is a product for which there is great opportunity for improvement–an an under-achiever in a growing market. A "dog" is a product with little potential.

B.O.T.B. *See* British Overseas Trade Board.

bottomry bond. A bond that pledges a ship as security. This type of bond may only be taken out by a captain who cannot contact the shipowners and who needs money urgently to complete his voyage. It is a last resort that is only used if money cannot be obtained against the shipowner's credit. A holder of a bottomry bond loses his money if the ship founders. The ship itself cannot be disposed of until all bottomry bonds are paid out.

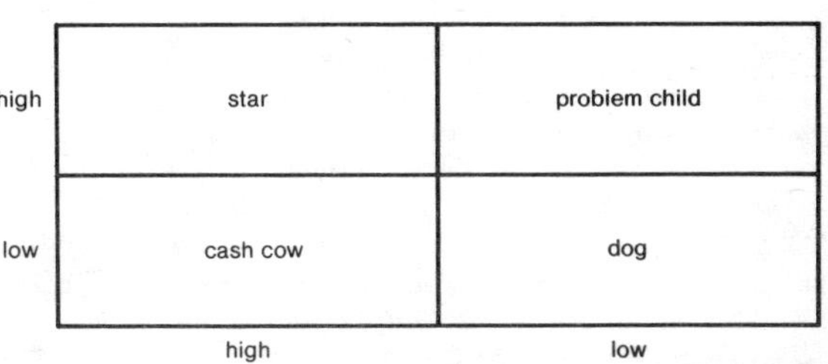

Boston matrix

bought note. A *contract note sent by a stockbroker or commodity broker to his client to confirm a purchase made on his behalf. It will give the details of the purchase, the broker's commission, and the date on which payment has to be made. It will also show any *stamp duty that has been incurred.

bourse. The generic name given to a stock exchange in continental Europe. The term is of French origin but is not restricted to the Paris market.

brackets. *See* income tax.

branch banking. A system of banking in which a small number of banks have a great many branches. The British banking system is a good example, having grown by amalgamation between banks, so that now the big four–Barclays, Lloyds, Midland, and National Westminister–each have thousands of branches and immense reserves. These reserves make for greater stability than the system of *unit banking that operates in the U.S. *See also* state bank, national bank.

brand leader. The most widely sold variety of a product. Its prestige and familiarity to the public are valuable assets that competing firms will vigorously attempt to obtain for their own products. They will often imitate the marketing policies of the brand leader's firm in the hope of similar success. In rare cases the brand leader is so widely known that its tradename becomes synonymous with the name of the product. *See also* price leadership.

brand name. A name by which a good of a certain producer is distinguished from those of other producers in the same industry. It is a prerequisite for product differentiation and is closely linked to the advertising of the product since the name often incorporates some of the characteristics the product is alleged to embody.

break-even point. The price at which the *marginal cost curve of a producer meets the average total cost curve. Assuming the producer is acting in a perfectly competitive market he will set his marginal cost equal to the price, which is also equal to the minimum value of average total cost. At a price any lower than this he will begin to lose money, although possibly not as much as he would if he ceased operations and *indirect costs continued. *See* shut-down point.

break-up value. *See* asset value (per share).

Bretton Woods Conference. An international conference held in 1944 in Bretton Woods, New Hampshire, U.S., by the governments of Canada, the U.S., and the U.K. It sought to establish a new postwar system of international monetary control and led to the establishment of the *International Monetary Fund and the *International Bank for Reconstruction and Development. *See also* American Plan, Keynes Plan.

bridging loan. A short-term loan made to enable a borrower to complete a purchase before he receives funds from another source, for example to buy a new house before he has received payment for his old house.

British Export Board. *See* British Overseas Trade Board.

British Institute of Management. *See* management.

British Insurance Association. The principal association of insurance companies in the U.K. Founded in 1917, its membership is open to all insurance companies authorized by the Department of Trade to transact insurance business in the U.K.

The aim of the association is the protection, promotion, and advancement of the common interests of all classes of insurance business and its main function is to represent the views of insurers in matters affecting their interests. It performs public relations activities in respect of the industry and it maintains constant contact with government departments and other bodies.

The association does not interfere in the underwriting policy or rates of a member, nor does it provide any guarantee of the solvency of any of its members.

British National Export Council (B.N.E.C.). An agency that was set up in 1964 to supersede the Export Council for Europe, the Council for Middle East Trade, the Western Hemisphere Exports Council, and the Commonwealth Exports Council. It was itself superseded by the British Export Board in 1971, called the *British Overseas Trade Board since 1972.

British Overseas Trade Board (B.O.T.B.). An agency of the Department of Trade set up in 1971 as the British Export Board, by which name it was known until 1972. It superseded the *British National Export Council. Its members are businessmen and government representatives from the Department of Trade and Industry and the Foreign and Commonwealth Office. It is concerned with export promotion by trade fairs, export marketing research, aid to British firms operating abroad, etc.

British Standards Institution (B.S.I.). An institution whose purpose is to lay down standards for engineering, building, textile, and chemical products in order to ensure that they are manufactured to a minimum standard of quality and to avoid the manufacture of an uncontrolled multiplicity of designs, sizes, and patterns. The B.S.I. is also active in the fields of units of measurement and technical terminology. It collaborates closely with the International Standards Organization and its publications include glossaries that give precise definitions of units and technical words.

Products that comply with certain standards are entitled to use the *Kite mark as a symbol of quality, provided that the manufacturers agree to regular inspection and control of the product.

The B.S.I. was founded in 1901, received a Royal Charter in 1929, and took its present name in 1931. It is independent of the government, but receives government financial support.

British Technology Group. A U.K. body formed in 1981 by the merger of the *National Enterprise Board (N.E.B.) and the *National Research and Development Corporation (N.R.D.C.). The aim of the group is to combine the technical expertise of the N.R.D.C. with the more commercially orientated N.E.B. to provide a stronger force for stimulating innovation and financing investment in high-technology industries, mainly through joint ventures as opposed to equity investment in companies.

British Textile Confederation. An organization set up on January 1972 to replace the *Textile Council. It encompasses the cotton, wool, man-made fibre, and textile converting sections of the textile industry. Its purpose is to represent textile manufacturers in negotiations with the government and the E.E.C.

broker. An agent employed by a principal to buy or sell goods or services for his account, usually because the broker has specialized knowledge of the market in which he operates or because the principal wishes to conceal his identity. Brokers receive a commission for their services (brokerage) related to the value of the transaction from the buyer, the seller, or both, according to the custom of the trade. *See also* stockbroker, commodity broker, bill broker, insurance broker, shipbroker.

brokerage. The service fee charged to a client by a broker for executing purchase or sale orders in securities, commodities, insurance, etc.

Brookings Institution. An independent U.S. organization that was founded in 1927. It conducts research into the policies and structure of government, foreign policy, economics, and the other social sciences. Its most notable achievement in the U.K. was its report on the U.K.'s economic prospects (1968), which subjected the U.K. to a more intensive analysis than had previously been attempted.

B.S.I. *See* British Standards Institution.

budget. 1. A prediction of the financial behaviour of a business enterprise over a specified period of time. Firstly, a forecast of those external factors that affect the enterprise has to be made and on the basis of this the future level of output and the development of the enterprise must be decided. Once this decision has been made, a budget becomes a detailed analysis of costs (by *cost centres or *cost units) that will be incurred as a result of the determined future trends. Normally these budget figures will be incorporated into the accounting system of control, acting as a monitoring and early-warning device when actual performance deviates from plan. *See also* capital budget, operating budget, principal budget factor.

2. A prediction of government expenditure and revenue for the coming financial year. In the U.K. it is drawn up each year, normally in April, and presented to Parliament by the Chancellor of the Exchequer. In times of financial crisis a budget is sometimes drawn up at other times during the year. The budget is used as an instrument of economic policy, particularly through changes in taxation. *See also* balanced budget.

budget account. An account opened by arrangement with a bank to enable a customer to meet his annual household bills. He lists his major outgoings, divides the total by 12, and instructs the bank to transfer the resulting amount each month from his current account to the budget account. The bank, having a copy of the list, will pay cheques drawn to meet items on it even if in some months the budget account is overdrawn. A similar system is operated by some department stores.

budgetary control. An effective method of monitoring the progress of a business. Initially targets are discussed and agreed for such parameters as output, efficiency, cost minimization, sales, cash flow, etc., for every department in the organization. The actual results achieved, during the course of the year, are compared with these budgets. Any deviations so discovered can be rapidly corrected or the budget altered without waiting for formal accounts to be prepared. The use of computers has greatly extended the scope of budgetary control.

budgetary policy. *See* fiscal policy.

Budget Day Price. The price of a share from which *capital gains (or losses) are assessed for purposes of capital gains tax. Budget Day Price is, for any particular share, the higher of the following two prices: the share's *middle price on the London Stock Exchange *Official List for 6 April 1965 and the *mean of the marks tabulated in the Official List for 6 April 1965 (referring to deals done on that day) and the marks tabulated in the Official List for 7 April 1965 (referring to deals done on the previous day). Marks recorded at special prices are excluded. Budget Day Price is of course relevant for the computation of capital gains tax only when a holding in a share dates from before 6 April 1965.

budget deficit. A budget in which less revenue is raised through taxation, customs duties, etc., than is used in expenditure. Its consequence will be to stimulate the economy and so is used to combat depressions. In practice, most of the budgets in the U.K. in the postwar era have run deficits, the balance being funded by an increase in the *National Debt. *See* balanced budget, budget surplus.

budget equation. An equation representing those "bundles of goods" that may be purchased for a given money income. In partial equilibrium analysis it is represented by the line, the slope of which is the negative of the price ratio, that meets the axes at the points representing possible consumption if all expenditure is concentrated on one good. In general equilibrium analysis it is represented by the line, the slope of which is the negative price ratio, that passes through the bundle of goods that represents the initial allocation of the consumer. It is of importance because under the assumption of no *bliss point it is the constraint that limits the consumer as he seeks to maximize his total satisfaction.

budget line (budget constraint). A straight line on a graph, charting the combinations of goods that a consumer could buy. It shows the maximum combinations of goods that the consumer could obtain with his income, given the prices of the goods. The line intersects each axis at the point at which the greatest amount of each product could be bought, so that nothing is spent on the other. Its slope is determined by the price ratio of the two products. If a consumer buys a combination of goods that places him on a point inside the area bounded by the axes and the budget line, he is not spending all of his income. Points beyond the budget line cannot be reached since they would cost more than the consumer's income. Changes in the level of income will not affect the slope of the budget line, since this is governed by the ratio of the prices of the products. Instead it will cause the budget line to move in or out parallel to the original budget line according to whether income decreases or increases. A change in the price of one good will cause the price ratio to change and therefore the budget line will pivot inwards or outwards according to whether the good becomes more expensive (enabling less to be bought) or less expensive (enabling more to be bought). *Utility maximization occurs when the consumer chooses that combination of goods that places him on the budget line at a point tangential to the highest possible indifference curve. *See diagram at* utility maximization.

budget surplus. An excess of revenue over expenditure in the national budget. Its effect will be to reduce the level of activity in the economy. *See* balanced budget, budget deficit.

buffer stock. A stock of a raw material, built up by a government or trade organization, with a view to stabilizing prices and damping out exaggerated swings in price. The buffer-stock manager is provided with funds enabling him to buy the commodity in question if it falls below a fixed price. This is to ensure that the price never falls below a profitable level for production of the commodity, thus helping to ensure continuity of supply. If the price should rise above an upper fixed price, the buffer-stock manager is empowered to sell the commodity on the open market to hold the price down, thus helping to restrain the commodity from pricing itself out of the market. Although buffer stocks are not always completely effective in containing prices during slumps and booms, they have in some cases proved themselves remarkably efficient. The buffer stock maintained by the International Tin Council is an example of an effective buffer stock. *See also* international commodity agreements.

building society. An institution that accepts deposits from the investing public at a rate of interest, and uses the funds so obtained to lend on mortgage, at a higher rate of interest, to people who wish to purchase their own houses. These loans are repaid by monthly instalments over a term of years. The operations of building societies are regulated by Acts of Parliament (1834, 1874, and 1962), and are controlled by the Registrar of Building Societies. Interest paid to building societies may be deductible from taxable income in certain circumstances, and interest earned on deposits is not subject to ordinary income tax. Rates of interest paid by building societies vary according to the rate of interest paid by banks and to the type of account. Some larger societies have recently challenged the *banks by providing investors with cheque accounts on which they pay interest and on which they make no charges if a minimum sum is kept in the account.

built-in obsolescence. *See* obsolescence.

built-in software. Programs that are sold as part of the computer, for example text editing and financial planning programs.

built-in (automatic) stabilizers. Policies or institutions that automatically act to dampen fluctuations in income, employment, etc., without specific government intervention. If the national income falls then income tax receipts fall, so increasing the budget deficit and having an opposite but necessarily smaller effect on income (a decrease in taxation will stimulate spending and thus stimulate the economy). A rise in unemployment raises total payments of unemployment benefit, which has a reflationary effect on income and employment.

Built-in stabilizers are a very desirable item in the management of an economy, but are difficult to design and are not usually very effective.

bulk carrier. A ship designed specifically to carry a particular bulk cargo (ores, coal, grain, etc.), which is generally homogeneous, of relatively low value, and capable of being loaded by gravity.

bull. 1. A person who expects prices, especially of shares and commodities, to rise.

2. An operator on a stock exchange or commodity market who expects prices to rise and therefore buys in the hope of selling (often in the near future) for a gain. A stale bull is one who has made such a purchase but is unable to liquidate his holding profitably either because the market has declined or remained static or because there are no buyers. *Compare* bear.

bullion. Gold and silver in bars. The word is also used when referring to large quantities of coins by weight. Until 1925 when the Gold Standard Act became law, anyone had the right, provided that the value was not less than £20,000, to take bar gold of sufficient fineness to the Mint and have it coined, but since that Act the right is confined to the Bank of England.

bull market. A market in which price are rising, enabling bulls to operate profitably.

bull position. *See* position.

buoyancy. The rising of government revenue in times of inflation. During an inflationary period the yield from direct taxation and ad valorem indirect taxation will rise as nominal incomes and prices increase. It is often asserted that governments favour mild inflation as a useful means of increasing revenue, without the need to increase tax rates.

burden of debt. The size of the interest payment due on the *National Debt passed on to future generations. The debt arises from the government's financing of a deficit by borrowing through the issue of government bonds. There is some dispute as to whether such a debt really causes a burden if it is completely owed to citizens of the country, since the interest is paid from tax receipts and further borrowing, which represents a *transfer payment within the country rather than a usage of real resources. It effects some change in the distribution of income but even this is limited since the holders of government stock earning this interest are usually in the higher income tax brackets so that their income tax is in part returned to them in the form of interest. It is thus an internal loan and leaves output unchanged, and as such it does not impose a burden on future generations. If, however, the financing of government deficits through loan finance (i.e. the issue of bonds) lowers saving relative to the amount of saving when tax finance is used, then the stock of capital passed on is lower and real output in the future will be lower. The part of the National Debt that is owed to other countries does constitute a burden since the balance of payments is adversely affected by the interest payments.

Bureau of the Mint. *See* mint.

business cycle. *See* trade cycle.

Business Expansion Scheme. A scheme introduced by the British government in 1983 to encourage investment in small expanding businesses by offering substantial tax advantages to investors. Under the scheme private individuals can claim tax relief at their top rate on investments in new equity in unquoted companies up to a maximum of £40,000 per year. In addition to single investments made by private individuals a number of financial institutions have established special funds making it possible for investors to pool their capital and spread the risks involved over a number of small business investments.

business interruption policies. *See* consequential loss policies.

business reply service. A service provided by the Post Office to enable firms to receive cards or letters from their clients without putting the clients to the expense of paying the postage. The firm must first apply to its local head postmaster for a licence and will usually be required to deposit sufficient money to cover the likely cost of the postage. The reply-paid coupon used by the client must take the form of a card, envelope, folder, or label of a specified design and size. Postage is charged on the number of replies received.

buy earnings. To buy a share that has a low or unattractive *yield but an impressive record of earnings growth. Such a share might well have a high *cover. An investor who buys earnings is thus taking a medium to long-term view: he hopes that the high earnings growth will continue and that the ploughing back of profits contingent on a low dividend pay-out ratio will accelerate the growth in the asset value of the share so that at some point in the foreseeable future an enhanced dividend yield will emerge and the capital gain shown by the share price will be greater than would have been the case with a lower-growth share.

buyer's market. A market in which supply exceeds demand and buyers can dictate the prices. If, however, they are only prepared to buy at prices that are too low, there may cease to be any sellers. The market may then become a *seller's market.

buying in. If a seller of shares, commodities, etc., fails to deliver the documents or goods that he has contracted to sell on a particular date, the buyer has the right to buy in the missing shares or commodities against him, debiting him with any market differences or unavoidable expenses incurred. In practice, this process will serve to establish a claim against the defaulter but is unlikely to make good the loss as the seller would not have defaulted if he could have met the market differences.

byte. A unit of information used in computer technology. It is equal to eight *bits. One character of information can be held in one byte. 1024 bytes equal one *kilobyte*, abbreviated to *kB* or simply *k*. One million bytes equal one *megabyte* (*MB*).

C

C. A programming language developed in 1972 and now widely used. The language is operationally very efficient and was originally designed as a language in which the operating system Unix could be writen; this made Unix more easily portable between different machines.

C.A.C.M. *See* Central American Common Market.

C.A.D. *See* cash against document.

calculus. An analytical branch of mathematics concerned with rates of change between related variables. Two areas of calculus can be distinguished: differential calculus (differentiation) and integral calculus (integration). The former is concerned with the rate at which a dependent variable changes as its explanatory variable (or variables) changes. Consider the consumption function, which postulates aggregate consumption to be a function of aggregate disposable income. The rate at which consumption changes as disposable income changes is Keynes's marginal propensity to consume, which is normally considered to be positive but less than one. The marginal propensity to consume is thus the *first derivative*, or the *differential*, of the consumption function: the fact that it is positive indicates a direct correlation between consumption and disposable income while the convention that it is less than unity implies that consumption changes proportionately less than disposable income. Conversely, a negative first derivative would indicate an inverse correlation, as between the speculative demand for money and the average level of interest rates. Thus the sign of the first derivative indicates direct or inverse correlation while its magnitude indicates the proportionate relationship between the dependent and independent variable. Differential calculus can be carried beyond this first stage and the *second derivative* can be calculated. The second derivative represents the rate of change of a dependent variable with respect to an independent variable to which it is related. It can be interpreted as representing whether a dependent variable rises or falls at an accelerating or decelerating rate as an independent variable changes. Integral calculus is the reverse of differential calculus: it involves finding the primary relationship (the *integral*) between a dependent and independent variable from a knowledge of the rate of change of the former with respect to the latter. Geometrically, an integral can be represented by an area under a curve; this interpretation is especially useful in that part of statistical theory dealing with the probability distributions of continuous variables. Economic applications of integral calculus include the calculation of a total function from a marginal function, the computation of the time path of capital formation given a rate of investment flow and an initial capital stock, and the derivation of the present value of a continuous cash flow. In statistics integral calculus is applicable to operations involving continuous variables whereas summation is applicable in the case of discrete variables. There are well-established mathematical techniques for calculating derivatives and integrals for any explicit function. Calculus, both differential and integral, is widely used as a tool of analysis in economic theory, in statistics, and in econometrics. To it has been added in more recent years the techniques of *matrix algebra and these two–calculus and matrix algebra –now comprise the basics of quantitative analysis in economics.

called-up capital. The portion of a share's price that is immediately payable. When a company issues shares, it may only ask for a proportion of the nominal price to be paid initially, perhaps 60p for every £1 share. This is the called-up capital. The remaining portion, in this case 40p per share, is a reserve that may be called upon later, perhaps to finance additional investment. This practice has now become rare.

call money. 1. Usually appearing under the heading *money at call and short notice* in the balance sheet of a bank, it is one of the more liquid assets, being the money lent to discount houses, bill brokers, and stockbrokers and jobbers. It is repayable on demand or, in the case of the bill market, within seven days. Money lent to the Stock Exchange is repayable within fourteen days. **2.** Money paid for a call *option on the London Stock Exchange or for a commodity.

call option. *See* option.

call over. A method of trading, used in some *commodity markets, in which dealers and brokers meet together at fixed times during the day to call over the prices of the commodity. The commodities traded in this way are those that can be graded accurately and sold on the basis of a standard sample (e.g. sugar, coffee, cocoa, metals, etc.): those that cannot be graded are usually sold by *auction. The call-over method is usually restricted to trading in futures (*see* futures markets) in which there may be substantial daily price fluctuations. Traders form a circle (for this reason this method of trading is sometimes called *ring trading*) and call out the prices at which they are willing to buy or sell each future position; in some markets they also specify the quantity. When there are both buyers and sellers at the same price, business is concluded. The rules of each market differ slightly, but all transactions are verbal and are based on a standard contract, which is exchanged after the call over. Payment is usually by differences through a *clearing house.

call up. *See* partly paid shares.

c. & f. *See* cost and freight.

C.A.P. *See* Common Agricultural Policy.

capital. An artificial factor of production, developed from *land, whose creation involves a sacrifice of present consumption. Its use in the productive process increases efficiency and output and this increase is the reward for abstention from consumption. Capital may be divided into fixed or concrete capital, circulating capital, and wealth. Fixed capital are those goods that lose comparatively little of their value during each cycle of production. Examples are plant, machinery, and tools. Circulating capital comprises stocks of raw materials, finished goods, etc., which will rapidly be used up. Wealth, in this sense, is paper capital, i.e. stocks, bonds, debentures, money, etc. The variation in the stock of capital in a country is explained by a *depreciation in the value of existing capital together with an addition to capital provided by investment. Investment is usually greater than depreciation so that the stock of capital normally increases.

capital account. *See* balance of payments.

capital allowances. The allowances that can be claimed by a company for tax purposes against the cost of fixed assets, e.g. machinery, plant, motor vehicles, industrial buildings, hotels, agricultural buildings, patents, etc. These allowances vary from time to time and in the U.K. major changes took place in 1972 and 1984. Capital allowances encourage investment and thus increase the level of production.

capital asset. *See* fixed asset.

capital budget. A long-term *budget relating to predictions and developments that take place over a greater time period than those considered by an *operating budget.

capital commitments. The capital expenditure that a firm has committed itself to but has not actually paid. For example, a new piece of machinery may have been ordered but not paid for or delivered. Such capital commitments must, according to the Companies Acts (1948–1981), be shown in the accounts of all U.K. companies.

capital consumption. Aggregate depreciation of all physical capital in an economy during a specified period of time. Capital consumption is the item that is deducted from gross national product and gross domestic product to obtain net figures. Its calculation is one of the most difficult statistical problems in national income accounting.

capital, cost of. The cost to a firm of all existing and potential sources of capital, measured as a rate of interest calculated by weighting the proportions of each source. Even though a firm may finance one project with one type of finance and another with a different type it is the overall mix of financing that is important. All sources of finance (including retained earnings) have a cost, including an *opportunity cost (the rate of return on an investment should be at least comparable with that for other projects).

Some authorities favour using the cost of capital as the discount rate when applying the discounted cash-flow technique in deciding whether or not to make an investment.

capital deepening. Capital stock growth in which capital is caused to grow at a greater rate than the labour force, causing the *capital-labour ratio to rise.

capital expenditure. The purchase of fixed assets, e.g. plant and machinery, for the purpose of increasing future production. Unlike *capital formation it does not involve an increase in the assets of a country, there merely being a transfer of assets from one individual or organization to another.

capital formation (capital accumulation). The increase of a country's stock of fixed capital assets (plant and equipment), either replacing old stock or adding new stock, and excluding repairs and maintenance. Net capital formation is the gross value of capital formation with depreciation deducted. Capital formation comes from savings, used directly for the purchase of materials and labour or indirectly through the purchase of securities or as bank deposits (which may be loaned out to industry). Initial capital formation is the most difficult stage in the industrialization of underdeveloped countries. However, once some capital has been accumulated, further accumulation becomes easier: as output increases so it becomes more feasible to increase capital.

capital gain. A realized increase in the monetary value of an asset. Capital gains tend to arise when demand for the asset exceeds supply over a period of time and when the asset does not depreciate through wear and tear. During periods of inflation monetary capital gains tend to arise even when there is no secular movement in demand-supply relationships. Capital gains derived from inflation are not necessarily real gains and it can be argued that it is inequitable to tax such gains; since 1982 in the U.K. the original cost of assets being sold can be scaled up by indexation (i.e. in proportion to the retail price index). Examples of assets on which capital gains might be expected to accrue are real estate, property, works of art, and stocks and shares. The Finance Act (1962) imposed tax on short-term capital gains, i.e. gains arising on assets resold within six months of purchase. The Finance Act (1965) extended the short-term nature of such gains to 12 months and introduced separate and less onerous taxation on long-term gains, i.e. gains accruing from assets sold more than 12 months after purchase. This distinction between short-term gains and long-term gains has now been abolished (except in connection with *gilt-edged securities) and a single tax rate of 30% now applies to all capital gains, after the first £5600 (1984/5 figures), which is tax free. Exemptions from this tax include gains on the sale of personal belongings, notably principal dwelling houses, and also on the sale of gilt-edged securities where such sale takes place at least 12 months after purchase. All gains arising from share transactions are assessable for capital gains tax, although *capital losses are deductible from the assessment.

capital gains tax. *See* capital gain.

capital gearing. *See* gearing.

capital goods (producer goods). Goods that are used in the production of other goods rather than sold to consumers, e.g. industrial machinery, raw materials, transportation equipment, factories, etc. *Compare* consumer goods.

capital-intensive industry (firm). An industry or firm in which a high proportion of the costs are due to the purchase, maintenance, and amortization of capital equipment and in which a relatively low proportion is due to labour. Printing is a capital-intensive industry, whereas publishing is a *labour-intensive industry.

capitalism (free *or* **private enterprise).** An economic and political system in which individuals are free to transact business on their own account, in order to maximize their profits, and to own capital and the means of production. An important aspect is the freedom of choice of consumers: what they choose to consume is what will be produced. Under pure capitalism there would be no state interference in the economic sphere but in all capitalist countries today there is some state intervention, for example in running certain industries that are not attractive to private enterprise since they may offer no certain profit. In addition, monetary and fiscal policies are applied in order to achieve such objectives as price stability or sustained growth.

Karl Marx viewed capitalism as a historical stage in political development, following feudalism and to be succeeded by socialism and finally communism. He believed that revolution was inevitable under capitalism. However, although Marx predicted that the living standards of the working classes must inevitably decline under capitalism, they have in fact risen greatly. *See also*communism, mixed economy, socialism.

capitalization. 1. *See* market capitalization.

2. The structure and amount of the long-term capital of a company. This will comprise issued ordinary shares and any of issued preference shares, debentures and loan capital, capital reserves, revenue reserves, and (in the case of a group of companies) capital supplied by *minority interests. Bank overdrafts may be included as part of a company's capitalization although they are not technically long-term sources of capital.

3. The conversion, as by a *bonus issue, of reserves into issued shares.

capitalization issue. *See* bonus issue.

capitalized value. The capital equivalent of periodic income (usually property income) as assessed by reference to an appropriate rate of interest and the annual amount of the income. Thus the capitalized value of an asset yielding £100 per year is £1000 if the rate of interest prevailing for such assets is 10% p.a. If this rate were to fall to 5% p.a., then the capitalized value of the income would rise to £2000; i.e. £100/0.05. Capitalized value is not necessarily a satisfactory method of valuation; for example, the market value of a plot of land with development potential might greatly exceed the capitalized value of the present rental income accruing to the owner.

capital-labour ratio. The proportion of capital to labour in an aggregate economy. It is most important in an economy with two factors of production and a constant-returns-to-scale *production function. In this case production per head may be regarded as a function of the ratio of capital to labour only, not of their absolute levels. Furthermore, the marginal rate of technical substitution is constant along a ray through the origin, a line along which the capital-labour ratio is constant. If Y is output, K is capital, and L is labour, then:

$$Y/L = F(K,L)/L = F(K/L, L/L) = f(K/L).$$

This representation is important in neoclassical models of balanced growth, such as the *Solow model.

capital levy. A tax on private capital rather than on income. It is regarded as a form of robbery by the wealthy and as a fair means of redistributing wealth by the poor. Governments are rarely inclined to resort to it, but the U.K. government's thinly disguised surtax surcharge of 1968 amounted to a miniature capital levy, as it taxed the highest rate of unearned income at over 100%. No capital levy could provide the government with a significant source of revenue: it is usually regarded as a possible means of redistributing income or reducing the *National Debt. Capital levies are unlikely to be imposed in the U.K. in the near future because of the excessive costs of collection, and the possibility of a dislocation of the capital market causing an outflow of foreign capital, which in turn would exacerbate the balance of payments difficulties.

capital loss. A realized decrease in the monetary value of an asset. The term is not applied to assets that depreciate through time or through wear and tear, such as motor cars or industrial plant and machinery. Rather it is used in connection with the same type of assets on which *capital gains are made. Capital losses as defined in this way can be established as *tax losses, i.e. are deductible from any assessment for capital gains tax.

capital malleability. The possibility of a change in use of a capital good after it has been incorporated into the *capital stock. Perfectly malleable capital may be used in any production process or in varying relative intensities to other factors regardless of past use. Departures from perfect malleability occur, for example, in a two-sector model, where capital initially used in one sector cannot be transferred to the other, or in models of *fixed proportions where relative levels of factors in a production process may not be varied after the investment has been made. *See also* putty-clay.

capital market. The market for long-term sources of capital. The demand side of the market is represented by industry, commerce, the government, local authorities, etc., which require long-term funds for fixed investment; the supply side is represented by stock exchanges and by savers and saving institutions, such as insurance companies, unit trusts, pension funds, and banks (although bank overdrafts are not normally considered to be capital market products). In terms of company balance sheets, the share capital and long-term debt items will have been obtained from the capital market. Capital markets are not of course solely concerned with the provision of new sources of capital, but also with the exchange of, and dealings in, claims to existing sources. In the U.K., the London Stock Exchange is no longer important as a source of capital although it does of course retain singular importance as far as the exchange of existing claims, namely stocks and shares, is concerned. Most developed capitalist nations have sophisticated and inter-dependent capital markets, but their absence or elementary development in developing nations is a major obstacle to the economic progress of such countries. *See also* money market.

capital movements. The transfer of funds from one nation to another by private individuals or companies. Capital movements may be for either long-term or short-term gains. Capital movements that fall into the first category are mainly for investment purposes, e.g. when a U.K. firm creates a subsidiary abroad or when a foreign organization invests in U.K. securities. Short-term movements are mainly speculative, e.g. to take advantage of changes in interest rates or to benefit from, or avoid, a revaluation (or devaluation) of a currency.

capital profit. A profit that arises from the sale of assets rather than as a result of trading or the practice of a profession.

capital reserves. The funds in a company that may not be distributed to shareholders. It includes share premiums, etc.

capital reversing. A condition arising in constructing the *factor price frontier when, as the rate of profit decreases, technique on the *envelope curve switches to another method of production with a lower level of capital per head instead of a higher one. If a *surrogate production function is constructed in such a case, it will show *isoquants concave to the origin and the results justifying an aggregate approach to the distribution of income between the factors will be invalidated.

capital saturation. The state that occurs when capital reaches its *intensive margin relative to labour. At this point the marginal productivity of capital has fallen to zero. That is, the capital-labour ratio is so high that further increases of it do not lead to an increase in output per head. If the distinction is made between gross output and output net of depreciation then capital saturation occurs when additions to the capital-labour ratio generate increases in output not greater than the level of depreciation.

capital-saving invention. An industrial invention that reduces the amount of capital required in a process. Such inventions cause less industrial unrest than labour-saving inventions but are very much less frequent. Most inventions tend to reduce the labour content of a process with only an incidental saving of capital.

capital stock. The accumulated stock of past purchases of capital goods after deducting depreciation and the amount scrapped because of *obsolescence. It is the total capital available to a firm, industry, or economy, and it is the relevant quantity to enter into the *production function. The contents of the capital stock may be of different ages and so of different efficiencies, but an asset of whatever age will be kept in use until the *net present value of its future earnings becomes zero.

capital structure. The composition of the long-term capital reserves of a company. It will vary with the methods used in raising the capital (in rights issues, debentures, loans, etc.), which in turn will be governed by other considerations (liability to taxation, anticipated profits, future policies, etc.).

capital transfer tax. A U.K. tax, introduced by the Finance Act (1975) and designed to replace *estate duty. It applies to all transfers of capital from one person to another during the donor's lifetime and at death. It is a progressive tax. For transfers made within three years of death and at death, the following rates apply (1984/5 figures):

£0–£64,000	nil
£64,001–£85,000	30%
£85,001–£116,000	35%
£116,001–£148,000	40%
£148,001–£185,000	45%
£185,001–£232,000	50%
£232,001–£285,000	55%
£285,001 and above	60%

For transfers made earlier than three years before death, the first £64,000 is still exempt and the higher rates are half those given above. There are certain exemptions, particularly those between husband and wife, transfers of not more than £3000 by any one person in each year, gifts of not more than £250 to one person in each year, wedding gifts by parents (up to £5000), grandparents (£2500), and others (£1000), and transfers to charities in certain circumstances. If the annual exemption of £3000 is not used up in one year the remainder can be carried forward to the following year only. The tax is generally payable by the donor (except for transfers at death) unless there are specifications in the gift to the contrary.

capital turnover. The ratio of the annual sales of a company to its invested capital.

capital widening. A type of capital stock growth by which capital is caused to grow at the same rate as the labour force. The two factors, then, grow in the same proportion, keeping the *capital-labour ratio constant, while the economy increases in scale.

cardinal utility. A concept that ascribes a quantifiable measure of utility to each good. It holds that a definite number of units of satisfaction (often known as *utils*) flow from each good. A play might yield 30 utils for a consumer, whereas a film might yield 10 utils, so that the consumer would choose to see the play. *Ordinal utility is invariably preferred to cardinal utility, since its assumptions are less open to question and it has equal predictive power.

card punch. *See* punched card.

card reader. *See* punched card.

cargo insurance. A form of insurance in which a shipper or consignee covers risks to his cargo. The insurance of cargo is arranged on a voyage basis, whether by sea or by air. However, an organization that is regularly shipping goods abroad will usually make arrangements for *open cover or for a *floating policy to provide automatic cover on the basis of a declaration made after shipment.

The question of who arranges and pays for the insurance of cargo depends on the conditions of sale. On an F.O.B. contract, the seller's responsibilities end once the goods are loaded aboard the carrying vessel and thereafter the consignee takes over responsibility for the goods, including the responsibility of arranging whatever insurance he considers necessary. On a c.i.f. contract, the seller has responsibility for arranging the shipment of the goods to the port of destination and of providing insurance cover. On a c. & f. contract, the seller is responsible for the shipment, but it is the buyer's responsibility to cover the insurance.

Cargo may be covered *free of particular average* (F.P.A.) or *with average* (W.A.). F.P.A. insurance covers the goods against total loss by sea perils or loss attributable to fire or collision. It includes cover for any contribution payable in the event of general *average. This type of insurance is usually employed for goods that are not easily damaged. W.A. insurance covers these risks and additionally the risk of damage or partial loss by sea water or heavy weather. Although W.A. does provide better protection than F.P.A., cover is still limited and it is customary to include such supplementary risks as damage by fresh water, oil, hooks, etc., or to insure on an *all risks* basis. Most cargo insurance policies are based on the *Institute cargo clauses. It is also usual to include *war risk* as set out in the Institute war clauses as well as the strikes, riots, and civil commotions clauses.

CARICOM. *See* Caribbean Community.

carriage costs. The cost of delivering goods within the U.K. may be borne by the seller or the buyer. If the seller pays the cost of delivery, by road, rail, etc., the price quoted will include the statement *carriage paid* (or *carriage free*, if he is using his own delivery service). If the buyer has to bear the cost of delivery the price will be *carriage forward.*

Caribbean Community (CARICOM). A group of Caribbean nations linked by a treaty signed in 1973 establishing a common market and a common external tariff. Aims are economic integration, cooperation in other areas, such as health and education, and coordination of foreign policy. Members are Antigua, Bahamas, Barbados, Belize, Dominica, Grenada, Guyana, Jamaica, Montserrat, St. Kitts-Nevis, St. Lucia, St. Vincent and the Grenadines, and Trinidad and Tobago. The Community has its headquarters in Guyana.

carry-over. 1. The quantity of a commodity remaining in the hands of producers at the end of one crop or season. The prices of such commodities as sugar, grain, coffee, jute, etc., in the absence of imposed controls, depend on supply and demand. The supply at a particular time consists of

the yield from the current or next crop plus the carry-over from the previous crop. In any system for predicting prices the anticipated carry-over must be taken into account as well as the anticipated yield of the next crop.
2. *See* contango.

cartel. An association of businesses formed for the purpose of regulating prices, outputs, or market conditions in an industry. The cartel may be national or international but the purpose is generally to exercise certain aspects of monopoly power in order to secure greater profits for its members. These activities are not always, however, illegal or undesirable. International cartels may operate between national government monopolies or regulated industries. Examples of these are the International Air Transport Association (I.A.T.A.) and the steel and munitions cartels headed by Krupp in the 1930s in Germany.

Cartels that are created solely to increase profits are regarded as being inherently unstable as eventually the more efficient members would profit by breaking the constraints. This in turn would lead to the cartel's destruction.

cascading. A description applied to a tax or tariff that is imposed on total value at various stages of production. The result is that a good passing between producers in several countries during the course of production is taxed at a higher rate than one that does not. *V.A.T. and the policy of *drawbacks are intended to offset this effect.

cash. Money in the form of notes and coins, still the most widely used method of payment. The term is also used for immediate payment as opposed to credit.

cash against document (C.A.D.). A method of payment for goods exported. The shipping documents are sent to a bank or agent at the port of destination and are given to the consignee when he pays the sum due. Having paid for and obtained the documents the consignee can obtain the goods when the ship arrives. This is also known as *documents against presentation.*

cash book. A book containing a detailed record of all the cash payments and cash receipts of a company. At the end of each period, usually a week or a month, the balance on the cash book (or books) should be reconciled to the balance as shown by the bank statement (or statements). This is normally considered an essential check on the accuracy of the records.

cash dealings. Dealings on the Stock Exchange to be settled the following day.

cash discount. *See* discount.

cash dispenser. A form of slot machine for supplying cash. It is a time- and labour-saving device, which when installed by a bank is operated by the customer inserting a plastic card on which his personal code is embossed enabling his account to be debited with the amount of cash obtained.

cash flow. Movement of money into and out of an enterprise, consisting of all its receipts and payments of cash. Given the adoption of the *accruals concept this is not necessarily the same as measuring the profit or loss of a company and frequently can be very different from it. However, cash flow projections (the anticipated rate of actual money movements) are of considerable importance in the making of management decisions. Obviously a company cannot make a decision requiring the outflow of sums of money that it either does not have or cannot borrow.

cash on delivery (C.O.D.). A service provided by the Post Office to enable businesses (especially mail-order houses) to send parcels by post for payment by the purchaser to the postman on delivery. The service is available to some overseas countries, the maximum amount to be collected not exceeding £50 (or £350 if the parcel is collected from the nearest post office).

Some businesses and stores also provide a C.O.D. service, using their own delivery vans.

cash ratio. The amount of cash reserve (in hand or deposited at the Bank of England) that a bank considers it necessary to keep in order to satisfy the demands of its customers for ready cash, in relation to the total of its liabilities made up of customers' credit balances on all types of accounts. Although there is no legal cash ratio imposed on U.K. banks the Bank of England agreed that as from 1 January 1947 the daily ratio should be on the basis of 8%. By open market operations the Bank of England can change the cash reserves of the commercial banks and thus their credit policy can be controlled because of the necessity for them to maintain their cash ratios.

In the U.S., the Federal Reserve authorities have power to vary cash ratios (which are not the same throughout the country) as they consider necessary.

catastrophe risk. An insurance risk in which the potential loss is of catastrophic proportions, e.g. a nuclear power station disaster.

Cauchy distribution. A statistical *distribution involving a continuous variable. A Cauchy variable is the ratio of two sums of observations on two independent standard normal variables. It is also a special case of *Student's t distribution with one degree of freedom. It is a relatively obscure distribution with a mean only in a restricted sense and no higher moments.

caveat emptor. (Latin for: let the buyer beware.) A rule of English law, stating that the seller of any goods has no obligation to point out to a purchaser any defect in the goods. It is up to the purchaser to inspect them and if he buys them without doing so, or without noticing a defect, he can recover nothing from the seller. This rule has been eroded in recent years by certain statutes, such as the Defective Premises Act (1972), which gives the purchaser of a defective house certain remedies, and the Sale of Goods Act (1979), which implies in contracts for the sale of goods that the goods are of a certain standard. Some court decisions are also contrary to the principle; for example, a manufacturer of goods is now liable to compensate the ultimate consumer of the goods if he is injured as a result of a lack of care in their manufacture; the seller also has a duty to warn the purchaser of known dangerous defects in the goods, which are not apparent from inspection.

C.B.I. *See* Confederation of British Industry.

C.C.A. *See* current cost accounting.

census. An official enumeration usually carried out for the purpose of providing demographic, economic, or social information. Censuses of population have been carried out in the U,K. every ten years since 1801; from 1966 there has been a supplementary one every five years after the major census. *See also* Census of Distribution, Census of Production.

Census of Distribution. A census of wholesale and retail distribution and certain other service trades, first carried out in 1950 and repeated approximately every five years since then.

Census of Production. A census of the output of all manufacturing industries, mines, quarries, building trades, and of all public utility services. Since 1968 a Census of Production has been taken each year. The census provides information used in the formulation of indices of industrial production and of wholesale prices and in the estimation of national income aggregates. *See also*Index of Industrial Production.

Central American Common Market (C.A.C.M.). A customs union resulting from a succession of treaties, the last being signed in Managua in 1960. It came into effect the following year, establishing a common market between El Salvador, Guatemala, Honduras, and Nicaragua. Costa Rica became a full member in 1962. It has been successful in abolishing 97% of intrazonal tariffs and coordinating a common external tariff on 98% of items of trade. Conflict between El Salvador and Honduras in 1969 led to an interruption of trade between the two and the withdrawal of Honduras from the common market in 1970.

central bank. A bank that works closely with its country's government to implement the monetary policy of the country. It acts as banker to the government and the commercial banks, controls the gold reserves and the note issue, and regulates the supply of credit. Most countries now have a central bank. The *Bank of England has gradually become a central bank, Germany and France have had central banks since the 1800s, and in the U.S. the *Federal Reserve System, established in 1913, acts as a central bank.

central limit theorem. A statistical theorem by which it can be demonstrated that the mean of a random sample drawn from a population with any distribution will itself tend towards the normal distribution as the sample size increases indefinitely. The central limit theorem is important because it enables hypotheses concerning the mean of any distribution to be tested by methods requiring a normally distributed variable, provided that large samples are taken.

central processing unit (C.P.U.). The part of a *digital computer in which the data is processed.

Central Statistical Office (C.S.O.). A U.K. government department responsible for the collection and coordination of statistics relevant to the national economy. Its purpose is the preparation and analysis of national income aggregates and social accounts as a basis for government financial and economic policy and for publication in the *Blue Book.

central unit. *See* Treasury.

certificate of incorporation. *See* incorporated company.

certificate of origin. A document that states the country from which a shipment of goods has originated. Most important trading countries agree to accept certificates of origin issued by official authorities or by organizations designated by their respective governments to issue such certificates. The organizations designated by the U.K. government are chambers of commerce affiliated to the Association of British Chambers of Commerce.

Determination of origin is not always easily decided. For example, a raw material may be shipped from India and processed in the U.K. When the U.K. processor comes to export it to, for example, a Common Market country he may obtain a preferential tariff if he is able to provide a U.K. certificate of origin; this would not be applicable if the country of origin was India. Origin is decided by various regulations or is at the discretion of the issuing authority.

certified accountant. *See* accountant.

cesser of action. The stopping by one court of proceedings pending in another court. This usually applies to bankruptcies in which a bankruptcy court may stop proceedings pending in another court against the bankrupt.

C.E.T. *See* common external tariff.

ceteris paribus. (Latin for: other things being equal.) A constraint introduced into an economic argument when one wishes to examine the changes induced by a variation in one of the variables alone, holding the others constant.

chain stores. A group of shops belonging to the same firm and selling the same range of products. They are usually situated in the principal towns of a country and may be large department stores or smaller shops that specialize in a limited range of products (such as food stores, chemist shops, shoe shops, etc.).

chairman. **1.** A person who presides over a meeting. In a formal meeting all remarks are addressed to the chairman, rather than to others participating in the meeting.

2. The most senior office in a public or private company. Very often the chairman is a figurehead who does not take an active part in the day-to-day decisions and is frequently a past managing director. Sometimes the offices of managing director and chairman are combined in the same person, especially in a small company in which that person is the majority shareholder.

chamber of commerce. An organization existing in most industrial towns with the purpose of representing and protecting the interests of its members: local manufacturers and merchants. The *Association of British Chambers of Commerce* acts for its members on a national scale and the largest chamber in the U.K., the *London Chamber of Commerce, acts as an examining board for certain commercial courses. Chambers of commerce exist in other countries and there is also an *International Chamber of Commerce.

chamber of trade. *See* National Chamber of Trade.

characteristics of goods. The attributes of the goods themselves. One approach to demand theory emphasizes that consumers are interested in the separate characteristics of goods. In this case utility is only indirectly a function of the goods consumed, and directly a function of the characteristics contained in them. For example, some of the characteristics of fresh fish are its taste, nutritional value, ease of preparation, appearance, etc. It is these characteristics that people wish to purchase, not the fish itself.

The approach is not a radical departure from previous demand theory, since it matters little whether the demand for goods is taken as the derived demand for characteristics or as a direct demand. However, as a conceptual framework it helps to explain the concepts of substitution and complementarity. The possibilities for negative or undesirable characteristics can also enter the analysis.

character printer. A device for printing the output of a computer one character at a time, also called a *serial printer*. They are considerably slower than *line printers. *Daisywheel printers are character printers.

charge. A security over the assets of a borrower, usually a company. Certain or all of the assets of the company are secured against certain amounts of money lent to the company. Often this money is specifically lent in the form of debenture stock, with specified interest rates and specified dates of redemption. The charge can, however, be created to secure other forms of borrowing, such as a bank overdraft. The charge can be either *floating* or *specific*. A floating charge is one that is generally secured over all the assets and a specific charge one that is secured against a specific asset or group of assets.

charges forward. An instruction denoting that all delivery charges are to be paid by the consignee of goods, when he receives them.

charges register. *See* registered land certificate.

chartered accountant. *See* accountant.

chartered company. An organization or body of persons given a legal status by a royal charter granted by the Crown. The company is thereafter treated as a person in law; it can sue or be sued in its own name in the courts, and has all the powers of an individual person. However, if the company pursues activities beyond the bounds of those envisaged in its charter, the charter may be forfeited.

An organization usually obtains a royal charter by addressing a petition to the Privy Council, outlining the powers required. The Privy Council will then advise the Crown whether or not to grant the requested charter.

In the past, chartered companies were used to further the development of new countries, e.g. the Hudson's Bay and East India Companies, but now they are mainly confined to non-commercial corporations, such as the Institute of Chartered Accountants and the Chartered Institute of Secretaries; municipal and county boroughs are also incorporated in this way.

chartist. An investment analyst who bases forecasts of share price movements on a study of charts, i.e. graphs on which are plotted past movements of individual share prices, of P/E ratios, and of these statistics relative to their stock market averages. Chartists claim that such charts of the share prices of most companies conform to one of a small number of familiar patterns and that from a study of the share's past movements the correct pattern can usually be identified and reliable forecasts thereby made. They thus ignore a company's fundamentals, i.e. factors relating to its present and future trading position. Chartism as a technique of investment analysis is more prevalent in the U.S. than in the U.K. It is a controversial system and in its strict form (i.e. the study of charts to the complete exclusion of fundamentals) has many more opponents than adherents. *See also* investment analyst.

chattels. Goods that are movable items of property. As soon as such items become fixed to the ground or to buildings, so that some damage will be caused by their removal, they cease to be chattels and become items of immovable property, or fixtures.

cheap money. *See* easy money.

cheque. As defined by the Bills of Exchange Act (1882), a bill of exchange drawn on a banker payable on demand. Cheques are the usual method of withdrawing money from a current account with a bank. To complete a cheque the drawer inserts the name of the payee and the amount he is to be paid in words and figures, and dates and signs it. The cheque may be either open or crossed (*see* crossed cheque). If it is open it may be cashed at the bank and branch on which it is drawn, but if crossed it must be paid into a bank account. Each cheque has a cheque number (numbered consecutively in the drawer's cheque book), a bank/branch number, and an account number printed on it. A payee may transfer his interest in a cheque by endorsing it and handing it to another person, but the drawer may restrict the negotiability of a cheque by crossing it. A bank customer must exercise reasonable care in drawing a cheque as if he draws it in such a manner as to facilitate fraud he will be responsible for any loss his banker sustains through such negligence. Although cheques are not legal tender, they are generally accepted for the payments of debts and may be regarded as *near money.

cheque account. An account, held at a bank or building society, on which cheques can be drawn.

cheque card. A card issued by a bank to approved customers, enabling them to make purchases on credit from traders who have joined the scheme and also to draw cash from any of the bank's branches up to a specified amount. The traders are reimbursed by the issuing bank, who render an account each month to the customer and any amount not paid off by him attracts debit interest. A similar scheme is operated by a number of large stores and suppliers using what is known as a *credit card. Originating in the U.S., this form of credit is increasingly being used in the U.K.

Chicago School. *See* quantity theory of money.

chief economic advisor's sector. *See*Treasury.

child benefit. A cash payment made by the Department of Health and Social Security to all U.K. families at a rate of £6.85 (1985) for each child, with an additional benefit payable to one-parent families.

children's assurance. A type of assurance devised for the welfare of children. Two of the most common are as follows: (a) *Child's deferred assurance.* This type of policy is effected on a parent's life for a specified number of years terminating at an *option date when the child attains vesting age. Until this time the premium is paid by the parent, but then the child has the option of having the assurance vested in his name and on his life as a normal whole life or endowment policy, irrespective of his medical condition.

If the child should die before the vesting age, the premiums are returned to the parent, often with interest. Should the parent die before the option date, no further premiums are payable and the option can still be exercised by the child at the appropriate time (vesting age). If it is decided not to continue the policy beyond the option date it is treated as a form of endowment that has matured and a cash sum is then payable.

(b) *Educational endowment.* An ordinary endowment assurance maturing in instalments to provide amounts to meet school or university fees. This policy is usually on the life of a parent.

chi-square distribution. A statistical *distribution involving a continuous variable. It is derived from the *gamma distribution by placing restrictions on both the latter's parameters: the gamma parameter γ is put equal to 2 and the parameter α is put equal to $\nu/2$, where ν is the chi-square distribution's *degrees of freedom. The distribution is characterized by the fact that its variance is equal to twice its mean. It is used very extensively in statistical analysis, especially in connection w:th testing hypotheses about and obtaining confidence limits for the variance of a normally distributed variable and also in connection with testing *goodness of fit. The graph of a chi-square density function will usually be a peaked curve with a positive skew although, for low degrees of freedom, it may be a negatively sloping curve without a peak. *See also* contingency table.

choice. The position that arises on the London Stock Exchange when a stockbroker can buy a certain share from one stockjobber at the same price that he can sell it to another.

chose in action. A property right that is enforceable by law but is held by a person other than the one in possession of the item of property in respect of which the right exists. A chose in action may be sold or assigned to a third party as long as the person in possession of the property is notified. Examples are debts, mortgages, negotiable instruments (e.g. cheques), and insurance policies. *See also* chose in possession.

chose in possession. An item of property or money that a person has in his possession. The term includes all assets apart from *choses in action.

c.i.f. *See* cost, insurance, and freight.

C.I.P.E.C. *See* International Council of Copper Exporting Countries.

circular flow of income. The flow of income from households to firms in the form of expenditure on goods and services and back again to households from firms in the form of payment for factors of production (see diagram). The flow can also be viewed in physical as opposed to money terms (goods and services, and factor inputs). This simple model can be developed to incorporate *withdrawals* from and *injections* into the system: in the real world not all income is spent, but savings are injected back into the system as investment expenditure, thus completing the circuit. Besides savings, withdrawals also include taxation and purchases of imported goods; these would result in a reduction of the circular flow of income unless matched by injections (investment, government expenditure, and exports), which increase it. An equilibrium level of national income exists when withdrawals and injections are equal, or, looked at in another way, when *aggregate demand equals *aggregate supply: this equilibrium level is not necessarily, however, full employment level.

In national income accounting, total income, expenditure, or (value-added) output can be used as by definition these should equate with each other because of the circular flow of income. *See also* income-expenditure model.

circular letter of credit. An instruction to a bank's agents abroad that they may honour sight drafts on the issuing bank up to the amount stated in the letter. It is issued at the request of a bank's customer, who is named in it and who carries it with him together with a *letter of indication* on which he has given a specimen of his signature, and should therefore be kept apart from the letter of credit. The customer pays for the credit when it is issued and it enables him to obtain foreign currency when travelling abroad. The amounts as drawn are entered on the letter of credit thus enabling the amount still outstanding to be calculated. *See* letter of credit.

circulating capital. *See* working capital.

City. The City of London, with reference to the complex of financial markets located there. The City contains the major parts of the U.K.'s capital market, money market, foreign exchange market, commodity exchanges, shipping exchange, and international insurance market, together with a large contingent of foreign financial institutions. City institutions account for several hundred million pounds worth of invisible exports (mainly from the insurance industry and espe-

consumption
expenditure
final goods and
services (= gross
national product)
households
businesses
factor inputs
factor payments (wages etc)
(=national income)

Simple circular flow of income model

rest of world
withdrawals
government
injections
imports
exports
taxation
government expenditure
capital market
investment expenditure
saving
consumption
expenditure
households
businesses
income

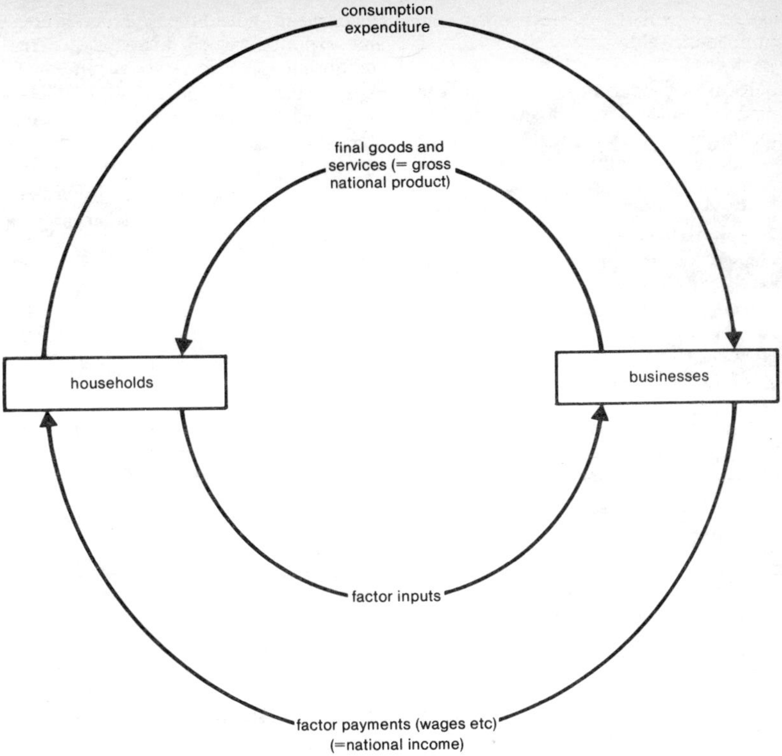

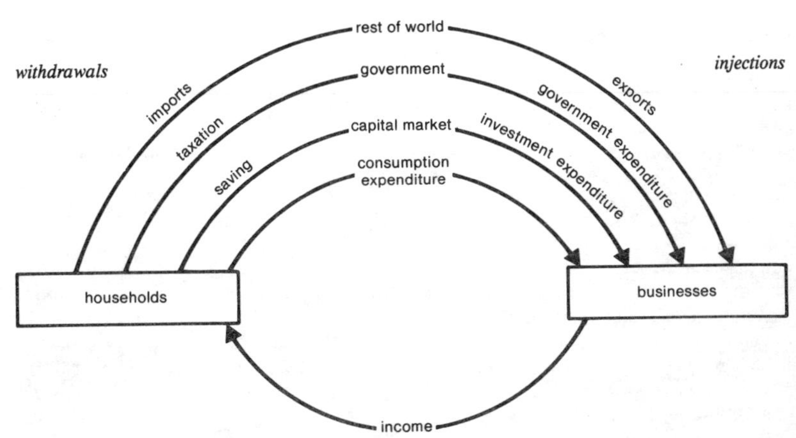

Refined circular flow of income model

cially Lloyd's), on which account the U.K. has a large invisible balance of payments surplus. The City has been a centre of international merchanting and insurance since the Middle Ages although its major growth commenced in the seventeenth century with merchant banking activities, which grew with the U.K.'s development as a trading nation. The London Stock Exchange became prominent during the nineteenth century, preceding the growth of corporate capitalism. In the twentieth century London's continuing status as a premier international centre brought about an influx of overseas representation, a trend that has so far resisted the U.K.'s post-war economic decline. The City remains easily the largest financial centre in Europe and the second largest (after New York) in the world. The Stock Exchange, although it has become a less significant part of the U.K. capital market, retains its international status. The City's largest institutions today are the clearing banks and the insurance companies.

City Code (on Takeovers and Mergers). A code laying down a number of principles of "good conduct" to be observed in takeover and mergers transactions in the U.K., with the general objective of providing equal treatment for all shareholders involved. In the late 1960s the larger City institutions, encouraged by the Bank of England, formed the *Panel on Takeovers and Mergers* to regulate takeover activity and in 1968 the Panel published the first City Code, which has since been revised and strengthened several times. Although its powers are not statutory, it can admonish offending companies in private or in public, or it can refer offenders to their own professional bodies (where relevant) for disciplinary action.

civil law. *See* law of contract.

classical model. The full-employment model of the economy characterized by price and wage flexibility. It assumes that the free and unhindered workings of the laws of supply and demand would always ensure full employment in the economy, provided only that all savings were invested. Consequently, any increase in unemployment would automatically be corrected by market forces. However this model completely failed to explain the length or severity of the Depression, while policy recommendations based upon this model (usually for a greater degree of *laissez-faire) generally worsened the situation. For these reasons the Keynesian model gained rapid acceptance. It explained those aspects that were unintelligible in terms of the classical model. Subsequently Arthur Cecil Pigou (1877–1959) rehabilitated the classical model by setting out conditions under which severe long-term unemployment might persist (*see* Pigou effect) although L. Metzler and others argued that this saved the classical model only by destroying a second important classical assumption–that real factors are determined solely by real factors. (In the Pigou effect the rate of interest is partly determined by the quantity of money in the economy.) Nevertheless, the classical model has regained popularity, especially with those who favour the limited governmental role implied.

classical range. The vertical segment of an *L.M. curve. In the classical model of the macroeconomy it was believed that neither the demand-for-money curve nor the supply-of-money schedule was affected by the rate of interest. This set of conditions would make the L.M. curve vertical: a change in the money supply would shift the L.M. curve by the same amount at any level of the rate of interest. *See* classical model.

classical school. A school of economic thought said to begin with the publication of Adam Smith's *Wealth of Nations* in 1776 and to reach its climax in J. S. Mill's *Principles of Political Economy*, published in 1848. Although it was influenced by continental economists, it was primarily a British school of thought, numbering among its members Malthus, Senior, James Mill, McCulloch, and perhaps most influentially David Ricardo. Its philosophy, while not as purely capitalistic as its detractors claimed, was by comparison with the restrictive doctrines of the mercantilists (*see* mercantilism) generally optimistic about the efficiency of a freely competitive system, incorporating Smith's doctrine of the *invisible hand. Total output was divided among the three factors of production: land, labour, and capital, of which the first two were the primary factors. Indeed, in the labour theory of value (as advocated by Ricardo), in order to yield a basis for the comparison of the value of goods at different times and places independent of the price level, labour alone was seen as the primary resource. The return to land was rent, which was seen as a windfall income, in the sense that the price of, for instance, wheat was set by the marginal plot of land (the least fertile) and so more productive land received a surplus of revenue over costs, output being higher per unit of cultivation. The short-run wage bill was to be determined by the wages fund theory and in the long run by subsistence arguments, such as that of Malthus. Profits, which supplied the wage fund, were a residual: the role of capital and capitalists, while certainly acknowledged, was not given a place of prominence. The theory dealt mainly in aggregates and so was macroeconomic in nature. On the other hand it did not seek to determine the level of output (the concern of modern macroeconomics), relying upon *Say's law to fix this as a datum, but rather sought to establish the determinants of the distribution of income (the preserve of modern microeconomics).

Clayton's case. A law case decided in 1816, which is considered to be the leading authority upon the appropriation of payments. From this case the rules derived are: (1) a debtor has the right to specify which of several debts due to the same creditor shall be discharged by a payment made by him; (2) if he does not so specify then the creditor has the right to make the appropriation; (3) if neither of them makes such an appropriation then in law the first item on the credit side of an account is applied to discharge or reduce the first item on the debit side. In certain circumstances, such as the death of a guarantor, a banker will stop operations on an account and open a new account, in order to avoid the consequences of this rule.

clean bill of lading. A *bill of lading is said to be clean if the goods it refers to have been loaded in apparent good order and condition. If the goods or packages are in any way defective the master or mate of the ship will add an endorsement to this effect. *See* dirty (or foul) bill of lading.

clean floating. *See* exchange rate.

clearing bank. A bank that is a member of the London *bankers' clearing house.

clearing house. An institution that undertakes the settlement of indebtedness between members. For example, traders in certain commodity markets use a clearing house to avoid the passing of cheques between brokers, dealers, etc. All sales and purchases are registered with the clearing house, which sends difference accounts to the traders, usually on fixed accounting days. The best known clearing house is the *bankers' clearing house.

close company (U.S. **closed company**). A company that is under the control of five or fewer participants, or of participants who are directors. This type of special status was introduced in the U.K. by the Finance Act (1965). Tax legislation was aimed at preventing the avoidance of income tax by not distributing profits as dividends to the shareholders. If 35% or more of the shares are held by the public the company does not fall into this category.

closed economy. An economy that neither imports nor exports. It is thus immune from any chain reactions affecting other nations, such as world inflation. The concept is useful as an extreme case, analysis of which can yield valuable information. Although there are no closed economies in the real world, some nations can be regarded as close approximations. The U.S. is the prime example, as its *foreign sector is relatively small. Consequently the U.S. government can virtually ignore the economic policies of foreign governments when making its own policy decisions. The countries of Western Europe, which are all *open economies, are very largely affected by the policies of other nations.

closed indent. *See* open indent.

close price. A share price characterized by a narrow margin between a stockjobber's *bid and *offer prices. Blue chips tend to have close prices relative to other stocks. A company thought to be in trouble is likely to have its shares quoted with a wide margin between the bid and the offer.

closing prices. Prices prevailing at the end of a day's dealing in a market. The term is usually used in connection with a *commodity or *stock exchange. On the London Stock Exchange, closing prices are those prevailing at the official close of business at 1530 hours; business transacted afterwards is known as *after-hours dealing*.

cluster sample. A sample taken by dividing the population into several strata and then selecting an entire stratum. Thus the pupil population of a school might be sampled by selecting every child in one class.

C.M.E.A. *See* Council for Mutual Economic Assistance.

Cobb-Douglas production function. A function relating output to inputs in which, based upon the assumption of competitive market pricing, the *elasticity of substitution is equal to one. In 1927 Douglas noticed that when the change in the logarithm of output was plotted on the same graph as the change in the logarithm of capital employed and the change in the logarithm of labour employed, the curve of output remained a fixed percentage distance between the curves of capital and labour, even though capital grew at a faster rate than labour. Cobb realized that such a function would be of the form:

$$Y = aK^{\alpha} L^{1-\alpha}$$

where Y is output, K is capital, L is labour, and $0 \leq \alpha \leq 1$. Under the assumption of *profit maximization the Cobb-Douglas production function has the property that the relative shares of income, capital, and labour are constant when they are paid their value of marginal product (i.e. the elasticity of substitution is equal to unity). In fact, the share is equal to the exponent of the input in the production function so that capital and labour receive α and $1 - \alpha$ per cent of the total value of the product respectively. From their real series of capital, labour, and output Cobb and Douglas estimated the value of α to be 0.25. This they then were able to check by examining the value data of shares of wages and profits in money terms. The share of capital again appeared to be 0.25 and the original estimate was in part verified.

COBOL. A high-level *programming language used especially for business applications and the most widely used in mainframe computers. Instructions are written in easy nontechnical English words and phrases. The name is an acronym for *co*mmon *b*usiness-*o*riented *l*anguage.

cobweb theorem. One of the earliest dynamic analyses of stability in a simple supply and demand situation, applying particularly where there is a large time lag between production and sale, as in agriculture. As seen in the graph, in the first period, expecting price p_0 the producer supplies quantity q_1, which then sells at price p_1 owing to the excess demand. In the next period he produces q_2 expecting price p_1 to prevail but finds he has over-supplied and sells at price p_2 instead, and so the process continues. In the case illustrated the process eventually leads to the equilibrium price and quantity p and q, but this is dependent on the relative slopes of the two schedules. It is possible that the prices and quantities might instead spiral outwards, never reaching equilibrium, or alternatively that they might oscillate between two sets of prices and quantities; this will depend upon the relative elasticities of the supply and demand curves.

The model is rather simplistic since it assumes that the producer never learns that the price he sold at over the last period will not be the same in the next, that he can keep taking losses without going bankrupt, and finally that the short-run supply curve in each period, or on market day, is completely inelastic and that he will have to sell everything during that period at whatever price.

Cocoyoc declaration. A declaration made at a symposium on development and resources held in Cocoyoc in Mexico in 1974. The declaration

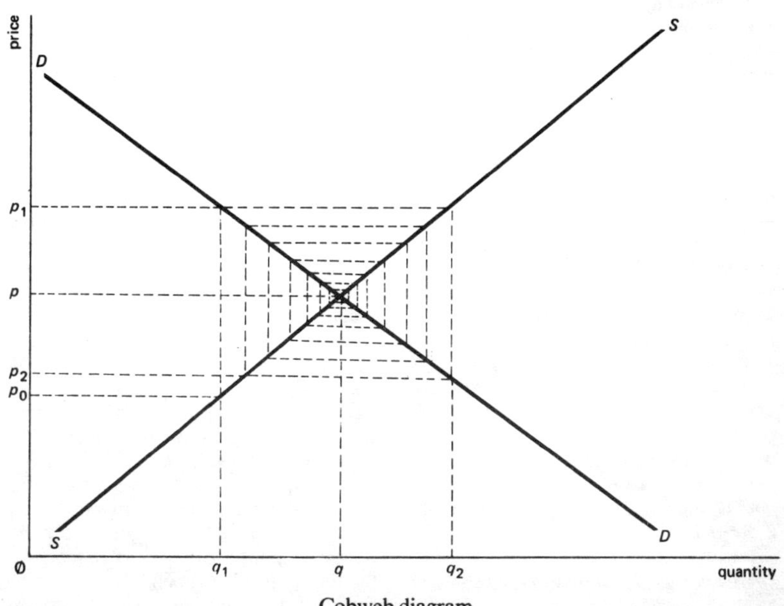

Cobweb diagram

emphasized that the gulf between the rich and poor people of the world cannot be solved by the present policies of the developed nations. Furthermore, it rejected the growing preoccupation of the developed nations with ecology, asserting that poverty is the greatest evil and that it can be solved without harming the environment. The symposium was under the chairmanship of Barbara Ward, a British economist, and was organized by the United Nations Environment Programme (UNEP) and the *United Nations Conference on Trade and Development (UNCTAD). The declaration also stated that the present crisis is not caused by population growth, but by economic and social misuses. It must, therefore, be solved by economic and political means. The declaration proclaimed that the purpose of growth is to satisfy the five basic needs: food, shelter, clothing, education, and health. It denied that the existing economic order can satisfy these needs, because the gap between the rich and poor nations is widening rather than narrowing. It advocated the need for a diversity of development methods coupled with national self-reliance. *See also* New International Economic Order.

coefficient. Any constant term in a function or model. For instance, in the demand function:

$$D = a + bP + cY + dX_1 + eX_2 + U,$$

where D is the quantity demanded (of a particular commodity), P is its price, Y disposable income, X_1 and X_2 substitutable or complementary commodities, and U a stochastic disturbance, the terms a, b, c, d, and e are coefficients. One of the major purposes of statistics and econometrics is the estimation of such coefficients. A coefficient is sometimes referred to as a *parameter*.

coefficient of determination. *See* correlation.

coefficient of multiple determination. The square of the coefficient of multiple correlation between three or more variables. The coefficient of multiple determination can be interpreted as the proportion of the total variation in the dependent variable explained by the independent variables. *See also* regression, multiple regression, multiple correlation.

coefficient of partial correlation. *See* partial correlation.

coefficient of variation. A measure of relative *dispersion calculated by expressing the standard deviation (σ) as a percentage of the arithmetic mean ($\bar{x}$). That is:

$$V = 100\sigma/\bar{x},$$

where V is the coefficient of variation. It is useful because it is independent of the units in which the basic variable is measured. Thus it can be used to compare the dispersions of distributions denominated in different units, such as steel output per day and electricity output per day, and also of distributions denominated in the same units but of such wide divergence that absolute measures of dispersion could not meaningfully be compared, such as the weights of oil tankers and the weights of dinghies.

coinage. The metallic currency in use in an economy. Material used for coins needs to be useful and of value, easily portable, indestructible, homogeneous, stable in value, and easily recognized. Consequently metal of some kind has been found to be most suitable, with gold and silver best of all. Early records show that metal was weighed when being exchanged but this was so inconvenient that it came to be divided beforehand into small pieces each of a certain weight. Later, in order that anyone might recognize that each portion was of a stated weight, a public stamp was placed on them. Coins have been of many different shapes but the circular ones have proved most convenient and popular. They may be intrinsically worth their full face value or be merely tokens, as are all the U.K. coins in current circulation.

co-insurance. Insurance cover on the same risk provided by several separate insurance companies. *See also* contribution.

collateral security. Security taken by a bank in support of its lending to customers. Colloquially it is used to describe impersonal security, such as a life assurance policy or stocks and shares, as differing from personal security, such as a guarantee. It is also used to describe security deposited by a third party, but by the terms of the Stamp Act (1891), it means additional or secondary security as opposed to the primary security. The Stamp Act allows collateral security (for example one of two mortgages) to be stamped at a lower rate than the primary security. *See* stamp duties.

collecting banker. When a banker collects cheques that a customer has paid into his account he is acting as an agent for that customer. As such, provided he acts in good faith and without negligence, he is afforded protection in law if the cheques have been stolen or misappropriated. Such cheques are not cleared until they are received and paid by the banker on whom they are drawn.

collecting society. *See* friendly society.

collective bargaining. The process of negotiating wages and conditions of employment that takes place between representatives of management and of employees through their trade union; the fundamental principle on which trade-union activity is based. The advantage to the employee of wage negotiations carried out on a collective basis is that it greatly strengthens his bargaining power. For the employer, the attraction is that one negotiation, however harassing, is less time-consuming and more efficient than negotiating individually with each employee. However, for the results to be effective both sides of industry have to accept the bargain struck by their representatives whether it applies nationally throughout an entire industry, to a single company, only to a particular craft, or even within a particular shop. *See also* trade union, wage drift.

collectivism. An economic system, practised in communist countries, in which the means of production are collectively owned by the community and in which there is extensive economic planning by the state. *See also* communism. *Compare* individualism.

collusive duopoly. A model of duopolistic competition in which the producers combine to act as one monopolist, then bargain between themselves over how to divide the profits. This can also be achieved by a quota system on each of the producers. The set of collusive duopolies, or core, is analogous to the contract curve in the *Edgeworth-Bowley box. It will be the set of tangency points between the iso-profit curves. Since the profit extractable from a market is dependent only on cost and demand factors, this monopolistic solution maximizes the total profit the duopolists can hope to attain together, though not individually.

Colombo Plan. A plan formulated at Colombo, Sri Lanka, in 1950 to improve the economies and living standards of South and Southeast Asian nations. Aid has been provided by the U.S., the U.K., Canada, Australia, New Zealand, and Japan to the Asian nations participating in the scheme, which were originally Afghanistan, Bhutan, Burma, Cambodia, India, Indonesia, Iran, Korean Republic, Laos, Malaysia, the Maldives, Nepal, Pakistan, the Philippines, Singapore, Sri Lanka, Thailand, and South Vietnam. The aid has been mainly concentrated in technical and educational development.

combination carrier. A *bulk carrier that can carry either oil or a dry bulk cargo, such as grain, ore, or coal.

combinations. The number of unordered arrangements of a specified total of items within a larger total. Thus, the sequence of letters a b c d provides the following six two-way combinations: ab,ac,ad,bc,bd,cd. *Compare* permutations.

combinations in restraint of trade. Illegal collusive agreements between firms to fix prices, output, or market conditions in order to exert a certain degree of monopoly power over the market with a view to increasing profits.

COMECON. *See* Council for Mutual Economic Assistance.

commercial bank. *See* joint-stock bank.

commercial codes. Codes used by international traders to reduce the cost of sending cables. Most commercial codes consist of five-letter groups representing a whole phrase; for example, in the *Acme Commodity* and *Phrase Code* the group IHOFZ means "We offer him c.i.f. subject to reply here by Monday our time, this is the best that can be done . . . ". The codes usually have mutilation tables enabling one-letter cabling errors to be identified and corrected. The other codes in common use are *Bentley's Second Phrase Code* and the *ABC Code*. The codes used by a particular company are often displayed in their letter head so that correspondents know which codes they may use. For firms that are in constant telegraphic contact it is often better to use a private code, which precisely meets the needs of the trade in question. Private codes are also usually based on five-letter groups; they have the added advantage of providing an element of confidentiality, but unless they are carefully compiled, with adequate check letters, they can be dangerous as mutilations in transmission can lead to serious errors.

commercial English. A form of written English that evolved in correspondence between nineteenth-century merchants. By reducing commercial correspondence to an exchange of formulaic phrases and sentences, the businessman is saved the time and trouble of thinking out what he has to say. The devotees of this style may begin their reply to a letter: "I have to acknowledge receipt of yours of the 3rd ultimo, contents of which have been duly noted." A simple acknowledgement of an order may read: "The esteemed order from your good selves will receive our best and most careful attention." Even when goods are not paid for, commercial English has a ready euphemism: "We regret that our account remains unpaid. Unless you can see your way clear to honour us with your cheque we shall have no alternative but to put the matter in other hands for collection." The style is always effusive, always servile; but by modern standards it is both too garrulous and too far from spoken English to find favour with any but the most pedantic.

commission. A sum of money paid to a salesman or an agent acting on another person's behalf, often calculated as a percentage of the value of the goods involved. An example is the sum charged by a stockbroker on shares that he buys or sells for his clients. Whether the commission is paid by the buyer or the seller depends on the custom of the trade. For example, in the U.K. an estate agent's commission is paid wholly by the seller, whereas in some commodity markets the commission is shared between buyer and seller.

committee of inspection. A committee that may be formed when a company is being wound up by the court in the U.K., with a primary function of giving directions to the *liquidator in the methods chosen to wind up the company. On liquidation, the creditors of the company have to decide whether to appoint a liquidator in place of the *Official Receiver and whether to form a committee of inspection to act with the liquidator. If the creditors do decide to elect certain of their members to a committee, then this committee will hold a general power of attorney for all the persons it represents. The committee should meet either at predetermined times or, if no specific arrangements exist, once a month.

commodity. **1.** (In economics). A *good that is tangible and can be transported. *Compare* service.

2. (In commerce). Any article of trade, but especially such raw materials as grain, sugar, cocoa, coffee, tea, rubber, jute, sisal, and metals. *See* commodity markets, international commodity agreements.

commodity broker. A *broker who specializes in the commodity trade, especially one who trades on behalf of producers, users, and dealers on a *futures market. The customs of each commodity trade are different and brokers fulfil slightly different functions in each case. Usually, however, they work for a brokerage, do not take up an open position in the market for their own account, and are not responsible for the solvency of their principals. In some trades they are required to pass names, i.e. state the name of their principals; in others they are not obliged to do so. As commercial commodities (other than metals) are sometimes called *produce*, commodity brokers are often called *produce brokers*.

commodity exchange. A market in which dealings are transacted in ownership titles to commodities; it is no longer general practice for there to be an actual physical exchange of commodities, although samples may be examined. Most sophisticated commodity exchanges of today have both spot markets and futures markets; the latter enable dealers to hedge against spot price fluctuations. *See also* London Commodity Exchange.

commodity markets. Although marketing arrangements for primary commodities vary from product to product, in most commodity markets price stabilization relies to a large extent on *futures markets, usually situated in user countries or such financial centres as London or New York. However, the relationship between commodity prices and the traditional market forces of supply and demand is a contentious political issue. Commodity producers in developing countries in Africa, Asia, and South America have often experienced a decline in the value of their commodity exports in relation to the cost of their manufactured imports. Their attempts to stabilize commodity prices by trade agreements (*see also* international commodity agreements) and such regulatory mechanisms as minimum export prices have not been particularly successful as the industrialized countries, who purchase the raw materials, have been opposed to such intervention. They object to interference to free market forces on the grounds that such agreements fail to satisfy the interests of either buyers or sellers and that the more efficient producers are, under market pressure, able to undercut fixed prices by private arrangements of one kind or another. Some of the poorer producing countries believe that an equitable solution to these conflicting interests will only be achieved by the *New International Economic Order proposed at the United Nations session on raw materials in 1974. According to this charter, developing countries should be encouraged to control the marketing of their own natural resources by regulating prices and insisting on a fair relationship between the costs of commodities and manufactured goods. The industrialized countries, for their part, fear that any move to raise commodity prices would aggravate the existing problems of world inflation. On the other hand, it is accepted that if commodity prices to the producing countries are depressed there will be inadequate investment in productive capacity, mineral exploration, etc., which will inevitably lead to world shortages of essential raw materials. One possible solution to this dilemma is that producers should be encouraged to process more of their own raw materials.

Common Agricultural Policy (C.A.P.). A policy, agreed by member states of the E.E.C., for fixing the prices of such agricultural products as milk, butter, meat, cereals, etc. The level of market prices for cereals is maintained by varying import levies so that the price of imports from nonmember states never falls below an agreed *threshold price*. At the same time, the home market is supported by the *European Commission, which is empowered to buy surplus cereals at an agreed *intervention price* (slightly below the threshold price) to help producers in the member states to achieve the official *target price* (this is intended to be an average price, rather than a guaranteed price). The Commission will also pay an *export subsidy* (or *restitution*) to producers of cereals who sell to nonmember states, in order to bridge any gap between the world market price and the intervention price. For beef and veal, the European Commission sets a *guide price*, which acts as a form of target price. If necessary, E.E.C. producers are helped to achieve this price by import controls and intervention on the home market. For pig meat, eggs, and poultry, the European Commission fixes a *sluice-gate* price every quarter. If goods are imported from nonmember states below this price, levies are paid. For fruit and vegetables, the Commission may fix a *reserve* (or *fall-back*) *price* for each commodity and is empowered to call upon the funds of the E.E.C. to ensure that produce reaches its reserve price.

The Common Agricultural Policy also provides subsidies from its common budget for the modernization of farms. It also lays down a common policy for exports of all produce to nonmember countries.

common budget. *See* European Commission, Common Agricultural Policy.

common carrier. A person or firm who undertakes to transport goods from one place to another for anyone willing to pay a reasonable charge. He cannot refuse to carry goods when asked to do so unless he has previously advertised any limitations to his service, unless his vehicles, vessels, etc., are full, unless the nature of the goods would involve him in an exceptional risk, or unless the consignor is unwilling to pay a reasonable charge.

He is obliged by law to carry the goods safely and securely and is liable for any loss or damage, unless the loss or damage is a result of some *inherent vice of the goods or a result of an act of God or the Queen's enemies (provided that the loss or damage could not have been foreseen and avoided).

The consignor must advise the carrier if the goods are in any way dangerous and if he fails to pay the carrier, the carrier has a particular *lien on the goods entitling him to retain them until the charges have been paid.

Common Commercial Policy. A policy agreed by members of the *European Economic Community that lays down regulations for member states concerning *common external tariffs, trade agreements, export subsidies, protective measures against dumping, etc. *See also* Common Agricultural Policy.

Common external tariff (C.E.T.). Import duties charged by all the members of a trading group of nations (such as the E.E.C.) on some or all of the goods entering any of these nations from nonmember countries.

Common Fisheries Policy. A policy that regulates the amount of fishing taking place in the coastal waters of E.E.C. member states. On January 1 1983 a new 20-year agreement in the interests of conservation set total catch limits on an annual basis for the major species of fish (principally herring and cod) and allocated catch quotas for members and also nonmembers (e.g. Norway) who have traditionally fished in E.E.C. waters. Each member state has an equal access zone, established in 1976, extending to 200 nautical miles from its coast, within which any other member state is allowed to fish. However, since 1983 each state also has a 12-mile exclusive zone to which it alone has access. Certain states, however, can fish for particular species within 6 to 12 miles of the coast of another member state, these exceptions having been defined in 1983.

common law. The part of English law deriving from the common law courts. It was originally based on the customs of the country and now consists largely of previous court decisions. *Compare* statute law.

Common Market. *See* European Economic Community.

Common stock. *See* stock.

Commonwealth Preference. A system by which certain goods could formerly be imported into the U.K. from Commonwealth countries at preferential rates of customs duties. It also applied to certain exports from the U.K. to Commonwealth countries. The goods to which it applied, the amount of the reduction, and the terms in which the preference was granted varied with each Commonwealth country.

The system was originated by the Finance Act (1919) and developed within the British Empire until the Second World War (it was formerly called *Imperial Preference*). It was restricted by trade agreements made under *GATT and as a result of the U.K.'s entry into the Common Market it was finally ended in 1977.

communism. A political and economic system under which all of a country's means of production, distribution, and exchange are owned and controlled by the state. All economic decisions are made ultimately by the state rather than resulting from the interplay of market forces and the profit motive of capitalism is abolished. Central planning enables many specific economic objectives to be achieved that would not be possible in a freer society. For example, a fast rate of economic growth can be obtained by directing resources towards the production of capital goods at the expense of consumer goods, thereby creating a high rate of investment at a sacrifice of a lower present standard of living. Although the efficiency resulting from competition and the free play of market forces is sacrificed, this is to some extent compensated by the absence of the inefficiencies and waste of resources that often characterize monopolistic competition.

Communism is the final stage, in Karl Marx's (1818–83) view, of the evolution of society from primitive culture through the stages of feudalism, capitalism, and socialism. It is created by the revolution of the exploited workers against the power of the capitalists and by the establishment of a temporary dictatorship of the proletariat. Marx distinguished two phases of communist society. The first, during which society is adjusting after its emergence from capitalism, is characterized by continuing pay differentials but the disappearance of inequalities derived from property ownership. The second phase to emerge involves the complete eradication of inequality, the ruling principle being "from each according to his ability, to each according to his needs", and the withering away of the state. The latter phase evolves gradually from the former and has never been put into practice.

The first communist party to be named as such was Lenin's Bolsheviks, after the 1917 revolution in what is now the U.S.S.R., to distinguish it from the Mensheviks and foreign socialist parties. During the twentieth century, however, various forms of socialism and communism are being practised by countries with vastly different political and economic systems. All those associated with the word communism have a one-party totalitarian system in which the freedom of the individual is sacrificed for the good of the state. *See also* socialism, capitalism, mixed economy.

company. A commercial organization formed to enable a number of people with access to capital to carry on a business together. Although the trading name of some *partnerships has included the words "and company", the use of these words now usually implies a *limited company. In the U.K. there are three types of company: *chartered companies (set up by royal charter), *statutory companies (set up by act of parliament), and *registered companies (registered with the *Registrar of Companies). Most British companies are registered companies, which include limited companies. A company is a legal entity that can enter into contracts, sue, and be sued. *See also* private company, public company, joint-stock company, limited company.

company law. The branch of English law that applies to corporations and companies, whether registered or chartered. It is mainly contained in the Companies Act (1948), which consolidated all the previous statutes relating to companies. It contains very detailed regulations as to how companies are to be run. A number of important amendments and additions to the law are contained in the Companies Acts of 1967, 1976, 1980, and 1981, the two latter Acts being concerned mainly with adjusting English company law so that it concurs more closely with the standards of the European Economic Community.

company secretary. The officer of a U.K. company who is responsible under the Companies Acts for seeing that the legal obligations of the company are complied with. He may or may not be a director of the company, but he is responsible for taking and keeping the minutes of both company meetings and board meetings. He also keeps the share register and is responsible for ensuring that dividends and interest payments are correctly made. Details of the secretary are recorded in the register of directors.

comparative cost principle. Nations will mutually benefit from trade if there is a difference in the comparative costs of production. For example, if two nations, A and B, are both producing and trading in two goods (say, machinery and wheat) and if A is able to produce machinery more efficiently than B, and B is able to produce wheat more efficiently than A, it would be to both nations' advantage to specialize: A in machinery and B in wheat. As a result more of both products would be produced.

Trade will be worthwhile even if one nation can produce both goods more efficiently. For example, assume that A can produce 80 units of machinery and 100 units of wheat when allocating half of its resources to the production of each and B can produce 60 units of machinery and 90 units of wheat, also dividing its resources equally. Aggregate production will then be 140 units of machinery and 190 units of wheat. A produces both machinery and wheat more efficiently than B. If A specializes in the product in which it has the largest comparative advantage, i.e. machinery, leaving wheat to be grown by B, aggregate production would be 160 units of machinery and 180 units of wheat. Thus 20 units of machinery have been gained and 10 units of wheat have been lost (when compared to the original situation). This is a net gain, for 20 units of machinery represent approximately 7% of resources whereas 10 units of wheat represent approximately 3% of resources. The nations have gained more than they have lost.

Although this is an example of a two-nation two-good economy the comparative cost principle is equally valid in the more complex real world. *See also* absolute advantage.

comparative statics. A common form of economic analysis in which different equilibrium states associated with different values of *exogenous variables or parameters are compared as, for instance, in an examination of the effect of a change in government expenditure levels on the equilibrium level of national income. Comparative static analysis may be qualitative or quantitative. Qualitative analysis is the simpler of the two and seeks to determine the direction of the change in equilibrium contingent on a specified change in an exogenous factor; quantitative analysis is concerned with the magnitude of the change. (Quantitative analysis will of course provide for the direction of the change as well as its magnitude). Although it takes into account changes in those exogenous variables and parameters that statics takes as constants, comparative statics disregards the process of adjustment of the endogenous variables; it assumes that the new equilibrium is both attainable and stable. Despite these limitations, comparative statics is the form of analysis underlying many of the economic hypotheses that have tentatively been accepted; it is probably the most common form of analysis currently in use. The major technique of comparative static analysis is differential calculus. *Compare* statics, dynamics.

Compensation Fund. *See* hammering.

compensation principle. An attempt to formulate an objective rule for determining the socially preferable option when judging alternative proposals for economic change, without recourse to value judgments or interpersonal comparisons of utility. The compensation principle was first advanced by Baron Nicholas Kaldor (*b.* 1908) and has three main forms. The Kaldor criterion is that A is preferable to B if it is possible for those individuals who benefit from state A relative to B to compensate those individuals who are worse off in state A so that the gainers remain better off than in B and the losers are no worse off. It is important to note that this compensation is not necessarily paid. The Indians dispossessed of Manhattan could be easily compensated from the economic advantages generated, but have not been; however, the action is socially preferred by the Kaldor criterion. The Hicks criterion states that A is preferable to B if the losers in A relative to B cannot bribe the gainers in A relative to B to remain in state B. The Scitovsky criterion imposes both the Kaldor and the Hicks conditions, since it is possible under either single criterion for A to be preferred to B and B to be preferred to A. However, this ranking itself is not necessarily transitive, that is A may be preferred to B and B may be preferred to C and C preferred to A. If it is required that the compensation actually be paid, then the system reduces to the Pareto case (*see* Pareto-optimal). For these reasons, apart from the difficulty of actually doing the accounting, the system is not practical. Furthermore, the basic assumption that value judgments should not be made to distinguish between different states is foreign to the political process of decision. *See also* cost-benefit analysis.

competition. A situation in a market in which a number of producers are attempting to increase their own profits at the expense of rival producers. This leads to *price wars, attempts to increase market shares, *product differentiation, etc. Competition is most keen under conditions of *perfect competition and is totally absent under *monopoly. In real markets, competitive forces will usually be midway between these two extremes.

Competition Act (1980). An Act of Parliament that extended monopoly legislation to cover potentially anti-competitive practices, such as refusal to supply, exclusive dealing, and price discrimination. Under the Act, the Office of Fair Trading (*see* Fair Trading Act (1973)) can itself take action to prevent a firm from operating an offending practice, or it can refer it to the *Monopolies and Mergers Commission for further investigation. Prior to the Act anti-competitive practices could be investigated only within the context of a wide-ranging investigation of suspected monopolies, whereas the Competition Act enables individual firms to be investigated, irrespective of whether the firm concerned is a statutory monopolist or not.

competition and credit control. A set of Bank of England proposals first published in May 1971 and implemented in September of the same year. The objective was to change both the financial structure and the conduct of monetary policy. Bank rate was abandoned and replaced by the minimum lending rate. This was determined by the size of the tender for the government bills on sale in the week. The larger the tender (on a Thursday) relative to the number of bills to be sold, the higher the price of bills. The higher the price of bills, the lower is the interest rate on them (*see* bonds). This interest rate then became the rate at which the Bank of England was willing to act as *lender of last resort and it was a key rate in determining the structure of interest rates. Since 1978 the rate has, however, been fixed by administrative decision. An attempt was also made to introduce more competition into banking by abolishing the clearing banks' interest rate cartel. This allowed banks to compete with each other for deposits. Cash and liquidity ratios were also abolished and replaced by a single cash reserve requirement, but this new requirement was very complicated and probably led to the ensuing excess money supply expansion.

compiler. *See* programming language.

complements. Goods whose characteristics are interrelated so that an increase in demand for one usually leads to an increase in demand for the other. Examples of these are bread and butter, cameras and film, or fish and chips. Accordingly one would suppose there to be an inverse relationship between the change in price of one good and the demand for its complements, as opposed to the direct relationship which exists between * substitutes.

As with substitutes, complements can be weak or close as the strength of interrelation between their characteristics varies. There are also net and gross complements; the former depend only on the substitution effect, the latter also take the income effect into account. Fish and chips, for example, are normally net complements. *See* substitutes.

composite demand. Demand for a good that arises from diverse sources who require it for different uses. In general, primary products have more alternative uses than manufactured goods.

composite hypothesis. *See* hypothesis.

compound interest. Interest compounded continuously from a point in time with reference to a specified time period and a specified rate of interest. The compounding process treats time as a continuous variable. For instance, £100 compounded at the rate of 5% per six months would after six months be worth 100[1 + 0.05] = £105 and after one year the sum would be worth $100[1 + 0.05]^2$ = £110.25. On the other hand, £100 compounded at the rate of 10% p.a. would after one year be worth 100[1 + 0.1] = £110 and after two years be worth $100[1 + 0.1]^2$ = £121. The capital sum plus accrued interest grows exponentially, not linearly. The general formula is $I = P(1 + r/100)^n$, where I is the interest, P the principle, r the rate of interest, and n the term. *Compare* simple interest.

comprehensive insurance. *See* motor insurance.

comptroller. A senior executive of a company who is responsible for the financial control of the company, including accounting and budgeting.

compulsory purchase. The acquisition of property under statutory powers without the consent of the owner. It must be distinguished from *requisitioning*, which is the compulsory taking of possession from the owner without a change in ownership. Examples of such statutory powers are those given by the Land Clauses Consolidation Act (1845) and the Compulsory Purchase Act (1965). The powers are given to certain government departments and public bodies, e.g. Water and Electricity Boards, for specific purposes. There are detailed rules as to the procedure to be adopted and the amount of compensation to be paid to the owner. There is also a right of appeal and in some cases public inquiries are held.

computer. A piece of equipment for storing data and performing operations on it according to a predetermined set of instructions (the *program). By far the most commonly used type is the electronic *digital computer*, so called because it accepts and handles data in the form of discrete digits, usually in *binary notation.

Modern digital computers are complex assemblies of electronic circuitry and electromechanical components. The raw data, which may be sets of figures, lists of words, catalogue entries, etc., is fed into the device via an *input device and held in a *storage device. The instructions for processing the data are also fed in and stored. This program controls the operations of drawing data from the store, performing the necessary processes on it in the *central processing unit, and returning it to the store. It delivers the results through an *output system in the form of printed characters, visual display, etc.

Within the system, information is handled in digital form: numbers, letters, and other symbols can be assigned a code consisting of binary digits 1 and 0. These digits can be represented by the presence or absence of some signal–for example by the presence or absence of a pulse of electric current, or of a magnetized region of a surface, or of a voltage on a transistor component. This use of discrete states of the equipment is the characteristic feature distinguishing digital computers from *analog computers.

Modern computers are capable of performing very complicated arithmetical computations but they are not simply large adding machines. Firstly, they are capable of storing very large quantities of data. Secondly, the use of a stored program enables whole sequences of operations to be performed. Thirdly, computers are not restricted to handling numerical data, nor is the processing restricted to arithmetical computation. The circuits in the central processing unit can also perform *logic functions*, including comparison of items. Thus the computer can make decisions (on the basis of conditions specified by the program) and sort and collate information. Finally, digital computers work very quickly, performing in minutes tasks that would take many years of tedious manual and mental effort.

Because of their speed, capacity, and versatility digital computers have many industrial and business applications: performing complex calculations, storing and retrieving information, sorting and collating statistical data, keeping accounts, paying employees, controlling industrial processes, machine tools, etc. They can be used for predicting market trends, forward planning of industrial production, etc.: the field of *operational research, for example, owes its importance to the development and availability of digital computers. Computer technology has advanced rapidly in recent years, especially in the area of *microcomputers. For most commercial and industrial uses, program packages can be purchased to enable normal functions to be carried out on a firm's own computer.

computer operation. The function of day-to-day running of computer programs after they have been written by the computer programmer. Computer operators are also responsible for the correct working of the computers themselves. *See also* systems analysis, computer programming.

computer programming. 1. The composition of a computer program.

2. The preparing of detailed instructions for a computer program within the specifications laid down by the systems analyst and ensuring that the program is correct and accurate in its performance. *See also* systems analysis, computer operation.

concealed unemployment. *See* disguised unemployment.

concept test (in marketing). The interviewing of a small sample of potential customers in a target market, to obtain their reactions to a proposed new product.

concessions. Circumstances in which a stockbroker can reduce, or remit altogether, the commission he charges to an investor. One of the most important concessions is the free to close rule, under which an investor who buys and sells the same shares within the same *account pays no commission in respect of the sale *bargain. There is a similar concession in the case of dealings in gilt-edged securities, transactions in which are made for immediate cash settlement. The free to close rule is applicable in this case if resale is made within 28 days of purchase. The other concession commonly granted is the graded reduction of commission rates according to the size of the bargain–the larger the bargain, the lower the commission rate (subject to a commercial minimum). Concessions are theoretically discretionary rather than mandatory, i.e. a stockbroker may, rather than must, grant them in appropriate cases. In practice, any concession that is available will be granted.

conditional bill of sale. A *bill of sale in which title to the goods referred to does not pass absolutely; the transferor reserves the right to retake the title under specified conditions. It has to be witnessed, but not necessarily by a solicitor.

conditional distribution. The statistical *distribution of a variable when a related variable is given a fixed value. The concept of a conditional distribution arises only when the two variables concerned do not have the property of independence: the conditional distribution of a variable given the value of an independent variable would simply reduce to the *marginal distribution of the (first) variable. A conditional distribution can be calculated by dividing the joint distribution of the two variables concerned by the marginal distribution of the second variable (i.e. the variable whose value is specified in the definition of the conditional distribution).

conditional probability. The probability of occurrence of one event or one value of a variable, given the outcome of another event or variable. Conditional probabilities can be represented by a conditional distribution.

Confederation of British Industry (C.B.I.). An organization representing the management of British industry on questions varying from labour relations to government trade policy. It was formed in 1965 from an amalgamation of the Union of British Employers Confederation, the Federation of British Industry, and the National Association of British Manufacturers. It represents over 300 000 companies, many trade associations, and all the nationalized industries. Membership is completely voluntary and members' subscriptions are geared to the number of their employees.

The Confederation has regional and local councils as well as the central council, which is democratically elected by the members.

As well as serving as a pressure group vis-à-vis the government, the Confederation maintains links with the *Trades Union Congress and other organizations. It also provides services and advice to its members on matters of technical legislation, industrial regulations, and export. However, its chief aim is to promote prosperity in British industry.

conference lines. Shipping lines that have formed an association to agree freight rates and passenger fares on liners (*see also* shipment of goods). Not all shipping lines belong to the conferences (there are separate conferences for different areas of the world) and nonconference freight rates tend to be lower than conference rates. Nonconference lines are often members of the communist bloc.

confidence interval. An interval of values within which the true value of a parameter of a population is hypothesized to lie with a specified degree of probability. The procedure for formulating a confidence interval begins with the point estimation of the parameter from a random sample drawn from the population and then, depending on the size of the sample and the nature of the distribution of the population, the calculation of an interval by the application of techniques derived mainly from Student's t distribution, the chi-square distribution, or the normal distribution. The probability associated with the interval is determined by choice and is conventionally set at 95%, 99%, or 99.9%. Thus one can speak of a 95% confidence interval for the mean of a normally distributed variable, where the confidence level of 95% is the probability that the interval does in fact contain the true value of the mean. A confidence interval is an interval estimate and is generally superior to point estimates. *See also* estimation.

confidence limit. One of the two end points of a *confidence interval.

confirmed letter of credit. *See* letter of credit.

confirming house. A domestic organization that places orders with local exporters on behalf of an overseas buyer. The confirming house acts on behalf of the overseas buyer and is sometimes regarded by the exporters as principal to the contracts and sometimes as agent. The overseas buyer has all the advantages of having a local agent: knowledge of domestic conditions, close supervision, ability to negotiate the best prices, insurance cover, shipping rates, etc. The advantages to the exporter are that the contract is enforceable in his own country, payment is made in his own currency, information on conditions in the overseas market is easily obtained, and dispatch, documentation, etc., is speeded up.

conglomerate. A *group of companies that pursues different activities in different industries. Unlike horizontally or vertically integrated firms it cannot build up reserves of specialist knowledge of productive processes. It can, however, build up a fund of financial and management expertise. Other advantages include minimization of risk, as the group is not dependent on the health of one industry, and access to more sources of knowledge, which should enable resources to be reallocated more efficiently than in a specialized company or group.

consequential loss policies. The physical loss or damage caused by fire and other major disasters can be compensated by the cover referred to under *fire insurance. However, in addition to material damage, almost invariably there are other losses to commercial firms, resulting from disruption of business activities and loss of production whilst repairs are in hand or suitable alternative premises are sought. Loss-of-profits insurance when arranged on a proper basis can remedy this situation by paying:

(i) any net profit loss;

(ii) all standing charges (i.e. expenses that are still incurred during the period of disruption, such as salaries, certain wages, rates and rents, etc.);

(iii) any necessary additional expenses. *Also called* loss-of-profit policies or business interruption policies.

conservativism (in accountancy). The use of the *prudence concept in accounting techniques.

consideration. 1. A profit or benefit given to one party to a contract by the other, in exchange for a promise made by the receiver of the consideration. Such a promise is not enforceable by law unless given in exchange for consideration or unless made in a *deed. The usual form of a consideration is the payment of money or an undertaking to pay it.

2. The money paid for the purchase of a number of shares before adding commission, stamp duty, fee, and V.A.T.

consignment. A shipment or delivery of goods. *See also* on consignment.

consignment note. A document made out by the sender of goods, handed to the carrier, and countersigned by the consignee on delivery as proof that delivery has been made. It gives a full description of the goods, marks and numbers (where appropriate), and the gross weight. It also gives the names and addresses of the sender and the consignee and states who is responsible for the carriage charge and the insurance.

consistency. A statistical estimator (*see* estimation) is said to be consistent if it can be shown mathematically that for large samples the estimator tends to be close to the true value of the parameter being estimated. Consistency is one of the desirable properties of estimators.

consistency concept. A fundamental *accounting concept in which accounts of an enterprise are treated in a similar manner and on the same basis from one *accounting period to the next.

consolidated accounts. The accounts, the balance sheet, profit and loss accounts, and notes thereto of a company and its subsidiaries, which must be consolidated to present the situation of the group as a whole at the end of a financial year. There are, however, certain exceptions to this rule as laid down by the Companies Acts (1948–1981). These are that group accounts need not be presented if the holding company's directors are of the opinion that it is impracticable or would be of no real value to the members, that the results would be misleading or harmful to any part of the group, or that the business of the subsidiary and holding company is so different that they cannot be treated as a single undertaking.

consolidated annuities. *See* Consols.

consolidated fund. The account of the Exchequer, held at the Bank of England, into which taxes are paid and from which government expenditure is made. It derives its name from the fact that several government funds were consolidated to form it in 1787.

consolidation. The action of reinvesting a *capital gain made on a speculative share in a more conservative security. The term is also sometimes used to mean the selling of equities at a gain and reinvestment of the proceeds in fixed-interest securities.

Consols. Funded government securities that need never be redeemed (although they can be, at the discretion of the government). Consols were first issued as a result of the consolidation of the national debt during the eighteenth century. Their (nominal) rate of interest was initially 3% p.a.; it was later reduced to 2¾% p.a. and now stands at 2½% p.a. Their true rate of interest (i.e. their annual return in relation to the actual price at which they can be traded) will be in line with the yield offered on comparable (long-dated) gilt-edged securities; it has in fact been well above 2½% for most of the time during the past 20 years. Consols is an abbreviation for *consolidated annuities*. *See also* irredeemable security.

consortium. An association of independent firms, formed to quote for and, if successful, to undertake a project that requires skills and resources not possessed by any of them individually. A consortium is usually formed to undertake one project; a more lasting association would be a *syndicate.

conspicuous consumption. A form of abnormal market behaviour in which a consumer derives utility from impressing others by purchasing some ostentatious good rather than from satisfaction afforded by his actual consumption of it. Goods so purchased tend to be highly priced. *See* Veblen effect.

constant capital. Marx's term for the sum of *depreciation on fixed capital plus resource inputs.

constant elasticity of substitution (C.E.S.) production function. A *production function for which the *elasticity of substitution, under assumptions of competitive pricing, is constant for changing levels of inputs, though not necessarily equal to unity. In 1961 Arrow, Chenery, Minhas, and Solow introduced the concept of the C.E.S. production function to economists. They had begun by the observation that the logarithm of output per capita is a linear function of the logarithm of the wage rate. However, the coefficient of the wage term, in fact the elasticity of substitution, was observed to vary from unity, the Cobb-Douglas case. Integration revealed the form of such a function to be:

$$Y = \gamma(\delta K^{-\rho} + (1 - \delta)L^{-\rho})^{-1/\rho}$$

where Y is output, K is capital, and L is labour employed. The interpretation of the parameters is: γ is the efficiency parameter since it changes the production function in scale; ρ varies as the elasticity of substitution, σ, i.e.

$$\rho = (1 - \sigma)/\sigma;$$

and δ is the distribution parameter, which reflects the distribution of income between the two factors for a given wage rate. Particular examples of the C.E.S. are: $\sigma = 1$, when it becomes

$$\gamma K^{\delta} L^{1-\delta}$$

the Cobb-Douglas; $\sigma = 0$, when there is a *fixed proportions production function.

constant returns. *See* returns to scale.

constructive total loss (in marine insurance). A ship that is not an *actual total loss, but has been damaged beyond economic repair, may be abandoned by its owners and declared a constructive total loss. In this case, the insured gives notice of *abandonment to the insurers, who then assume all rights to the property. The same procedure may be adopted for a cargo that is damaged to such an extent that it has become useless for all practical purposes.

consular invoice. A special form of invoice, legalized by a consul in an importing country. Consular invoices are often required by the customs of a country to confirm the country of origin. They are used extensively in South America.

consumer credit. Any form of borrowing by consumers, hire purchase being the principal source. In recent years *credit cards and personal loans granted by banks have created considerable credit. Most of the U.K. banks have a subsidiary hire purchase company to whom they refer customers in need of credit for the purchase of consumer goods, and to whom they lend money. The Consumer Credit Bill (1974) gives greater protection to borrowers and, amongst other things, obliges lenders to specify in writing the equivalent annual flat rate of interest.

consumer durables. Goods purchased by consumers for use over a relatively long period. The term can be restricted to such products as cars, washing machines, furniture, etc., or may also include broader categories, such as clothing and money. The distinction between a durable and nondurable is one of degree, especially as the former may contain an element of built-in obsolescence. Durables are of interest for two reasons. Firstly, their durability poses problems in demand analysis, which can only be resolved by resort to capital theory; secondly, the aggregate of durable purchases is both unstable and difficult to predict; it is, therefore, of great interest to macroeconomic policy-makers. In some circumstances, large fluctuations in such an important expenditure category can destabilize the economy, in others it can be controlled for policy purposes (as in the use of hire-purchase regulations, etc.).

consumer good. A commodity bought for household or personal use. *Compare* capital goods.

consumer nondurables (disposables). Goods that are completely used up at the moment of consumption. The purchases of these goods, such as food, tobacco, and drink, exhibit very regular tendencies and they tend to follow the course of purchases implied by demand theory when prices or income change.

consumer research. *See* market research.

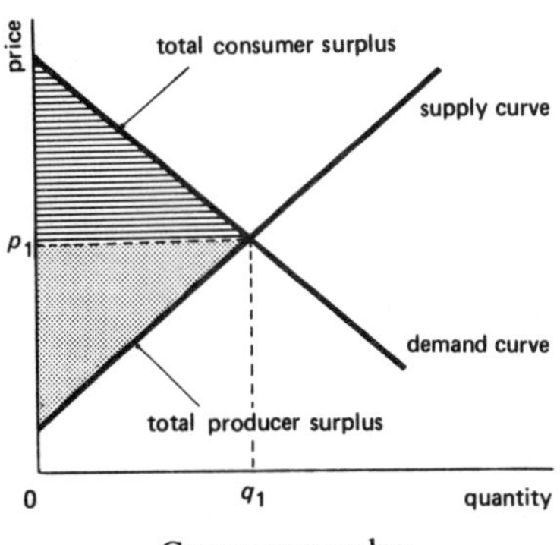

Consumer surplus

consumer surplus. The consumer's benefit from trade. In standard *partial equilibrium analysis the intersection of the supply and demand curves determines the price of a good and the quantity of it that is sold. At this point, the utility from the marginal unit of the good is just equal to its price; it follows that the previous units of the good were worth more than their price to the consumer (*see* diminishing marginal utility). This excess satisfaction is the consumer's surplus. Graphically, it is measured by the area bounded by the vertical axis, the price line, and the consumer's demand curve and is the difference between the maximum the consumer would have paid rather than give up the good and what he actually pays.

This concept is of some use in examining the welfare implications of the effects of monopoly and taxation in an industry. For instance, the creation of a monopoly where a competitive industry previously existed always leads to a reduction in the amount of goods supplied, an increase in price, and a reduction in consumer surplus. There are drawbacks, however, particularly the problem of measurement and those associated with partial equilibrium analysis in general, i.e. the impossibility of considering one sector of the economy in isolation from the whole. *Compare* producer surplus.

consumption. The expenditure of a nation or individual on consumer goods and services. It does not include expenditure on capital goods. Private consumption is regarded as being expenditure by consumers on goods and services such as food, drink, and entertainment. Public consumption is the current expenditure of the government on such items as health, education, and defence. Total consumption accounts for approximately 80% of national income (the remaining 20% being spent on investment).

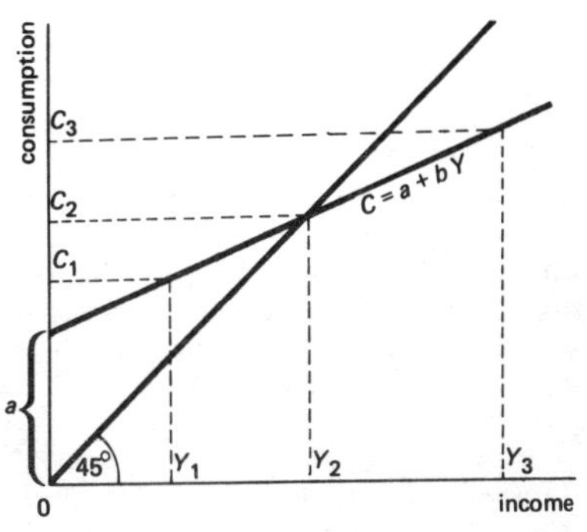

Consumption function

consumption function. A relationship between the size of national income (Y) and the proportion of income that is spent on consumption (C) rather than saved. It was first advanced by Keynes who believed that the level of consumption (and hence of saving) is dependent more on the level of income than on the interest rate. The most commonly used type of consumption function is the linear equation:

$$C = a + bY,$$

where a is the minimum amount of purchasing that will take place at any level of income and b is the *marginal propensity to consume. At income level Y_1 (see diagram), the amount of consumption is C_1. Consumption is greater than income so that past savings are being used up. At income level Y_2, the amount of consumption is C_2. As the point C_2Y_2 falls on the 45° line, it indicates that this is a point at which income equals consumption. At income level Y_3, the associated amount of consumption is C_3. At this point consumption is less than income so that saving takes place. *See also* multiplier.

containerization. A method of freight-handling in which general cargo is packed into large rectangular containers and carried in this form from a factory or inland loading depot by lorry to a port, where it is loaded onto a ship with much greater speed and less pilfering and damage than with conventional handling methods. Thus it can be moved to its final destination without being unpacked. Although it involves a large capital outlay, fewer ships are needed because they have a greater capacity than conventional general cargo ships and spend less time in ports.

contango. 1. A charge in the form of an interest rate paid by a *bull speculator for deferring, from one *account day to the next, final * settlement on account of shares purchased. **2.** The practice of such deferment. **3.** To buy a certain share but defer settlement on it. The contango rate of interest is usually ½%–1% higher than the appropriate money market rate and is levied on the contangoed share's *middle price at the close of business on the penultimate day of the *account in which the share was bought. **4.** A rate of interest received by a *bear speculator who wishes to defer settlement (perhaps because he has sold short). Such a rate of interest would be ½%–1% lower than prevailing money market rates. However, whether a bear receives contango at all will depend on the balance of bulls and bears at the end of the account; if there is an excess of bears over bulls the former may not only not receive contango, they may even have to make a payment themselves (known as *backwardation). When making contango arrangements, a speculator deals with his stockbroker and it is between stockbroker and client that contango money is passed. Contango arrangements are usually made when a bull hopes to make a resale; their purpose is to give the nature of an *inter-account deal to a transaction that straddles more than one account. The contango payment usually makes this a viable proposition when the deferment is for one or two accounts only. Contango is sometimes called *continuation* or *carry-over*.

contango day. The day on which a *contango on the Stock Exchange is arranged. Contango day was formerly the first day of a new *account; it is now the last day of the old account.

contemptuous damages. *See* damages.

Contents of Recent Economics Journals. A weekly publication of the Department of Industry Library Services. It gives the tables of contents of the world's main English-language journals in economics, finance, and taxation.

contingency insurance. A type of insurance that covers a multitude of risks, usually remote. It tends to be issued when the proposer prefers insurance protection to any legal remedy, which may be very slow, uncertain, and possibly nonexistent. Examples include restrictive covenant indemnities, missing beneficiary indemnities, and missing document indemnities.

contingency table. A table used for comparing the goodness of fit of the cross-frequencies of two variables that are believed to be related. For instance, one may postulate the hypothesis that a person's income is related to the length of his full-time education. One could then take a large random sample of individuals and allocate each according to his rating on income and education. The results of this would be displayed on a contingency table as a preliminary to the actual test, which, under certain limiting conditions, is based on the chi-square distribution. The null hypothesis to be tested here is that of no relation between the variables (or that the variables concerned have the property of independence).

contingent annuity. An *annuity that becomes payable if a particular contingency or pre-agreed set of circumstances arises. Thus a married man may purchase an annuity for his wife, which only becomes payable should he die before her. It is sometimes known as a *reversionary annuity*.

contingent liability. *See* liability.

continuation. *See* contango.

continuous variable. *See* variable.

contract. An agreement enforceable by law (provided that, in certain cases, the prescribed formalities are observed) between two or more persons to do or abstain from doing some act or acts. Generally there are no necessary formalities and a contract may be written or oral, as long as some *consideration is present. However, some contracts are unenforceable unless in writing (for example, contracts for the sale of land, for marine insurance, for the transfer of shares in a company, or for hire purchase) and some are unenforceable unless made by *deed (e.g. contracts purporting to transfer shares in statutory companies or U.K. ships). Moreover, contracts are unenforceable if they are illegal. Examples of illegal contracts are gaming contracts in which persons stand to win or lose as the result of a game, contracts to carry out immoral or fraudulent acts, contracts made by a minor, or contracts entered into by one party under a fundamental misapprehension of its terms. Some contracts are voidable, that is they may be cancelled by one of the parties. Examples are contracts entered into under duress or as a result of misrepresentation of facts.

contract curve. A set of points on an *Edgeworth-Bowley box diagram showing situations in which one person cannot be made better off without others being made worse off. The points are therefore *Pareto optimal. If the economy is trading (or producing) at any other point, the utility of any one of the traders (or the production of one of the goods) could be increased without making the other trader worse off (or producing less of the good) by exchanging a different combination of goods (or producing different outputs). In production, if in the Edgeworth-Bowley box diagram the contract curve lies on the side of the diagonal that is closer to the capital input axis the good will be produced using capital-intensive methods, while if it is closer to the labour input axis labour-intensive methods are used. *Compare* offer curve.

contract guarantee insurance. Insurance against the failure of the contractor to carry out his obligation to perform the task within the contractual terms. To protect himself, the person who places the contract can obtain a guarantee bond from an insurance company, which is an undertaking to accept responsibility for the performance of the terms of the contract. Examples include performance bonds, bid bonds, customs bonds, supply bonds, and advance payments bonds.

contract note. A document sent by a stockbroker or commodity broker to his client to confirm a purchase (*bought note) or sale (*sold note) made on his behalf. It will give full details of the purchase or sale, the broker's commission, and the date on which payment must be made. It will also show any *stamp duty that has been incurred or any other charges or discounts.

contra proferentem rule. (Verba chartarum fortius accipiuntur contra proferentem. Latin for: the words of a contract are construed more strictly against the person proclaiming them). This rule ensures that if a written contract is ambiguous, it will be interpreted in the way least advantageous to the party who drew it up.

contribution. 1. (in insurance) Where two or more insurance contracts of indemnity that are in force cover the same interest in a common subject matter in respect of the same risk, the law does not permit the insured to recover under both and so make a profit on his loss. Where the insured is over-insured because of increasing the insurance, the respective insurers must share the loss in rateable proportion. If one of the insurers has paid more than his proportion he is entitled to the appropriate contribution from the other insurers.

2. (in accountancy) The difference between sales and variable costs in *marginal costing. This amount contributes towards the recovery of fixed overheads, the remainder being profit.

contributories. The members and past mnembers of a company that is being wound up are all potential contributories to help cover the liabilities of the company and the costs of winding up. Past members are generally only considered as contributories if they have ceased to be members within a year of the winding-up, and would then only be liable in so far as present members were unable to meet their contributions. In the most common case of a company limited by shares, the maximum contribution required from a member could not exceed any amount uncalled on the shares that he holds.

control accounts. Accounts intended to check the accuracy of the posting of a large number of individual items to a large number of individual accounts. For example, in the case of cash received from trade debtors the total of all cash posted to all the individual accounts at each posting would be posted in total to the control account. A similar exercise would be conducted on the totals of all invoices billed to each trade debtor. As a result, the balance on the control account would show the total amount owed by trade debtors, which should be reconciled periodically to the sum of all individual balances.

control chart. *See* quality control chart.

conversion (in law). Wrongful interference with another person's property, thereby depriving that person of his right of possession. A banker who collects a cheque for a person who hasnot a good title to it is guilty of conversion but whether he is liable to the true owner for such conversion depends upon whether he has observed the rules laid down for his protection in the Cheques Act (1957).

conversion issue. An issue of a new security for the purpose of replacing one already in issue that will shortly become due for redemption, not for the purpose of raising money. Conversion issues may be either of gilt-edged securities by the government or of equities by a company; in the latter case shares are issued to holders of convertible debentures who wish to exercise their conversion rights at the appropriate time.

convertibility. The extent to which a currency can be freely exchanged for gold or for foreign currencies. Most western nations' currencies are now convertible in foreign currencies, if not in gold.

convertible debentures and loan stock. Corporate debentures and loan stock that, at the holder's option, may be converted on certain specified terms into the ordinary shares of the company.

convertible term assurance. A normal term assurance with the provision that the assured has the option to convert such a policy into a *whole life or *endowment assurance without the necessity of supplying medical evidence of health. This option must normally be exercised within a specified number of years during the duration of the assurance.

Because of the advantage of not having to supply medical evidence of health on conversion it is the normal practice of assurers to load (increase) the premium to some extent from the date the convertible term assurance is effected.

convex. A function is convex if a line segment between any pair of points on the curve of the graph lies above the arc of the curve between the two points. As an example of its importance, convexity is an essential characteristic of indifference curves, reflecting the fact that the *marginal utility of a good declines as its quantity increases.

conveyance. A *deed by which ownership of land and buildings in England and Wales is transferred, not including registered land (*see* land registration), for which a different system operates. In 1984 conveyances can only be drawn up by qualified solicitors although a parliamentary committee has made recommendations for the regulations and qualifications required by non-solicitors to perform conveyancing should legislation to this effect be passed.

cooperative movement. A movement first successfully launched in 1844 by the Rochdale pioneers, a group of 28 weavers, for the benefit of members. Profits were shared amongst the members by the payment of a dividend in proportion to the amount of the member's purchases. The consumers' cooperatives also own manufacturing and wholesaling concerns and associated building and insurance societies. Cooperative societies exist in many countries.

copyhold land. *See* freehold.

copyright. The exclusive right to use or authorize others to use literary, dramatic, musical, and artistic works, sound recordings, films, or radio and television broadcasts. In the U.K. the law relating to copyright is contained in the Copyright Act (1956).

core. *See* memory.

corner. A situation in which one person, firm, or cartel buys up all the supplies of a commodity and is then able to name its own selling price. This situation has been achieved successfully on rare occasions in international *commodity markets for a short period. The high prices that result usually bring out further supplies or substitutes to break the corner. Corners are usually associated with the activities of *profiteers and can often be mercilessly antisocial. For example, in the 1940s one Indian firm managed to create a corner in rice: as a result many thousands of Indians died of starvation. Corners can usually be avoided by government restrictions on monopolies and anti-trust laws.

corner solution. A situation that occurs on any graph when a decision-maker's best course of action places him on one of the axes. For instance, assume that a consumer must divide all his income between spending and saving. A corner solution would exist if he spent as much as possible and saved nothing, since graphically this would be represented by the point at which the *budget line meets the spending axis, i.e. at the corner.

Corn Exchange. A wholesale *commodity exchange located in the City and dealing in seeds, cereals, fertilizers, and animal feeding stuffs. It is the largest distribution centre for these commodities in the U.K. and was founded in 1749.

corporate management. Management with respect to the effects of current decisions upon the long-term performance of an undertaking. In the case of a company, the board of directors is responsible for:

(i) Formulating the company's corporate objectives.

(ii) The company's long-term viability and profitability.

(iii) The provision and allocation of the resources, e.g. capital, at their disposal.

(iv) Evaluating and selecting alternative policies.

(v) Complying with legal obligations.

corporate objectives. Those objectives that aim at the attainment of a desired future course for the company as a whole, providing motivation, guidelines for action, and values for the conduct of the business and a basis for measuring performance. If the objectives are to be of any use to management it is considered essential that they should be quantifiable, achievable, and clearly ranked to indicate priorities. However, all businesses have a multiplicity of objectives, many of which are noneconomic (e.g. social objectives) and subjective.

corporate (strategic) planning. The systematic review of an organization's long-term future prospects by management. This analysis should provide information from which it is possible to identify any gap between objectives and forecast, for example, based on the resources available. Such a *gap analysis* could indicate that the company should search for new products and/or new markets, and if the gap cannot be closed the company will have to amend its objectives. Current management decisions should take into account corporate planning.

corporate structure. The organizational structure of personnel necessary for implementing management decisions. Responsibilities are defined and lines of authority are established in such a way that coordination is fostered both vertically and horizontally and feedback channels are open to and from the decision makers.

corporation. A group or association of people recognized in law as an individual entity able to sue or be sued in its own name. A corporation may be a *corporation aggregate* or a *corporation sole*. Examples of the former are *chartered companies, *registered companies, *statutory companies, and local councils. A corporation sole is an individual holder of an office, such as a reigning monarch or a bishop, who enters into contracts in his official capacity. These contracts do not bind him personally when he retires from office but they do bind all successors to that office.

corporation tax. The tax charged on a company's profits as assessed for tax purposes. This profit assessable for tax is the profit of the company for an *accounting period modified in a variety of specified ways, such as by *capital allowances for fixed assets purchased, the removal of various expenses (e.g. some types of entertaining) that are disallowed for tax purposes, and the removal of various types of income, such as *franked investment income, which are taxed under different arrangements. In the U.K. the rate of corporation tax is determined each year by the Chancellor in the *budget and is paid in two portions: advance corporation tax (A.C.T.) and mainstream corporation tax.

correlation. A statistical technique for calculating the degree of association in variations in the values of two or more variables. Positive or direct correlation takes place when high values of one variable are associated with high values of the others (and similarly with low values), while inverse or negative correlation occurs (in the two-variable case) when high values of one variable are associated with low values of the other (and vice versa). Thus positive correlation might be postulated between consumption, disposable income, and wealth or between the stock of physical capital in a country and its income per head, while inverse correlation might be measured between interest rates and the level of commitments for capital investment. The most important uses of correlation are in the discovery of possible connections between variables, which can then be put to further analysis using the techniques of statistical inference, and in the refutation of hypotheses thrown up by the process of statistical inference. It is important to note that correlation techniques have limited value in the verification of hypotheses and no value at all in the demonstration of causal connections, because there may be a variable outside the analysis that affects equally those being correlated or, alternatively, because a correlation between two variables may be completely spurious or due to chance factors *(nonsense correlation)*. In particular, one should always be suspicious when two variables appear to be highly correlated with each other over a long period of time. Correlation is measured by a coefficient graded between plus one and minus one: a value close to plus one indicates a high degree of positive correlation, a value close to minus one indicates a high degree of inverse correlation, and a value close to zero indicates poor correlation. This correlation coefficient is normally calculated by the product-moment formula in which (in the two-variable case) the covariance between the two variables is divided by the product of their respective standard deviations. If it is desired to correlate two attributes (which cannot be measured), they can be ranked and then correlated by means of Spearman's coefficient of rank correlation. The product-moment coefficient can, however, be reduced to Spearman's coefficient. The square of the correlation coefficient is called the *coefficient of determination. See also* multiple correlation, partial correlation. *Compare* regression.

correspondent bank. A *clearing bank that acts as an agent for nonclearing banks. In the U.K. nonclearing banks are rare and therefore correspondent banks are of minor importance. In the U.S., however, the majority of banks are nonclearing and so the correspondent banks are much more important.

corresponding principle. A principle asserting that to each comparative statics analysis there corresponds an implicit dynamic system whose specification and stability conditions justify the results of the analysis.

cost. The amount (usually measured in money) that has to be spent or given up in order to produce or acquire something. An important distinction is made between *economic costs and accounting costs. *See also* private costs, social costs, direct costs, indirect costs.

cost accountant. An accountant who is concerned with money as a means of measuring economic performance rather than as a means of economic production (*compare* financial accountant). His task is to identify the various monetary costs incurred in the running of a business with the various processes of production required in the operations of the business. Thus a cost accountant would have the problem of identifying what costs had been incurred in producing an item of finished stock. By identifying costs the relative efficiency and importance of a business's constituent parts can be observed.

cost and freight (c. & f.). When goods are shipped from one country to another the contract is usually based on one of three sets of shipping terms. It may be a *free on board (F.O.B.) contract, a *cost, insurance, and freight (c.i.f.) contract, or a cost and freight contract. A cost and freight contract is very similar to a c.i.f. contract except that the buyer, rather than the seller, is responsible for the cost of the insurance.

cost-benefit analysis. A set of techniques that have been developed in order to examine and evaluate the desirability of investment projects. Cost-benefit analysis seeks to obtain an estimate of the net present value of such a project by discounting the project's costs and benefits to society. As such, cost-benefit analysis is analogous in principle to the present value method of ordinary investment appraisal used by the cost accountants of a private firm, but there is one fundamental difference. Whereas cost accounting is interested only in monetary revenues and outlays contingent on the project (no matter what their time scale), cost-benefit analysis seeks to evaluate all phenomena associated with the project that can be said to have a utility or disutility. Thus a cost-benefit analyst examining a railway project would include as costs not only the money outlays involved in the construction, maintenance, and repair of the railway but also such disutilities as destruction to the environment and the noise nuisance; on the benefits side he would measure not only commercial revenue but also reductions in the travelling time of commuters and in congestion costs to motorists. A private firm has no interest in such social costs and benefits except to the extent that they affect the performance of its own employees. Since social costs and benefits are denominated in a variety of physical units (minutes, decibels, pollution per cubic metre of atmosphere, etc.), it is necessary to reduce them to a common unit of account–namely, money. This is the major problem of cost-benefit analysis: putting a money value on such costs as pollution or noise, or measuring in money terms the extra cost in human life of a motorway compared with an ordinary road. Various devices have been employed to assess a monetary valuation for these items; for instance the Roskill Commission, whose terms of reference were to find the best site for the third London airport on the basis of cost-benefit analysis, put a value on noise by selecting a sample of people who lived close to the proposed sites and asking them how much money they would wish to receive in compensation for the noise nuisance of an airport (*see* compensation principle). Apart from the possibility of bias, such methods are rather crude and in the last resort the arguments must be presented to the government or a governmental agency for political decision. The role of cost-benefit analysis in delineating all relevant costs and benefits, specifying the alternatives to the project under examination, and quantifying what reasonably can be quantified permits of a much superior basis for political decision and is at least instrumental in the valuation of nonmonetary costs and benefits.

cost centre (in accountancy). Any area of a business enterprise to which costs can be ascribed. This centre can be geographical or it can be an item of equipment, a person, or a department. The use of cost centres is often a viable alternative to a *cost unit as a means of identifying and cataloguing costs. It is useful in supplementing the idea of cost units. The obvious advantage of a cost centre over a cost unit is that various indirect costs become more readily identifiable.

cost effectiveness. A system of accounting when planning that seeks to determine the maximum amount of a service that may be provided for a given level of expenditure. If a firm also has a method of estimating the benefits of probable actions it can combine both techniques to help plan its optimum course of action. *See also* cost-benefit analysis.

cost function. A function of prices and output that determines a firm's lowest cost for producing a given output at fixed prices. Formally, the optimization problem is solved to determine the amounts of inputs as functions of prices and then these functions are substituted into the *iso-cost line* equation yielding a function independent of the level of inputs.

cost, insurance, and freight (c.i.f.). When goods are shipped from one country to another, the contract is usually based on one of three sets of shipping terms. It may be a *free on board (F.O.B.) contract, a *cost and freight (c. & f.) contract, or a cost, insurance, and freight (c.i.f.) contract. In the last case the seller pays for delivery of the goods to the port of shipment, loading the goods onto the ship, freight from the port of shipment to the port of destination, and insurance of the goods up to the port of destination. On a c.i.f. contract the seller must supply the buyer with all the documents he requires to take delivery of the goods at the port of destination. These include a *bill of lading, an insurance policy, a commercial invoice, and any other special documents he may require, such as a certificate of origin, export licence, etc. The buyer is obliged to pay for these documents when they are presented to him (usually through a bank) and title to the goods passes when the documents have been paid for. It is sometimes said that on a c.i.f. contract the buyer is buying documents not goods: this is because, if the documents are in order, the buyer is obliged to take them up (pay for them) even if the vessel has been lost en route. Moreover, he has to pay for the documents before he has had an opportunity of examining the goods.

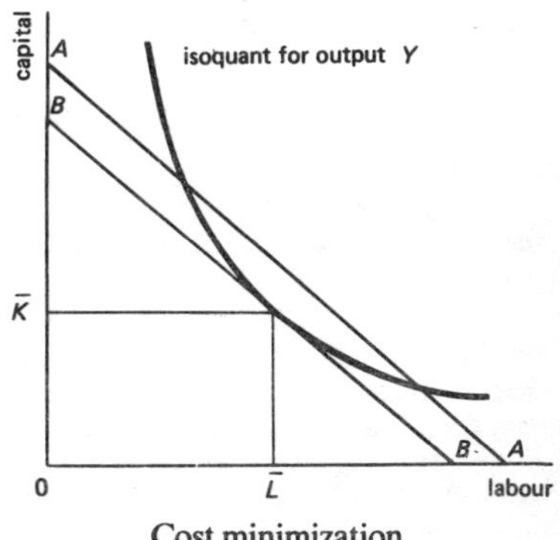

Cost minimization

cost minimization. The process of finding the combination of inputs that requires the least expenditure by the firm to produce a given output. Providing the partial derivatives of the production function exist this requirement is satisfied when the marginal rate of technical substitution (as shown by the isoquant) equals the slope of the iso-cost line at a point of tangency. In the case of competition this reduces to the familiar marginal rate of technical substitution being equal to the price ratio where prices are constant and so the iso-cost line is a straight line. The rate at which a firm can exchange one input for another on the market is just equal to the rate it can technically exchange inputs keeping output constant. For instance if the marginal rate of technical substitution were greater than the price ratio, then the firm can get more in terms of output than it pays for by substituting labour for capital and so it can reduce costs by moving to a more labour-intensive position. Two exceptions can occur to the tangency conditions. The isoquant may be kinked (*see* fixed proportions) and so the cost-minimizing position may not be tangential or the cost-minimizing solution may be a *corner solution. The process of cost minimization may be viewed as a *Lagrangian optimization. Cost is minimized subject to the constraint that output remains fixed at a given level. In this case the Lagrange multiplier can be interpreted as the marginal cost of producing another unit of output. Convexity plays an important role here for if the law of diminishing returns is broken and the isoquants are concave to the origin, then the point of tangency will correspond to a point of cost maximization.

cost of capital. *See* capital, cost of.

cost of living index. *See* Retail Price Index.

cost-plus. A form of contract in which goods and services are supplied at cost plus an agreed percentage or an agreed lump sum. This form of contract is used when it is difficult to estimate costs, but the contractor has an incentive to inflate costs rather than to keep them to a minimum.

cost price. The price of a good offered for sale at the price the seller had to pay for it, i.e. without any profit.

cost-push inflation. A theory of *inflation that attributes the cause to rising costs in the economy. Unions or businessmen (or both) are assumed to be able to increase the price paid for their services or goods in the absence of excess demand for them. This implicitly assumes some form of administered or monopolistic pricing on the part of the producers. Faced with increased prices for goods, consumers try to increase their income to maintain previous consumption by demanding higher wages and profits, which in turn increases costs.

If true, a major weapon to combat inflation would be a rigorous *incomes policy that would prevent the initial increase in prices and costs. However, there is no general agreement on the main cause of the inflation that has persisted since the war. *Compare* demand-pull inflation, monetary inflation.

cost unit (in accountancy). The cost ascribed to a single identifiable unit, which can be a material unit, a service unit, a unit of production, or any other identifiable unit. In the case of a raw material unit, for example a screw, the cost unit is the price at which that screw was produced. Identification of the costs of a unit on which work has been done can be more complicated, as direct and indirect costs have to be ascribed to it.

Council for Mutual Economic Assistance (COMECON *or* **C.M.E.A.).** An organization for economic cooperation formed in 1949 and consisting of the

Iron Curtain countries: Bulgaria, Czechoslovakia, Hungary, Poland, Romania, and the U.S.S.R. Albania, the German Democratic Republic, Mongolia, Cuba, and Vietnam have since become members, although Albania ceased to attend in 1961. Yugoslavia has agreed to participate in the work of some technical and economic bodies associated with the Council. Afghanistan, Angola, Ethiopia, Laos, Mozambique, and the Republic of Yemen attend as observers. Its original purpose was to facilitate coordination of the central planning of the economies of the region and to consolidate Soviet influence in the area. It therefore did not seek trading contracts outside the group, attempting to establish a relatively self-sufficient economic system. Recently the organization has permitted some greater liberalization of trade between member countries and the West to stimulate growth and earn foreign exchange. *See also* Marshall Plan.

Council for the Securities Industry. A regulatory body formed in the U.K. in 1978 after increasing concern about developments in the securities industry (e.g. *over-the-counter market dealings, *Ariel, and the growth of the *Eurobond market) that were outside the scope of the Stock Exchange and the *Panel on Takeovers and Mergers. Its powers are not statutory but it has the backing of the Bank of England and the financial institutions of the City.

counter bid. *See* offers, bids, and quotations.

counter offer. *See* offers, bids, and quotations.

countervailing credit. *See* back-to-back credit.

countervailing duty. A special additional import duty imposed by a country to counteract dumping, foreign export subsidies, or other unfair competitive practices by foreign firms or governments. It may also be levied to prevent imports gaining an advantage from bearing no domestic taxation (duties on foreign spirits are levied to equal the tax on Scotch whisky, brandy, etc.). Countervailing duties are usually allowed in trade agreements.

coupon. One of a set of warrants attached to a bearer bond. In order to obtain payment of interest or dividend when due, a coupon must be detached and presented to an accredited agent by the owner of the bond (or on his behalf). *See also* talon.

coupon yield. The *yield provided by a *bearer bond.

Cournot aggregation. A relationship derived from *utility maximization theory stating that the weighted average of the price elasticities of all goods with respect to a particular good's price (the weights being the budget shares of the individual goods plus the budget share of the particular good chosen) equals zero. Assuming that consumption takes place along the budget line, the condition can be interpreted as saying that the income released from the expenditure on the given good by a fall in its price is entirely spent upon all the goods, including the one whose price had changed (Antoine Augustin Cournot, 1801–77).

Cournot duopoly. A model of duopolistic competition in which each producer assumes that the other will hold his production constant in the next period, when he himself is deciding how much to produce. The model is dynamic and has more than one possible equilibrium solution, only one of which is stable.

court bond. A document issued by an institution of undoubted probity and financial standing, such as an insurance company, and agreed by the person applying for the bond, guaranteeing that the latter will faithfully carry out the duties entrusted to him by a court of law, comply with any regulations made by the court, and make good any financial loss caused by failure on either count. Examples of court bonds are those required when administering an intestate's estate, or the bond a receiver will require when appointed to look after the affairs of a mentally incapable person.

covariance. A measure of the degree to which two variables are associated. The covariance is a characteristic parameter of multivariate distributions and can be calculated as the expected value (or arithmetic mean) of the products of the deviations of corresponding pairs of the variables from their respective means. Thus the covariance between the variables X and Y can be written as

$$\mu_{xy} = E[(X - \mu_x)(Y - \mu_y)]$$

where μ_x and μ_y are the means of X and Y respectively. The covariance is encountered frequently in correlation analysis; indeed, it is a constituent part of the formula for the coefficient of correlation. It is also used to some extent in more general regression analysis and in econometrics. Variables that have the property of independence have zero covariance and thus zero correlation.

covenant. *See* deed.

cover. The number of times a public company's profit available for distribution (i.e. its profit after tax and after prior charges such as the preference dividend and *minority interests' share of profit) exceeds the actual dividend distribution declared in respect of ordinary shares. Thus if a company's pretax profit is £lm., its tax liability £500,000, and the dividend in respect of preference shares and minority interests' share are both £100,000, then the company's earnings or profit available for distribution is £300,000: if the company declares a dividend in respect of ordinary shares amounting to a total sum of £30,000, then this latter dividend is said to "be covered 10 times" (by earnings). Before the introduction of the imputation system of corporate taxation, a company's dividend cover was normally calculated by reference to its gross dividend; under imputation tax, however, which raises a company's tax rate but offsets this with an imputed tax credit for shareholders, the cover is often calculated in respect of net (i.e. net of imputed tax) dividend. Given the *quality of the earnings, a share's dividend cover is obviously an index of the degree to which a dividend can be considered safe; the higher the cover, the safer the dividend and the greater the scope for increases in it. Dividends occasionally exceed earnings, as when a company has a bad year with sharply reduced profits but nevertheless decides to maintain its dividend; such a dividend is said to be *uncovered.* Some companies deliberately operate a high retention ratio (implying a high cover) in order to maximize future earnings growth. A high cover, however, often implies a low *yield, especially when the share is considered to be of high quality and is rated at a premium to the market.

covered bear. *See* bear.

cover note. A slip of paper giving proof of the existence of insurance, issued when there is some delay between the time the contract becomes binding and the issue of the policy. In several classes of insurance business these are used quite extensively. They have particular importance in motor insurance since they provide evidence to the police that the bearer complies with statutory insurance requirements until such time as the policy and insurance certificates are to hand.

C.P.U. *See* central processing unit.

craft union. *See* trade union.

crawling peg. *See* exchange rate.

credit. 1. Purchasing power created by bank lending. Bank loans and overdrafts to customers increase both their purchasing power and that of their creditors. It is important that the monetary authorities should be able to control the creation of credit; in the U.K. this is partly achieved through the Bank of England, which can raise its interest rates call for *special deposits from banks, and carry out *open-market operations. **2.** Direct or indirect lending enabling a person to take possession of goods for future payment. The creditor (a bank, shop, etc.) allows the customer the use of the capital involved until some specified time when the payment becomes due: sometimes interest is charged for this facility. **3.** Positive assets, such as money in a bank account. Credit entries are made on the right-hand side of an account in double-entry book-keeping. **4.** *See* letter of credit.

credit card. A card issued by some large stores and other institutions to approved applicants, which enables them to obtain goods and services on credit at specified suppliers. The system is similar to that of the *cheque card.

credit control. 1. *See* credit, competition and credit control.

2. The system by which companies ensure that debtors pay the amounts due from them within a reasonable time. It includes credit policy, credit vetting, credit administration, recording, and the chasing of outstanding accounts.

credit insurance. A type of insurance that protects firms by identifying doubtful customers and by the speedy replacement of working capital if unforeseen bad debts are sustained. Export credit insurance can also protect against any loss arising from the frustration of deliveries or nonpayment by an overseas buyer due to political or commercial causes. *See also* factor.

credit note. A document issued by one party to a transaction to the other to inform him that his account has been credited with the amount shown. The credit may arise as a result of an inadvertent overcharge or of a faulty consignment that has been returned. Credit notes are usually printed in red.

creditor. A person or institution to whom any person, company, or other legal entity owes money. On a *balance sheet the most common type of creditor shown is the trade creditor, to whom money is owed for the purchase of goods and services. This sort of creditor is known as a *current liability as the money has to be paid immediately or in the near future. Some creditors, such as the holders of debenture stock redeemable in several years, are known as deferred creditors. The shareholders of a company may be considered the ultimate creditors of that company.

creditors' voluntary liquidation. The *liquidation of a company that is unable to meet its debts and, consequently, is unable to continue to trade. The stages of going into liquidation differ from those in the case of a *member's voluntary liquidation, especially with respect to the declaration of solvency, which cannot apply in this case. The main difference is that the creditors of the company are in control of the liquidation and appoint the liquidator. The calling of the various meetings is also different.

credit rating. The extent to which a person or firm will grant credit to some other person or firm depends on the credit rating of the latter. This information may be built up by bank or trade references or from confidential directories that list the creditworthiness of firms.

credit squeeze. A restriction by the government on the provision of credit from retailers to consumers. Typical measures would be a restriction on lending by banks, an increase in deposits for articles bought on hire purchase, and a reduction in the time allowed for repayment. Credit squeezes are used by governments to reduce the economic activity of the economy.

credit transfer (bank giro). A means of payment into a creditor's account by completing a form with the name of the creditor together with the name and branch of his bank and then handing it into a bank. This method of payment has increased to such an extent that the clearing banks established a credit clearing system in 1960 similar to their cheque clearing system: this enabled all credit transfers to be cleared through the *Bankers' Clearing House,

criminal law. *See* law of contract.

critical-path analysis. A set of techniques designed to locate the lowest cost method of executing a project that consists of several activities, some or all of which have to be performed consecutively. Its procedure is to determine the time required for each activity and the manner in which different activities are related, any sequence of consecutive activities defining a *path.* The critical *path* is the path with the longest time to completion; efforts at achieving the optimum combination of cost and time will then revolve around the substitution of noncritical paths and activities that are not on the critical path for critical-path activities. The traditional application of critical-path analysis is in the planning and control of construction programmes for heavy industrial projects, although it has also been used more recently in the context of such problems as work-layouts in an office and the design of clerical systems.

critical region. *See* hypothesis testing.

crossed cheque. A cheque marked with two parallel lines across the face, indicating that it must be paid into a bank account. Sometimes the words "and company" are added (these have no legal significance) and sometimes the words "not negotiable" (*see* negotiability). All these are general crossings, but other words, such as the name of a bank, may be added, which restrict the negotiability of a cheque and are known as *special crossings.*

cross-elasticity of demand. The reaction in the demand for a product (x) following a change in the price of another (y), It is quantified as the value of the proportional change in the quantity of x bought, divided by the proportional change in the price of y:

$$\eta_{xy} = \frac{p_y}{q_x}\frac{\partial q_x}{\partial p_y} = \frac{\partial \log q_x}{\partial \log p_y}$$

A positive cross-elasticity of demand indicates that the goods are substitutes; for example, a fall in the price of fresh vegetables will reduce the demand for frozen vegetables. A negative cross-elasticity of demand indicates that goods are complements; a rise in the price of petrol will reduce the number of cars purchased. A high value, either positive or negative, signifies a strong relationship between the two products, whereas a value close to zero signifies a weak relationship.

cross rate. *See* indirect parity.

cross-section analysis. Analysis of heterogeneous data relating to one time period. Thus an analysis of demand for a particular product might proceed by the stratification of consumers into different income groups and the examination of demand behaviour in each stratum at a particular point in time. Cross-section analysis is often used in combination with time series data in econometric studies; time series analysis by itself is inferior when the data under consideration has a wide dispersion (such as income per capita); however, cross-section data may be costly or difficult to obtain. *Compare* time series.

crude birth (death) rate. *See* birth rate, death rate.

C.S.O. *See* Central Statistical Office.

cubic function. A function containing at least one independent variable that is raised to the third power but none raised to any greater power, e.g:

$$w = ax + by^2 + cz^3.$$

The graph of a cubic function with one independent variable will characteristically display two curves.

cum. (Latin for: with; inclusive of (in connection with securities). A share quoted *cum dividend means that a purchaser will be entitled to receive a dividend shortly to be announced or paid. Similarly cum interest means with current interest, cum rights means with rights recently issued, cum bonus or cum capitalization means with a bonus recently declared. The sale of a security cum all means with all advantages accruing to the purchaser. *Compare* ex.

cum dividend. Denoting the price of a share on the stock exchange when it includes the right to receive the next dividend payable. Shares are normally taken to be cum dividend, unless they are purchased within one month of the payment of the dividend. *Compare* ex dividend.

cumulative distribution (in statistics). A *distribution of *cumulative probabilities. One of the most frequent applications of cumulative distributions in applied statistics is for the purpose of comparison, for instance to compare the weight distributions of several different groups of school children. A simple method of comparison using cumulative distributions is by graphs. *See also* ogive, distribution function.

cumulative frequency distribution. A *frequency distribution in which the frequencies are cumulative.

cumulative probability. The *probability that a random variable takes a value below or (less commonly) above a specified value.

currency. 1. The money in circulation in a country, originally gold, silver, and copper, but now also including bank notes, bills of exchange, cheques, and other substitutes for coins.

2. The period that has to run before the maturity of a bill of exchange.

currency appreciation and depreciation. Increases and decreases in the *free exchange rate of a currency. *See also* devaluation, revaluation.

current account. 1. *See* bank account.

2. *See* balance of payments.

current assets. The working capital of a company, i.e. those assets, such as stock (either raw materials or finished products), used to generate more income, and other assets, such as cash with a bank or money owed to the company. Current assets represent the comparatively liquid assets of a company by which it is able, at least in the short term, to finance the cost of generating further income. An essential difference between the nature of current and *fixed assets is that the former should be continually turning over, whereas the latter should be relatively static.

current cost accounting. *See* inflation accounting.

current liabilities. Liabilities that become due for payment within a year. They are distinguished from *deferred liabilities by the time of payment. Typical examples are trade creditors (usually on one to three months' credit), dividends declared, and taxation, although the same balance sheet can show different tax liabilities as both current and deferred. This distinction between liabilities on a balance sheet is useful since a comparison can then be made between current assets and liabilities to assess the short-term position.

current purchasing power accounting. *See* inflation accounting.

current ratio. The ratio of the current assets of a business (including stock and work-in-progress) to its current liabilities. The ratio gives an idea of the status of a business in terms of cash flow and the adequacy of the working capital. It is usually thought that the value of the ratio should exceed two for comfortable trading. However, if the saleability of the stock is in question, the *liquid ratio is a more accurate measure.

current yield. *See* flat yield.

curriculum vitae. (Latin for: the course of one's life.) A brief account of one's qualifications and career often required by employers from job applicants. *See* personnel selection.

Customs and Excise. A U.K. government department that collects and administers *indirect taxation (*compare* Inland Revenue), including value added tax; duties on tobacco, hydrocarbon oil, and alcoholic drinks; protective duties; and betting and revenue duties. It is responsible for preventing and detecting evasion of the revenue laws. It performs a wide range of nonrevenue agency work for other departments, such as the enforcement of prohibitions and restrictions on the import and export of certain classes of goods, exchange currency control, and the compilation of U.K. overseas trade statistics from import and export documents. The uniformed branch (the Customs Waterguard Service) are stationed at ports and airports and are concerned with the prevention of smuggling.

customs assigned number. A number allocated to a registered exporter by H.M. Customs and Excise, permitting goods to be exported without going through the *pre-entry procedure. The customs assigned number has to be notified to the shipping company or airline before loading and the number must appear on the bill of lading or the air waybill.

customs union. Two or more countries that agree to have no trading or customs barriers between them. They also usually agree to a common external tariff against states that are not members of the union. The *European Economic Community is a customs union.

cut-throat competition. A market situation resulting from oligopoly or duopoly, when the oligopolist (or duopolist) continues to cut prices until price is less than marginal cost, hoping to sustain losses in the short run but eventually to capture a larger market share for himself by driving out some of his competitors.

cyclical unemployment. Unemployment caused by fluctuations in the *trade cycle. Unemployment will increase in a recession and will decrease in the subsequent economic recovery. In recent years the trade cycle has become irregular, due largely to governmental policy, and as a result this type of unemployment has become less important.

D

daisywheel printer. A type of *character printer providing letter-quality output from a computer. The printable characters are located at the end of stalks radiating from a central hub; hence the name and its alternative, *petal printer*. The daisywheel containing the characters may be easily changed enabling the use of several fonts and character sets.

damages. Compensation that a court in a civil (as opposed to criminal) case decides should be paid by one person to another, either because the former has broken a contract with the latter or because he has committed a civil wrong or tort against the other.

Damages may be *liquidated*, i.e. certain in amount, as when a contract provides that a certain amount is to be paid to the aggrieved party in the case of a breach, or *unliquidated*, i.e. uncertain in amount, in which case a court, if it decides that damages must be paid, must also decide upon the amount. The damages may, in this latter case, be *contemptuous*, when the court decides that the person bringing the case is technically right but should be awarded ludicrously small damages to show that they think that the case should never have been brought; *nominal*, if the court decides that the person bringing the case is right but that he has not suffered any loss for which he ought to be compensated; *substantial*, in which the court awards such amount to the person bringing the case as it estimates will place him financially in the same position as he would have been had the wrong not been done to him or the contract had not been broken; or exemplary, in which the court awards damages far in excess of what is needed to compensate the aggrieved party in order to punish the wrongdoer. Substantial damages may include *specific* damages, i.e. damages of an exactly assessable amount, such as medical expenses incurred as a result of an injury suffered by the aggrieved party, and *general* damages, i.e. damages not exactly assessable, such as damages for loss of life expectancy.

danger money. *See* occupational hazard.

database (data bank). Data organized in direct access *storage devices in such a way that up-to-date information is immediately available. The software that is used to create, maintain, and access the database is known as the *database management system* (DBMS).

data file. *See* file.

data processing. Operations performed on data by a computer system in order to rationalize such data or to extract information from it. The data processing department of an organization will include management, systems analysis, computer programming, and computer operation in its functions. It will also embrace *organization and methods and certain operations research activities and will function according to a set of standard procedures.

dated securities. *See* redeemable security.

day books. Books of account in which all the purchases and sales of a business are listed individually on the day on which they occur, before being posted to the appropriate ledger. Day books are used as part of the journal system of identifying debits with the equivalent credits. It is usual to keep separate purchases day books and sales day books.

days of grace. The three days that are allowed before a bill of exchange is actually due if it is not payable on demand. Days of grace have been abolished in nearly all countries except England. *See also* due date.

A larger number of days of grace are allowed by insurance companies within which premiums due on life and fire insurance policies may be paid, although the due date of a premium is that specified in the policy.

D.E.A. *See* Department of Economic Affairs.

deadweight debt. Any debt that is not incurred in return for a real asset. Most of the *National Debt is a deadweight debt as it was accumulated in waging war.

deadweight tonnage. *See* tonnage.

dealer. (esp. in the U.S.) A *stockjobber.

dealing for the account. *See* inter-account deal.

dear money. Money that can only be borrowed with difficulty and at a high rate of interest. *See also* open market operations, easy money.

death duties. Taxes paid to the government at, or by reason of, the death of any person. In the twentieth century in the U.K. the main type of death duty has been *estate duty. However, it was abolished by the Finance Act (1975) and replaced by *capital transfer tax, which includes the transfer of a person's property on his death to his executors.

Although capital transfer tax and capital gains tax are often incurred as a result of a person's death, and can therefore be called death duties, they both also apply to lifetime transactions. There is, therefore, no longer any form of tax that is charged solely at death.

death rate. The crude death rate for any given year is the number of deaths per 1000 of the average population for that year. The crude death rate has the same disadvantages as the crude *birth rate and, like the latter, can be calculated for a section of the population or standardized. The *infant mortality rate, for instance, is an age-specific death rate. The tendency shown by the populations of the advanced nations to rise during and soon after the process of industrialization was attributed more to falling death rates among the younger sections of the population than to rising birth rates.

debenture. A document setting out the terms of a loan, usually to a company. The term is also used for the loan itself or for each unit of the loan (in the U.K., usually £1). When debentures are issued to many different people, the debenture document is usually held by a trustee on their behalf. Debentures may be secured or unsecured. A *secured debenture* may be secured by a fixed charge or by a floating charge. In the case of a fixed charge, the security is a particular item of the company's property, which the trustee may sell for the debenture-holders if they have not been repaid by the repayment date. A floating charge is a charge on all the assets owned by the company, any of which may be sold to repay the debentures. In the case of an *unsecured debenture*, the debenture-holders, if they have not been repaid by the repayment date, must wait until the company has been wound up. They will then have priority over all shareholders for the repayment of their capital.

The other main distinction between a debenture-holder and a shareholder is that the former is entitled to fixed, regular, and predetermined payments of interest, whereas the latter is paid a dividend that may vary with the profits of the company. A *perpetual debenture* cannot be redeemed on demand; an *irredeemable debenture* cannot be cashed at any time and is bought solely for the interest payments.

debit note. A document issued by one party to a transaction to the other to inform him that his account has been debited with the amount shown. A debit note is usually supplementary to an invoice and may refer to an inadvertent undercharge on the invoice.

debt. A sum of money or some other asset owed by one person or group to another. Debts result from deferral of payment for a good or from borrowing to purchase a good or service. *Debt servicing* is interest repayment on a debt. Certain debts, such as bills of exchange, can be assigned to other people by the creditor and become negotiable instruments. *Compare* credit. *See also* National Debt.

debtor. A person or institution that owes money to an individual, company, or other legal entity. The most common type of debtors to companies are trade and sundry debtors: these represent current assets on the balance sheet, as these debts are expected to be realized within one year. Trade debtors are those individuals or companies to whom a sale has been made, but who have not yet paid. Sundry debtors are also usually current and could consist of items arising from factors ancilliary to the company's main business, such as a loan to an employee to help cover moving expenses. *See also* bad debts.

decile. One of nine values dividing a statistical distribution into ten equal portions when it is arranged in order of magnitude. Thus the first decile has 10% of the items in the distribution falling below it, the second has 20% below it, and so on. *See also* percentile, quartile.

decimal currency. Currency in which the standard unit is divided into 100 subunits. This facilitates arithmetic calculation. The first state to adopt decimal currency was the U.S. (in 1792), quickly followed by many European states during the Napoleonic era. Most Commonwealth countries changed to decimal currency in the 1950s and 1960s, for example Australia adopted it on 14 February 1966 and New Zealand followed on 10 July 1967. The U.K. switched to decimal currency on 15 February 1971. However, since the pound is an uncommonly large standard unit of currency, it was felt that 100 subdivisions would not be enough to prevent excessive price increases. Accordingly, the halfpenny was retained until 1985. The U.K. decimal coins are the penny and two-pence pieces (of bronze) and the five-pence piece, ten-pence piece, and fifty-pence piece (all made of cupro-nickel). The £1 coin (made of nickel brass) was introduced in 1983. Most countries in the world now have decimal currencies.

decimal notation. *See* binary notation.

decision model. A *model used primarily as a source of control, as in an industrial process. The dependent variable is often called the *outcome* or *output* of the model while the independent variables (or inputs) are divided into controllable decision variables and noncontrollable (but not necessarily constant) parameters. There must be a causal functional relationship connecting the outcome of the model with the decision variables and parameters and there will often be constraints on the decision variables. The independent variables must include at least one decision variable, otherwise the model would be of no use as a source of control.

declaration day. The last day in any *account on which a share *option may be taken or *declared* for *settlement in respect of that account. Declaration day is always the penultimate day of the account.

decreasing marginal cost. *See* marginal cost.

decreasing returns. *See* returns to scale.

decreasing term assurance. A type of *term assurance with the sum assured in the event of death decreasing each year. While this type of policy is utilized for many purposes it is probably most commonly used in connection with mortgages on a house purchase. The sum assured can be arranged in connection with the original loan so that it reduces as the loan is repaid by the borrower. By this method the amount outstanding on the loan is covered at all times and would be cleared by the sum assured in the event of a premature death.

decree of sequestration. *See* sequestration.

deductible. Another word for excess (*see* excess policy). It is used frequently in fire insurance and is most commonly used in the U.S.

deductions at source. The deduction of income tax from income before it has reached its recipient. The individual or organization deducting the tax will then pass on the tax to the Inland Revenue. This is a common practice in the U.K. since it is an economical method of collection and prevents evasion.

deed. A document under seal, i.e. one signed by the party or parties to it in the presence of witnesses, then sealed. (The seal was originally made by impressing the personal marks or signets of the parties on hot red wax attached to the document.) It is then delivered to the person in whose favour it is made. The observance of these formalities ensures that any promises (usually in this instance called *covenants)* contained within the document are legally enforceable, even if completely gratuitous and made for no *consideration. However, in the U.K. the official stamp of the Inland Revenue must be impressed upon the document and the appropriate amount of stamp duty (50p) paid before it can be produced before a court as evidence. The old method of sealing a deed with hot wax and a signet has now largely died out and has been superseded by the use of *wafer seals.* These are small circular pieces of red adhesive paper, which are merely attached to the document opposite the signatures of each party. Most companies, however, still have their own seals and impress their own individual emblems on deeds to which they are parties.

deed of arrangement. A document setting out the terms of an agreement between an insolvent debtor and some or all of his creditors. The agreement is designed to enable each creditor to be paid off in whole or in part without making the debtor bankrupt. The form, content, and registration of these deeds are governed by various rules, mainly contained in the Deeds of Arrangement Act (1914). The deed may take various forms, e.g. an assignment of some or all of the debtor's property to a trustee for the creditors (*deed of assignment*), an appointment of inspectors to run the debtor's business as a going concern or with a view to eventually winding it up (*deed of inspectorship*), an agreement that no creditor will take legal proceedings against the debtor until he has had a certain time to pay (*let-*

ter of licence), or an agreement that each creditor will accept a certain percentage in settlement of the whole debt (*deed of composition*). A deed of arrangement is usually made before a bankruptcy petition is presented to a court, but may be made afterwards if the court consents.

deed of covenant. A *deed by which a person promises to pay another a sum or sums of money. If such a deed provides for regular payments to be made for a period exceeding six years, the payer may reclaim from the Inland Revenue any income tax paid on such sums.

deep-pocket view. An argument that a subsidiary may have access to more funds than an independent firm of equivalent size. The subsidiary might then be prepared to suffer large losses in a price war to drive competitors out of the industry and establish a monopoly. However, this is not the best strategy to maximize profits, as the funds would be financing an unprofitable activity when they could be utilized profitably elsewhere. In addition, the independent should be able to borrow funds to survive the price war.

default. A failure to comply with the terms of a contract. The seller may default by not delivering whatever it is that he has contracted to deliver. He may ask for extra time but if this is not granted he goes into default. A buyer may default by failing to take up and pay for goods that he has contracted to buy. In most contracts a default procedure is laid down. This will normally refer the parties to an arbitration as a prerequisite to litigation.

deferred annuity. An *annuity that requires the payment of a single premium or a series of annual premiums some years before the annuity is due to start. The bulk of these are sold in connection with approved pension schemes.

deferred assets. Assets that are neither fixed nor current.

deferred liabilities. Liabilities that are not current.

deferred rebate. A rebate made by a shipping company to shippers to encourage them to support a particular line. It is made at stated periods, often on the understanding that all goods shipped to a particular destination are shipped by that line. *See also* aggregated rebate scheme.

deferred taxation. The tax liability that, under present circumstances, will eventually come due by a company but is not at present considered in the tax assessments made by the tax authorities on the company. It may arise from the excess in the current accounting year's profit over taxable income. Provisions would also be made for the potential chargeable gain tax liability on the revaluation of assets held (such as land) and for tax payments deferred by means of *roll-over relief. The amount of deferred taxation must be disclosed in the notes to the *published accounts of companies.

deficit financing. A planned excess of governmental expenditure over the revenue raised by taxation, the gap being financed by borrowing. It is a common fiscal method of stimulating the economy as extra money is pumped into the economic system. Deficit financing was first advocated by John Maynard Keynes (1883–1946) and has become an accepted part of the policies of post-war governments.

deflation. 1. A reduction in the general price level due to a decrease in the economic activity of a nation. The price level as well as national income, output, and employment will all fall. During the twentieth century the only sustained period of deflation in the U.K. existed between 1920 and 1938 when the general price level fell by almost 50%. Governments introduce deflationary policies for several reasons: to decrease the rate of inflation, to cut the volume of imports, or to prevent the economy from becoming *overheated. Among the deflationary policies available to the government are increases in the interest rate, increases in level of taxation, and *credit squeezes (*see also* deflationary gap, disinflation).

2. The conversion of a factor (such as a wage, the cost of raw materials, etc.) from a nominal to a real amount, when measured in monetary terms. For example, the nominal incrcase in the price of consumer durables must be divided by the rate of inflation to arrive at the real increase in the price.

deflationary gap. The difference between the amount that is actually spent in an economy and the amount that would have to be spent in theory in order to maintain output at a level corresponding to full employment.

defunct company. A limited company that has ceased to operate and has been wound up. It is removed from the Register of Companies and included in the Register of Defunct Companies (often referred to as the Dead Book).

degrees of freedom. A parameter of the chi-square distribution, Student's t distribution, and the F distribution. When a test of hypothesis is made using formulae or techniques based on any of these three, the correct degrees of freedom must be calculated and taken into consideration when determining the significance of the results. Degrees of freedom represent the number of changes that can be made to a group of numbers while still satisfying any external constraint. For example, one can select three numbers that must add up to a total of 16. Two of these numbers can be of any value but the third is then restricted so that the total comes to 16: if the first two numbers are four and eight then the third must be four, and if the first two numbers are 24 and 28 then the third must be -36. In this case there are two degrees of freedom. Usually the degrees of freedom appropriate to any test will be equal to the number of items in the random example on which the test is based, minus one.

de-industrialization. A dramatic decline in the relative importance of a country's manufacturing sector. As a country reaches economic maturity it is not uncommon for the manufacturing sector to decline relative to other sectors of the economy, in particular to the service sector. This development tends to reflect changes in the pattern of final demand. De-industrialization, which occurs as a result of a country's increasing uncompetitiveness vis-à-vis trade partners, can constitute a serious problem, bringing with it a loss of output and rising unemployment.

del credere agent. An agent who in addition to obtaining orders on behalf of his principal also guarantees that the customer will pay for the goods. Agents who accept the del credere risk charge an extra commission to cover this risk.

delegatus non potest delegare. (Latin for: a delegate cannot delegate.) An agent who has contracted to undertake work has no implicit right to delegate to another. This is often applied to situations in which the personal abilities of the agent are of paramount importance. However, in many fields delegation is customary; for example, in the building industry subcontracting is commonplace.

delivered pricing. A pricing system in which the producer undertakes to deliver his product, or to have it delivered, and includes transportation costs in the quoted price.

It allows the producer to discriminate between geographical areas by quoting price differentials that do not reflect the true differentials in transport costs. Geographical price discrimination is more difficult under a system of *mill pricing.

delivery note. A document that usually accompanies the delivery of goods. It is often similar to an *advice note, but is usually prepared in duplicate so that the customer or his representative can sign one copy to provide the vendor with evidence that the delivery has been made. As it lists the quality, quantity, and marks and numbers (if applicable) of a consignment it also serves as a check to the customer that he has received what he ordered.

demand curve. A curve that relates the amount of the good a consumer wishes to buy with the maximum he is willing to pay for it, on the assumption that income and all other prices remain fixed. It is the graph of the *demand function, holding all variables other than the price of the particular good constant. It is customary to plot price on the vertical axis and quantity on the horizontal axis. From the demand curve one can read off what quantities will be demanded at various prices.

Unless the good is a *Giffen good, the curve will slope downwards to the right, showing that a greater quantity will be demanded at a lower price. Changes in the prices of other goods and income will shift the curve on the graph. For example, an increase in income will shift the demand curve to the right if the good is a *normal good, to the left if it is a Giffen good. An increase in the price of another good will shift the curve to the left or right depending on whether it is a gross *complement or gross *substitute. Finally, a change in tastes will alter the form of the demand function, with results according to the changes specified.

The demand curves of individual consumers may be added together to obtain an aggregate or market demand curve. Graphically this is done by displacing one graph to the left by the quantity demanded at each price level by the other. The resulting demand curve tends to be less steeply sloping. The intersection of the demand curve with the *supply curve indicates the equilibrium price of a good.

Demand curves may also be drawn relating the amount of one good a consumer wishes to purchase and the maximum price he is willing to pay for some other good, the prices of these goods, as well as income, being held constant. The curve will rise to the right in the case of a substitute and fall in the case of a complement.

demand deposit (in the U.S.). A bank deposit on current account that can be withdrawn on demand without notice.

demand function. A mathematical relationship between the quantity of a good that a consumer wishes to buy and the variables that affect this choice. The main variables will be the price of the good itself, the prices of all other goods (especially close *complements and *substitutes), the size of the consumer's income, and the tastes of the consumer. It is represented geometrically by the *demand curve.

demand-pull inflation. A theory of *inflation that attributes price rises to increases in aggregate demand over and above available supply at full employment level.

Studies of the U.K. economy have indicated that most of the inflation arising in the U.K. in the last 30 years has been created by demand-pull rather than by cost-push factors, especially as it has frequently been deliberate government policy to take action to stimulate the economy in an attempt to maintain full employment. *See also* inflationary gap. *Compare* cost-push push inflation.

demand theory. The branch of *price theory that deals with the way in which the consumer makes his choices for consumption with a given income and set of prices. It is essentially a *partial equilibrium analysis (*see* utility maximization).

demarcation dispute. An industrial dispute between trade unions or between sections of the same union regarding who should perform certain functions when the work involves more than one type of worker. Such disputes often arise when a new process is introduced, since there is no clear-cut division between the different parts of the work and no established precedent. Demarcation disputes were prevalent in the U.K. in the 1960s, but have declined following the creation of a Demarcation Disputes Tribunal by the T.U.C.

demography. The statistical study of human populations. This encompasses an examination of the total size of a population, its composition by age, sex, location, occupation, etc., and its birth and death rates within these categories. It also includes such sociological features as migration, the average size of a family, and the average age at marriage. Demographic data is recorded by censuses of population and by registration of births, marriages, changes of address, etc. The frequent inadequacy or inaccuracy of such statistics in developing countries is a major problem because, in the case of highly populated countries such as India, a viable population policy is a matter of urgent necessity. Demographic studies can be inductive as well as descriptive. Prediction is usually based on extrapolation.

demurrage. A penalty payment provided for in a contract to compensate one party if the other is late in performing his obligation. It is usually calculated as a certain amount for each day that performance (usually the loading of a ship or completion of a building) is delayed. Even if the actual loss caused by the delay is less than the demurrage provided for in the contract, the full amount of the demurrage must still be paid.

denationalization. *See* privatization.

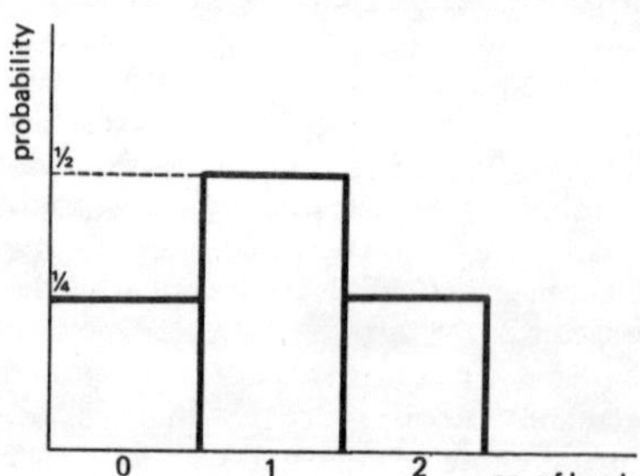

Fig. 1: Density function of a discrete variable

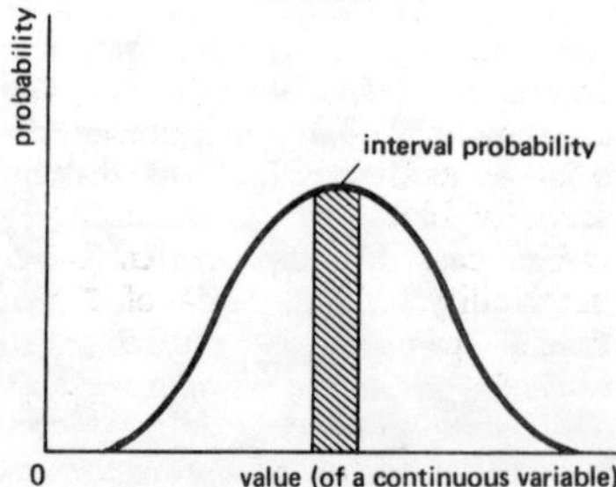

Fig. 2: Density function of a continuous variable

density (frequency) function. A function that defines the numerical probabilities of an event or random variable for each value or interval of values that the variable can take. For instance, the probability of getting two heads, one head, and no heads when two coins are tossed is respectively a quarter, a half, and a quarter. These results can be represented geometrically as in Fig. 1. It will be observed that the above probabilities add up to one, and this will always be the case when the probabilities of all possible values that a discrete variable can take are enumerated. Such a range of probabilities can also be represented functionally and in fact the number of heads obtained in the tossing of unbiased coins follows the binomial distribution and can be written:

$$[2!/x!(2-x)!](\tfrac{1}{2})^x(\tfrac{1}{2})^{2-x}$$

where x represents the variable concerned (0, 1, and 2: the number of heads obtained) and ! is the factorial sign (0! = 1). Continuous variables present a rather different situation for probability analysis as compared with discrete variables because the probability, for instance, that a man is six feet tall is infinitesimally small if the measurements are absolutely exact. However, one can visualize the assessment of probabilities of values of a continuous variable; thus we can find the probability that a man's height is between 71.9 inches and 72.1 inches (or any smaller interval) rather than that it is 72 inches exactly. Geometrically the density function of a continuous variable is represented as a curve, as in Fig. 2, rather than as a series of blocks, as in the discrete variable case in Fig. 1. An interval probability, such as that of a man's height, can be interpreted as the shaded area in Fig. 2 calculated as a percentage of the total area under the curve. Calculation and manipulation of continuous variable probabilities involve integral calculus; discrete variable probabilities involve summation. The term density function is now used in connection with both discrete variables and continuous variables although, strictly speaking, it relates more to the nature of continuous variables; the terms *frequency function* or *frequency probability function* are sometimes used in connection with discrete variables. *See also* probability, distribution.

Department of Economic Affairs (D.E.A.). A U.K. government department created in 1964 to take over the major part of the Treasury's responsibility for economic planning and coordination. Great emphasis was laid on the fact that the department stood for the interests of the economy as a whole and had no narrow departmental interests to defend. Relations with the Treasury were uneasy as respective roles were never clearly defined, leading to clashes over policy. The creation of the D.E.A. was followed by a series of economic crises culminating in the devaluation of November 1967. As a result, the National Economic Plan (prepared in September 1965) was recognized as obsolete and discarded. The staff at the D.E.A. consisted of a high concentration of economists, statisticians, and industrialists. The D.E.A. was disbanded in 1969: its economic functions were taken over by the Treasury and its industrial functions were transferred to the Ministry of Technology.

Department of Employment. A U.K. government department that is responsible for the efficient use of manpower resources. Its network of Employment Offices provide a free service in matching employers seeking labour and workers seeking employment. In addition it administers the Government Training Centres (which teach skilled crafts), the Industrial Rehabilitation Units (for training the disabled and handicapped to re-enter employment), and the Youth Employment Service. It also deals with the payment of unemployment benefits, the repayment of income tax to unemployed workers, the collection and publication of labour statistics, and provides a liaison service with the *International Labour Organization.

Until 1968, the department was known as the Ministry of Labour and from 1968-70 as the Department of Employment and Productivity. In 1974 some of its responsibilities were transferred to the newly created *Manpower Services Commission and the * Health and Safety Commission.

dependent variable. 1. A *variable whose value is determined by the value assumed by the relevant *independent variable or variables. The dependent variable is normally placed on the left hand side of an equation.

2. A variable that does not have the property of *independence in connection with another variable under consideration.

deposit. 1. The amount a customer has to pay to reserve an article for future purchase.

2. The amount of the first instalment in hire purchase. It has become an instrument of monetary policy for the government to increase or decrease the legal amount of this first instalment, according to whether it wishes to decrease or increase the demand for goods.

deposit account. *See* bank account.

deposit society. *See* friendly society.

depreciation. 1. The decrease in value of an asset through wear and tear, obsolescence, or any other factor that decreases its usefulness. In accounting, when a *fixed asset is bought by a company, its total cost is not charged immediately to the *profit and loss account for that accounting period on the basis that this asset will be used over a longer period of time as part of the company's means of earning profits. Consequently a fixed asset is depreciated in the accounts over its useful life; a certain proportion of its cost value is charged each year to the profit and loss account, correspondingly reducing the value of that fixed asset in the balance sheet. The proportion so charged is determined by the estimated useful life of the asset concerned. At the end of this period the whole asset should have been charged to the profit and loss account.

2. A drop in the value of the floating rate of exchange of one currency in terms of another. *See* devaluation.

depression (slump). The stage of the standard *trade cycle that is characterized by the under-utilization of all the factors of production (i.e. when there is excess capacity and unemployment) and a reduced level of demand. Prices tend to fall, confidence in the future is lacking, and investment is reduced. This is usually taken to be the lowest point of the business cycle. The next stage in the cycle is the *recovery. The period 1929–33 is often referred to as the *Depression*.

derived demand. The demand for a good that is due to its use as a factor of production for another good. For example, few people want chickens for pets but they are very much in demand since they produce eggs and meat. The demand for chickens is the demand derived from that for eggs and meat. If the demand for either of these should drop, so presumably would the farmers' demand for chickens. The demand for all the factors of production is a derived demand. No one wants capital goods for their own sake, but for the consumer goods they produce.

devaluation. The reduction in the value of a currency in terms of the supporting monetary metal (usually gold) or in terms of another country's currency, i.e. a decrease in the value of its fixed exchange rate. Devaluation is sometimes forced upon a country by a massive adverse trade balance and is intended to remedy the situation by stimulating demand for its exports by making them cheaper and discouraging imports as foreign goods become dearer. However, as devaluation causes other countries to lose confidence in the country devaluing, it cannot be resorted to frequently and member countries of the *International Monetary Fund are obliged to consult their fellow members before a devaluation. Additionally, if several countries devalue simultaneously much of the benefit may be lost. The pound sterling was devalued in 1949 and 1967. *Compare* depreciation. *See also* J-curve.

developing (underdeveloped, less developed) country. A country whose level of economic development is not yet sufficiently advanced to generate the savings necessary to finance the investment needed to further industrialization. The developing countries earn their foreign reserves mainly from *primary production and are therefore vulnerable to changes in world prices for primary products and to deteriorating *terms of trade. Many are heavily dependent on a single product, which increases their vulnerability to world markets. The problem of overpopulation is acute in many of the developing countries and tends to nullify the effect of increases in national income, keeping the average standard of living at a low level. The developing countries, with about 70% of the world's population, are usually considered to include all Africa except the Republic of South Africa and possibly Zimbabwe, all Asia except Japan and the U.S.S.R., all Central and Latin America except Argentina, the Caribbean and Pacific Islands, and sometimes South Eastern Europe. The criteria usually used to distinguish the developing countries are national income, net average per capita income, energy available per head, literacy, etc. Certain characteristics are common in all developing countries: poverty, inadequate diet, disease, illiteracy, an agricultural economy, high fertility, and institutional arrangements that hinder economic growth. The developing countries are attempting to achieve in one or two decades the level of economic development of the Western countries, which took several centuries to reach. They rely to a large extent on international aid, both in the form of capital and in technical knowledge. *See* United Nations Conference on Trade and Development, New International Economic Order, Cocoyoc Declaration.

development areas. Depressed areas in which the level of business activity, as reflected generally by the level of employment, is lower (and unemployment higher) than some specified percentage of the national average. These areas are so distinguished in order that special programmes (such as *investment incentives) can be implemented to encourage new industries into them. Development areas are mostly areas of traditional heavy industry, such as coal-mining and steel production.

differential calculus. *See* calculus.

digital computer. *See* computer.

dilution. The reduction in control and/or earnings suffered by existing shareholders of a company when new issues of shares are made.

diminishing balance. *See* reducing balance.

diminishing marginal utility. The law of diminishing marginal utility states that after a certain point successive equal units of a commodity being consumed yield less and less satisfaction. For example, the more chocolate one eats the less the added enjoyment of the last piece. The mathematical significance is that the first partial derivative of the marginal utility will be negative.

diminishing returns (diminishing marginal product). The law of diminishing returns states that as more and more of one input is added, keeping the others fixed, after some point one will move farther and farther from the best input mix, and consequently the returns in physical terms from each additional unit of input will grow less and less. The law assumes that the units of input being increased are identical and that technology does not change. The mathematical significance is that the first derivative of the marginal product will become negative after some point.

direct access. *See* storage device.

direct costs (variable costs, prime costs). Costs that vary directly, though not always proportionately, with the volume of output. The principal direct costs are labour, raw materials, and power. In accounting, direct costs are identifiable as directly arising from and relating to the various *cost units or *cost centres being used as a means of analysing costs. For example, if a sales department is being used as a cost centre, then a direct cost would be the wages of those working in that department. *Compare* indirect costs.

direct debits. An extension of the *credit transfer system in which a supplier, by agreement with the purchaser, credits his own bank account to the debit of the purchaser's account with the cost of goods or services supplied. It is convenient for such transactions as the delivery of petrol by the oil companies to garages, as the cost and quantity delivered are not constant.

direct labour. The part of the workforce in a business that is directly concerned with the manufacture of goods or the provision of a service. *Compare* indirect labour.

direct-mail shot. *See* direct selling.

directors. Those persons who are appointed to run a company and have the responsibility of thereby fulfilling all the statutory obligations, both of the directors and the company. In the case of smaller private companies the directors are frequently the major shareholders. As companies grow larger and are offered for sale to the public, shareholders and directors tend to become separate persons. The first directors of a company are normally appointed from the *articles of association of the company with successive directors being appointed under the terms of these articles. *See also* corporate management.

direct production. The production of a commodity without the use of machinery and without the division of labour into various specialized tasks. *Compare* roundabout production.

direct-response selling. *See* direct selling.

direct selling. The selling of goods by the producer to the consumer without the intermediary of either whosesaler or retailer. It usually involves door-to-door selling or direct-response promotion, either by advertising in newspapers, magazines, etc., and including a reader-reply form in the advertisement, or by *direct-mail shot* (posting sales literature direct to potential customers). In direct-mail selling the seller acquires a list of potential customers to whom he posts his advertising literature direct, usually including a postage-paid reader-reply card. Some businesses specialize in direct selling, even though they are not themselves the producers of the goods offered, and there is a trade in lists of potential customers. A seller may build up his own list for a direct-mail shot or he may rent a list *(list renting*). As list renting is often confined to a single direct-mail shot, it is usual for the owner of the list to carry out the mailing so that the hirer cannot copy it for subsequent use. To ensure that the mailing is correctly carried out, the hirer may include addresses known to him (called *sleepers*).

direct taxation. Taxation levied on individuals or corporations and paid by them to the taxation authority either directly or through an employer (*see* P.A.Y.E.): this form of taxation contrasts with *indirect taxation, which is levied on goods and services. Direct taxation includes income tax, capital gains tax, corporation tax, and capital transfer tax. It has the advantage of being related to the ability to pay the tax and the disadvantage that it may sometimes be a disincentive to working and saving. It is therefore usual for governments to raise their revenue by a mixture of both forms of taxation. As the rate of direct taxes usually increases with income or capital they are progressive taxes (*see* income tax) and as they are more immediately apparent than other forms and not so easily shifted (*see* shifting) they are more politically significant.

dirty (foul) bill of lading. A *bill of lading that bears an endorsement by the master or mate of a ship to the effect that the goods referred to in the bill arrived for loading in a defective condition. *Compare* clean bill of lading.

dirty float. A policy in which the exchange rate of a currency is nominally allowed to float freely, but the monetary authorities surreptitiously intercede in order to stabilize and influence the movements in the rate. The U.K. pound was the subject of a dirty float in the early 1970s, when its depreciation was partially arrested by government intervention on the foreign exchange markets.

disc. *See* disk.

disclosure. At common law the duty of disclosure remains in force throughout all negotiations leading up to the formation of the contract of insurance. Once the contract is in force it is subject only to ordinary good faith. However, this position may be amended by specific provisions in the contract. For example, at common law a person arranging a personal accident assurance would not have to disclose the fact that during the contract's duration he changed his occupation to one that was more hazardous. However, these types of contract normally contain the condition requiring the insured to notify the insurer of any such change in risk. Where the contract is not arranged on a long-term basis (these are usually insurances other than life assurances) a duty to disclose any change of a *material fact may arise on the contract's renewal. *See also* utmost good faith.

discount. **1.** A deduction from the price of an article, as allowed by a wholesaler to a retailer (*trade discount*) or by a retailer to a member of the public who pays in cash (*cash discount*).

2. To purchase a *bill of exchange for less than its face value. The party discounting the bill has the advantage of receiving the money before the bill matures, the amount of the discount depending on the length of the unexpired portion of the bill and the risks involved. Bills are usually discounted with a bank or a *discount house.

3. The amount by which the price of a security stands below its par or paid-up value. For example, a gilt-edged security standing at 98½ is said to be at a discount of 1½%.

4. The amount by which the price of a recently issued share stands below its issue price.

5. A share, on the London Stock Exchange, is said to be at a discount to the market when its *P/E ratio is below that of the market average. In this sense, the shares of a company may stand at a discount to those of other companies in the same industry or a sector of the market, as a whole, may stand at a discount to the rest of the market. These discounts reflect market sentiment regarding the outlook for the profits of the company or sector concerned.

6. To take into consideration an anticipated development. For example, an anticipated economic recession might be discounted by a stock exchange before it took place so that prices may be marked down even while companies were enjoying buoyant trading conditions. Similarly, publication of good results by a company may cause the price of its shares to remain unchanged or even to fall because the good results had been anticipated and reflected in an earlier rise. The good results are then said to have been discounted.

7. The amount by which a particular currency stands below par on the foreign exchange markets. *Compare* premium.

discounted cash flow (D.C.F.). *See* discounting back.

discount house. A financial institution that specializes in discounting *bills of exchange. Discount houses form part of the *discount market.

discounting back. Assessing the present value of a benefit or stream of benefits that will accrue in the future. For instance, what would it be worth to pay now to obtain an asset that will be worth £100 in three years time, or to obtain a security that will yield £100 a year for ever? The interest rate must be known before the solution can be found. The formula used is:

$$V_p = B_0 + B_1/(1 + r) + B_2/(1 + r)^2 + \ldots B_n/(1 + r)^n$$

where V_p is the present value of the asset, B_0 is the initial net benefit, B_1 is the net benefit accruing after one year, B_n is the net benefit in year n, and r is the interest rate. Accountants often describe this as a *discounted cash flow (D.C.F.).*

discount market (bill market). The London discount market deals principally with bills of exchange. When bills were the main means of payment for foreign and internal trade it was necessary that they should be readily negotiable. Consequently *accepting houses of known integrity accepted approved bills and the *discount houses readily discounted bills so accepted. These discount houses in turn borrowed from the commercial banks at call (*see* call money), and when the banks were unwilling to lend they borrowed from the Bank of England as *lender of last resort. All these institutions constitute the discount market. The market is now mostly in *Treasury bills as by agreement the commercial banks do not tender for Treasury bills but buy those they require from the bill brokers.

discount rate. 1. The rate at which a bill of exchange can be discounted. *See* discount (def. 2). **2.** The U.S. equivalent of *minimum lending rate.

discrete variable. *See* variable.

discretionary trust. *See* trustee.

discriminating monopoly. A form of monopoly in which a monopolist sells his products or services to two or more groups of consumers at different prices. As a result he obtains a greater profit than would otherwise be the case. An example is the Electricity Board's levying of different prices for electricity according to whether its use is domestic or industrial. If industrial users were forced to pay the higher domestic price so many would transfer to other forms of power that the net profit accruing from that sector would decrease due to the reduction in sales. If domestic users were allowed to pay the lower industrial price, the increase in sales would be insufficient to compensate for the reduction in profit on each unit and again the profit accruing from that sector would fall. By segmenting the market the monopolist thus increases his profit by charging what each part of the market will bear; in each sector, price is increased until the *price elasticity of each segment equals one. It is a necessary condition for this to succeed that arbitrage between segments cannot occur, e.g. factories cannot pipe electricity to neighbouring households. The difficulty of ensuring this is the main reason for its relative scarcity. Price discrimination is forbidden by restrictive practices legislation in many countries.

discriminating tariff. A tariff that is not applied equally to all the trading partners of a country. This is the basis of such custom unions as the E.E.C. The prohibition of these tariffs is one of the key features of GATT, except for those organizations attempting to promote long-term regional economic integration (such as the E.E.C.).

diseconomies of scale. *See* economies of scale.

disembodied technical change. *See* vintage model.

disequilibrium. A state in which *equilibrium has not been reached. *See also* stability, fundamental disequilibrium.

disguised (concealed) unemployment. The unemployment of those who are willing and able to work, but who are not actively seeking employment. For instance, in a recession there would be housewives who would like to obtain jobs but who have no opportunity to do so; there would also be pupils who had originally intended to leave school, but who now continue their education since no vacancies are available. These people are unemployed, but will not be included in the U.K. unemployment figures, which are collations of all those who register for work at the various employment offices. Thus the U.K. unemployment statistics invariably slightly underestimate the true number of those unemployed. This is not the case with the U.S. unemployment figures, which are calculated by a different method based on polls.

dishonour. A bill of exchange can be dishonoured either by nonacceptance (when the drawee refuses to accept the bill) or nonpayment (when the acceptor fails to pay it on the day on which it is due). A foreign bill so dishonoured must be protested (*see* protest) in order to preserve the holder's recourse against the drawer or endorsers, but this is not necessary for an inland bill. A cheque is dishonoured when the drawer's bank refuses to pay it because of insufficient funds in the drawer's account.

disinflation. The limiting or curbing of inflation by mildly deflationary measures (*see* deflation) in order to maintain or increase the purchasing power of the monetary unit. Disinflationary policies include restricting consumer expenditure by hire purchase controls, credit squeezes, the raising of interest rates, etc. Such policies have to be administered with care in order to avoid deflation.

disintermediation. A situation on the financial markets that arises when, owing to a change in interest rate, a *financial intermediary finds itself unable to continue *intermediation. For instance, if a building society has its borrowing rates fixed externally, a large rise in the market rate of interest leaves it unable to attract new funds because it will be paying those from whom it borrows less than other institutions. If it cannot attract new funds it cannot fulfil its function as an intermediary because it has no extra funds to lend to new borrowers. It is then in a situation of disintermediation.

disinvestment. Insufficient gross investment to cover the total of capital loss from wear and tear. Net investment is negative and the capital stock of the economy falls. This only normally happens when there is a deep depression in the economy. *See* investor, inventory investment.

disk. A direct access computer *storage device consisting of a flat disk coated with magnetic material. Information is stored on concentric tracks and access is effected by rotating the disk on a spindle and reading with a moving head. *Floppy disks* or diskettes looking like pliable record discs and varying in size from 3 to 8 inches diameter are common on business *microcomputers; they can typically hold 1 megabyte of information and are relatively inexpensive. A *fixed disk* is one that cannot be physically removed from the system. *Mainframes commonly use disk packs with several disks stacked on one spindle.

dispersion. The degree to which the items of a statistical distribution (or set of values) are scattered about their mean. Dispersion is one of the major parametric characteristics of a distribution, the others being location (measured by the mean), *skewness, and *kurtosis, and a mean should be considered in isolation from a measure of dispersion of the items to which the mean relates. There are several measures of dispersion, easily the most important of them being the *variance or its square root, the *standard deviation.

displacement tonnage. *See* tonnage.

disposable income. The amount of income left to an individual for spending and saving. It is the income that remains after direct taxes have been deducted.

disposables. *See* consumer nondurables.

distributable reserves. Reserves out of which a company makes a *distribution, usually its revenue reserves. The distinction between distributable and nondistributable reserves of a company is important, especially since certain reserves are specified by statute as being nondistributable.

distributed processing. A system in which several computers are used in different locations communicating with one another or with a central computer.

distribution. 1. The payment made by a company out of its distributable profits or reserves to interests outside that company. The most common form of distribution is the payment of a dividend to shareholders of the company, although other types of distributions do exist, notably in the case of *close companies.

2. (probability distribution). The range of probabilities associated with different values (or intervals of values) of a random variable. There are discrete and continuous distributions according to whether the variable is discrete or continuous, and one can talk of the distribution of a population, which refers to all the values that a variable can take, or a *sampling distribution*, which is the distribution of a random sample drawn from the population. A distribution can be defined algebraically or geometrically by a *density function and will have a series of characteristic coefficients called moments, which include the distribution's mean and variance; a formula for these coefficients can be derived from the distribution's density function. The concept of a distribution is an essential first step in the application of probability theory since a distribution can be formulated for any variable which can take different values and to which one can therefore attach probabilities that it takes such different values. Although the variety of possible distributions is infinitely large, there are in fact a dozen or so well-known distributions within the framework of which most empirical and theoretical work in statistics can be done. The two most frequently encountered distributions are the *normal distribution (which is continuous) and the *binomial distribution (which is discrete). *See also* probability.

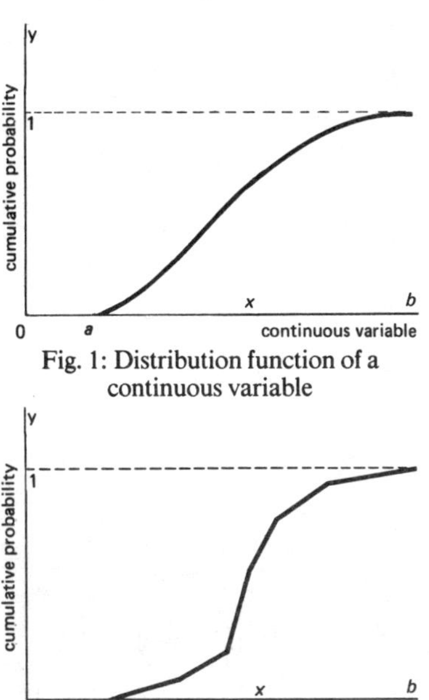

Fig. 1: Distribution function of a continuous variable

Fig. 2: Distribution function of a discrete variable

distribution function (cumulative distribution function). A function that defines the *cumulative distribution of a random variable. A variable's distribution function is closely related to its *density function and either can be derived if the other is known. When the random variable is discrete, the distribution function can be obtained by adding the *probabilities as given by the density function in cumulative fashion, while the distribution function of a continuous variable is found by integrating the density function. A distribution function has a characteristic shape on a graph: Fig.1 illustrates a distribution function for a continuous variable. The random variable x ranges in value from a to b as indicated. When $x = a$ the variable's cumulative probability is zero; when $x = b$ it is one. Fig.2 illustrates the same distribution function for a discrete variable, in which case the function is a series of connected points rather than a curve. *See also* distribution. *Compare* ogive.

diversification. Expansion of an existing firm into an industry with which it had previously been unconnected. It may occur for several reasons. It may be undertaken to minimize the risk of depending upon the health of one industry, which might be relatively harder hit by events than the economy as a whole. It might be undertaken as a means of avoiding seasonal or cyclical fluctuations in the initial industry, e.g. a firm producing ice creams could also produce Christmas confectionery in the autumn in order to keep its staff fully occupied. Another reason for diversification might be to increase growth rate. For instance, a company might find that it can expand more easily in a new industry rather than by fighting to increase its market share in the present industry, especially if the size of its present industry is static or declining. An extreme example might be a monopolist who has saturated his market without exhausting all possible economies of scale. The monopolist's only means of fully using these economies would be to produce goods for a totally different market that could be produced fairly easily with existing plant. Any such economy of scale would reduce costs of production and so increase competitiveness. Examples would be a marketing organization that was previously operating below peak efficiency or the application of the results of research and development to other products.

Unlike *vertical integration, diversification cannot increase the monopoly power of any firm. Indeed, it can markedly increase competition by challenging apparently entrenched monopolies, which might have little to fear from small firms without access to large sums of capital. The development of a complete product line does, nevertheless, make it easier for a firm to tie retail outlets to it and so create barriers to entry through its marketing organization.

dividend. **1.** A share in the profits of a limited company paid to shareholders. The rate of dividend is declared at the *annual general meeting of the company and will depend on the profit made during the preceding year. The dividend is expressed as a percentage of the nominal value of the shares. For example, an 8% dividend on 50p shares will pay 4p per share to the shareholders. If the shares are standing at 80p, the *yield is only 5% (50/80 × 8), If the company has made little or no profit or wishes to use what profit it has made for reinvestment, it is not obliged to pay a dividend, though companies that pass their dividend are unlikely to find favour with their shareholders. Although dividends are declared annually it is quite common for companies to pay an *interim dividend* on account during the year.

2. Cooperative societies pay dividends to their members out of their profits. The dividend is paid in proportion to the amount the member has spent and is expressed as a number of pence in the pound. For example, a dividend of 5p in the pound would entitle a member who had made purchases of £15 during the year to a dividend of 75p.

dividend cover. *See* cover.

dividend equalization reserve. An account to which a company that wishes to maintain steady yearly dividends, in spite of significant yearly fluctuations in profit, may allocate profits in varying amounts from the profit and loss account. From this account a relatively steady flow of dividends may be declared. It is, however, a relatively uncommon type of company account.

dividend limitation. A policy in which companies are forced to limit any increases in their dividends by government order. It usually forms part of a prices and incomes policy to curb inflation and is offered as a quid pro quo to workers who have had their wages frozen. This type of policy was first imposed in the U.K. in 1969.

dividend policy. Company policy, formulated by the board of directors, deciding how the profits are to be divided between the shareholders (by way of dividends) and the company (as retained profits) for reinvestment purposes. Some of the profits may have already been reinvested and are therefore not available for distribution to shareholders.

dividend warrant. A cheque issued by a limited company to a shareholder in payment of the *dividend to which he is entitled. It is usually attached to a statement showing how the amount of the cheque was arrived at, i.e. the number and type of shares held and the rate of dividend. It also shows the tax liability on the dividend at the standard rate and whether or not the tax has been deducted.

dividing society. *See* friendly society.

divisia index. An index number in which the rate of change of the aggregate is the *weighted average of the rates of change of the summarized variables, where the weights are the value shares of the individual variables in total value. The index may be considered to be an instantaneous adjustment to either a *Paasche or *Laspeyres index. It is useful in the measuring of productivity changes by means of aggregate output and input, as under perfect competition and constant returns to scale a zero rate of real technical progress will be reflected by an estimated aggregate rate of technical progress of zero.

division of labour. Specialization of tasks within a production process. More generally it can refer to the disintegration of the market between, as well as within, industries. In Adam Smith's *Wealth of Nations* it was treated as the characteristic that distinguished economic behaviour and was a major source of relative material abundance in civilized society. By allowing a worker to concentrate on only a small part of the production of a good, it encouraged *increasing returns and enabled mass-production methods to be adopted. Smith's example of a pin factory emphasized the benefits of the division of labour to even the most apparently simple tasks. Furthermore, as *technological change and innovation would be encouraged by insights gained by specialists, division of labour can be seen as a prime motive force for economic growth.

dock receipt. A receipt for goods that have been delivered to a dock warehouse for shipment.

documentary bill. A *bill of exchange to which are attached such documents as a bill of lading, invoice, insurance policy, dock warrant, etc.

documentary credit. A method of financing foreign trade. An exporter not certain of the creditworthiness of an importer may request him to open a credit at a bank in favour of the exporter. Bills of exchange can then be drawn in favour of the exporter, and the bank will advise him of the terms of the credit and what documents must be attached to the bills. *See also* letter of hypothecation.

document of offer for sale of shares and debentures. When a company allots its shares to an intermediary institution, such as a merchant bank, for eventual sale to the public, any documents offering the shares for sale to the public constitutes a *prospectus and must meet all the conditions and requirements of a prospectus.

documents against acceptance. A method of payment for goods exported. The shipping documents attached to a draft for the sum due are sent to a bank or agent in the port of destination. The documents are released to the consignee when he accepts the draft.

documents against presentation. *See* cash against document.

dollar gap. The shortage of dollars resulting from sustained balance of payments deficits of Western European countries after World War II. In the post-war period Europe's devastated stock of capital assets was insufficient to rebuild the economies and sustain the level of consumption that people could afford, and this demand was met chiefly by American suppliers. European dollar and gold reserves were drained and the U.S. accumulated massive reserves of gold. The dollar gap persisted until the mid-1950s. *See also* Marshall Aid Programme.

dollar stocks. A general term for U.S. and Canadian securities.

domain. The set of all possible values that an independent variable can take in a specified function. *Compare* range (def. 2).

domestic credit expansion (D.C.E.). A measure of the change in the money supply used by the *International Monetary Fund. It is the change in the money supply minus the change in the government's net foreign currency holdings (the change in reserves minus the amount of government borrowing from abroad). This is a measure of little economic significance for policy or prediction purposes because it is the change in the unadjusted money supply that affects the level of output and the rate of inflation. The concept gained prominence in 1968 when the International Monetary Fund used control of the D.C.E. as a condition on a loan to the U.K. government.

domestic economy sector. *See* Treasury.

domestic element. *See* rate support grant.

double-entry book-keeping. An integral part of most systems of accounting, in which the various accounts in a company have two sides, a debit and a credit. A debit entry in an account indicates that the company is owed a certain amount whereas a credit indicates that the company owes this amount. For example, in the cash-at-bank account, a debit entry indicates that cash has been, or should have been, received into the company's bank account and a credit entry indicates that cash has been paid out of that account. The general principle is that every debit has a credit, i.e. where a debit entry is made in one account a corresponding credit entry must be made in another: if cash has been received the company must owe this to someone, even if this is only the shareholders. At any time the sum of all the debits and credits in the various accounts must equal each other, i.e. the *books of account must balance.

double option. *See* option.

double pricing. Displaying two prices for a product, the higher one being deleted to show the prospective buyer that the price has been reduced. This practice is discouraged as the higher price may be misleading.

double switching. A condition arising in the construction of the *factor-price frontier where a production technique combining a certain proportion of capital and labour produces the highest rate of profit at two different wage levels, with another technique yielding a higher rate of profit at a wage rate in between. If double switching between production techniques occurs the factor-price frontier cannot be used to justify the use of a production function that treats heterogeneous capital as an aggregate with an interpretable marginal productivity proportional to the rate of profit. *See* surrogate production function.

double taxation. *See* overseas income taxation.

Dow Jones Averages. Four index numbers representing movements on the New York Stock Exchange. There is one index each for home bonds, for transportation stocks, for industrial stocks, and for utilities. The most famous of these is the Dow Jones Industrial Average which, although it is calculated differently, is in other respects very similar to the Financial Times Industrial Ordinary Index. It is based on 30 leading industrial stocks and its base year is 1928.

downside. A term used with reference to the probability of or potential for downward movement in the price of a share on a stock exchange. To say that a particular share has limited downside or little downside potential means that it is thought that there is little risk that the share price will fall independently of the rest of the market. The term is frequently used in the recommendations of stockbrokers to their clients. *Compare* upside.

draft. A written order to a bank to pay a specified sum to the person named on the draft. *See also* bank draft.

drawback. A repayment of the customs duties paid on imported materials when the materials are re-exported. The materials may be re-exported in the same form as they were imported, if they are part of an entrepôt transaction, or they may be processed before re-export. In the former case payment of duty and claiming of drawback can be avoided by storing the goods in a *bonded warehouse.

drawee. The drawee of a *bill of exchange is the person to whom it is addressed, who is expected to accept it and pay it on maturity: the drawee of a cheque is the banker on whom it is drawn, i.e. the bank holding the account of the person signing the cheque or of the company on whose behalf it is signed.

drawer. The drawer of a *bill of exchange is the person who signs it and orders the drawee to pay the amount for which it is made out, i.e. he is the creditor; the drawer of a cheque, however, is the debtor, signing it and ordering his bank to pay his creditor, the payee.

drum. *See* magnetic drum.

dual capacity. Denoting the system of stock exchange dealings in which stockbrokers and stockjobbers are not divided into separate firms. The British Stock Exchange is the only one to keep a distinction between brokers and jobbers (the *single capacity* system), and has operated this system since 1910; declining numbers of stockbroking and stockjobbing firms have, however, undermined the competitive nature of the stock market and proposals have been made to abandon the system.

due date. The date on which a *bill of exchange is payable. If payable on demand, at sight, or on presentation, no *days of grace are allowed, but they are allowed on a term bill. If a bill is drawn payable a number of months after date, no account is taken of the irregular number of days in the months, e.g. if drawn three months after 9 January the due date of the bill is 12 April. *See also* bank holidays.

dummy variable. A variable used in econometric work to allow for shifts in functions contingent upon temporal circumstance (such as war or a change in political regime) or attributes (such as sex or marital status). Thus it might be thought that there is a downward shift in the consumption function in wartime as compared with peacetime or that there is a higher demand for cars among men than among women. In such cases a dummy variable can be inserted into the function and given a value of one when the shift in the function is thought to take place and a value of zero when it is thought that no shift occurs. In this way an extra coefficient (the one attached to the dummy variable) is brought into the analysis when the shift occurs and two (or more) functions can then be formulated.

dumping. The practice of selling goods abroad at a price below their marginal cost, i.e. at a loss. The purpose of this could be to maintain a stable or oligopolistic domestic market structure by disposing of temporary surpluses abroad, or as a means of disrupting the domestic market of a foreign competitor. Tariffs designed to prevent the effects of dumping are allowed under GATT and the practice is either prohibited or discouraged by most trade agreements.

duopoly. An industry that has two producers and a large number of purchasers. Each producer has some control over the price and output, but he must consider the possible reactions of his one competitor.

Depending on the assumptions each makes concerning his rival, different equilibria are possible. In general, the total profits in the industry are less than would be achieved if the two colluded (*see* collusive duopoly) and acted as one monopolist, and more than if they were to set price equal to marginal cost. The problem can be usefully approached by game theory methods. *See also* Cournot duopoly, Stackelberg duopoly, Bertrand duopoly, Edgeworth duopoly.

duopsony. An industry with two purchasers and many producers: the demand counterpart to duopoly.

durables. *See* consumer durables.

Durbin-Watson d statistic. A statistic used in econometrics to test for *autocorrelation. Its computation has a standard formula. Although exact levels of significance for the statistic are not available, two statisticians (Durbin and Watson) have tabulated upper and lower boundaries for it for various values of the number of observations and the number of independent variables. If in any particular case the statistic was calculated and found to be above the upper boundary, then the hypothesis of autocorrelation could be rejected; if it was found to be below the lower boundary, autocorrelation would be suggested, and a value between the two boundaries would be inconclusive. The formula for testing positive autocorrelation differs from that for testing negative autocorrelation, but both involve the Durbin-Watson d statistic and its boundaries.

dynamics. The economic analysis of the time paths through which a model's endogenous variables pass in disequilibrium situations, and the question of whether or not the variables will converge to equilibrium or diverge away from any equilibrium. In the latter case the system represented by the model is said to be unstable. A central feature of dynamics is the dating of the variables and this introduces into the analysis a consideration of the time factor. Time can be treated either as a continuous variable or as a discrete variable, although the former is usually the more realistic. The best-known example of a dynamic analysis is probably the Domar growth model, which attempts to delineate the time path required of the rate of investment flow per year if there is to be equilibrium between potential productive capacity and aggregate demand through time. Dynamics is more advanced than *comparative statics or *statics but economic realities are sometimes poorly represented by dynamic models because of the complexity of forces that interact on economic variables in the real world. The most common quantitative techniques used in dynamic analysis are integral and differential calculus. The benefit of using dynamic models is that some idea is given of the amount of time required before reaching the new equilibrium, whether it will reach it at all, and what value the system's determinates will assume in that time.

E

E.&O.E. *See* errors and omissions excepted.

early bargains. *See* after-hours dealings.

earned income. Income derived from paid employment, either as an employee or as a result of self-employed activities. An additional U.K. tax on unearned income, termed investment income surcharge, was abolished in 1984/85. Thus the distinction between earned and unearned income becomes immaterial in terms of tax. Salaries, director's fees, profits, and royalties are regarded as earned income but dividends, even from a company of which one is a director, are not.

earnings per share. *See* available earnings.

earnings yield. The hypothetical *yield that a shareholder would obtain if all the *available earnings of the company in whose shares he had invested were to be distributed as dividend. In this sense it is the reciprocal of the *P/E ratio, expressed as a percentage. The term is also sometimes used in the context of fixed-interest securities to mean the *flat yield.

easement. A right of the present owner of a particular piece of land to use in some way, or take something from, a neighbouring piece of land (*positive easement*), or to prevent the owner of that neighbouring piece of land from using his land in a particular way (*negative easement*).

Examples of positive easements are a right of way or a right to take water; an example of a negative easement is a right of light, by which the owner of the easement can prevent his neighbour from building anything that obstructs the light reaching his windows. Easements may be created in a *deed or by prescription, i.e. the continuous use of the right for 20 years without objection from the neighbour.

easy (cheap) money. Money that can be borrowed at a low rate of interest because of monetary expansion. When the monetary authority wishes to induce an expansion in the level of activity in the economy, it increases the amount of money in the banking system. This increases the reserves of the *financial intermediaries who are able to increase their lending at lower rates of interest without loss of profit. *See also* open market operations.

E.C.G.D. *See* Export Credits Guarantee Department.

E.C.I. *See* Equity Capital for Industry.

econometrics. The application of statistical techniques to economic theories. Applied econometrics is concerned both with forecasting and with investigating the validity of economic theories. The normal procedure is to develop a mathematical model, apply statistical methods to the available data to obtain estimates of the model's parameters, and use the methods of statistical inference to decide whether or not the hypotheses underpinning the model can be accepted. If the model is not rejected, then tentative forecasts can be made on the basis of such techniques as extrapolation. The more theoretical side of econometrics is concerned with the formulation of a corpus of mathematical and statistical theory designed for the use of economic data. Most of the problems of econometric theory devolve from the application of this statistical theory, which involves assumptions of some stringency, to economic data for which such assumptions do not necessarily hold, together with associated difficulties, such as *autocorrelation and *multicollinearity. Economic theory supplies the models used in econometrics. Most econometrics is based on *regression and *correlation and does not therefore say anything about the causation of economic phenomena.

economic cost. The total sacrifice involved in performing an activity. It is thus the *opportunity cost of using factors of production in one activity rather than another. Economic cost will usually be greater than *accounting cost*, which is the total money outlay involved in an activity.

Consider a firm that operates a factory for one year. Accounting cost would include the price of raw materials, rent, interest payments, labour costs, etc. Economic cost would be the sacrifice involved in not using these factors in their most profitable alternative use; i.e. using the raw materials, land, capital, etc., in the next most profitable way. If the firm was not borrowing money and paying interest but using its own capital, accounting procedures would not make any deductions for interest charges. Economic procedures, on the other hand, would make an interest charge, as a sacrifice (equal to the interest that could be earned) is involved in not lending the money.

Economic cost is preferred to accounting cost (at least by economists), because it represents the real sacrifice involved in commercial activities whereas monetary outlays merely approximate to it. The concept of economic cost highlights the fact that mutually exclusive choices are continually being made in the productive process; money must be spent in one way or another but not in both ways. The cost of something is equal to the cost of what must be given up to acquire it.

Economic Development Committee (E.D.C.). *See* National Economic Development Council.

economic effects of taxation. Taxation is used by governments to raise revenue and to influence the economy; for example, in the U.K. selective employment tax was primarily designed to encourage workers to move from the service industries to the manufacturing industries. This latter purpose is relatively new, having first been used in the twentieth century. All taxes affect the economy to some extent and these effects must be taken into account when new taxes are imposed or tax rates altered. For instance, income tax reduces the net wage rate. This causes an *income effect, which will increase work effort (people will work harder to protect their standard of living), and a *substitution effect, which will decrease work effort (people will feel that it is not worthwhile to work long hours). The net effect is unpredictable. However, it is possible to be more specific for some groups; the net wage of working mothers is often so low that an increase in income tax will discourage many from entering the work force.

Saving is directly related to disposable income and so an increase in income tax will decrease the level of savings. Furthermore, the average amount saved rises with income so that the imposition of a *progressive tax would decrease savings more than the imposition of a *proportional tax, even if both yielded an equal amount of revenue.

The effects of indirect taxes differ. Taxes on goods used at work (e.g. safety clothing) will reduce work effort more than taxes on leisure products (holidays, caravans), which reduce the value of leisure. Taxes on such items as food and clothing are generally neutral with regard to work effort. Taxation on business profits will usually reduce investment unless there are compensating measures, such as capital allowances or investment credit.

economic good. *See* good.

economic growth. The expansion of the output of the economy (national income). This expansion may or may not follow a steady course but in the West, for the last two centuries, there has been a continuous tendency for the level of income to rise.

There are no firm conclusions about the causes of growth or about the reasons why growth rates differ but the major factors involved can be outlined. Economic growth may result from growth in the population, which provides a larger growth in the labour force. This augments the quantity of factors of production available as does investment in physical capital. Technological improvements in the quality of capital resulting from innovation can also be important in the growth process, but not all technological improvement is embodied in the capital stock. For example, improvements in the stock of knowledge or investment in human capital are important sources of growth in output.

Growth rates differ between nations mainly because of differences in the rates of factor augmentation (investment, population growth) or because of differences in the rates of factor improvement (technical progress). For instance, the U.K. probably experienced slow growth in the post-war period because of a slow rate of factor augmentation (low population growth and low investment). This may have happened because individuals preferred consumption now to consumption in the future (a high rate of *time preference in consumption) and so did not wish to undertake the high levels of saving necessary for a temporarily high growth rate.

The subject has aroused so much debate, both for and against growth, because of its welfare implications. A higher growth rate will produce a higher level of income in the future and this could make people happier, but this will only be achieved by settling for a lower present standard of living than would otherwise result. The heavy concentration on economic growth as an objective of economic policy has been much criticized because of external effects on the environment associated with growth, e.g. increased pollution, which decreases the standard of living although it may not be allowed for in any index. However, many believe that these effects can be interpreted as a failure of the pricing mechanism rather than a direct result of growth.

Growth theory as an area in economics is rather abstract and mechanical, with models such as the *Harrod–Domar model paying a great deal of attention to mathematical solutions and properties and taking little notice of the choice processes involved. This indicates that much of the theory has sprung from the internal development of the subject rather than from factors observed in the real world, such as underdevelopment and differences in relative growth rates. These problems have stimulated a different and more institutional literature. The theory has produced few results except in the area of balanced growth (*see* steady-state growth path), in which the rate of growth is given by the rate of technological progress and the rate of population growth.

It is important in discussing growth theory to distinguish between the rate of growth and the rate of growth per capita, the latter being the relevant measure of welfare change. In an underdeveloped economy the rate of growth in output may appear high, but it will often be associated with rates of population growth in excess of 2%, which will double the population within a generation. *See also* optimal economic growth.

economic profits. The difference between a firm's income and costs, broadly defined as in accounting. However, in economics the opportunity costs are included, especially those of the entrepreneur and his capital investment. In the simplest case these could be determined by the prevailing wage for a man of his qualifications and the interest rate on his bank deposits or blue chip investments. Thus, a shopkeeper who has invested £10,000 in his shop might make £3000 a year profit in the accounting sense. However, given a prevailing interest rate of 10% and a job offer of £2500 to work for a competitor, he actually loses £500 per year in the economic sense. This example does not include such factors as pride in ownership or security, but the economist believes that these may be given a value and added to the balance sheet for the final computation of economic profits. It is these profits that the economist refers to when he speaks of profits reducing to zero under perfect competition. *See* normal profit.

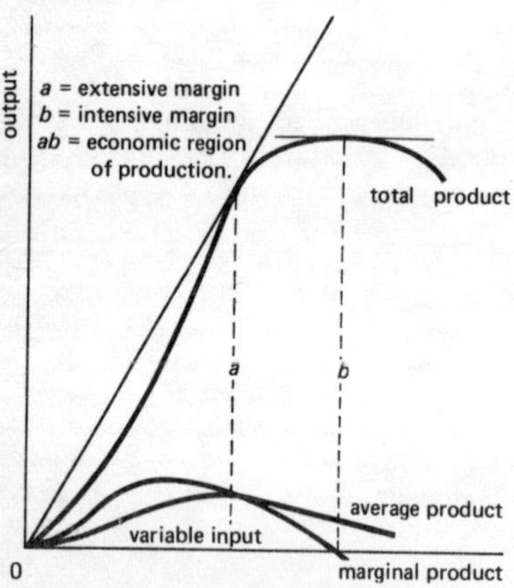

Economic region of production

economic region of production. The various mixes of inputs that will be employed by a cost-minimizing firm, lying in the area of an *isoquant map between the ridge lines, where the marginal products of all factors are zero or positive. For a variable factor of production, with all others fixed, the economic region of production involves the use of the amounts of the factor that lie between the *extensive and the *intensive margins. If production were to take place beyond the intensive margin, for instance, then more could be produced by using less of the variable input, thus decreasing costs, while up to the extensive margin more could be produced by using less of the fixed factor, keeping the variable factor constant. Some of the fixed factor would be thrown away, increasing both the marginal product of the variable factor and production with variable costs left unchanged.

economics. A social science concerning the production of goods and services and their distribution, exchange, and consumption as well as the interrelationships between these processes. The most widely accepted definition is that of Professor Lionel Robbins who believes economics to be "the science which studies human behaviour as a relationship between ends and scarce means, which have alternative uses". People's desires are almost infinite while the resources which they use to satisfy them are very definitely finite. Each must attempt to satisfy some wants while discarding others and must allocate resources accordingly. Economics is the discipline that analyses these decisions. It can be broadly subdivided into *microeconomics (which concerns the situation confronting a single unit, whether person, firm, or industry) and *macroeconomics (which concerns the economy as a whole, for example the balance of payments, the level of employment, and the rate of inflation). Many areas, e.g. *public finance, will overlap into both areas, but this division is valuable since decisions and policies that are logical for an individual can be harmful for an economy.

Economics is positive rather than normative; it does not state what should be done but only what can be done. For instance, economics cannot decide whether it is desirable to reduce inflation; it can only attempt to predict the results of each policy and leave the choice to others. Value judgments are dispensed with as much as possible even in areas such as *welfare economics; if two situations are both *Pareto-optimal then economics has no criterion for selecting one in preference to the other. This is a political rather than an economic decision.

economic sanctions. Embargoes on the export of goods, services, and capital to a particular nation. They can be used in addition to military operations, as in the blockades of the U.K. and Europe in the Napoleonic Wars; or as a substitute for war, e.g. the ban by members of the League of Nations on the export of certain products to Italy in 1936 and the U.N.'s similar embargo on Rhodesia, which started in 1965.

economic statistics. Data and indices relating to macroeconomic variables, such as prices, production, population, incomes, employment, etc. As a subject, economic statistics is a branch of applied statistics, mainly of a deductive rather than inductive nature: the data is analysed in order to establish significant relationships and trends.

economies of scale. Phenomena that cause the average cost of production to decline as output increases. *Diseconomies of scale* exist when the average cost rises with increased production. In the standard theory of the firm, as firms increase production they pass through an early stage in which there exist economies of scale and a later stage in which there are diseconomies. At the cross-over point, average cost reaches its minimum and is equal to marginal cost. When economies of scale predominate in an industry, marginal cost remains below average cost over the relevant range of outputs so that with marginal cost pricing the producer would obtain an abnormally high profit. This tends to result in a natural monopoly as one firm expands to reach optimum size, capturing the entire market. Again in the standard theory of the firm, diseconomies are presumed to exist at higher outputs so that the market supply curve is rising when it meets the demand curve.

Economies of scale can either be internal or external. Internal economies are those that arise within the firm itself; they are usually caused by technological and organizational factors and are closely associated with the concept of returns to scale. External economies arise from the effect of a firm's expansion on market conditions and on technology, such as the creation of common facilities for *research and development.

Internal economies and diseconomies can be ascribed to two basic causes: the technology of efficient size of operation and the distribution of indirect costs. Each process in a firm can be considered as an entity in itself with its inputs bought from some other process and its product sold to yet another. For one of these entities the externalities are clear: a machine has a certain rental that is spread over the number of units produced; the more units, the less the average cost. It also has a certain efficient operating size, which may increase with the size of the machine. When the entities are combined, the degree of their interrelation and their individual economies and diseconomies will determine the firm's economies and diseconomies as a whole. For example, it may be that the optimum size of plant requires a large and cumbersome administration.

External economies and diseconomies are of two kinds: pecuniary and technological. The former arises from market conditions. Hence external pecuniary economies of scale would arise when an increase in production increases the demand for some input whose price falls because of internal economies in the production of that factor. A pecuniary external diseconomy would arise if the price were to rise from internal diseconomies. Even under constant returns to scale, increased demand causes the resources used in its production to become more in demand and hence to command a higher price due to scarcity.

An example of a technological economy might occur if an expansion of farming enabled a common irrigation system to be installed. A technological diseconomy would exist where an increased demand on the existing water supplies caused a drought.

E.C.S.C. *See* European Coal and Steel Community.

E.C.U. *See* European Currency Unit.

Edgeworth–Bowley box diagram. A device named after its inventors, Francis Edgeworth (1845–1926) and Sir Arthur Lyon Bowley (1869–1957), used to demonstrate the most efficient allocation of resources between two producers, or of goods between two consumers. It is widely used in international trade theory, where the producers and consumers are nations. Various refinements of the diagram allow for the restrictions and abnormalities that can arise in international trade.

The basic framework is a rectangle, the parallel sides of which indicate the total amount of the two goods or resources available to the system. From diagonally opposite corners (usually the lower left and upper right) a set of *indifference curves may be drawn for each consumer, or isoquants for each product. In the case of two consumers, the amount of the good consumed by the first consumer is measured along the bottom and left hand sides. His indifference curves are drawn in convex to the lower left corner; the farther away from that corner the indifference curves are, the greater the utility he obtains. Similarly, the amount consumed by the second consumer is measured along the top and right hand sides; his indifference curves are drawn in convex to this corner.

Each point in the box gives a possible allocation of the goods. Suppose the box is five units high and ten units long with goods A and B represented on the vertical and horizontal axes respectively. Suppose further that consumer I's indifference curves go out from the lower left and consumer II's come down from the upper right. The point two units up from the lower left and seven units across allocates two units of A and seven units of B to consumer I and places him on an

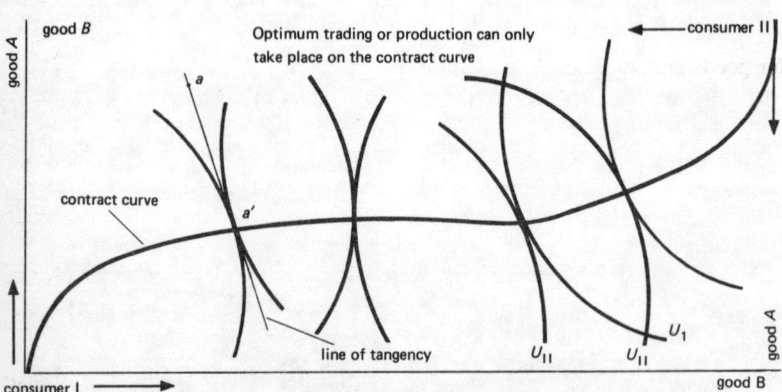

Edgeworth-Bowley box diagram

indifference curve u_{I}. At the same time it allocates three units each of A and B to consumer II and places him on indifference curve u_{II}. Since u_{I} and u_{II} curve in different directions, unless they are intersecting at only one point (called a point of tangency), each cuts across higher indifference curves of the other. Thus there is a point on u_{I} that puts consumer II on a higher indifference curve (u_{II}) without making I any worse off. The original allocation is therefore not efficient. The set of all these points of tangency are the *Pareto-optimal points. They form a curve that runs from the lower left to the upper right-hand sides of the box; efficient allocation can only take place along this curve, which is called the *contract curve.

An additional interpretation can be attached to the line of tangency between the indifference curves of the two consumers along this curve. It is a budget constraint and its slope indicates the relative prices of the two goods (*see* budget equation). Given any initial endowment between I and II, for instance a point *a* not on the contract curve, I and II will bargain perhaps by some *tâtonnement process until they have found a point *a′* such that the line of tangency passes through *a*; the difference between *a* and *a′* is the amount that will be traded between the two.

By substituting isoproduct curves for indifference curves and resources for goods one can find the set of efficient allocations of resources between two producers and determine efficient relative prices.

This one diagram illustrates all the major features of standard microeconomic theory. However, many results that are easily proved in a two-person two-good model do not necessarily extend to all persons and goods of the real world. Nevertheless proofs based on an Edgeworth-Bowley box diagram are as rigorous as any mathematical alternatives, given the assumptions on which it operates.

Edgeworth duopoly. A model of duopolistic competition devised by Francis Edgeworth (1845–1926), in which each producer assumes that the other will hold his price constant but that he is unable to supply the entire market. Thus, unlike the *Bertrand duopoly model, the producer might maximize profit by charging a higher price than his competitors and exploiting his monopoly power over the remainder of the market. In such an industry, with two prices and a homogeneous good, it is more appropriate to consider the situation as a variant of price discrimination, and as such it is generally assumed that arbitrage does not take place between the two categories of buyers in the simplest case.

education endowment. *See* children's assurance.

E.E.C. *See* European Economic Community.

effective demand. Demand for a commodity backed by the money to purchase it, i.e. actual expenditure. In the Keynesian system, effective demand determines output, which in turn determines the level of employment. It can be divided into two components, consumption and investment. Effective demand is generally assumed when demand is discussed in economics.

effective rate of protection. *See* implicit tariff.

effective tax rate. The average rate of taxation. In a progressive tax system this tends to rise faster than the increase in taxable income since the rate of taxation increases disproportionately with a rising taxable income to a certain level.

efficiency. 1. The utilization of resources in the most effective manner. Efficiency can be of two sorts: technological and economic. One firm is technologically more efficient than another if it can produce the same output using fewer inputs or an equal number of inputs with less of at least one input being used. All firms are not comparable in terms of technological efficiency since, because of different production processes, one firm might always use more of some input than another while the second always uses more of some other input than the first. In this case there is no immediate criterion for deciding which is technologically more efficient, and one must turn to the question of economic efficiency.

Economic efficiency consists of efficiency in production, distribution, and allocation. *Efficiency in production* exists when inputs are utilized to produce a given level of output at the least possible cost. Unlike technological efficiency, it enables diverse assets, processes, etc. to be compared. In terms of the *Edgeworth-Bowley box diagram, production is efficient if carried out along the *contract curve, or in general if it is not possible to produce more of any one good while maintaining production of all others at the same level through a reallocation of resources and a change in technology.

Efficiency in distribution results when a particular set of products are divided amongst the consumers in such a way that no one person could be made better off without making another worse off. This is more commonly called Pareto optimality (*see* Pareto-optimal) and the points equivalent to efficiency points on the Edgeworth-Bowley box contract curve are called the *Pareto-optimal points.*

Allocative efficiency results when inputs are optimally divided among various products.

2. A statistical *estimator is said to be efficient if it can be shown mathematically that its *variance is less than the variance of any other estimator of its class. If this property can be shown only for large samples, then the estimator is said to be asymptotically efficient. Efficiency is one of the desirable properties of estimators.

EFTA. *See* European Free Trade Association.

elastic. Denoting a curve whose *elasticity at a point is greater than one: the proportionate change in the dependent variable is greater than the proportionate change in the independent variable. If a good is price elastic, it implies that a fall in the price of the good induces a sufficient increase in demand for expenditure on that good to increase. If the income elasticity of a good is greater than one, the good is income elastic and the share of expenditure of the good increases as income increases. In perfect competition the demand curve faced by a firm, being horizontal, is perfectly elastic: the firm can sell all it wants at the going price, or alternatively if the firm raises its price above the market price it loses all the demand for its product.

elasticity. The change in a dependent variable in response to a change in an independent variable. It is a function of the shape and position of a curve. For example, if the curve is relatively flat, a small change in the independent variable will correspond with a relatively large change in the dependent variable and the curve is said to be *elastic. If the curve is relatively steep the reverse occurs and the curve is said to be inelastic. When elasticity (E) is perfectly elastic, it is equal to infinity; when it is perfectly inelastic, it is equal to 0, and when elasticity is equal to one a change in the independent variable induces a proportionate change in the dependent variable. An elasticity may be either an arc elasticity or a point elasticity. The former is the elasticity for a discrete change along a curve. For such there are problems in defining the denomination of the proportional rate of change to allow symmetry in going from one point to another and back. A common formulation is:

$$(\Delta x_1/x_1)/(\Delta x_2/x_2)$$

which can be transformed into:

$$(\Delta x_1/\Delta x_2)(x_2/x_1).$$

A common case is where x_1 represents the quantity of a good bought and x_2 represents its price. A definition for point elasticity is:

$$(dx_1/dx_2)(x_2/x_1).$$

Elasticities, as opposed to simple slope calculations, are of use to economists because they are pure numbers which do not depend upon the units in which the variables are measured. The slope of a demand curve measured in pence is one one-hundredth of the equivalent slope in pounds, while the elasticity of demand at equivalent points is identical. Thus comparisons can be made across countries with different units of account.

elasticity of substitution. The extent to which other goods or factors of production will be substituted for one whose price has increased. Perfect elasticity of substitution would occur if two goods were identical. The elasticity of the capital/labour ratio with respect to the input price ratio was first introduced by Hicks as:

$$\sigma = F_K F_L / F_{KL},$$

where output:

$$Y = F(K,L),$$

and F_K and F_L are the partial derivatives of the production function with respect to capital and labour, and F_{KL} is the cross-partial derivative. It is perhaps more transparent in the form independently introduced by Joan Robinson:

$$\sigma = (w/r) / (K/L).\partial(K/L) / \partial(w/r).$$

The two definitions are equivalent under conditions of competitive pricing and constant returns to scale. Reference to the Robinson definition reveals the significance of the elasticity. If $\sigma > 1$ then the capital/labour ratio, in response to an increase in the input price ratio, rises proportionately faster than the price ratio. This implies that the share of income accruing to capital increases. On the other hand if $\sigma < 1$, labour's share of income rises when the wage/rental ratio increases. Only if $\sigma = 1$ (in the *Cobb–Douglas production function) does a change in the input price ratio leave the relative shares of capital and labour the same. The elasticity cannot be less than zero as this would imply isoquants concave towards the origin.

eligibility rule. A criterion as to which bills the Banks of England will rediscount when functioning as *lender of last resort. Eligible paper consists of Treasury bills, gilt-edged securities whose redemption date is less than five years away, and first-class commercial bills.

embargo. **1.** A prohibition on the export of certain goods or classes of goods to certain countries, usually for political reasons. For example, there is an embargo on the export of strategic materials from the U.S.A. to the U.S.S.R.

2. A prohibition on the import of certain goods or classes of goods, especially on goods coming from a country with which the government is in political disagreement. For example, after Rhodesia's unilateral declaration of independence in 1965 an embargo on the import to the U.K. of certain goods from Rhodesia was imposed.

3. An agreement by the members of a trade union not to unload goods shipped from certain countries, usually for political reasons.

embezzlement. The appropriation by an employee of money belonging to his employer. This was formerly a separate statutory offence under the Larceny Act (1916), but it is now subsumed in the Theft Act (1968) and is no longer a separate offence.

employers' liability insurance. A form of insurance, now compulsory in the U.K., that provides cover for employers in the event of liability to employees arising from industrial fatality, disease, or injury. The Employers' Liability (Compulsory Insurance) Act (1969) requires all employers to be insured up to at least £2,000,000 against liability to their employees arising from any one occurrence, although most policies provide unlimited cover. This form of insurance gives employees protection in addition to that provided by National Insurance.

Employment Acts (1980, 1982). U.K. Acts of Parliament that gave individual employees improved rights and job protection, but at the same time reduced the legal powers of trade unions. In particular, it became illegal to engage in secondary industrial action, including *secondary picketing.

employment agencies. Organizations that attempt to bring employers with vacancies into contact with prospective employees. Commercial employment agencies obtain their revenue by charging a fee for every applicant hired. Governmental agencies, of which there are two types–the *Employment Exchanges* and the *P.E.R.* (Professional and Executive Recruitment Agencies) provide their services free or for a nominal charge related to the employee's time with the firm and his salary.

Employment Protection Acts (1975, 1978). U.K. Acts of Parliament that gave greater security of employment to individual union members and improved rights relating to such matters as compensation and maternity leave for women employees. The 1975 Act also established the *Advisory Conciliation and Arbitration Service* (*ACAS*) to settle industrial disputes between employers and trade unions.

E.M.S. *See* European Monetary System.

endogenous variable. A variable whose value is determined by one of the relationships specified by the model under consideration. Endogenous variables are frequently referred to in the context of simultaneous models. For instance, in a model of income determination, consumption expenditures and (usually) investment as well as income will be regarded as endogenous to the model. The concept of the endogenous variable is similar in nature to that of the dependent variable and it is true that the dependent variable of each relationship in the model will be endogenous, but an endogenous variable can also appear as an independent variable in other relationships in the model (give rising to the model's simultaneous nature). Each endogenous variable in a model will have its own functional relationship and the number of equations in a model will be equal to the number of endogenous variables in it. *Compare* exogenous variable.

endorsement (indorsement). A signature on a *bill of exchange or a cheque, usually upon the back of the document, by which it is transferred to another party. Previous to the passing of the Cheques Act (1957), all cheques payable to the order of the payee had to be endorsed, but this is now unnecessary when the payee pays such a cheque into his own bank account. However, if he transfers it to another person he must endorse it. Bills of exchange still require to be endorsed, as do foreign cheques and cheques cashed across a bank counter.

endowment assurance. A type of policy providing for the sum assured to be paid either at death or after a fixed number of years, whichever event occurs first (the assured selects the number of years when effecting the policy), unlike many *life assurance policies in which the assured can never benefit while the life assured is still alive. This type of policy can be with profits (*see* with-profits policy). *Compare* pure endowment assurance.

Engel aggregation. A relationship derived from *utility maximization theory where the *weighted average of the income elasticities for each good, the respective budget shares being the weights, equals unity. It results from the assumption of nonsatiation, which implies that all income is spent, and can be interpreted as saying that any additional money earned is completely spent. The sum of the marginal propensities to consume the individual goods equals unity.

Engel curve. A curve on a graph showing that the quantity of a good demanded is a function of total income, all other things (prices) being held constant. On a graph that shows the indifference curves and budget line of an individual it may be constructed by observing the effects upon demand for a good of a parallel shift of the budget curve, representing a change in money income, prices being held constant. Engel curves are important in aggregation analysis since if they are linear and of the same slope irrespective of the individuals studied, an aggregate demand curve may be employed irrespective of the distribution of income.

Engel's law. The proportion of income spent on food diminishes as income increases, other factors remaining constant. The law was formulated by Christian Lorenz Ernst Engel (1821–96), a nineteenth-century Prussian statistician. On the basis of this law *Engel curves have been developed, which are important for the analysis of family expenditure patterns.

enterprise zone. A small district in the U.K. singled out by the government for special financial assistance to combat economic decline. Eleven zones were established in 1980 to attract new investment, and 14 more were planned. *See also* development areas.

entrepôt trade. Trade in which goods are shipped to one port and subsequently re-exported and shipped to another port. For example, the tea trade is largely centred in London and tea is sold by auction in London after tasting and inspection. London is therefore the natural centre of the entrepôt trade in tea, substantial quantities being re-exported to European countries. If customs duty has been paid on imported goods that are later re-exported, the duty may be claimed back (*see* drawback); alternatively the goods may be re-exported directly from a *bonded warehouse, in which case the import duty does not have to be paid.

entrepreneur. The decision-maker, risk-taker, and organizer in a commercial enterprise. His functions are to supply risk capital, decide on what to produce at what scale of production with what combination of inputs, to manage the enterprise, and to bear the risks. In the twentieth century, the entrepreneur has become less prominent as industrial organizations have grown more complex. He is found in sole proprietorships, partnerships, and perhaps in those companies in which one individual owns a large proportion of the shares and provides the motive power in the direction of the company. Formal entrepreneurial functions are now normally split between those who make the decisions and those who supply the capital. In the case of a limited company, the board of directors and the management make the decisions while the shareholders ultimately bear the risks, since they supply the capital. In the case of a nationalized industry, it is the relevant government department that is the decision-maker, although it usually delegates its powers, and the tax-payers who bear the risks.

Entrepreneurship is regarded as the fourth factor of production, together with land, labour, and capital, with profits being its reward. It is assumed that the entrepreneur aims to maximize profits although in practice he may not always act with this sole aim, especially in the short run. The entrepreneurial spirit is, however, an essential component in a profit-based economy. Indeed, it has been claimed that the inefficiencies of state-owned or nationalized industries are a direct result of the replacement of entrepreneurs by high-ranking civil servants. One of the problems of a mixed economy is to maintain sufficient incentives to encourage entrepreneurial activity.

entropy. A concept taken from information and communications theory and used in the measurement of *industrial concentration. It originated in thermodynamics and is a measure of the disorder or randomness of a system. The formula:

$$H = \Sigma^{m}_{k=1} p_k \log p_k$$

enables the randomness of a system to be predicted. Here p_k is the probability associated with the kth of m categories. When all categories are equally probable, i.e. $p_k = 1/m$, H achieves its maximum value log m, and the system is completely random. When one category is completely certain $p_k = 1$, H achieves its minimum value of zero and the system is completely predictable. The advantage of entropy over other measures of industrial concentration is that one may use it between various industries to indicate the monopoly power of some conglomerate or multinational firm, whereas other measures of concentration must be used within a single market.

entry and exit. The facility with which new firms become established in an existing industry or old firms leave through liquidation or bankruptcy. These are important considerations for the theories of *perfect and *imperfect competition. *See* barriers to entry, monopolistic competition, monopoly.

envelope curve. The curve that is tangential to a point of each curve in a family of curves indexed by a continuous variable. The major example in economics is the long-run average cost curve, which is the envelope of the short-run average cost curves. Each short-run curve is determined by the size of the *capital stock, which is fixed in the short run but continuously variable in the long run.

equilibrium. A situation in which there is no inherent tendency for change. In a product market, equilibrium is reached when the quantity of products supplied exactly equals the quantity demanded. An industry is in equilibrium when firms are neither entering nor leaving the industry, i.e. when normal profits are being earned. In classical economics it was assumed that the economy would inevitably move towards an equilibrium point at a condition of *full employment of resources, although it is now felt that it could be in equilibrium at less than full employment, as happened in the Depression (*see* depression). Once equilibrium is reached the conditions will remain unchanged unless or until there is some disturbing outside influence. *Static economics* studies these points of equilibria. In reality, equilibrium is rarely achieved, although there are movements towards and away from it (*see* cobweb theorem). *See also* multiple equilibrium.

equi-marginal principle. People will allocate their expenditure among goods in such a manner that the ratio of *marginal utility to price for each good is identical. In this way a consumer with a finite income will maximize the utility he can gain. If he deviated from this combination by buying more of some goods and less of others he would lose more utility than he would gain.

equitable interest. A right to enjoy possession of, or to receive income from, an item of property of which the legal ownership is vested in another person. *See also* beneficial interest.

equitable mortgage. An agreement by a borrower that an equitable interest in a property shall be transferred to a lender as security for the debt. It arises when title deeds are handed over either with or without any document of charge, or when a memorandum of charge is given without being supported by the deeds. Unlike a legal mortgage it does not vest a legal estate in the lender, but the memorandum, if taken, usually includes an undertaking by the borrower to grant a legal mortgage when requested.

equity. 1. Net assets attributable to the ordinary shareholders of a company.

2. (*pl.*) Ordinary shares. Equities represent a form of investment in which the degree of risk and the possibility of capital gain is high relative to investment in fixed-interest securities.

3. The system of English law developed in the seventeenth to nineteenth centuries by the chancery courts and administered by the Chancellor of England to temper the sometimes unfair and harsh results brought about in the king's courts. The rules of common law, which were used in the king's courts, were by this stage rather rigid and inflexible. The law relating to *trusts is an example of the law developed in this way. The rules of equity were merged with the rules of common law by the Judicature Acts (1873-75), which resolved most cases of conflict and provided that, in any cases in which there was still a conflict, the rules of equity should prevail.

Equity Capital for Industry (E.C.I.). A financial organization established in 1976 by several City institutions and the Bank of England to assist in the supply of equity capital to small and medium-sized U.K. industrial companies unable to raise new equity from traditional market sources. *See also* Industrial and Commercial Finance Corporation.

equity-linked policies. Insurance policies that are linked to a fund consisting solely of equities. *See also* unit trusts.

equity switchings. *See* switching.

ergonomics. The scientific study of work situations in industry. The object of ergonomics is to determine the optimum physical environment in work places so that the productivity of labour and capital is maximized. This involves arranging the methods of work, the layout of factories, and the design of processes and machines according to a plan. Ergonomic principles have been increasingly applied in recent years within large companies, especially those of American parentage.

error (in statistics). The difference between an observed value and a true value or expected value. When such an error occurs in a statistical investigation based on random samples, it is caused merely by chance, i.e. it is a random deviation and there is no implication of mistake by human agency.

errors and omissions excepted (E.&O.E.). An expression often included at the end of an invoice to safeguard the creditor against clerical mistakes.

escalation clause. A provision in a contract to increase the price charged for goods or services if costs rise above a stated limit. Escalation clauses are common in contracts for long-term projects in periods of high inflation.

escape clause. A clause in a contract that allows one party to evade the consequences of some onerous clause in certain circumstances.

escrow. A contract, deed, or other document that is held by a third person and that does not become effective until some specified condition has been fulfilled. For example, shares in a company held *in escrow* by a third person are held on trust until a specified condition has been fulfilled.

estate duty. A tax introduced by the Finance Act (1894), whereby a certain percentage of the value of the property owned by a person at his death became payable to the Inland Revenue. It was never a very satisfactory tax and was often known as "the voluntary tax" because there seemed to be so many loopholes that it was always possible for the ingenious citizen to find ways of managing his affairs so that estate duty was often almost completely avoided. In fact, between 1894 and 1975 (when estate duty was finally abolished) the Inland Revenue attempted to close up more and more ingenious loopholes that had been discovered. An early remedy was simply to give away one's property shortly before one's death, but this was soon brought within the scope of the tax. A loophole that proved more difficult to close was the transfer of property to a family company. As the company did not die it could not be made to pay an estate duty until certain legislation was introduced to close this loophole. Estate duty applied to deaths occurring before March 1974, since when it has been replaced by the *capital transfer tax. Estate duty was charged on an ascending scale of rates so that generally the richer a person was when he died, the higher the rate of estate duty on his assets would be.

estimation. A branch of *statistical inference concerned with setting a value to a parameter of a population. The value calculated is called an *estimate,* and the function or equation used to calculate the estimate is the *estimator.* The estimator itself will contain no parameters but only ascertainable statistics. An estimate may be a point estimate or an interval estimate. A point estimate is the simple inference of a population parameter by the corresponding sample value; for instance, the mean height of adult males in London may be estimated by calculating the average height of a random sample of adult male Londoners. An interval estimate is found by taking the point estimate and setting confidence limits to it; the series of values between the limits then forms the interval estimate. The calculation of an interval estimate involves, in the case of a mean, the standard deviation of the random sample and statistics derived from Student's t distribution. Interval estimates are naturally more reliable than point estimates. The most common methods of estimation are *least squares estimation and *maximum likelihood estimation. It is desirable for point estimates to have certain properties, notably those of *unbiasedness, *consistency, *efficiency, *sufficiency, and *invariance.

estimator. *See* estimation.

estoppel. A rule of evidence originating in the Chancellor's Court in the seventeenth or eighteenth century (but since 1875 applied in all courts). According to this rule a person is prevented from denying the truth of a statement previously made by him or implied by his conduct when another person has acted upon the statement.

An example is a statement by a person A that another person B is his agent and may make contracts on his behalf. If a third person C hears that statement (or forms a reasonable conclusion in view of A's conduct that B was his agent), and makes a contract with B because of this belief, A cannot later in court deny that B was his agent, even though it was not in fact the case. A will be personally bound by the contract with C.

Euler's theorem. A mathematical result for homogeneous-of-degree-k functions, which states that the sum of the products of the partial derivatives with respect to each independent variable, with that variable, is equal to k times the function itself.

$$\Sigma_i(\delta f/\delta x_i)x_i = kf(x_1, \ldots, x_n)$$

The major economic significance of this result is in the product exhaustion theorem, which states that under constant returns to scale, payments to inputs just equal receipts from the sale of the output. The crucial factor is that input price equals *marginal revenue product.

Euratom. *See* European Atomic Energy Community.

Eurobond. An interest-bearing stock denominated in a *Eurocurrency. Eurobonds are issued by foreign governments, companies, or international syndicates. Information about them (e.g. quotations and yields) is published by the Association of International Bond Dealers, established in 1969. The Eurobond market developed in the 1960s and operates outside the stock exchanges.

Eurocurrency. Currency of one of the major industrial and financial countries held in bank deposits outside its country of origin. The Eurocurrency market differs from the foreign-exchange market as it is not concerned with buying and selling foreign exchange but accepting deposits and making loans (Eurocurrency credits or Eurocredits) in foreign currencies. For example, a deposit may be made with a bank and denominated in a currency other than that of the country in which the bank is situated: the bank can lend this money to any company or bank, which may then use it to obtain any currency it needs on the foreign-exchange market. Transactions are normally in sums of at least six figures and loans are made for periods ranging from overnight to several years; they are used to finance balance of payments deficits, for commercial transactions, and industrial development. They have also provided a mechanism for recycling the petrodollars of the OPEC countries. The market developed from the *Eurodollar market in the late 1950s and the main markets were in Europe (London being the biggest)–hence the name–but others have since developed, especially the Asian Dollar Markets in Hong Kong and Singapore as well as others in the Middle East and the Caribbean. The international nature of this market and its enormous size have led to increasing concern because it is outside the control of any particular country or organization.

Eurodollar. An international currency medium in the form of claims to U.S. dollars held by institutions outside the U.S. The Eurodollar market has expanded rapidly since 1957 as dollars became more plentiful in Europe owing to foreign aid and investment by the U.S., and have been increasingly used to finance international trade. The market is outside the control of any national authority both because transactions take place outside the country whose currency is being dealt in and because the markets were established comparatively recently. *See also* Eurocurrency.

European Atomic Energy Community (Euratom). The organization set up by the Euratom Treaty (1957) to promote the peaceful uses of nuclear energy by members of the E.E.C.

European Coal and Steel Community (E.C.S.C.). An association of nations (originally Germany, France, Italy, and Benelux) formed to create a free market in coal and steel. Although it was created in 1951 to regulate the coal and steel industries of Western Europe, it served as a prelude to greater European economic and political integration, not simply for the formation of a European free trade area. The E.C.S.C. was the immediate predecessor of the E.E.C. One of the principal ideals behind the organization was that with such close interdependence in coal and steel, the backbone of heavy industry, war would in future be impossible between the member states.

European Commission. The body, based in Brussels, that controls the workings of the *European Economic Community. It employs some 10 000 staff and is controlled by 14 Commissioners (with no more than two members from an individual country serving at any one time), who are appointed for four-year terms by the unanimous agreement of all the states. It formulates proposals for decision by the Council of Ministers and implements the decisions when they are made. It controls the common budget, into which all duties are paid and from which all subsidies are made.

European Currency Unit (E.C.U.). A unit of account consisting of combined European Economic Community currencies used as a reserve asset within the *European Monetary System. The E.C.U. is essentially bookkeepers' money, having no life of its own. It is created by member countries when they swap 20% of their gold and foreign currency reserves for E.C.U.s.

European Development Fund. *See* Lomé Convention.

European Economic Community (E.E.C., Common Market). A customs union founded by the *Treaty of Rome* in 1957, signed by France, West Germany, Italy, the Netherlands, Belgium, and Luxembourg, which had previously combined in the *European Coal and Steel Community. On 1 January 1973 the U.K., Eire, and Denmark joined under the Treaty of Accession, while Norway decided against joining after a national referendum. In June 1975 the U.K. also held a national referendum because of internal disagreement but the result was in favour of remaining in the E.E.C. Greece became a member in 1981; Portugal and Spain are expected to join in 1986, Turkey at some later date. The population of the E.E.C. is 290 million, which makes it the largest *trade bloc in the world.

The purpose of the Community is to promote free economic activity and increase productive efficiency by removing restrictions on trade and on movements of labour and capital between its members. Such restrictions include quotas or levies (customs duties between members are being dispensed with), monopoly practices, and dumping. The aim is to integrate economic policy in agriculture, transport, and industry and to establish a common level of external tariffs. The enlarged market area available to an industry can provide the incentive for large-scale investment and the advantages of economies of scale.

The Community is controlled by the *European Commission, who implement the policies decided by the Council of Ministers, which consists of one minister from each member country. The European Parliament has, as yet, little political power but the far-reaching question of political union is the ultimate aim of the community. The Parliament can pass laws affecting all members, chiefly of a commercial nature, but each member of the Council of Ministers has the power of veto. The *European Investment Bank was set up as a fund to aid in the development of economically backward regions, to establish enterprises necessitated by the formation of the Community, and to finance projects that are of common interest to member states. The European Court of Justice meets at The Hague. The *Common Agricultural Policy (C.A.P.) seeks to increase agricultural earnings and productivity and to eliminate fluctuations in prices and supplies. Products are guaranteed an intervention price: if the market price falls below this the Community guarantees to purchase excess supplies at the intervention price. The Common Market is protected from outside competition by a variable tariff, which keeps the price of foreign goods above a threshold price slightly above the intervention price. The C.A.P. consumes two thirds of the Community budget.

Entry and exit visas and work permits between member countries are no longer required but passports and residence permits are still needed. People moving to another member country have the same social security rights as its nationals.

European Free Trade Association (EFTA). An association that came into existence after the signing of the Stockholm Treaty (1959). Its members, Austria, Denmark, Norway, Portugal, Sweden, Switzerland, and the U.K., joined together after negotiations for a broader free trade area had broken down with the establishment of the *European Economic Community. These countries preferred a free-trade area to a customs union for reasons of sovereignty, colonial connections, or (in the case of Switzerland, Sweden, and Austria) traditional or imposed neutrality. Between 1960 and 1967 tariffs were abolished on all industrial goods but without close cooperation in the formulation of social and economic policy. Finland joined EFTA in 1961 and Iceland in 1970. However, the entry of the U.K. and Denmark into the E.E.C. in 1973 seriously weakened the organization, its remaining members signing bilateral trade agreements with the E.E.C.

European Fund. *See* European Monetary Agreement.

European Investment Bank. An *investment bank set up by the Treaty of Rome (1958) to make grants and loans for projects of common interest to members of E.E.C., especially the development of backward regions, such as S Italy. Capital for the bank is provided by member states in proportions laid down in its statute.

European Monetary Agreement (E.M.A.). An arrangement, established by members of the O.E.E.C. in 1958, when the Western European countries restored the convertibility of their currencies after the post-war recovery period. The object was to facilitate clearance of balance of payment deficits between the countries and to maintain the *European Fund*, a fund built up to provide two-year loans to countries with short-term balance of payment difficulties.

European Monetary Cooperation Fund (Fecom). *See* European Monetary System.

European Monetary System (E.M.S.). The currency arrangement that came into operation in March 1979, replacing the *snake for coordinating the exchange rates of member countries of the European Economic Community. Membership of the E.M.S. is voluntary and some countries, notably the U.K., have chosen to stay out. Exchange rate movements are controlled by a parity grid. Each currency is given a central rate expressed in terms of a new kind of money–the *European Currency Unit. Currencies can fluctuate against each other within a band of ±2¼% (±6% for Italy) around their central rates; the central rate itself can also be altered (devalued or revalued) if necessary. The E.M.S. is administered by the *European Monetary Cooperation Fund*, known as *Fecom* from its French initials.

European Recovery Programme. *See* Marshall Aid Programme.

European Regional Development Fund. A fund established in 1975 by the E.E.C. to further its general policy of promoting "regional balance". The fund makes disbursements to E.E.C. national governments, mainly on a quota basis (Italy currently receives 40% of the fund and the U.K. 28%), to finance selected investment projects in industry and for selected infrastructure projects. The areas that qualify for assistance are limited to those already covered by member states' own regional aid programmes (i.e. it is intended to supplement, not replace, member governments' own contributions).

ex. (Latin for: without, exclusive of.) A share quoted ex dividend or ex div means that a purchaser will not be entitled to receive the share's current dividend. Similarly one can buy a fixed-interest security ex interest, meaning without current interest, or shares ex rights or ex bonus (or ex capitalization), meaning respectively without rights recently issued and without a bonus issue recently declared. Dealings in a security ex all means with all such supplementary advantages accruing to the seller. *Compare* cum.

ex ante. (Latin for: from before.) Concepts and theories that look at the world from before the event and generally deal in plans or expectations. Thus, at a given ex ante price, a supplier may wish to sell a certain quantity of goods, but if a market is not in equilibrium this might not be possible. In the real world trading will still take place before the price finally adjusts to equilibrium, but it is only at equilibrium that desired ex ante supply equals the ex ante demand. *Compare* ex post.

excess capacity. Excess capacity exists in a firm that produces at an output at which marginal cost is less than its average cost, for then it is still possible to decrease average cost by producing more goods. Excess capacity may thus be measured as the increase in present output that is needed to reduce average cost to a minimum. Although equality of marginal cost and average cost is desirable, it is not always possible, especially when significant economies of scale exist, as in a *natural monopoly. Excess capacity is a characteristic of *monopolistic competition. *See also diagram at* monopolistic competition.

excess demand. The difference in a market between the total amount of a good demanded at a particular set of prices and the amount supplied. The prices mentioned are those for all goods and not just the one under consideration. Excess demand is positive when demand exceeds supply, negative when demand falls short of supply, and zero when the market clears.

excess policy. A type of insurance policy in which the policyholder is responsible for a specified sum in each claim. If the policy is subject to an excess of £50, the policyholder is responsible for the first £50 of every claim. This excess may be compulsorily applied by the insurer, or the insured may agree voluntarily to such a provision. Normally when there is an excess the premium is reduced. *See also* deductible.

excess supply. The difference in a market between the total amount of a good supplied and the amount demanded at a particular set of prices. It is equal in magnitude but opposite in sign to *excess demand.

exchange control. The control by a country of the extent to which its currency can be exchanged for that of another country. It is usually introduced to help a government keep its balance of payments in equilibrium and maintain the value of the nation's currency. Exchange control regulations are imposed to restrict the outflow of capital from a country. Maintenance of currency values is particularly necessary in countries that impose a fixed exchange rate on their currencies. Restrictions on the outflow of capital make it necessary for permission to be sought from the government or its agencies for the export of currency for purposes of foreign investment, living abroad, and even holidays abroad. Some countries also insist that permission must be sought for the purchase of foreign currencies, or the export of domestic currency, to pay for goods bought abroad. These measures require very stringent policing if they are to be effective. Exchange controls in the U.K. were abolished in 1979.

Exchange Equalization Account. An account established in 1932 and managed by the Bank of England on behalf of the Treasury with the object of stabilizing the international value of sterling. The managers of the Account were authorized to buy or sell foreign currencies or gold as necessary to counteract the operations of speculators, seasonal fluctuations, and other effects unconnected with trade. Other countries have established similar accounts. With the outbreak of war, by the Currency (Defence) Act (1939), the government's total gold resources were concentrated in the Account, as were all private holdings of gold, foreign exchange, and foreign securities, so that the Treasury had control of the total foreign monetary resources of the country. Although exchange controls were abolished in 1979 the Bank of England continues transactions to hold the exchange rate steady.

exchange rate. The price at which one currency can be exchanged for another, i.e. the price of a currency in the foreign exchange market. When considering the variations in terms of a particular country's currency it is customary to use that country's currency as the numeraire and evaluate the exchange rates for all other currencies in terms of it. The desire to exchange domestic currency for that of a foreign country has its origins chiefly in the desire to invest in, or import from, that country. Similarly there are those in the foreign country seeking the home country's currency in order to purchase its exports or make investments, and this determines supply. At the equilibrium exchange rate these two will balance out. The equilibrium equation is thus linked to the balance of payments. When the balance of payments is running at a deficit, i.e. there are accommodating capital inflows, there will be pressure on the exchange rate to fall or depreciate. When it is running at a surplus the pressure will be towards appreciation of the domestic currency. Exactly how the price will respond to this pressure depends on whether the exchange rate is fixed or floating, or is some mixture of the two, such as the sliding peg.

Under a *floating exchange rate*, the exchange rate will be allowed to vary until supply and demand in the exchange market are in equilibrium (*clean floating* refers to the completely unfettered operation of market forces). Under a *fixed exchange rate* the government will attempt to keep the price fixed in the short run by accumulating or depleting its foreign exchange reserves, or by borrowing abroad. With a *sliding* (or *crawling*) *peg* the exchange rate moves in response to supply and demand conditions, but only by limited amounts each month (*see* snake).

If, under fixed exchange rates, such policies as tariffs fail to eliminate disequilibrium, it will be necessary to alter the exchange rate of the currency (*see* devaluation, revaluation). The argument in favour of floating exchange rates is that they provide an immediate means of bringing the balance of payments into line. The arguments against it centre around the inhibiting effects on trade of uncertainty and the destabilizing effect of speculation. The arguments for fixed exchange rates are that they induce confidence and stability. Against them is that they have an opportunity cost in terms of holding exchange reserves and also that the government is forced to restrict its use of the exchange rate as a policy instrument. A delicate judgment is required in deciding whether particular circumstances are best served by employing fixed or floating exchange rates.

Since 1972 most of the world's currencies have been floating. *See also* European Monetary System.

exchange restriction. A limitation on the purchase and sale of foreign and domestic currency. It is a form of *exchange control imposed by the state to maintain an artificially high *exchange rate for its currency.

Exchequer and Audit Department. A U.K. government department headed by the Comptroller and Auditor General, who authorizes all issues from the Consolidated and National Loans Funds after satisfying himself that Parliament has given authority for them.

excise duty. 1. A duty levied on goods (such as alcoholic drinks and cigarettes) that are produced in the same country as they are sold. Excise duties are distinguished from customs duties as the latter are levied on imports. In the U.K., excise duties are collected by H.M. Customs and Excise.

2. (In the U.S.). An indirect tax levied on business rights or privileges; it is measured by the money value of sales or goods involved.

exclusive events. Events that cannot occur simultaneously. The probability that one of several exclusive events will occur is the sum of their individual probabilities of occurrence. *Also called*: mutually exclusive events.

ex dividend. Denoting the price of a share on the stock exchange when it does not include the right to receive the next dividend. The dividend is retained by the seller or is returnable to the seller even if it is paid to a buyer, who bought the shares after they had gone ex dividend. Shares usually go ex dividend one month before the payment of the dividend, when the price of the share usually drops by an amount equivalent to the dividend per share, other things being equal. *Compare* cum dividend.

executor. A person who has been appointed to administer the estate of a testator as instructed in his will. Institutions may also be appointed by the testator and most banks have departments willing to act in this capacity. Where two or more executors are appointed the acts of any one of them are deemed to be the acts of all, except that they must all join in the conveyance of real estate or the transfer of stocks and shares. If after a period of time a trust commences under the terms of the will, they then become trustees of the will and must all join in any disposal of the testator's assets. *See also* letters of administration.

exemplary damages. *See* damages.

exempted dealers. Individuals or organizations that are allowed by the *Prevention of Frauds (Investments) Act to buy securities for their own account. Examples are banks and insurance companies.

exhaustive events. A set of events, one of which must occur in any context or problem. The sum of the probabilities of occurrence of exhaustive events is one.

exogenous variable. A variable whose value is not determined by any of the relationships in the model under consideration. For instance, two of the determinants of aggregate income are the level of government expenditures and external demand (expressed through exports), variables usually regarded as exogenous to the theory of income determination. It should be noted that the distinction between endogenous and exogenous (or predetermined) variables is valid only for the purposes of model construction and is not meant to portray the economy as it is in the real world. An exogenous variable will always be an independent variable in any of the model's relationships in which it occurs, although some of the independent variables in any relationship may be endogenous. *Compare* endogenous variable.

expansion path. The locus of cost-minimizing combinations of factors for a given factor-price ratio as the level of output is increased. For a constant returns to scale or homothetic production function the expansion path is a straight line through the origin, corresponding to fixed input ratios, since along such a ray the marginal rate of technical substitution is constant and so is equal to the constant price ratio, fulfilling the cost-minimizing conditions.

expectations. Beliefs about future events with regard to business activity, thought by Keynes to be one of the major influences on investment. It is necessary to form expectations when taking rational economic decisions. Many economic theories predict that certain events will occur in response to exogenous changes when other things, such as expectations, are held constant. Since expectations cannot be directly observed, a theory of expectation formation or direct extraneous information on them is needed. In many tests of economic theories the theory of expectations is taken as part of the maintained hypothesis, but this may lead to error. A commonly used theory of expectations is that they are formed adaptively, i.e. current expectations equal past expectations plus some proportion of the error in prediction made in the past. This theory is very difficult to check. For instance, the degree of inflation that union officials expect in the next year will probably affect their negotiations with management over pay increases, but it will be so inextricably linked to other factors that its importance would be difficult to estimate. *See also* term structure of interest rates.

expected inflation. A rate of change in the price level that is anticipated by all individuals in the economy. When their expectations are correct the inflation is fully anticipated. If all individuals expect inflation then all contracts will be negotiated so as to take it into account; there will consequently be no resource misallocation. As an example, when considering the prevailing interest rate, adjustment to expected inflation can be represented as the difference between the money rate of interest (the amount actually paid) and the real rate (the amount paid minus the expected rate of inflation, which just equals the depreciation on the real capital involved) that is incorporated into contracts. The real rate is the relevant variable for decisions except in the money market, and because the money rate of interest exceeds the real rate, less real money balances will be held. This may make individuals feel worse off and induce a *real balance effect on savings. This is the only way an expected inflation can affect real variables in the economy. *See also* unexpected inflation.

expected payoff. A notional payoff arising from the selection of a mixed strategy in *game theory. The expected payoff can be calculated as a *weighted average of (pure) payoffs, using as weights the proportions in which the player selects different courses of action in his overall mixed strategy. If the opponent is also pursuing a mixed strategy, the solution to the expected payoff can be found by linear programming techniques.

expected value. The arithmetic mean of a random variable or the mean of its distribution. Since the arithmetic mean is easily manipulated algebraically, expected value operations are frequently encountered in statistics. An expected value is conventionally denoted by the letter E; thus the symbol for the expected value of X is $E[X]$.

explanatory variable. *See* independent variable.

exponential distribution. A statistical *distribution involving a continuous variable. The exponential distribution is the *gamma distribution when the latter's α parameter is restricted so that the distribution's mean equals its standard deviation. The graph of an exponential density function is a negatively sloping curve.

exponential function. A function of the form $y = b^x$, which is monotonically increasing provided that the base is greater than one; if the base is less than one but greater than zero, then the exponential function will be monotonically decreasing. The base most frequently taken is the irrational number e = 2.71828 . . . . Exponential functions have a limited application in economics, mainly in the field of dynamics in which many growth rates follow an exponential time path.

exponential smoothing. A means of making short-term forecasts on a time series by the exponential weighting of moving averages. Moving averages by themselves cannot be used for forecasting purposes because of the gap at the end of the reduced moving average series. Exponential weighting consists of closing the gap by assigning weights that are biased in favour of the more recent values of the time series. This extended series can then be projected to make the forecast.

Export Credits Guarantee Department (E.C.G.D.). A government department, set up in 1919, to provide insurance for U.K. exporters against the major risks of nonpayment by their overseas customers. Cover is also provided for U.K. banks that finance exports. Since 1972 the E.C.G.D. has operated a scheme offering U.K. investors up to 15 years' protection against political risks in respect of new investment overseas.

Most of the insurance provided by the department is under short-term guarantees, covering standard goods sold on up to six months credit, and under extended-term guarantees, covering production engineering goods sold on credit terms up to five years. Projects may be covered under specific guarantees. The insurance covers up to 90 or 95 per cent of loss due to insolvency of the buyer, the action of a foreign government preventing performance of a contract, war, cancellation of a U.K. export licence, or exchange control difficulties.

The E.C.G.D. is non-profit-making, although it is intended to be self-supporting.

export-import bank. A bank established by the U.S. government to make loans to foster international trade with the U.S.

export incentive. Government aid intended to promote exports. It can be either directly tied to the amount of exports of a particular firm or applied more indirectly by aiding an industry that relies primarily on exports for its market. This aid can take the form of subsidies, tax incentives, or credit facilities. The government's purpose in such a policy is to bolster the level of economic activity and to help the balance of trade. This aid is generally regarded as giving an unfair competitive advantage to its recipients and is either specifically prohibited or discouraged by most trade agreements, including GATT.

export leasing. A procedure by which a leasing company enables a foreign buyer to take delivery of plant or equipment without paying for it (either because he is short of funds or cannot obtain an import licence or exchange control permit) and for the local manufacturer or exporter to receive payment in full. The plant is purchased by the leasing company, who pays the manufacturer, and leased to the overseas buyer.

export multiplier. The ratio of the increase in domestic national income to the increase in exports that caused it. This ratio is dependent upon the *marginal propensity to save of those people whose income has increased as well as the aggregate propensity to import that exists in the domestic country. *See also* multiplier, foreign trade multiplier.

exports. Goods and services that are sold to foreign countries. Goods are classified as visible exports (*see* visibles) whilst services, such as banking, insurance, tourism, etc., are invisible exports (*see* invisibles). Exports and *imports together form the *foreign sector of an economy.

All countries seek to increase the volume of their exports as much as possible to finance the purchase of their essential imports. Governments frequently attempt to encourage exporters in a variety of ways (*see* export incentives), which may or may not be prohibited under GATT and other international trade agreements. An example is the *export subsidy* provided under the *Common Agricultural Policy of the E.E.C.

The U.K. has consistently exported more invisibles than it has imported, but this has not been so for visibles. In total, the growth in U.K. exports has been slower than that of its industrial competitors for a number of reasons: loss of relatively protected pre-war markets, concentration in comparatively slowly growing markets, and labour problems.

ex post. (Latin for: from after.) A concept that describes the results of actions after they have happened rather than their expected results. For instance, a producer might expect to be able to sell all his goods for £20 each, but find that in practice he has to reduce them to £10 to clear his stock. In these circumstances his *ex ante price is £20 and his *ex post price is £10. In a perfect world ex ante and ex post prices would be identical, since everyone would be able to predict accurately future conditions in the market. In fact, the disparity between them is responsible for many fluctuations in the economy. *See also* comparative statics, statics, dynamics, cobweb theorem.

ex quay. Denoting a contract for the sale of goods in which the seller pays freight charges to the port of destination, unloading onto the quay, and loading onto rail or road vehicles from the quay. The buyer is responsible for all subsequent transport charges.

ex ship. *See* free overboard.

externalities. Goods and services whose costs and benefits are not properly accounted for by the price system. As a result, the production of externalities is never at the optimum level for the economy as a whole and the *Pareto-optimal marginal conditions that consider social benefit and cost cannot be substituted into the price system.

Examples of externalities in the system could include the costs of clearing a street covered by litter and the displeasure it gives to other street users. As examples of externalities in production, company A trains computer programmers who are then free to work for company B; company B can offer higher wages since it has not borne the costs of training. An oil company would like to reduce production from a field to conserve supplies, but the neighbouring company could then get more from the field by continuing production at full capacity. Smog is the product of many firms emitting smoke into the air, but each of them individually does not contribute a significant amount and does not pay compensation for the damage it causes. Each firm is therefore powerless to put a stop to the nuisance by independent action and sees no need to reduce its output independently. Externalities can be either beneficial or harmful: in production they are called *external economies* and *diseconomies*, respectively.

extraordinary general meeting. Any meeting of a company other than the *annual general meeting. It may be called by the directors or by the holders of not less than ten per cent of the voting shares.

extraordinary items. Accounting items that occur outside the normal course of business and are both material and not expected to recur regularly or frequently. For example, if a property company lost part of its property portfolio in an earthquake in a zone that was previously considered safe, it would be reasonable to assume that this fact would be reflected in the accounts as an extraordinary item. A distinction is made between extraordinary and *exceptional items*. The latter, although significant, are the results of the ordinary course of business.

extrapolation. The projection of a series of historical data (especially time series data) into the future for purposes of prediction or forecasting. Thus if an index number is constructed for food consumption per head every ten years and the trend has been a 10% increase every ten years, e.g. 100 in 1960, 110 in 1970, 121 in 1980, then the index for 1990 might be extrapolated to be 133. Extrapolations have most validity when there are no current circumstances from which it may be inferred that the historical trend will be broken or interrupted; furthermore the historical data themselves should contain no item that may have been affected by extraordinary events (such as World War II). In the case of the output of cyclical industries (or economies), extrapolation can only be used in respect of the secular (long-term) trend and even then is of uncertain validity. *Compare* interpolation.

ex warehouse. *See* spot goods.

ex works. Denoting a contract for the sale of goods in which the buyer is responsible for all delivery charges, except loading onto the road or rail vehicles for which the seller is responsible.

F

face value. *See* par value.

factor. 1. A firm that will, by arrangement, purchase the trade debts of its clients and collect them on its own behalf. The purchase price will be a percentage (usually 80%) of the face value of the debts, but the balance remaining (less a service charge) will be paid to the client when the debt has been collected. The factor has the right to select the debts he will service and may not be prepared to make advances against debts that he considers doubtful. The factor's function is to help to provide the trade with working capital. He may also operate a nonrecourse facility on selected debts, i.e. for an extra charge he may be prepared to offer a form of *credit insurance, guaranteeing payment to the trader even if the debtor fails.

2. An individual or firm in certain trades that buys in bulk and sells on a wholesale basis.

factorial. A mathematical notation written ! and indicating that the number to which it is attached should be multiplied by all the integers below it (down to one). Thus: $5! = 5 \times 4 \times 3 \times 2 \times 1 = 120$. Zero factorial (0!) is conventionally given the value of 1.

factor-price frontier. A schedule showing the highest technically possible rate of return to capital given a fixed wage rate. In an economy with many techniques of production the factor-price frontier is the upper envelope of the curves for each technique. The factor-price frontier was an analytic tool developed by Paul Samuelson (*b.* 1915) in the debate on the aggregation of capital, in order to defend the use of aggregate models where heterogeneous capital goods are treated as if they were homogeneous. The *elasticity of the curve at any point determines the relative shares of income between labour and a suitably defined aggregate for capital. If the factor-price frontier satisfies certain conditions then it may be used to derive a *surrogate production function, the marginal products of which determine the rates of return to capital and labour as if the heterogeneous capital stock of the real world could be represented as homogeneous "jelly", as in the simple aggregate models. The appropriate level of capital "jelly" may be derived from knowledge of prices and the amount of labour used. However, if *double switching or *capital reversing are present the analogy breaks down as the conditions to ensure a production function is well behaved, i.e. convex to the origin to yield meaningful economic profit maxima, are invalidated.

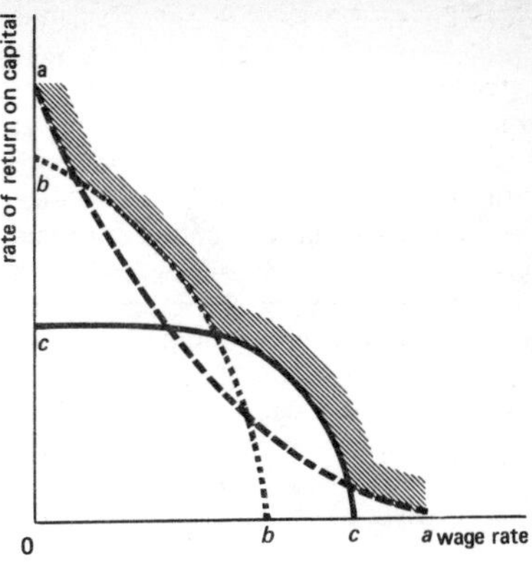

Factor-price frontier

factors of production. Resources used as inputs in the production of a good. They are broadly grouped into land (including natural resources), labour, and capital, and sometimes also entrepreneurship.

factory costs. The sum of the *direct costs and the *indirect costs in a manufacturing business. The factory cost of a good is the cost of manufacture before mark-up for profit.

Fair Trading Act (1973). An Act of Parliament that consolidated existing monopoly legislation and also extended it in a number of ways. The Act created a new post, the Director-General of Fair Trading, and a new office, the Office of Fair Trading, to implement and coordinate all aspects of monopoly control. The Director-General took over the functions of the Registrar of Restrictive Trading Agreements (*see* Restrictive Trade Practice) and became responsible for referring monopoly and merger investigations to the *Monopolies and Mergers Commission.

The Act lowered the market share criterion for monopoly situations from one third to one quarter, extended the legislation to include public-sector monopolies, and provided for the registration of restrictive agreements relating to the supply of commercial services. In addition, the Act provided for tighter control of unscrupulous trade practices (e.g. misleading money-back guarantees or trade descriptions) and established a Consumer Protection Advisory Committee.

fall-back price. *See* Common Agricultural Policy.

family allowances. *See* child benefit.

Family Income Supplement (F.I.S.). A payment that can be claimed by U.K. residents in full-time work, who have at least one child in the family and whose total family income is below a certain level. Those drawing F.I.S. are also entitled to other benefits, such as free prescriptions, dental treatment, glasses, milk and vitamins, school meals, and legal aid.

F.A.O. *See* Food and Agricultural Organization.

f.a.q. *Abbrev. for* fair average quality. Denoting a quantity of a commodity that is offered not on a particular quality specification but on the basis that it is equal to the average quality of the current crop, recent shipments, etc.

f.a.s. *See* free alongside ship.

fate (in banking). The payment or dishonour of a cheque. When a banker is requested by another bank to advise fate, he is being asked to state whether or not he has paid the cheque to the debit of his customer's account.

F.C.I. *See* Finance Corporation for Industry.

F distribution. A statistical *distribution involving a continuous variable. An F variable is the ratio of two chi-square variables and has two sets of degrees of freedom corresponding to those of its numerator and of its denominator. Like Student's t distribution, the F distribution is important as a vehicle for hypothesis testing. It can be used to test the equality of two variances, in analysis of variance, and as a joint test on two regression coefficients. Like the Student's t tests, the F tests do not depend on population parameters but unlike the case with the t tests, the F test for the equality of two variances does require both variables to which the two variances relate to be normally distributed.

feasibility study. The analysis of a proposed project with reference to its technical, economic, and financial features. The purpose of a feasibility study is to ascertain the project's potential for commercial success before any large capital outlays are made.

Fecom. *See* European Monetary System.

Federal Reserve System. The banking system of the U.S. that acts as its central bank; it was established by the Federal Reserve Act (1913). There are 12 *Federal Reserve Districts* in the U.S., each with its own *Federal Reserve Bank*, whose activities are coordinated and controlled by the *Federal Reserve Board* in Washington. This is headed by a Board of Governors, who are advised principally by the *Federal Reserve Open Market Committee* and the *Federal Advisory Council.* Commercial banks that are members of the Federal Reserve System maintain reserves with the Federal Reserve Banks and their reserve requirements are determined by the Federal Reserve Board. The country's monetary policy is implemented by the Federal Reserve System.

fertility rate. The number of live births in any given year per 1000 women aged between 15 and 44 inclusive. Fertility rates can be calculated for women aged within a sub-category of this span. The fertility rate is considered superior to the crude birth rate because it is more sensitive to a population's age composition; in fact, the fertility rate in the U.K. has shown a trend similar to the crude birth rate.

F.F.I. *See* Finance for Industry Ltd.

fiat money. Any object that has been declared to be legal tender by the government although it is not backed by reserves. Paper money is fiat money since it can no longer be redeemed for gold and its intrinsic worth is almost nil.

fictitious assets. Entries that have to appear in a balance sheet for accounting reasons, although they have no realizable value. A trading loss is an example. *Compare* intangible assets.

fidelity guarantee insurance. A type of policy effected by an employer insuring him against the possibility of the dishonesty of an employee or employees.

fiduciary issue. A government-authorized issue of bank notes, which is backed by government securities and not by gold. Instituted by the Bank Charter Act (1844), it was then £14 million; when the Bank of England took over the note-issuing rights of the commercial banks (as these lapsed) and the Treasury issue in 1928, it was in that year raised to £260 million. With the Second World War and the transfer of nearly all the gold held by the Bank of England to the *Exchange Equalization Account, the fiduciary issue was increased to £1400 million. As a result of inflation it has since increased substantially (12 820 million on 2 January 1985) and represents virtually the whole note issue. Although it fluctuates, being higher at times when there is an increased demand for cash, e.g. Christmas, it is only likely to be reduced by the greater use of means other than notes for debt settlements, e.g. cheques, credit transfers, giro, etc.

field. *See* file.

FIFO. *See* first in, first out.

file. A set of information stored on a computer *storage device. A file consists of *records*, which in turn consists of *fields*. A purchase ledger computer system, for example, might contain a supplier's file with a record for each supplier; each record would contain fields, such as the supplier's name, supplier's address, etc.

final dividend. The final distribution of profits declared by a company in respect of a particular trading period, usually one year. *See also* interim dividend.

final invoice. *See* pro-forma invoice.

Finance Corporation for Industry (F.C.I.). A subsidiary of *Finance for Industry Ltd. established in 1945 by the Bank of England and the English and Scottish clearing banks to provide medium- and long-term loans to larger industrial companies. Its purposes are to encourage productive investment in fixed assets, support working capital, and encourage investment to increase exports. *See also* Industrial and Commercial Finance Corporation.

Finance for Industry Ltd. (F.F.I.). A holding company for a group of U.K. agencies, including the *Finance Corporation for Industry and the *Industrial and Commercial Finance Corporation, which together provide loan and equity finance to industry. F.F.I. was established in 1973 and by 1982 had committed some £750 million to industry. Its share capital is held by the Bank of England (15%) and the English and Scottish clearing banks (85%).

finance house (finance company). An institution whose main business is hire-purchase finance. A number of the larger companies formed the *Finance Houses Association* in 1945, to protect the interests of its members. Most of the commercial banks have considerable interests in these houses, providing funds as required: in addition, the finance houses accept deposits from the investing public, usually at a higher rate of interest than the banks' deposit rate.

financial accountant. An accountant who is concerned with the application and control of money, treating money as an economic factor of production (*compare* cost accountant). His field embraces the whole system of administering and accounting for the movement of money, with all the rigorous cross checking that this will entail. He is concerned with the level of cash of the company, bank balances, the means of paying creditors, dividend policy, the age of debts and overdue accounts, and investment of spare cash.

financial intermediary. An institution that acts as an intermediary between those individuals or firms who wish to lend and those who wish to borrow. The existence of financial intermediaries reduces risks by allowing specialist institutions to evaluate the creditworthiness of borrowers. Because of their greater wealth they are more able to stand a run of defaults on debts, a principle known as *gamblers ruin,* because it is probable that eventually the wealthier gambler will win. This risk reduction may encourage lending and thus reduce the interest rate if most individuals are risk averters. Institutionally it is common to distinguish between banks and nonbank financial intermediaries. The importance of the former is that their liabilities enter the common definition of the money supply. The liabilities of nonbank financial intermediaries may enter some money supply definitions or they may be classed as *near money (depending on their liquidity). Examples of nonbank intermediaries listed in terms of decreasing liquidity are: building societies, savings banks, hire purchase companies, insurance companies, pension funds, and investment trusts. *See also* intermediation, disintermediation.

Financial Times Actuaries Share Indices. A series of 54 share indices published daily except Monday in the Financial Times together with historical highs and lows and comparative indices for each day of the previous working week and for the corresponding day of the previous year. The indices are compiled each day by computer in cooperation with the Institute of Actuaries in London and the Faculty of Actuaries in Edinburgh. They are *Laspeyres-type arithmetic indices (unlike the Financial Times Industrial Ordinary Index,

F.T.—Actuaries Share Indices

Equity Groups	*No. of Indices*	*No. of Securities*
Capital Goods	8	178
Consumer Goods (Durable)	4	56
Consumer Goods (Nondurable)	12	168
Other Groups	4	94
INDUSTRIAL GROUP	1	496
Oils	1	4
500 SHARE INDEX	1	500
Financial Group	10	100
Investment Trusts	1	50
ALL-SHARE INDEX	1	650
Commodity Groups	6	53
Fixed Interest	5	57
TOTAL	54	760

which is a geometric index). The 54 individual indices comprise 760 securities taken to be representative of the entire London Stock Exchange and drawn from each individual sector of the market. The table indicates the broad breakdown of the indices as they appear in the Financial Times. The Capital Goods Group, for example, has indices for Building Materials shares, Heavy Engineering shares, and five others as well as an overall group index, while the Financial Group has similar subsections for Bank shares, Discount House shares, and so on. Only the shares of the larger quoted companies are included in the indices; however, the constituents of the All-Share Index represent some 80% of the market in terms of capitalization. The base date from which the indices of the securities are calculated is 10 April 1962. The Financial Times Actuaries Share Indices are used extensively by institutional investors.

Financial Times Industrial Ordinary Index. An index number of share prices (1935 = 100) comprising 30 constituents chosen to be representative of U.K. industry and commerce (but not finance). The index is a geometric index, so that it gives less weighting to extreme movements among the constituents than would an arithmetic index; it is assessed hourly by the Financial Times, which publishes it each day as it was at the close of (Stock Exchange) business on the previous day. The constituents of the index (1985) are the shares of the following companies:

Allied-Lyons, Associated Dairies, Beecham, B.I.C.C., Blue Circle, Boots, B.P., British Oxygen Company, British Telecom, B.T.R., Cadbury-Schweppes, Courtaulds, Distillers, G.E.C., G.K.N., Glaxo, Grand Metropolitan Hotels, Hanson Trust, Hawker Siddeley, I.C.I., Imperial Group, Lucas, Marks and Spencer, National Westminster Bank, P. & O., Plessey, Tate & Lyle, Thorn E.M.I., Trust House Forte, and Vickers. These 30 constituents are altered occasionally to reflect the changing composition of U.K. industry; it is generally automatic for them to be assigned *blue-chip status in investment matters. The Industrial Ordinary Index, widely referred to as the *30-share index* or simply *the index*, is easily the best-known barometer of the London Stock Exchange, sensitive as it is to the "mood" of the market hour by hour. It is a constituent index of the Financial Times Stock Indices although not of the Financial Times Actuaries Share Indices.

Financial Times Stock Indices. A series of *Laspeyres price indices published each day except Monday in the Financial Times. Included are the indices for government securities (1926 = 100), for fixed-interest securities (1928 = 100), for gold mine shares (1955 = 100), and for industrial ordinary shares, i.e. the *Financial Times Industrial Ordinary Index (1935 = 100). The series also includes the average dividend *yield, the average *earnings yield, the average *P/E ratio for ordinary shares, and the number of (Stock Exchange) dealings marked. These statistics are all listed as at the close of business of each of the last six trading days and of a year ago. Historical highs and lows of the indices together with indices of Stock Exchange activity (1942 = 100) are also listed.

financial year. An accounting period of twelve months, which for a business can start on any date. It is usual, however, for businesses to start their financial year on the same day as the calendar year (1 Jan.) or the *fiscal year (6 April). The Companies Acts (1948–1981) use a wider definition, referring to a financial year as the period covered by the profit and loss account of business, whatever the length of the period.

fine trade bill. A *trade bill that is backed by an established bank or finance house whose creditworthiness is beyond dispute. When acting as a *lender of last resort, the Bank of England will only accept fine trade bills as security.

fine tuning. The use of monetary and fiscal policy to regulate short-term fluctuations in output or to control inflation or the balance of payments. The tendency to attempt to use fine tuning to regulate the economy has been strongly criticized as ineffective because the following three types of lag may delay the results of the policy until the policy becomes counterproductive: (i) the lag between the occurrence of an event and the publication of the relevant statistics; (ii) the lag between the receipt of information and its interpretation and action by the government; (iii) the lag between a policy decision and its actual effect. All these lags are also very unpredictable. However, the alternative to fine tuning, which is rigid adherence to a strategy decided upon much earlier, also has obvious drawbacks, caused by its inherent inflexibility. The choice between these two alternatives often reflects a political opinion as to how much intervention should take place in the economy. *See also* built-in stabilizers.

fire insurance. Insurance providing compensation for loss or damage caused by burning. To form a valid claim under the policy there must be actual ignition, which was accidental as far as the insured was concerned. The standard fire policy, which is prepared for virtually all commercial risks, also covers damage by lightning and, to a limited extent, explosion.

For an additional premium the standard fire policy may be extended to cover any of the following:

(i) bursting or overflowing of water tanks, apparatus, or pipes;
(ii) earthquake;
(iii) explosion (the cover is wider than in the standard policy):
(iv) flood;
(v) hail;
(vi) impact damage by vehicles, animals, or articles from the air, including aircraft;
(vii) riot or civil commotion (the latter would include damage done by strikers, locked-out workers, and some forms of malicious damage);
(viii) storm and tempest;
(ix) spontaneous combustion, self-heating, or fermentation;
(x) subsidence and landslip:
(xi) thunderbolt.

It is increasingly becoming the practice amongst insurers to grant policies that cover many or all of the policies referred to above and also to include certain accident insurance risks, such as burglary, public liability, etc.

firm offer. *See* offer.

firmware. *See* microcomputer.

first in, first out (FIFO). A method of valuing company stock on hand. It is based on the assumption that older stock, i.e. stock that has been longest on the premises, is used before the stock purchased at a later date. It is necessary to adopt such a method of valuation when stock of an identical type, for example screws of a similar gauge, is placed together in a bin. Stock is normally valued at its cost value and, as over a period of time the price of a stock item rises, there will exist in a pool of stock similar items at different cost values. This type of valuation tends to push up the valuation of the balance of stock in a situation where prices are rising. *See also* last in, first out.

first-loss policy. An insurance policy in which both parties know and accept that the sum insured represents less than the value at risk, but where *average is not applicable.

These policies are used frequently in burglary insurance. The justification for them is that there are some areas in which the possibility of a total loss is extremely remote, such as the theft of all of the contents of a large department store. Therefore with this type of risk it is permitted to insure for a fraction of the actual value, with a view to covering the estimated largest probable loss.

first of exchange. The principal copy of a *bill of exchange. When it has been presented and honoured, copies are cancelled.

F.I.S. *See* Family Income Supplement.

fiscal drag. The effect of fiscal policy in restraining the autonomous expansion of the economy when taxes are progressive. A rise in income will raise tax receipts and may reduce government expenditure by reducing unemployment benefits, etc. This rise in net government receipts will reduce the level of aggregate demand below that which would have been reached without fiscal drag. Therefore upturns in the economy will be slower and of smaller magnitude. In downturns there is an automatic expansionary effect because the counterpart to fiscal drag is a *built-in stabilizer.

fiscal (budgetary) policy. Government taxation and expenditure policy designed to regulate the level and composition of output. The government has some control over the level of aggregate demand in the economy through its use of budget deficits and surpluses (*see* I.S. curve, budget, unbalanced budget). If the government believes that unemployment is too high, it can stimulate the level of aggregate demand by increasing the budget deficit. This raises the level of government expenditure and by a multiplier process raises income by more than the initial increase in the budget deficit. Alternatively, if the government believes that the level of aggregate demand is too high, it can reduce it by decreasing the budget deficit. A stimulus to the use of budgetary policy came from the work of J. M. Keynes in *The General Theory of Employment, Interest, and Money* published in 1936. He advocated the use of fiscal policy to cure the high level of unemployment in the Depression. His work has had a great influence on the conduct of post-war economic policy in the West. However, attempts to use his policy prescriptions (made in relation to massive unemployment) as a guide to the policy necessary for *fine tuning have created doubts as to whether fiscal policy is completely effective for these purposes. Since the late 1970s *monetary policy has replaced it as the main control measure of the U.K. government.

fiscal year. The twelve months covered by Budget estimates and constituting the year of account of the government. In the U.K. it runs from 6 April to 5 April twelve months later and in the U.S. it starts on 1 July and ends on 30 June twelve months later. *See also* financial year.

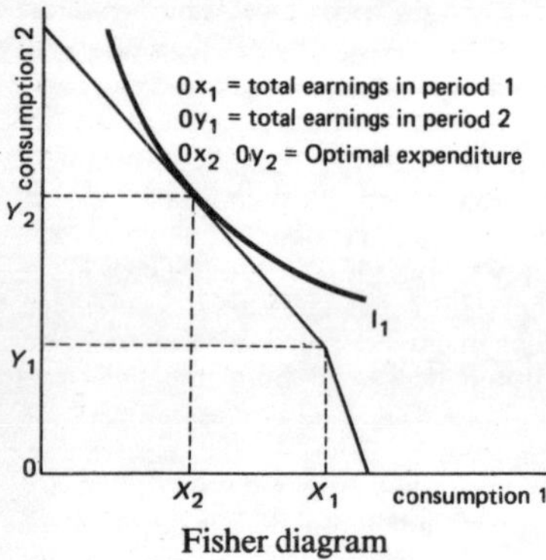

Fisher diagram

Fisher diagram. A graphical method devised by Irving Fisher (1867–1947) used for illustrating time preference in consumption between two periods. Consumption between periods one and two is plotted on the axes and indifference curves on the graph represent the combinations of consumption in the two periods between which the consumer is indifferent. The budget constraint is found by taking the line between the amount of income receipts in period one plus those of period two discounted by the rate of interest, and the income in period two plus that of period one augmented by the rate of interest. These are plotted on the axes for consumption in periods one and two respectively. The line then represents all the possible amounts a person can spend in the two periods by saving present income or borrowing against future income. The fact that a person might have greater difficulty borrowing than lending is shown on the graph as a change of slope in the section of the line that represents the combinations in which he will be borrowing. The person maximizes utility over time at the point at which an indifference curve is tangential to the inter-temporal budget constraint. If this point dictates an expenditure greater than his income in period one he will borrow to finance the difference: if less, he will lend.

Fisher's index. An index number calculated by taking the geometric mean of the relevant *Laspeyres and *Paasche indices. Fisher's index, which was devised by Irving Fisher (1867–1947), has been recommended as "ideal" because it falls between the Laspeyres index, which is an overstatement, and the Paasche index, which is an understatement. Furthermore one can obtain the value index by taking the product of the Fisher price index and the Fisher volume index whereas, using Laspeyres and Paasche indices, the value index can be obtained by either multiplying the Laspeyres price index by the Paasche volume index or by multiplying the Laspeyres volume index by the Paasche price index. This, of course, requires that the respective Laspeyres and Paasche indices should be based on the same data and calculated from the same base period. However, Fisher's indices are less widely used than Laspeyres indices.

fixed (capital) assets. Assets purchased by a company that are not intended for immediate consumption, but rather as a means of production. For example, a fixed asset could be a new piece of machinery purchased for the plant of a manufacturing company, or more indirectly it could be a typewriter enabling an ancillary service to be performed. Due to wear and tear and to obsolescence all fixed assets are only of use for a limited length of time; for the purposes of accounts, provision for this wear and tear (*see* depreciation) has to be made. *See also* current assets.

fixed costs. *See* indirect costs.

fixed disc. *See* disc.

fixed exchange rate. *See* exchange rate.

fixed-interest security. A *security the return on which is fixed in absolute terms. Thus bonds, debentures, gilt-edged securities, and preference shares are all fixed-interest securities, but ordinary shares are not (because the dividend *yield can be altered from year to year). The price of fixed-interest securities tends to vary inversely with the general level of interest rates, as determined by government monetary policy, although this relation becomes weaker as redeemable fixed-interest securities approach their redemption date.

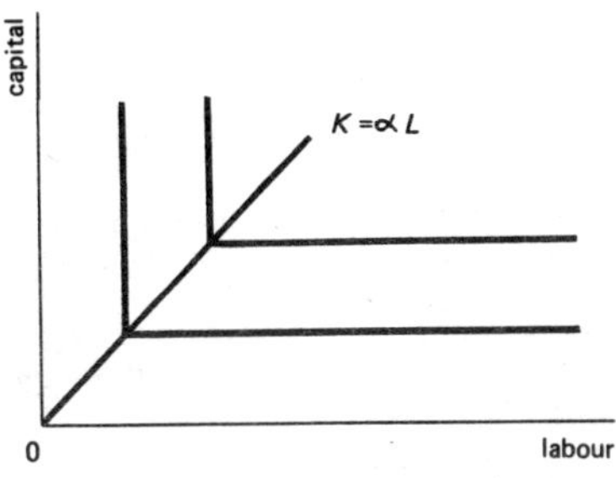

Fixed proportions production frontier

fixed proportions production function. A *production function relating output to inputs where the *elasticity of substitution is equal to zero, the inputs being in a constant ratio to one another and there being no substitution between factors.

On a graph of capital plotted against labour, efficient production can occur only along the line whose equation is:

$$K = \alpha L,$$

$$\text{then } Y = \beta \min (K/L, \alpha L),$$

where Y is output, K and L are capital and labour (in general any inputs) and β represents the scale of production. The function min (a,b) equals the lesser of a or b. The isoquants are lines parallel to the axes; they meet on the line with capital/labour ratio α. The *Harrod–Domar model depends upon such a production function to produce its knife-edge problem and the Leontief input-output system describes such a set of production processes with many interrelated goods.

fixed trust. A type of *unit trust in which the managers are limited in their investment to a fixed list of securities. These trusts, which were the original types of unit trust, have been operated since the 1930s, with the object of pooling small savings in order to invest them in the Stock Market. They were said to "offer the small investor a stake in British industry". *Compare* flexible trust.

flag discrimination. The tendency of a nation to insist on its own fleet carrying its own trade.

flag of convenience. The registration of a ship under the flag of a nation to which it does not belong in order to avoid heavy taxation and strict regulations concerning the crew. Some *tramp steamers are registered under flags of convenience but the practice is becoming increasingly widespread. Flags of convenience are offered by Liberia, Panama, Lebanon, Honduras, Haiti, Singapore, and Cyprus.

flat yield. A *yield as calculated by expressing the current gross annual interest payable as a percentage of the purchase price of a fixed-interest security, without taking into account any capital gain (or loss) on redemption. It is sometimes referred to as a running yield, current yield, or earnings yield. *Compare* redemption yield.

fleet rating. The rating of a fleet of motor vehicles under one insurance policy. Where there are at least ten motor vehicles (or at least five high-risk vehicles, such as coaches or heavy goods vehicles) under one ownership, insurers are prepared to consider fleet rating of the risk. This permits the risk to be rated on its own merits. A fleet can consist of an assortment of vehicles, and can also apply to ships or aircraft.

flexible trust. A type of *unit trust in which the managers are at liberty to change the portfolio. The unit-holders are usually notified at each distribution of dividends of the pattern of the trust's investments at that time and they will thus be able to see what changes have been made to the portfolio. *Compare* fixed trust.

floating charge. A *charge that does not become fixed until the occurrence of some event. An example is a debenture given by an incorporated company to secure its indebtedness to its bankers, which comprises a fixed charge upon its property and a floating charge upon its stock, book debts, etc. This allows the company to trade and alter the composition of these assets, the charge floating until the company goes into liquidation or breaks some condition specified in the debenture, when the current value of these assets becomes the fixed amount charged to the bank.

floating debenture. *See* debenture.

floating debt. A short-term section of the U.K. unfunded *National Debt that consists of *Treasury bills and *ways and means advances. The Treasury bills are either sold on the open market or held by various government departments. Ways and means advances are usually made by governmental departments or the Bank of England to the Treasury. *Compare* funded debt.

floating exchange rate. *See* free exchange rates, exchange rate.

floating policy. A type of insurance policy used by a person, such as a builder, all of whose work is of a similar nature. An annual estimate is required of the value of the work to be undertaken, which is then rated according to the category in which the insured risk falls. At the end of the year the estimate is compared to the value of the work actually undertaken and the premium is adjusted accordingly.

Such a policy can also be used to cover goods of changing value and in different locations. In marine insurance it is used by traders who make frequent shipments of cargo. The sum insured is generally set at a figure sufficient to cover a large number of shipments and a provisional premium is paid, based on this figure. As the shipments are made they must be declared to the insurer immediately (or at regular intervals) and the sum insured is reduced by the amount of each declaration. When the original sum insured has been exhausted the insurer will adjust the premium according to the declarations at the agreed rates, and another policy must be taken out to provide continuing cover. *See also* open cover.

floating warranty. A guarantee or warranty given by a person that induces another to enter into a contract with a third person. Such a warranty may in certain circumstances be enforceable against the warrantor, even though he is not a party to the contract. An example is a guarantee given by a motor dealer, inducing a customer to enter into a contract to buy a motor car on hire purchase from a finance company. If the car proves defective, the customer may recover damages from the dealer.

floor trader. A member of a stock exchange, commodity market, Lloyd's, etc., who is entitled to trade on the floor of the exchange.

floppy disk. *See* disk.

flotation. The raising of capital through public subscription by a new company, or on behalf of a new company by a merchant bank.

flow concept. A quantitative concept in economics, which requires the dimension of time to give it meaning. Typically, though not necessarily, it is the rate of change of some *stock concept. Investment can be regarded as the rate of change in capital stock, while income, defined as a person's receipts over the period of a year, has no such obvious stock counterpart. Nevertheless they are both flow concepts.

flurry. A sudden surge of activity, often speculative, on one of the financial markets, notably the foreign exchange market. The borderline between a flurry and a crisis is a matter of opinion.

flying picket. *See* picketing.

F.O.B. *See* free on board.

Food and Agricultural Organization (F.A.O.). A special agency of the United Nations, founded in 1945 at a conference in Quebec, with the principal objects of carrying out research and providing technical assistance to countries around the world in agriculture, forestry, and fishing. Its headquarters are in Rome. At its inception it was entrusted with other responsibilities, such as promoting commodity agreements. Among its major operations have been the 1960 Freedom from Hunger Campaign and the 1969 indicative world plan for agricultural development up to 1985.

F.O.Q. *See* free on quay.

F.O.R. *See* free on rail.

forced loan. **1.** A compulsory loan levied on the subjects or certain classes of subjects of a nation by the ruler or government. Well-known examples are the forced loans of Charles I's reign, which contributed to his downfall.

2. A loan arranged to meet some exigency; for example, a loan that has reached maturity but cannot be repayed by the borrower might have to be renewed.

forced saving (forced frugality). A reduction in the consumption of consumer goods enforced on consumers by the government, as by increased taxation or by the raising of prices relative to incomes.

forecasting. The delineation of a trend or series that it is estimated a variable will follow in the future. The distinction should be made between long-term, or secular, forecasting and short-term forecasting (which, in respect of economic magnitudes at least, is likely to be affected by cyclical considerations). There are several techniques of forecasting, such as extrapolation of time series, extrapolation of various growth curves, regression, etc., the common feature of which is that they are all approximate in their accuracy. Some writers use the term *prediction as though it were synonymous with forecasting in this sense; however, it is usual to retain the more general definition for forecasting and to restrict the definition of prediction to the precise assessment of the value of a variable under specified conditions.

foreclose. To sell property that has been mortgaged as security for a debt that is not paid. Foreclosure may only be carried out with the permission of the court.

foreign bill of exchange. A *bill of exchange that is neither drawn nor payable within the U.K. In common with all bills of exchange the use of foreign bills has declined, but they are still required when a *documentary credit is opened.

foreign exchange. The system of dealing in and converting the currency of one country into that of another. When *exchange rates are allowed to fluctuate freely the use of paper money and token coins complicates these rates as they are not a true indication of the value of the metal content as between the coinage of countries but are an indication of the confidence felt in their respective governments and the balance of payments position. However calculations are further complicated by restrictions imposed by governments seeking to protect their trade (*see* exchange control). The *International Monetary Fund was set up to prevent wide fluctuations in exchange rates, which destroy confidence and restrict foreign trade. All the joint-stock banks have separate departments dealing in foreign currency.

foreign exchange broker. A broker who buys and sells foreign currencies on the *foreign exchange market, usually on behalf of a bank or some other institution.

foreign exchange market. The international market in which foreign currencies are traded. Transactions are carried out by telephone, telegraph, or telex. From 1931 (when the U.K. finally left the gold standard) to 1932 the market was free and sterling was permitted to find its own level. However, after sterling had lost about one third of its value in the free market, the British government established the *Exchange Equalization Account (in March 1932) to stabilize the market by buying sterling to support it when it was weak and selling it when it was strong.

foreign investment. The acquisition of foreign physical assets, securities, or bank deposits. During the nineteenth century the U.K. invested widely abroad and the income from these investments enabled the U.K. to run a deficit on its *balance of trade since this was made up by invisible items in the *balance of payments. However, many of these investments had to be sold after World War II.

foreign judgment. A decision of a foreign court, usually referring to whether or not a debt is owed by one person to another. Such a judgment is not enforceable in the U.K. unless the creditor (if it was in his favour) applies within six years for it to be registered with the high court. If it is so registered, it may be enforced in the U.K.

foreign sector. The part of the economy concerned with dealings with the outside world. This includes not only importing and exporting but also short-and long-term capital flows. The introduction of a foreign sector does not change the traditional I.S.-L.M. model (*see* I.S.-L.M. analysis) unless one assumes a flexible exchange rate and perfect capital markets. In this case the government is unable to change the money supply or the interest rate because both are fixed by the outside world. An attempt to raise the interest rate will induce large inward capital flows forcing the interest rate down again. An attempt to raise the money supply will lower the interest rate and induce large outward capital flows, which will continue until the interest rate and the money supply have returned to their previous levels.

There has been increased interest in these problems of macroeconomics during the last few years, mainly associated with the names of H.G. Johnson and R. Mundell.

foreign trade multiplier. The effect on a country's foreign trade of an increase in home demand. It is influenced by: (1) the increase in demand for imports as well as home-produced goods: (2) the possible increase in demand for the country's exports by foreign countries whose income has increased because their exports to the domestic country concerned have risen. *See also* export multiplier.

foreign trade zone. *See* free zone.

forestalling. A government policy designed to curb trends in the economy that might ultimately disrupt planned objectives.

forfeited shares. Shares in a company that have to be surrendered by the shareholder because he cannot pay for them in full, or pay for any balance outstanding, when called upon to do so by the company. *See* partly paid shares.

forgery. The making or alteration of any document to the prejudice of another person. Cheques on which the signature is not valid or on which the amount has been altered without the authority of the drawer are forgeries. Where the signature on a cheque or bill of exchange is forged no person can obtain a good title to it.

for the account. Denoting a purchase of shares on the London Stock Exchange that the purchaser intends to close out with an equivalent sale within the same account. In this way he will not have to pay for the shares but will receive a difference account showing his profit or loss. The same procedure applies to a bear sale. Buying and selling for the account are speculative operations.

FORTRAN. A high-level *programming language used especially for scientific and mathematical applications. Instructions are written using simple English words and mathematical formulae. The most common version is FORTRAN IV. The name comes from *for*mula *tran*slation. It was developed in 1956, and was the first widely used programming language.

forward dating. *See* post dated.

forward exchange. Foreign currency bought or sold for future delivery. Dealers quote a spot rate for immediate transactions and rates for dealings one, two, or three months ahead. These enable a trader to be certain of the cost of foreign currency that he may require to complete an overseas purchase, without being at risk of fluctuations in exchange rates.

forwarding agent. A person or firm concerned with collecting goods from a factory, warehouse, etc., and delivering them to a port of shipment, airport, or railway terminus for onward transportation to their destination. Forwarding agents specialize in supplying or arranging for road vehicles to pick up the goods, dealing with customs authorities, booking freight, etc. on behalf of their clients.

forward integration. The amalgamation of a manufacturing business with a firm that markets its products.

forward marketing. Contracting to buy (forward purchasing) or sell (forward selling) goods or securities at some date in the future at a price agreed at the time the contract is made. In *commodity markets, forward trading is used extensively as a means of hedging against sharp fluctuations in price. *See* futures markets.

foul bill of lading. *See* dirty bill of lading.

founders' shares. Shares that are taken up by the founders of a company. They often receive the residue of distributed profits after the fixed dividends to ordinary shareholders have been paid.

F.P.A. Free of particular average. *See* cargo insurance.

fractional banking. The system of banking in which the bank keeps a definite ratio between its cash reserves and its total deposits. *See* cash ratio.

franchise. 1. A licence to manufacture or market a product with an established trade name or to operate a service, the equipment or supplies for which are manufactured by a monopoly producer. The *franchisee* (or holder of the licence) makes an initial payment or pays a royalty on the product to the *franchisor* (or grantor of the licence), or promises to buy specified equipment or supplies exclusively from the franchisor. Franchises are often given for a particular area. In the case of manufacturing under licence, the franchisee is often provided with the know-how and sometimes the finance to set up a factory to manufacture a particular product.

2. A clause in a *marine insurance policy that disallows claims below a fixed minimum sum unless the ship is stranded or sunk. If the claim exceeds this minimum it will be paid.

franchise policies. Like *excess policies, these insurance policies are designed to eliminate small claims. With a £50 franchise, for example, the insured would be responsible for any claims not exceeding that amount, but if the cost exceeded £50, the insurer would pay in full.

franco. Denoting an export contract or quotation based on delivery terms in which the seller is responsible for the cost of delivering the goods to the importer's warehouse. For example, if a British exporter makes a price of £50 franco Milan for his product, this price includes the cost of the goods, all sea and rail (or air) freight charges, insurance during the whole voyage, and delivery from the Milan railway terminal (or airport) to the buyer's warehouse in Milan.

franked investment income. Income receivable that has already been subjected to corporation tax. The most general case of franked investment income arises when a company receives dividends from another company. Dividends are distributed from a company out of its taxed profit and are therefore treated in a different way in the tax computation of the recipient company's profits. As this income has already been subjected to corporation tax once, it is removed from the recipient company's profits assessable for corporation tax. Such franked investment income will bear a tax credit representing the *advance corporation tax (A.C.T.) payable by the distributing company, which can be offset by the recipient against any A.C.T. that it has to pay.

franking machine. A machine supplied under licence from the Post Office to a business in order that it can frank its own mail. Mail so franked is handed into the Post Office and weekly readings of the total amount used in postage are submitted to the Post Office. Franking machines that print the name of the business or an advertisement are also available.

fraternal insurance. *See* friendly societies.

fraud. Dishonesty resulting in personal gain. Fraud is usually a criminal offence under the Theft Act, for which the penalties may be severe, but it also has wide implications in the law relating to contracts. If a person makes a statement without caring whether it is true or false, and thereby induces another to enter into a contract, this is known as a *fraudulent misrepresentation* and it enables the other person to rescind the contract. This person may also take court action against the person perpetrating the fraud for compensation for any loss it has caused him.

fraudulent conveyance. The signing away of property by a bankrupt in order to evade creditors.

fraudulent preference. If within the months of becoming bankrupt a person makes a payment to one of his creditors with the intention of giving preference to that creditor over the others, then such a payment is fraudulent and becomes void. This is known as fraudulent preference, but the burden of proof of the bankrupt's motives lies upon the trustee in bankruptcy.

fraudulent trading. The continuation of business after a company has been wound up (*see* winding up). In these circumstances the directors of the company become liable without limit for the debts of the company.

free alongside ship (f.a.s.). Denoting an export contract or quotation based on delivery terms in which the seller is responsible for the cost of delivering the goods to the quay at the port of shipment, but not for the cost of loading them onto the ship.

free banker. A banker who takes the view that the practice of obtaining collateral security against overdrafts and loans should be less stringent.

free capital. Capital in the form of liquid cash.

free competition. An economic system in which private enterprise exists without any state interference. Prices are reached purely by the market forces of supply and demand. *See also* perfect competition.

free depreciation. A *depreciation allowance from the government to private industry in which firms are allowed to write off the original costs of their assets over whatever time limit they choose. This system provides great flexibility for firms and allows them greater freedom of action. For instance, firms can choose to delay their tax payments until years in which they earn high profits. Two disadvantages are that the government has less advance knowledge of, and control over, the revenue that is raised from tax and no longer has power to stimulate or discourage investments by variations in the allowance. *See also* accelerated depreciation.

free docks. Denoting an export contract or quotation in which the exporter pays for transportation of the goods as far as the docks from which they are to be shipped.

free economy. An economic system in which market forces, without any state intervention, determine what is produced, the allocation of factors of production, and the distribution of income. However, the state intervenes to differing extents in every country and even in nonsocialist countries there has been a trend in recent decades for the state to assume more and more responsibility in economic matters. *See also* mixed economy.

free (*or* private) enterprise. *See* capitalism.

free entry. The absence of *barriers to entry.

free (floating) exchange rates. Exchange rates that are determined by the supply and demand for the currency on the *foreign exchange market. It has been argued that free exchange rates have an unsettling effect on international trade. They do, however, tend to keep a country's balance of payments in balance, since if its currency appreciates in terms of others, its exports will fall, and if it depreciates its exports will rise and imports fall, until an equilibrium is reached. *See* exchange rate.

free good. *See* good.

freehold. A type of ownership or tenure of land, which applies to all land that is owned outright. The only other type of tenure now is *leasehold tenure. The term *freehold tenure* was used under the feudal system to describe land owned by freemen who owed no duties to any lord of the manor. Other land (that occupied by serfs who owed a large variety of duties to the lord of the manor) was known as *copyhold land.* Copyhold tenure survived into the twentieth century, although in the early years of this century in most cases sums of money were paid to the lord of the manor in lieu of the performance of duties. Copyhold land was converted into freehold land by the Law of Property Act (1925). *See also* land registration.

free issue. *See* bonus issue.

free list. A list of goods that can be imported free of duty.

free market. 1. A market in which the price of a commodity is determined by the market forces of supply and demand without intervention from the state or elsewhere. The stock market comes nearest to being a free market in the U.K. and the U.S. The commodity markets are often controlled to some extent by restrictions on price fluctuations.

2. (On the London Stock Exchange.) A situation in which a particular stock or share is freely available in relatively large quantities.

free of all average. Denoting a marine insurance policy that provides only for claims made for total loss, excluding *general average and particular average losses. *See also* cargo insurance.

free of capture. Denoting a marine insurance policy in which no cover is provided for the capture of ships or mutiny. Free of capture or seizure refers to a policy taken out in times of war, when the insurance company disclaims liability for such losses.

free of particular average (F.P.A.). *See* cargo insurance.

free of stamp. A security (share, debenture, etc.) that can be dealt in free of *stamp duty. On the London Stock Exchange, stamp duty has to be paid on the purchase (but not the sale) of all securities except new issues, bonus shares, rights issues, etc., which are said to be free of stamp.

free on board (F.O.B.). When goods are shipped from one country to another the contract is usually based on one of three sets of shipping terms. It may be a free on board contract, a *cost, insurance, and freight contract, or a *cost and freight contract. In the first case the seller's responsibility ends with the delivery of the goods to the port of shipment and the cost of loading them onto the ship, It is the buyer's responsibility to provide or nominate the ship and to arrange the insurance cover, but the seller must notify the buyer that the goods have arrived at the port in order that he may arrange insurance cover. Payment is usually made as soon as the goods have been loaded, against commercial invoice and *mate's receipt.

free on board and trimmed. Denoting a *free on board contract in the coal trade, in which the seller must ensure that the coal is properly stowed in the ship.

free on quay (F.O.Q.). Denoting shipping terms for goods to be exported, in which the exporter delivers the goods free of charge to the quay from which they will be shipped. The buyer takes all responsibility for shipment and insurance from then on.

free on rail (F.O.R.). A basis for the delivery terms of a contract, similar to *free on board except that the seller is responsible for delivery of the goods to a railway station and paying for them to be loaded onto a train. The insurance of the goods is the responsibility of the buyer, who also pays the railway freight charge.

free overboard (free overside, ex ship). Denoting shipping terms for goods to be exported. The exporter pays for all charges up to the port of destination, including unloading from the ship, but not any *lighter charges.

free port. A port at which goods for re-export can be landed without the payment of customs duties, thus permitting an entrepôt trade. *See also* free zone.

free reserves (in U.S. banking). Excess reserves held by the banks above the legal reserve requirements.

free trade. International trade taking place without the imposition of tariffs or quotas on imports by any individual country. According to the theory of *international trade, the maximum advantage from trade to the world as a whole would come from free trade, but such an ideal situation has never existed. In the mid-nineteenth century there was the nearest approximation to it, but many factors, not least the rise of nationalism and industrialization in underdeveloped countries, have contributed to its decline. Since 1945, however, many countries (e.g. the E.E.C.) have made agreements to form *free trade areas* within which free trade can take place, though tariffs and quotas are retained for imports from the rest of the world.

freeze. *See* wage freeze, rent freeze.

free zone (free trade zone). An area in or near a port or airport in which goods for re-export or for manufacture into goods for export can be imported free of customs duties. In the U.S. such a zone is also known as a *foreign trade zone*. *See also* free port, bonded warehouse.

freight. The cost of shipping a particular cargo for a particular voyage. For all general cargo, freight rates were formerly quoted on the basis of one freight ton of 40 cubic feet or 20 cwt, whichever was the greater. This is usually described as *weight or measurement (W/M), ship's option*. With metrication, however, rates are now more frequently quoted on the basis of 1 tonne (1000 kilos) or 1 cubic metre, with separate rates for weight and measurement. Certain cargoes are quoted on a weight only basis and valuable cargoes are sometimes quoted on an *ad valorem basis, usually as a percentage of the F.O.B. value. Air freights are usually quoted on the basis of 1 kilogram or 7000 cubic centimetres, whichever is the greater.

freight forward. Denoting a shipment on which the freight is payable at the port of destination.

freight insurance. A form of *marine insurance in which a shipper or consignee covers himself against loss for sums paid out in freight (hire of a ship or cargo space). Under the terms of section 16 of the Marine Insurance Act (1906) the insurable value for freight is the gross freight at risk (including profit) plus the cost of insurance.

Freight Integration Council. A council established by the Transport Act (1968) in order to advise the Minister of Transport on the coordination of freight transport by the various national transport bodies.

freightliner. A nationwide container rail service linking the U.K.'s chief industrial centres with container ports. The service was the outcome of the Beeching Report published in 1963. Containers are loaded by the user at his own factory, sent by road to a freightliner terminal, and transported by rail to another terminal, from where they are delivered to their destination by road. It is thus a door-to-door service.

freight note. A document issued by a shipping company detailing the charge for shipping a particular consignment of cargo for a particular journey.

freight release. When freight has been paid in advance, the shipowner or his agent can endorse the bill of lading with a freight release, which enables the importer to take immediate delivery of the goods.

Frequency Distribution

Income	*Frequency*
£1000 p.a. or under	150
£1001–£2000 p.a.	300
£2001–£3000 p.a.	250
£3001–£4000 p.a.	100
£4001–£5000 p.a.	50
£5001 or over	150
Total no. of households =	1000

frequency distribution. A *distribution of frequencies or classifications of items according to some variable or attribute. A frequency distribution is constructed by dividing into classes the range of values taken by the variable and then assigning each of the items to these classes. For instance, to construct a frequency distribution of 1000 households (the items) according to their incomes (the variable), six classes of income could be defined and each of the 1000 households allocated into one of six classes as shown in the table. The frequency for any individual class is the number of items falling in it (the relative frequency is this number divided by the total number of items) while the distribution of these frequencies is their arrangement as given in the table. One drawback to such frequency distributions is that they often have an open-ended class. In the table the sixth class listed is open-ended because it does not have a maximum and its large frequency appears to interrupt the pattern set by the rest of the distribution. The solution to the problem of such open-ended classes is to split them up further, so that they have such small frequencies that they do not upset the distribution as a whole. If this can be done then wide and sweeping *hypotheses can be made concerning the entire *population of the items in question. Frequency distributions are used very extensively in applied statistics for purposes of the presentation of data. For example, one could construct a frequency distribution of industrial companies according to capital employed. Their usefulness lies in the manner in which they can present large amounts of data while not losing sight of the major characteristics of such data, especially their mean, their variance, and their degree of skewness. Frequency distributions are purely empirical devices and are applied only in connection with collected groups or samples of items and should therefore be distinguished from an ordinary (probability) distribution, which applies to whole populations of items.

frequency function. *See* density function.

frequency polygon. A diagram based on a histogram having equal class intervals. It is constructed by joining the midpoints of the class intervals one to the next; the heights of the ordinates are given by the heights of the histogram's blocks (these heights being proportional to the class frequencies when the class intervals are equal). The extreme points are joined to the horizontal axis where the midpoints of the next section would have been.

frequency probability function. *See* density function.

frictional unemployment. Unemployment resulting from the time involved in workers changing jobs. There may be enough vacancies for everyone but there are time lags between workers leaving jobs and taking up others and so even in times of full employment there are always unemployment figures resulting from frictional unemployment.

friendly society. A mutual benefit insurance association, formed voluntarily to assist members (in sickness, old age, widowhood, etc.), who make regular contributions to a fund from which claims are paid. Friendly societies existed in the U.K. in the seventeenth century and were widespread in the Industrial Revolution, when little help was available from other sources for workers who fell on hard times. The National Insurance legislation of 1946 placed the administration of National Insurance under a central government body, causing many of the friendly societies to close down. Friendly societies still exist, however, in the U.K., Germany, France, Belgium, Denmark, Sweden, Switzerland, and the U.S. (where the insurance provided is known as *fraternal insurance*). Registered friendly societies in the U.K. are supervised by the Chief Registrar of Friendly Societies, an office established by statute in 1846.

Before 1800 friendly societies were small local bodies, often operating from the village inn. After that large centralized societies appeared, either *affiliated societies*, consisting of largely autonomous local bodies legally affiliated to the central managing body, or the completely integrated societies working from a head office or through local agents. Some were formed exclusively to cover burial expenses. Many later became known as *collecting societies* because of their method of house-to-house collection of subscriptions. These share the *industrial insurance business with insurance companies.

The friendly societies basically operate on accumulative, deposit, or dividing principles. *Accumulative societies* keep a constant fund for meeting claims as they come due. *Deposit societies* allocate all or most of their funds annually to the credit of the individual members, who thus have insurance benefits while saving at the same time. *Dividing societies* periodically divide between members funds remaining after claims have been met.

fringe benefits. Something given by an employer to his employees to supplement normal wages and often used in wage negotiations as an alternative to increasing wages. Such benefits include luncheon vouchers, the opportunity to purchase goods produced by the firm at a cheap rate, expense accounts, company cars, pension schemes, subsidized canteens, etc. Since these things are not liable to income tax, they are of more value than their monetary equivalent in wages.

front door. *See* back door.

front-end loading. *See* rule of 78.

frozen assets. Assets that cannot, at least without great difficulty or loss, be converted into money. *Compare* liquid assets.

frustration of contract. Making the performance of a contract impossible through some occurrence that is no fault of the parties to that contract, e.g. the burning down of a concert hall shortly before a performer has contracted to perform there. Prior to 1943 the loss lay where it fell, the contract became void, and neither party could recover anything from the other. This led to unfair results in some cases (e.g. if the concert performer had already been paid in full for his performance) and the situation was changed by the Law Reform (Frustrated Contracts) Act (1943). Any money paid can now be recovered, although expenses incurred can be deducted. It is also possible to deduct the value of any work already carried out of which the party seeking to recover the money has had the benefit.

F.T. index. *See* Financial Times Actuaries Shares Indices, Financial Times Industrial Ordinary Index, Financial Times Stock Indices.

full-cost pricing. The fixing of the price of a good by a manufacturer by calculating the direct cost per unit of output and adding a mark-up for overheads and profit. The overheads are calculated for less than full capacity operation of the plant to allow for fluctuating levels of production. Since the demand curve for a particular product is impossible to calculate precisely, this cannot be used to establish a marketing cost.

full employment. The level of employment at which everyone able and willing to work is employed and the only unemployment is *frictional unemployment. The full employment level of the economy indicates full capacity output, i.e. all resources are employed. As defined by Lord Beveridge, full employment means that no more than 3% of the U.K. working population are unemployed. *Over-full employment* occurs when there are more jobs available than people seeking work. This creates an inflationary situation, as the labour shortage means that employment has to be given to less capable workers who bring down the average standard of efficiency in industry. In addition, the wage-bargaining power of employees is strengthened by the fact that the employer would find it difficult to replace them, and employers have to bid up wages to obtain a necessary labour force.

The classical economists assumed that market forces tend to keep the whole country at a level of full employment although there would be temporary bouts of unemployment. However, Keynes pointed out that this is not necessarily always the case and he stressed the need for government intervention, for example by investing public money to supplement private investment where this is insufficient to maintain full employment.

fully paid shares. Shares whose full value has been paid, either at issue or later. They thus represent no liability to the shareholder in respect of calls made by the company for payment of any balance unpaid. *See also* partly paid shares.

function. A quantitative relationship expressed in the form of an equation in which one or more independent variables, together with their coefficients, uniquely determine the value of the function's dependent variable. An increasing (or direct) function has a positive graphical slope and is one in which the dependent variable is positively correlated with the independent variable (or variables). Conversely, a decreasing function has a negative graphical slope and is characterized by an inverse correlation between dependent and independent variables: the Keynesian speculative demand for money is a decreasing function of the average level of inter-

est rates. A function may be increasing and decreasing over different parts of its range or else it may be increasing (or decreasing) throughout its entire range; in the latter case it is said to be *monotonic*. A distinction is sometimes made between an explicit function and an implicit function. In the following two functions:
(1) $y = 2x/(1 - x)$
(2) $y - xy - 2x = 0$
equation (1) is an explicit function of the variable x in that the dependent variable y is explicitly delineated in terms of its explanatory variable (x); equation (2), which is the same relation as equation (1), is an implicit function of x (assuming x is the independent variable) because any change in x now merely implies an offsetting change in y required to maintain the equality. It is sometimes desirable in econometric problems to put functions in implicit form before the application of *matrix algebra.

functions of money. Three attributes of money that cannot be found in a barter economy. Money acts as a *medium of exchange, a *unit of account, and a *store of value.

fundamental disequilibrium. A disparity between the official exchange rate and the actual value of a currency of so great a magnitude that the only remedy is an alteration in the exchange rate. Such policies as deflation or reflation of the economy would be inadequate. Fundamental disequilibria can only occur when exchange rates are fixed, since floating exchange rates would always stay in parity with the actual value through the working of supply and demand.

fundamental term. A term of a contract that is so basic that the contract would be a nonsense without it. For instance, in the case of the sale of a motor car, it is a fundamental term that the car will have an engine. The important difference between fundamental terms and the less important terms of a contract (known as *conditions* and *warranties*) is that the latter may be excluded if one party wishes whereas fundamental terms implied in a contract may not be excluded.

funded debt. The part of the U.K. National Debt that the government has no obligation to repay by a fixed date. It is almost entirely made up of securities quoted on the Stock Exchange, the most important being 3½% War Loan (1952 or after). Approximately 10% of the National Debt is funded debt. *Compare* unfunded debt, floating debt.

funding loans. The name of various U.K. government stocks forming part of the *funded debt. Examples are 6% funding loan 1993 and 6½% funding loan 1985-7.

funding operations. Actions to convert short-term debts (*see* floating debts) into long-term debts (*see* funded debts). It is normally used to describe the management of the National Debt by the National Debt Commissioners, but can also be applied to the manoeuvres of the Bank of England in their dealings in Treasury bills and government bonds. Private firms can also undertake funding operations to convert their short-term debts, such as overdrafts, into long-term debts, such as debentures.

funds. *See* government bonds.

futures markets. Markets in which consumers of and dealers in commodities can buy and sell the raw materials in which they are interested for future delivery. There are two main functions of such a market: the first is to provide a medium for *hedging operations and the second to provide an opportunity for speculation. The two aspects are complementary and both are necessary if the market is to be successful in steadying prices and reducing the effects of price fluctuations resulting from gluts and shortages of crops, harvests, etc.

Modern futures trading was probably originated by sixteenth-century whalers who sold their catch before sailing (to finance their voyages) and it developed rapidly during the nineteenth century, principally in the cotton market. For an effective market, the commodity must be capable of being graded so that the goods do not have to be inspected before they are bought or sold. In fact, delivery of goods contracted for on a futures market is rarely effected. In practice, a buying contract is usually settled out by an equivalent selling contract so that money differences, rather than actual goods, pass between the contracting parties. For example, a tyre manufacturer may place a large contract for natural rubber with a producer for shipment from origin in six-monthly quantities. By placing such a large contract he may obtain exceptionally good terms and will ensure the continuity of his supplies. Although he would be likely to place such a contract when he considered the market price to be low, he would be aware that other factors during the six-month shipment period might intervene to depress the price further. He might therefore decide to hedge his purchase by selling an equivalent (or smaller) quantity of rubber on a rubber futures market. If the price did fall in this period he would make a profit when buying back (covering) his short sale on the futures market. This profit would offset the higher price he had paid for the actual rubber. If the price rose, however, he would make a loss when covering his short sale, but by successfully playing the market might still end up with a cheap purchase of actual rubber (compared to the current high price). *Options, *arbitrage, and other market operations enable users of futures markets to hedge their stocks without taking an uncovered (open) position in a commodity that may be prone to wide price fluctuations. Speculators are necessary operators in these futures markets as they are willing to take a view of the market and to expose themselves to an open position.

G

gains from trade. The benefits that a country receives from entering into international trade rather than producing and consuming in isolation. It is a broader term than *comparative cost, since it includes those gains possible even when both countries have identical production functions and factor endowments but differing tastes.

These can be demonstrated graphically on a *transformation curve. Given terms of trade between two outputs the consumption possibilities under trade are not just those of the curve itself but those lying on and within a line drawn at a tangent to the curve, whose slope is determined by the *terms of trade. A clear gain is always possible under normal assumptions, including perfect competition, although the welfare implications of trade are more complicated, since the change in production brought about by trade will probably alter the income distribution.

galloping inflation. *See* hyperinflation.

game theory. A body of mathematical theory concerned with situations of conflict. It is concerned with games of strategy rather than games of chance (such as throwing dice). A game of strategy is a situation in which two or more participants are faced with a choice of courses of action, or *strategies, by which each can achieve gains or losses according to the strategies chosen by the other contestants. The losses may be absolute, as in the case of a *zero-sum game, or relative. The situation is one of uncertainty because each participant has incomplete information concerning the intentions of the others. The final outcome of the game will be determined jointly by the strategies selected by all the players and may involve a situation of stable equilibrium, unstable equilibrium, or no equilibrium at all. Game theory evaluates the effect on this final outcome of different behavioural patterns on the part of the contestants. In the case of two participants and a constant sum to be distributed between them according to their strategies, game theory analysis is relatively simple; in other cases, much more sophisticated analysis is required. Game theory is used to analyse certain situations in the social sciences, notably those relating to the theory of the oligopolistic firm and to business studies, where managerial psychology can play an important part. The analogy between rivalry in games and business competition, from which game theory has been derived, was first developed by von Neumann and Morgenstern in 1944.

gaming contract. A contract between two parties who stand to win or lose money (or property) depending on the result of a game. Both *wagering contracts and gaming contracts were made void by the Gaming Act (1845), but the Betting, Gaming, and Lotteries Act (1963) legalized certain types of gaming if practised according to the provisions laid down in the Act.

gamma distribution. A statistical *distribution involving a continuous variable and dependent on two positive parameters, usually written α and β. Such variables as the length of life of industrial equipment follow a gamma distribution. The distribution's mean is the product of the two parameters $\beta\alpha$ while its variance is given by the expression $\beta^2\alpha$. The graph of the gamma density function will depend on the value of the two parameters but will usually be a curve with a positive skew. The *exponential and *chi-square distributions are special cases of the gamma distribution, which is also related to the *beta distribution.

gap analysis. *See* corporate (strategic) planning.

garnishee order. An order by the court on behalf of a judgment creditor attaching funds of the judgment debtor that are in the hands of a third party, known as the *garnishee.* Bankers are probably the most usual recipients of such orders, which warn them not to make any payments to the debtor until sanctioned by the court.

gatekeeper. A name used in management for an employee who is in charge of an "information junction". The gatekeeper may stop information passing through the information junction for a variety of reasons, and is able to exercise control over certain flows of information. Thus the gatekeeper determines what management will and will not see, or what information may be passed on to parent or subsidiary companies.

GATT. *See* General Agreement on Tariffs and Trade.

gaussian distribution. *See* normal distribution.

Gauss–Markov theorem. A theorem demonstrating mathematically that, under certain assumptions, least squares estimation provides estimators that are the best among all linear unbiased estimators in the sense that they are efficient (or have minimum variance). The necessary assumptions are that the mean of each of the stochastic disturbance terms must be zero, the covariance between any two of the stochastic terms must be zero, and the variance of each of the stochastic terms must be constant. There will of course be as many stochastic disturbances as there are observations. The Gauss–Markov theorem is not limited by the number of independent variables although if there are more than one, then there must in addition be at least as many observations as there are parameters to be estimated and furthermore there must be no exact linear relationships between any of the independent variables. The Gauss–Markov theorem is one of the most important in econometrics and a large section of elementary econometric theory is concerned with the implications for least squares estimation if one or more of the above assumptions do not hold. *See also* least squares estimation, autocorrelation, heteroscedasticity, multicollinearity, unbiasedness, efficiency.

G.D.P. *See* gross domestic product.

gearing. The degree to which a company's *capitalization is represented by debt, as opposed to shareholders' interest. Gearing can be measured either by the percentage of such debt to total capital or by the percentage of such debt to shareholders' funds, i.e. total capital minus debt. When examining a company's gearing from the point of view of its ordinary shareholders, it is usual to treat preference share capital as part of the company's debt (because it carries a fixed-interest charge) and also, in the case of large quoted companies, to include bank overdrafts in the debt total (because bank overdrafts tend to be a regular source of capital for large companies although they are technically items of short-term credit). High gearing, i.e. a high proportion of debt in a company's capitalization, tends to have, as its name indicates, a gearing effect on (available) earnings; that is, high gearing is beneficial to ordinary shareholders when the company is enjoying buoyant trading conditions and high trading profits, but detrimental to them when the company faces a dull demand situation. The maximum degree of gearing that it is commercially prudent for a company to operate depends on the nature of its trading situation, its labour contracts, and most of all on the *quality of its profits. In stock exchange terms, a period of rising interest rates will tend to depress the prices of shares of highly geared companies rather more than those of others.

General Agreement on Tariffs and Trade (GATT). An international organization that serves as a centre for multilateral tariff negotiations between member states, now numbering more than 80, and who amongst themselves account for about 80% of the world's trade. At its inception in 1947-8 it had been intended as an interim measure until the *International Trade Organization (I.T.O.) could be established, but since none of the 23 signatories ratified the charter of the I.T.O., GATT continued as a focus for international initiatives in multilateral tariff reductions. It now possesses a secretariat and a permanent headquarters in Geneva.

GATT has conducted seven major rounds of talks, which have produced substantial tariff reductions, the most significant of these being the *Kennedy Round (1962–67) and the *Tokyo Round (1973–79).

Its three guiding principles in the promotion of world trade are multinational negotiations, nondiscriminatory reductions (*see* most favoured nation clause), and dismantling nontariff trade constraints, such as *import quotas, *subsidies, and *import surcharges. GATT does, however, permit the imposition of tariffs to counteract unfair competition (*see* dumping).

Apart from expected obstacles with protectionist sentiment, three factors have caused difficulty for GATT. In certain commodities exemptions have to be granted. These arise, especially in agriculture, where governments are pursuing a policy of price support. Secondly, developing nations felt that their interests were not being adequately catered for within the framework of GATT; they were granted a provision allowing the most favoured nation clause to be waived in the case of dealings with developing countries. The *United Nations Council on Trade and Development (UNCTAD) was organized specifically to deal with their problems. Finally, regional trade groupings, such as the E.E.C., have largely overshadowed the effectiveness of GATT.

general average. *See* average (def. 2).

general damages. *See* damages.

general equilibrium analysis. An economic theory or argument that considers the interactions of all sectors in the economy. The results arrived at may concern all sectors or just one, but in principle they take into account all possible feedback from the economy. Input-output models and the income-expenditure models are examples of this type of approach. Because of the complexities of the interrelations and the sheer number of variables in an economy, a general equilibrium analysis either requires highly simplifying assumptions concerning the structure of the markets and the behaviour of the economic agents or it deals in highly aggregated quantities. For example, a typical assumption is that all agents are price-takers or that transaction costs do not exist. The income-expenditure model deals only in very large aggregates, such as consumption and income, not distinguishing between quantities to any greater extent than between durables and nondurables, or investment goods and consumption goods.

A general equilibrium analysis involves a fairly sophisticated level of mathematics; the fewer assumptions made, the more complicated the mathematics. In deciding whether a general or *partial equilibrium analysis is appropriate for a single-sector problem, one must weigh the degree of interaction of that sector and the restrictiveness of the assumptions implicit in a partial equilibrium analysis against the restrictiveness necessary for those in a general equilibrium analysis and the extra difficulty of the latter. Often, although a general equilibrium analysis is logically more correct, it is only marginally so and a partial analysis is quite satisfactory.

general index of retail prices. *See* Retail Price Index.

general offer. Any offer for sale made to the general public rather than to a restricted number of persons. For example, goods on display in a shop are on general offer and any member of the public is entitled to purchase them at the offered price. On the other hand, a car offered for sale privately by one man to another may not be on general offer; a third party has no right to assume that he too could purchase the car at that price if the man to whom it was offered does not wish to purchase it.

general partner. A person engaged in business with others as part of a partnership in which the liability of some or all of the other partners to contribute capital to the firm is limited to a certain amount but in which his own liability is not. Such a partnership is governed by the Limited Partnerships Act (1907), which severely restricts the rights of the *limited partners to have control over the running of the partnership. These restrictions do not apply to the general partners, who therefore have control of the partnership, the limited partners being not much more than investors. *See also* partner.

general strike. A withdrawal of labour by all or most trades with a view to securing some common object by paralysing the economy. The only general strike in British history lasted from 3 May to 12 May in 1926. The primary cause was the failure of the government to deal effectively with the coal industry. One million miners were already on strike and another million men (railwaymen, dockers, transport workers, printers, steel and iron workers, builders, and electricity and gas employees) were called out in sympathy by the T.U.C. The strike was short-lived for a number of reasons: the government's emergency plans proved effective in minimizing hardship, little effect was felt outside the large towns, demonstrations tended to be local and lacked coordination, and the General Council of the T.U.C. had gone further than they had intended to go. After the strike the government passed the Trade Disputes and Trade Union Act (1927), which made all sympathetic strikes illegal and attacked the political use of union funds. This Act was repealed by the Labour government in 1946.

general union. *See* trade union.

geographical mobility. *See* mobility.

geometric mean. The *n*th root of the product of a set of *n* numbers. The geometric mean is used to calculate the average of ratios, and its major statistical application is in the calculation of index numbers. It is less affected by the larger numbers in the set being averaged than the arithmetic mean and more affected by the smaller numbers. The effect of this is that the geometric mean is always less than the arithmetic mean (unless all the numbers in the set are identical). The geometric mean cannot be calculated for a set of numbers one or more of which is zero or negative. *Compare* arithmetic mean, harmonic mean, quadratic mean, median, mode.

geometric progression. A mathematical series in which the difference between each consecutive value rises by a constant multiple, e.g. 2, 6, 18, 54, 162. *Compare* arithmetic progression.

Gibrat's law. The principle that the logarithms of personal incomes are distributed normally. When charted on a graph with axes representing population and income, income distribution is positively skewed (*see* skewness) rather than being normally distributed. Consequently Pareto (1848–1923) rejected chance as being insufficient to explain variations in income. However, R. Gibrat believed that income distribution is related to another unknown factor (e.g. ambition or capability), which is normally distributed, i.e. governed by chance, so that:

$$u = \text{a} \log Y + \text{b}$$

where u is the unknown factor, Y is income, and a and b are constants. In that case, income distribution is indeed randomly distributed, albeit indirectly.

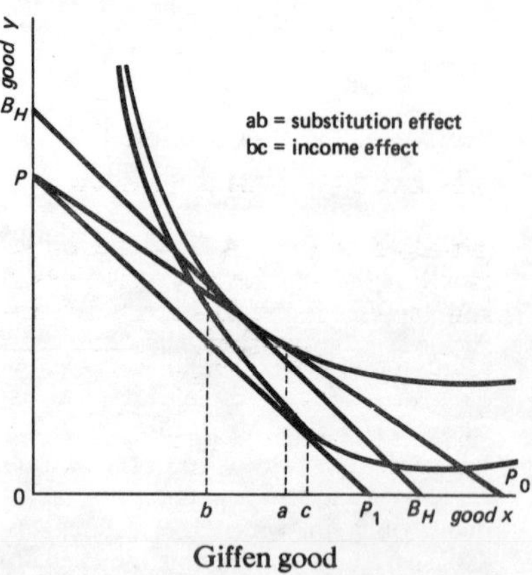

Giffen good

Giffen good. A good for which the quantity varies directly with the price: demand increases when price increases. It violates the law of demand. The good is an *inferior good for which the *income effect dominates the *substitution effect. The classic example is that of potatoes in Ireland. An increase in the price of potatoes led to an increase in their consumption, since the added expenditure on potatoes required to maintain subsistence consumption meant that consumers could no longer afford more expensive substitutes, such as meat, and consequently had to eat even more potatoes for nourishment. Because the budget share of potatoes was so high, the increase in price lowered the amount of income available for expenditure on other goods, and this effect led to reduced consumption of other goods and increased consumption of potatoes. This phenomenon, known as the Giffen paradox, was observed by Sir Robert Giffen (1837–1910).

gift. A transfer of the ownership of property from one person to another, otherwise than in exchange for other property, money, or any other benefit accruing to the giver. A gift over a certain value now attracts *capital transfer tax, under which the giver must pay tax calculated according to the amount by which the gift diminishes his total assets.

gifts tax. *See* capital transfer tax.

gilt-edged security. A fixed-interest security issued by the U.K. government and traded on the London Stock Exchange, In total they constitute *government stock.* They may be irredeemable, such as *Consols, or redeemable, usually at par, at a specified date or dates. *Short-dated gilts* are those having less than five years to redemption, *medium-dated gilts* have between five and fifteen years to redemption, while *long-dated gilts* have in excess of fifteen years to redemption. They are considered very safe in the sense that it is unlikely that the government will renounce its debts. This does not mean that gilt-edged securities are necessarily safe or good investments; indeed they are poor investments in times of rising interest rates (because their prices move inversely with the level of interest rates) and in times of inflation, as are all fixed-interest securities. However, there are certain advantages in dealing in gilt-edged securities on the Stock Exchange: there is no stamp duty payable on purchases of them, stockbroker's commission is lower than in the case of equity dealings, and finally any capital gains resulting from sales made more than 12 months after purchase are exempt from capital gains tax.

giro. A banking system for the settlement of debts. It is a cheap and simple system used on the Continent for many years. In 1968 a similar system was established in the U.K. by the Post Office, known as the *National Giro.* Customers give their instructions to any post office, as all accounts are kept at one centre in Bootle, Merseyside. Debts are settled between account-holders by transfer from one account to another, or giro cheques may be drawn for payment to others. The joint-stock banks have a similar system in operation. *See* credit transfer.

glamour stocks. *See* growth stocks.

gnomes of Zurich. An informal name for the heads of Swiss banks, most of whom work in Zurich. In some circles they have been accused of exerting political pressure by influencing the confidence of investors in the monetary and economic policy of a government.

G.N.P. *See* gross national product.

go-go. Denoting a unit trust or a share on the stock exchange that is likely to provide growth rather than income. *See also* growth stocks.

going concern concept. A fundamental *accounting concept in which it is assumed that an enterprise will continue its business in the foreseeable future. This means specifically that no liability will be shown in the profit and loss account and balance sheet of the enterprise for the cost of liquidation or for the curtailment in the level of business.

gold bloc. Those countries remaining on the *gold standard after it had been abandoned by the U.K. and more than 40 other nations in 1931-32. The countries were France, Switzerland, the Netherlands, and Belgium. Gold flooded into these countries until 1934, when the U.S. dollar was devalued and stabilized. Gold continued to flow into the U.S. until World War II, when it was halted by American loans and military expenditure.

gold bullion standard. *See* gold standard.

gold clause. A clause in an agreement between a government and potential creditors. It guarantees that loans will be repaid at the gold equivalent of the currency at the time the loan was made. For instance, if the value of a currency has fallen by 10% by the date of redemption, then the cost of repayment will correspondingly increase. Without this clause nations suffering high rates of inflation might find loans difficult to obtain.

gold coin standard. *See* gold standard.

golden age. A term originating with Joan Robinson (1908–83) that denotes an economy in a state of *steady-state growth, when Harrod's (Sir Roy Forbes Harrod, 1900–78) condition of the *warranted rate of growth equalling the *natural rate of growth is met and near full employment is sustained. It is so named as it is the fastest sustainable rate of growth.

gold exchange standard. *See* gold standard.

golden handshake. *See* severance payment.

golden rule. In a model in which the rate of investment is a decision variable, the golden rule yields the growth path that maximizes sustainable consumption per head along a *steady-state growth path. The rule states that the share of profits (calculated under competitive conditions) should equal the saving rate and therefore, along the golden rule steady-state path, total investment is equal to total competitive profits: workers never save, capitalists never consume. An alternative statement (remembering that the warranted rate of growth must equal the realized rate of growth which must equal the *natural rate of growth for a *golden age) is that the rate of return for capital equals the natural rate of growth.

gold market. A market in which gold is traded. As a metal market the gold market has exceptional significance because of the reserve status of gold in the international monetary system. The industrial applications of gold are insignificant and its commercial usage is restricted to such applications as jewellery and dentistry. However, when the international monetary system moves into crisis or when international inflation becomes disturbingly excessive, speculative demand for gold becomes strong. The effects of this are to weaken the major currencies and, on stock exchanges, to weaken prices of *fixed-interest securities while promoting strong upward pressure on the prices of gold-mining shares. The most important gold markets in Europe are in Zurich and London.

gold (specie) points. The points marking the upper and lower limits of the disparity between the exchange rates of two currencies when measured by the *gold standard. If the difference passed beyond these limits it would become profitable to exchange one currency for another, perhaps pounds for francs in Paris, then convert the francs into gold to be shipped back to London for conversion into pounds. Because of the small shipment costs and the certainty of conversion, this activity operated efficiently and tended to keep the exchange rate between the gold points. However, this form of *arbitrage acted directly upon the *money supply, thus having an inflationary or deflationary effect. In the above example, the money supply in France would decrease while the U.K. money supply would increase, unless sufficient large *buffer stocks of gold were held by the central banks.

gold pool. An organization of countries whose purpose was to prevent an increase in the price of gold above a certain amount. It was formed in 1961, its initial members being Belgium, France, Italy, the Netherlands, Switzerland, the U.K., the U.S., and West Germany. Whenever an increase in the price of gold above $35.19875 seemed imminent the organization intervened to sell bullion on the London gold market. France withdrew in 1967 and the gold pool ended in 1968. Instead a two-tier price for gold was introduced: the price of gold to central banks was held at $35 per ounce while its price to other consumers was determined by market forces. This two-tier system was abandoned in 1971 following the collapse of the Bretton Woods fixed exchange rate regime and the advent of *free (floating) exchange rates. *See* International Monetary Fund.

gold standard. A monetary system in which the value of the basic unit of a country's currency is fixed in terms of gold. Currency is freely convertible into gold and the free import and export of gold is allowed. Under the *gold coin standard*, gold coins of fixed weight and fineness are minted. A gold reserve is maintained by the central bank to back the currency. The gold standard fixes exchange rates between countries in terms of gold, in which all international payments are made. If exchange rates varied from the *mint par of exchange, it would be profitable to import or export gold in exchange for currency, depending on the direction of variation, provided that the variation exceeded the cost of transporting and insuring the gold (*see* gold points). Thus a stable rate of exchange could be established under the gold standard.

In classical economic theory the gold standard was the mechanism by which imbalances in international trade were automatically ironed out. If a country's balance of payments was in deficit, its gold reserves were depleted since more gold is paid out for imports than is received from exports. The central bank had to contract the money supply in order to cover its liabilities to currency-holders. This resulted in falling prices, which would increase exports, and falling wages, which would check the demand for imports, and thus correct the deficit. The reverse occurred in response to a balance of payments surplus. The country could not allow its currency to deflate as it would then be profitable to exchange currency for gold, further depleting gold reserves. Therefore in a situation of chronic balance of payments deficits due to a country's unbalanced trade structure, economic policies such as raising the bank rate would be necessary to induce foreign capital into the country to offset the deficit.

The U.K. was formerly on the gold standard from the early nineteenth century: previously both gold and silver were used as standards. In the U.S. the Gold Standard Act of 1900, reaffirming an early act of 1873, finally made gold the single standard and defined the dollar in terms of gold: henceforward all money issued in the U.S. was to be maintained at a par with gold. Most financially important countries were on the gold standard between 1900 and 1914 but were unable to maintain it during World War I, when international movements of gold no longer operated freely. The U.K. returned to it in 1925 in a limited form known as the *gold bullion standard*, under which there was no gold coinage and individual bank notes were no longer convertible into gold, but unminted gold bars of 400 ounces each were bought and sold by the Bank of England. Other countries adopted either this system or (particularly the Scandinavian countries) the *gold exchange standard*, under which the central banks would exchange home currency for that of some country on the gold standard rather than for gold. During this period much government intervention was necessary and the operation of the gold standard was further hampered by restrictions on international gold movements resulting from the war. It foundered for many reasons: countries found that they could not deflate sufficiently to the extent that gold was flowing out (especially as their economies were already suffering under the Great Depression), short-term speculative capital movements made the difficulties worse, and the fact that the U.K. had adopted the pre-1914 parity with the U.S. dollar made the pound grossly overvalued in the trading situation in which the U.K. found itself after the war. The gold standard was abandoned by the U.K. in 1931 and most other countries followed suit. Those retaining the gold standard were known as the *gold bloc. After World War II the *International Monetary Fund established par values of member countries' currencies in terms of gold and these could not be changed without consultation with the I.M.F.

Gompertz curve. *See* growth curve.

good (in economics). A *commodity or *service that satisfies some human want. *Economic goods* are goods that are useful as well as being scarce in relation to the uses to which they could be put. Such goods bear a price, as compared with *free goods*, such as air, which are naturally occurring, in abundant supply, and need no conscious effort to be acquired. Freely distributed items are not free goods in this sense if someone has made an effort to produce or acquire them. *See also* Giffen good, normal good, inferior good, luxury good, necessary good.

goodness of fit. The degree to which the observed frequencies of any frequency distribution are compatible with the theoretical frequencies that external factors would lead one to expect. For instance, if men's weights were thought to follow the normal distribution, then a random sample of 1000 men could be selected from the population and measured for weight and the resultant observed distribution could then be tested for goodness of fit with the (theoretical) normal distribution. Under certain limiting conditions, hypotheses concerning goodness of fit can be tested using techniques based on the chi-square distribution.

goods in transit insurance. The insurance of goods while they are in transit within the U.K. In general, insurance cover is taken out by the consignor, the consignee, the carrier (*see* common carrier), or the forwarding agent. This type of cover is called for in the case of: imports in transit from docks or airport to final destination; exports in transit to the docks or airport, especially when sold on an *F.O.B. contract (*see* cargo insurance); inland transit of goods by road, rail, or post.

Certain carriers, such as British Rail, are classified as publicly owned carriers and as such are obliged to operate under fixed conditions of carriage, which specify their liabilities for loss or damage to goods in transit.

goodwill. The value of a business in excess of its asset value. It consists mainly of the good reputation of the business and the expectation that old customers will continue to patronize the firm. This is a saleable asset when a business is sold. It is difficult to quantify and is usually a matter for negotiation.

go slow. A form of industrial protest in which employees work at a deliberately slow pace. It is generally regarded as a breach of the implied duty of cooperation.

Gossen, Three Laws of. Laws concerning consumer behaviour formulated by Hermann Heinrich Gossen (1810–58), which encapsulated the essence of marginal utility theory. The first law states that the satisfaction obtainable from the consumption of an additional unit of a good diminishes as more is consumed until there is satiation (the law of diminishing marginal utility). The second law states that for satisfaction to be maximized, the marginal utility from the consumption of the final unit of money's worth (i.e. all income now having been spent) of each good consumed must be equal for each good. In other words, the marginal rate of substitution equals the price ratio. The third law, derivable from the first two, states that the subjective value of every additional unit of a commodity consumed diminishes progressively until it reaches zero.

government actuary. A U.K. government official controlling a small team of actuaries. Their task is to estimate the statistical probabilities of future events so that appropriate action may be taken. For example, an estimate of the number of people of pensionable age in 1990 may influence the choice by the government of the size of National Insurance contributions now. *See* actuary.

government bonds. The U.K. government borrows from the investing institutions and public by the issue of bonds under a number of names: Consols, exchequer bonds, treasury bonds, victory bonds, war loans, etc., collectively known as the *funds.* They are dealt in on the Stock Exchange, and to some extent through the Post Office and Trustee Savings Bank Accounts.

government broker. The stockbroker through whom the U.K. government markets *gilt-edged securities. The government broker was until August 1984 the senior partner of the old established stockbroking firm, Mullens & Co.; when this firm merged with another, arrangements were made for two partners in the firm to join the Bank of England and operate from within the Bank as government broker, remaining an *ex officio* member of the Council of the Stock Exchange.

government sector. The part of the economy concerned with the transactions of the government. The government influences the economy by its ability to tax and its desire to spend. If the government moves into budgetary deficit (spending exceeds tax revenue) aggregate demand will be increased; if it moves into surplus the reverse happens. Studies of the government sector of macroeconomic models analyse these effects (*see* I.S. curve, fiscal policy, policy mix, budget).

government securities. All borrowing by the government on which a fixed rate of interest is paid. They include the *funded debt and *Treasury bills.

Government Statistical Service (G.S.S.). The statistics divisions of all U.K. government departments as well as the Business Statistics Office and the Office of Population Censuses and Surveys (which collect the data), and the *Central Statistical Office (which coordinates the system). Although its primary aim is to provide information for the government it regularly publishes a large volume of statistics of which the *Monthly Digest of Statistics*, quarterly *Business Monitors*, and the annual *National Income and Expenditure Blue Book* are examples.

government stocks. *See* gilt-edged securities.

graduated pension scheme. A graduated addition to the U.K. government's *retirement pension brought into operation in 1961. It consisted of 2.5p per week for each £7.50 of all graduated contributions paid by a man (£9.00 for a woman). These graduated contributions were payable by all employed people aged 18-70 (65 for a woman) who earned more than £9 a week, unless they had contracted out of the scheme. From 6 April 1975, as a result of the Social Security Act (1973), the National Insurance flat-rate and graduated contributions ceased to be payable for employees and were replaced by contributions wholly related to earnings. *See* pensions.

grant of probate. *See* letters of administration.

grants-in-aid. Grants from the U.K. central government to the local authorities to help finance services, such as the police, hospitals, and roads, that are not covered by the *rates support grant. These grants are not paid by the Treasury but must be sanctioned and paid by the appropriate ministries.

graph. A two-dimensional diagram, generally depicting the relationship between two variables by means of continuous curves or lines. Conventionally the independent variable is represented on the horizontal axis while the vertical axis represents the dependent variable (note, however, that price-quantity diagrams depicting demand and supply curves are an exception). A graph may have four quadrants, representing combinations of positive and negative values of each of the two variables; in economics, however, it is usual to display only the familiar northeast quadrant of a graph because negative values of either variable are rarely of interest. It is possible, though difficult, to draw a three-dimensional graph (to represent the relationship between three variables).

green card system. An international extension of the concept behind the formation of the Motor Insurers' Bureau. This applies to virtually all European countries in which are established bureaux similar to the M.I.B. Motorists intending to visit other European countries are provided with a green card issued by their national bureau through a member insurer, as evidence that their insurance is sufficient to comply at least with the minimum requirements of the countries listed.

The foremost intention of this system is to ensure that injured nationals shall be compensated within the scope of the national legislation when injuries are caused by visiting motorists. This system implies that the national bureau will guarantee any payment due recovering in due course from the bureau of the visiting motorist, which in turn recovers from the insurer involved or from the motorist personally.

green pound. The pound sterling in terms of the *green rate of exchange* fixed by the E.E.C. by reference to

European units of account rather than by market foreign exchange rates. This green rate is used to convert farm prices into national currencies so that they are in principle the same throughout the E.E.C., regardless of movements in actual exchange rates. A country's green rate can only be revalued or devalued if other member countries agree. The differences arising between green rates and market rates of exchange have necessitated the payment of *monetary compensatory amounts. Green rates were first introduced in 1969.

Gresham's law. The axiom stating that bad money drives out good. The maxim has been falsely attributed to Thomas Gresham, a financial councillor to Elizabeth I of England. The principle behind it is that where there are two different types of money in circulation, for example gold and silver, particularly if one is being, or is thought to be being, debased and falling in value relative to the other, this increases the scarcity of the more valuable coin, accelerates the drop in relative value of the other, and adds to the incentive to hoard. This continues until the more valuable type is almost entirely driven from circulation.

gross domestic fixed capital formation. Total investment expenditures on fixed capital during a specified period of time in a country. Gross domestic fixed capital formation is one of the constituents of gross national product (G.N.P.); it excludes expenditures on maintenance and repairs and on inventory investment. It includes investment expenditures in the economy by nonresidents but excludes investment expenditure by residents outside the economy. It is gross in the sense that capital consumption is not deducted.

gross domestic product (G.D.P.). *Gross national product (G.N.P.) excluding net property abroad. Thus G.D.P. is an estimate of incomes accruing to residents and generated within the country only. Although G.N.P. is the more global statistic, G.D.P. is much more frequently used in reference to sectoral industrial analysis. G.D.P. can be calculated either at factor cost or at market prices in exactly the same manner as G.N.P. G.D.P. is sometimes referred to as *gross value added.*

gross finance charge. The interest repayment of a loan being repaid over a fixed period of time, calculated normally at a flat interest rate. A certain varying percentage of this gross finance charge is allocated to each instalment received over the life of the debt.

gross income. A person's income from all sources. Deduction of outgoings and expenses gives the *total income* for tax purposes. Deduction of allowances from the total income gives the *taxable income.

gross interest. The total amount of interest yielded by an investment before tax is deducted. *Grossing up* is calculating the amount of an investment subject to tax that would be needed in order to produce the same income as one not subject to tax.

gross investment. The total of all investment expenditures in the economy or in a firm. In the economy as a whole, gross investment can never be negative. It includes expenditure on replacing worn-out or obsolete equipment, and the least that can happen in the economy as a whole is that the worn-out equipment is not replaced. In that case total investment is zero. It is gross investment that is relevant for macroeconomic analysis.

gross national product (G.N.P.). The value of all goods and services produced in the economy during a specified period of time; it is the national

income of that country. It can be computed in three ways.
(i) The sum of all incomes accruing to residents of the country as a result of economic activity. This embraces wages, salaries, rents, interest charges, incomes of professional and self-employed individuals, pay of the armed forces, dividends, retained profits (gross of depreciation), and net property incomes from abroad. This definition excludes *transfer payments.
(ii) The sum of the *value added by each industry in an economy minus indirect taxes plus subsidies and plus net property income from abroad.
(iii) The sum of all expenditures; i.e. consumption expenditure plus gross domestic fixed capital formation, the value of any physical increase in stocks, government expenditure, and exports minus imports. From this total must be deducted net taxes on expenditure and to it must be added net property income from abroad.
Each of the three methods should yield the same figure but statistical imperfections in the measurement of various relevant items prevent this. Major problems arise in connection with producer consumption (including owner-occupied houses), unpaid services (such as housework) and the movements of this item, and the division of the figure for changes in the value of stocks into stock appreciation (or depreciation) and the value of any physical change in stocks. Inflation brings about a divergence between money G.N.P. and real G.N.P.; the latter can be obtained either by deflating money G.N.P. by some price index–an approximating procedure –or else by attempting to measure physical G.N.P., an enormous task in view of the diversity of physical units and the problem of assigning physical units to service commodities. Comparisons of real G.N.P. for different years have these difficulties compounded by the presence of changes in the quality of goods and services marketed and the introduction of entirely new goods and services. It can thus be seen that national income aggregates such as G.N.P. and its derivatives are by no means perfect measurements; however, they are the best indicators of economic growth and changes in national prosperity and, as such, they are widely referred to in economic, statistical, industrial, and commercial terminology. Gross national product can be measured at factor cost or at market prices; the former state relates to values net of direct taxes and subsidies and thus at genuine economic costs. G.N.P. at market prices is equivalent to G.N.P. at factor cost plus indirect taxes minus subsidies. Gross national product is gross in the sense that capital consumption is not deducted from it.

gross profit. **1.** The trading profits of a business concern before deducting the expenses (to give the *net profit). For a manufacturer, gross profit equals the total sales revenue less the total *factory costs, taking into account differences in the value of the stock at the beginning and end of the period. For a trader, it is the difference between total sales and total purchases taking stock changes into account.

2. In the retail trade the gross profit is sometimes taken as the difference between the selling price and the buying price: in this context it is the same as the markup (*see* markup price).

3. In some contexts the pre-tax profit is regarded as the gross profit and the profit after deducting tax as the net profit.

gross (register) tonnage. *See* tonnage.

gross value added. *See* gross domestic product.

gross weight. **1.** The total weight of a package including the contents and the packing material. It is the sum of the *net weight and the *tare.

2. The total weight of a road transport vehicle or railway wagon and the goods that it is carrying, when weighed on a weighbridge.

3. The total weight of an aircraft including crew, fuel, cargo, and passengers.

ground rent. A sum of money paid periodically by the owner of a building to the owner of the land on which the building stands. The landowner is said to have a *freehold interest, which can be bought and sold, the building owner to have a leasehold interest (*see* lease). This leasehold interest must be limited to a particular term of years after which it will expire. The landowner then becomes entitled to possession, not only of the land but also of the building on it, as under English law an owner of land is deemed to own anything growing, placed, or erected on or in it. He may then, of course, grant a new lease to whoever had owned the building.

group life assurances. Assurance policies taken out on a collective basis, assuring the lives of a particular group, such as the employees of a company. Often the individual members are not required to contribute towards the premiums (which are paid by the employer or by the group organization). These are very often associated with private occupational pension schemes and often form the basis from which a pension scheme grows in the size and type of benefits.

Often potential members are encouraged to join because of the opportunity of large life cover without having to supply medical evidence as to their health.

group of companies. An association of companies that are linked by some degree of common ownership. It is often composed of one *holding company and several *subsidiary companies. A group of companies may operate totally within one industry, in which case they will either be horizontally or vertically integrated or they may operate in several different industries in which case the group would be a *conglomerate. A feature of the last 40 years has been the growth of the *multinational company or group of companies (which itself may be horizontally or vertically integrated or be a conglomerate).

Group of Ten (Paris Club). Ten countries (the U.S., U.K., West Germany, France, Italy, the Netherlands, Belgium, Sweden, Canada, and Japan) who signed an agreement in 1962 to make increased funds available to the *International Monetary Fund. They cooperate with the *Bank of International Settlements in giving assistance to member countries who have balance of payments deficits.

group relief. A form of tax relief applicable to a group of companies, i.e. a number of companies that are owned by another company or are fellow subsidiaries of the same holding company. In so far as some of these earn profits assessable for U.K. corporation tax and others suffer losses, which are also so assessable, these losses in one company can be offset against profits in another. This form of relief is only applicable to losses and profits earned in the same period of time, during which time the companies concerned must have been members of the same group. An election for group relief must be made formally to the Inspector of Taxes.

growth curve. Any of a set of curves used to represent a variable as a function of time and hence describing its growth process. They may be used to illustrate the growth of an individual, of a country's population, of the sales of a new product, etc. A *Gompertz curve* defines a growth rate that declines at a constant rate (and tends to zero as the time variable be-

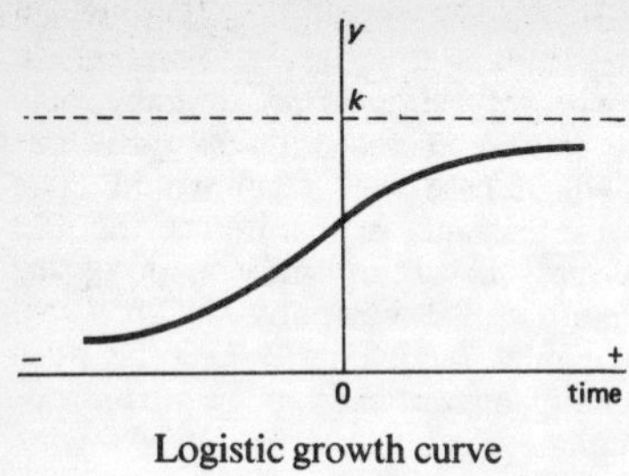

Logistic growth curve

comes infinitely large); its expression is:

$$y = ae^{-bt},$$

where a and b are parameters, e is the mathematical base 2.71828, y is the dependent variable, and t is the time variable. If the growth rate declines at a constant rate but tends to a positive constant c as t becomes infinite, then a modified exponential curve is formed, given by the expression:

$$y = c + ae^{-bt}.$$

A logistic curve is given by:

$$y = k(1 + ae^{-bt})$$

and denotes growth, which develops slowly at first and then takes off and finally levels off, as indicated in the diagram.

growth stocks. Ordinary shares of companies whose profits are thought to have exceptional growth potential. Such *stock will be rated on a stock exchange at a *premium to the rest of the market. Growth stocks are frequently referred to as *glamour stocks* or *go-go stocks.*

growth theory. *See* economic growth.

G.S.S. *See* Government Statistical Service.

guarantee. 1. A banker may be willing to lend to a customer against the undertaking (a *guarantee*) of a third person (the *guarantor*) to repay the debt to the bankers should the customer fail to do so. The banker usually requires some form of security to be deposited by the guarantor to support his guarantee.

2. *See* warranty (def. 3).

guaranteed stocks. Stocks issued by the U.K. nationalized industries (either to the former owners in compensation or to increase their capital) that are guaranteed by the government. They are thus *gilt-edged.

guide price. *See* Common Agricultural Policy.

H

half-commission man. A person who works with a stockbroking firm on the London Stock Exchange, introducing clients to the broker in return for half (or some other share) of the broker's commission.

hammering. The formal announcement (on the floor of the London Stock Exchange) that a member or member firm is unable to meet his obligations. Hammerings are infrequent and tend to unsettle share prices; they usually arise either because of large bad debts or because member firms have engaged in the practice of arranging large loan facilities to clients on collateral represented by shares, which fall substantially in value. The Stock Exchange operates a guarantee fund (*Compensation Fund*) out of which members of the public are reimbursed (at discretion) if affected by the failure of member firms; members of the Stock Exchange generally have unlimited liability.

Hang Seng Index. An index number of share prices on the Hong Kong Stock Exchange.

hard currency. A currency that is in great demand and in short supply on the foreign exchange markets. Following World War II with the slow recovery in production by the European countries there was a great demand by them for exports from the U.S. so that the term was applied particularly to the U.S. dollar. *Compare* soft currency.

hardware. The physical components or machinery that makes up a computer system: the memory input and output devices, central processing unit, etc. *Compare* software.

harmonic mean. The reciprocal of the arithmetic mean of the reciprocals of a set of numbers. Thus the harmonic mean of the numbers 10, 15, 30 is given by:
$1/(1/3)(1/10 + 1/15 + 1/30) = 15.$
The harmonic mean has certain limited applications, notably when finding the average speed over two journeys of the same distance. The harmonic mean is always less than the arithmetic mean and geometric mean unless all the numbers in the set being averaged are identical. *Compare* arithmetic mean, geometric mean, median, mode, quadratic mean.

Harrod–Domar model. An analysis of growth in an economy that was conceived independently by Sir R. F. Harrod (1900–78) and E. D. Domar (*b.* 1914). In its crudest form it is a development of the *income-expenditure model that allows certain of the variables to be varied exogenously over time. It sought to discover whether an economy could grow continuously at a constant rate (**steady-state* growth) or whether imbalances in the growth of sectors of the economy would inevitably occur, causing cyclical fluctuations in the economy. In Harrod's model the *marginal propensity to save (s) and the capital-output ratio (c) are fixed. If investment equals savings, output and the stock of capital grow together in the proportion s/c and steady-state growth exists. However, if investment only equals savings initially the situation becomes more complicated. The level of investment determines the amount of demand in the economy through the *multiplier. In its turn, investment is affected through the accelerator (*see* accelerator principle) by firms' expectations as to the prospects for future demand. If the level of investment is initially too high due to an incorrect expectation as to the future level of demand, then there will be a continuing growth in excess capacity leading to a growth in unemployment and an eventual recession. If the level of investment is initially too low there will be a growing inability to satisfy demand with a concurrent increase in inflation. Only if savings equal investment at every period of time will the economy grow at the equilibrium growth rate (*warranted growth rate*). Success in this model is separated by only a *knife-edge* from failure. Harrod also extended the model to determine at what level the economy would need to grow to keep pace with the increase in the growth of the labour force.

Since 1939, work on the model has been directed to relaxing the restrictive assumptions in an attempt to escape the possibilities of the model not being exactly right and to make the model more realistic. For example, models now have variable savings rates or the possibility of substitution between capital and labour. *See* Solow model.

haulage. A charge for transporting goods by road. It usually does not include the cost of loading and unloading.

head lease. A *lease of land granted by the person entitled to the *freehold interest in that land. The person to whom the head lease is granted may himself grant a lease to a third party, this being called a *sub-lease.*

Health and Safety Commission. A U.K. body representing employers, trade unions, and local authorities set up under the Health and Safety at Work Act (1974) to protect people at work and the general public from industrial hazards. It has taken over the responsibility of the government inspectorates for developing and carrying out policy on health and safety measures covering factories, mines and quarries, explosives, nuclear installations, and alkali works. The Commission encourages the development of voluntary organizations within each industry at national level for the consideration of safety matters and the formulation of policy on accident prevention.

Heckscher–Ohlin model of trade. A model of trade that, unlike the *comparative cost model of David Ricardo (1772–1823), bases its explanation for world trade principally on differing factor endowments and factor cost considerations rather than on the degree of effort necessary to produce a good. It states that trade arises because nations possess factors of production in different proportions, which in turn leads to differences in the relative costs of production. Nations that are relatively well endowed with capital will have a comparative advantage in the production of capital-intensive goods and will export these and import labour-intensive goods, while nations rich in labour will do the opposite. When deciding whether a nation is, for example, rich in capital it is insufficient to consider the amount of the factor endowments in physical terms alone, since demand conditions might offset this. If a nation consumes above-average amounts of the capital-intensive good then it may import that good rather than export it, even though it has large amounts of capital.

The basic assumptions of the model are that: costs of transportation are nil; there is perfect competition inside the economy; there are identical production functions in all nations.

hedging. A commercial operation undertaken by a trader who wishes to protect himself against price variations over which he has no control and which he is unwilling to attempt to predict. The operation is widely used in commodity markets, especially those offering the hedging facility of a *futures market. For example, if a manufacturer enters into a contract to sell twelve separate monthly quantities of his product and if the cost of the product depends heavily on a constituent commodity that is known to fluctuate in price, the manufacturer may wish to hedge his sale by simultaneously buying monthly quantities of that commodity on the futures market. In this way he is protected against any rises in price of the commodity throughout the year. Similarly, purchases may be hedged by making sales on a futures market (*see also* option).

The term is also used in the context of protecting one's capital against inflation (*hedging against inflation*). It may be thought that equities (ordinary shares) provide the best hedge against inflation, as a decline in the purchasing power of money should be balanced by a rise in the value of equities. In the inflation of the first half of the 1970s, however, there was a decline in both the value of money and the value of equities on most western stock exchanges.

hereditament. A plot of land, originally just big enough to support one family. It must, on intestacy, devolve on an heir. It is now used for a plot of land in general, excluding what is above, below, or annexed to the soil (e.g. buildings).

heteroscedasticity. The condition of inconstant variances in the random variables of a series of observations. When the random variables in question are the stochastic disturbances of a regression model, the presence of heteroscedastic variances transgresses one of the assumptions underlying the Gauss–Markov theorem and ordinary least squares estimation will provide inefficient estimators. If the variance-covariance matrix is known, then the variables can be transformed to eliminate the heteroscedasticity when least squares estimation will be valid. *Compare* homoscedasticity.

hexadecimal notation. *See* binary notation.

hidden price increase. A reduction in the quantity or quality of a good or service while its price remains unchanged. The substitution of vegetable matter for meat in sausages or a reduction in size of cigarettes or bars of chocolate would be examples of hidden price increases.

hidden (secret) reserve. An undisclosed reserve, i.e. one that is not evident from scrutiny of the balance sheet of a company. It arises when the assets of a company are deliberately undervalued or the liabilities are deliberately over-valued. For example, the stock-in-trade of a business may be shown on the balance sheet at its cost price instead of its market price (when the latter is the higher). The shareholders and tax authorities would then be unaware that realization of the assets would show a larger profit than that disclosed by the balance sheet. It is not permitted by law for limited companies to have such hidden reserves.

hidden tax. A tax that is included in the price of a product. The tax is said to be hidden, because its presence and size is not disclosed to the consumer. All indirect taxes are hidden taxes, unless they are specified (as in V.A.T.).

hidden unemployment. A number of people who are employed although their productivity does not justify the wage they receive. This is often found in the agricultural sectors of developing countries where each farm is owned by a family. If there are no prospects of work elsewhere, relatives may remain on the farm even though they are not contributing to production.

Higher National Certificate and Diploma. *See* national certificates and diplomas.

histogram. The graph of a frequency distribution. A histogram is constructed with a series of rectangular blocks representing the class frequencies in such a way that the areas (not the heights) of the blocks are proportional to the frequencies. The width of the blocks on the horizontal axis will differ if the class intervals differ, and will do so proportionately. Open-ended classes are either omitted or allotted arbitrary boundaries. Histograms are used most commonly where the subject is discrete rather than continuous, for instance to illustrate variation in the years spent in education rather than variation in the height of the population. *See also* frequency polygon.

historical cost accounting. A method of preparing accounts in which the historical cost (i.e. original cost) of an asset is entered in the balance sheet, depreciation being charged in the normal way. In an inflationary period this can lead to an inadequate allocation from profits to replace the asset. *See* inflation accounting.

Historical School. A mid-nineteenth-century German school of economic thought that disputed the methodological and behavioural validity of much current economic thought. In the works of Roscher and Schmoller it held that economics was an inductive rather than deductive science. Fundamental economic laws were to be inferred by historical observations of trends and not deduced from premises based upon assumptions on the individual nature of man as an economic animal. It saw nonmaterial and group motivations as important in determining behaviour. In this respect it defended nationalism and saw a rationale in mercantilist doctrines (*see* mercantilism) on the basis that protectionism would strengthen the state's defences, which was more important then, rather than increase its wealth.

H.N.C. *Abbrev. for* Higher National Certificate. *See* national certificates and diplomas.

H.N.D. *Abbrev. for* Higher National Diploma. *See* national certificates and diplomas.

hoarding. Retaining money rather than spending or investing it. Some people or businesses might increase their holdings of cash because of an increased *liquidity preference. This would reduce the supply of funds available for investment. If hoarding took place on a large enough scale, the market rate of interest would be distorted and an imbalance would be created in the economy.

holder. A holder of a *bill of exchange is the person in possession of it. He may be simply the holder, a *holder for value*, or a *holder in due course*. A holder may be the payee, an endorsee, or the bearer of the bill. A holder for value is one who holds a bill of which value has at any time been given, as regards the acceptor and all those who were parties to the bill before such value was given. To be a holder in due course, which is a legal term and which affords certain rights, he must have taken it for value before it was due for payment, in good faith and without notice of any defect in the title of the person from whom he took it.

holding company. A company that controls another company or companies (*see* subsidiary company). Under British law control of another company is deemed to exist if one company controls the board of directors of another or owns more than 50% of the nominal share capital of that company. The growth of the number of holding companies in modern times has been the result of a continuing trend of acquisition as a means of growth and also the setting up of new companies by existing companies to develop in new fields.

holiday and travel insurance. Usually a package insurance, covering costs due to unavoidable cancellation, baggage and personal effects, medical expenses, compensation for accidents, and in some instances legal liability to third parties for bodily injury or damage to property caused by the insured's negligence.

This type of insurance can be arranged also under individual sections so that the cover can be tailored to meet individual personal requirements.

home computer. *See* personal computer.

home service assurance. *See* industrial life assurance.

homogeneity of degree k. A description of any function in which, when all independent variables are increased in proportion λ, the dependent variable increases by λ^k. Economically constant-returns-to-scale *production functions are homogeneous of degree one and demand functions that depend only upon price ratios are homogeneous of degree zero.

homogeneity test. A test used to examine the homogeneity of the results of several similar experiments, i.e. the extent to which the results indicate that the different experiments are merely independent versions of the same experiment. For instance, a homogeneity test could be applied to a set of daily random samples (of the same size) of a manufactured product with a certain number of defective items in each sample. Homogeneity tests are an application of the chi-square distribution.

homogeneous product. A product of which any one unit is indistinguishable from any other, at least in the eye of the consumer. It is also often required that a homogeneous product be perfectly divisible, meaning that for every decimal fraction there is that quantity of the good available.

Homogeneity is a simplifying concept of considerable use as an approximation to the real world, although it is rarely found in actuality. However, it is a necessary condition for *perfect competition. *See* product differentiation, advertising.

homoscedasticity. The condition of constant variances in the random variables of a series of observations. The Gauss–Markov theorem requires as one of its assumptions homoscedastic variances of the stochastic disturbance terms. *Compare* heteroscedasticity.

homothetic. Denoting an increasing function of a function that is homogeneous of degree one. For such a production function the marginal rate of technical substitution is constant along a ray of constant input ratios from the origin as in the homogeneous case. The *expansion paths for constant input price ratios are also rays from the origin.

horizontal integration. The extent to which the producers in the same stage of production in an industry come under some unified control. In a monopoly there is complete horizontal integration, in an oligopoly a great deal, but the unified control need not be vested in one company or producer: it may be through a permanent association of producers, such as a cartel, or collusive agreements (either overt or tacit) between members of the industry. A degree of horizontal integration in an industry is a prerequisite to the exercise of monopoly powers in that industry. *See also* vertical integration.

horizontal mobility. *See* mobility.

hot money. Money that moves substantially, rapidly, and at short notice from one country's financial centres to another's. The motives behind the movement of hot money are either for the purpose of arbitrage, as when money is attracted to relatively high short-term interest rates, or speculative, as when money shifts in anticipation of a possible revaluation or devaluation. The arbitrage function of hot money enables a government to strengthen its balance of payments and its exchange rate (if the latter is a floating rate) by manipulating its monetary policy so that interest rates in the country are higher than in other countries. Such expedients are inadvisable except for very short-term purposes since hot money is highly volatile. Hot money is controlled by financial institutions and industrial corporations rather than by individuals.

household insurance. A type of insurance applying to the structure of a dwelling and to the household contents. A comprehensive type of policy is now often marketed under this heading and this usually covers the dwelling against the risks of: fire, lightning, explosion, etc.; bursting of water pipes; riot, civil commotion and malicious damage; storm or flood;

theft; impact damage; accidental breakage of fixed glass; owners liability to the public; loss of rent. Where damage has occurred, architects' and surveyors' fees are also covered.

The *contents* are usually covered for the same risks as the dwelling and in addition for: temporary removal (in certain instances); breakage of mirrors; the insured's liability as a tenant; the insured's legal liability as a private householder.

hull insurance. The insurance of a vessel and its machinery during construction, and thereafter at sea. Hull policies are generally extended by adding to the insured perils losses arising from a number of other causes including accidents caused by the master, crew, or pilots; accidents in loading, discharging or shifting cargo or fuel; bursting boilers, breakage of shafts, or any latent defect in machinery or hull; and contact with aircraft. *See* marine insurance.

human capital. The education and training in skills that is embodied in the workforce. It is similar to other types of capital investment in that current consumption is foregone to acquire means to increase future consumption. However, unlike other forms of capital it becomes embodied in the individual and cannot be repossessed in settlement of a debt. For this reason banks, finance houses, etc. dislike providing loans for educational purposes. The concept of human capital is used to explain the variation in earnings throughout the population: unskilled labourers will reach their peak wages at a fairly early age, professional men would earn their highest salary much later in life. Although the lifetime earnings for these two groups could be identical there would be great inequality in any year.

hypergeometric distribution. A statistical *distribution of a discrete variable, which is usually the proportion of a sample from a finite population having a specified attribute. If, for example, ten women are selected from a group of fifty with a view to discovering the percentage of the group that takes contraceptive pills, the probability of selecting a woman who takes contraceptive pills will clearly not remain constant as the ten successive individuals are sampled and thus the necessary condition for the application of the binomial distribution will not be fulfilled. If the sample size is very small relative to the population size, the results given by the hypergeometric distribution will be close to those given by the binomial distribution. The mean of the hypergeometric distribution is equal to the mean of the corresponding binomial distribution but the variance is smaller.

hyperinflation. Dramatically high levels of *inflation, invariably lasting only a few months or less but usually accompanied by social disorder. It is often assumed to begin when price increases exceed 50% a month. For this reason the persistent high levels of inflation (20–30%) a year experienced in certain South American countries are not considered to be hyperinflations. Examples of hyperinflations were those experienced in Germany, Austria, and Poland after World War I, and Greece and Hungary at the end of World War II. Here inflation was measured in hundreds and thousands of percentage points. The argument is often made that inflation leads to hyperinflation and then to social breakdown, but there is no evidence yet to support this theory. It is more likely that social breakdown leads to hyperinflation, and that its roots are to be found more in political than economic causes. *See* inflation.

hypermarket. A very large *supermarket, usually with a minimum of 25 check-out points. In addition to household products, food, and drink, a hypermarket often sells clothing and sometimes furniture. They are usually situated outside towns and provide extensive car-parking facilities.

hypothecation. *See* letter of hypothecation.

hypothesis. 1. (In statistics). An assertion concerning some characteristic of a population, such as its mean or its density function. If a hypothesis specifies values for all the parameters associated with a population, it is called a *simple hypothesis*; if not, it is called a *composite hypothesis*. The hypothesis towards which a statistician will direct his enquiries in a test is referred to as the *null hypothesis*, and a test of hypothesis will have in addition to the null hypothesis an *alternate hypothesis*, which will specify values mutually exclusive to those specified by the null hypothesis. Whether a null hypothesis is accepted or rejected will depend on the result of the test and the *critical region. If the null hypothesis is rejected then the alternate hypothesis is corroborated. *See also* hypothesis testing.

2. (In any science). A theoretical proposition postulating a rule of behaviour among any set of phenomena. Hypotheses may be correct or false (a proposition that is always correct is a tautology) and must be capable of refutation. A hypothesis can be proved wrong (by being refuted) but can never be proved right. If tests fail to refute a hypothesis, then the hypothesis is said to be verified or corroborated. In the social sciences, which are concerned with the behaviour of human beings rather than of inanimate matter, there are very few hypotheses that even appear to have been demonstrated beyond question and hypotheses in economics, for instance, must be viewed critically.

hypothesis testing. A branch of statistical inference concerned with the testing of an assertion or a *null hypothesis concerning the parameters of density functions. The null hypothesis may take the simple form of specifying a value for the mean or variance of a distribution, it may postulate equality of two means or two variances, or it may assert *goodness of fit of an observed frequency to a theoretical distribution. Frequently hypothesis tests are only valid if the population with which one is dealing has a normal distribution. A hypothesis test will be *one-tailed* or *two-tailed* according to the nature of the *alternate hypothesis. If the alternate hypothesis states that the value of the parameter under investigation is above but not below (or below but not above) the value stated by the null hypothesis, then the hypothesis test will be one-tailed; if, on the other hand, the alternate hypothesis specifies that the parameter can have any value other than that stated by the null hypothesis, then the hypothesis test will be two-tailed. The results of a test of a simple hypothesis can be incorrect in two ways: it can reject a true null hypothesis or it can accept a false null hypothesis. The first type of error is commonly referred to as a *Type I error* and the second a *Type II error.* The size of the Type I error, or the probability of its occurrence, is usually fixed at five per cent and the best test is then evidently the one that minimizes the size of the Type II error, given this level of the Type I error. A hypothesis will be rejected if the result of the test falls into its *critical region*, which will be selected so that the values inside it correspond to the values of the random sample that are least congenial to the null hypothesis. Hypothesis tests are carried out mainly with the use of the *chi-square distribution, the *F distribution, and *Student's t distribution, while critical regions are selected by such theoretical instruments as the *Neyman–Pearson Lemma and the *likelihood ratio test. *See also* hypothesis, estimation, power (of a statistical test).

I

I.A.M. *See* Institute of Administrative Management.

I.B.R.D. *See* International Bank for Reconstruction and Development.

I.C.F.C. *See* Industrial and Commercial Finance Corporation.

I.C.F.T.V. *See* International Confederation of Free Trade Unions.

I.D.A. *See* International Development Association.

identification. The problem of determining whether or not the coefficients of the individual relationships in a simultaneous model can be estimated. For any relationship this will depend on two necessary conditions–the order condition and the rank condition. The order condition states that the number of predetermined variables not represented in the relationship must be at least as many as the number of endogenous variables included minus one; the rank condition relates to a property of the matrix of the coefficients of the reduced form. If these conditions are not fulfilled the relationship in question is said to be unidentified; if they are fulfilled exactly the relationship is exactly identified; and if they are fulfilled in excess the relationship is said to be overidentified. Different relationships in the same model can be unidentified, exactly identified, or overidentified; there is no need for them all to be either identified or unidentified. The coefficients of an unidentified relationship cannot be estimated whereas those of identified (or overidentified) relationships can be. The identification problem frequently causes trouble in applied econometric work. *See also* simultaneous model.

I.F.C *See* International Finance Corporation.

illegal partnership. A *partnership that is disallowed by law. The main examples are partnerships formed to carry out a business or acts that are unlawful, and partnerships of more than twenty partners (except partnerships in certain professions, e.g. of solicitors, accountants, and stockbrokers, in which limited companies are not allowed).

I.L.O. *See* International Labour Organization.

I.M.F. *See* International Monetary Fund.

immediate annuity. An *annuity that gives the investor immediate payments as soon as the investment is received by the insurance company.

immediate holding company. A company or corporation that holds a controlling interest (by holding a majority of the shares) in another company. The immediate holding company may itself be controlled by a third company, which will be regarded as a holding company of both.

immigrant remittances. Money sent by immigrant workers to their native countries and consequently an adverse invisible item in the country of work's balance of payments. Although usually an insignificant drain on the country of work, these sums can be a valuable source of foreign exchange for the country of origin of the immigrants. For example, Yugoslavs, Greeks, and Turks working in the E.E.C. send home significant sums.

impact day. The first day on which any publicity may be given to a new share issue from which over £3 million is being raised. The Bank of England controls the timing of such issues.

impact effect. The immediate effect of a sudden change in demand during which all the factors of production are fixed. Since the supply cannot readjust immediately the price must rise unless rationing is introduced. This is a temporary phase as the abnormally high profits being earned will attract new firms into the industry. These new firms will expand the output and the price will begin to fall. The impact effect occurs immediately prior to the *short run.

imperfect competition. *See* monopolistic competition.

imperfect market. A market that does not fulfill all the conditions of a *perfect market. There may be few buyers or sellers, a heterogeneous product, inadequate information regarding the prices of competitors, significant costs of transport, or *barriers to entry. All markets are imperfect to some degree in the real world.

imperfect oligopoly. An industrial structure consisting of a limited number of firms producing a similar but slightly different product. By its actions each firm can affect the price and total quantity of the product that is sold. Unlike perfect oligopoly, the product of each firm has one or more unique characteristics. The difference may be promotion of a brand name, attractive packaging, or a minor difference in quality or location. For instance, the cost of buying petrol from two identical garages in a small town would differ for each consumer because of the cost of time and transport in reaching them; in these circumstances one garage could slightly increase the price of its petrol without losing all its custom. *See also* oligopoly, perfect oligopoly, duopoly.

Imperial Preference. *See* Commonwealth Preference.

Imperial units. Units of measurement used in the English-speaking world. They include yards and miles; pounds, hundredweights, and tons; gallons; British thermal units; etc.

Imperial units are being superseded by metric units, especially by *SI units. *See also* U.S. customary units.

impersonal account. A ledger account that deals with assets or capital (*real account*) or with revenue or expenditure (*nominal account*) but not with debtors or creditors (*personal account*).

implicit tariff. The real tariff that is placed on a particular industrial process when a country charges a lesser tariff on inputs than on outputs. If the inputs into making sandals are 50% labour and 50% leather, and if leather is admitted duty free while sandals face a tariff of 10%, then the true tariff on the value added by foreign sandal makers is 20%, i.e. one fifth of the value of the leather used in the process. This is also called the *effective rate of protection* and is distinguished from the manifest tariff.

implied terms. Terms of a contract that are not expressly stated but that the law regards as necessary to make sense of the contract or to give effect to the intentions of the parties. These are usually terms that would have been included had the parties thought necessary, but that were in fact taken for granted.

Certain statutes also imply terms in particular types of contracts. For example, the Sale of Goods Act (1979) implies a number of terms in a contract for the sale of goods to the effect that the goods will be of reasonable quality and fit for the purpose for which they are being purchased.

Implied terms may always be excluded from a contract if both parties agree on this and express such agreement in the contract. There are a limited number of cases of statutorily implied terms that may not be so excluded, e.g. a number of nonexcludable terms implied in hire purchase contracts by the Consumer Credit Act (1974).

import deposit. A method of restricting imports to a country, in which the government calls on importers for a money deposit when the goods arrive at the port of entry. This method was first used in 1968 by the U.K. as an alternative to raising import duties which it had agreements with GATT and EFTA not to do), and lasted until 1970. The import deposit required then was 50% of the value of the goods except food and raw materials.

import duties. *See* tariff.

import entry form. A form filled in by an importer of goods and submitted to the Customs and Excise. The form is used for calculating any import duty and, when passed by Customs, as a warrant to allow the goods to be removed from the port of entry.

Import-Export Bank. A U.S. bank set up in 1961 to provide export credit insurance for U.S. exporters. It performs a similar function to the U.K. Export Credit Guarantee Department, except that the U.S. bank provides cover against some political risks.

import licence. A permit that allows an importer to bring a certain quantity of foreign goods into a country and allows him to purchase the foreign currency required to pay for them. Import licences are required when imports are restricted by import quotas or by currency controls. *See also* imports.

import quotas. *See* imports.

import restrictions. The primary import restrictions are tariffs and quotas. Other more subtle restrictions do exist, including preferential purchasing on the part of state agencies and the creation of differentials in industrial standards designed to discourage importers. The differentials might arise either in standard checks to which domestic goods are not subjected or standards that would require a major retooling for a prospective importer. Also taxes can be imposed on characteristics peculiar to foreign imports.

imports. Goods and services purchased from a foreign country. In order to control its *balance of payments, a country must sometimes restrict imports. It may also wish to restrict imports to protect its own producers from foreign competition, or to prevent goods that are illegal to use or possess from entering the country. The methods used to control imports are: a) *prohibition*, b) *import duties* (*see* tariffs), c) *import quotas*, d) *currency restrictions*. Balance of payments restrictions and protection of home producers may involve all four methods of controlling imports. Preventing the entry of illegal goods normally involves only prohibition. Import duties are taxes levied on the imports to a country. There may be an overall rate for all imports or the tax may depend on the type of import. Import quotas restrict imports by imposing a limit on the quantity of goods that can be imported from a particular country in a particular period. Quotas are usually controlled by the issue of *import licences. Control of imports may alternatively rely on restricting the supply of foreign currency to importers, a measure that also usually involves the issue of import licences.

Import restrictions (except those used to prohibit illegal imports) have to be used by governments with care and discretion if they are not to involve reprisals from other countries, which can have a serious effect on their exports. For example, the U.K. imports a relatively high proportion of foreign cars, but is prevented from imposing prohibitive restrictions on these imports because it fears that such reprisals will affect the export of its home-produced cars. The international control of tariffs and tariff barriers is the function of *GATT.

import specie point. The level of exchange rates at which it becomes profitable for a country on the *gold standard to import gold rather than buy foreign currency on the foreign exchange market. The import specie point is one of the *gold points.

import surcharge (import tax). An addition to tariffs that are already levied on imports. It has been imposed by the U.S., the U.K., and others when they wish to increase their tariffs temporarily, usually in response to pressure on the balance of payments, but do not wish to appear too blatantly in violation of their obligations under GATT and other international agreements.

imprest account. A self-checking account in which the balance must always match a specified figure. An imprest system is often adopted for petty cash purposes. If under such a system the petty cash balance is £100, then at any time the balance of cash in the till plus any petty cash vouchers on which a reimbursing cash cheque has not been drawn must total £100.

impossibility of rejection. *See* public good.

impulse buying. Buying a product on impulse from a retail outlet as a result of seeing it on display, rather than setting out to purchase a specific product.

imputation system of taxation. A system of taxation, introduced into the U.K. on 6 April 1973, which entails a two-stage payment of corporation tax for the liability arising from any one *accounting period. A charge for any distribution made, such as a dividend paid to the shareholders of a company, known as *advance corporation tax* (*A.C.T.*), reduces the mainstream corporation tax charge made on the profit relating to that period, within limits. The difference between this and the traditional system of corporation tax is that the former encourages a company to distribute its profits. Under the traditional system a company had to pay tax on its distributions, which could not be offset against corporation tax. On the other hand, the rate of corporation tax tended to be lower in the past.

imputation theory. The market mechanism for price-setting of the *Austrian School, where the producer imputes the consumer's *marginal utility response to his actions in order to construct a *marginal product. The process had application in the fixed-proportions production function used by the Austrians where the usual marginal physical product, and therefore the price-equals-value-of-marginal-product relation of profit maximization, is meaningless. However, the mechanism is difficult to interpret in a positive economic manner where producers are divorced from the consumers of their products. In the Austrian model prices may be determined by linear programming techniques under the assumption of competitive *free entry, and the imputed value of goods can be given the normative interpretation of a measure of social gains and costs of the producer's actions. It is the precursor of *opportunity cost.

imputed cost. A monetary estimate of the *opportunity cost of using resources that are already owned and so have no formal price. It is thus an estimate of the sacrifice involved in not using an input in its next-best use. For instance, the imputed cost of liquid assets is the maximum interest that could be earned elsewhere. Imputed cost must be added to actual outlay if a true estimate of the cost of production is to be arrived at.

incestuous share dealing. Buying and selling shares in associated companies to secure tax advantages. This may be legal or illegal.

incidence of taxation. *See* tax incidence.

income, circular flow of. *See* circular flow of income.

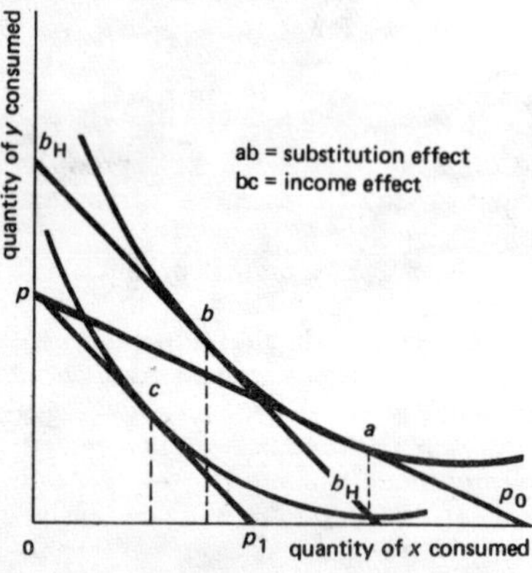

Income and substitution effects

income effect. That portion of the total response to a change of a price that results from the fact that *real income is affected by it. The income effect may be derived by finding the point of tangency of a line with the new price ratio to the *indifference curve at the old level of utility and subtracting the difference from the total change. The term may be represented, for small changes in price, as the quantity of the good whose price is changing (the amount of income necessary to keep utility unchanged) multiplied by the marginal propensity to consume that good (the rate at which the new income would be spent on the good). The fact that the income effect plus the *substitution effect together equal the total effect of a price change is known as the *Slutsky decomposition*. A good is a *Giffen good when the income term is sufficiently large and opposite in sign to the substitution effect to dominate it and violate the law of demand.

income elasticity of demand. The *elasticity of the variation of quantity demanded of a good to total income. Its sign and magnitude characterize goods as *inferior or *normal, *luxury or *necessary goods.

income-expenditure model. A theory of income determination derived from the work of J. M. Keynes (1883–1946) in *The General Theory of Employment, Interest and Money*. Production of goods and services, and therefore the level of national income, depends on the level of aggregate demand, which is determined in turn by the level of personal income, as shown by the *consumption function, and by the level of taxation and investment. In its simple form the model splits variables into those that are endogenous (income, consumption) and those that are exogenous (investment, government budget). Equilibrium is achieved when the level of withdrawals from the *circular flow of income (savings, imports, taxation) just equals the level of injections into the flow (investment, government spending, exports). The equilibrium may well occur at a level that is less than full employment.

The income-expenditure model can be demonstrated with the Keynesian cross diagram. The *savings schedule is used to indicate the level of withdrawals associated with each level of income and the level of exogenous injections is included. If there were none of these there would be an equi-

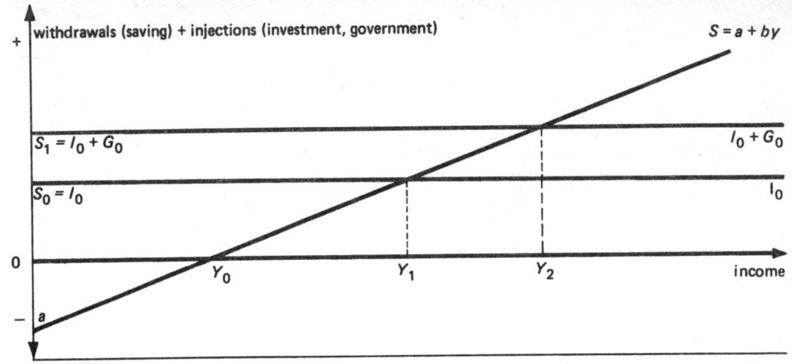

Income-expenditure model

librium level of income at Y_0, where $S = 0$. If a sum of money is then invested, I_0, the equilibrium level of income must rise to Y_1 before savings equal investment. The increase of income from Y_0 to Y_1 is greater than the amount invested because a fraction of income will be spent rather than saved. If another exogenous variable, government expenditure, is introduced into the model at a level of G_0, income must increase to Y_2. Here equilibrium is again reached since the amount of exogenous injections (I_0 + G_0) equals the amount of endogenous withdrawals (S_1).

This approach to macroeconomic behaviour has been criticized as being an inaccurate representation of Keynes's view and an inadequate description of the real world. This latter criticism can be justified because its predictions do not appear to work well when there are important changes taking place in the economy, such as an increase in the rate of inflation. Other criticisms are that it ignores the monetary sector and also unduly minimizes the effect of the interest rate on the level of savings. Despite these criticisms, a more complex form of this apparatus is the basis for most large-scale models.

income profit. A profit that arises as a result of trading or the practice of a profession. *Compare* capital profit.

income redistribution. The result of *transfer payments that shift income from one group in the community to another, usually from higher incomes to lower. The major tools for the transfer are *progressive taxation and *welfare payments. The primary rationale is the same as for *ability-to-pay taxation, and the desire to provide each individual in the community with an income that will support an adequate standard of living. The goal is to achieve, in some sense, a more equitable distribution of incomes.

incomes policy. A government policy that attempts to limit the rate of increase in wages and salaries without increasing unemployment; *dividend limitation and price controls are also sometimes included. The main aim of an incomes policy is to reduce the rate of inflation although there may be subsidiary aims, such as the redistribution of income.

Many believe that without an incomes policy, measures designed to reduce inflation have the effect of creating unemployment, as shown by the *Phillips curve. Incomes policies have also been advocated as a method of altering expectations as to the future rate of inflation. If people believe that the policy will drastically cut inflation, they will be prepared to settle for less than they otherwise would have done. Proponents of *demand-pull inflation regard an incomes policy as merely a useful supplementary weapon to fiscal and monetary policies. Believers in *cost-push inflation, however, maintain that increases in labour costs are mainly due to union strength, especially since the government's commitment to full employment lessens the onus on unions to safeguard their members' jobs. It is these economists who advocate an incomes policy as the major instrument to curb inflation. Finally, there is the monetarist view that inflation is caused by the growth of the money supply and that incomes policies are totally irrelevant.

The success of incomes policies in the U.K. has been mixed. The first was initiated by Sir Stafford Cripps in September 1948 and was a voluntary curb on wage and price increases. It was fairly successful until 1950, when it broke down under the pressure on prices caused by the Korean War. The next attempt was the Macmillan Price and Wage Plateau, which lasted from March to December 1956. Prices were held down in the private sector and firms were encouraged to resist wage demands. From August 1961 to October 1964 the government implemented three successive policies; this was the first time that norms were set to indicate what wage increases should be. The next (Labour) government also imposed incomes policies, the climax being a complete wage freeze in 1966. The 1970 (Conservative) government initially rejected incomes policies but was forced by the deteriorating situation to adopt one (phases I, II, and III) from 1972. The following government also adopted a voluntary incomes policy (the social contract) followed by a £6 pay limitation policy after the failure of the social contract, but this ended in 1977. In general, U.K. incomes policies have been imposed during economic crises, have been short lived, and have rarely been totally successful. They are extremely difficult to maintain. If an employer offers a higher wage increase than is permitted, no union negotiator feels able to refuse it. If a union supports an incomes policy it must cooperate with employers in blocking their members' demands–a situation that is both invidious and anomalous. Even if the T.U.C. agrees to a policy an individual union can disagree and might be able to destroy the policy. For example, a large number of unions settled under phase III of Mr. Heath's policy, but the miners did not. They were sufficiently strong to cause the policy to fail: Mr. Heath emerged from the conflict as a backbench opposition M.P. Finally, while it is in everyone's interests that a prices and incomes policy should succeed, it is difficult to impose because many groups try to make themselves exceptions to the policy, often on good grounds: however, once the policy has been breached it is quickly eroded into total failure. *See also* prices and incomes policy.

income tax. The tax applied to the income of individuals or families. The rate charged varies with the level of *taxable income. Usually a certain amount can be earned without being taxed, the size of this amount depending on the number of dependants, etc., and then succeeding ranges (or *brackets*) are taxed at increasing *marginal rates of taxation. This type of *progressive tax is common to virtually all countries so that those persons who have higher incomes bear a higher burden of taxation in proportion to their incomes, and consequently the inequality of the distribution of net incomes within the economy is reduced. The current rate in the U.K. (1984–5) is 30%, rising progressively to 60%.

income-tax allowances. *See* personal allowances.

income tax year. In the U.K., a period of a year from 6 April to 5 April the following year for which income tax calculations are made.

income velocity of circulation. The average number of times that a unit of currency is used in transactions in a given period. An increase or decrease in the velocity of circulation has the same effect on the economy as an increase or decrease in the quantity of money. If £X of business was transacted throughout the country in one day followed by £$2X$ of business on the second day (with the quantity of money static) the income velocity of circulation would have doubled. The income velocity of circulation for a specific period can be estimated from the formula: $v = Y/M$, where v is the income velocity of circulation, Y is the level of national income, and M is the supply of money available in the economy. It is usually considered to be a constant with a value slightly under three, but recent research suggests that it does vary, albeit extremely slowly. Its most important appearance is in the Fisher *quantity of money equation.

inconvertible paper money. Paper money that cannot be converted into gold. Since 1931 all bank notes issued by the Bank of England have been inconvertible. Prior to that, with the exception of some war years, they were convertible. *See* convertibility.

incorporated company. When a company is formed it must be registered with the Registrar of Companies who issues a *Certificate of Incorporation*. A *Memorandum of Association and *Articles of Association have to be drawn up to define the objects and powers of the company and its directors. Not until all formalities are completed will the Certificate of Incorporation and a certificate to commence business be issued. Creditors of a company must sue it in its own name, should such action become necessary, as the members of a company are only liable to the company, or in case of *winding-up to the liquidator.

increasing marginal cost. *See* marginal cost.

increasing returns. *See* returns to scale.

incremental costs. The additional costs incurred as a direct result of taking on a new project. The inverse of this would be referred to as *incremental income/savings*.

indecomposable. Denoting a set of production techniques in which the production of each good depends, as an input, on all other goods either directly or indirectly, i.e. requires a good that in turn requires another good. A stew does not require pesticide directly, but uses it indirectly in the production of vegetables. The concept is generally used in analysis where the production process is represented as a matrix, [aij], where the typical member is interpreted as the amount of good i used in producing one unit of good j. Such a matrix is decomposable if it can be arranged such that there exists a number k, where aij = 0 for i > k, j ≤ k. This may be interpreted as dividing the economy into two sectors: the goods 1, . . . , k; and k + 1, . . . , n, where n is the number of goods. Then the first sector depends neither directly nor indirectly on the second sector for inputs, but the second sector still may require goods from the first as inputs, so the two sectors are not independent. If no such arrangement exists then the set of production techniques is indecomposable.

indemnity. An undertaking to afford protection against damage or loss. Bankers frequently give indemnities on behalf of customers in respect of lost share certificates, bills of lading. etc., and take counter indemnities from the customers.

Insurance contracts other than insurances of the person are contracts of indemnity, i.e. the insurer undertakes to make good the insured's loss. If there is no loss there is no payment due. The measure of indemnity, subject always to the policy limits, is the amount of the insured's liability to the third party. The insurance contract itself may contain specific provisions regarding the amount to be paid by the insurer. Normally indemnity would be calculated in the following ways:

(a) *Property insurance.* The indemnity will equal the intrinsic value of the article immediately prior to the loss or damage. This would have to take into account any appreciation or depreciation on the original cost, and insurers are only liable up to their sum insured.

(b) *Liability insurance.* Indemnity here is much more easily measured, as it consists simply of the amount of damages awarded to (or negotiated with) the third party, plus any legal costs involved.

(c) *Rights* or *interest insurance.* In this case indemnity consists of the financial loss involved with the infringement of rights or prejudice of financial interest, such as default by a book-keeper insured under a *fidelity guarantee policy.

There are four basic methods of providing an indemnity:

(i) Cash.

(ii) Replacement. In this case the insurer finds it more advantageous to replace an article rather than to pay cash.

(iii) Repair. An adequate repair constitutes an indemnity. This form of settlement is very common in motor insurance.

(iv) Reinstatement. In fire insurance, this usually refers to the restoration or rebuilding of premises to their former condition.

indenture. A *deed to which there is more than one party. The name derives from the indented or rough edges of the document of indenture (as opposed to the straight edges of a deed poll), which were caused originally by the tearing of two or more copies of an indenture (one for each party to retain) from the same sheet of paper, leaving each piece with rough or indented edges. Since the exact tear could not be matched this method was a guard against forgery.

independence. An important statistical property that determines the probability treatment of two or more variables. Two variables are said to be independent if the outcome of one does not affect the outcome of the other. If two cards are drawn from a pack of cards, the two variables represented by these two draws will be independent only if the first card is replaced before the second card is drawn. If this is not done, then the probability of obtaining a spade on the second draw will differ according to whether or not the first card drawn was a spade, and in either case will be different from the probability of obtaining a spade on the first draw. In many areas of statistics, the independence of the variables is an important consideration; a random sample, for example, must comprise independent selections from a population. *Independent variables are generally easier than *dependent variables to handle in statistical analysis; many formulae and theorems that have been developed are applicable only to variables that are independent. Analysis encompassing variables that are not independent involves *conditional distributions. *See also* marginal distribution.

independent variable. 1. A *variable whose value is not determined by the model or equation under consideration but whose value does determine or partly determine the value of a *dependent variable. Independent variables are normally placed on the right hand side of an equation. An independent variable is sometimes called an *explanatory variable*.

2. A variable that has the property of statistical independence.

indexation. The linking of payment of money wages, government spending, a rate of interest, etc., to the rate of change in the price level. It would ensure automatic compensation for the effects of inflation so that individuals or institutions could receive the same real payment for their services despite price level changes, and it would tend to curb inflation if wage increases above this indexed level were only paid if productivity increased. It would counteract the inequity that results from the fact that in the transition period to an *expected inflation some groups are slower to adapt than others (or are prevented from adapting). However, since it is possible that this arrangement might destabilize an otherwise stable economy by further fuelling inflation it is not universally approved.

index-linked. Denoting a price, wage, cost, etc., linked to an index that measures changes in the price level of an economy. Thus, for example, a 2% index-linked savings certificate would pay a rate of interest of 2% plus the current rate of inflation as given by the Retail Price Index. *See* indexation, escalation clause.

index number. A single number that measures the average percentage change in the price, volume, or value of a set or 'basket' of related items during the time between some elected base period and the current period. A *price index measures the average percentage change in the prices of a given physical volume of commodities. Thus, to say that the *Retail Price Index is currently 350 (Jan. 1974 = 100) is to say that the retail prices of a set of major consumer goods, weighted according to the relative importance of the individual commodities within the set, have on average risen by 350% since January 1974. Other examples of important price indices are the Wholesale Price Index and the *Financial Times Industrial Ordinary Index. A *volume index* (or *quantity index*) seeks to find a weighted average of the changes in the volumes of the commodities under consideration, with the weights again arranged to reflect the relative importance of the different commodities. Examples of important volume indices are the *Index of Industrial Production and the Indices of Exports and Imports at constant prices. A *value index* shows the overall net effect of both price and volume changes in the commodities included in the index; the Index of Consumers' Expenditure at current prices is a value index. A value index is the easiest to calculate and a volume index the hardest. There are basically two methods by which index numbers can be calculated: by means of a weighted aggregative or a weighted average of *relatives. A weighted price (or volume) aggregative is the ratio of the sum of current-year prices (or volumes) to base-year prices (or volumes), which is then weighted by either current-year values or base-year values. Indices calculated by this method are better known as Paasche indices and Laspeyres indices. A value index can be calculated by dividing the sum of current-year values of the commodities (current-year prices multiplied by current-year volumes) by the sum of their base-year values (base-year prices multiplied by base-year volumes). A price index can be calculated by either of the two methods outlined above. A volume index, however, has special difficulties because the volumes of the different items in the index may be denominated in different physical units (unlike their prices, which are all denominated in money). The classic illustration of this is a volume index of chemical production that includes dyes, drugs, pharmaceuticals, plastics, etc., and therefore involves such units as gallons, tons, cubic feet, and so on. The usual solution to this problem is to take the relevant value index and "deflate" it, using some suitable price index as a deflator. The difficulty of assigning a unit of output to a service is evident. This problem concerning the specification of the unit of output is frequently referred to throughout statistics and economics as the *index number problem*. Other problems relating to index numbers devolve upon the choice of weights: the allocation of weight is an essential feature of an index number and yet there is an element of subjective judgment involved in their selection because they reflect consumer tastes. Furthermore, to leave the weights unchanged for a long period of time assumes unchanged tastes and ignores both the introduction of new products relevant to the index and increases in the quality of goods already in the index (which tend to reduce their volume but should cause an increase in their weight). *See also* Laspeyres index, Paasche index.

Index of Industrial Production. An index compiled by the *Central Statistical Office to provide a monthly measure of changes in the volume of industrial production in the U.K. The index charts the growth in production for each major industry and for the economy as a whole.

From a base level of 100 in 1975, industrial production in the U.K. had risen to 109 in 1983. In the U.S. production rose from a base level of 100 in 1975 to 125 in 1983.

indicator. A measurable variable that is used as an index of a different variable to which it is related and that is difficult or impossible to measure directly. Thus the Retail Price Index is used as an indicator of the cost of living, although there are many items relevant to the average family's cost of living that are not included in the Index. Also, when constructing a model of inflation, it may be considered that one determinant of the level of wages is employers' demand for labour. The best way to obtain data on this variable is to use an indicator such as the level of vacancies or the level of unemployed. Indicators are very common statistical devices in empirical economics and econometrics.

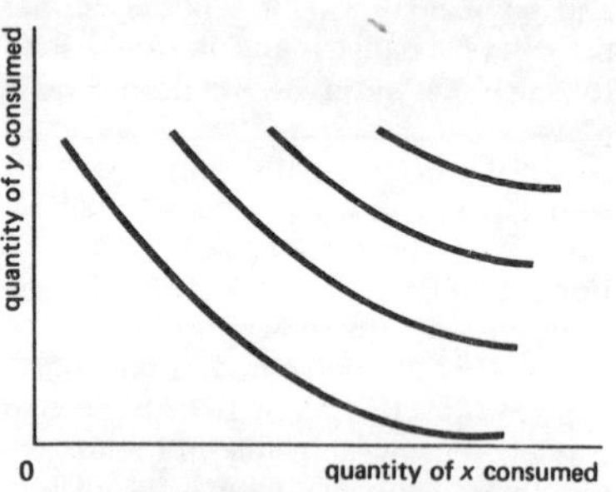

Indifference curves

indifference curve. A curve on a graph (that charts all possible combinations of goods available to a consumer) connecting all combinations between which the consumer has no preference, so that they provide equal utility. To simplify the construction of diagrams it is generally assumed that the consumer can only choose between two goods.

Normal indifference curves slope downwards from left to right showing that the reduction in quantity of one good must be compensated for by an addition to the second good if total utility is to remain unchanged. Unwanted goods, such as rubbish or goods providing rapid satiation provide exceptions (*see* bliss point). Curves that are furthest from the origin are preferred as otherwise utility could be increased simply by throwing goods away. Indifference curves are convex with respect to the origin since the marginal utility of a good declines as the quantity of it that is bought increases. Consequently, if the quantity of one of the goods is continuously reduced, progressively more of the second good must be added to compensate for the loss. This can be seen in the diagram by the flattening of the curve as it approaches the axes. Finally, it is assumed that indifference curves are "dense", occupying every point in space and that they cannot intersect. The concept of the indifference curve provides a simple but effective tool to analyse consumer behaviour under constraints (*see* utility maximization) without the assumption of measurability or of comparability of individuals' indifference curves.

indirect costs (fixed costs, overhead costs, supplementary costs). Costs of production that do not vary significantly with the volume of output and can only be changed in the long run. Examples of indirect costs include interest charges on loans, costs of maintaining equipment, rent and rates, and administration costs (in the short run). In accounting, indirect costs are not easily identifiable against any of the various *cost centres or *cost units being used in the analysis of costs. For example, if a sales department is being used as a cost centre, an indirect cost would be the proportion of the rates paid relating to it. *Compare* direct costs.

indirect labour. The part of the work force in a business that is not directly engaged in the manufacture of goods or the provision of a service. Such labour includes office staff, salesmen, night-watchmen, etc. *Compare* direct labour.

indirect least squares. A method of econometric *estimation used to provide estimators for the coefficients of simultaneous model relationships. The procedure is used first to obtain the reduced form of the model, then to estimate the coefficients of the reduced form by ordinary *least squares estimation, and finally to obtain estimates of the coefficients of the original model by appropriate arithmetical operations on the reduced-form estimates. Estimates provided by indirect least squares will not be unbiased; they will however be consistent. Indirect least squares can only be used to estimate relationships that are exactly identified. *See also* identification. *Compare* two-stage least squares.

indirect parity. A situation that arises when the direct rate of exchange between two currencies is not the same as the *cross rate*, i.e. the rate of exchange between the two currencies as calculated through a third currency. In these circumstances there is an opportunity for *arbitrage. For example, if the pound moves up against the French franc but down against the U.S. dollar, while the rate between the dollar and the franc remain unchanged, it would be possible to carry out a profitable arbitrage. This would involve using pounds to buy francs, using the francs to buy dollars, and converting the dollars back to sterling.

indirect production. *See* roundabout production.

indirect taxation. Taxation levied on goods and services. This is illustrated in the purchase of petrol: a large portion of the cost of petrol for the consumer is accounted for by the tax levied on it. Various forms of indirect taxation exist, a common one at present in the U.K. being *value added tax, which replaced purchase tax. In so far as indirect taxation is levied on necessities rather than luxury goods it is said to be regressive. *Compare* direct taxation.

indirect utility function. A *utility function in terms of prices and income, not goods consumed, which shows the maximum utility that can be achieved at the given price levels. The *utility maximization problem is solved to yield demand functions in terms of prices and income and these in turn are substituted into the utility function to yield the indirect utility function.

Individualist School. A school of economic thought that regards the freely pursued self-interest of individuals as the most beneficial actions for mankind. This view was upheld by Adam Smith and Jeremy Bentham but has lost popularity since the latter part of the eighteenth century. The economic system consistent with this belief is the *laissez-faire economy. *Compare* collectivism.

indorsement. *See* endorsement.

inducement to break a contract. An act by which a person who is not a party to a particular contract persuades one of the parties to the contract to break that contract in an unlawful manner. Any other party to the contract who suffers damage as a result of this inducement may sue and recover damages from the inducer, unless the latter is a trade union.

Industrial and Commercial Finance Corporation (I.C.F.C.). A subsidiary of *Finance for Industry Ltd. established in 1945 by the Bank of England and the English and Scottish clearing banks to provide equity and loan finance for small and medium-sized companies. *See also* Finance Corporation for Industry.

industrial bankers. 25 of the smaller *finance houses that formed the Industrial Bankers' Association in 1956. They obtain their funds mainly from the investing public, and attract them by offering a higher rate of interest than that paid by the commercial banks and the larger institutions.

industrial concentration. *See* concentration ratio.

industrial democracy. *See* workers' participation, profit-sharing.

industrial development certificate (I.D.C.). A certificate issued by the Department of Industry permitting the industrial development of sites in certain parts of the country. I.D.C.s are not required in Special Development Areas or Development Areas but are required in London, Southeast England, and the Midlands. First issued in 1948, they enable the government to control the location of industries to a certain extent but are independent of planning permission. An I.D.C. has to accompany an application for planning permission in the relevant areas.

industrial espionage. An attempt by one business organization to obtain the commercial secrets of another. Often illegal methods, such as bugging and wire tapping, are used. Devices such as paper-shredding machines in offices are often used to avoid the leakage of company secrets.

industrial estate (trading estate). A planned area of factories and warehousing that is usually segregated from the residential areas of a town. The first industrial estates (then more frequently called trading estates) were built in the nineteenth century, Trafford Park near Manchester being built in 1896. They offered factory sites and premises, which were well provided with services and thus enabled businesses to be founded at a much reduced initial capital outlay. These early estates (for example, those at Trafford Park and Slough) were operated by commercial companies. Some were developed in conjunction with housing schemes. The success of these commercial industrial estates in attracting light industry encouraged the government to build its own estates on the same lines. The purpose of the government estates was to offer factories at a low rental in areas of high unemployment: for instance, the Team Valley (Gateshead) industrial estate, one of the most well-known government estates, was built in the 1930s. The *Industrial Estates Corporations* are government-financed and controlled public corporations, which build factories for rent or sale, sometimes to the specification of a particular firm and sometimes of a standard type.

industrial injuries benefits. Benefits payable under the U.K. national insurance scheme to those employees who suffer incapacity, disablement, or death caused by accidents at work or by specified industrial diseases. There are three types of benefit: injury benefit, disablement benefit, and death benefit.

industial life assurance. A type of life assurance that had its beginnings in the industrial or working classes created by the Industrial Revolution, especially during the nineteenth century.

The working classes were for the most part ignorant of life assurance and generally could scarcely have afforded the annual premium. Nevertheless there was still the desire and need to provide for the cost of premiums, to meet which many hundreds of *friendly societies were created. In addition to legislation applicable to insurance generally this type of business is affected and governed by many Industrial Assurance and Friendly Society Acts. While industrial life assurance and ordinary life assurance basically are the same types of business, industrial life assurance necessitated certain differences in practice:

a) Premiums are payable weekly or fortnightly.

b) Premiums are collected by an agent of the assurance company from the assured's home.

c) Premiums are generally very small.

d) Sums eventually payable are limited (the sum assured was originally intended only to cover funeral costs).

e) The unit of cover is the premium (i.e. the assured decides what he wants to pay and this consequently indicates the cover obtained).

f) The agent collecting the premium is usually employed by the assurer and he is remunerated partly by commission. *Compare* ordinary life assurance.

industrial market research. *See* market research.

industrial organization. The branch of economics concerned with the reasons for, and the factors affecting, the behaviour of individual firms and the structure of industry as a whole. Among the topics covered are: *advertising, *diversification and *vertical integration, the reasons for and the results of *monopoly, *price and *output policies, and the involvement of the state in industrial production through the *location of industry, *nationalization, etc.

Industrial Reorganization Corporation (I.R.C.) A U.K. body established by Act of Parliament in 1966. The I.R.C.'s main role was to encourage and support structural reorganization, particularly by promoting mergers that would not otherwise have taken place. The need for greater concentration and rationalization was specifically linked to the promotion of greater efficiency and competitiveness. The I.R.C. was abolished in 1971.

industrial union. *See* trade union.

industry. **1.** Producers generally, or those of a particular range of goods in which case they are often named after the principal product, e.g. the meat industry.

2. (In economic theory). The market framework for the partial equilibrium analysis used in discussing perfect and imperfect competition. The supplier is taken to be the producer of the good and the demander either its consumer or a producer at a further stage of production using the good as an input.

inelastic. Denoting a curve with *elasticity less than one: a change in the independent variable induces a proportionately smaller change in the dependent variable. If a demand curve is price inelastic then an increase in price leads to an increase in expenditure on the goods as demand does not fall fast enough to compensate for the increase in price. An income-inelastic demand curve implies that the percentage of a consumer's total expenditure that is devoted to one particular good decreases as income increases. The short-run supply curve, taken as vertical, is said to be perfectly inelastic since a variation in market price induces no change in quantity supplied.

infant. A person under the age of 18. Infants are afforded certain protections in law. Money lent to an infant cannot be recovered in the courts, so that bankers have to be especially careful in the conduct of accounts of infants.

infant industry. A new industry for which there is an argument for providing short-term protection (usually by tariffs). The main thrust of the argument is that the internal economies, technological improvement, and increased investment generated would lead to a decrease in the costs of production enabling competition to be successfully faced, so that in the end the increased benefits derived from an efficient and expanding industry would more than outweigh the losses (such as higher prices) incurred in the short term by the imposition of the tariff.

A properly functioning capital market would ensure the same result, but it is argued that a common characteristic of developing countries is the weakness of the capital markets so that new industries in these nations will need initial protection. Furthermore, it is argued that there are external social benefits of increased technological expansion that will not be taken into account by the firm's actions. As a counter to these arguments it is often maintained that a proper programme of taxes and subsidies would have the same effect, but without the welfare loss implied by a tariff.

inferior good. A good for which income elasticity of demand is less than zero. As income increases consumption of the good falls as preferable higher-priced substitutes can be afforded. If the income elasticity of an inferior good is relatively large compared to the price elasticity, then the good is a *Giffen good.

infinite series. A mathematical series that can be extended indefinitely according to the nature of its progression. An infinite series is either divergent, in which case its value does not tend towards any finite number, or convergent, when its value does tend towards a finite number, which can usually be computed algebraically. The following is an example of an infinite series: $1 + x + x^2/2! + x^3/3! + \ldots$ (The ! is the factorial sign). This series is convergent for any value of x: for the case of $x = 1$ the series adds up to 2.71828 . . . , the number represented in mathematics by the letter e. Generally, for any value of x, the sum of this series is (e^x).

inflation. A general increase in the price level that is sustained over a period of time and does not reflect real factors. An increase in price alone is not inflation. For instance, as a result of a crop failure or an increase in the price of imported oil there might be significant increases in the prices of food, petroleum products, or imported goods in general, relative to the rest of the economy. People are worse off but this is not in itself inflation, although it may be inflationary if other sectors of the economy struggle to maintain their relative shares of income or former consumption patterns. Also, an economy might show a slight rise in prices as it is recovering from a recession. These phenomena are self-limiting and do not alone justify the term inflation.

The actual cause of inflation is a much debated question with one school centring on the demand and cost factors (*see* demand-pull, cost-push inflation, inflationary gap), while the other concentrates on monetary factors (*see* monetary inflation).

A further complication arises in the actual measurement of inflation over a period of time, which can be biased by the choice of price index and the changes in the quality of goods used in that index.

It has also been suggested that inflation is a persistent phenomenon that can only be reduced by decreasing aggregate demand in the economy at the expense of higher unemployment. *See* Phillips curve.

inflation accounting. A system of accounting that takes inflation into account, in terms of either general or specific changes in prices. There are a number of techniques for converting the accounts prepared by *historic cost accounting conventions into inflation-adjusted accounts and there is still debate over the best method to be used, but the system used for published accounts in the U.K., as defined by the Statement of Standard Accounting Practice introduced in 1980, is mandatory for all listed companies and for large unquoted companies. This *current cost accounting (C.C.A.)* system is required to show the impact of inflation by means of an adjusted profit and loss account and balance sheet, which can supplement or take precedence over the historical accounts. Assets are stated at their value to the business based on current price levels; current costs are matched instead of historic costs against revenues. Adjustments are made for changes in specific (rather than general) prices. An amount equal to all the adjustments necessary to convert the historical cost accounts to current cost accounts will be transferred to a current cost reserve account.

Current purchasing power (C.P.P.), or *general purchasing power* in the U.S., accounting adjusts historic costs to take changes in general price levels into account, using a retail price index.

The opponents of historic cost accounting base their arguments on the premise that the business should be regarded as an economic entity that is required to retain a sufficient surplus of funds to maintain the undertaking intact in real terms and not simply in terms of monetary units. However, many accountants continue to use historic methods.

inflationary gap. The excess demand for output at full employment in the simple income-expenditure model. As a result of either too high investment or a continuing government deficit, the savings schedule intersects the investment and government expenditure schedule at a level above that of full employment (*see diagram at* income-expenditure model). In the diagram assume that full employment occurs at Y_1 but that equilibriim occurs at Y_2. The inflationary gap is the difference between Y_1 and Y_2. Thus the equilibrium state is physically unattainable by the economy and persistent excess demand causes prices to rise steadily until either savings increase or investment and government expenditure decrease. The analysis underlies most demand-pull theories of inflation, but not all, since such inflation may only exist at full employment.

inflationary spiral. Any form of inflation that is self-sustaining. A typical form is one in which price rises generate successful demands for wage increases, which raise costs and so cause further price rises and wage demands. In such a situation the rate of inflation tends to increase continuously as people begin to expect, and allow for, future bouts of inflation.

inflation tax. 1. The transfer of real resources from the private sector to the government purely through inflation. Inflation increases the nominal value of goods, savings, incomes, etc., and under a progressive tax system this would ensure that a higher percentage of real income would be collected by the government. This effect is enhanced by the fact that many people who were previously free from income tax (because of very low earnings) would now be brought into the net.

2. A proposal of the British Liberal Party that the benefits of inflationary wage settlements should be taxed at a punitive rate and that the offending firms should also be penalized. Employers who made inflationary wage settlements would pay a heavy tax on the full amount in excess of the agreed limit. It was felt that this penalty would strengthen employers' resolve not to agree to such settlements. In addition, employees who negotiated inflationary wage settlements would have the excess payments taxed away, thus rendering large wage claims futile.

informative advertising. *See* advertising.

infrastructure (social overhead capital). The capital assets of a country available for public use, including roads, housing, public utilities, amenities, etc. The term sometimes includes the *human capital embodied in the population. The infrastructure of a region is often of considerable importance in the planning of investment by companies; one location may be preferred to another for the building of a new plant because of its superior infrastructure.

inherent vice. A property of certain goods that makes them an exceptional risk to a carrier or an insurer. If this property is not apparent and if the carrier or insurer has not been warned of it, the carrier is not liable for damage to the goods arising solely from inherent vice while in transit, nor is the insurer liable when covering the goods. For example, certain fibres have an inherent tendency to rot during shipment, certain resins melt into one solid lump, and certain oilseed products have a tendency to spontaneous combustion; these are all examples of inherent vice.

inheritance tax. A tax on the wealth received by the individual heirs to an estate, usually varying inversely according to the nearness of the relationship of the heir to the deceased. Inheritance taxes, besides constituting a significant source of revenue to the government, are also intended to reduce the inequality of wealth in a nation. In the U.K. inheritance taxes are now covered by *capital transfer tax.

injections. *See* circular flow of income.

injunction. A court order addressed to a particular person to do or not to do a particular thing. Such orders are often made in cases in which mere award of damages would not be satisfactory, e.g. an action brought by a person for the removal of an unlawful obstruction of a right of way to his house. The court may order the person who caused this obstruction to remove it; if he fails to do so, he may be fined or imprisoned for contempt of court.

Injunctions may also be used in cases in which a court hearing is pending, to stop anything happening in the meantime to prejudice the trial; in this context they are called *interim injunctions.* For example, where there is an action pending to decide a dispute as to the ownership of a parcel of goods, the court may make an interim injunction to prevent the person in possession of the goods from shipping them abroad out of the court's jurisdiction.

inland bill. The Bills of Exchange Act (1882) defines an inland bill as one that is or on the face of it purports to be, both drawn and payable within the British Islands (excluding Eire) or drawn within the British Islands upon some person resident therein. Any other bill is a foreign bill.

Inland Revenue, Board of. In the U.K., *direct taxes (income tax, capital gains tax, capital transfer tax, stamp duty, etc.) are assessed and collected by the Board of Inland Revenue, whereas *indirect taxes are assessed and collected by H.M. *Customs and Excise.

input device. Any of several devices for feeding information into a digital *computer. Input devices convert the data into the electrical signals handled by the machine. In some systems this is a fairly direct process: for example, input devices exist for reading conventional characters printed in magnetic ink (as on bank cheques) and for reading ordinary printed text (*see* optical character recognition). More usually the information is first converted into some less conventional form, such as *punched cards, *punched tape, or *magnetic tape, using special keyboarding apparatus. This is then read by the appropriate input device.

input-output analysis. The analysis of interindustry relations by techniques of *matrix algebra. Although it is obvious that different industries in the economy are interdependent in respect of their techniques and volumes of production, the interrelationships contingent upon the large number of industries in an advanced industrial economy were too complex and involved for detailed examination until the development of computing. Input-output analysis is a technique developed by Wassily Leontief (*b.* 1906) by means of which such interrelationships can be analysed quantitatively, empirically, and in some detail. It proceeds with the formulation of simultaneous equations for each industry; each equation represents the equality between the total output of the product of an industry and the sum of all the demands for that product in the economy–demands both from industries who require the product as an input (including its own industry) and from final consumers. Labour inputs and final consumption patterns can be treated either as exogenous (and fixed) items, or else conceptually as other "products", with final consumption of other products representing the "inputs" of labour, and labour services representing the "outputs" of labour. The coefficients that appear in the simultaneous equations represent the percentage unit of one product necessary as an input for the unit production of another. Thus the equation:

$$z = a_1w + a_2x + a_3y + a_4L$$

means that the production of one unit of z requires a_1% of a unit product w, a_2% of a unit of product x, a_3% of a unit of product y, and a_4% of labour service units (L). In this equation the output is z, the material or capital inputs are w, x, and y, L is labour input, and a_1, a_2, a_3, and a_4 are input-output coefficients which are determined by technical conditions derived from empirical data and assumed to be constant. These simultaneous equations can be represented in total by an *input-output matrix* with a row for each output and a column for each input. Given the input-output coefficients and further assumptions that the products of each industry are homogeneous and that there are constant returns to scale in each industry, it is possible to locate "correct" levels of output for each industry in the context of a specified final consumption pattern and to determine the effects of a change in final consumption patterns or in production techniques (i.e. in input-output coefficients) on the input-output structure of the entire economy. Despite the simplifying assumptions involved, input-output analysis has been applied very widely in economics.

input-output matrix. *See* input-output analysis.

inputs. The *factors of production used in the production of a good.

insanity. To protect himself, a banker will not allow any more transactions on the account of a customer once that person is proved mentally incapable, except for payment for necessaries. The Court of Protection will make an order for the administration of the person's property and affairs, and usually a receiver is appointed to manage these.

inscribed (registered) stock. Stock for which certificates are not issued, ownership being recorded in a register. The names of each stockholder and quantity held are inscribed by erasing one name and inserting a new one. Inscribed stock is usually government stock but transfer complications make it unpopular.

inside money. Money based on the debts that are part of an economic system itself. In an advanced economy, most money is a creation of the private banking system so that the ownership of money (a credit) by one individual or group is matched by the debit of another. The net financial holdings of the private sector consist only of *outside money, because the inside money is offset in the process of *balance sheet consolidation. It is possible to have a pure inside money economy, a pure outside money economy, or a mixture of both. Patinkin proves that if an economy has only inside money there can be no wealth effects (*see* Pigou effect) of a price level change. There can only be substitution effects as the level of real balances becomes sub-optimal.

insider. A person, such as a director, who has foreknowledge of information likely to affect the share price of a particular company prior to the publication or general dissemination to the public of such information. Thus, if a company is about to report unexpectedly poor results, a situation that could lead to a sharp fall in its share price, then the directors and other insiders will be able to sell shareholdings in the company before publication of the results and possibly to buy them back after publication, thus avoiding the *capital loss. Conversely, share purchases will be feasible prior to the publication of unexpectedly good results. Such transactions are referred to as *insider deals* and were made illegal in the U.K. under the Companies Act (1980).

insolvency. The inability of an individual or company to pay its debts when they become due. Although this may lead to *bankruptcy or *liquidation it is not the same thing. An individual may have valuable assets that cannot be realized when they are needed to meet his debt: he is then insolvent but not necessarily bankrupt.

instant. Of this month. For example, in commercial English it is quite common to write: 'Thank you for your letter of the 3rd inst.' Inst. is the usual abbreviation. *Compare* ultimo.

Instinct. An automated share-dealing system that has been introduced in the U.S.A. The U.K. *Ariel system has been developed using Instinct as a model.

Institute cargo clauses. Clauses devised by the Institute of London Underwriters for use in marine insurance policies. *See* cargo insurance.

Institute of Administrative Management (I.A.M.). A U.K. professional body dealing with all aspects of management. Until 1972 it was known as the *Institute of Office Management.*

Institute of Marketing. A U.K. professional body dealing with and setting examinations in *marketing. Founded in 1911, its headquarters are at Cookham, Berkshire.

Institute of Office Management. *See* Institute of Administrative Management.

Institute of Personnel Management. *See* personnel management.

institutional investors (institutions). Organizations whose business causes them to receive funds that need to be invested. Such organizations include insurance companies, banks, pension fund investment trusts, unit trusts, and commercial/industrial concerns that administer their own pension schemes (or have available other funds). The share of the stock market owned by institutional investors has increased rapidly since the war in both London and New York, and sentiment in both markets is now dependent on the investment policies of the institutions. Institutions can also build up a shareholding in a particular company that gives them an important voice at shareholders' meetings, especially during takeovers.

insulation. *See* sterilization of gold.

insurable interest. A financial or other involvement that constitutes an insurable risk or provides the legal right to insure. The insured must stand to lose should the eventuality insured against occur.

The law has always regarded possession of an insurable interest as a necessary prerequisite for insurance. Without an insurable interest any apparent insurance contract would be nothing more than a wager, which may not necessarily be illegal, but which is definitely not an enforceable agreement. The essentials of insurable interest are:

a) There must be life or limb, property, potential liability, rights, or financial interest capable of being covered.

b) Such life or limb, etc., must be the subject matter of the insurance.

c) The insured must be in a legally recognized relationship with the subject matter of the insurance, whereby he benefits from its continued safety or the absence of liability and is prejudiced by its damage or destruction, or the creation of liability. In general, insurable interest must exist both at the inception of the insurance and at the time of the loss, except in respect of *marine insurance (it must exist at the time of the loss) and life assurance (it must exist when the contract was effected).

insurance. A system for providing financial compensation for the effects of misfortune or loss, the payments being made from the accumulated contributions of all the parties participating in the fund or scheme. All participants pay a calculated contribution (usually called a *premium*), based on the calculated probability of the risk insured against occurring. In return, they have the right to call on the fund or pool for any appropriate payment should the event insured against occur, the amount having been calculated by a claims assessor unless it is a sum agreed in the policy. Insurance companies or *Lloyd's underwriters act as the fund holders; brokers or agents act as intermediaries between them and those seeking insurance. Many types of insurance policies are available, though the most common are *motor insurance, *fire insurance, burglary, *marine insurance, and *life assurance. The government organizes insurance against unemployment, sickness, and old age (*see* National Insurance) in the U.K. and some other countries. *Compare* assurance.

insurance agent. A person who puts anyone wishing to be insured in touch with an insurer, sometimes being empowered to commit the insurer. Insurance agents perform this function usually only as a sideline, dealing with only one or two insurance companies, and are in a trade or profession, such as banking, which frequently brings them into contact with people seeking insurance.

An industrial insurance agent is usually quite different in that he is normally employed by the insurer. He is generally remunerated partly by commission on the business acquired and partly by salary.

insurance broker. A person who negotiates insurance cover with an insurance company or underwriter on behalf of a client. He normally obtains a commission from the insurers (which sometimes takes the form of a fee) but being independent of them can advise his clients on which insurer is offering the most favourable terms for his particular purpose. The broker may also handle claims, loans against policies, and general insurance advice.

insurance policy. The document setting out the exact terms on which an insurance cover has been provided. The policy is evidence of a contract but does not in general constitute a contract.

insurance premium. *See* premium.

insured. The person who has the legal right to call on the insurer for any appropriate payment should the event insured against occur. *See also* assured.

intangible (invisible) assets. Those assets of a company that although of value to the company and contributing to the level of a company's sales, have no physical substance. For example, in the balance sheet of a company *goodwill might appear under assets. This indicates that the company places a value on its name or on the goodwill of its clients whom it may have serviced over a long period of time. Another example of an intangible asset would be a patent or a trademark. *Compare* fictitious assets.

integrated software. Software that allows several operations to be carried on with the same program, sometimes displaying different programs in separate sections of the computer screen.

intelligent terminal. Any computer input or output device that is capable of carrying out processing. It is usually equipped with a *visual-display unit.

intensive margin. The point in production beyond which marginal product is negative, given one variable factor with all others fixed. There is too much of the variable input for the amount of fixed inputs. *See diagram at* economic region of production.

inter-account deal. A speculative transaction on the London Stock Exchange involving both the purchase and sale of the same amount of the same stock within the same *account. Because of the account system of settlement, under which the actual transfer of monies due from dealings in any particular stock is reduced to a net figure and deferred until *account day, an inter-account deal is characterized by the transfer only of a gain (or loss), adjusted for stockbroker's commission. Thus a bull speculator can buy £100,000 of ABC Co. Ltd. shares on one day and sell the same shares a few days later (but within the same account) without ever having to advance £100,000. If the price of ABC Co. Ltd. shares rose between purchase and sale, the speculator will have made a gain (before paying stockbroker's commission) and vice versa. Conversely a bear operator can sell short, i.e. sell stock that he does not have with the intention of buying back after the price has fallen. If the end of the account intervenes before the prices of the shares have moved and if the investor remains confident that the price will move in the desired direction in the near future, it may be possible to arrange for a *contango or *backwardation, to extend the essential characteristics of the inter-account deal over two (or more) accounts. There is no payment of the transfer stamp or fees in the case of inter-account deals, although the stockbroker's commission is payable.

interactive. Denoting a method of computer operation in which the user can communicate with the computer during processing, modifying the program or changing the data.

inter-bank market. A section of the London money market in which financial institutions borrow and lend usually large sums of money for short periods, including overnight loans. The *Inter-Bank Offered Rate* is the rate of interest charged on loans and the *Inter-Bank Market Bid Rate* is the rate paid on deposits. This market developed in the 1960s.

interest. The money paid by a borrower for the use of the lender's money. If the rate of interest is 9% per annum then for each £100 lent nine pounds is payable as interest at the end of a complete year, and for each part of £100 or part of a year the amount of interest payable is in proportion. Simple interest is calculated upon the principal sum only, whereas compound interest is calculated upon the principal plus any interest due at a date when it is agreed it should be added to the outstanding loan. The formula for calculating simple interest is $I = Prt$, when I is the amount of the interest, P is the principal sum, r is the rate of interest, and t is the time period. For compound interest the formula is more complicated:

$$I = P[(1 + r)^n - 1],$$

where n is the total number of conversion periods and r is the rate of interest for each conversion period. For example, if £300 is invested at 8% per annum and compounded quarterly for 5 years, r will be equal to:

$$8/100 \times 1/4 = 0.02$$

and n will be equal to:

$$4 \times 5 = 20$$

The interest will therefore be:

$$300[(1.02)^{20} - 1] = £145.80.$$

The rate of interest quoted will depend upon the money supply and demand, the risk to the lender, and the agreed duration of the loan.

interest arbitrage. Transactions in currency between at least two financial centres, that take advantage of differentials in interest rates. It is responsible for at least some of the difference between *forward and *spot rates. For example, if the three-month interest rate in London was higher than the rate in New York by 2%, but the forward and spot rates in London were the same, then it would pay arbitrageurs to borrow dollars in New York and exchange them for pounds, then lend in London and arrange to buy back dollars three months later. This would provide a profit of 2%, less expenses. Assuming that the U.K. interest rate is not forced to a parity with the U.S. rate, the forward market in London would be flooded with demand for dollars, causing the forward price of the dollar to rise above the spot price until the percentage premium on the dollar is equal to the interest differential. Alternatively, if the U.S. interest rate was higher, the percentage discount would be equal to the differential. In practice interest rate arbitrage is not the only determinant of the difference between spot and forward rates. Hedging and speculation are also important.

interest test. A *psychological test sometimes used in *personnel selection or vocational guidance to obtain information about a person's interests, leisure activities, etc. Together with other tests, it can be used to help to decide how a person would be best employed, both for maximum job satisfaction and to make the maximum use of his interests and talents.

interim dividend. Any distribution of profits declared by a company in respect of a particular trading period, usually one year, other than the *final dividend. Most U.K. quoted companies declare an interim dividend after six months of their financial year with a final dividend coming after the full twelve months. It is rare in the U.K. for more than one interim dividend to be paid in any one year. *See also* interim report.

interim report. A short statement published by a *quoted company in connection with the trading results appertaining to the first six months of its financial year. The interim report will always contain details of the company's pretax profit, estimated taxation, *available earnings, and *interim dividend for the relevant six-month period together with comparative figures for the first six-month period of the previous financial year and for the full previous financial year. Frequently, too, there will be details of the company's sales turnover and interest payments and some comment on the figures with perhaps some mention of prospects for the second six months of the financial year. There are no details of balance sheet figures in the interim report. The six-monthly profit figures given in interim reports are unaudited, unlike the full year's figures published in the company's annual report. The term *interim* is frequently used as a shortened form of both interim report and interim dividend.

intermediate good. A good that is neither an initial resource nor a final product. It is produced by the economy in order to be used as an input in the production of some other good. The same type of good may be regarded as both an intermediate good or a final good in different processes. For instance, brandy may be consumed directly, as a final good, or may be employed to flavour a sauce, as an intermediate good.

intermediation. The activity in the money market of an institution (*see* financial intermediary) that accepts deposits and uses them to grant loans. It acts as an intermediary between an individual saver (or firm) who wishes to delay his consumption (or physical investment) and an individual (or firm) who wishes to bring forward his consumption of his income (or physical investment). The intermediary pays interest on deposits and charges it on loans. The former is usually much less than the latter, the difference accruing to the intermediary. This may be used as a measure of capital market imperfection, because if these markets were perfect then by definition each individual would have perfect knowledge about all other borrowers and lenders and therefore would not require an intermediary to evaluate the creditworthiness of others. It is this ignorance about the reliability of borrowers or the patience of lenders that allows intermediation to take place. *See also* disintermediation.

internal audit. The continuous auditing of the accounts of a business by internal staff rather than outside accountants. The purpose is to check the efficiency and profitability of the organization and to avoid undetected fraud and theft.

internal control. The means by which a company arranges for its business to be conducted in an orderly manner, to safeguard its assets and to ensure the accuracy of its financial records. Two important but not comprehensive methods for ensuring this are *internal audit* and *internal check*. The latter means that the system of accounting is such that each person's work is checked and corroborated automatically by an independent person.

internal rate of return. The rate of interest that, when used as the discount rate, reduces to zero the *net present value of the flows of costs and benefits associated with an investment project. It is claimed that this gives an adequate rule for investment decisions, the rule being to undertake a project only if the internal rate of return exceeds the rate of interest on the market. Unfortunately the internal rate of return criterion will not provide a unique solution if there is more than one period when net losses are incurred, as for example when there are heavy outlays initially and at the end of the project. In those cases the internal rate of return will equal zero at more than one interest rate. A unique solution will occur if the project can be terminated at will, but this is impossible for most projects. Another problem arises from the fact that this method is only a mechanical rule rather than an intrinsically correct principle; when the discount rate alters over time there is no single rate of interest with which the internal rate of return can be compared, whereas the present value method can still be applied. Thirdly, this method can give wrong or misleading results when a choice must be made between two mutually exclusive projects, especially if the projects differ in size or duration. This arises because a lower internal rate of return may be associated with a higher net present value. This problem can be overcome by calculating instead the rate of return on the differences between each pair of projects being considered. This becomes a very complex operation as the number of projects being considered increases. The concept derives from the work of Irving Fisher (1867–1947) on the theory of interest, and was used by John Maynard Keynes (1883–1946) under the name of *marginal efficiency of investment. *See also* marginal efficiency of capital.

International Bank for Reconstruction and Development (I.B.R.D., World Bank). The principal organization in the *World Bank Group, the other two being the *International Finance Corporation and the *International Development Association, both of which have close ties with the I.B.R.D.

Together with the *International Monetary Fund and the *International Trade Organization, the I.B.R.D. originated at the *Bretton Woods Conference and was intended as one of the three pillars of international economic organization after World War II, beginning operations in 1946. Although its original aim was largely to assist the economic recovery of countries that had been crippled by war, its present operations are largely in the making and guaranteeing of loans to underdeveloped countries and the provision of technical assistance. Only members of the I.M.F. can become members of the I.B.R.D. and their subscriptions are determined by a quota system. Quotas were doubled in 1959 and more than doubled in the case of members, such as Japan, whose original contributions were out of line with their economic importance and subsequently there have been further increases in subscribed capital. Of the subscribed capital only a certain amount is available for immediate call by the bank. This was 20% at its inception and 10% (1% in gold or dollars and 9% in national currency) after 1959. The remainder is used to enhance the bank's guaranteeing capacity for specific projects. The bank's operating capital is raised primarily through the sale of bonds. In its lending capacity the bank deals either directly with governments or with projects for which some government will act as guarantor. Furthermore there are restrictions upon how the bank may utilize the national currencies placed at its disposal, these restrictions being designed to ensure that the Bank will not upset the balance of payments equilibrium of the countries concerned. The headquarters of the I.B.R.D. is in Washington.

International Chamber of Commerce. An organization founded in 1920 for the purpose of exchanging information between local chambers of commerce on matters of international interest. It is situated in Paris.

international commodity agreements. Agreements designed to minimize fluctuations in the prices and outputs of commodities. International *commodity markets have traditionally been very sensitive to fluctuations in supply and demand; as the economies of primary commodity-producing countries are very dependent on the export earnings of the commodities, a series of agreements was made after World War II with the intention of smoothing out those price fluctuations. Broadly these agreements fall into one of the three categories. Some, such as the *International Wheat Agreement*, depend on a series of multilateral contracts between producers and consumers according to which trading is confined within certain minimum and maximum prices. Others, such as the *International Coffee Agreement*, operate a quota system for the exporting countries outside a certain price range. Above this range producers restrict exports and below it consumers are rationed. The *International Tin Agreement* is an example of the third type of arrangement: according to this agreement an international buffer stock is established for use if the price falls below or rises above a fixed price range.

International Confederation of Free Trade Unions (I.C.F.T.U.). An international association of noncommunist trade unions that was created in 1949 when the noncommunist unions withdrew from the *World Federation of Trade Unions. Its headquarters is in Brussels.

international credit unions (clubs). Reciprocal agreements between finance houses in Europe to provide credit facilities for international trade.

International Development Association (I.D.A.). A member of the *World Bank Group, affiliated to the *International Bank for Reconstruction and Development. It started operations in 1960 for the purpose of supplying low-interest long-term loans to underdeveloped countries. The repayment schemes offer very favourable terms, one aspect being that the loans may be repaid in the national currency of the borrower, a currency that is generally much weaker than would be acceptable to most creditors as a mode of repayment. Loans are made mainly for the development of economic *infrastructure. Membership of the Association is open only to members of the I.B.R.D. and voting rights are determined by capital subscription. A distinction is made between developed and less developed members. The former are required to pay up fully in gold or convertible currencies, the latter only 10% in this form and the balance in national currencies. Furthermore, there are restrictions on the application of the capital acquired in these national currencies so that the balance of payments of these countries is not upset. The Association is allowed to sell bonds and borrow to obtain funds, additional funds being obtained only through further capital subscriptions, called replenishments. The headquarters of the I.D.A. is in Washington.

International Finance Corporation (I.F.C.). A member of the *World Bank Group that is permitted to invest directly in private companies, make loans to private investors, or guarantee such loans; its equity holding in any one company, however, must not exceed 25%. Established in 1956, it is an affiliate of the *International Bank for Reconstruction and Development and only members of the I.B.R.D. may participate in the Corporation. The capital of the I.F.C. is much smaller than that of the I.B.R.D., but it is fully paid up in gold or dollars. Unlike the I.B.R.D. the I.F.C. operates mainly from this capital, though it is allowed to raise money from the sale of bonds and through loans. The headquarters of the I.F.C. is in Washington.

International Fund for Agricultural Development (IFAD). An agency proposed at the World Food Conference in 1974 and established in 1977 with the aim of providing additional funds for the agricultural development of developing countries, particularly for the benefit of the poorest rural population. Its headquarters are in Rome.

International Labour Organization. (I.L.O.). An organization founded in 1919 under the auspices of the League of Nations for the purpose of improving working conditions throughout the world and promoting social legislation. In 1946 it passed into the structure of the United Nations. Its operations are limited in that it can only make recommendations, publish statistics, draft models for international social legislation, and provide technical assistance. Countries are represented in theory by four delegates, one each from the employers and workers and two from the government. Recently, however, the social organization of some countries has rendered such a representation scheme impractical. The I.L.O. headquarters is in Geneva.

International Monetary Fund (I.M.F.). A fund set up by the U.N. as a result of the *Bretton Woods Conference in 1944. It came into operation in 1947, with headquarters in Washington. Its aims are the promotion of international monetary cooperation, the expansion of world trade through the removal of exchange controls and other means, the stabilization of exchange rates, and the making available of funds to enable countries experiencing short-term balance of payments difficulties to maintain their exchange rates. The resources of the Fund come from capital subscriptions by member states. The exact quotas are decided upon at reviews every five years, principally on the basis of the economic importance in international trade of the country. In addition, there are reviews of individual countries' quotas and across-the-board percentage increases in subscriptions, the latter becoming more and more frequent with the progress of world inflation. Voting rights on almost all issues are related to the size of the quota. The quotas are paid 25% in reserve assets (formerly gold) and the balance in the members' own currencies. Countries with balance of payments difficulties may purchase currency from the fund up to a limit of 125% of their quota. For the first 25% of their quota, called the *reserve* (formerly *gold*) *tranche*, no objections are made; for the second 25% advice may be given by the fund but restrictions are minimal; after that the country must accept the Fund's advice on how to correct its disequilibrium. After the reserve tranche, interest charges are imposed on these purchases, and I.M.F. regulations constrain borrowers to buy back their own currency reasonably quickly, usually within three to five years. On the other hand, countries with increased foreign exchange reserves are required to sell them to the Fund for their own currency. When additional resources are required in the very short term, these are acquired through loans from the *Group of Ten (the *Paris Club*). The machinery for these loans was set up under the General Arrangements to Borrow, concluded in the early 1960s and renewed periodically since then. In addition, the introduction of *Special Drawing Rights (S.D.R.s) as an international paper money have further increased the resources of the Fund; since 1972 the standard unit of account in the Fund has been the S.D.R. The Fund has also established a number of drawing facilities to assist primary producers and countries experiencing longer term liquidity problems arising from oil price increases.

The Fund has a broad code of conduct relating to exchange rates, originally centred on the par value (fixed exchange rate) system, but now adapted to a regime of floating exchange rates. Until 1971 members fixed par values for their currencies in terms of gold, with a limited degree of spot flexibility (1% either side of the par value). A country could alter its exchange rate only if it was in fundamental disequilibrium–a situation of chronic (long-term) deficit or surplus on its balance of payments. Devaluations and revaluations of a currency amounting to over 10% required the Fund's approval. Since 1971 most of the world's major currencies have been floating. (Members of the *European Monetary System operate a fixed exchange rate system between themselves, but float against non-members.) A country's exchange rate is "managed" by its central bank, but within rules of good conduct laid down by the Fund.

International Standards Organization (I.S.O.). An organization founded in 1946 and situated in Geneva for establishing international industrial, commercial, and scientific standards. The *British Standards Institution and the *American National Standards Institute Inc. are members.

International Telecommunications Union (I.T.U.). An organization founded ded in 1865 (as the International Telegraphic Union), which changed its title in 1934 and is now an agency of the United Nations. It is situated in the Palais des Nations in Geneva and is concerned with the control of international regulations, use, and development relating to telephone, radio, and telegraph services.

International Trade Organization (I.T.O.). One of the three institutions intended to be the pillars of international economic reconstruction after World War II, the other two being the *International Bank for Reconstruction and Development and the *International Monetary Fund. I.T.O.

was to deal with problems in trade and in the long run bring the world to a more liberal free-trade economy. However, the organization was never created since the founding charter was never ratified by the U.N., the main dissenter being the U.S. Instead, GATT has taken over the purposes of this body, not as an active organization in its own right, but primarily as a forum for multilateral bargaining.

interpolation. The projection of a series of historical data (especially time series data) within consecutive items of the data. For instance, if the country's population had been measured by census every tenth year and one wished to obtain an estimate of it in 1925, then the procedure would be to interpolate between the figures for 1920 and 1930 by making an estimate in line with the trend of the entire historical series; one would not, for example, take the middle figure between the 1920 census and the 1930 census in the above example unless the population was growing in an arithmetic progression. *Compare* extrapolation.

interpreter. *See* programming language.

intervention price. *See* Common Agricultural Policy.

intestacy. The state of an individual's affairs if he has died without having made a will or not having specified in it his wishes as regards part of his property (a *partial intestacy*). When a person dies intestate his nearest relative may then usually apply for *letters of administration, i.e. the High Court's authority to dispose of all the dead person's assets. These must be distributed in accordance with certain strict rules. Under these rules the widow or widower is given a fixed lump sum out of the proceeds of sale of the deceased's property (fairly large if there are no surviving children of the marriage, but smaller if there are such children), plus a life interest in half the remainder of the property. The rest is then divided equally amongst the deceased's children or, if there are none surviving, his parents or, failing them, more remote relatives.

intrinsic value. The innate value of a commodity before it has been processed or manufactured into a marketable form. In economics, a commodity has no innate value, its price being a reflection only of its supply and demand, not of any innate property of the material itself. *See also* free good.

introduction. An offer to the public of a new issue of shares through the London Stock Exchange. The requirements of an introduction are that there should be no large *bargains (relative to the issue) involved in marketing the shares, that there should be a large number of shareholders, and that shares should be made available in which to start a market. Unlike other forms of offer, an introduction avoids the complicated procedure involving an application form and prospectus. *Compare* offer for sale, offer by prospectus, offer for sale by tender, placing, rights issue.

invalued policy. *See* marine insurance.

invariance. One of the desirable properties of statistical *estimators. An estimator is said to be invariant if a *monotonic function of the parameter being estimated can itself be estimated by the same function of the estimator. For instance, the maximum likelihood estimator of a standard deviation (which is the square root of a variance) can be found by taking the square root of the maximum likelihood estimator of the relevant variance. *See also* estimation.

inventory. **1.** A complete list of the stocks of raw materials, components, work-in-progress, and finished goods held by a business. Such a list would show the amount, unit price, and total value of each type of stock held. A formal inventory is made annually by a business concern for accounting purposes but many firms keep a perpetual inventory, on which day-to-day changes are entered, to facilitate *stock control. In the U.S. the term is also used for the stocks themselves, or their value.

The building up (or running down) of inventories (stocks) is called *inventory investment (or disinvestment). When this occurs unintentionally it indicates that sales and production levels are not properly matched. When it is deliberate, the reason is usually related to general economic conditions and it is believed to be a cause of the *trade cycle (national income is determined by changes in stocks as well as sales). When prices are falling the level of stocks will be run down and production is scaled down accordingly; if prices are rising production is stimulated and stocks are increased. As in the case of capital investment, this works through the *accelerator principle: if firms maintain a fixed ratio between sales and their level of stocks, an increase in sales will be reflected in inventory investment; if sales subsequently remain constant, output for the following period will decline because nothing extra is needed to add to stock. Fluctuations in stock are also associated with the prevailing rate of interest, since stocks represent tied-up money. The optimum level of stocks to hold in any given conditions can be determined mathematically by techniques known as *inventory analysis*.

2. An itemized list of the furnishings, fittings, and fixtures of leased furnished property. The items are described and a note of their condition may be given. The inventory is checked when the lease is taken up and checked again on termination of the lease.

inventory and valuation policy. A type of insurance policy that, like a *valued policy, is based on an independent expert's valuation. Such insurances are normally on household goods and personal effects and cover a list of articles drawn up by the insured and a professional valuer, who states the sum to be insured under each item. The main difference between these policies and valued policies is that the sum insured is not necessarily paid in the event of a loss. The sum insured is accepted as the original value at the commencement of the policy, but the amount payable takes into account wear and tear and depreciation.

inventory investment. An increase in the stocks of unsold products. Unintentional inventory investment, which occurs when anticipated sales do not materialize, is often the first indication to a firm that the *boom is ending. *See* inventory.

inventory turnover. *See* stock turnover.

inventory valuation adjustment. An adjustment made to the value of inventories at the end of an accounting period in the calculation of the *gross national product. This adjustment takes into account a change in the value of inventories due to a price change rather than any change in physical quantity.

investment. **1.** Expenditure on productive *capital goods: usually physical capital, such as machinery or plant, although investment in *human capital can be included. Investment may be divided into *net investment and *gross investment; the former is the amount by which the total physical capital stock is increased and the latter is the total spending on physical capital including depreciation. In a Keynesian model, investment is a major source of fluctuation in the economy (*see* trade cycle).

2. The spending of money for purposes other than consumption in order to earn income from it or to realize a capital gain at a later date. In general financial usage, investment includes the purchase of stock-exchange securities, government stock, life assurance policies, etc., or the depositing of money in interest-bearing bank or building-society accounts. The purchase of any asset that is expected to increase in value, for example houses, antiques, or works of art, can be regarded as investment.

investment allowances. *See* capital allowances.

investment analyst. A person professionally employed in the forecasting of share prices. The technique most commonly used in investment analysis is an examination of the present and likely future trading position of a company (or of an entire sector of the stock market, such as banks or the motor component industry) with a view to forecasting its future profits. This forecast will be related to the company's present share price (or the sector's current rating) and the resultant ratio compared to the same ratio for other companies in the sector (or other sectors of the market) and for the market as a whole. On this basis it will be possible to determine whether the company (or the sector) is to be considered cheap (i.e. that its shares should be bought), dear (i.e. that its shares should be sold), or fairly valued (in which case shareholdings should be maintained). Investment analysts may be asked to make a forecast on the probable state of the market in one year, two years, five years, etc. It is naturally easier to develop a forecast on a shorter view; however most *institutional investors build up their holdings on a medium-to-longer view. Investment analysts are employed by large firms of stockbrokers (who compete for institutional clientele) and by major institutional investors, i.e. insurance companies, pension funds, clearing banks, merchant banks, investment trusts, and unit trusts. A minority of investment analysts use *chartist techniques.

investment bank. A bank that specializes in providing finance for industrial companies by buying shares (especially new issues) in the companies, often selling the shares in small lots to investors. The term is widely used in the U.S., but in the U.K. this function is usually fulfilled by *merchant banks. In France, investment banks are called *banques d'affaires. See also* European Investment Bank.

investment club. A group of people interested in making stock-exchange investments on a joint basis. By pooling their resources they are able to make more regular and larger investments than any of them could make individually. They are also able to build up a safer and more profitable portfolio than they could expect to own as individuals. Rules vary from club to club but there are often national asseciations of investment clubs, which offer advice on how to set up and run such groups.

investment grant. A form of investment incentive in which money is paid directly to a firm that undertakes new investment in order to lower its net cost and therefore induce more investment.

investment incentives. A scheme of governmental encouragement and aid to the private sector designed to encourage the increase of *capital stock. These may take the form of tax incentives, such as a *capital allowance, or direct subsidies, such as an *investment grant. The incentives may be applied to certain *development areas only, as a spur to local employment, or more generally, as a fiscal measure to induce a *multiplier effect on national economic activity.

investment income. Income derived from securities held, rather than from trading.

investment portfolio. A list of the investments held by an individual or an institution, such as an insurance company or an investment trust. The investor or investment manager has to decide to what extent he will permit his portfolio to include high-risk securities, and to what extent it will include gilt-edged securities and *blue chip securities. In spreading the risk over the whole portfolio, he will have to take into account whether he requires high income, high growth, or a mixture of both.

investment-saving curve (I.S. curve). A curve drawn through all the points on a graph in which combinations of income and the rate of interest provide a goods market in equilibrium. This occurs when investment (which varies with the rate of interest) equals savings (which vary with the level of income).

As the investment schedule in the first diagram indicates, a higher rate of interest (r) will produce a lower amount of investment (I). For instance, the interest rate r_1 will produce I_1 investment. This amount of investment is plotted on the second diagram, which is an *income-expenditure model. This contains a saving function showing the level of income (Y) needed for savings (S) to equal investment. In this instance it is Y_1. Transferring to the third diagram, the intersection of r_1 and Y_1 is charted and the process is continued until the I.S. curve is constructed.

In this model a fall in r induces a higher level of I, which in turn increases Y through the multiplier process, so increasing S. Equilibrium in the goods market is achieved when an increase in I just generates an increase in Y large enough to produce the exact level of saving needed to match I and vice versa for an increase in r. In more advanced analyses the goods market contains the government and foreign sectors. This does not change the analysis as government expenditure and exports have effects that are similar to investment, while taxation and imports have effects that are similar to saving.

The I.S. curve and the *liquidity-money curve when used together provide the standard tools of macroeconomics: they illustrate the effects of changes in exogenous variables on the endogenous variables. For instance, a change in government expenditure will shift the whole of the I.S. curve because it is an exogenous variable. A shift in the curve of this kind must be distinguished from a movement along the curve induced by a change in the interest rate. For an explanation of I.S. curve shifts see the liquidity-money curve. *See also* I.S.-L.M. analysis.

investment sector. The total set of investment decision-makers in macroeconomic models of the economy. It encompasses all investment in durable capital goods, but excludes investment in securities, bonds, etc., which is part of the *money market. The investment sector is one of the most volatile areas of the macroeconomy and is usually regarded as the immediate source of most *trade cycle fluctuations.

investment trust. The aim of investment trusts is to give the investor of limited means the opportunity of spreading his money over several securities. One kind is a company formed to invest in the shares of other companies or other securities, whose own shares are dealt in on the stock exchange. The other kind is a unit investment trust usually known as a *unit trust, in which the unit-

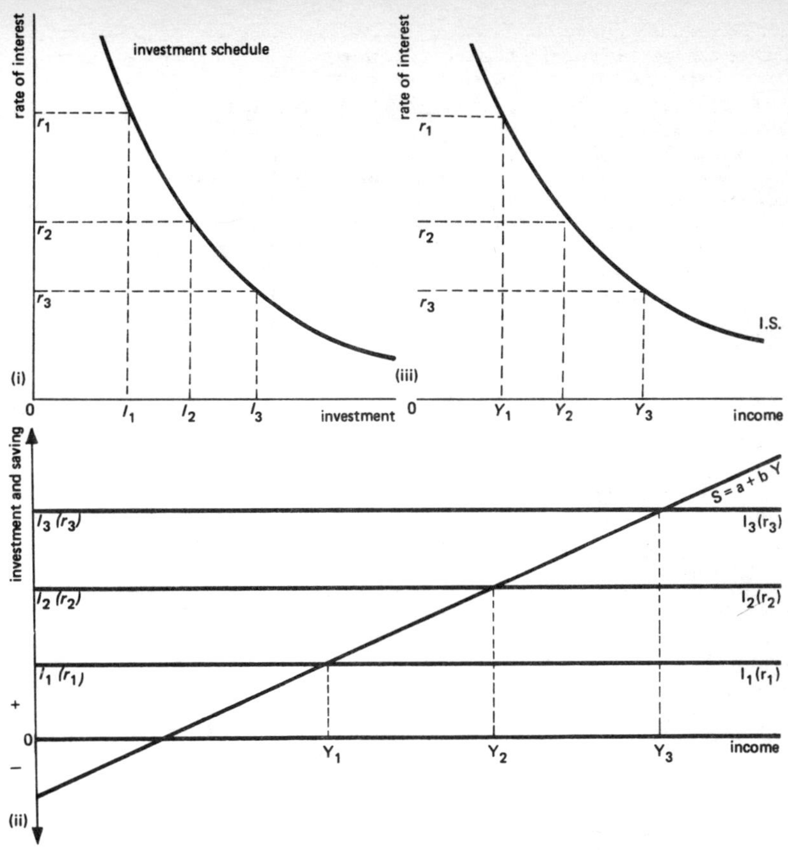

Investment-saving curve

holder is not a shareholder of the investing company.

invisible assets. *See* intangible assets.

invisible balance. *See* invisibles.

invisible hand. A metaphor used by Adam Smith to describe the action of *market forces in bringing the market to equilibrium and equating aggregate supply and aggregate demand. Through its operation the common good could be achieved by each working in his own interests.

invisibles. Payments and receipts accruing from international trade in services as opposed to goods. Examples of invisible items are earnings from shipping, insurance, banking, tourism, aviation, etc. Invisibles also include interest on overseas investments, profits remitted from factories set up by U.K. firms abroad, government expenditure abroad, etc. The *invisible balance* (i.e. balance of payments and receipts from invisibles) in the *balance of payments of a country is important as it can enable the country to run at a deficit on the *balance of trade (visible balance) while keeping a healthy balance of payments. The adverse balance of trade of the U.K. has for a long time been partially or totally offset by a favourable invisible balance.

invitation to treat. A request to a person to enter into negotiations with a view to making an offer, the acceptance of which would form a binding contract. There is a very fine, but legally important, distinction between making an offer and making an invitation to treat. The making of an offer holds one to a binding contract if it is accepted (*see* offers, bids, and quotations) and the making of an invitation to treat does not. The placing of goods in a shop window with a price ticket on them is a mere invitation to treat, and the shopkeeper is not bound to sell them at that price, although he may commit an offence under the Trades Description Act if he does ask a higher price. However, if he states to a particular customer that he will sell the goods for a certain price, then he is making an offer to which he can be held.

invoice. A document supplied by the seller of goods informing the buyer how much he owes, how and when the goods were dispatched, what the payment terms are, and who is responsible for the insurance of the goods while in transit. The invoice will also list the goods bought, giving a commercial description of them, and stating their price. An invoice may be regarded as a demand for payment, but in some cases this function is provided by a statement of account.

invoice discounting. *See* factoring.

I.O.U. A non-negotiable evidence of a debt consisting of a written document beginning with the words "I owe you . . .". It does not require to be stamped unless it includes a promise to pay.

I.R.C. *See* Industrial Reorganization Corporation.

irrational behaviour. Behaviour by a consumer or producer that does not maximize his utility or profit. G.S. Becker has shown that the normal negatively inclined market *demand curve can be derived even if there is widespread irrationality by consumers. *See* rational behaviour.

irredeemable debenture. *See* debenture.

irredeemable security. A security on which there is no date for the redemption of the capital sum. *Consols are an example of irredeemable securities. A characteristic of (fixed-interest) irredeemable securities is that they maintain permanently the exact inverse relation between their prices and the general level of interest rates; in the case of redeemable stocks this relation would become weaker as *redemption date approached. All corporate ordinary shares are irredeemable. Irredeemable securities are often referred to simply as *irredeemables*.

irregular industrial action. Any industrial action, short of a strike, taken by a group of workers in furthering an industrial dispute. The object is to prevent or reduce the production of goods or the provision of services and includes working-to-rule and going slow.

irrevocable documentary acceptance credit. A form of irrevocable and confirmed *letter of credit in which an overseas buyer opens a credit with a bank in the country of the seller. The bank will then issue a letter of credit to the seller guaranteeing to accept bills of exchange drawn on it on presentation of the appropriate shipping documents.

irrevocable letter of credit. *See* letter of credit.

I.S. curve. *See* investment-saving curve.

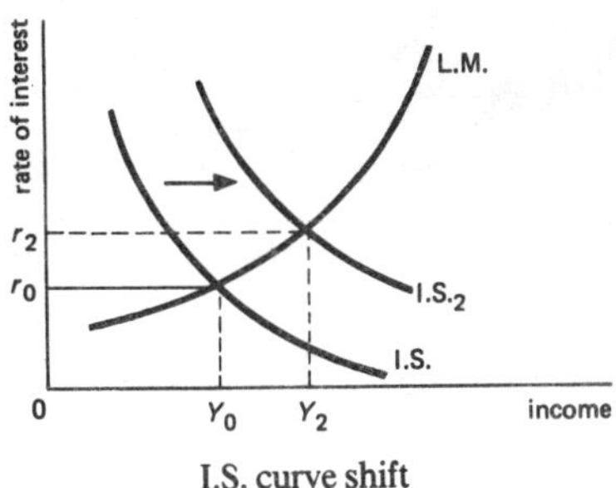

I.S. curve shift

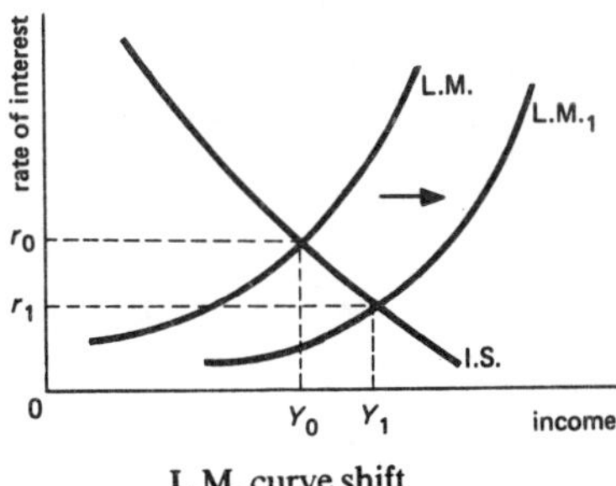

L.M. curve shift

I.S.-L.M. analysis. Analysis involving the manipulation of both the *investment-saving curve and the *liquidity-money curve. This forms the core of modern macroeconomics. The I.S. curve associates income and the rate of interest negatively; the L.M. curve associates them positively. At their point of intersection there is simultaneous equilibrium in the goods and money markets, since each curve charts all the equilibrium points in each of these markets. The intersection determines the equilibrium rate of interest and level of income–any other combination of rates of interest and levels of income would mean that one or both markets would be in disequilibrium. The analysis is used to predict the effect of changes in exogenous variables, such as government expenditure or the money supply, on the endogenous variables (which are the rate of interest and the level of income). For instance, from the first diagram it can be seen that an increase in the quantity of money will shift the L.M. curve to the right, because higher levels of income are needed to return the money market to equilibrium at each rate of interest. This is because the increase in supply must be met by an increase in demand, which is determined in turn by the level of income. This will occur automatically since the increase in the money supply will cause interest rates to fall, thus stimulating investment and income. At the new equilibrium point the rate of interest has fallen from r_0 to r_1, while the equilibrium level of income has risen from Y_0 to Y_1. In the second diagram it is the I.S. curve that has shifted to the right, perhaps because more favourable expectations as to the level of future profits have been created so stimulating investment at all rates of interest. If interest rates remained unchanged the new equilibrium level of income would be greater than Y_2. However, the increased demand for money caused by the upsurge in transactions would force the rate of interest up to r_2, which would in turn limit the increase in income to Y_2.

The addition of assumptions about the aggregate *production function and conditions in the labour market complete the model and allow us to derive predictions. For instance, an increase in the money supply at full employment will create excess demand and raise prices in the same proportion as the initial increase in the money supply; an increase in the level of government expenditure at a time when there is unemployment will raise income, employment and the rate of interest.

Different assumptions about the shape of the I.S. or L.M. curves will give us different models and generate different policy recommendations (*see* classical range, liquidity trap).

I.S.-L.M. analysis is derived from Sir John Hicks's (*b.* 1904) exposition of the work of Keynes.

I.S.O. *See* International Standards Organization.

isocost curve. A line on a graph that shows all the combinations of two different goods that can be bought for the same total expenditure. If the prices of these goods are fixed (i.e. the buyer cannot affect their prices by his purchases) it is a straight line with its slope being equal to the negative of the price ratio between the two goods. In this case, it is exactly equal to the *budget line. However, in some instances the purchases of the buyer can affect price–perhaps through discounts for bulk-buying or by driving the price up through increased demand. The isocost curve will then be distorted over at least part of its range.

iso-outlay curve. A line on a graph that links all combinations of capital and labour that produce a given output at the same cost.

isoproduct curve. *See* isoquant curve.

isoprofit curve. When a firm produces a range of products, the isoprofit curve charts all variations in the output of each product at which total profit is the same. It is assumed that the firm cannot maximize its profit on one product without decreasing its profit elsewhere.

isoquant (isoproduct) curve. The locus of points that link the different combinations of capital and labour that yield the same level of production. Isoquants are usually convex towards the origin to reflect *diminishing returns to each factor, all other factors being held fixed. The isoquant map may be found if the *production function is known, by fixing the output as a parameter to be held constant while inputs are varied. Then the isoquants are seen to represent the contours of the production function surface projected onto the plane of the inputs.

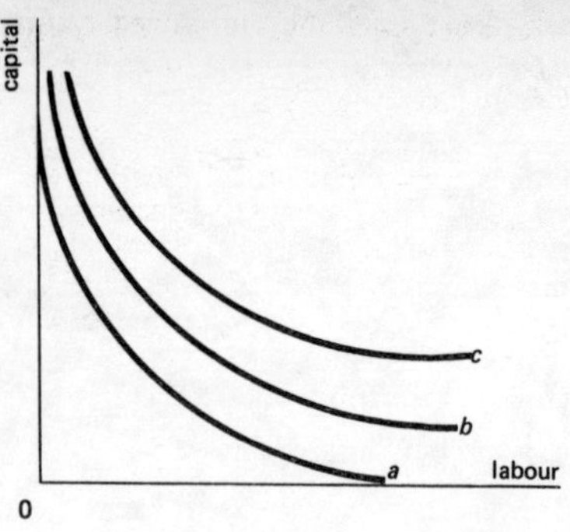

Isoquant

issue. 1. The amount of stock or the number of shares in a company offered to the public at any particular time.

2. The number of bank-notes printed at any particular time. *See also* fiduciary issue.

issue by tender. The process of issuing stocks or shares in which applicants have to put in a tender stating the price at which they would be willing to purchase them. The stocks or shares are then issued to the highest bidders. It is usual for the issuers to state the minimum price that they would be willing to accept.

issued (subscribed) capital. The amount of a company's capital that is issued to shareholders. This may be less than the *authorized capital. The company can at any time issue new capital up to the value of the authorized capital. If it wishes to issue capital in excess of the authorized capital it has to apply to the *Registrar of Companies.

issuing house. An institution that specializes in the business of making new issues of stocks or shares of public limited companies. To enable the company to obtain capital immediately the issuing houses usually take up (*see* underwriting) all the issue or a large part of it and then offer the shares to the public at a higher price. They need to be expert at judging the market otherwise a large part of the issue may be left on their hands.

I.T.O. *See* International Trade Organization.

I.T.U. *See* International Telecommunications Union.

J

J-curve. The shape of a line on a graph that plots the fluctuation in the balance of payments over time after a devaluation of the currency. After devaluation exports will become cheaper and imports will become more expensive. Through inertia, however, the same volume of imports and exports is likely to be bought since people take time to alter their sources of products. Since imports are dearer and exports are cheaper the net initial effect will be a worsening of the balance of payments (the downward stroke of the J). Eventually people will switch from the more expensive products to their cheaper equivalents and the balance of payments will improve (the upward stroke of the J).

jerque. To search a ship to ensure that it contains no cargo that has been omitted from the captain's list or from that submitted to the customs authority. A *jerque note* is the certificate issued by a customs officer stating that he is satisfied that the cargo is in order.

jettisons. Goods or objects deliberately thrown overboard to lighten a ship in order to save it from sinking in a storm or in other dangerous circumstances. When the goods jettisoned form part of an insured cargo they constitute a general average loss (*see* marine insurance).

job analysis. An analysis of the most efficient method of carrying out a particular job, especially with reference to the skills required by the person carrying it out. The object is to increase the efficiency and profitability of a process or to increase the job satisfaction of the employees. This may be achieved by using the results of job analysis to improve the design of the finished product or the manufacturing equipment, to devise better training methods, to assist in *personnel selection, or as an aid to *job evaluation.

jobber. *See* stockjobber.

jobber's turn. The difference between a stockjobber's *bid and *offer prices. Thus, if a share is quoted 250p-260p, the jobber's turn is 10p. *See* stockjobber.

jobbing backwards. Reflecting profitlessly, and usually with some dismay, on past decisions that would have been made differently in the light of subsequent information.

job costing. A method of using *cost units, which is generally used when the cost units are all different and each unit has to be costed separately. For example, a central-heating firm would account for each job undertaken separately, allocating costs where possible to the specific jobs to which these related. This would supply the necessary information as to the *profitability of the various types of jobs.

job evaluation. An assessment of the qualifications and skills required to perform the various jobs in an industrial operation and an evaluation of the relative worth of these jobs. Job evaluation is often used as a basis for wage agreements and differentials.

job-knowledge tests. A test, often used in *personnel selection, to test a person's skill or range of skills in a particular field of activity. In conjunction with *psychological tests they may be used to predict the future performance of an applicant for a job.

joint account. A bank account in the names of two or more persons (often husband and wife) on which all the parties thereto must operate jointly, unless otherwise provided by an authority given to the bank. On the death of one party the benefit of any credit balance passes to the survivor (s) except in the case of partnership, executor, or trustee accounts.

joint and several liability. Where two or more persons have a joint liability to a bank, the bank will insist that they must also be severally liable so that it can then look to each one individually for the total amount of the debt and can have as many rights of action as there are debtors.

joint consultation. Discussions between management and employees to promote understanding, improve relations, and define policy. This is not the same as *collective bargaining, which is concerned with negotiating the terms of employment.

joint (complementary) demand. Demand for two or more goods that are used together. If a change in the demand for one good causes a positive change in the demand for a second good, they are said to be complements. Examples are cars and petrol, knives and forks, and bread and butter. Although the quantity demanded of both goods will move in step with each other, prices may not. If the supply of A can be varied more easily than the supply of B, then an increase in demand will raise the price of B more than that of A.

joint density function. A *density function defining probabilities that two or more random variables will take values (or intervals of values) within their respective ranges.

joint distribution. *See* multivariate distribution.

joint industrial council (Whitley council). A council composed of representatives of the employers and trade unions in an industry. It meets to negotiate wages, conditions of work, means of increasing productivity, etc., and to arbitrate in disputes. These councils were created on the recommendation of the Whitley Committee in 1917. They are mainly found in circumstances in which the government is the employer, such as the civil service.

joint life and last survivor annuities. Annuities providing a higher level of income when both husband and wife are alive, dropping to a half or two thirds on the first death.

Sometimes a husband (as a member of an approved pension scheme) has the option to take a reduced pension for his own and his wife's lifetime, which on his death (if his wife is still alive) will continue to be paid to her for the duration of her lifetime. *See also* annuity.

joint production. *See* joint supply.

joint-stock (commercial) bank. A bank that is a public limited company, thus differing from a private bank, which is a partnership. With the many bank failures and the reduction in the number of private banks during the 1800s, the joint-stock banks opened many more branches and by amalgamations became institutions of great strength commanding massive reserves. They deal with the general public, unlike *merchant banks and many other financial institutions, which are more concerned with trade.

joint-stock company. The original (seventeenth-century) name for the type of business now known as a limited company. A modern limited company has three principal characteristics: the liability of members is limited to the nominal value of their shareholding, the profits are divided between shareholders in proportion to their shareholding, and the company itself exists as a separate legal entity.

The first act of parliament (1720) to control the formation of joint-stock companies followed the debacle of the South Sea Bubble. This act laid down that companies had to be formed by Royal Charter (a *chartered company) or by Act of Parliament (a *statutory company). However, as the number of companies increased during the eighteenth century it became necessary to simplify the formation of such companies and after the act of 1825 it became possible to form a limited company by registration (*registered company), with a *Registrar of Companies to ensure that the formation procedure was adhered to. The vast majority of U.K. companies are now registered companies.

joint supply (production). The situation that exists when an increase or decrease in the production of one good is matched by a similar change in the production of another. Examples of goods in joint supply are wool and mutton and petrol and heavier oils. When there is an increase in demand for one of the goods, production of both will be increased with the result that since the demand for the second has not increased its price will fall.

joint tenants. Two or more persons who have a common interest in the same piece of land, whether *leasehold or *freehold, and who have the right of survivorship. According to this right the surviving joint tenants have the right to take equally between them the share in the property of one of their number who has died, until only one of the joint tenants remains, and he then holds the property absolutely. This distinguishes joint tenants from tenants in common.

joint tenure. A form of partnership, now not widely used, in which the period of the partnership is limited to a defined period.

judgment creditor. A person who holds a court order showing that he is owed money by another person. If the *judgment debtor continues to withhold payment, the judgment creditor may return to the court to ask it to levy execution on the debtor, i.e. send its bailiffs in to seize and sell some of the debtor's goods in order to pay off the debt.

judgment debtor. A person whom a court has ordered to pay money to a *judgment creditor.

judgment summons. The process used to procure the committal of a person against whom judgment has been given for a sum of money.

just price. A concept of the *scholastics of a fair price that reflects society's evaluation of the worth of a given good or service. The formation of the just price was never fully considered, but it was related in time to costs of production duction and individual satisfaction, and may possibly be thought of as a competitive price. The main point is that the just price was conditional on the tastes of the community; it was not an objective valuation of the good. As such it removed the discussion of price from theology into the social sciences. Even if the just price was never strictly defined, it did rule out monopolistic pricing practices by insisting that price charges should reflect the standards of society.

K

k (kB). *See* byte.

kaffirs. A colloquial name sometimes given to South African gold-mining and related shares on the London Stock Exchange.

kangaroos. A colloquial name sometimes given to Australian mining, land, and tobacco shares on the London Stock Exchange.

keelage. A fee that becomes payable when a ship enters and stays in certain ports.

Kennedy Round. A round of multilateral tariff negotiations conducted in the *General Agreement on Tariffs and Trade. It was the sixth of such rounds and by far the most comprehensive. Impetus for it came from President Kennedy's administration, which put the *Trade Expansion Act* through the U.S. Congress in 1962. This act allowed the reduction of tariffs by 50% on all commodities and 100% on those commodities in which the U.S. and the E.E.C. accounted for 80% of the world trade. Provisions were also made for other reductions. This authority was in some cases tied to reciprocity on the part of the E.E.C.

Despite high expectations in the U.S. there was little enthusiasm among the Europeans. Negotiations began in 1964 and were only just completed before the lapse of the special powers of tariff reduction granted by the act. Although significant reductions were obtained, they were not as extensive as those hoped for. *See also* Tokyo Round.

key money. *See* premium (def. 9).

Keynesian analysis. The major contribution of Lord John Maynard Keynes (1883–1946) to economics, described in his *General Theory of Employment, Interest, and Money* (1936), which has had a profound effect on economics (*see* income-expenditure model, liquidity preference). Using Keynes's analysis as a basis, governments have used budgets not only to pursue specific programmes, but also as a means of determining the level of production and hence the level of employment, in the hope of averting a repetition of the Depression. Many believe that the most important innovations in the analysis were the *consumption function and the introduction of the *speculative demand for money. Keynes also introduced the idea of inflexible money wages and prices, which explained the causes of long-term unemployment.

His discovery, the consumption function, showed that a decreasing proportion of income was spent as income increased. This fact, coupled with Walras' law, led through the action of the *multiplier to the possibility that an insufficient level of demand in an economy might cause too low a level of effective demand, allowing an unemployment equilibrium to exist. This can be contrasted with *Say's law, which considered this situation to be logically impossible, and with the flexible-price model of the *neoclassical school, in which there was only a stable equilibrium at full employment. Whether Keynes's unemployment equilibrium is of a long- or a short-run nature is still a matter of debate among economists.

Keynes Plan. A plan put forward by J. M. Keynes in 1943, while working for the U.K. Treasury, for the reorganization of the world monetary system after World War II. He proposed the establishment of a world clearing bank and the creation of an international currency, which he called bancor. Deficits or surpluses in international transactions could be financed by the clearing bank. If the surplus or deficit of a country passed a certain limit, which would depend upon the sum of its exports and imports, then a penalty would be paid by both surplus and deficit countries alike. Thus an incentive towards equilibrium was to be established for both surplus and deficit countries. This move to equilibrium could be accomplished either by managing the economy or the exchange rate or by surplus countries lending capital to deficit countries. Thus a tendency was to be established for a more liquid and balanced world monetary system. In the *Bretton Woods Conference the Keynes Plan was rejected in favour of the more modest proposals for the *I.M.F.

key punch. *See* punched card.

key sector. *See* local loans.

key task analysis. A form of work study in which a key task (one that controls the total time taken for a particular job) is subjected to a detailed analysis in terms of the skill required to perform it, the best way of doing it, and the time taken to carry it out.

key worker. A highly skilled worker who is able to train other employees, install plant or machinery, or form a nucleus around which a labour unit can be built.

kilobyte. *See* byte.

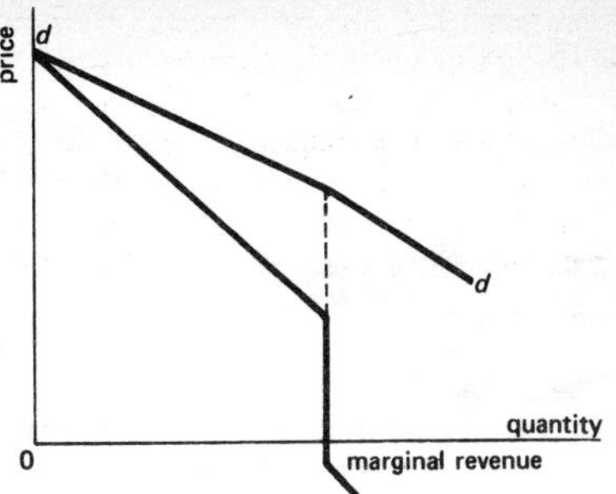

Kinked demand curve

kinked demand curve. The demand curve faced by an oligopolist in a model of oligopoly formulated by P. Sweezy. The demand curve is kinked at some average industry price. Above this price he faces a relatively elastic demand for his output since his fellow oligopolists are reluctant to follow him in a price increase, preferring to pick up the business he loses. Below this price he faces a relatively inelastic section as his fellow oligopolists will follow him in price cuts in order to maintain their market shares. The marginal revenue curve derived from this demand curve has a vertical segment at the quantity at which the kink occurs. This is used to explain the prevalence of administered prices since the price at the kink will be profit-maximizing over a range of variations in the marginal cost along this segment. Marginal cost and marginal revenue could intersect anywhere on the vertical section without affecting the price charged or quantity demanded. The greater the kink in the curve, the greater the range of variations permissible. The weak point in the model when applied to oligopoly is that it does not explain the origin of the kink price, or the mechanism by which price changes. Price leadership is offered as one explanation.

The curve can also occur in international trade where a monopolist in his home market is protected by a tariff barrier. The kink then occurs at the price at which foreign competitors can compete economically in the market.

kite. An *accommodation bill. *Kiteflying* is raising money by such bills.

Kite mark. The symbol used by the *British Standards Institution to indicate that a product complies with its standards. Its use, under licence from the B.S.I., requires agreement to regular inspection and control of the product.

knock-for-knock agreement. A collective agreement between various motor insurers to the effect that if there is damage to a policyholder's motor vehicle then questions of responsibility for the accident will not be pursued, but each insurer will pay for the damage to his own policyholder's motor vehicle, provided such damage is covered by the policy.

krugerrand. A coin containing one ounce of pure gold produced by the Chamber of Mines in the Republic of South Africa and used as a means of buying gold in those countries in which the general public are not permitted to buy bullion but are allowed to buy gold coins. Krugerrands have never been a currency coin and are minted purely as a means of evading restrictions on the purchase of bullion. Since the early 1970s they have been purchased by investors as a hedge against inflation. In the U.K. they are available for purchase from bullion dealers, banks, and stockbrokers; import restrictions were lifted in 1979 when exchange controls were abandoned. *See also* sovereign.

kurtosis. The degree to which a statistical distribution has a high peak around its mode. It is one of the essential characteristics of a distribution, although its application is more limited than that of skewness.

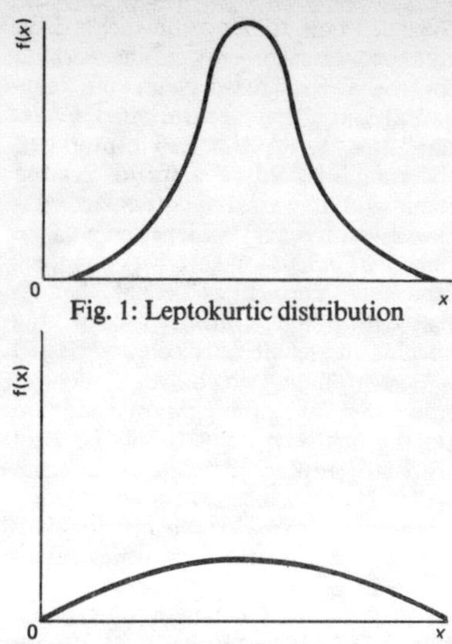

Fig. 1: Leptokurtic distribution

Fig. 2: Platykurtic distribution

Fig. 1 illustrates a *leptokurtic* distribution, or one with a narrow base and a high peak. The distribution of the height of ballet dancers, which is normally set within narrow limits, would have such an appearance. The broad flat-topped distribution in Fig. 2 is said to be *platykurtic*. Kurtosis is measured by a coefficient based on the fourth moment about the mean, and the kurtosis coefficient of distribution is often evaluated by comparing it with the normal distribution, which has a kurtosis coefficient of three.

L

labor union. The U.S. name for a *trade union.

labour. The sum total of human effort that is used in the productive process, whether it is the creation of goods or the provision of services. It includes both the total number of hours worked and the physical strength and skill that is expended in the process. Although there are many diverse forms of labour, it is normally assumed to be a homogeneous input. The entrepreneurial activity is sometimes regarded as a specialized form of labour and sometimes as a completely distinct factor of production. *See also* human capital.

labour-intensive industry or firm. An industry or firm in which a high proportion of the costs are due to labour and a relatively low proportion due to the purchase, maintenance, and amortization of capital equipment. Publishing is a labour-intensive industry, whereas printing is a *capital-intensive industry.

labour market. The market in which the quantity of labour employed and the wage rate per unit of labour are determined. It is made up of many smaller interacting labour markets dealing in different skills at different locations. The demand for labour is indirect, being derived from the demand for the product through the production function. Alfred Marshall (1842–1924) specified four conditions that would determine the demand for labour. The demand for labour would become increasingly inelastic: (i) the more inelastic is the demand for the product; (ii) the smaller is the elasticity of substitution with other factors of production; (iii) the lower labour costs are as a proportion of total costs; (iv) the more inelastic is the supply of labour. These conditions would help to explain why, for instance, airline pilots earn more than shop assistants. The supply of labour depends on the overall rate of population growth, on the distribution of tastes and abilities, on the costs of training for a particular industry, on the differences in earnings, etc. The aggregate labour market is one of the four markets analysed in traditional macroeconomics. It is a vital market in a macroeconomic model, because it is used with an aggregate production function to derive an aggregate supply curve. If money wages rather than real wages determine the quantity of labour, or if *money illusion exists in the labour market, then the possibility of a Keynesian unemployment equilibrium arises.

labour theory of value. The theory that the value of a good equals the sum of the amounts of labour used in its production, either directly or indirectly, so that an absolute value can be attached to any product, independently of any other product. Thus, assuming equal quality of labour, a product that takes two hours to manufacture is twice as valuable as a product that takes one hour to manufacture. David Ricardo (1772–1823) used this theory to explain the determination of prices and this point was developed by Karl Marx (1818–83); prices were presumed to be proportional to embodied labour value. This has several major weaknesses. For instance, workers must receive payment during the process of production, i.e. before the product is sold. These payments (perhaps advanced from a *wages fund) must earn interest charges or else they will not be made and so the value of the product is composed of interest payments as well as payments for labour. Also the use of capital equipment, which contains embodied labour of different ages, poses complex problems. Another difficulty arises when two goods have different *capital–labour ratios; different levels of wages will produce different price ratios between the two goods. But since labour value is constant, relative prices are not in simple proportion to it. *See* Ricardo effect, transformation problem.

laches. A rule of law originating in the courts of equity (*see* beneficial interest) stating that a person forfeits rights when he has delayed more than a reasonable length of time in enforcing them. The rule applies only when the court is being asked to apply to the situation a remedy that originated in the courts of equity (e.g. an injunction or specific performance). Where a remedy originating in the courts of common law is sought (e.g. damages) the fixed time periods laid down by the Statute of Limitations are applied instead (*see* limitation of actions).

The doctrine of laches on the other hand does not prescribe any fixed periods. It is up to the court to decide whether or not the delay has been reasonable in the circumstances.

labour turnover rate. The rate at which employees leave a particular department, employment, or industry. It may be calculated as the ratio of the number of employees leaving to the average number on the payroll, expressed as a percentage.

laesio enormis. (Latin for: extraordinary injury.) A legal doctrine derived from Roman law, and now included in some continental legal systems based on Roman law. It states that the price payable under a contract must be fair and reasonable, otherwise the contract may be rescinded. No such rule exists in English law.

LAFTA. *See* Latin American Free Trade Association.

lagged relationship. A functional relationship between one variable in the current time period and another variable or variables in previous time periods. Thus it might be postulated that current investment expenditures depend on the consumer demand levels of the previous year.

Lagrangian optimization. A mathematical technique for determining the optimal value of an objective function when the independent variables are related with one or more constraints. Primary economic examples are *utility maximization, subject to a budget constraint, and *cost minimization, subject to a production function being satisfied. The Lagrangian multiplier so determined has economic significance, in the former instance as the marginal utility of money and in the latter as the marginal cost. In these cases it acts as a *shadow price.

laissez-faire. (French for: free to act.) The theory that trade and industry is most profitable when left to free enterprise, without state regulation. It is based on the belief that man is motivated by self-interest and that a natural balanced system of production and exchange, of mutual benefit to all, will result if men are not regulated in their economic activity. Adam Smith (1723–90) advocated the withdrawal of trade restrictions imposed by the mercantilists in his day, basing his argument on the principle of laissez-faire. Most economists believed in laissez-faire by the beginning of the nineteenth century but its failings, especially with regard to the great inequality of wealth, the harsh treatment of the workers, and the growth of monopolies, soon became apparent. Consequently in western economies today the state is playing an ever-increasing role; such economies, since they no longer adhere to strict laissez-faire, are termed *mixed economies. *See also* capitalism.

L.A.N. *See* local area network.

land. A natural resource that has no cost of production and without which production is impossible. Land consists of such natural resources as fields, minerals, forests, wild game, the sea, fish, climate, the air, etc., as well as space itself (for building on, etc.). The amount of land is more or less fixed, but it can be switched from less to more profitable uses; fens can be drained for cultivation, farmlands built on, etc. Land is regarded as one of the *factors of production in economics.

land bank. 1. *See* agricultural bank.

2. The amount of land owned by an estate developer that he has in reserve.

land certificate. *See* registered land certificate.

landed. Denoting the price of an export contract in which the exporter pays all freight and insurance costs (*see* c.i.f.) and in addition pays for the cost of landing the goods from the vessel. He does not, however, pay delivery charges to the buyer's factory or warehouse (*see* franco).

landing account. An account sent by a dock warehousing company to the owners of goods that have recently been landed from a vessel. The account shows the quantity and condition of the goods and the date that warehouse rent starts (if the goods are to be stored in the company's warehouse). A landing account is usually accompanied by a weight note.

landlord and tenant. The rights of the landlord and tenant in English law are primarily laid down in the lease itself, but in recent years an enormous amount of legislation has affected these rights, giving the tenant in many cases the right to continue in occupation of the land even after the expiration of the fixed length of time for his occupation laid down in the lease. The most important statutes affecting the relationship of landlord and tenant are the Rent Acts (1968 and 1974) relating to residential property, offices, shops and factories, and the Agricultural Holdings Act (1948) relating to farming land.

land registration. A system by which the title to each particular piece of land in the U.K. is registered and the owner issued with a *registered land certificate. The system has been in force since the last century and has been gradually extended so that it now covers approximately two thirds of the country. From time to time government orders are made designating new areas of compulsory registration, in which transfer of ownership must be registered with the *Land Registry. Thus the system of land registration is gradually being extended.

Land Registry. A U.K. government department, administered under the Lord Chancellor by the Chief Land Registrar, responsible for *land registration. It was set up by the Land Registry Act (1862). The transfer of ownership of registered land is made much simpler, cheaper, and quicker by the work of the Land Registry.

land waiter. A customs officer responsible for examining and sampling goods entering or leaving the U.K. and for ensuring that the correct amount of taxes and duties has been paid.

Laplace criterion. One of the *strategies analysed for its effect on the outcome of game theory situations. The Laplace strategy is the course of action that has at a maximum the sum of the *payoffs for all possible outcomes. The criterion is suitable as a midway strategy between optimism and conservatism and assumes that there is an equal *probability that the opponent will select any of the strategies available to him. *See also* game theory, payoff matrix. *Compare* maximax, minimax regret, maximin.

LASH. A method of cargo handling first operating in the U.K. in 1969, in which barges carrying cargo are lifted onto the ship by a crane on the ship's deck. Very large amounts of cargo can thus be loaded and unloaded quickly, with a minimum requirement for port facilities. LASH is an acronym for *l*ighter *a*board *sh*ip.

Laspeyres index. An index number that uses base period values as weights. Thus a Laspeyres price index is given by the formula:

$$\Sigma_n P_1 Q_0 / \Sigma_n P_0 Q_0,$$

where P_0 and P_1 represent base-year and current-year prices respectively, Q_0 represents base-year volumes, and n is the number of commodities bought. Conversely, the Laspeyres quantity index is given by the formula:

$$\Sigma_n Q_1 P_0 / \Sigma_n Q_0 P_0$$

where Q_1 represents current-year volumes. Laspeyres indices tend to overstate price or volume rises but they have the advantage over Paasche indices in that a series of them can be compared and also in that less information is required to compute such a series. *Compare* Paasche index, Fisher's index.

last in, first out (LIFO). A method of valuing company stock. Generally stock is valued at cost and in certain cases, where the cost of stock items is changing over a period of time, stock of the same type will contain items of different prices. It is necessary to make some assumption about the value of items removed from stock. In this method of valuation it is assumed that the items removed first from stock were the items bought last. *Compare* first in, first out.

lateral integration. *See* horizontal integration.

Latin American Free Trade Association (LAFTA). An organization founded in 1960 with the intention of establishing a free trade area between its members, which were originally Argentina, Brazil, Chile, Mexico, Paraguay, Peru, and Uruguay. It was extended later to include Colombia, Ecuador, Venezuela, and Bolivia. Agreements were later reached in principle to extend this to a Latin American customs union, together with the *Central American Common Market, but nationalism and a tendency to form subregional groupings stood in the way. In 1969 a customs union called the *Andean Pact* was formed consisting of Bolivia, Chile, Colombia, Ecuador, and Peru; in 1981 LAFTA was terminated and replaced by the *Latin American Integration Association.*

law. 1. A rule or a system of rules, especially those by which a country is governed. In England these were originally devised and administered by the King or Queen. These powers gradually became delegated to others: the administration and interpretation of laws to the King's judges, and the making of laws to the representations of the Lords and the common people in Parliament.

The word *law* is also used to distinguish the system of rules used in the sixteenth to nineteenth centuries in the Common Law Courts, which were the King's courts, from the system used in the Chancery Court, controlled by the Chancellor. The latter system is known as *equity*. The two were fused in 1875, and it was decreed that whenever they conflicted, the rules of equity should prevail.

2. A consistent relation between cause and effect deduced from experiment and empirical study.

law of contract. The branch of English law that governs agreements, whether written or oral, between one person and another. The law of contract, together with the law of *tort, forms what is known as the *civil law*, i.e. the law governing judicial proceedings taken by one citizen against another, as opposed to the *criminal law*, in which the state takes action against an individual. Most of the law of contract is derived from the common law, i.e. based on previous decisions of the English courts, many dating back to the seventeenth century or even earlier. However, there are a number of statutes that govern particular aspects of the law of contract, e.g. the *Sale of Goods Act (1893), the Law Reform (Frustrated Contracts) Act and the Misrepresentation Act. The Unfair Contract Terms Act (1977) is also very important and enables terms contained in a written contract which are unfair to the consumer to be struck out or disregarded. Equity also plays a part, especially where the remedy being sought by someone making a claim under a contract is an equitable one, e.g. specific performance.

law of large numbers. The tendency of a group of individuals to show greater uniformity of behaviour than an individual and of such uniformity to increase as the size of the group increases. The law is one of the basic postulates of statistics, which deals with aggregates rather than single individuals.

law of markets. *See* Say's law.

law of proportions. A variation in the proportions in which the factors of production are combined will cause an increase in returns if the change is towards the optimum and a decrease if it is away from it. A variation in the original combination may be made for a number of reasons; for example, a reduction in the costs of machines relative to the cost of labour would encourage more capital-intensive methods.

law of statistical regularity. The tendency of a random sample taken from a larger group to reflect the characteristics of the larger group. Exceptions will occur, as in the case of a population with a few abnormal items, but such irregularities can be discovered by means of comparing different samples or by increasing the sample size. The law of statistical regularity is a central hypothesis of applied statistics.

lay days. The number of days on which a vessel may load or unload in a port without incurring charges. The days may be counted as *running days* (including weekends, etc.), as *working days* (excluding Sundays and public holidays), or as weather working days (days on which the weather permits working to proceed). If the lay days are exceeded the shipowner becomes liable for *demurrage.

lay-off. A situation in which an employer has to suspend or terminate the employment of a number of workers through lack of work. A lay-off may be caused by a strike at a supplier's factory, which results in a shortage of a particular component.

lay-off pay. The U.S. term for redundancy pay.

lead. The first Lloyd's underwriting syndicate to put its name to a risk. Once a large syndicate has acted as a lead by putting its name on the slip, brokers find it easier to persuade smaller syndicates to take a share of the risk.

leads and lags. Advances and delays in the repayment of international debts. If a devaluation is expected, domestic debtors to overseas creditors will hasten (lead) their repayments to avoid a heavier bill when the devaluation occurs. At the same time, overseas debtors will delay (lag) their payments in order to reduce their real value when the devaluation occurs. Both actions will cause a net outflow of currency, which will worsen the balance of payments and perhaps create a self-fulfilling prophecy by causing a devaluation where, in fact, none was intended. An anticipated revaluation will set this process into reverse.

Overseas debtors will lead with their repayments while domestic debtors will lag with them creating a net inflow of currency, which will strengthen the balance of payments and perhaps be the cause of a revaluation. Leads and lags were blamed for aggravating several sterling crises in the 1960s.

learning curve. A graph in which the rate of progress of a trainee learning a particular task is plotted against time. If the task involves manufacturing a single component, the rate of progress can be measured by the number of production units produced in a fixed time. In more complicated set-ups, other means have to be devised for measuring progress. In all cases, however, it is usual for the curve to have an initially high slope indicating a fast rate of learning. Thereafter the curve typically flattens out to form a learning plateau, which in some cases at least represents a period during which learning is consolidated. The curve then rises again until it finally flattens out at the level of the experienced worker.

lease. A contract by which the owner of a building or a piece of land grants to another the right to exclusive possession of that building or land for a fixed time (term) in return for periodic payments of money (rent), thus creating the relationship of *landlord and tenant. It is also the name of the document by which such a grant is made.

If the term is more than three years, the lease must be in the form of a *deed; otherwise it is known as a *tenancy* agreement or an agreement for a lease, the effect of which is, however, almost identical.

It was formerly possible to grant a lease to a person for his life or a perpetual lease, but the Law of Property Act (1925) converted the former into a lease for 99 years, and the latter into a lease for 999 years. It is therefore no longer possible to have anything other than a fixed-term lease. The grant of a lease creates a *leasehold interest* in the particular building or piece of land and this interest, especially if the term of the lease is fairly long, can be bought, sold, and mortgaged. A company must show in its account as a capital asset all its leasehold interests, although it must distinguish between those leases having more than 50 years to run and those having less. Accounts must also show leasehold properties separately from all *freehold land owned.

At the end of the term of the lease, subject to the many statutes that allow a tenant to extend his stay, the tenant must return the land or building to the landlord and must repair or pay the landlord compensation for any damage (*dilapidations*) that has occurred during his tenancy. *See also* landlord and tenant.

lease-back. An operation in which the owner of property sells it to another on condition that the former owner can lease it back for a fixed period of time at a specified rent. In this way *liquid capital can be obtained for other uses.

leasehold land. Land that is occupied by a person as a result of the grant to him of a *lease and for which he pays *ground rent to the owner of the *freehold.

least squares estimation. A method of statistical *estimation of the parameters of a model when the model is put in the form of a regression. A simple two-variable economic hypothesis is that the demand for money is inversely dependent on the average level of interest rates: if this hypothesis was correct we could say that, since monetary demand adds to inflation, high interest rates can be regarded as anti-inflationary. Letting M represent the demand for money and

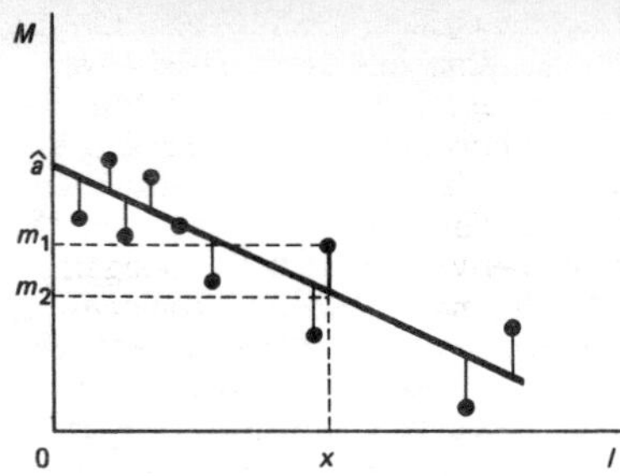

Least squares estimation

I represent the average levels of interest rates, we can write:

$$M = a + bI.$$

Note that least squares estimation requires the regression equation to be of linear form–if the relationship between the variables is thought to be nonlinear, then it must be made linear by some appropriate transformation, such as the logarithmic or reciprocal transformation. The nature of an economic relationship, as represented on a scatter diagram, requires the insertion of a stochastic disturbance. This implies that the actual observed demand for money (however it is measured), written M, will differ in random residual fashion from the level as stipulated in the hypothesis:

$$M = a + bI.$$

The regression parameters a and b are normally written $\hat{a}$ and $\hat{b}$ in the estimation equation to distinguish the model parameters from their estimators. Thus the regression equation to which least squares estimation is to be applied is written:

$$\hat{M} = \hat{a} + \hat{b}I + e,$$

where e is the stochastic disturbance. The principle of least squares estimation is to determine solutions for $\hat{a}$ and $\hat{b}$ by minimizing the sums of the squares of these stochastic disturbances. Least squares estimation can be illustrated diagrammatically.

The estimator $\hat{a}$ is the intercept of the function on the axis of the dependent variable while $\hat{b}$ is the gradient of the function. In the case of an inverse relationship, such as the one postulated here, $\hat{b}$ will be a negative number. Sometimes in the case of a positive relationship, $\hat{a}$ will be zero or negative; this will occur when the function begins at or below the origin. The stochastic terms are represented by the vertical lines between the scatter points and the function. For instance in the diagram, the average level of interest rates is x%, the actual observed demand for money $\hat{M}$ is m_1, while the theoretical demand for money $\hat{M}$ according to our hypothesis is m_2. Clearly, then, the stochastic terms e are simply $\hat{M} - M$, the differences between the actual and theoretical levels of the demand for money corresponding to any average level of interest rates. Least squares estimates of $\hat{a}$ and $\hat{b}$ are then found by minimizing Σe^2–the sum of the squares of the residuals–and then solving for $\hat{a}$ and $\hat{b}$ using the techniques of calculus and, in the case of more than one independent variable, matrix algebra. If the hypothesis were reversed, and it were postulated that the average level of interest rates depends inversely on the demand for money, so that the demand for money became the independent variable and the average level of interest rates the dependent variable:

$$(I = c + dM),$$

then least squares estimation would require the minimization of the sums of the squares of the horizontal distances between the scatter points and the function. The result would be a different fit. Least squares estimators $\hat{a}$ and $\hat{b}$, once calculated, can be tested by reference to the economic theory behind the hypothesis using methods of statistical inference. Least squares estimation is applicable to single linear functions with any number of independent variables and it can be demonstrated mathematically by the Gauss–Markov theorem that, under certain assumptions, least squares estimators are the best statistical estimators. Least squares estimation and its derivatives, such as *indirect least squares, are the most common forms of estimation in econometrics although they are used somewhat less frequently than maximum likelihood estimation in statistics generally. *See also* multiple regression, regression, two-stage least squares, normal equations. *Compare* maximum likelihood estimation, method of moments, Bayesian estimation.

ledger. A book in which accounts are recorded, usually using the methods of *double-entry book-keeping. Depending on the organization of the business, separate accounts will be kept in separate ledgers, e.g. *purchase ledger, *sales ledger, etc. *See* books of account.

legal reserve. The reserve of money that building societies, insurance companies, etc., are obliged by law to keep as security for the benefit of their customers.

legal tender. Money that a creditor is legally bound to accept from his debtor in settlement of the debt. To be legal tender the exact sum of the debt must be tendered. In England, Bank of England notes are legal tender up to any amount, cupro-nickel or silver coins worth more than 10 pence up to £10, coins of not more than 10 pence up to £5, and bronze coins up to 20 pence.

lender of last resort. One of the functions of a *central bank is that it should be willing to lend when the commercial banks are not; it thus becomes a lender of last resort. The Bank of England performs this function, lending to the discount houses when they are "forced into the Bank", against bills deposited as security. To discourage such borrowing it charges a higher rate of interest than the market rate.

Leontief model. An economic model of the economy devised by Wassily Leontief (*b.* 1906) employing an *input–output method of analysis. The method allows for explicit consideration of *intermediate goods and the problems of interindustry dependency. There are two types of Leontief economies: closed and open. In the closed economy there are no unused factors of production and demand for goods is generated internally. Labour is paid a *subsistence wage, in that it is treated as a good produced by fixed household consumption as an input to other processes. There is no joint production. Then the problem is to demonstrate the existence of a positive level of production that generates sufficient output to supply the inputs needed to produce that output. The mathematical assumption necessary for this is the Hawkin–Simons condition, which basically states that the production of any good does not require, directly or indirectly, a higher level of input of itself to produce a given output. For example, less than one gallon of petrol is required to transport, process, and construct the capital equipment necessary for the production of one gallon of petrol. The model may be further extended to yield a competitive price vector, with zero profits, under the same assumption. The model may be made more general by the admittance of nonproduced primary resources and to allow for explicit production and choice of final goods.

less developed country (L.D.C.). *See* developing country.

lessor. The grantor of a *lease. *See* landlord and tenant.

letter of allotment. A document stating the amount of stock or the number of shares that have been allotted to an applicant for a new issue or a *rights issue. *See* application and allotment.

letter of credit. A letter from a banker to his agent abroad or to a foreign bank authorizing the payment of a specified sum or sums to a person named in the letter.

Commercial letters of credit are extensively used as a means of payment in overseas trade. Very often a contract for the sale of goods stipulates that payment shall be by letter of credit. This requires the purchaser to apply to his bank (the credit-issuing bank) to open a letter of credit, negotiable at a bank (the negotiating bank) usually nominated by the seller (the beneficiary), in favour of the seller. On presentation of the documents stipulated in the letter of credit, payment will be made by the negotiating bank to the beneficiary. The stipulated documents usually include the bill of lading, insurance policy, commercial invoice, quality guarantee, weight note, certificate of origin, and licence. Letters of credit have a fixed term and cannot be negotiated after the expiry date although by mutual consent they can be extended.

An *irrevocable letter of credit* is one that cannot be revoked (cancelled) by the purchaser or the issuing bank before the expiry date, without the consent of the beneficiary.

A *confirmed letter of credit* is one in which the negotiating bank guarantees payment to the beneficiary should the issuing bank fail to honour it. The safest form of credit is a confirmed irrevocable letter of credit opened at a first-class bank. Unconfirmed or revocable letters of credit have much less value. A *circular letter of credit* is addressed to all the agents of the issuing bank and a *direct letter of credit* to only one.

letter of hypothecation. A form of authority given to a banker, often in connection with a documentary bill, authorizing him to sell the goods that have been pledged to him, if the bill is dishonoured by nonacceptance or nonpayment.

letter of indemnity. 1. A letter provided by an exporter of goods stating that he will be responsible for any losses arising from faulty packing or shortweight at time of loading. This letter is provided to avoid bills of lading being claused to the effect that the packages were delivered to the ship in a damaged or faulty condition or that the goods did not weigh what they were said to weigh. If the shipping documents are accompanied by a letter of indemnity the shipping company will usually issue a clean bill and thus enable the exporter to receive payment for the goods without difficulty.

2. A letter requesting a company's registrar to issue a replacement share certificate for one that has been lost, the holder indemnifying the company for any loss that might result, and usually it must be countersigned by a bank or insurance company.

letter of indication. A letter issued by a bank to a customer to whom they have also issued a *circular letter of credit. The letter of indication provides a specimen of the customer's signature and has to be produced to the paying bank with the letter of credit. The letter of indication should be carried separately from the letter of credit.

letter of licence. A written offer by creditors to a debtor giving him a certain period to settle his debts before they take court proceedings to enforce payment. This is a type of *deed of arrangement; if properly completed and registered in accordance with the Deeds of Arrangement Act (1914) it is binding on the creditors.

letter of regret. A letter stating that an application for a new issue or a rights issue of stocks or shares has been unsuccessful.

letter of renunciation. A letter in which a shareholder renounces his right to stocks or shares allotted to him. *See* renunciation.

letter of set off. *See* set off.

letters of administration. An order sealed by the High Court authorizing the person to whom it is addressed to deal with and distribute the property of a deceased person who has not appointed anyone to do this in his will. If he had, the person appointed would be known as an executor, and would obtain a very similar order from the High Court known as a *grant of probate.*

The person who is given letters of administration is known as the *administrator* and must either administer the deceased's estate in accordance with the deceased's last will, if he has left one (in which case a copy will have been attached to the letters of administration), or, if no will has been left, in accordance with the rules of *intestacy.

letters patent. The documents that grant a *patent to an inventor.

level of confidence. *See* confidence interval.

level of significance. *See* significance.

level premium. *See* mortality table.

leverage. The U.S. term for *gearing.

liability. Any form of debt. In accountancy, liabilities are divided into *current liabilities and *deferred (long-term) liabilities. A *contingent liability* is one that may arise as a result of some future event. A *secured liability* is a debt against which the borrower has pledged sufficient assets to safeguard the lender against loss. *See also* limited liability, medium-term liabilities.

liability insurance. *See* indemnity.

licence. A document giving a person a right that he would not otherwise have. The term mainly applies to documents issued by a government, such as licences to use radios or television, to keep a dog or a gun, to drive a motor vehicle on a public road, to import or export certain goods, to sell alcoholic liquor or tobacco, or to use public premises for dancing or singing. In the U.K. all these actions are illegal without a licence, but most of these licences can be obtained merely on payment of a prescribed fee. For some, however, applicants must pass tests of competence and responsibility.

The term also extends to documents made by private persons or companies, for example giving others rights to use their land, although such rights must not amount to the giving of exclusive occupation of the land, in which case the document would be known as a *lease. *See also* franchise.

licensed dealer. A stockbroker who is not a member of a stock exchange but who is licensed by the Department of Trade and Industry to buy and sell stocks and shares on his own account as an *outside dealer*. He usually buys a line of shares on the stock exchange and sells them in small lots to private investors.

lien. A right to retain possession of the property of another until liabilities, such as a debt due to the holder of the goods by the owner of them, are satisfied. In addition a banker's lien, which is a special form of general lien, includes a right of sale after reasonable notice has been given.

life assurance. An important branch of insurance, with a large choice of policies available. There are four main types: *term assurance, *whole life assurance, *endowment assurance, and *annuities.

With a policy in which payment is due at the death of the *life assured, assurance companies sometimes require a medical examination. If the life assured was suffering from a serious illness at the time of taking out a policy, unknown to the assurance company, the latter may disclaim liability.

Policies may be *with profits (with higher premiums) or without profits, or they may be *unit-linked or *equity-linked. In the U.K. for life assurance contracts made after 13 March 1984 there is no longer income tax relief on premiums. *Compare* industrial life assurance. *See also* assurance.

life assured. The person whose life is the contingency against which the assurance is effected.

life cycle hypothesis. *See* saving.

LIFO. *See* last in, first out.

lighter. A barge, usually one that is without means of propulsion and has to be drawn by a tug, in which goods are transported within a port or along a river. The charge for transporting goods by lighter is the *lighterage.*

likelihood function. The *joint density function of all the random variables selected in a random sample. This will simply be the product of their individual density functions. Likelihood functions are necessary in the determination of maximum likelihood estimators. *See also* maximum likelihood estimation.

likelihood ratio test. A statistical method for determining the best critical region in the case of a composite hypothesis. The method involves a ratio of two *likelihood functions. *See also* hypothesis testing.

limit. An instruction given by a client to a *stockbroker in respect of the maximum price at which the latter can execute a purchase order or the minimum price at which he can execute a sale order. A time limit for this instruction (e.g. good till cancelled) is also required. An order placed at limit is sometimes called a *limit order* or a *limited order. See also* at limit.

limitation of actions. The barring of a person's legal rights in the courts, if he does not enforce them within a certain time. This applies only where a common law remedy is being sought rather than an equitable one (*see* laches). The time limits only run from the date on which the person becomes aware of the facts that give rise to his right to apply to the courts, or from the date on which his claim was last acknowledged by the person against whom he is claiming.

In the case of a claim for recovery of a debt, part-payment by the debtor will give the creditor a fresh period of time in which to enforce his claim. The time limits are laid down in the Limitation Acts (1939, 1954, and 1963) and vary according to the nature of the claim. Moneylenders only have one year to recover money and the interest on it, while persons claiming damages for breach of contract or for personal injuries in *tort have three years; persons seeking to recover land or other property have twelve years, and persons with most other types of claim have six years.

limited by guarantee. The liability of some professional organizations is limited by the guarantee of the members. This applies to one form of limited liability company as laid down by the Companies Act. *See* company.

limited company. A *company, either private or public, whose shareholders' liability is limited to the amount they have paid for shares (*see* limited liability). Unlimited companies are rare. A company limited by guarantee is often formed by non-profit making organizations to secure the benefits of incorporation and limited liability; the founder members or an executive committee are liable for debts only up to a fixed nominal limit. *See also* joint-stock company, public limited company.

limited letter of credit. A *circular letter of credit that is payable in a limited number of places. No letter of indication is required as the issuing bank circulates a copy of the signature of the payee to its agents in these places.

limited liability. A company arrangement whereby the liability of the owners of the company, the shareholders, is limited to the amount they have subscribed for shares plus any uncalled capital on shares in issue. The liability of a limited company itself, however, is not limited. It is liable for every penny it owes and when it is unable to meet its commitments, it is put into liquidation and its assets divided up among creditors, generally on a pro rata basis. The distinction between a company and its shareholders as separate legal entities was established in the nineteenth century. Without limited liability each person who shares in the ownership of a company is jointly liable for that company's debts to the full extent of his private resources.

limited market. The situation in respect of a particular share that arises when there is difficulty in buying or selling it. For instance, it may be difficult to buy a share because of a large parent holding. The term is usually used in connection with *institutional investors, which deal in large blocks of shares relative to private investors.

limited partner. A person who enters into a *partnership but whose liability for the debts of the partnership is limited to the amount of capital he has invested in it. In a limited partnership there must be at least one full partner with unlimited liability. A limited partner cannot withdraw his capital without the consent of the full partners.

limit-pricing. A policy of restricting prices to discourage the entry of new firms into an industry that can be implemented when *barriers to entry exist in the form of *economies of scale. Limit-pricing occurs when the existing monopolist lowers his price (and increases output) to such an extent that no new entrant could possibly sell enough to cover its large initial costs. This strategy makes the likelihood of competition arising very improbable, but since it permanently lowers the level of profits it is unlikely to be the profit-maximizing strategy. It might be more profitable to maximize profits in the short run and wage periodic price wars to drive out all competitors that have entered the industry. In any case, limit-pricing depends on so many factors: no *product differentiation, no access to funds for the new entrant, no long-term contracts for it, etc., that it should perhaps be regarded as being part of *game theory.

l'impôt unique. *See* physiocratic system.

line. A large quantity of shares (or loan stock) of a particular company available for purchase or sale on a stock exchange. The term is normally used in connection with the dealings of *institutional investors.

line and staff management. A concept of management based on a military model. It consists of two main relationships: the line management being concerned with the main activities of the company (manufacture, retailing, etc.) while the staff management is concerned with essential support services (such as accounting, transport, plant maintenance, etc.) for the line management. The line manager usually forms part of a chain of command, from top executive down the line to junior manager. Staff managers, in a large organization, may have their own hierarchy in their own field of activity, but this line has no direct connection with the main line management.

linear expenditure system. A set of demand curves indicating that the amount spent on each good increases proportionately with income after the subsistence level has been passed (assuming that prices are constant). In this case, the *Engel curve will have a positive uniform slope of 45°, although it will not necessarily pass through the origin. The linear expenditure system is primarily used in empirical work.

linear function. A function in which none of the independent variables are raised to a power greater than one. A simple linear function with only one independent variable can be represented on a graph as a straight line, as:

$$y = a + bx.$$

The coefficients a and b are represented on the graph by the intercept of the function on the y axis and by its slope respectively.

line management. *See* line and staff management.

linear programming. A mathematical technique designed to locate optimum solutions for problems involving *linear functions and constraints. The optimum solution to a linear program is usually one of maximization of profit or minimization of cost. For example, if an industrial firm produces two products with different profit margins (the two products require for their unit production different amounts of labour input, of machine input, and of storage space, the more profitable of the two products being more expensive in at least one input), what is the firm's optimum (i.e. most profitable) output mix, given that the firm's resources permit only of a certain maximum amount of labour, a maximum amount of machine time, and a maximum amount of storage space? The constraints are an essential feature of the problem, otherwise the firm's optimum output would involve infinitely large quantities. Linear programs are frequently used by economists, statisticians, and industrial analysts.

linear regression. *Regression carried out on the basis of a linear function.

line printer. A device for printing the output of a computer one line at a time, rather than character by character. Line printers can print up to 3000 lines per minute.

liner. A ship operating on a scheduled service between fixed points, carrying either cargo or passengers. *Shipping conferences fix freight rates for liners operating on particular routes. Cargo carried on liners is usually assorted and tends to consist of part-processed or finished goods. Bulk cargo is sometimes carried as "bottom cargo" (in the bottom of the hold) but is usually in bags. *Compare* tramp.

liquid assets (liquid capital). Assets that have a fixed monetary value and can easily be converted into money at that value. Money is the most obvious liquid asset. Bank current account deposits are another example. Liquid assets are thought to be a possible determinant of consumption. *See also* liquidity.

liquidated damages. The damages that a party to a contract agrees to pay as compensation if he fails to fulfil his obligations under the contract. Liquidated damages are estimated and agreed at the time the contract is signed; they are not related to the actual loss sustained by the breach. *See also* penalty clause.

liquidation (winding-up). The termination of a company when it has completed the business for which it was created, when the members of the company decide to withdraw from business (*see* members' voluntary liquidation), or when the company is unable to meet its obligations (*see* creditors' voluntary liquidation).

A liquidator of the company will be appointed who will take charge of all the assets of the company and dispose of them in an orderly manner, obtaining the best prices he can and using the proceeds to repay the creditors of the company in a manner defined by law, any surplus at the end being repaid to the members. A company may be wound up by a court if it has passed a special resolution to this effect, if it defaults in delivering the *statutory report to the registrar or in holding the *statutory meeting, if the company does not commence business within a year from incorporation or suspends business for a year, if the number of members is reduced below the statutory minimum, if the company is unable to pay its debts, or if the court is of the opinion that it is just and equitable that the company should be wound up. *See also* Official Receiver.

liquidator. A person appointed to take over the control of a company that is to be wound up and to realize its assets and distribute the funds so realized to the creditors of the company, normally in a well-defined sequence, with any balance remaining being distributed among the members of the company. A liquidator can be appointed either by the members of a company, the creditors of the company (if it appears that the company is not going to meet its debts), or by the court. *See also* Official Receiver.

liquid capital. *See* liquid assets.

liquidity. The proportion of assets held in a liquid form (*see* liquid assets). For example, a firm is said to be highly liquid if it has a large proportion of liquid assets.

Banks must maintain a definite ratio between the total of the deposits made with them (their liabilities to their customers) and the amount of their liquid assets (cash, *money at call or short notice, and bills discounted). The most remunerative item for a bank is money lent to customers, but this is the least liquid asset, so that when money is lent the proportion of easily realizable assets has to be maintained to meet any increase in the demand for cash. The present liquidity ratio maintained by British banks is 28%. *See also* cash ratio.

liquidity-money curve (L.M. curve). A curve joining all combinations of income and the rate of interest at which the money market is in equilibrium. The supply of money is determined by the interaction of the government, the Bank of England, and the banking system. In the first diagram this is completely fixed. The curves that cut the vertical line representing the money supply are demand for money schedules at various levels of income. It can be seen that the demand for money is positively related to the level of income, since the curves move outwards from the origin; and inversely related to the prevailing rate of interest as shown by their negative slopes (when the interest rate increases, the opportunity cost of holding ready money rather than interest-bearing securities also increases and the demand for money declines). Since the quantity of money is fixed in this case, the rate of interest must adjust to bring the money market back into equilibrium. At a level of income Y_1, the equilibrium interest rate is r_1, at Y_2 it is r_2, and so on. The L.M. curve is derived by plotting

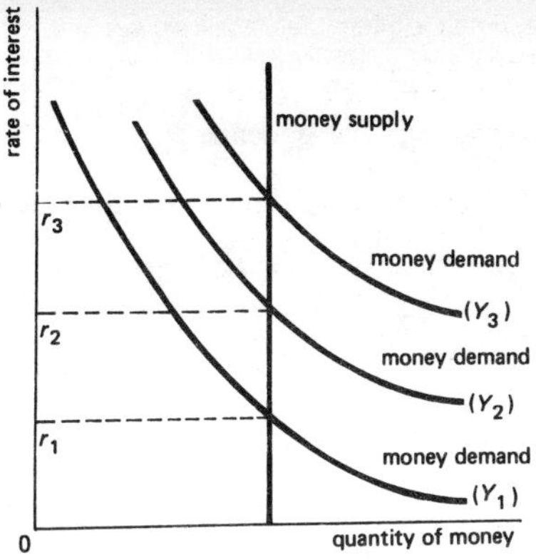

Money market

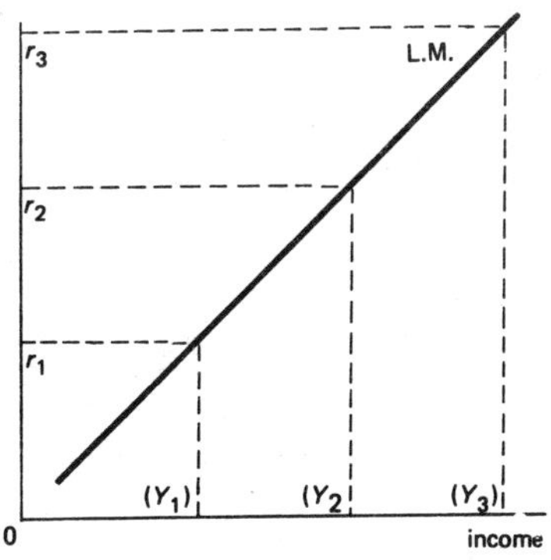

L.M. curve

these points on to the second diagram. As a higher level of income is associated with a higher rate of interest, the L.M. curve slopes upwards.

The money market is essential to Keynes's analysis of macroeconomics. He believed that there was a possibility that the L.M. curve could become perfectly interest-elastic at low income levels so that the rate of interest would remain at too high a level to ensure full employment (*see* liquidity trap). Combined with the *I.S. curve we get *I.S.-L.M. analysis, the standard tool of macroeconomics. It is different assumptions about conditions in the money market that give different predictions of the effectiveness of monetary policy. An extreme Keynesian, who believes that the L.M. curve is perfectly horizontal, would deny any use for monetary policy at this point because of the liquidity trap. An extreme monetarist, who believes that the L.M. curve is perfectly vertical, would deny any use for fiscal policy in manipulating interest rates at this point. *See* classical range.

liquidity preference. The desire to hold liquid money as opposed to investing it. It is a concept originated by Keynes to explain the demand for money. Three important components of the liquidity preference of the private sector can be differentiated–the *transactions demand for money, the *speculative demand, and the *precautionary demand. Of these, the precautionary demand is quantitively insignificant relative to the other two. Transactions demand depends upon the level of national income and the price level. The total relationship is often expressed in terms of the demand for real cash balances, which is a function of the level of the real national income and the real rate of interest. So:

$$M/p = f(Y,r),$$

where M is the stock of money, p is the price level, Y is real national income, and r is the rate of interest. It is generally accepted that this equation determines the rate of interest, at least in the short run. Changes in the money stock will cause a change in the rate of interest necessary to maintain the equality. In conditions of full employment, changes in the money stock may be reflected also by some change in the price level, but the price level would not be expected to take up the whole effect. There has been considerable empirical work on estimating liquidity preference functions of the above form, using post-war data, but none have been very successful.

liquidity trap. A situation in the economy that arises when the rate of interest is so low that *liquidity preference is high enough for investors to prefer holding cash to bonds. The rate of interest will not fall below this level (between 2% and 4% according to Keynes) as people already want to hold as much cash as possible. Indeed, the interest rate is so low that everyone expects it to rise in the near future. Therefore the price of bonds, which is inversely related to the interest rate, is bound to fall so that if bonds are held capital losses could be expected. At this level liquidity preference is infinitely elastic, shown on a graph as a horizontal *L.M. curve. Monetary policy is ineffective in changing the rate of interest or level of income, since increasing the supply of money will not reduce interest rates below this already low level, thus stimulating investment, but will result in more money being held as cash. However, although very plausible this phenomenon has never been definitely proved to have existed, even in the Depression.

liquid (acid-test) ratio. The ratio of current assets less stock and work-in-progress to current liabilities. This ratio gives a better indication of a company's health than the *current ratio, because it does not rely on the value of stocks or work-in-progress that may be unsaleable.

listed company. *See* quoted company.

listed security. A security quoted by a stock exchange and thus available for trading on that exchange. *Compare* unlisted securities.

list price. The price of a product to the consumer, without any discount. For example, in a recession car dealers may be willing to sell new cars below list price in order to attract business. When a wholesaler quotes the list price to a retailer it is usually understood that the price is subject to the usual trade discount.

list renting. *See* direct selling.

lists closed. Application lists for new issues of shares to the public on the London Stock Exchange are open for a specified time only; *lists closed* is the term used when this time expires or when the offer is fully subscribed. For a popular issue, the lists may be open for as little as a minute.

livery companies. The medieval guilds of the City of London are sometimes called livery companies on account of the elaborate dress worn by their members on ceremonial occasions. Although in the main they no longer perform useful functions in their individual crafts, they remain influential City institutions with fine banqueting halls. Apart from their ceremonial and social activities, many of them are involved in education: some were responsible for founding well-known public schools (such as the Haberdashers and the Merchant Taylors) while others administer the funds of public schools on behalf of the founder. For example, when Dean John Colet founded St. Pauls School in 1509, he entrusted the financial endowment of the school to the Mercers' Company, who still administer it. In 1878, the livery companies joined with the Corporation of London in forming the City and Guilds of London Institute to promote education in technical subjects.

livestock and bloodstock insurance. The insurance chiefly of horses or cattle, under which the market value of the animal is paid up to the sum insured in the event of death during the period of insurance from accident, sickness, or disease occurring or contracted within such a period. Usually death from lightning or fire is also included.

Lloyd's. A London association of underwriters best known for marine insurance although all kinds of insurance are undertaken. It originated as a group of underwriters who met in a London coffee house under the proprietorship of Edward Lloyd in the seventeenth century. In 1871 Lloyd's was incorporated by Act of Parliament. As a corporation Lloyd's does not underwrite insurance business. This is all transacted by the individual underwriting syndicates (*see* Lloyd's underwriter). *Lloyd's List and Shipping Gazette* is a publication of shipping news for marine insurance purposes (Edward Lloyd published similar information for his customers in a publication called *Lloyd's News*).

There are *Lloyd's agents* in almost all the world's important ports.

Lloyd's broker. An insurance broker who is a member or subscriber of *Lloyd's and is empowered to obtain business for Lloyd's underwriters. He is the only channel through which the public can insure with Lloyd's. There are over 200 Lloyd's brokers.

Lloyd's Register of Shipping. A society formed by *Lloyd's to inspect and classify ocean-going vessels of 100 tons or more. The society produces annually the *Lloyd's Register of British and Foreign Shipping*, which lists details of virtually all the world's ships. Ships are given periodic surveys by Lloyd's surveyors—those achieving the highest classification are known as "A1 at Lloyd's", the letter indicating the condition of the hull and the number the condition of the trappings.

Lloyd's underwriter. An individual transacting insurance on his own behalf as a member of Lloyd's. Lloyd's itself is a corporation, but it merely provides facilities for its members to transact business and is in no way responsible for liabilities incurred by the underwriters, who must deposit a substantial sum of money in order to become Lloyd's underwriters. The public are not permitted to deal direct with Lloyd's underwriters, but only through a Lloyd's broker. There are over 6000 underwriting members. Because of the large numbers and the complexity and size of present-day insurance transactions, members are organized into syndicates, consisting of from just a few to a few hundred members: syndicates share the risks incurred, accepting unlimited liability. Each *name on a syndicate is directly responsible to the policy-holder to an extent represented by his share of the risk.

L.M. curve. *See* liquidity-money curve.

load line. The line running round a ship above which the ship must not be immersed. It prevents overloading of the ship and was introduced by Samuel Plimsoll M.P. in 1876; it is therefore sometimes known as the *Plimsoll line.* The load line includes a number of marks showing the depth to which the ship may be safely loaded in a variety of seasons and salinities.

loanable funds theory. The theory that the rate of interest is determined by the demand for and supply of funds available for lending. Loanable funds are required for investment and for the enlargement of cash holdings (hoarding), while the supply of loanable funds is composed of personal and business savings as well as of bank credit. This theory was developed in detail by Knut Wicksell (1851–1926) and the *neoclassical school.

loan account. If a banker agrees to lend to a customer by way of a loan instead of by way of an *overdraft, then the full amount of the agreed borrowing is at once debited to a separate loan account and credited to the customer's current account. *Interest is then charged on the full amount of the loan. *See also* bank advance.

loan capital. The part of a company's capital that does not form part of its *share capital and earns a fixed rate of interest rather than a share of the profit. It is usually secured by mortgage on the company's property or by a guarantee. Loan capital is often raised by *debenture.

Loan Guarantee Scheme. A scheme introduced by the British government in 1981, in collaboration with 30 banks and lending institutions, to assist in the expansion of small businesses. Under the scheme the government is prepared to guarantee up to 70% of approved loans to small businesses provided that the lending bank will underwrite the balance.

loan stock. *See* debenture.

local area network (L.A.N.). An arrangement in which several computers in the same building can share resources (storage devices, output devices, input devices) and communicate with one another.

Local Employment Acts. A series of U.K. acts of parliament (1960, 1970, 1972) providing for a system of grants and loans to companies providing employment in areas in which there is high unemployment.

local loans. Borrowing undertaken by U.K. local authorities for financing such capital expenditure as the acquisition of land, erection of buildings, etc. For capital expenditure in the *key sector*, which includes such services as education, housing, and principal roads, local authorities may borrow only in respect of specific approvals granted by the appropriate government department. For the *locally determined sector*, which includes such services as libraries, parks, swimming baths, and council offices, a block loan sanction is allocated annually to each local authority, which is then free to decide which projects to undertake and what sums to borrow within the permitted amount. Local authorities may issue long-term loans by means of private mortgages, by issuing stock on the Stock Exchange, and by bonds that may or may not be quoted on the Stock Exchange. Authorities also have access to the *Public Works Loan Board, the rates of interest of which are fixed by the Treasury. Loans may be repaid in yearly or half-yearly instalments or in a lump sum at the end of the period.

location of industry. The factors influencing the location of industry can be divided into the following categories: natural, economic, social, and political. The natural factors are geographical and geological: these would apply mainly to extractive and processing industries, or those requiring special facilities, such as proximity to a port or other transport facilities. The economic factors include transport costs, labour costs and the type of available labour, proximity to cheap power, and external economies (local infrastructure, complementary industries, etc.). The social factors would include the amenities of the area under consideration, the prestige of certain regions (particularly a capital city), and industrial inertia (unwillingness to move once established in a particular region). In the political category, government regional policy and defence considerations would have to be taken into account.

Before World War I one of the major locating factors, particularly for heavy industry, was nearness to a coalfield and nearness to a supply of raw materials. However, since then the increasing use of other forms of power has freed industry from the need for access to nearby coal and improved transport, especially the road network, has reduced the need to be near to raw materials. As the proportion of light industry has grown, requiring few specific localized needs, industry has in general become much less tied to specific areas and proximity to markets is now probably the principal locational influence for most industries.

The expression *planned location of industry* was used in the Beveridge Report (1944) to denote a government policy of diversifying industry in each area, to reduce the consequences of changes of demand causing heavy *structural unemployment in the areas of traditional localized industry. It also included the policy of checking the concentration of new industries in the southeast of the U.K. In 1945, certain areas of highly localized traditional industries were designated Development Areas, into which new industry was encouraged to move. Various investment grants and other financial incentives have been in operation to attract industry to these areas. The *Regional Economic Planning Councils were established to help reduce the imbalance in industrial structure and the *Location of Offices Bureau provides help and encouragement to firms with offices in London to relocate in the provinces or at least outside the London area. The new towns have been built to rehouse overspill population from London and the other conurbations and to provide premises and amenities for light industry.

Many theoretical models of location have been constructed, some of them based principally on the models of Von Thünen and Weber, who concentrated on finding the least-cost location for economic activity (agriculture in the case of Von Thünen's model and industry in the case of Weber's).

Location of Offices Bureau. A U.K. government bureau, set up in 1963, to encourage firms to move out of central London. The bureau provides advice on suitable locations, directing some firms to the suburbs and others to different parts of the country.

location quotient. A measure of the extent to which a particular economic activity is represented in a particular region, given as a percentage of the degree to which it is represented in the national economy. If the quotient is over 100, there is some degree of specialization in that region in that activity. It is usually calculated using employment figures.

loco. Denoting the price of goods at a specified place, often an exporter's warehouse. If a contract is based on a loco price, the buyer has to pay all the charges of transporting and shipping the goods to his own factory or warehouse.

lock-out. Industrial action in which employers refuse employees access to their place of work unless they agree to accept the terms laid down by the employers.

lock-up. An investment that is expected to prove profitable in the long term rather than the short term. The capital is thus "locked-up" in the investment for a considerable period.

locus poenitentiae. (Latin for: an opportunity to repent.) The doctrine that an illegal contract, which would otherwise be void, can be saved if the parties change their minds and decide not to carry out the illegal purpose.

logarithmic (ratio) chart. A graph on which the scales of the axes are obtained by plotting the logarithms of the variables. The effect is to render equal intervals on the axes equivalent to equal percentage changes (not equal absolute changes) so that a linear function represents continuous compound growth. Logarithmic charts are suitable when there are abnormally high and low items, when it is desired to examine relative movements rather than absolute movements, or when the series increases more or less in geometric progression. The axes of a logarithmic chart start at one; it is not possible to show zero and negative values.

logarithmic function. A function of the form:

$$y = \log bx.$$

Logarithmic functions are monotonic and are closely related to exponential functions.

logistic curve. *See* growth curve.

logistics. *See* marketing logistics.

Lomé Convention. An agreement signed in 1975 in Lomé, the capital of Togo, between the E.E.C. and 46 African, Caribbean, and Pacific developing countries; it was enlarged in 1979, when there were 60 developing countries involved. Its aim was to provide aid by removing customs duties (on a non-reciprocal basis) on most of their imports to the E.E.C., directing funds to the Lomé countries through the setting up of the *European Development Fund*, and to give technical assistance.

London Chamber of Commerce. The largest *chamber of commerce in the U.K.; situated in the City, it provides the usual services for business, trade, and industry. In addition, it provides secretarial and administrative staff and facilities for a number of trade associations and acts as an examining board in commercial and business subjects.

London Commodity Exchange. A *commodity market in the City of London situated, since 1973, in Corn Exchange Building, Mark Lane. The area of the City around Mincing Lane and Mark Lane has been a centre for commodity trading since the tenth century, a formal market being established in 1811 in the London Commercial Sale Rooms in Mincing Lane. After the destruction, in World War II, of the building in which this market was housed, the London Commodity Exchange was established in Plantation House, Mincing Lane, in 1954, where it remained until 1973.

The commodities dealt in include sugar, coffee, cocoa, rubber, soya bean meal, vegetable oil, and wool. For each of these commodities the London Commodity Exchange is responsible for the leading world *futures (terminal) market, providing hedging facilities and an indication of world values for up to 15 months ahead. Trading in most of these commodities for futures is by *call over on the floor of the Exchange at regular times during the day. For most commodities there is also a spot market in which goods are bought and sold for immediate delivery. In some commodities a shipment market, based on a standard c.i.f. contract, is also provided on the floor of the Exchange.

London Metal Exchange (L.M.E.). An exchange in which dealings are carried out in the metals copper, tin, zinc, lead, and silver. These commodities are the most important nonferrous metals used by U.K. manufacturing industry and since they are not mined in the U.K. (the only internal supply being scrap) their price movements on the L.M.E. are an important determinant of industrial costs. Dealings on the L.M.E. are mainly in futures. The exchange was founded in 1881.

London School of Economics and Political Science (L.S.E.). A school of the University of London that is mainly concerned with the teaching of the social sciences. The school has steadily expanded since its foundation in 1894 by Sidney Webb. Its library, the British Library of Political and Economic Science, is one of the finest social science collections in the world.

London Stock Exchange. The London Stock Exchange was founded in 1773, having developed slowly during the years prior to that date from informal transactions between merchants in the City of London's coffee houses. The present Stock Exchange has a professional membership of some 3500, who alone may deal and who are divided into a declining number of stockbroking and stockjobbing firms. The Stock Exchange is governed by a Council of some 46 elected members plus the government broker, who is a non-voting member. The Council regulates procedures with a view to safeguarding the interests of both members and public. In terms of *equity capitalization the London Stock Exchange is now the third largest in the world after New York and Tokyo, although dealings in government and local authority stocks are considerably greater in London than on any other exchange in the world. About 7000 securities are listed. In March 1973 the amalgamation of the London Stock Exchange and the provincial exchanges took place. *See also* stockbroker, stockjobber, account.

long-dated gilt. *See* gilt-edged security.

long end of the market. The section of the stock market for *fixed-interest securities that is concerned with transactions in long-dated issues.

long position. A *position in which a security or commodity is held in excess of amounts contracted for delivery. A dealer with a long position is a *bull speculator. He expects the price of his stock or commodity to rise thus enabling him to make a gain. *Compare* short selling.

long run (long period). A period of time that is sufficiently long for all the factors of production to be varied, enabling the most efficient combination of factors to be chosen. Its importance is that it corresponds to the situation facing a newly created firm that can select the optimum combination of factors, i.e. all the factors are variable. Once it has made its choice some of these factors will be fixed and its decisions must then be carried out in the *short run.

longs. A term used on the London Stock Exchange with reference to fixed-interest securities, mainly gilt-edged securities, with redemption dates more than 15 years into the future. *Compare* mediums, shorts.

long-term capital. **1.** The liabilities of a company that may run for a long period before they have to be repaid. It is usually assumed that they are used for financing long-term capital projects. Long-term capital is usually provided by institutions, such as commercial or merchant banks.

2. International capital flows that finance investment in plant and machinery. They are provided by companies from abroad and the investment can be sold at any time. It can be argued that it is not worthwhile distinguishing between short- and long-term capital flows in international economics: the same criticism also applies at the level of the firm. The essence of the definition is in the length of the commitment entered into, but in practice the length of the commitment can often be negotiated and altered.

long-term debt. Long-term loans and debentures, i.e. long-term sources of finance other than equity.

long-term liability. A loan that does not have to be repaid within three years. In an accounting context, it is sometimes taken as a loan that does not have to be repaid in the current accounting period. *See also* liability.

long ton. *See* ton.

Lorenz curve. A curve showing the spread in the ownership of economic variables. The cumulative percentage of the variable is plotted as an ordinate against the cumulative frequency distribution of the owners. For instance, a Lorenz curve for wealth distribution could be constructed if it were known that the wealthiest 10% of the population owned 50% of the nation's wealth, the top 20% owned 70% of it, the top 30% owned 80% of it, etc. The Lorenz curve for wealth distribution for a country that had an exactly equal distribution would be a straight line through the origin at an angle of 45%. The amount of curvature of a Lorenz curve thus indicates the degree of inequality while its form (i.e. whether it is concave or convex from below) indicates whether the skewness of the distribution is positive or negative. A Lorenz curve is interesting not only for its total shape but also for the difference in the gradients of its different segments. Applications of the Lorenz curve other than wealth distribution include income distribution and the size distribution of firms.

loss adjuster. A professional who negotiates the settlement of insurance claims between the insurer and the policyholder on behalf of the insurance company.

loss leader. A product or service sold at a loss in order to attract customers to buy other products that are expected to make a substantial profit. A supermarket, for example, may offer one product at less than cost price in order to attract customers into the store. This practice is illegal in the U.K. under the Resale Prices Act (1976). However, it is a common practice for retail stores to offer certain products at a reduced profit in order to attract customers.

loss-of-profit policies. *See* consequential loss policies.

loss ratio. The total of all the premiums paid to an insurance company divided by the total of the money paid out in claims.

L.S.E. *See* London School of Economics and Political Science.

Ltd. Abbrev. for limited. All private *limited companies must include the word limited in their title; public companies now include *p.l.c.

Luddites. The bands of workers who, during the period 1811-16, smashed industrial machinery in the belief that it was causing unemployment. The word comes from the name of a workman, Ned Ludd, who smashed an industrial machine in a temper in Leicester at the end of the eighteenth century.

lump sum. **1.** A sum of money paid on retirement in addition to a pension under some contributory pension schemes.

2. A sum of money paid to a dependant (or dependants) on the death of an insured person in place of a pension or annuity.

3. A sum of money paid for freight, irrespective of the quantity of the cargo.

lump-sum tax. Any tax that is a fixed amount and so does not vary with the amount or size of the factor being taxed. A lump-sum tax that is levied on a firm will increase its *fixed costs, but will leave its marginal costs unaffected. Therefore, the profit-maximizing level of production will remain unchanged in the short run, since it is determined by marginal cost and marginal revenue. This is still the optimum level of output although profits have been reduced.

In the long run, prices and output may be affected depending upon the state of the industry. If the industry is an absolute monopoly output and the price charged will remain unchanged. The monopolist cannot pass the tax on to the consumers or he would have done so already in order to maximize profits. An exception would be if the tax is so large that it reduces his profit to nil in which case he ceases production. A second exception could occur if a monopolist had not maximized his profits previously for fear of encouraging firms to enter the industry (*see* limit-pricing). After the imposition of the tax it might increase price (and reduce output) to preserve the same level of profits. In that case the consumer would bear the cost of the tax. The situation is different in a perfectly competitive industry in which profits have already reached a minimum. The imposition of the tax would cause losses to be suffered and the industry would contract as firms left the industry. Eventually the number of firms would be few enough for collusion to take place and the price would rise until firms were again covering costs. Thus in this case the consumers bear the tax. *See also* incidence of taxation.

lump system. A system of employment in which workers, especially in the building industry, are paid a daiiy lump sum or a lump sum for an agreed amount of work. In the U.K. this form of employment is frowned upon as it enables workers to avoid taxation.

luncheon vouchers (L.V.s). Vouchers given to employees by some employers who do not provide canteen facilities. The vouchers may be used towards the cost of meals in many restaurants but may not be exchanged for cash. Certain specialist firms supply the L.V.s to the employers at cost plus a small commission, later redeeming them from the restaurants at a small discount. The discount and the commission together provide for the expenses and profit of the specialist firm.

Lutine bell. The bell taken from the vessel *Lutine*, which sank in the North Sea in 1799 with a cargo of bullion. The bell now hangs in the underwriting room at *Lloyd's and is rung on rare occasions before important announcements are made–once for bad news and twice for good news.

luxury good. A good on which an increasing proportion of income is spent as income increases; its *income elasticity of demand is greater than one. Examples are holidays and *consumer durables. *Compare* Giffen good, necessary good, normal good.

M

M_0 A very basic measure of the U.K. money supply. It is composed of all notes and coins held outside the banking sector plus banks' till money and operational balances at the Bank of England.

M_1. A measure of the U.K. money supply. It is composed of all notes and coins held outside the banking sector plus all current accounts of U.K. residents minus 60% of the net value of items in transit. This definition attempts to include all the generally acceptable means of payment. It is a narrower definition than M_3.

M_3. A measure of the U.K. money supply. It is composed of all notes and coins held outside the banking sector plus the current and deposit accounts of U.K. residents plus the estimated holdings of sterling certificates of deposit by U.K. residents minus 60% of the net value of items in transit. It is a broader definition than M_1.

machine-down time. A period during which a machine cannot be used because it has broken down or is being repaired or serviced. *Compare* machine-idle time.

machine-idle time. A period during which a machine cannot be used because of a shortage of labour, input materials, or orders. *Compare* machine-down time.

machine language. *See* programming language.

macroeconomics. The study of aggregate economic behaviour. From theories about the aggregate effects of individual behaviour on goods, money, and labour markets, macroeconomic theory derives predictions about the level of real income, the level of prices, the rate of interest, the level of saving and investment, the rate of growth, the balance of payments, and the level of unemployment. It is fluctuations in the latter that have been of central interest in the development of the subject. This difficulty of reconciling the large-scale unemployment of the Depression with the predictions of classical theory stimulated J. M. Keynes (1883–1946) to write his *General Theory of Employment, Interest, and Money*, and the book found a wide audience amongst those concerned with the need for policies to control the level of unemployment. Modern macroeconomics is regarded as dating from this publication. The determinants of macroeconomic phenomena in the usual model are the level of investment, the amount of consumption, government taxation and spending, the quantity of money, and the exchange rate.

magnetic disc. *See* disc.

magnetic drum. A direct-access computer *storage device consisting of a cylinder coated with magnetic material. Information is stored on parallel tracks around the cylinder and access is achieved by rotating the drum and reading with a number of fixed heads. With the advent of cheaper *memory and faster *discs, drums are becoming less common.

magnetic tape. A sequential-access computer *storage device consisting of a strip of plastic tape coated with magnetic material. Tapes have large capacities (up to 10 million bits per reel) but slow access times.

mail order. A method of marketing in which buying and selling is carried out by post. Producers, companies specializing in mail order, or their agents advertise their products, usually including a postage-paid reader-reply card, or they send out a direct-mail shot to consumers (*see* direct selling). Some mail-order houses have a wide range of goods in stock and send out catalogues to their prospective customers. Payment is either cash with order, cash on delivery, or by instalment. The low marketing costs often allow the seller to include instalment terms for little extra charge.

mainframe. A large conventional digital computer as compared to a *minicomputer or a *microcomputer. Mainframe computers are used by government and other large organizations for storing and manipulating large volumes of data, such as details of banking transactions, national records, etc.

main store. *See* memory.

mainstream corporation tax (M.C.T.). The difference between a company's total liability to corporation tax and *advance corporation tax.

maintenance. 1. (In law). The financial provision by a husband for his wife or ex-wife and children.

2. A financial contribution by a person towards the cost of a lawsuit in which he does not have a particular legal or moral interest. A contract to make such a contribution is illegal.

make a price. A stockjobber is said to make a price for a particular stock when he quotes to stockbrokers *bid and *offer prices at which he is prepared to deal.

Malthusian theory. The Rev. Thomas Robert Malthus (1766–1834), an early English economist, wrote *An Essay on the Principle of Population as it affects the Future Improvement of Society* (1798), in which he attempted to disperse the aura of optimism that had enveloped economic science since Adam Smith's "invisible hand" had promised to guide the economy to efficient wealth; as a result of Malthus' writings on population growth, economics became known as the "dismal science". He observed the tendency of populations to grow geometrically while the supply of food can only grow arithmetically, so that the former will eventually overtake the latter. Since the supply of land is fixed, the law of diminishing returns must take effect as more people attempt to work the same amount of land. The wage rate, which is determined by the marginal physical product of labour, will thus decline as population grows, achieving equilibrium at the minimum subsistence level in the absence of checks on population growth. Malthus distinguished the *positive* checks of disease, famine, and war, from *preventive* checks, by which he meant moral restraint, as he did not condone birth control. Above this equilibrium level population would increase and below it population would decline through death from starvation. In 1803 Malthus published a revised edition of his book in which he held out more hope for the maintenance or improvement of living standards by advocating late marriage and sexual abstinence to control population growth. Malthus's predictions did not, however, come true since technological advance enabled production to increase so that wages could rise. Moreover, the cultivation of new land increased the food supply. He did not foresee the stabilizing and subsequent fall in the birth rate, which followed industrialization, and the associated increase in wealth in the western world. (Immediately prior to World War II the fear in the U.K. was of a falling population rather than one that rose rapidly, although after the war the birth rate underwent an upsurge.) However, the situation Malthus feared approximates closely to the overpopulated developing economies of India and Africa; there is no certainty that the birth rate in these countries will level off as they become industrialized as it did in the western world.

managed currency. A currency whose exchange rate is influenced by government action in the foreign exchange markets. This is inevitable for a currency with a *fixed exchange rate, but can also apply when the exchange rate is floating. *See* dirty float.

management. 1. The control, coordination, and planning of an organization in order to achieve maximum efficiency. Management is often considered to be a factor of production, along with land, labour, and capital. The principles and techniques of management are taught at colleges, universities, and business schools: the entrepreneurial activities associated with management (making profitable use of opportunities, foreseeing market trends, and being a persuasive negotiator and advocate) are less easily acquired through formal education. The *British Institute of Management* was set up by the Board of Trade in 1947 to promote management studies and to provide information to members.

2. The people responsible for performing these tasks.

management accountant. An accountant who combines the techniques of the *cost accountant and *financial accountant and on the basis of the information so provided is able to assist management decisions affecting the development of his business. From cost accountancy information the management accountant is able to analyse the detailed makeup of the business, and from the financial accountancy information he will be provided with an overall picture of the business.

management audit. A systematic, critical, and unbiased review and appraisal of an organization's operations. This may be performed by outside consultants and is concerned with production methods, control systems, etc. *See also* marketing audit, position audit.

management by exception. The use of variance analysis in budgetary control and standard costing to identify items that are out of line with those that were planned. Highlighting such variances enables management to concentrate their efforts on those items.

management consultant. A professional advisor on the techniques of management. Consultants are often called in to advise the board of directors of an ailing company on ways of improving efficiency and profitability. Although they lack detailed knowledge of a particular business, they are able to provide an objective outside view that is totally uninfluenced by personal relationships. Consultants usually offer advice on the use of manpower, industrial relations, managerial structure and techniques, utilization of resources, and long-term policy and planning. Most U.K. management-consultant firms are members of their trade association, the *Management Consultants' Association;* the professional body for individual consultants is the *Institute of Management Consultants.*

management information system (M.I.S.). A centralized pool of information within a company forming a *data bank from which authorized company personnel may extract relevant data, thus ensuring that the same basic data is used by all departments.

managing director. The director of a public or private company who has ultimate responsibility for the day-to-day management of the company, for supervising the implementation of the decisions of the board of directors, and for the long-term planning of the company's policy. He is the most senior executive of the company, with the exception of the *chairman. The U.S. equivalent of the managing director is the president.

mandate. An authority in writing signed by the *mandator* empowering another person (the *mandatory*) to act on his behalf. If this is to act in respect of a bank account the banker must be supplied with a specimen of the mandatory's signature on the mandate. A mandate is determined by the death, bankruptcy, or mental incapacity of the mandator.

manifest. A list of the cargo carried by a ship. It is made out or signed by the captain and also gives details of the ship and its destination. It must be left with the customs before the ship leaves port and copies are sent to the ship's agents at the ports of destination. A similar document is also required for aircraft cargo.

manpower. The total labour force of a country, including both men and women. If there is a *manpower surplus* there are more people than jobs; in a *manpower deficit* there are more jobs than people. *Manpower requirements forecasting* uses statistical techniques for determining future numbers of workers of each level and type of skill that will be required, esp. in accordance with development planning in less developed countries, and it is a much used approach to educational planning.

Manpower Services Commission (M.S.C.). A body set up under the Employment and Training Act (1973) to manage the government's employment and training services. It started operations in January 1974. It exercises its responsibilities through two agencies: the Employment Service Agency and the Training Services Agency. These agencies are statutory organizations, each headed by a chief executive appointed by the M.S.C. The main object of the change is to transfer direct control from the government to representatives of employers, employees, and local government and educational interests who, together with the chairman, form the ten members of the M.S.C. The main duty of the M.S.C. is to make the appropriate arrangements for assisting people to select, train for, obtain, and retain employment and for assisting employers to obtain suitable employees.

manufacturer's agent. A commission agent who has a *franchise to market a manufacturer's products in a particular area, usually for a stated period.

margin. 1. The difference between the sale price of a good or service and its cost to the seller. The margin thus includes expenses and profit.

2. The minimum profit that enables a transaction to be economically sound.

3. The final unit of an economic factor, such as is used in production or consumption.

4. The difference between the amount of a loan made available to a speculator by a stockbroker and the current value of the security deposited as collateral, the latter of course being greater than the former. "Trading on margin" by a speculator is thus making share deals on the strength of any margin in excess of the minimum permitted by the broker. The security deposited as collateral usually takes the form of holdings in gilt-edged securities or blue-chip shares. When the margin, expressed as a percentage of the current value of the collateral, falls too low (as may occur when the prices of the securities deposited as collateral fall sharply), the stockbroker will demand part repayment of the loan.

marginal analysis. Economic analysis in which the profit or utility maximizing behaviour of economic agents is decided by the benefit of the last unit of production or consumption, i.e. by the behaviour at the margin. It is assumed that individuals and organizations will attempt to maximize their aims–utility or profit. To do so it is the marginal alterations to the total that must be considered. Marginal analysis thus uses differential calculus extensively. In mathematical terms the profit or utility functions are usually approximated by continuous differentiable functions, sometimes with constraints, and the last unit, or the marginal rate, becomes the first derivative of this function. The conditions for maximizing behaviour at the margin are all equivalent to first order conditions for maxima, and while these conditions must hold for the maximizer, they are not sufficient to guarantee a maximum. To guarantee sufficiency one looks at the second order conditions, which put further constraints on the marginal rates, such as the law of decreasing marginal utility. Marginal analysis is the primary tool of most *partial equilibrium analysis.

marginal cost. The extra cost of increasing output by one unit of production. It is entirely made up of *direct costs. Given a continuous differentiable cost function its mathematical equivalent is the first partial derivative of that function with respect to output. A condition for profit maximization is that production takes place at the level of output at which marginal cost equals price.

marginal costing. (In accountancy). The ascertainment of marginal costs and of the effect on profit of changes in volume or type of output by differentiating between fixed costs and variable costs.

marginal distribution. The statistical distribution of a variable, as contrasted with a *conditional distribution. The product of a conditional distribution and the marginal distribution of the variable whose value is fixed in the conditional distribution is the joint distribution of the two variables concerned.

marginal efficiency of capital. The *internal rate of return that would reduce to zero the net present value of a marginal increment or decrement in the capital stock. It is claimed to have a stable and declining relationship with the quantity of capital, and is the only theoretically acceptable marginal efficiency relationship. Lerner and others have used this fact to criticize Keynes's concept of the *marginal efficiency of investment.

marginal efficiency of investment. Keynes's term for the *internal rate of return. He used it as the basis of his investment theory, deriving a marginal efficiency of investment schedule by ranking projects in order of their internal rates of return and using the criterion "invest if the internal rate of return exceeds the market rate". Unfortunately there is no reason for the change in the level of investment to bear a predictable relation to changes in interest rates. Investment is the flow change in capital, and it is the capital stock which is affected by the rate of interest. *See* marginal efficiency of capital.

marginal physical product. The physical output that the last unit of an input adds to total product, with all other units held constant. With a continuous differentiable *production function its mathematical equivalent is the partial derivative of that function with respect to the selected input. One condition for profit maximization is that production occurs in the range in which marginal product decreases as input of the selected factor of production increases.

marginal propensity to consume (M.P.C.). *See* propensity to consume.

marginal propensity to save (M.P.S.). *See* propensity to save.

marginal rate of substitution (M.R.S.). A ratio of the marginal utilities of two goods. It is represented by the slope of the indifference curve between the two goods. To maximize his utility, when consuming two goods, a consumer must equate the ratio of the marginal utilities of the two goods to the ratio of their prices. If the ratios do not tally, the consumer will substitute one good for another until they do. Distribution of available goods in an economy is at the optimum when the marginal rates of substitution for all consumers are equal. If they also equal the *marginal rate of transformation of the two goods (which is the equivalent term in production) the economy is in equilibrium.

marginal rate of taxation. The amount of tax imposed as a percentage of an additional unit of income.

marginal rate of technical substitution. The ratio of *marginal products of two factors in a particular product, i.e. the slope of the *isoquant at that input mix. It is the counterpart in production of the marginal rate of substitution in consumption. The conditions for productive efficiency are that for all products these ratios should be equal to each other and also to the ratio of prices for the two factors of production. On an *Edgeworth–Bowley box diagram this appears as the condition that the price line intersecting the contract curve be tangential to both isoquants at that point.

marginal rate of transformation. The rate at which the production of one good can be replaced by the production of another as a result of a reallocation of inputs. Graphically it is represented by the slope of the *production possibility curve at the point of original production. The ideal combination of goods and the ideal level of output is produced when the marginal rate of transformation of the goods equals the ratio of their price.

marginal relief. Relief granted by a tax authority if the strict application of the rules would impose a heavy burden on a taxpayer who only marginally falls within a higher tax bracket or category.

marginal revenue. The change in total revenue resulting from the sale of an additional unit of production. Under imperfect competition a firm cannot sell any more of a product without reducing price. Marginal revenue is thus the extra revenue gained from the sale of the marginal unit minus the revenue lost on the preceding units by the reduction in price. For example, a manufacturer produces 10 000 bottles, which he sells at 10p each. Total revenue is thus £1000. If he produces an extra unit of 1000 bottles, he can only sell his whole production at 9.5p each; total revenue is therefore £1045. Marginal revenue is thus £45 and not £95 (1000 × 9.5p). Under perfect competition, price need not be reduced to sell more of a product, since each firm's output is too small to affect price. If the bottle manufacturer was in a perfectly competitive market he could increase production without decreasing price.

marginal revenue product. *Marginal revenue multiplied by *marginal product. It is the yield obtained from using an extra unit of input, say one more machine or another shift of workers. If possible, each input will be increased until its marginal revenue product equals its marginal cost.

marginal social cost. The cost of an additional unit of production to society as a whole, taking into account external economies or diseconomies (*see* externalities) so that *Pareto-optimal conditions can be formulated using the marginal social cost rather than the individual's marginal cost in the industry. Then, by a programme of taxes and subsidies, an attempt can be made to alter the marginal costs of individual firms until they equal the marginal social cost causing an increase in welfare for society as a whole.

marginal utility. The increase in total utility derived from the last unit of a good consumed. The mathematical equivalent is the first derivative of the utility function. One condition for utility maximization is that the marginal utility of a good divided by its price must equal the marginal utility of money for all goods. The marginal utility of a product determines the price that people are willing to pay for it.

Marginal utility can be used to explain the *value paradox. Although water has a high total utility, it has a low marginal utility in the relevant range, hence its price is low. Diamonds, on the other hand, have a low total utility but a high marginal utility, hence a high price.

marginal utility of money. The increase in total utility derived from an additional unit of money to spend on consumption. Its mathematical equivalent is the partial derivative of the indirect utility function with respect to money. It is held that the marginal utility of money diminishes as income increases and this is one justification for progressive taxation; thus each person sacrifices an equal amount of utility.

marine insurance. Insurance against risks arising from maritime trade and ventures: this is probably the oldest form of insurance. A phrase found in nearly all marine insurance policies is "perils of the sea". These include storm, tempest, collision, theft, stranding, fire, and a number of other less likely perils (such as detention by foreign princes, barratry of the master, and dangers occasioned by pirates). Marine insurance consists of three separate types of policy: *hull insurance, *cargo insurance, and *freight insurance. Policies may provide cover for a single voyage, a specified length of time, or a combination of both (*see also* open cover, floating policies). Marine policies are provided by *Lloyd's underwriters and the insurance companies that specialize in this type of business.

In marine policies a distinction is made between an *actual total loss and a *constructive total loss (*see also* abandonment): many of the policies insuring cargo are based on the *Institute cargo clauses. Policies may be *valued* or *unvalued.* A valued policy specifies the value of the subject matter and the holder of such a policy receives this specified sum in the event of a total loss (irrespective of its value at the time of the loss). An unvalued policy provides for claims based on the value of the subject matter at the time of the loss. The question of partial losses is of great importance in marine policies. *See* average, free of particular average, free of all average, with average.

maritime industrial development area (MIDA). An area of industrial development adjacent to deep water, consisting of interdependent plants and processes. Such an area must have a large acreage of level land suitable for industrial development and it must have a favourable location in relation to communications and markets. Rotterdam and Marseilles, for example, have maritime industrial development areas, but in the U.K. the idea has not been officially pursued.

marked cheque. A cheque marked as "good for payment" by a bank on whom the cheque was drawn at the request of another bank in the same town, or at the request of the drawer. This was once a frequent practice but has now practically ceased. The abolition of local exchanges, and the decision of the London Clearing Bankers in 1920 that instead of "marking" a cheque a bank draft should be issued, avoided the bank having to take into consideration the amount of the marked cheque when deciding if other cheques drawn on the customer's account should be paid.

market. 1. The existing or potential demand for a product.

2. (In economic theory). The arena of the activity of trading or exchanging goods of a certain type, possibly for other goods but generally for money. In a sense it is an abstraction of the market place. Suppliers are assumed to produce or procure commodities elsewhere and bring them onto the market where demanders are waiting to exchange commodities or money for them. Then through some market mechanism a market price is arrived at, at which suppliers and demanders make their exchanges.

Markets can be in equilibrium or disequilibrium, depending on whether or not aggregate supply equals aggregate demand. A market need not and generally does not have only one physical location, but when it does not market imperfections often result, arising from ignorance of prices elsewhere, difficulties of communication, etc.

marketable security. Any security that can be bought or sold on a stock exchange.

market assessment. *See* marketing.

market capitalization. The on-going value of a company as determined by the market value of its entire issued share capital, i.e. the number of shares in issue multiplied by the stock market price of such shares.

market forces. The forces of supply and demand, representing the aggregate influences on price and quantity of the activities of the economic agents in a market. In general excess demand is assumed to cause prices and quantities supplied to rise and excess supply to cause price and quantities supplied to fall, although the end result of the action of these forces depends on the specific market mechanism and the shape of the supply and demand curves.

market imperfections. The conditions of a market in which the economic agents have imperfect knowledge about the offers made by other agents. For instance, school-leavers might be ignorant of job opportunities and accept wages at less than they could earn elsewhere or alternatively they may expect wages to be higher elsewhere and refuse jobs at the going wage.

Costs of transport, especially when there are differences between suppliers, may also be considered as market imperfections or, equally validly, as factors leading to product differentiation, causing imperfect competition to prevail in an industry that would be otherwise perfectly competitive. Market imperfections are not necessarily permanent but can often be overcome at a price (the *transactions cost).

marketing. The management function concerned with the identification and evaluation of a company's market (*market assessment*), carrying out research to provide information on the size of the market and the price that a particular product or service should command (*see* market research), and subsequently packaging, promoting, selling, and distributing the product on a profitable basis. Marketing also includes the provision of any after-sales service and has an important part to play in ensuring that the product is so designed as to satisfy market requirements.

marketing logistics (physical distribution management). The distributive activity involved in ensuring that the products offered actually reach the market, i.e. the place component of the *marketing mix.

marketing audit. That part of the *management audit particularly concerned with the marketing environment and marketing operations. It is a means by which an organization can identify its own strengths, weaknesses, threats, and opportunities in this area.

marketing information system. An arrangement to tap flows of information within a firm, enabling it to gather, process, and utilize information in the relevant area. It consists of four subsystems: internal accounting, marketing intelligence, marketing research, and marketing management science.

marketing mix. The four major elements of marketing (the four *P*s): product, price, promotion, and place. The right product must be found to satisfy consumer needs at the right price and be made known and available in the right market area.

marketing research. *See* market research.

market leader. A company that has the largest share of a particular market for a particular product or service. A market leader is also usually the most profitable company in the field.

market mechanism. The means by which the market forces direct the movements of price and quantity sold in a market. These vary greatly according to whether one uses a static equilibrium analysis (*see* tâtonnement) or a dynamic analysis. In the dynamic case the speed of adjustment in the market, and possibly even the stability of equilibrium, is dependent upon the exact mechanism specified.

market penetration. Entering a particular market and gaining as large a share of the market as possible (*see* market share). The firm may deliberately under-price its product at first in order to familiarize the consumers with the product name.

market price. The unique price at which commodities are exchanged in a market for each other or for money at a particular time. It may happen in an industry that very similar goods sell at different yet comparable prices. A weighted average of these prices is not, strictly speaking, a market price: each of the prices separately is a market price and each good would sell in its own market. As with many concepts in theoretical economics the term is exact, yet highly abstract; it is therefore often used very loosely.

market rate of discount. The rate at which bill brokers will discount approved bills of exchange of not more than three months' currency. It is usually lower than the rate charged by the bank of England acting as *lender of last resort.

market research. Research carried out by surveys to assess the size of market and the price that a particular product or service should command on it. Research into the market for consumer goods, which may be carried out by a firm's own marketing staff or by a market research agency, is called *consumer research*. Research into the sale of industrial products is a separate activity known as *industrial market research*. The U.K. professional body for market research is the *Market Research Society*.

Marketing research is a term now used for a broader field of activity; it includes the information provided by a market-research survey as well as details of alternative products on the market, the sales strategy of competitors, and the current economic background. Marketing research provides management with the information required to determine marketing policy for a particular brand of product.

market segmentation. Natural groups or segments within a market in which customers exhibit the same broad characteristics. These segments tend to form separate markets in themselves to which a product may be targeted, for example mothers of young children.

market share. 1. The percentage of total sales in an industry accruing to one firm. It is one of the principle variables used to measure industrial concentration.

2. The percentage of sales of a particular commodity or service out of the total in its class, for example bikinis, out of total sales of swimwear. *See also* market penetration.

market skimming. A policy of entering into a market at a high price and then, later on if necessary, lowering the price to gain acceptance in other price segments. Thus only a small section (the "cream") of the market is aimed at initially, but the brand name is established.

market value. The price at which a security can be dealt in on a stock exchange at any specified time. Thus if a company had issued 5p shares in 1850 at par and they were now quoted at 350p, then the par value of the shares is 5p but their market value is 350p. *Compare* par value.

marking names. A list of finance houses, *stockjobbers, or *stockbrokers kept by the London Stock Exchange authorities in whose name U.K. owners of U.S. and Canadian shares can have the latter registered for ease of dividend collection.

markings. Details of the prices at which *bargains in particular shares are transacted on the London Stock Exchange. Markings are entered on special slips by unauthorized clerks or *blue buttons and this information is used for entering into the Official List details of the day's business.

Markov chain. A sequence of events characterized by the condition that the probability of any specified outcome at the *n*th stage of the sequence is dependent only on the outcome at the $(n - 1)$th stage and is independent of the outcomes of all previous stages. The Markov chain has certain limited applications, but its main importance lies in the implication of this state of affairs for the estimation of probabilities at different stages in the sequence.

markup price. A price reckoned on the basis of cost plus a fixed percentage markup.

Marshall Aid Programme (Marshall Plan). The scheme instituted by George Marshall (1880-1959), the U.S. Secretary of State, in 1948 to aid the economic recovery of Western Europe after World War II. Officially called the *European Recovery Programme*, it provided for the the infusion of capital from the U.S. into Europe on a vast scale to finance investment and consumption. Marshall Aid was administered by the European Cooperation Administration in the U.S. and by the *Organization for European Economic Cooperation in Europe. It lasted for three years.

Marshallian stability. A comparative statics stability condition for a market (named after Alfred Marshall, 1842–1924), which assumes that the quantity demanded is a function of price, stability resulting when producers raise their output in response to a demand price that exceeds the supply price or when they lower their output when the opposite is true. The conditions agree with the *Walrasian stability when supply and demand curves have slopes of opposite sign, i.e. one slopes up and the other down, but the two are inconsistent when the curves slope in the same direction. For example, if both supply and demand curves are positively sloped the equilibrium is stable in the Marshallian sense if the demand curve is more steeply sloped, and stable in the Walrasian sense if the supply curve is more steeply sloped.

Marshall–Lerner condition. A condition that indicates whether a devaluation will correct or worsen a balance of payments deficit. The condition is set in terms of import and export *elasticities. In its simplest form it states that the balance of trade deficit will improve or worsen according to whether the sum of the demand elasticity for imports into the devaluing country plus the demand elasticity in the rest of the world for its exports, is greater or less than one. For instance, if imports consist of necessities (so that demand elasticity is low) there will be little reduction in the volume that is imported, despite their increase in price. Therefore, the deficit might worsen. Usually, the demand elasticity is sufficiently high for devaluation to narrow the deficit. There is also a further refinement which incorporates supply elasticities into the calculations.

Marshall Plan. *See* Marshall Aid Programme.

Marxian economics. Karl Marx (1818–83) published the first of the three volumes of his major work *Das Kapital* (Capital) in 1867. Apart from the polemic it contained, the work represented a major theoretical attempt to counteract the works of the Classicists, whom Marx saw as apologists for the capitalist system. Borrowing from Ricardo, whose work formed the starting point of his theory, Marx used the *labour theory of value as a basis for a discussion of the exploitation of the workers by the capitalists in the form of *surplus value. According to this argument, workers are paid a subsistence wage but the goods they produce are valued by the labour time involved in their production; the difference in value accrues to the capitalist as profit. Over a period of time, however, wages will tend to be bid up as capitalists attempt to expand using their accumulated profit; this would reduce profits. To counteract this capitalists would employ labour-saving technical innovations creating a *reserve army of the unemployed to reduce wages. But capital is non-productive, its cost reflecting its future production, labour being the sole source of profit in the system. So the problem will in fact be intensified by an action that is intended to solve it. Marx predicted that this contradiction in the capitalist system would lead to its inevitable collapse; he also predicted that capitalism would be replaced by socialism, under which workers would control the means of production thus avoiding the inherent paradox of capitalism. However, the labour theory of value has analytical problems in that it ignores the effects of capital on price, the source of the transformation problem; also the assumption that workers do not save for investment is crucial to his analysis of accumulation.

mass production. The manufacture of a product in large quantities to a standard specification, with the maximum use of machinery and automation and the maximum division of labour. The product may have a high degree of engineering excellence but will involve little or no craftsmanship. The use of labour is usually confined to monotonous simple assembly tasks on an assembly line.

While mass production formerly implied a standardized product, modern techniques have enabled mass-production methods to be used to assemble standardized components into a more diversified range of products.

material fact (in insurance). A fact that would influence the mind of a prudent underwriter in assessing a risk. What is material is a question of fact to be decided by the courts of law, if necessary. There are certain facts, however, that are quite obviously material to an insurance contract: for example, in life assurance, the fact that the proposed life assured has diabetes and in motor insurance that a standard model has a specially tuned engine. At common law a person cannot be penalized for not revealing facts that he does not know and cannot reasonably be expected to know. There are certain known facts and many others that need not be disclosed (*see* disclosure). They may be summarized as follows:

a) facts that improve the risk.

b) facts that the insurer may be presumed to know (i.e. common knowledge, such as the existence of a state of war).

c) matters of law.

d) facts capable of discovery by the insurer from information supplied.

e) facts that the insurer's representative fails to notice on a survey.

materiality. An accounting concept that ignores insignificant data. What is significant, however, will depend upon the size and nature of the undertaking. For example, a stock of stationery could be regarded as of such insignificant value that it is just written off against the profits of the current accounting period and not carried forward as stock in hand.

mate's receipt. A document signed by the mate of a ship stating that the goods described in the document have been loaded onto his ship. This document may be required as proof of delivery in a *free on board contract.

mathematical economics. The application of mathematical techniques to economic variables in order to discover or demonstrate functional relationships between them. Mathematical economics is distinct from econometrics in that it is confined to theoretical analysis in economics whereas econometrics, although it has its own theory, relates to the empirical testing of economic theories. Thus mathematical treatment of demand theory, growth theory, monetary theory, international trade theory, and various other aspects of economics have been formulated. There is some controversy among economists as to the suitability of mathematical analysis in economics. Some maintain that the inexact nature of economics (as compared with the physical sciences) leads theorists using mathematical techniques to misrepresent economic relationships by oversimplifying them (i.e. by making them too exact) and to ignore consciously or otherwise variables that are not amenable to mathematical representation and circumstances or conditions that render mathematical analysis invalid. The mathematical school, however, holds that although mathematics is not a perfect instrument of analysis in economics, the advantages of its use, especially that of rendering advanced theories comprehensible to a wide audience, greatly outweigh the disadvantages. The major instrument of analysis used in mathematical economics is calculus.

matrix. A rectangular or square array of numbers in rows and columns in the following fashion:

$$\begin{bmatrix} 4 & 1 \\ 2 & 3 \end{bmatrix} \quad \begin{bmatrix} 9 & 0 \\ -11 & 7 \\ 3 & -5 \end{bmatrix} \quad \begin{bmatrix} 0 & \frac{1}{2} & -2 \\ -6 & 16 & -\frac{3}{4} \end{bmatrix}$$

The individual numbers are referred to as the elements of the matrix. Generally, in analysis in econometrics or mathematical economics, matrices are denoted by letters of the alphabet, so that a matrix would be written as:

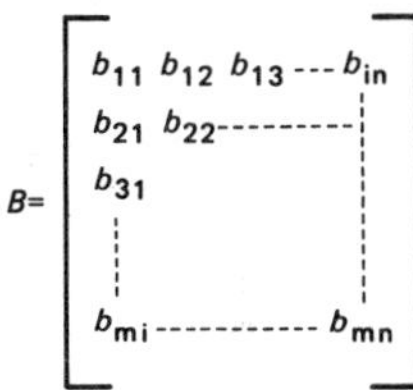

Each element of the matrix now has two subscripts, one of which (conventionally the first) denotes the row in which the element appears while the second denotes the column. The matrix B above has m rows and n columns, and would therefore be said to be of order m × n. Matrices are of substantial importance in *econometrics, both in the theory and in its application; matrices simplify the presentation and facilitate the estimation of economic models.

matrix algebra. A branch of mathematics concerned with the conditions under which certain operations, such as addition, subtraction, multiplication and inversion, can be performed on matrices. It is also concerned with the analysis of different types of matrix and of different types of algebraic expression involving matrices. Matrix algebra has very considerable application in economics, especially in empirical economics, because many economic models permit of mathematical representation by matrices and the techniques of matrix algebra often provide great insight into such models because of their power and simplicity. Apart from model estimation, matrix algebra is used in such areas as econometric theory, input–output analysis, and linear programming.

matrix printer. A computer printer that builds the characters it prints from a matrix of dots. It is very fast but the final quality is inferior to a single character printer.

maturity. The date on which some document, such as a stock, bill of exchange, insurance policy, etc., is due to be exchanged for cash. *See also* term structure of interest rates.

maximand. The variable which it is desired to maximize in, for example, *linear programming. An industrial firm might be interested to discover that level of output, subject to its productive capacity and the prices and availability of its raw materials, which maximizes its profits. Thus profit is the maximand. *Compare* minimand.

maximax. One of the *strategies analysed for its effect in the outcome of a game theory situation. The maximax strategy is that course of action whose best outcome is better than the best outcome of all other courses of action. The maximax player is thus maximizing his maximum payoff. Maximax is the most optimistic of the strategies. *See also* game theory, payoff matrix. *Compare* maximin, minimax regret, Laplace criterion.

maximin. One of the behavioural patterns analysed as a *strategy for its effect on the outcome of a game theoretic situation. The maximin strategy is the course of action whose worst outcome is better than the worst outcome of any other course of action. The player who follows the maximin strategy is thus maximizing his minimum *payoff. The maximin strategy has been suggested as suitable for conservative contestants. *See also* payoff matrix. *Compare* maximax, minimax regret, Laplace criterion.

maximum likelihood estimation. A method of statistical estimation in which a random sample is taken from a population whose parameters are to be estimated and estimators of the parameters are then derived in a manner that maximizes the likelihood or probability of selecting the random variables that were in fact sampled. This is done by means of the *likelihood function, which can be maximized by standard calculus, often with a logarithmic transformation. This maximization process permits of a solution for the desired estimator. Maximum likelihood estimation, unlike *least squares estimation, does not require a linear or linearized function. Maximum likelihood is the most powerful technique of estimation that has been developed and is the most widely used in statistics generally. Maximum likelihood estimators have the desirable properties of asymptotic efficiency, consistency, sufficiency, and invariance, but they are not necessarily unbiased. *See also* estimation, likelihood function. *Compare* Bayesian estimation, method of moments.

M.B. *See* byte.

M.C.T. *See* mainstream corporation tax.

mean. *See* arithmetic mean.

mean deviation. The arithmetic mean of the deviations of all the items in a distribution or set of numbers from their arithmetic mean, where all such deviations are taken as positive numbers. For instance, in the set of numbers 7, 11, 14, 9, 13, 6 the arithmetic mean is 10 and the deviations of each of the numbers from the mean are −3, 1, 4, −1, 3, −4 respectively. Making all these deviations positive and taking their arithmetic mean gives 16/6 = 2.67, which is the mean deviation of the original set. The full name of the mean deviation when it is measured like this is the *mean deviation from the mean*. The mean deviation can also be measured from the median of the distribution, when it is at a minimum, or from the mode of the distribution or from any other point on it. As a measure of dispersion the mean deviation is much more scientific than the range or the semi-interquartile range since it uses all the items in the distribution, but it cannot be applied for further calculation or algebraic operation and is therefore rarely used. *Compare* range, semi-interquartile range, standard deviation.

mean price. The arithmetical mean of two prices, such as the mean of a stockjobber's buying and selling prices of a security. It is sometimes taken as the market price.

means test. A method of establishing the right of a claimant to a *welfare benefit. The claimant must have a sufficiently low income or have certain personal circumstances for eligibility. Programmes that are means-tested may be contrasted with universal programmes, such as pensions or the health service. Means tests are defended as a way to lower the cost of welfare programmes by paying benefits only to those people who need them. On the other hand the administration of means tests, besides being costly, can be a way of conveying stigma and constitute an invasion of privacy.

mean-variance analysis. The making of decisions when there is *uncertainty in the outcome. It is particularly used in examining how an investor will organize his *portfolio. In this model it is assumed that the determinants of an individual's choice are the expected return and the variability of the return (which is calculated by some estimate of the variance of the distribution of possible outcomes). The individual's choice as to how he will arrange his investments can be plotted on a graph with the expected return on the vertical axis and the variance on the horizontal. There is usually one certain alternative; for example, holding money at a fixed interest rate. This is represented by a point on the vertical axis, i.e. zero variance. The other investment possibilities are also placed on the graph. If there is only one other possibility, then the line between the certainty point and the investment point will give the possibilities between which a person can choose by diversifying his portfolio. A set of indifference curves can be drawn on the diagram, their shape depending on the individual's attitude towards risk. For a normal risk averter they will be convex towards the lower right hand side of the diagram.

The major criticism of this approach is that it reduces investment to just two criteria: the mean and the variance. There is also a symmetry about the distributional possibilities: this arises in the case of a reverse lottery. Using mean-variance analysis there is no distinction between paying a pound for a one-in-a-thousand chance of winning £1000 and being paid a pound to undergo the one-in-a-thousand chance of having to pay out that amount. The analysis can be extended to include the possibility of borrowing and of more than one possible investment. *See also*state preference theory.

measured daywork. A form of wage structure in which a daily target of production is set, an agreed wage being paid for each day that the target is reached. If the target is not reached a proportion of the agreed full wage is paid. Targets are set for measured daywork using a work measurement technique, such as time study or work sampling.

measurement tonnage. *See* tonnage.

mechanization. The replacement of manual labour by machinery in industrial and agricultural processes. Mechanization started on a significant scale in the Industrial Revolution and still continues with the increasing use of automation and computerization in industry and the increasing use of mechanized equipment on the land.

median. The value that divides a set of numbers into two equal portions. The median can be found by arranging the set of numbers in descending order and taking the middle number (if there is an odd numher of items in the set) or the arithmetic mean of the two middle numbers (if there is an even number of items in the set). It is one type of average; other common averages are the *arithmetic mean and the *mode.

medical insurance. *See* private health insurance.

media research. Analysis of the relative advertising potential of television, radio, newspapers, etc.

mediation. The use of an independent third party to assist in the settlement of an industrial dispute. The mediator calls the representatives of both sides together and assists them in reaching a compromise without loss of face.

medium-dated gilt. *See* mediums.

medium of exchange. Anything that is widely acceptable as payment for debts and thereby fulfils the principal function of money. In primitive economies the medium of exchange may have some intrinsic value but modern economies use money, in some form, for all transactions.

mediums. A term used on the London Stock Exchange with reference to fixed-interest securities, mainly gilt-edged securities, with redemption dates ranging from between 5 years and 15 years into the future. *Compare* longs, shorts.

medium-term liabilities. Liabilities that have to be met within two to four years. They are not as imminent as *current liabilities or as distant as *deferred liabilities.

megabyte. *See* byte.

member bank. 1. A U.S. bank that is a member of the *Federal Reserve System. It includes all national banks and many state banks; member banks are the U.S. equivalents of *commercial banks.

2. A U.K. *commercial bank that is a member of the *Bankers' Clearing House.

member firm. A firm of stockbrokers or stockjobbers whose directors or partners are all members of the London Stock Exchange.

members' voluntary liquidation. The *liquidation of a company resulting from a decision of the members to wind up their company and realize any assets. In order to achieve this, a special resolution must be passed to wind up the company. However, before this occurs the directors have to make a statutory declaration that the company is solvent and able to pay its debts in full within a twelve-month period from the commencement of winding up. Within 14 days of the passing of the special resolution the company must publish a notice of the winding up in the London Gazette.

Memorandum of Association. One of the documents that must be drawn up when a company is formed (*see* incorporated company). It sets out the title of the company, whether or not its liability is limited, and gives its registered address, particulars of the types of business the company may undertake, the amount of its authorized capital, and particulars of the shares forming this capital. The document must be signed by the founder members (a minimum of two for a private company and seven for a public company) and lists the number of shares for which each has subscribed.

memorandum of satisfaction. A signed document stating that a mortgage or charge on property has been repaid in full.

memory (main store). A computer *storage device for holding information that is directly required for processing. Memories are of two types. Magnetic memories consist of a large number of rings of ferrite (a magnetic material) threaded on wires. These rings (called *cores*) each store one bit of information. Core memories are now being supplanted by semiconductor memories. Computer memories are direct-access devices with low access times and usually have associated backing stores.

mercantile agent. A commercial agent with the authority to buy or sell on behalf of his principal.

mercantile law. The branch of law that is concerned with trade, especially international trade, shipping, etc.

mercantilism. A school of economic thought that developed between the sixteenth and eighteenth centuries. In response to the growth of national mercantile economies it attempted to discover the source of national wealth and the policies that would maximize it. It saw bullion (or specie) as the prime measure of the wealth of a nation and advocated governmental action to increase this store. Domestically, it promoted the interests of the mercantile classes with monopoly licences and the depression of wages. The essence of the mercantile tradition was in international trade. To increase its store of bullion it was necessary for a country to enjoy a surplus in its *balance of trade. To this end tariffs were imposed to protect home export industries and exclude foreign goods. Exports of finished goods were encouraged and cheap markets of raw materials were secured by the colonial system. Classical economists, following David Hume (1711–76) and Adam Smith (1723–90), reviled the restrictive nature of mercantilist doctrine seeing it as serving the self-interest of the merchant classes. Real wealth, they believed, was to be equated with the full-employment level of production of goods and services. They also attacked mercantilism on analytic grounds by demonstrating the *specie flow mechanism to dispute the efficacy of mercantilist policy in achieving mercantilist aims. Long after its demise mercantilist dogma received a boost from Keynes when he showed that an underemployment equilibrium could receive an addition to effective demand from a surplus in the balance of trade, thus raising the real wealth of a nation.

merchandising. A branch of *sales promotion concerned particularly with retail activities, such as sampling, free gifts, and the strategic placing of goods or advertising displays (commonly known as a *point-of-sale* display). As well as promoting certain goods it is used by large retail organizations simply to induce potential customers into the store. *See also* loss leader.

merchantable quality. *See* Sale of Goods Act (1893).

merchant bank. A banking institution whose financial business gradually evolved from its merchant business. The merchant bankers' local knowledge of the countries with which they traded made them specialists in estimating the creditworthiness of their customers, which in turn enabled them to accept bills of exchange and arrange loans at the request of foreign traders (*see* accepting house). Their business has now extended beyond normal banking transactions to include dealings in foreign exchange, the issue of long-term loans for governments and companies abroad, acting as company advisers, underwriting new issues and managing takeover bids, insurance business, unit trust management, etc.

merger. The amalgamation of two or more firms to form one new company. A merger may serve to increase efficiency by removing excess capacity and by enabling firms to take advantage of *economies of scale, but they may also increase monopoly power. In the U.K. mergers can be investigated by the *Monopolies and Mergers Commission to determine whether or not they are in the public interest. In the U.S.A. the position is safeguarded by the *anti-trust laws. *See also* takeover, horizontal integration, vertical integration, diversification.

merit rating. A method by which an employer can assess the value of employees, especially with reference to rates of pay and promotion. A merit-rating chart for each employee is compiled with points being awarded for skill, initiative, willingness, punctuality, absenteeism, attitude to management, etc. The large number of people involved in making the assessments minimizes the influence of personal likes and dislikes. Merit rating is often only one of several factors involved in making pay and promotion decisions.

method of moments. A method of statistical estimation in which a parameter of a particular density function that is also a *moment (or a function of a moment) of that density function is estimated by taking a random sample from a population having that density function and calculating the corresponding sample moment (or a function of it). The method of moments has limited value as a method of estimation both because of its narrow scope (the parameter being estimated must be a moment or a function of a moment) and because it does not necessarily provide estimates with the properties of unbiasedness and efficiency. *See also* moment, estimation. *Compare* maximum likelihood estimation, least squares estimation, Bayesian estimation.

method study. *See* work study.

metrication. The process of converting from a nonmetric to a metric system of units: for example, conversion from *Imperial units (foot, pound, second) to the c.g.s. (centimetre, gram, second) system or to *SI units.

metric ton. *See* ton.

metrology. The study of units of measurements. Weights and measures have always been a subject of great importance to commerce, as most transactions for goods are based on an exchange of money for a measured quantity of the good. *See also* metrication, SI units, Imperial units.

microcomputer. A small *computer using *microprocessors and silicon chip based *memory. The memory is classified as *ROM* (read only memory) and *RAM* (random access memory). ROM has very fast access times and may not be overwritten. Programs resident in ROM are called *firmware* and typically consist of basic system software. RAM is memory that may be overwritten. Microcomputers can be operated in a normal office environment by staff untrained in computer technology.

microeconomics. The branch of economics concerned with the problems and choices that confront the individual person, firm, or industry. Topics that are dealt with include the theory of utility, analysis of the price mechanism, perfect competition and monopoly, the demand for and supply of goods and services, and the theory of the firm. In each case one individual, organization, or sector of the economy is considered in isolation from the rest of the economy. *Compare* macroeconomics.

microprocessor. A *central processing unit based on the semiconductor capabilities of silicon chips. Microprocessors are widely used to control equipment ranging from washing machines to power stations.

MIDA. *See* maritime industrial development area.

middleman. An intermediary between buyer and seller, producer and consumer, etc. Middlemen are sometimes regarded as unnecessary adjuncts of the capitalist free-enterprise system, who make a profit at the expense of the consumer without making a useful contribution to society. This view is not, however, consistent with the laws of supply and demand: if middlemen did not supply a service for which there is a demand they would be unlikely to be able to make a profit. In general, middlemen provide such services as finance, a distribution network, price stabilization, introducing buyer to seller, etc. *See also* wholesaler.

middle price. The midway level between a share's *bid and *offer prices on a stock exchange. Thus if a share is quoted 250p-260p (meaning that it can be sold at 250p and bought at 260p), the middle price is 255p. Most newspapers publish only middle prices.

mill pricing. A pricing system in which the buyer undertakes the responsibility for transporting the product from the mill or factory and the producer quotes a price exclusive of transport costs. Under such a system it is more difficult for the producer to practise price discrimination between geographical areas than with *delivered pricing.

minicomputer. A small digital computer. The distinguishing line between *microcomputers and minicomputers is vague. A minicomputer will normally be able to support many more *storage devices and *input/output devices than a microcomputer.

minimand. The variable that it is desired to minimize in any problem. A conglomerate manufacturing group, for instance, might wish to know what arrangement of its different products, subject to demand and the maintenance of its overall profits, minimizes the amount of its raw materials it has to scrap. In this case, scrap is the minimand. *Compare* maximand.

minimax regret. One of the *strategies analysed for its effect on the outcome of game theoretic situations. The minimax regret strategy is that course of action which has at a minimum the maximum loss that the player can sustain if his opponent chooses the best course of action from his own point of view. The minimax regret player is thus minimizing maximum regret. The minimax regret criterion, sometimes called the Savage criterion, is a relatively conservative strategy. *See also* game theory, payoff matrix. *Compare* maximax, maximin, Laplace criterion.

minimum lending rate (M.L.R.). The advertised minimum rate at which the Bank of England would discount approved bills of exchange (of not more than three months' currency) or grant short-term loans, when acting as *lender of last resort. In October 1972 the minimum lending rate replaced bank rate, which was originally regulated by the supply and demand for money but was later used as an instrument of government policy, being set at a high rate to check inflation or at a low rate to stimulate the demand for goods in a period of depression. The minimum lending rate influenced all other money market and discount rates and was itself linked to the Treasury bill rate by formula. It was altered at the Bank of England's discretion when the difference between the two rates exceeded half a per cent, the M.L.R. being the higher. The M.L.R. was abolished in August 1981 as part of the monetary authorities' plans to adopt a more flexible approach to interest rate policy. *See also* base rate, Treasury bills.

minimum sacrifice. *See* sacrifice.

minimum subscription. The minimum amount of money that the directors consider necessary in order to launch a new company. It is usually stated in the *prospectus.

minimum wage. A stated payment per hour below which employment is prohibited. In the U.S., federal law specifies the minimum wage rate that is payable throughout the nation, whilst in Canada minimum wages for most types of factory employment have been set in all the provinces. In the U.K. although there is no universally applicable minimum wage, wage minima are set for various industries and employments by orders made under the authority of the Wages Councils Act (1979). Minimum wages have been advocated as a socially just measure designed to protect and improve the standard of living of the poorest sections of the community. It is often argued however that since the minimum wage would have to be higher than the existing wage to have any effect, it would cause the demand for labour to fall and so create unemployment. If so, it would be the poorest members of the community who would be made redundant.

minority interest. When the holding company (or companies) of a group do not hold 100% of the ordinary shares of the group's subsidiaries, there will be minority interests in the group. For instance, suppose Company A holds 90% of Company B, 60% of Company C, and 98% of Company D: the four companies represent a group in the accounting sense but there are minority interests (of 10% in Company B, 40% of Company C, and 2% of Company D). Minority shareholders are of course entitled to their full share of profits and dividend, although their voting rights will be of no importance.

mint. A place in which metal coins are manufactured. In the U.K. the government department of the *Royal Mint*, under the control of the Chancellor of the Exchequer, has been the sole legal manufacturer of coins since the mid-sixteenth century. It also manufactures medals and foreign coins. In 1968 it was moved from London to Llantrisant, South Wales. In the U.S., coins are manufactured by the *Bureau of the Mint*, a branch of the Department of Treasury, which operates several mints and supervises various assay offices and depositories.

mint par of exchange. The rate of exchange between currencies as determined by the amount of pure metal each standard unit of currency contains. On the *gold standard, rates of exchange were determined by the amount of gold contained in the coins. *See* par of exchange. *See also* gold points.

M.I.S. *See* management information system.

misfeasance summons. An application to a court by a *liquidator, shareholder, or *creditor involved in the winding up of a company, or by the *Official Receiver, to examine the conduct of a present or past director of the company and, if necessary, to force him to repay or compensate the company for any money misappropriated or misapplied.

misrepresentation. An untrue statement of fact that induces a person to enter into a *contract. The misrepresentation may be fraudulent, i.e. deliberately intended to deceive, in which case the injured party can obtain damages and also rescind the contract, or it may be innocent, i.e. made as a result of a genuine mistake by a person who believes the representation to be true. In this case the injured party formerly had no right to claim damages, but could only rescind the contract; however, since the passing of the Misrepresentation Act (1967) a court may in the case of an innocent misrepresentation declare that damages are a more suitable remedy than *rescission of the contract, and award damages instead. Since the Misrepresentation Act, negligent or reckless misrepresentation may also give rise to a claim for damages.

mistake (in law). An error or misapprehension of fact that induces a person to enter into a contract. It does not necessarily invalidate the contract, although it may in certain circumstances do so. If the mistake is common to both parties (*mutual mistake*) it will have no effect if it is superficial, but it will make the contract void if it is fundamental. For example, in a contract for the sale of goods, a mistaken belief that the goods to be sold are in existence, when in fact they are not, will obviously nullify the contract. If the mistake is only made by one party (*unilateral mistake*) he may rescind the contract if the mistake was caused by misrepresentation or if the mistake is important and the other party was aware at the date of the contract that it was being made.

mitigation of damage. The minimization of a loss by the sufferer of the loss. If a court finds that a person is entitled to *damages for some loss, it will not usually order him to be compensated in respect of the whole loss unless it is satisfied that he has mitigated his damage as far as possible.

mixed economy. An economic system in which private enterprise and *nationalized industries exist alongside each other. In capitalist economies there is invariably some degree of government control over commerce and industry and in socialist economies some private enterprise often exists. Although the proportion of each type varies from country to country, almost all economies are to some extent mixed. In general, in a mixed economy the government seeks to control the basic industries (such as coal mining and steel production in the U.K.) as well as the public services, such as public transport, the post office, and the electricity and water utilities. In some cases public ownership is a matter of convenience (it would be impracticable to have more than one water company laying water mains in a district), in others the profit motive of private enterprise is inappropriate (as in providing an unprofitable train service as a public amenity), and in yet others the capital investment is too large for a private company. It may also become necessary for private-enterprise concerns to be taken over by the state for political reasons, for example to enable a failing company to continue to provide jobs or in the cause of promoting *industrial democracy. In Western Europe, mixed economies have been evolving during the course of the twentieth century as a means of maintaining the incentives of a capitalistic society without its worst features and of combining freedom of choice with a measure of economic planning. *See also* public sector, private sector.

M.L.R. *See* minimum lending rate.

mobility. The relative ease with which a factor of production can be transferred to a different use or a different location. Capital equipment often lacks mobility in that it can only be used for one specific purpose or is too expensive to transport. Land is obviously immobile geographically but it can generally be put to various uses. The mobility of labour is the degree to which workers are able or willing to change occupations (*occupational mobility*) or to move to a different area in the course of changing jobs (*geographical mobility*). *Horizontal mobility* refers to changes that do not result in a change in grading or status, whereas *vertical mobility* refers to changes that do. Prospects of an upward change will increase a worker's mobility but downgrading will reduce it. Highly skilled labour naturally lacks occupational mobility, whereas it is relatively easy for unskilled labour to change jobs. In general, however, labour tends to lack geographical mobility since many people prefer to stay in the area in which they have been brought up and made their homes. Mobility of labour is necessary for the elimination of disequilibrium in the labour market: if labour was perfectly mobile there would be no structural unemployment caused by technological progress and changes in demand. The U.K. government attempts to increase both occupational and geographical mobility by such means as retraining schemes, making information available about jobs in various parts of the country, etc. However, a great deal of expenditure is directed to encouraging firms to set up factories in areas of unemployment rather than relying on efforts to increase labour mobility.

mock auction. An *auction that is unfair in some way so as to make it illegal. The position is governed by the Mock Auctions Act (1961), which makes it a criminal offence to organize an auction at which any lot is sold at a price lower than one that is bid, or at which any part of the price is repaid to the buyer, or at which goods are given away to attract bidders for other items, or at which only those who have already bought lots are allowed to bid for further ones. *See also* ring.

mode. The value in a set of numbers that occurs most frequently. Thus in the set of numbers: 9, 15, 11, 13, 19, 15, 16, 11, 12, 13, 11, 18, 19, the mode is 11. There may of course be no mode or more than one mode; if there are two modes the set is said to be bi-modal; if more than two the set is said to be multimodal. Unlike the *arithmetic mean, the mode has no further application in statistical operations and is a tool of descriptive statistics only. *Compare* geometric mean, harmonic mean, median, quadratic mean.

model. A theoretical system of interlocking relationships designed to represent real-world phenomena and the connections between such phenomena, i.e. to serve as an instrument for explaining past and present events and for predicting and perhaps controlling future events. At its simplest, a model will consist of a single hypothesis that can be translated into a single functional equation with one dependent variable and one or more independent variables. For instance, one might postulate the microeconomic model that the demand for a particular commodity is a function of its price, disposable income levels, and the price of substitutes and complementary commodities. More commonly, however, a model will contain a series of hypotheses; the Keynesian theory of income determination, for example, will in simple form contain a consumption function. an investment function (the accelerator), a liquidity preference function, and a multiplier, while the supply of money (and therefore the rate of interest) and the level of government expenditure will be included as independent variables. It would not be possible to present a true image of the real world in a model because the real world (in the social sciences) is much too complicated; instead the model seeks to highlight the most important variables and to bring out the most important relationships. A model can usually be constructed and can sometimes even be analysed by argument but it is almost always convenient to present the model statistically by means of a series of functional equations before analysis is attempted. Correct statistical presentation requires as necessary antecedents correct definition of the variables (so that relevant observations can be made), correct measurement, and the ability to collect random samples (which means that the populations of the variables must be known and that an appropriate sample design must be arranged). Once the model is presented statistically, one can proceed to the estimation of the coefficients of the independent variables and from there, using techniques of statistical inference, one can analyse the implications of the model and decide on the basis of how close these implications are to the events of the real world whether the model can be rejected or provisionally allowed to stand. This analytical process, which is the logical development of a model, is much easier to carry out if it is done statistically (or mathematically) than if it is done without mathematical techniques, but the limiting necessary conditions mentioned above emerge only when a statistical analysis is attempted. In economics these conditions sometimes do not prevail, although there is no shortage of models or theories. It should be noted that statistics (and mathematics and econometrics) can never produce or even suggest economic models; this is the exclusive task of economic theory. Statistical and econometric techniques are simply instruments that aid in the analysis of the models. *See also* decision model, simultaneous model.

modified exponential curve. *See* growth curve.

moment. One of an indefinite number of characteristic coefficients derived from a distribution either from a *moment-generating function or by means of expected value operations being applied to powers of some function of the random variable whose distribution is under consideration. One can calculate moments about the origin, moments about the mean, or about any constant. To take two examples, the *n*th moment about the origin of the distribution of a random variable is found by taking the expected value of the *n*th power of the random variable; similarly the *n*th moment about the mean is given by the expected value of the *n*th power of the difference between the random variable and its mean. The first moment about the origin of a distribution is its mean while the second moment about the mean is its variance (the first moment about the mean is zero by definition). The third moment about the mean is an indicator of the skewness of the distribution while the fourth moment about the mean indicates the degree of the distribution's kurtosis. There are set formulae with which one can calculate moments about the mean from knowledge of the corresponding (and lower) moments about the origin. Moments above the fourth are rarely used.

moment-generating function. A function involving a mathematical series from the base **e**, from the expansion of which one can read off any desired *moment (about the origin, mean, or any constant). This process requires term-by-term integration in the case of a continuous density function.

monetarism. A school of economic thought developed mainly in the 1960s and 1970s, which holds that instability in an economy results from disturbances in the monetary sector, and therefore advocates the regulation of the money supply as the principal method of economic control. *See also* monetary theory.

monetary assets/liabilities. In inflation accounting, cash, debts owing and due, and loans that exist as money or money claims regardless of changes in price levels. In times of rising inflation it may be advantageous to have a high level of monetary liabilities, e.g. creditors, as their value in real terms is falling.

monetary compensatory amounts. Subsidies and border taxes used by the E.E.C. to bridge the gap betwen the green currency rates (*see* green pound) and real foreign exchange rates so that fluctuations in exchange rates are not reflected in farm prices. This keeps prices of agricultural produce comparable between member countries and prevents trading between them taking place purely as a result of exchange rate fluctuations, thus stabilizing the agricultural sector.

monetary economy. An economy in which money is the medium of exchange. Trade is obviously greatly facilitated by the use of money other than commodities for settling debts and the advantages of the division of labour can be exploited through the payment of money wages. *Compare* barter.

monetary inflation. A theory of *inflation that emphasizes the role of expansion in the money supply. It is closely associated with some variant of the *quantity theory of money, which links the money supply directly with the price level and the level of output. It emphasizes the role of expectations in inflation, especially in the short term, in which results not completely in accord with the theory can be explained through the adaptation of expectations to changes in rates of inflation.

monetary policy. The control of the supply of money and liquidity by the central bank through *open market operations and changes in interest rates to achieve the government's objectives of general economic policy. The control of the money supply allows the central bank to choose between a *tight money and an *easy money policy and thus in the short- to medium-run to affect the fluctuations in output in the economy. In an economy on a fixed exchange rate, a tight money policy will raise the rate of interest and induce capital to flow in to earn the higher interest. This will improve the balance of payments on capital account. Monetary policy may be used to control the level of employment, the balance of payments, the rate of economic growth, or the level of inflation, depending on the situation. It is claimed that in the post-war period in both the U.K. and the U.S. monetary policy has had a destabilizing influence because of the lags involved. These lags are said to be both long and variable and to make the effect of monetary policy very uncertain. This policy cannot be used for *fine tuning if this view of the economy is correct. Monetary policy can be distinguished from credit policy, which is the use of quantitative controls on borrowing and lending imposed by the government in an attempt to influence aggregate demand. *Compare* fiscal policy. *See* Radcliffe Report.

monetary reform. The introduction of a new unit of currency in a country, necessitated either by hyperinflation or inflation or by a policy such as decimalization (as in the U.K. in 1971).

monetary system. The policies and methods adopted by a country for the issue and control of its currency. The type of foreign exchange standard, the standard unit of currency and its divisions, monetary reserves, legal tender, convertibility, etc., would all constitute aspects of a country's monetary system. *See also* gold standard, bimetallism, monometallism.

monetary theory. The theory concerning the influence of the quantity of money in the economic system. It has received increasing attention over the last 30 years, in part because of the recent emergence of rapid inflation, but mainly due to the development of the subject. In many ways the implications of simple income-expenditure models, which had no monetary sector, were found to be lacking in the prediction of the behaviour of output and prices, and the use of ad hoc cost-push theories was found unsatisfactory. The major developments, both theoretical and empirical, have emanated from the U.S., especially from the University of Chicago and Professor Milton Friedman. The study of monetary phenomena has always been an integral part of macroeconomics, and before Keynes it constituted the whole of macroeconomics. It was only the development of small-scale empirical models of the economy that led money to be relatively ignored. The monetarist counterrevolution has been successful to the extent that the majority of economists now believe that the quantity of money has a significant effect on macroeconomic variables. *See* quantity theory of money.

monetary union. A group of nations that have agreed on exchange rates so as to make their currencies interchangeable. For example, the *Scandinavian Monetary Union*, lasting from 1873 until World War I, adopted the same monetary unit (the krone) and a single gold standard; its members were Sweden, Norway, and Denmark.

monetary unit. The standard unit of currency used in any country and quoted in its exchange rates, for example the dollar (U.S.), pound (U.K.), yen (Japan). The unit is related to the values of other monetary units by means of its exchange rate.

money at call and short notice. *See* call money.

money broker. A person or firm who, for a commission, deals in the money market in short-term loans and securities. He arranges for banks to lend to discount houses, etc., on a day-to-day basis.

money had and received. Money in the possession of one person that rightfully belongs to another. This may lead to a court action based upon a claim that money has been paid over to a person and that it would be unfair to allow him to retain it, either because it has been paid over upon false pretence, or he has totally failed to give any *consideration for it.

money illusion. The inability of an individual to realize that a *ceteris paribus increase in the general price level results in a fall in the value of any item that is measured in money terms and, in particular, earnings. Keynes suggested that workers suffer from money illusion, whereas employers do not. Hence, he sad, an increase in the price level when the money wage remains constant would increase employment and maintain the same perceived level of satisfaction of the workers, since they would not realize that their real wage is in fact lower. Empirical tests have tended to disprove this hypothesis, at least in times of high inflation. Hence, most modern models of the economy specifically exclude the possibility of money illusion from their equations. *See also* expected inflation, unexpected inflation.

money in circulation. The amount of money circulating in a country, excluding that held by the central bank (the Bank of England in the U.K. and the U.S. Treasury and the federal reserve banks in the U.S.). The amount of money in circulation is related to the volume of bank deposits, since a bank has to increase its cash holdings when deposits increase so as to maintain a constant ratio between its cash holdings and its liabilities to customers. *See also* income velocity of circulation.

moneylender. Any person wishing to carry on the business of moneylending in the U.K. must, under the Consumer Credit Act (1974), be registered and must take out a licence annually. These provisions do not apply to registered friendly societies, building societies, and bona fide banks and insurance companies. The 1974 Act also contains strict provisions insisting that the true annual rate of interest (known as the annual percentage rate or APR) be quoted in advance and in a particular way.

money market. The open market for lending or borrowing money at call or short notice (*see also* capital market). Institutions doing business in the money market are the discount houses, commercial banks, and the government, who deal in *bills of exchange, *Treasury bills, and *trade bills, which are the main items of exchange. The Bank of England is the *lender of last resort. The *foreign exchange market *bullion market, and the *accepting houses are sometimes considered to be part of the money market. The U.K. money market is in the City of London while the U.S. national money market is in New York.

money supply. *See* quantity theory of money, M_0, M_1, M_3.

money wages. Wages expressed in terms of money units (*compare* real wages). If prices and money wages change together there is no change in real wages in terms of what can be bought. If in this case the quantity of labour supplied changes there must be *money illusion in the labour market. This is the core of the neoclassical characterization of Keynesian macroeconomics. It is said that Keynes achieved his results by assuming that money wages were rigid downwards (i.e. wages do not decline in response to a slackening of demand for labour), and this irrational behaviour can produce unemployment equilibrium in the economy.

Monopolies and Mergers Act (1965). *See* Monopolies and Mergers Commission.

Monopolies and Mergers Commission. A commission established by the Monopolies and Restrictive Practices (Inquiry and Control) Act (1948) to investigate and report on monopoly situations. The Commission's terms of reference were later widened to cover mergers, in the *Monopolies and Merg-*

ers Act (1965) and individual anti-competitive practices, in the *Competition Act (1980). Cases for investigation are referred to the Commission by the Office of Fair Trading; *see* Fair Trading Act (1973).

Monopoly situations. The legislation defines a monopoly situation as one in which a single firm supplies at least one quarter of a particular good or service (scale monopoly), or in which two or more firms jointly supplying more than one quarter of a good or service agree to restrict competition between themselves (complex monopoly). The Commission is required to investigate monopoly suppliers to determine whether or not they operate in the *public interest.* The public interest is broadly equated with behaviour that is reasonable both with respect to consumers' interests (e.g. fair prices) and those of other suppliers (e.g. absence of practices designed to harm competitors) and which produces an efficient use of resources.

Mergers. The legislation covers mergers that create or intensify a monopoly situation or that involve the taking over of assets in excess of £15 million. The Commission is required to determine whether or not a merger is in the public interest, taking into account its possible advantages, such as improved efficiency, increased international competitiveness, etc., and balancing them against possible disadvantages in the form of increased market power, higher prices, etc.

Anti-competitive practices. The Commission has to decide whether or not such anti-competitive practices as refusal to supply, exclusive dealing, aggregated rebates, and price discrimination operate against the public interest.

monopolistic (imperfect) competition. A market situation under which the goods of the various producers are not perfect substitutes (i.e. it is a form of *imperfect competition*), al-

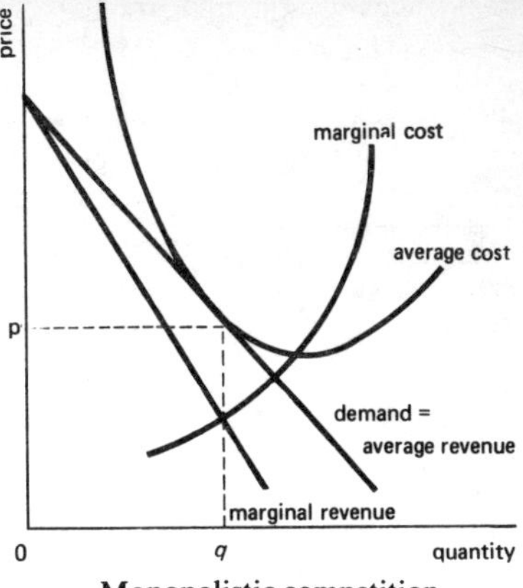

Monopolistic competition

though it is assumed that there are many producers and reasonable freedom of entry to the industry. The lack of perfect substitutability is due mostly to *product differentiation, *advertising, or locational factors. For example, other things being equal one prefers to buy milk at a shop 15 yards from home rather than from one 15 miles away, so that if a shopkeeper is the only one in an area he may charge a penny or two more than his distant competitor. This is shown graphically by the fact that the demand curve is downward-sloping rather than being perfectly horizontal as in *perfect competition.

In general, as a result of the lack of substitutability each producer may exert some small control over his price and so will act as a monopolist and adjust his output to set marginal cost equal to marginal revenue and this output will be less than the one at which marginal cost equals average cost. This difference in output is the degree of excess capacity that exists and the price charged is higher than marginal cost. The concept of monopolistic or imperfect competition as a midpoint between the extremes of *monopoly and perfect competition was devised independently by E. H.

Chamberlin in the U.S. and J. V. Robinson in the U.K.

monopoly. An industry in which there is only one producer and many con-

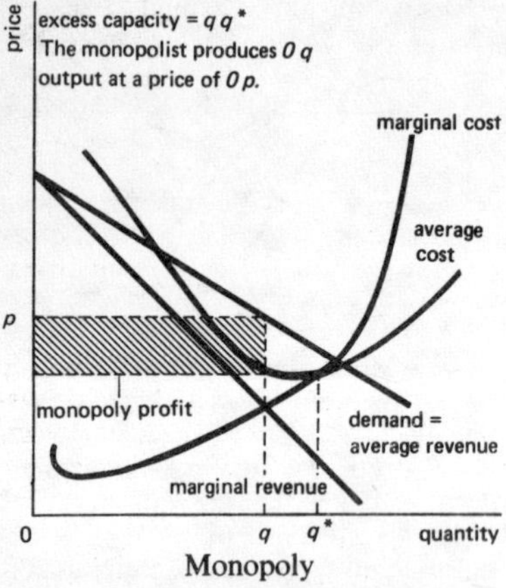

Monopoly

sumers. Hence the demand curve for this producer will be the industry demand curve, which is the aggregate demand curve for the product; this is assumed to be downward sloping. By contrast in perfect competition the assumptions imply that the firm faces a perfectly elastic horizontal demand curve, so sets his marginal cost equal to the price which will be the same as marginal revenue. In a monopoly, marginal revenue is not equal to price, but to $p(1 - 1/\varepsilon)$ where p is price and ε is the elasticity of demand and is greater than zero. Consumers then pay p/ε per unit above the marginal cost to the producer, and the proportion of that which is above the average cost is the monopoly profit. It is not true however that the existence of a monopoly price implies the existence of monopoly profit. High fixed costs relative to demand can mean that the monopoly only operates at the break-even point. Neither does the restriction of output in itself imply excess capacity. However there is a net loss in *consumer surplus that cannot be made up, even if a monopoly tax were to be imposed to redress the distributional effects of the monopoly and return monopoly profits to the consumer.

The continued existence of a monopoly with monopoly profits implies prohibitive barriers to entry, otherwise competitors would be attracted into the industry by those profits.

Because monopoly leads to a misallocation of resources through setting the marginal cost equal to marginal revenue instead of to price, government policy is generally opposed to monopoly, at least in the private sector. There are circumstances in which a government will support a private monopoly within its own country, often for purposes of national security, or to realize economies of scale, which will make the industry competitive in international trade. *See* rationalization. *See also* natural monopoly, patent monopoly, bilateral monopoly.

monopoly profits. The *economic profits that accrue to a monopolist as a result of his control over pricing and output in an industry; calculated as the difference between his average cost (including opportunity cost) and the price, multiplied by the output.

monopoly tax. A tax imposed by a government to redress the distributional distortions of monopoly. Since a monopolist decides on his output simply from considerations of his marginal cost and demand conditions, a *lump-sum tax, which does not alter his marginal cost curve, may return to the consumer by way of the government the surplus exacted by the monopolist in the form of monopoly profits. This does not, however, rectify the misallocation of resources and a dead-weight loss in consumer surplus remains.

Although theoretically appealing, the tax is almost impossible to apply in reality, simply because of the difficulties in calculating the monopoly profits since the costs and profits appearing on the accountants' books are not the same as economic costs and profits.

monopsony. An industry in which there is only one consumer or buyer, but many producers. It is the counterpart to monopoly. In this case the buyer sets his marginal revenue cost equal to his marginal utility or marginal revenue product, depending on whether the good is intended for consumption or, more frequently, is an intermediate good used as an input in a further stage of production. The distribution effects and welfare loss through misallocation of resources are analogous to those of monopoly, except that in monopsony the purchasers appropriate the producer surplus.

monotonic. A function is said to be monotonic if it either increases or decreases through its entire range but does not do both. Diagrammatically, the slope of a monotonic function will be either positive or negative throughout its range.

Monte Carlo study. An application of *simulation in which the probabilities associated with the various outcomes of a system or activity are calculated on the basis of repeated experiments with a model. Monte Carlo techniques are used in those cases in which the mathematical derivation of probabilities is either excessively cumbersome or extremely difficult because of the complexity of the system. They have received widespread acceptance in many areas of empirical quantitative analysis, notably operations research.

Monthly Digest of Statistics. A monthly publication of the U.K. *Central Statistical Office, covering major sectoral and industrial statistics, vital statistics, and national income statistics. *See also* Annual Abstract of Statistics.

moonlighting. Having a second job, especially one that is carried out in the evening or at night after leaving one's primary daytime job. The propensity to moonlight is considered to be a negative function of income and a positive function of family size.

moratorium. A period during which the payment of debts is suspended. It may consist of one government giving a foreign government authority to delay meeting its obligations. Alternatively it may occur if a whole market gets into difficulties as a result of exceptional circumstances; to avoid possible bankruptcies the whole market declares a moratorium during which the payment of market debts is suspended for a period in order to enable firms to make appropriate financial arrangements.

mortality rate. Another name for the crude death rate. *See* death rate.

mortality table. An actuarial table showing the life expectancy of a person of a given health disposition. The first series of tables was produced as early as 1693. A more important set was compiled in 1755 by Dodson, who showed that it was possible to charge the same premium per annum throughout a life assurance contract (a *level premium*), provided that it is graduated to the assured's age on entry.

mortgage. A transfer of land or any saleable property as security for a debt or the discharge of some obligation. The borrower is known as the *mortgagor* and the lender as the *mortgagee*. A *legal mortgage* vests a legal estate in the *mortgagee* with the power to sell the mortgaged property should the mortgagor default in payment of the debt. *Building societies lend money to house purchasers taking the property as collateral security. Mortgage regulations in the U.K. are governed by the Law of Property Act

(1925). *See also* equitable mortgage, second mortgage.

mortgage debenture. A *debenture issued by a company on a specified asset. It is used especially by property companies to raise capital. *See also* floating charge.

mortgagee in possession. A mortgagee who has taken over the mortgaged property on the default of the mortgagor in order to collect rents and manage the property. Should he wish to avoid the liabilities attached to the upkeep of the property he may appoint a receiver to manage the estate and collect rents.

most-favoured-nation clause. A provision in a commercial treaty by which two countries agree to extend to each other in the future the same treatment as they extend to the most favoured nation they are dealing with. Thus if A and B conclude a treaty today and tomorrow B concludes a more advantageous treaty with C (perhaps for a further set of tariff reductions), the conditions of the second treaty will automatically extend to A as well. This is the heart of the GATT policy of nondiscrimination, i.e. that all friendly nations should be allowed to carry on trade with a country on the same terms. However, since agreements on tariffs are usually made on categories of goods, de facto discrimination can and does occur through tariff differentials. Thus, if only country A exported copper and only B exported wool, a reduction in the tariff on copper or an increase on the wool tariff is clearly discriminatory. Waivers for the most-favoured-nation clause have been granted by GATT in cases of commercial treaties with under-developed countries, between countries intending to form a customs union, and for certain arrangements with colonial origins such as *Commonwealth preference.

motion. A proposal that is put to a meeting for discussion or debate. It is usual for those attending the meeting to receive a formal *notice of motion* before the meeting to enable them to decide whether or not they wish to speak at the meeting and whether they are for or against the motion. Changes to the motion may be discussed at the meeting in the form of amendments. If the meeting votes to incorporate an amendment into the original motion, the amended motion (called the *substantive motion*) is then discussed. When a motion has been debated and voted upon it becomes a *resolution of the meeting.

motivational research. A marketing study into the underlying psychological reasons consumers have for buying one particular product rather than some other product. It is usually the first stage in a campaign to stimulate sales.

motor insurance. Insurance for motor vehicles has been compulsory since the Road Traffic Act (1930) covering claims resulting from the death or injury of a third party caused by the vehicle. Compulsory cover was extended by the Motor Vehicles (Passenger Insurance) Act (1971) and the Road Traffic Act (1972) to include liability for the death of or injury to any passenger in the vehicle itself. Most drivers have either *third party insurance, covering the insured's legal liability towards third parties including passengers and damage to third parties' property, or *comprehensive insurance*, which provides the widest cover available. The full extent of the cover provided varies with the insurance company, but all comprehensive policies cover the driver, the insured vehicle, third parties, and sometimes the contents of the insured vehicle. There are also third party, fire, and theft policies. Insurance companies base their premiums on the type of cover provided, the size and value of the vehicle, the use of which it is to be put, the age and driving record of the driver, and the area of the country in which the vehicle will normally be driven. *No-claims bonuses reduce the cost of a premium and thus discourage the insured from claiming for small sums.

Motor Insurers' Bureau. A body that was created as a consequence of an agreement between almost all of the insurers transacting motor insurance and the Minister of Transport in 1946. It has a legally binding agreement with the government to satisfy judgements in respect of claims within the scope of the Road Traffic Acts, where the plaintiff has been unable to recover from the motorist involved any damages awarded. Hit-and-run drivers who could not be identified are within the scope of this agreement.

There is also a domestic agreement made between members of the Bureau which deals with cases where a policy issued by a member was in existence but for some reason was not effective in respect of the accident in question. The member who issued the policy makes any necessary payments without recovery from the main fund of the Bureau.

mountain. A surplus of agricultural produce that accumulates in the E.E.C. as a result of the operation of the *Common Agricultural Policy. The C.A.P., which is primarily designed to safeguard the income and standard of living of the farmers of the E.E.C., establishes minimum prices for most types of produce. If the market price of any crop falls below this guaranteed minimum, the farmers can sell instead to the Community, which must buy at the guaranteed minimum price. As a result the farmers can plan ahead in the knowledge that there will be a floor price at which they will be able to sell, and since this minimum price has to be fairly high to guarantee the farmers' incomes the system encourages overproduction. The gluts, or mountains, that occur are sold to the Community, which must dispose of them. Unfortunately it cannot sell them to consumers within the E.E.C. as this would depress prices; depressed prices would mean that even more produce would be offered to the Community, so further increasing the mountains. As destroying the produce is politically and morally unacceptable, the E.E.C. either disposes of the mountains by selling to groups who would be unable to afford such goods at their normal prices, such as old-age pensioners, or sells them to countries outside the E.E.C. at extremely low prices.

Notable surpluses have been the butter and beef mountains and the wine and milk lakes. Their existence has led some members, for example Germany and the U.K., to seek radical reforms in the C.A.P., but this has been vigorously resisted by other members, such as France, where the farming lobby is large and politically important.

In 1982 C.A.P. spending accounted for 63% of the E.E.C. budget, compared with 74.5% in 1975.

moving average. A series of arithmetic means calculated from groups of consecutive values in a time series. The groups of values from which the moving averages are computed are obtained by including the next value in the series and excluding the earliest. A moving average for the series 8, 14, 16, 12, 20, 24 might be obtained as follows:

$$(8 + 14)/2 = 11; (14 + 16)/2 = 15;$$
$$(16 + 12)/2 = 14; (12 + 20)/2 = 16;$$
$$(20 + 24)/2 = 22.$$

Thus the moving average in this case is given by the series 11, 15, 14, 16, 22. Moving averages of quarterly data are often calculated in order to eliminate seasonal factors; in this case the groups would contain four items each (representing the four quarters). Moving averages are used to smooth a time series in order to present its trend more clearly.

multicollinearity. The presence of substantial correlation between two or more of the independent variables in a regression. This makes it difficult to distinguish their separate influences and to estimate their individual relative effects. Multicollinearity vitiates one of the assumptions underlying the Gauss-Markov theorem and least squares estimators will thus not be satisfactory in a regression involving multicollinear variables. In the case of perfect multicollinearity, when two or more independent variables are connected by an exact linear relationship, least squares estimation will not even be possible. In the case of high but not perfect multicollinearity the variances of the regression coefficients will be very high and consequently their significance levels will be unsatisfactorily low. This is normally the means by which multicollinearity is discovered. Multicollinearity occurs quite frequently in econometric studies and its remedy is basically the acquisition of better data. Early studies of the demand function based on time-series data, for instance, ran into problems because of multicollinearity between two of the independent variables, prices and incomes. The solution was not found until the collection of cross-section income data, which gave a wider range of income variation and permitted the determination of a good income coefficient, which was then inserted into the time-series analysis. *See also* Gauss-Markov theorem.

multilateral trade. International trade in which each state trades with many other states and accepts a surplus or deficit in its balance of payments with individual states, although it attempts to keep its overall trading position in balance. The advantage of this form of trade is that it enables the total volume of trade to be greater than that with *bilateral trade, which leads to gains in efficiency through specialization.

Since 1947 GATT has been the principal body to encourage multilateral trade by seeking a general reduction in tariffs and the abolition of quotas.

multinational. A company with branches or subsidiaries in several countries. Multinationals are usually very large organizations with an international approach to commercial tactics.

multinomial distribution. A *multivariate distribution involving discrete variables. It is an extension of the binomial distribution to the case in which the results of independent trials of an experiment can be placed into more than just the two categories of success and failure. The multinomial distribution, however, is an awkward distribution to handle for the purposes both of analysis and of numerical calculation.

multiple. *See* P/E ratio.

multiple correlation. Correlation between three or more variables. Multiple correlation is thus an extension of two-variable correlation, although the arithmetic involved mushrooms as more variables are added. Multiple correlation does however differ from simple correlation in one respect other than the number of variables involved: its coefficient does not have a sign. This is because, in the case of three (or more) variables, one variable may be directly correlated with one of the others but inversely correlated with the third. The coefficient of multiple correlation can be calculated by a formula applied to the first-order correlation coefficients; that is, to the simple correlation coefficients as between individual pairs of the variables that are under analysis. Its square is the coefficient of multiple determination. Multiple correlation has limited value in statistical and econometric analysis and is used less frequently than *multiple regression. *See also* correlation.

multiple (non-unique) equilibrium. **1.** In theories of the firm that take into account objectives other than profit-maximization a firm can be in equilibrium at a number of levels of production. These theories hold that after a minimum level of profits has been attained, a firm may seek other targets, such as gaining a certain share of the market, a particular level of sales, or a maximization of growth rate.

2. If a firm has a marginal cost curve with more than one minimum point, the marginal revenue curve will cut the marginal cost curve from above more than once. The points at which this occurs will represent levels of output at which the firm is in equilibrium although it will be in disequilibrium at any point in between.

multiple exchange rates. A number of exchange rates that are quoted for a currency, each rate depending upon the purpose for which it is required. This system cannot operate without drastic exchange controls to prevent advantage being taken of the differences between rates.

The system was pioneered by Nazi Germany in the 1930s. At that time Germany was undergoing an ambitious programme of domestic expansion, especially in rearmaments, so that the Reichsmark was greatly overvalued. Multiple exchange rates enabled Germany to maintain her level of exports despite this overvaluation.

Multiple exchange rates were widespread in World War II and in the post-war years, when some countries gave preferential rates to tourists. However, they were condemned by the *Bretton Woods Conference and have become rarer, although they are still used in parts of South America and elsewhere.

multiple regression. *Regression applied to three or more variables; i.e. with two or more independent variables. The typical linear multiple regression equation will take the form: $Y = a_1 + a_2X_2 + a_3X_3 + \ldots a_nX_n + e$, where Y is the dependent variable, $X_2, \ldots X_n$ are the independent variables, $a_1, \ldots a_n$ are the regression coefficients, and e is a stochastic disturbance term. Estimation procedures, such as least squares, can be used to calculate values for the coefficients and the relationship between the X variables and Y will then take its form. Coefficients of (simple) correlation and of partial correlation can be calculated between Y and individual X variables and these, together with the regression coefficients, the coefficient of multiple determination, and the variances of the variables, form the basic tools of detailed regression analyses. They can be manipulated to determine such questions as the amount of variation in the dependent variable explained or unexplained by various permutations of the independent variables, and the increase in the explained variation of the dependent variable due to one of the independent variables. *See also* least squares estimation, coefficient of multiple determination.

multiple shops. A former name for *chain stores.

multiple taxation. Taxes levied by several authorities on the same basis. For instance a New Yorker pays income tax to the city of New York, the State of New York, and the U.S. federal government. If U.K. local rates were replaced by a local income tax, as has been suggested, income tax in the U.K. would become a type of multiple taxation.

multiplier. The number by which the amount of a specific capital investment (or change in some other element in aggregate demand) is multiplied to give the resulting total amount by which national income or employment is increased. The multiplier takes into account all the spin-offs into different trades and industries resulting from the investment (or other change in aggregate demand). It is expressed as the reciprocal of the *marginal propensity to save: the greater the marginal propensity to save, the smaller is the multiplier since relatively more money is being taken out of circulation rather than being spent and increasing the incomes of others. However, if an economy is already at full employment an increase in investment tends to raise prices and interest rates rather than increase real income. The multiplier concept was introduced by Richard Kahn in 1931 and was later used extensively by J. M. Keynes.

multivariate (joint) distribution (in statistics). A *distribution involving two or more random variables. A multivariate distribution can be defined by a *joint density function. For example, the incidence of a disease may vary according to age, sex, weight, and occupation; one could then formulate a multivariate distribution based on these four random variables and from it could be determined the probability that the disease would strike any particular individual according to his status with respect to the four random variables. (This assumes that the total incidence of the disease is also known.) *See also* density function.

mutilated cheque (bill, bank note). If a cheque or *bill of exchange is torn to such an extent that there is a possibility that it was intended to be cancelled then the banker on whom it is drawn will require the collecting banker to confirm that it was accidentally torn, if that was the case, before he will pay it. Bank of England notes having more than half the note with the whole of the promise to pay, some of the signature, and one complete serial number and part of the other on the fragment will usually be paid by the Bank of England on presentation through a bank or post office, but otherwise a full explanation of the circumstances will be required and payment will be delayed.

mutual funds. The U.S. name for *unit trusts.

mutuality. A rule of *equity preventing a court from granting a remedy to one party to a contract that could not be granted to the other party, were he to apply for it. For instance, if one party is entitled to goods the other must be entitled to payment. It applies especially to the remedy of *specific performance. Thus a court will not grant this remedy to a minor or person of unsound mind as it could not be granted against such a person.

mutual life assurance company. A company that has no shareholders. The funds come from members' contributions; apart from benefits and running costs there are no other charges on the funds. These companies grew from the Friendly Societies, which were based on mutual aid (people banding together to provide help for each other in times of personal misfortune).

mutual mistake. *See* mistake.

myopia. The short-sightedness of the individual in not acting in his best economic interests. This is usually due to a distorted *time preference, in that the individual prefers to spend his money now rather than saving some for future needs. There may, however, be other reasons, such as inadequate knowledge. Governments often act to correct this by such measures as the enforcement of a minimum period of education, compulsory provision for retirement, etc. The extent of the government's paternalism will vary with its political beliefs.

N

naked debenture. Another name for an unsecured *debenture.

name. A member of a *Lloyd's underwriting syndicate. Each name on the syndicate is directly liable to the policyholder for his share of any loss. Names do not take any active part in the underwriting process, but they have to show that they personally own substantial funds, a proportion of which has to be deposited with Lloyd's.

name day. *See* ticket day.

narrower-range securities. *See* Trustee Investment Act (1961).

National Advisory Council on Education for Industry and Commerce. A body set up in 1948 by the Minister of Education, which advises the Secretary of State on the national policy necessary for the full development of education in relation to industry and commerce, including training for management and design and the allied professions, within the field of further education. It maintains contacts with industry and commerce and appropriate professional bodies. It arranges consultations with the University Grants Commission on matters relating to education of university standard. The council is reconstituted every three years and has a chairman, up to 20 members nominated by the Secretary of State, and 52 members nominated by the ten Regional Advisory Councils for Further Education in England and Wales.

national banks. U.S. commercial banks that are established by federal charter, unlike state banks which are established by state charter. They were created by the National Bank Act (1863) and were originally empowered to issue notes as well as performing the commercial functions of a bank. Membership of the *Federal Reserve System is compulsory for national banks (though not for state banks).

National Board for Prices and Incomes (N.B.P.I. *or* **P.I.B.).** An independent board that was created by the U.K. government in 1965 to consider and report on the effects of proposed increases in prices, wages, salaries, and dividends that were referred to it by government departments. It emphasized productivity agreements as being justifications for above-average increases in earnings. The board was closed down in 1970, but its activities were taken over by the *Pay Board in 1973.

national certificates and diplomas. Higher education qualifications in the U.K., ranging up to degree standard, mostly in the fields of business studies, science, and engineering. Certificates (O.N.C. and H.N.C.) are awarded after part-time study, whereas diplomas (O.N.D. and H.N.D.) are awarded after full-time study.

Ordinary certificates and diplomas (O.N.C. and O.N.D.) achieve standards comparable to A-level. O.N.C. courses last three years and O.N.D. courses last two years for full-time students and three years for sandwich-course students. H.N.D. courses approach degree standard. The courses last from two to three years. H.N.C. courses are of a lower standard than H.N.D. courses, but can be raised to an H.N.D. level after an extra year of study.

National Chamber of Trade. A U.K. organization founded in 1897 to promote the causes of the distributive trades. Its members are either local chambers of commerce or trade or national trade organizations. It publishes the *National Chamber of Trade Journal* monthly.

National Coal Board (N.C.B.). The public corporation that controls the U.K. coal-mining industry. The nationalization of the industry had been recommended by the Sankey Commission in 1919 but was not effected until 1947, following the Coal Mines Nationalization Act (1946), which set up the N.C.B. The Act set out the N.C.B.'s policy as the production of coal at such prices and in such quantity as to further the public interest. It brought 1500 mines under the control of the N.C.B. and 400, each employing fewer than 30 underground workers, remained independent but operated under licence from the N.C.B. The coal industry is administered by nine regional Coal Boards and 48 area managements. Since 1946 many small mines have been closed in an attempt to rationalize the industry and other more profitable ones have been enlarged and automated.

National Debt. The debts that are owed by a central government both internally (owing to persons resident in the country concerned) and externally (owing to foreign creditors). Part of the U.K. internal debt is in the form of *National Savings Certificates and other forms of bonds issued through the Post Office to attract the savings of investors of limited means. The remainder is in the form of three-month *Treasury bills and borrowings from the Bank of England (the *floating debt) or in the form of the various *government bonds (the *funded debt). (*See also* unfunded debt.) The National Debt has greatly increased after every war, but is now lower, expressed as a percentage of national income, than it was immediately before World War II. It is managed to some extent by the *open market operations of the Bank of England through the *National Debt Commissioners. All interest on the National Debt has to be provided by taxation and the management of the National Debt is an important instrument of government monetary policy. The external debt, though smaller than the internal debt, is more important as payments of interest to other countries adversely affect the *balance of payments. The external debt mainly consists of debts that were incurred during the immediate post-war years from the U.S. and Canada.

National Debt Commissioners. The branch of the Bank of England that manages the National Debt. Its aim is to finance the National Debt as cheaply as possible by issuing bonds and repaying and converting those that have matured.

National Development Bonds. Bonds issued by the U.K. government in May 1964 to replace the Defence Bond, which had been introduced in 1939. They were available in units of £5 from savings bank post offices, trustee savings banks, commercial banks, and stockbrokers. They could be held by individuals, trustees, limited companies, and other bodies. They were replaced by British Savings Bonds in 1968.

National Economic Development Council (N.E.D.C.). A council of representatives of government, industry, and the unions in the U.K. under the chairmanship of the Prime Minister or a senior minister. *Neddy*, as the N.E.D.C. is sometimes called, was set up in 1962 with an independent secretariat to oversee development in different industries and regions with the aim of increasing the rate of economic growth in the U.K. In 1964 smaller sub-committees known as *Economic*

Development Committees (E.D.C.s or *Little Neddies*) were set up under its management to study and assist particular industries. This aspect of the N.E.D.C.'s work was further extended in the late 1970s, with the setting up of some 40 sector working parties.

National Enterprise Board (N.E.B.). A U.K. body established by the Industry Act (1975). The main purposes of the N.E.B. were to assist the economy and to promote industrial efficiency and international competitiveness. It was given access to £1000 million of public money to enable it to finance the establishment and development of individual firms, and to assist in the reorganization of an industry by promoting mergers and rationalization programmes. Major investments were made in British Leyland, International Computers, and the Inmos (microchip) project. In 1981 the N.E.B. was merged with the *National Research and Development Corporation to form the *British Technology Group. *See also* Industrial Reorganization Corporation.

National Giro. *See* Giro.

National Health Service. A comprehensive range of services provided free by the U.K. government for the prevention, diagnosis, and treatment of illness for all citizens. It includes the provision of hospitals as well as medical, dental, nursing, ambulance, maternity, and family-planning services. The National Health Service Act (1946), introduced by Aneurin Bevan, set out to provide a free medical service for all and took over the responsibility for the voluntary hospitals. The organization, established in 1948, was a tripartite structure corresponding to the three main parts of the service: the hospital service, the general practitioner service, and the local authority health service.

national income. The total annual value of all the goods and services produced by a country: it is equal to the *net national product at factor cost. Sometimes national income is calculated gross of capital consumption, in which circumstances it is equivalent to *gross national product at factor cost. In the U.K. the *Central Statistical Office publishes the *Blue Books giving the national income within that period. *See also* income-expenditure model, circular flow of income.

National Incomes Commission. A body appointed by the U.K. government in November 1962 to examine and report upon the repercussions on the national economy of specific wage agreements referred to it. It had no substantive powers, nor did the government take any powers to enforce its findings. Its establishment was opposed by the T.U.C. and it received no cooperation from any trade union. With the setting up of the National Incomes and Prices Board in 1965, the Commission was terminated. Its impact was minimal.

National Institute of Economic and Social Research. A research association set up in 1938 to increase knowledge of the economic and social conditions of contemporary society. It publishes the *National Institute Economic Review.*

National Insurance. A system of insurance benefits provided by the U.K. government to meet such specified contingencies as unemployment, sickness, old age, and widowhood. Benefits are paid for partly by the insured person's contributions, partly by contributions of employers in respect of their employees, and partly by a contribution made by the Exchequer out of general taxation. The National Insurance Act (1965) consolidated the National Insurance Acts (1946–64) and makes everyone over the minimum school-leaving age in the U.K. eligible. From April 1975 the flat-rate national insurance contributions and graduated contributions have been replaced by a system of earnings-related contributions. National Insurance should not be confused with supplementary benefits. The former provides for benefits dependent upon a person's contributions, the latter provides for benefits out of state funds because of need.

nationalized industry. An industry that has been brought under direct state control and ownership, such as the steel and coal industries in the U.K. The usual justifications for nationalization are that the social rate of return is higher than the private rate of return (for instance, the industry is loss-making, but as its products are vital to other industries it has to be subsidized) or that *economies of scale in organization and production exist within the industry. The nationalized industry thus may monopolize the market without the fear of *monopoly pricing practices. *See also* privatization.

National Plan. A plan, usually for a period of several years, formulated by a government for the economic development of its country. The U.S.S.R. successfully carried out two Five-Year Plans in the 1930s with ruthless determination; other countries have copied the idea, though not the method. A National Plan was drawn up in the U.K. in 1965 for the period 1965–70, though it had to be revised in 1968 because of the effects of credit restrictions. It detailed the investment and growth rate that would be required from each industry to achieve an increase in G.N.P. of 25% by 1970 and to correct the balance of payments deficit. These targets were rightly criticized at the time as being over-optimistic and this indeed proved to be the case.

National Research and Development Corporation (N.R.D.C.). A U.K. body established by the Development of Inventions Act (1948) to encourage and exploit inventions. The N.R.D.C.'s basic terms of reference were to promote the adoption by industry of new products and processes invented in government laboratories, universities, and elsewhere. Public money was made available both to finance individual projects and to establish joint ventures with industrial firms. In 1981 it was merged with the *National Enterprise Board to form the *British Technology Group.

National Savings Bank. A savings bank operated by the Post Office. There are two types of accounts: Ordinary Accounts and Investment Accounts, which pay a higher rate of interest.

National Savings Certificates. A method of borrowing by the U.K. government devised to encourage people of limited means to save by purchasing certificates, which are issued in small denominations through post offices, banks, and savings centres. The interest on them is free of income tax, but the number that can be held by any one person is limited. They were first issued in 1916 and called *War Savings Certificates.* The 28th Issue (introduced August 1984) pays 9% interest per annum. Inflation-linked National Savings Certificates are also available, paying a 3% (1984–85) supplement.

National Savings Stock Register. A list showing the U.K. government securities that may be bought through any post office. The securities that are available include consols, funding stock, Treasury loans, and British Savings Bonds. The prices of most of these securities are not fixed but vary from day to day. They are quoted on the Stock Exchange, through which they are bought and sold.

National Trust. An organization that maintains and preserves places of national importance, either for their natural beauty (coast lines, mountains, moorlands, fens, etc.), natural wealth (bird sanctuaries, areas of unique fauna and flora, etc.), or historic interest (stately homes, national monuments, ancient sites, etc.). The National Trust was founded in 1895 as a public company not trading for profit and was incorporated by Act of Parliament in 1907. The National Trust for Scotland was founded in 1931.

Although not directly subsidized by the state, the National Trust enjoys relief from taxation. Its revenue comes from members' subscriptions, donations, and income from its properties, which are either bought or bequeathed to it.

natural economy. A *barter economy, so called because money is an artificial invention that replaced the more "natural" barter system.

natural increase. The difference between the number of births and deaths occurring in a population during a given period. During the last 75 years in the U.S. the natural increase in population has been well over 100 million. This statistic, coupled with the net migration rate, are all that is needed to find the change in numbers of a population.

natural justice. The rules and procedure to be followed when arbitrating on (*see* arbitration) or adjudicating in disputes. The principles are that an arbitrator or adjudicator must declare any interest he has in the matter being disputed, that he should give each party an equal opportunity to state his case, and that no evidence should be heard without both parties or their representatives being present. All documents produced in evidence must be available for scrutiny by both parties. In fact, the arbitrator must act fairly, without bias, and in good faith.

natural level of unemployment. The level of unemployment that at any time is consistent with equilibrium in the structure of real wage rates. A lower level of employment implies an excess demand for labour, producing upward pressure on real wages relative to the *secular trend. A higher level implies the reverse. This controversial concept is used by M. Friedman (*b.* 1912), who introduced the term in 1968, to justify his claim that in the long run neither *fiscal nor *monetary policy can affect the level of unemployment. Thus, an economy could be at the natural level of unemployment with 25% inflation or 10% deflation. The only effect of policy in the long run is to change the price level or the rate of inflation.

natural monopoly. A monopoly arising when decreasing returns to scale make optimum plant size large relative to demand for the product and possibly, though not necessarily, greater than total demand at a price equal to the minimum average cost. In this case, the market will only support one firm. Indeed in such a case it may even be that the monopoly price is lower than the break-even point for smaller firms, so that new entrants would have higher costs than the monopolist.

natural rate of growth. The maximum sustainable long-run rate of growth in the Harrod-Domar model of the economy. It is directly related to the increase in the labour force and the rate of technological change and must equal the *warranted rate of growth if equilibrium in the economy is to be maintained.

natural rate of interest. The rate of interest at which the demand for, and supply of, loanable funds are in balance. In the real world the market rate of interest will deviate from the natural rate of interest because of excess credit creation by the banks (increasing the supply of loanable funds) or hoarding of cash by individuals (reducing the supply of loanable funds).

natural wastage. The depletion of a workforce through nonreplacement of those who leave, retire, or die. Once the decision to reduce a workforce has been taken, natural wastage is usually preferred by both management and employees to creating redundancies, although it often takes longer to have the desired effect.

N.B.P.I. *See* National Board for Prices and Incomes.

N.C.B. *See* National Coal Board.

near money. An asset that is transferable and therefore may be used to settle certain debts, but that is not acceptable when tendered for all transactions. For instance, banks may use short-term bills as a medium of exchange in certain circumstances, but an individual may not be able to do so. Near money is not included in the *money supply because, unlike bank notes, coins, and cheques, it is not in general use for the settlement of debts.

N.E.B. *See* National Enterprise Board.

N.E.D.C. (Neddy). *See* National Economic Development Council.

needs element. *See* rate support grant.

negative cash flow. A situation in which more cash is being paid out by an organization than it is receiving. This does not necessarily mean that it is making a loss; for example, it may be working on a contract to deliver goods in 10 months time. If the payment terms are that payment is made after delivery, it will be paying out money on this contract for 10 months without any income. During this period it may have a negative cash flow, but this may be restored to a positive cash flow, and a profit, when the goods are paid for. *See also* cash flow.

negative easement. *See* easement.

negative income tax (N.I.T.). An *income tax in which people who earn an income below a given cut-off point receive, rather than pay, taxes in proportion to the amount that their earnings fall short of the cut-off. In practice it is equivalent to giving a grant to each individual (and hence a guaranteed annual income) and then taxing all his earned income. The point at which the tax equals the original grant is the cut-off point. The system was proposed by Milton Friedman as a means of redistributing income to replace *welfare payments. As with *lump-sum taxation*, it is then argued that the market mechanism will lead to an efficient allocation that is equitable since incomes have a guaranteed minimum. It is also argued that it increases the incentive to work since someone receiving N.I.T. can increase his after-tax income by working since his *marginal rate of taxation is less than 100%, i.e. the amount of grant reduction is less than the additional earned income. This is contrasted with welfare benefits, such as unemployment insurance, with which any earnings result in a loss of all the benefit or at least an amount equal to the income increase (i.e. equal to 100% tax or more), which is a supposed disincentive to work (*see* poverty trap). Another name for this is *tax-credit system*.

negligence. The breach of a duty to take care, which causes loss or injury to the person to whom the duty is owed. The duty of care may arise in a number of ways. It is owed by a motorist to all other users of the highway, by a manufacturer to the consumers of his product, by a professional man to his clients, by a director to his shareholders, etc. The person aggrieved is entitled to an action in *tort to claim damages. When the negligence is committed by an auditor in incorrectly preparing a company's accounts, the only party aggrieved was formerly considered to be the company itself. However, recent decisions indicate that other persons are likely to be affected by the incorrect accounts, e.g. the company's creditors, and that they may also have a good claim against the auditor.

negotiability. The ability of a document, entitling the holder to a certain sum of money, to change hands. For a document to be negotiable it must permit: (1) legal ownership to pass to another person by delivery or by *endorsement and delivery; (2) the holder to bring an action at law if necessary; (3) the person to whom it is transferred to take it in good faith and for value (provided that he has no notice of any defect of title) and to acquire an indefensible title to it. The most common examples of negotiable instruments are bills of exchange and cheques, but these can lose their negotiability by being made payable to a certain person only, or marked not transferable, or by being restrictively endorsed, or by becoming overdue. A creditor may refuse to accept a negotiable instrument as payment for a debt and insist on legal tender. *See also* crossed cheque.

negotiable instrument. A document of title that can be freely negotiated, so that title passes with the document. It cannot, however, pass a better title than possessed by the holder. Examples are *bills of exchange, *bearer bonds, promissory notes, and bank notes.

neoclassical production function. *See* production function.

neoclassical school. A school of economic thought that was founded in the 1870s when the concept of marginal analysis was introduced by Menger, Jevons, and Walras. The work of the founders was carried on by Böhm-Bawerk, Marshall, Pareto, Clark, and Fisher. It is classical in the sense that it saw the central role of economics to be the explanation of the distribution of income, sharing with the classicists the opinion that competition led to an efficient allocation of resources. It departed dramatically, however, in its analytic approach, being essentially microeconomic. It used the principle of utility and profit maximization to derive demand and supply curves, which were combined in a general equilibrium to determine relative prices, and thus relative shares of output. It relied on differential calculus to demonstrate the basic rules of marginal analysis, which characterizes the optimality relationships of perfectly competitive economics.

neo-Malthusianism. The belief that Thomas Malthus (1766–1834) was correct in predicting that the geometric growth of population would outstrip the arithmetic increase in food production. Whereas Malthus advocated moral restraint and later marriages to restrict population growth, neo-Malthusians recommend the worldwide use of birth control.

net assets. The difference between the total assets of a firm and its current liabilities.

net book amount. The *written down value* of an asset after allowing for depreciation.

net current assets. *See* working capital.

net domestic product. The *gross domestic product less capital consumption.

net income. 1. Personal income after paying all personal taxes or business income after deduction of the cost of collection.

2. *See* net profit.

net investment. The change in the capital stock available to the economy or to a firm after investment has taken place. It is equal to *gross investment minus the amount needed to replace the worn out capital (depreciation). This is the investment quantity that has some welfare significance; it may be negative (*see* disinvestment).

net national product. Gross national product minus capital consumption.

net present value. The *present value of the benefits of a project minus the present value of its costs.

net price. The price paid by a buyer after all discounts have been deducted.

net profit. 1. The profit as shown by a *profit and loss account. This is calculated by deducting from the *gross profit all such expenses as rent, rates, insurances, interest charges, advertising, depreciation, etc.

2. In some contexts the profit after deducting tax is regarded as the net profit.

net profit ratio. The ratio of net profit to sales.

net reproduction rate. The number of female children in a population, expressed as a proportion of the number of female adults in the preceding generation. If the ratio is greater than unity the population is increasing; if the result is less than unity the population is declining. This statistic is a more sophisticated estimate of population trends than a comparison of the crude birth and death rates.

net (register) tonnage. *See* tonnage.

net tangible assets. Total assets less intangible assets and current liabilities.

net weight. 1. The difference between the *gross weight of a package and the *tare, i.e. the weight of the actual goods in the package.

2. The weight of the goods (including their packages) carried by a road-transport vehicle or railway wagon, but excluding the weight of the vehicle or wagon. When weighed on a weighbridge, the net weight is obtained by deducting the tare of the vehicle or wagon from the gross weight.

net worth. 1. The residual value of the assets of a company after all claims have been deducted.

2. *See* wealth.

neutral rate of interest. The equilibrium rate of interest at which the demand for, and supply of, funds will be equal.

New Deal. The domestic programme introduced by President Franklin D. Roosevelt in the U.S. during the period 1933 to 1939. Faced with the Depression, the New Deal was a series of pragmatic attempts to bring about immediate economic relief and reduce unemployment, coupled with wide-ranging reforms to avoid any repetition of the Wall Street crash. The New Deal faced bitter opposition for its "socialistic" tendencies with many of its measures being declared unconstitutional by the Supreme Court. However, most of its reforms were eventually accepted as necessary.

new entrants. 1. Those seeking work for the first time, e.g. school-leavers or housewives. If recruitment for the expanding industries is carried out among new entrants, while *natural wastage is allowed to operate in declining industries; the required redistribution of labour in the economy will occur with little friction. Such a policy takes a long time to work however, and usually firms must expand or contract more quickly than this method allows. **2.** Newly established firms in an industry. One of the conditions of *perfect competition is that there are no barriers to entry into the market for such firms.

New International Economic Order. A series of measures proposed and adopted by the U.N. General Assembly in 1974 with the object of achieving internationally a similar spread of wealth, income, and political power as the nations of Western Europe have achieved since World War II. The methods of bringing about this radical restructuring of world economic order are broadly those of the European social democracies: mixed economies, taxation of the rich for the benefit of the poor, restraint on the political influence of the rich, curbs on the activities of multinational companies and monopolistic enterprises, and the provision of international social services.

Because existing world economies tend to favour the industrialized nations at the expense of the developing nations, who supply the basic raw materials of industry, the most important measures in achieving the New International World Order must be concerned with the control of natural resources. Suggestions for creating an international public sector include exploitation of nonterritorial waters by an international agency, international taxation on the use of nonterritorial air- and waterways for the benefit of the poorer nations, increased processing of raw materials in the countries of origin, the creation of international buffer stocks of commodities to stabilize prices (*see* commodity markets, international commodity agreements), and a revision of the system by which aid is given to the poorer nations by the industrial nations.

new issue. An issue of shares or loan stocks that has recently been offered to and taken up by the public.

new time. When stockbrokers on the London Stock Exchange deal *for new time,* they are executing purchase and sale orders during the last two days of one account for *settlement in the next account, i.e. as though such deals were actually transacted in the next account.

New York Stock Exchange. *See* Wall Street.

Neyman-Pearson Lemma. A statistical theory concerned with the determination of the best critical region in the case of simple hypotheses according to the criterion of the minimization of the size of the *Type II error for a given size of *Type I error. *See also* hypothesis testing.

night safe. A means by which a customer can deposit cash and cheques in a bank outside banking hours. Night safes are set into the outside wall of the bank and are fitted with a locked cover to which the customer is given a key. A wallet with a key is supplied, into which the customer puts the cash and cheques, locks it, and places it in the night safe. When the cover is closed again, the wallet is deposited inside the safe within the bank. When the customer calls at the bank during business hours he is given the locked wallet, which he opens, and pays the contents into his account. Alternatively he may arrange to be supplied with a wallet that is opened by the bank cashiers and the contents credited to his account. Night safes were introduced in the U.K. in 1928.

Nikkei-Dow Average. An index number of share prices on the Tokyo Stock Exchange.

nil paid. Denoting new shares (esp. a rights issue) for which no money has yet been paid to the company.

no-claims bonus. A bonus deducted from an insurance premium if no claim has been made in the previous period of insurance. The system is used extensively in *motor insurance to discourage small claims, and may amount to as much as 60% of the premium. The insured has to decide on each claim whether it is cheaper for him to forfeit his no-claim bonus or not. The insured is eligible for the bonus provided he makes no claim; this is irrespective of whether or not he is to blame. Insurers stress that a no-claim bonus is not a no-blame bonus.

nominal account. *See* impersonal account.

nominal capital. The total of the face value of the shares of a company, i.e. the total nominal value of all the shares.

nominal damages. *See* damages.

nominal income. **1.** The amount of cash paid to a worker for his services. It is distinguished from the *real income.

2. The part of the total wage paid to a worker that consists of cash rather than other benefits, such as free meals or transport.

nominal ledger. The most important constituent of the *books of account of a company. It is a record of all the various accounts of the company, either in a detailed or a summary form, with the possible exception of the cash account. At the end of an *accounting period the balances of the various accounts are extracted from the nominal ledger and used to produce the figures for the balance sheet and profit and loss account. Prior to this the balances on the nominal ledger are listed in a trial balance, in which the sums of the debits and credits should be equal.

nominal partner. *See* partner.

nominal price. The estimated price of an article rather than its market price. The two might differ either because the market price has not recently been established or because supply and demand make the market price above or below the nominal price. A work of art might fall into the first category. A valuer may say that it is worth £1000, and this would be regarded as its nominal price. However, when put up for auction it may fetch only £750. This would be its market price. A product in short supply might provide an example of the second category. For example, the nominal price of a prestige car might be £15,000, but because the demand exceeds the supply, it may not be possible to buy one below £20,000.

nominal value. **1.** The current money value of any economic variable. For example, the nominal value of savings is a certain number of pounds, regardless of what the price level is. So, if the price level rises, the nominal value of savings remains constant. Similarly, the nominal value of total production is a certain quantity of money. If the general price level rises, then the nominal value of production will increase, even though production in terms of goods and services (in real terms) remains unchanged. Nominal value should be contrasted with *real value. For example:

$$M = pm,$$

where M is the nominal money supply, p is the price level, and m is the real money supply.

2. *See* par value.

nominal yield. The income received from a security expressed as a percentage of its *par value. *Compare* yield.

nominations. *See* assignment of life policies.

nominee shareholding. A shareholding purchased by an investor through a merchant bank, stockbroking firm, or some other nominee so that it is the name of the nominee, not the real investor (the *beneficial owner*), that appears on the shareholders' register (of the company whose shares are held). Nominee shareholdings are fairly prevalent and it is possible for a company that desires to take over a smaller company to build up a substantial and individual interest in shares that is concealed by being bought through nominees. Disclosure becomes necessary by law when one company's direct shareholding in another exceeds 10% of the other's issued share capital.

nonassented stock. *See* assented.

noncontributory pensions. *See* pensions.

nondurables. *See* consumer nondurables.

nonemployed. A U.K. *National Insurance category that covers those who are neither in full-time employment nor are self-employed. People in this category are entitled to all benefits except industrial injuries benefits, maternity allowance, sickness benefits, and unemployment benefits.

nonexcludability. *See* public good.

nonlinear programming. A mathematical technique designed to locate optimum solutions for problems involving constraints. The purpose of nonlinear programming and the context in which it is used are analogous to those of *linear programming with the single difference that, as the name suggests, there will be at least one nonlinear relationship. Nonlinear programmes are much more difficult than linear programmes to solve and consequently any nonlinear functions in these problems will be converted to linear form whenever the approximation is judged to be sufficiently close.

nonmarketable securities. That part of the unfunded *National Debt that cannot be bought or sold on the Stock Exchange. Approximately £4100 million of the debt is composed of small savings, such as savings bonds, national savings certificates, and premium bonds, etc. The balance is made up of terminable annuities and miscellaneous liabilities owing to other governments and international organizations.

nonmonetary advantages and disadvantages. An employee's subjective evaluation of his conditions of work. Examples of nonmonetary advantages might be pleasant surroundings and stimulating work, while disadvantages might include grimy conditions and an awkwardly sited location. These factors added to the monetary wage comprise the real wage, which can be greater or less than the monetary wage depending upon whether the advantages outweigh the disadvantages. *Nonpecuniary costs and benefits* is an alternative term.

nonpecuniary costs and benefits. *See* nonmonetary advantages and disadvantages.

nonprice competition. A form of competition that is different from all other forms of competition in economics, which is dominated by price-quantity relationships. In general, a producer finds himself in a situation in which he hopes to influence the shape of the demand curve to increase his profits, and often relies on this strategy totally, being unable or unwilling to alter the price of his product. The methods available include product differentiation and sales promotion (such as style changes), trading stamps, and contests and advertising. Other forms of nonprice competition, such as lobbying for government contracts, are not usually included.

nonrivalness in consumption. *See* public good.

nonsense correlation. *See* correlation.

nontaxable income. Income that is excluded before liability to income tax is assessed. Nontaxable income in the U.K. includes: a proportion of the interest on deposits with the national savings bank or trustee savings bank; redundancy payments up to a certain amount; income from scholarships, bursaries, and similar educational endowments; interest on national savings certificates; disability pensions; and certain other allowances.

In addition certain people and organizations are totally exempt from income taxes. These include some foreigners working in the U.K. if double taxation agreements have been concluded with their countries, certain literary and scientific institutions, certain friendly societies and trade unions, certain savings banks, and registered charities.

nonunique equilibrium. *See* multiple equilibrium.

nonvoting shares. Shares that do not endow the holder with the right to vote at company meetings. The purpose of issuing such shares is to raise further capital without diluting the control of holders of the voting shares. Nonvoting shares generally rank pari passu with voting shares in respect of other rights, such as divident payments. They are usually given the title of *A shares.*

Nordic Council. A consultative organization, formed in March 1952, consisting of Denmark, Finland, Iceland, Norway, and Sweden. Its aim is to provide a forum for discussion. Achievements of the Council have been the abolition of passports for travel between member states, the creation of a free labour market, and coordination of economic and social legislation.

no-rent land. A theoretical concept used by Ricardo to explain variations in the rent of different pieces of land. No-rent land was defined as a piece of land that it was only profitable to cultivate if no rent was paid. If more fertile land was available for cultivation, a prospective farmer would be willing to pay in rent the difference between the values of this land and no-rent land. He could not make a profit if he offered more and might be outbid if he offered less. Thus no-rent land acted as a base from which to estimate the rents of all other pieces of land.

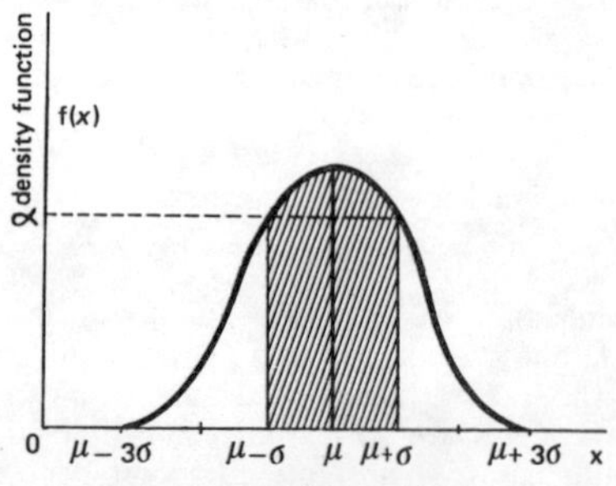

Normal distribution

normal (gaussian) distribution. A statistical *distribution of a continuous variable that is symmetrical around the variable's mean. The density function of a normal variable can be illustrated graphically by a bell-shaped curve as indicated in the diagram, where the horizontal axis is represented by the normally distributed variable *x* and the vertical axis is represented by the value of the variable's density function, f(x). Although a normal distribution is always symmetrical (and therefore always has zero skewness), its location with respect to the horizontal axis is defined entirely by the variable's mean and standard deviation. The mean of the variable, represented by μ in the diagram, is always directly beneath the peak of the distribution while the standard deviation, represented by σ, will have equal ordinates on either side of the mean. It can be shown that approximately 68% of the area under the curve lies between $\mu + \sigma$ and $\mu - \sigma$; thus any value of a normal variable has a probability of 0.68 of being within one standard deviation of the variable's mean. Similarly it can be shown that any value of a normal variable has a probability of 0.954 and 0.997 of being within two and three standard deviations respectively of the mean. Examples of an approximate normal distribution would be the height of a large group of men, or the accuracy of a large number of bullet shots. The normal distribution is the most important of all distributions because, at least in the social sciences, it is the most frequently encountered in the real world, and because the knowledge that a real variable is normally distributed greatly facilitates its statistical analysis. There are some statistical properties, such as independence between the mean and variance, which apply to the normal distribution but to no other. The normal distribution can theoretically be used directly to test a hypothesis about a mean, or to test a hypothesis concerning the difference between two means (or two proportions or two *coefficients of correlation); however, such tests frequently require both large samples and knowledge of the *population parameters and are therefore often either impractical or impossible in practice. An important concept relating to the normal distribution is that of the *standardized variable*: applying the property that a linear function of normal variables is itself normally distributed, the expression:

$$Z = (x - \mu)/\sigma,$$

where x is a normally distributed variable with mean μ and standard deviation σ, is itself normally distributed with zero mean and a variance equal to 1. Such variables as Z are said to be standardized or standard normal variables and are usually easier to handle both in theory and in empirical work. Certain mathematical relations exist between the normal distribution and other distributions.

normal equations. The equations resulting from the process of calculus in *least squares estimation. The normal equations will all be linear and the number of them will be the same as the number of parameters to be estimated. When there are more than two parameters to be estimated, it is usual to solve the normal equations by matrix algebra.

normal (necessary) good. A good for which the *income elasticity of demand is positive but less than one. Consumption of the good increases as income increases, but at a slower rate.

normal price. The equilibrium price of a good or service. The actual price of any commodity is influenced by numerous factors but in the long run, competition will ensure a return to the normal price, which just covers costs.

normal profit. The amount needed to keep an entrepreneur in a particular activity. Profit is the payment to the entrepreneur for his enterprise in the same way that rent is a payment for the use of land and interest is a payment for the use of capital. Normal profit will exactly compensate the entrepreneur for his services. If abnormally high profits were being earned new firms would enter the industry and the increased competition would decrease profits. If abnormally low profits were being earned firms would leave the industry to gain a better return elsewhere so allowing the industry's rate of profit to rise. In a perfectly competitive market only normal profits can be earned; in a monopoly, however, abnormally high profits can be gained since *barriers to entry prevent new firms entering the industry.

normative economics. The branch of economics that seeks to determine what ought to be, in the sense of making ethical judgements as to the desirability of different economic states. The statement that people with higher incomes should pay more tax is a normative statement, as are most government policy decisions. The question of the final shifting of the tax and who actually bears it is a positive question.

nostro account. An account conducted by a U.K. bank with a bank in a foreign country. *Compare* vostro account.

notary public. An official, usually a solicitor, who is legally authorized to attest documents. *See also* noting.

notice in lieu of distringas. A notice given by a shareholder and supported by a statutory declaration made by him certifying his interest in some shares to the company, thus preventing any attempted transfer of his shares. This procedure has replaced the now obsolete application to a court by a writ of distringas. If an application is later delivered to the company to register a transfer of the shares, the company will notify the person who has served the notice upon it and will only then register the transfer if he does not object within eight days. The procedure is used when a shareholder or a person having an equitable interest in the shares suspects forgery or fraud.

notice of abandonment. *See* abandonment.

notice of motion. *See* motion.

noting. A bill of exchange dishonoured by nonacceptance or nonpayment may be handed to a *notary public to be noted. The notary presents the bill again and if acceptance or payment is still not obtained he makes a note of the circumstances in his register with a cross reference written on the bill. Then, if necessary, the noting can later be extended to a *protest. Noting must be completed not later than the next business day succeeding that on which the bill was dishonoured.

notional income. The nonmonetary satisfaction that an owner derives from an asset. Governments rarely tax this because of the difficulties of quantification; costs of collection might easily exceed revenue gained. The most recent form of taxation of notional income in the U.K. was on owner-occupancy of houses under Schedule A. This tax was abolished in 1963.

not negotiable. A *bill of exchange marked with these words is not a negotiable instrument and the holder cannot have a better title to it than the person from whom he took it. It thus provides a safeguard in the case of theft. A cheque can be crossed with these words, but other forms of bill must have them inscribed on their face.

N.P.V. (no par value). *See* par value.

N.R.D.C. *See* National Research and Development Corporation.

N.T.P. Short for *not to press (for delivery)*, an expression used when a *stockjobber sells shares that he does not have and which he thinks may take some time for him to acquire.

The sale is then on the understanding that the purchaser is not to press for delivery. *See also* bear.

null hypothesis. *See* hypothesis (def. 1).

numbered account. A bank account that is identified by a number only, the name of the account-holder being kept secret. The Swiss practice of having numbered bank accounts lends itself to large sums of money being deposited there from all over the world, some of which is generally believed to have been acquired in questionable circumstances.

numeraire. The good in terms of which all other prices are expressed. Since only price ratios matter in determining economic behaviour, in an economy with n goods only $n - 1$ can be determined. So the price of one good, the numeraire, is fixed, thus fixing the level of all other prices. This good must not be a *free good.

nursery finance. Funds lent by *stockjobbers or *institutions to private companies that intend to go public within a few years.

O

objectivity. (in accountancy) The avoidance of personal judgment by establishing rules for the recording of financial transactions.

obsolescence. The depreciation in a consumer durable or capital good that is due to a change in technology or tastes rather than any actual physical deterioration. Thus new invention may make a machine uncompetitive or unsaleable even though it is still efficient. This is more noticeable in consumer durables in which there are continual style changes. For example, in cars, obsolescence is thought to induce people to buy new cars while their old ones are still working satisfactorily. The intentional outdating of a product is known as *planned obsolescence* or *built-in obsolescence.*

occupational hazard. A risk of accident or disease that occurs in certain jobs. These jobs usually command higher wages than comparable jobs without the element of hazards and they may command *danger money.* The legal aspects of occupational hazards are dealt with in the U.K. by the Health and Safety at Work Act (1974).

occupational mobility. *See* mobility.

O.C.R. *See* optical character recognition.

octal notation. *See* binary notation.

odd lot. A small and irregular number of shares or amount of stock. Because of inconvenience to a *stockjobber involved in dealing in such amounts, the price at which one can purchase shares (or stock) in odd lots is higher than it would be otherwise and the price at which one can sell is conversely lower. *Compare* round lot.

O.E.C.D. *See* Organization for Economic Cooperation and Development.

offer. The price or terms under which a person is willing to sell. In commodities an offer will include the quantity, quality, and price of the goods as well as the delivery or shipment and payment terms. An offer may be firm for a stated period or may not be firm (usually called a quotation). Once a *bid has been made against a firm offer it ceases to be valid.

On the London Stock Exchange the offer price is the higher of the two prices that a stockjobber quotes when approached by a stockbroker. *See also* counteroffer; offers, bids, and quotations.

offer by prospectus. An offer to the public of a new issue of shares or debentures made directly (through a prospectus) by the company in whose name the shares or debentures are registered. *Compare* introduction, offer for sale, offer for sale by tender, placing, rights issue.

offer curve. A curve on a graph that plots the amount of a good a country is willing to export in return for the imports of some other good. It is commonly used in the study of international trade. On the same graph it is possible to plot an offer curve for the second country, reading imports for exports on the horizontal axes and vice versa, then the intersection of these two curves will determine the terms of trade and the amounts traded.

This curve can be geometrically derived from the *transformation curve and the community indifference curves if the distributional aspects of changes in production are ignored.

A typical offer curve slopes increasingly upwards to the right when exports are plotted on the horizontal axis and imports on the vertical axis, indicating that a country will be prepared to export progressively less of its good in return for more imports. It is possible for the curve to become inelastic at some level of imports and for the offer curve to bend backwards after this point. This indicates that the country is willing to give less and less for its increased imports, taking advantage of the improved terms of trade.

Given the offer curve and the terms of trade, one can determine the level of imports and exports by constructing a line from the origin whose slope is the ratio of imports to exports. The point at which this intersects the offer curve represents a trading equilibrium. It is likely (unless the offer curve is completely elastic at the origin) that at certain terms of trade there will be no intersection. This is because at these terms of trade the country will begin importing the good it previously exported, and vice versa. A second offer curve could be drawn sloping up to the right and subsequently levelling off. In general, however, only the relevant sections of each country's offer curve are included on the graph. *See* Edgeworth-Bowley box diagram.

offer for sale. An offer to the public of a new issue of shares or debentures through an intermediary such as a merchant bank. The intermediary takes up the issue from the company itself and then offers the shares to the public at a price slightly higher than that at which it took up the new shares in the first place; the difference covers the intermediary's expenses and fee. *Compare* introduction, offer by prospectus, offer for sale by tender, placing, rights issue.

offer for sale by tender. A rare method of issuing shares. As with an offer for sale, the issue is purchased in the first instance by an intermediary, such as a merchant bank, which then invites tenders for the shares from the public on the basis of a prospectus in which a minimum tender price is stated. After receipt of the tenders, the intermediary then fixes the price at which the issue is to be sold. *Compare* introduction, offer for sale, offer by prospectus, placing, rights issue.

offers, bids, and quotations. In general usage these three words are often used to mean the same thing. In commerce, each has a precise meaning. An *offer* from one individual or firm to another is a declaration that they are willing to sell specified goods at a specified price, on specified terms. Offers are also usually firm for a specified period. An offer that is not firm for a specified period is called a *quo-*

tation. For example, one company may answer an enquiry for goods thus: "We quote, not firm, ...", whereas another may answer: "We offer, firm until withdrawn, ...". Or if they are offering on a fluctuating market: "We offer firm, for reply received here by 10 00 hours tomorrow morning, ...". Offers, in addition to stating the quality and quantity of the goods, should also state the delivery or shipment period, the delivery or shipment terms (who pays for cost of delivery or shipment and insurance), and the payment terms. For example, an offer might read: "We offer, firm for reply within one week, 100 tonnes of hand-picked and selected groundnuts for July shipment from origin at £300 per tonne, c.i.f. London, payment by irrevocable letter of credit opened at a first class London Bank".

If the recipient of the offer finds the price too high, or the shipment too late, for example, he may make a *bid* against the offer. Once the bid has been made the offer ceases to be valid. The bid itself however, if the market is fluctuating, should also state for how long it is firm. For example, a bid in reply to the above offer might read (after referring specifically to the offer): "Bid, firm for reply Thursday, £295 June shipment". The company who made the original offer now has a firm bid in hand, which it can accept, against which it can make a *counteroffer,* or which it can refuse without making a counteroffer. In the above case, the company may find the price acceptable for July shipment but not for June shipment. In this case, the counteroffer might read: "Counteroffer, firm for immediate reply, £295 July shipment". Usually, by this stage, business has been done or the parties have given up. However, the buyer may make a *counterbid,* which calls either for an acceptance or another counteroffer.

In international trade, especially in *commodities, these exchanges are made by cable or by telex. If cables are used, the cost of cabling is dramatically reduced by the use of *commercial codes. *See also* invitation to treat.

offer to purchase. *See* takeover.

Official Close. *See* after-hours dealings.

Official List. A list published by the London Stock Exchange at 5.30 p.m. on each trading day. The Official List contains details of all quoted securities with the exception of a few inactive stocks. These details include the latest dividend, the *ex dividend date (i.e. the date on which each share goes ex dividend), and date of dividend payment, and the prices (both *bid and *offer) of each security as at 2.15 p.m. These prices and the prices at which *bargains have been marked are extracted from the day's *markings. The full title of the Official List is the *Stock Exchange Daily Official List.*

official rate. The rate of exchange given to a currency by a government or its agencies. This rate may not be the same as the market rate on the foreign exchange markets. In order to impose the official rate on the exchange market a government has to be willing to buy or sell the currency to support or depress the market rate so that it coincides with the official rate.

official receiver. An official appointed by a court in the U.K. who administers the estates of bankrupts. He may act as the trustee in bankruptcy or some other person, who is answerable to him, may be appointed. He is also required to investigate the conduct of the bankrupt and report any misdemeanours to the court. An official receiver also supervises the compulsory winding up of a company, acting as provisional liquidator.

official strike. *See* strike.

off line. Not connected to a computer; denoting computer operations controlled by instructions that have been stored earlier. *Compare* on line.

Offshore Supplies Office. A department of the U.K. Department of Energy, set up in Glasgow in 1973, to assist and encourage the offshore oil and natural gas industries, especially by giving special credit terms to companies involved in developing oil and gas resources in the North Sea.

ogive. The graph of a cumulative frequency distribution. Taking a frequency distribution of 100 men according to their weight the cumulative frequencies are calculated by adding all the ordinary frequencies below the maximum weight of each class. Thus if there are 45 men out of the 100 under consideration who weigh less than 160lbs then this can be read off the ogive on whose vertical axis are the cumulative frequencies of the men. An ogive is usually drawn as a curve rather than as a series of connected points. *See also* distribution function, frequency distribution.

old-age pensions. *See* pensions.

oligopoly. An industry in which there are few sellers but many buyers, thus each seller has some control over his price and recognizes that the actions of his competitors will affect his profits. The product is usually assumed to be homogeneous (*perfect oligopoly*). Many of the possible hypotheses as to how such an industry operates are generalizations of *duopoly models, two in particular being the *kinked demand curve and *cut-throat competition. *See* monopolistic competition.

oligopsony. An industry in which there are few buyers but many sellers, thus each buyer has some control over the price of his purchase. It is the counterpart of oligopoly. *Compare* monopsony.

O & M. *See* organization and methods.

Ombudsman. *See* Parliamentary Commissioner for Administration.

on approval. A potential buyer may take goods away from a seller's premises on approval, with the seller's consent, in order that he may make up his mind whether or not he wishes to buy them. The buyer then becomes a *bailee, with an obligation to return the goods in perfect order if he does not purchase them. Many large shops allow their account customers to take goods home *on appro* and the practice is also common in some trades.

O.N.C. The abbreviation for Ordinary National Certificate. *See* national certificates and diplomas.

on consignment. Goods may be sent to an agent on consignment, i.e. with instructions to sell them on behalf of the principal as soon as possible, usually at a specified price but sometimes at the best market price. The agent does not usually pay for the goods until they have been sold, does not normally have title to them although he does have possession, and usually works for a commission. From the point of view of the principal, goods delivered to an agent on consignment can neither be regarded as stock nor sales.

oncosts. *See* indirect costs.

O.N.D. The abbreviation for Ordinary National Diploma. *See* national certificates and diplomas.

on demand. A *bill of exchange is payable on demand if the person to whom it is addressed will pay to the drawer or the bearer, on presentation of the bill, the sum of money specified. An uncrossed cheque functions as a bill payable on demand.

one-sector model. A totally aggregated economic model in which the one good produced is totally malleable for use as a capital or a consumption good. *Harrod's and *Solow's models are examples of one-sector models.

one-way price. A single price quoted by a *stockjobber in respect of a security at which he will either buy or sell. Usually, a jobber will quote two prices at the higher of which (the *offer) a stockbroker can buy and at the lower of which (the *bid) a broker can sell.

on line. Connected to a computer; denoting computer operations in which instructions are executed as they are generated. *See also* real time. *Compare* off line.

OPEC. *See* Organization of Petroleum Exporting Countries.

open cheque. An uncrossed cheque that can be cashed at the counter of the drawee banker.

open cover. A form of marine insurance in which the insurer agrees to insure all shipments of cargo made during an agreed period, usually 12 months. Premium rates are agreed at the outset and declarations of all shipments will be required, but there is no limit to the number automatically insured. The premium is payable after the declarations have been made, though a series of *floating policies may be issued under the open cover.

It sometimes happens that a shipment takes place before the shipper or the consignee is aware of it. In such a case, open cover provides for automatic protection.

open credit. A means by which a bank customer is able to cash cheques at a bank or branch other than that at which he keeps his account. A certified signature of the customer is sent by his bank to the paying bank or branch together with an authority to cash his cheques up to a specified amount. With the advent of the *cheque card open credits are no longer widely used.

open economy. An economy that includes a large foreign sector, which plays an important part in the operation of the economy. The U.S. can be considered a *closed economy as its foreign sector is small relative to the economy as a whole, whereas the U.K. is an open economy.

Policy making in an open economy is particularly difficult as the actions of other countries must be taken into account; for instance, the importance of short-term international capital (*see* hot money) places constraints on the use of monetary or other policies designed to affect the interest rate. An open economy is also highly susceptible to *trade cycles, as the effects of crises in other countries are transmitted to their trading partners. For instance, the effects of world inflation could be transmitted to a nation that had fixed exchange rates.

open-end trust. A form of *unit trust in the U.S. in which the operators of the trust may vary the investments without notifying shareholders.

open general licence. In general, the import and export of goods into and out of the U.K. requires licences. For goods on which there are no restrictions, open general licences are available.

open indent. An overseas order made to a domestic agent for the purchase of certain goods in which the choice of manufacturer is left unspecified. A *closed indent* also specifies the manufacturer.

opening prices. Share prices as quoted at the commencement of business on the London Stock Exchange (9.30 for commercial securities or 10.00 for gilts). Some opening prices may differ from the corresponding *closing prices of the previous day, as, for example, when there has been unexpected news concerning a company or an industry overnight.

open market operations. The purchase or sale of government stocks by the *central bank on the open market, in such institutions as the stock exchange, in order to expand or contract the volume of credit nationally available. Government securities are sold in order to reduce the supply of funds in the *money market and thus to force up market rates of interest; conversely, securities are purchased providing the market with an increase in liquid funds and lower interest rates. More recent techniques to control the amount of credit include adjusting the amount of *Treasury bills issued each week (*see* tap stocks) and the *special deposits called for from the commercial banks.

open policy. *See* floating policy, open cover.

open position. The position of a dealer or trader in shares or commodities who has made a purchase or sale without making an equivalent *hedging transaction at the same time (*see also* bull, bear). He is thus speculating on market movements: he closes his position and takes his profit or loss either by selling his holding, if he made a purchase, or by covering (buying back), if he made a sale. Alternatively, he may hedge his open position at a later date by a purchase or sale of similar but not identical shares or commodities or by taking out an *option or a *contango (on shares). *See also* futures market.

open-price agreement. A form of price collusion occurring in some oligopolistic markets. Firms agree to circulate details of the prices of their products (as well as future price changes) to each other so that they can achieve a measure of price conformity without the losses in revenue resulting from a *price war. *See also* price leadership.

operating budget. A short-term budget that lays down the detailed requirements needed for the running of an enterprise over a specified period of time, usually a year. Items of a capital nature are excluded from such a budget as they relate to the long term. *See* capital budget.

operating system. The fundamental *system software that controls the management of resources within a computer. Different manufacturers' mainframes have different operating systems. Many microcomputers utilize the same operating systems such as CP/M, MS-DOS, and UNIX: this enables different microcomputers to utilize the same programs.

operation job card. A form on which is inserted the total length of time spent by an employee on a task. By this method, the time consumed on each project can be easily monitored.

operations (or **operational**) **research.** A multidisciplinary area of activity concerned with the location of optimum solutions to problems relating to the performance of systems of men, money, materials, and machines. The procedure followed in operations research is to define the problem, formulate a model representing the system, and use various techniques by which the manipulation of the model can be made to represent different decisions or strategies in respect of the cost, quality, control, and direction of the system's variables. The solution that emerges from the model is then applied to the real problem. Operations research involves mathematicians, economists, and engineers and has wide currency in industrial management; its techniques include *linear programming, *game theory, *critical-path analysis, *present value calculations, and *simulation.

opportunity cost. The monetary sacrifice when a factor of production is not used in its most profitable alternative activity. If A owns a computer that he can lease out for £5000 p.a. this is the opportunity cost of using it for himself since it is what he is giving up. Opportunity cost constitutes the main difference between *economic costs and accounting costs. Every factor must always have an opportunity cost attached to it, since every factor always has an alternative use.

optical character recognition (O.C.R.). A system for feeding information into a computer in the form of conventionally printed letters, numbers, and other characters. The *input device (called an *optical character reader*) scans the text by a photoelectric method and converts each character into electrical signals. Specially designed typefaces are used with this technique, which are keyboarded on conventional golf-ball electric typewriters.

optimal economic growth. The rate of *economic growth that maximizes the sum of social welfare over time. A value judgment is required to decide on the optimal growth path. The government needs to decide how to weight the welfare of future as against present generations in the face of present political exigencies. When the weighting process has taken place the level of saving required is determined so that the rate of capital accumulation is known. This gives the future rate of output so that the future level of welfare is determined.

It is often argued that a higher rate of growth is to be preferred because the low weight attached to future generations is immoral. There has been much discussion of this problem in the philosophical literature (on the theory of justice), especially the work associated with Rawls of Harvard. The work on optimal growth stems from the influential work of Frank Ramsey of Cambridge in 1928; although highly mathematical it is somewhat less mechanical than the rest of the growth literature.

optimal quantity of money. It has been claimed that in a modern economy that makes use of credit money, the amount of money held by individuals is less than is optimal. The cost of producing money is nearly zero, whereas the cost of holding it is the nominal rate of interest. The claim derives from the simple Paretian welfare economics criterion that price should equal marginal cost. To engineer optimal money holdings it has been suggested by H. G. Johnson that a rate of interest be paid on money holdings, such as large notes and current accounts at clearing banks. Prof. Friedman has proposed that the government engineer a rate of deflation equal to the real rate of interest so that the real value of nominal money holdings should rise by this amount. Both proposals would induce individuals to hold more money and be in a preferred position at no resource cost to the economy.

optimum population. The level of population at which income per head is a maximum. If the population declines, the labour force would be too small to run the economy with maximum efficiency. If the population increases, there would be too many workers and the law of *diminishing returns would start to apply.

This concept is only of long-term value when formulating policy. For example, India is overpopulated but no action can be taken that will reduce numbers in the immediate future. However, its government is attempting to slow down the rate of increase by a variety of family planning methods. On the other hand, Australia is underpopulated and consequently has an active immigration policy. An additional complication to the implementation of demographic policy is that the optimum size of a population alters as technology improves. For example, in developing countries especially, the level of output increases as the country becomes more industrialized and a greater population can be sustained.

option. The right to buy or sell something at its current price, especially a line of shares on a stock exchange, a commodity on a *futures market, or property, if one decides to do so within a specified period. In general, the option to buy or sell costs a specified sum of money (the *option money*), which is forfeited if the option is not taken up. On commodity markets and the London Stock Exchange an option to sell is called a *put option* and an option to buy a *call option.* An option either to buy or sell is a *double option.* An option is a form of speculation: if a dealer believes that the price of a certain share or commodity is likely to rise he may purchase a call option. If the price of the share or commodity does rise in the specified period (usually three months on the London Stock Exchange, often three or six months on a commodity market) by more than the option money plus the broker's commission, etc., he can call his option and make a profit by simultaneously selling at the higher level. If the price does not rise by this amount he will not exercise his option and will lose only his option money. However far the price of the shares or commodity may fall he will only lose his option money. Put options work in the same way for operators who believe that prices will fall. Double options can be arranged for speculators who believe that the price of a share or commodity will move either up or down. For example, a double option might be arranged on a share or commodity that had recently risen and might be expected to rise further on the confirmation of some particular rumour or to fall substantially if the rumour was not confirmed. A director of a company is not allowed to buy or sell options in the shares of his company. Option dealings were frequent on the London Stock Exchange before World War II, but were suspended in 1939 and not resumed until 1958. Option deals are available on some, but not all, commodity markets.

option dealer. A stockbroker or stockjobber engaged in the sale of *options. Option dealers have the same function in respect of options as stockjobbers do in respect of the straightforward purchase and sale of shares. They are thus not permitted to deal directly with buyers of options but must act through the office of a stockbroker. If a stockbroker is registered as an option dealer then he can deal directly with the public only in his capacity as a stockbroker in the purchase and sale of shares; in his capacity as an option dealer he must deal through another stockbroker.

order cheque. A cheque that is made payable to somebody "or Order", requiring the endorsement of the payee unless he pays it into his own banking account. *See also* endorsement.

order statistics. Statistics based on the arrangement of a sample in ascending order of magnitude, such as the percentiles, the quartiles and the distance between them, and the *range (def. 1).

ordinal utility. Utility ranked in order of preference rather than being given a numerical value. A consumer cannot measure the satisfaction obtained from the consumption of many goods, but he can express a preference for some goods rather than others or his indifference between them. *Pareto showed that ordinal utility was all that needed to be assumed to construct a theory of rational consumer behaviour. People will always try to maximize their satisfaction and so will always seek goods with a higher level of utility than they already have. It is enough to know that the utility yielded by a set of goods is higher than that yielded by the present combination. To discover by exactly how much is unnecessary, since the consumer's behaviour will be unaffected by the knowledge. Ordinal utility rather than *cardinal utility is used in the construction of *indifference curves.

ordinary department. One of the departments of a U.K. Savings Bank. It holds all deposits that are repayable on demand or at short notice. Due to their extreme liquidity, these deposits earn very low interest rates.

ordinary life assurance. Ordinary *life assurance as opposed to *industrial life assurance, has the following basic general features:

a) The premium is usually payable annually (monthly, quarterly, or half-yearly instalments can be arranged but usually at an increased cost).

b) The premium is usually paid by cheque or banker's order direct to the assurer.

c) The premium usually consists of a considerable sum.

d) *Sums assured are normally in hundreds or thousands of pounds.

e) The unit of cover is usually the sum assured (i.e. the premium is calculated from the amount of cover required).

f) The agent need not be an employee of the assurer; he may be an insurance broker or a bank manager. *Compare* industrial life assurance.

Ordinary National Certificate and Diploma. *See* national certificates and diplomas.

ordinary resolution. A resolution that has been passed by a majority of more than 50% of those members of a company who are entitled to vote at a general meeting. The period of notice is normally determined by the *articles of association of the company but if these do not specify a minimum period then this period is taken as 14 days.

ordinary share. *See* share.

organization and methods (O & M). A set of business techniques involving the formulation and synthesis of the procedures, management, organization, and methods of control relating to any undertaking. It is more specialized than general administration.

Organization for Economic Cooperation and Development (O.E.C.D.). An organization formed after a conference held in Paris in 1960. Its original members were West Germany, the U.K., Ireland, France, Austria, Sweden, Canada, Iceland, Denmark, Italy, the U.S., Norway, the Netherlands, Turkey, Greece, Belgium, Portugal, Spain, Switzerland, and Luxembourg; the organization was subsequently joined by Finland, Japan, and Australia with Yugoslavia in an associate capacity. Its primary purposes are the encouragement of trade between its members, the increase of the national incomes of the members, and the coordination of aid to the developing countries. The O.E.C.D. has an active secretariat at its headquarters in Paris, which initiates studies on international economic problems such as monetary reform, and has extensive publications. The O.E.C.D. superseded the *Organization for European Economic Cooperation.

Organization for European Economic Cooperation (O.E.E.C.). An organization of 16 European countries established in 1948 to administer, in collaboration with the European Cooperation Administration in Washington, the *Marshall Aid Programme and to stimulate trade and economic cooperation within Europe. It was superseded in 1961 by the *Organization for Economic Cooperation and Development.

Organization of Petroleum Exporting Countries (OPEC). An international cartel of the oil-producing nations, founded in Iraq in 1960; present members are Indonesia, Ecuador, Venezuela, Algeria, Libya, Saudi Arabia, Kuwait, Iraq, Iran, Nigeria, Gabon, and the Persian Gulf States. In 1973 it succeeded in coordinating international action and achieving a dramatic rise in the price of oil, causing a large movement of financial resources from the developed countries to those underdeveloped countries with significant oil deposits. It has also encouraged a policy of nationalization of the oil-extraction and refining industries based in the member countries. The relative inelasticity of oil consumption has resulted in sustained balance of payments difficulties in many countries.

organized market. A market held at a specific location, where buyers and sellers can meet and trade. Under these conditions the methods of exchange and the transmission of relevant data can become highly sophisticated. Well-known organized markets are the stock exchanges and commodity exchanges.

origin. The country in which a commodity originates. The term is used in the expression *shipment from origin* to distinguish shipment from stocks of the commodity in some other country (usually a consumer country).

original-entry book. A book in which events and transactions are initially recorded before being transferred to a ledger. A purchases book and a sales book are both books of original entry.

original goods. Products of nature that are available without the need for capital investment. Examples are virgin land, wild fruit, mineral springs, and a navigable waterway. They have, however, no economic value until factors of production are applied to them, and dependence on original goods indicates a primitive or young society that has been unable to exploit them. *See also* land.

original producers. The owners of *original goods, who permit others to use them upon payment of rent. Labour is sometimes regarded as an original good, since it needs no capital to make it valuable, and therefore a labourer who offers himself for hire can be called an original producer.

Oslo Convention (1930). An agreement signed by the Netherlands, Belgium, Sweden, Norway, Denmark, and Luxembourg in December 1930 to provide for a greater measure of free trade among them.

other deposits. One of the liabilities of the Banking Department of the Bank of England as shown in the *weekly return. It consists of the deposits of the London clearing banks, the balances of foreign banks, and the balances of ordinary customers of the Bank of England.

outcome. *See* decision model.

Outer Seven. The seven countries that were in *EFTA, in contrast to the more compact group of countries in the *E.E.C.

outlay. The total expenditure needed to achieve an objective. An accountant would consider it to be synonymous with total cost but an economist would also add an estimate of *opportunity cost to arrive at total cost.

outlay taxes. *See* indirect taxes.

out of date. A *bill of exchange payable on demand must be presented for payment within a reasonable time after its issue in order to render the drawer liable and will be deemed to be overdue when it appears to have been in circulation for an unreasonable time. *See also* stale cheque.

output device. Any of several devices for obtaining the information processed or stored in a digital computer. The usual method is to print the data using a *line printer. Other forms of output include *magnetic tape, *punched cards, *punched tape, and the use of *visual-display units.

outside broker. A U.K. stockbroker who is a member of the Association of Stock and Share Dealers rather than a stock exchange. He functions as a middleman, buying from members of the Stock Exchange and reselling to investors. He is allowed to solicit business, unlike members of stock exchanges.

outside dealer. *See* licensed dealer.

outside money. Money issued by some agency that is exogenous to the economic system itself. When the debts and credits of different individuals in the private sector (*see* inside money) are consolidated so that they cancel, the next credit remaining is the quantity of outside money. This can, if it exists at all, be one of three types: non-interest-bearing government debt (paper money, fiat money), gold or other precious metals, or foreign currency. A change in the price level changes the real value of the outside money and may thus induce wealth effects in consumption (*see* Pigou effect, real balance effect). When both inside money and outside money exist in an economy together, the effect of a change in the amount of money will only be neutral when both types change in the same proportion.

outside tender. A tender for Treasury bills that does not come from a member of the London discount market. Outside tenders come from foreign and Commonwealth banks.

outturn. The actual amount of revenue raised by taxation, rather than the estimate embodied in that year's budget statement.

outworking. *See* putting-out system.

overcapitalization. A condition occurring in a company when its issued capital exceeds the value of its net assets, particularly when it ceases to be profitable because the issued capital is too large to earn a reasonable return. *See also* watered stock.

overdraft. A bank loan to a customer in which the customer's current account is permitted to go into debit, the balance varying with each debit or credit transaction. Interest is calculated on the debit balance on a daily basis. *See also* bank advance.

over-entry certificate. A document that enables excess duty to be reclaimed from the Customs. Duty on imports is paid on arrival. If too much has been charged, an over-entry certificate is issued. If too little has been charged, a post-entry duty is levied.

over-full employment. *See* full employment.

overhead costs. *See* indirect costs.

overinvestment. Excessive investment of funds in the production of capital equipment. Towards the end of a *boom, businessmen will have overoptimistic expectations of the future demand for their products. Consequently excessive investment will take place. Once the boom ends there will be a large amount of surplus capacity in capital equipment and current investment on capital goods will be drastically reduced. These reductions will create more unemployment so worsening the recession.

overnight loan. A loan made by a bank to a bill broker, to enable him to take up *bills of exchange, on the condition that the loan is repaid the following day.

overseas banks. 1. Banks whose head offices are in a foreign country but who have branches in the country concerned.

2. Banks whose main dealings are in foreign countries: these are usually separate departments of the commercial banks.

Overseas Development Administration. A U.K. government department responsible for Britain's policy of financial and technical assistance to developing countries. The aid programme provides both grants and loans, technical assistance in the form of British experts and equipment, the training of overseas personnel, and research services.

overseas finance sector. *See* Treasury.

overseas income taxation. Taxation that occurs when personal or corporate income is entitled to be taxed by more than one nation. For instance, an individual who earns part of his income abroad may be taxed on it both by the foreign and domestic governments.

This could be a substantial barrier to the movement of capital and labour and for this reason many countries have attempted to avoid the problem by signing double-taxation agreements. For example, a U.K. citizen who pays £*x* in tax on income earned abroad (to the country in which he earned it) will only pay U.K. tax minus £*x* if that country has an agreement with the U.K. Where £*x* is greater than his U.K. tax bill he will pay no U.K. income tax, although he will not receive a refund.

oversubscription. The position that arises when total applications for a new issue of shares exceed the number being offered. New share issues are nearly always oversubscribed or (less frequently) undersubscribed to some extent because it is very difficult for issuing intermediaries to estimate with precision the price at which a new issue will be exactly subscribed. One factor tending to lead to oversubscription is speculative purchases by *stags. When oversubscription occurs, all applicants are allotted a lower number of shares than they applied for. For instance, suppose a new issue is oversubscribed 100%, in this case all applicants could receive just half the shares they applied for. However, allocation is not always on a strictly pro rata basis. Sometimes small applications receive no shares and the larger applicants a higher proportion. Some companies, on the other hand, prefer to favour the small investor. Other companies prefer to allocate shares by ballot. It is quite common for a popular issue to be oversubscribed 10, 20, 50, or even 100 times.

over-the-counter market. An auxiliary stock market in which securities not quoted in the main market are dealt in. The term is more frequently used in the U.S. than in the U.K., where since the *U.S.M. was established, over-the-counter dealings are confined to small less actively traded unquoted companies and those quoted on a recognized overseas stock exchange.

overtime. Hours worked in excess of the contracted number. To encourage employees to work overtime the rate of payment is normally higher than the basic rate. Employers prefer to pay existing staff overtime, rather than to increase their workforce: there are fewer costs (e.g. National Insurance payments and training costs) and the man-hours worked can be varied more easily than by hiring and firing. Nevertheless there has been a persistent fall in the number of overtime hours worked in the U.K. in the post-war era, perhaps because leisure is a *luxury good. An increase in wage-rate can cause an increase or decrease in the length of overtime worked, depending upon the shape and position of each worker's indifference curves.

overtrading. Operating a firm beyond the capacity of its working capital. In this case, cash is not flowing in quickly enough to cover outlay, such as rent, wages, costs of materials, etc. In other words, the *cash flow is inadequate.

ownership. The ultimate right to possess an item of property. It is not, however, the same as *possession as there are many circumstances in which an owner may give up or lose possession of an item of property, e.g. to a bailee or a thief, and yet still remain the owner. In the case of land, there may be several owners all having different interests in the same piece of land, e.g. the owner of the *freehold interest, the owner of a *leasehold interest, the owner of a right-of-way over the land, and the owner of an *equitable interest. In the case of other goods, the legal owner of an article may differ from the owner of an equitable interest in the article, but no other type of ownership in it can usually exist. Ownership is transferred in a variety of ways, depending on the type of property. A company's shares are transferred by the handing over of a stock transfer form together with the share certificate, registered land by the handing over of a transfer deed and the land certificate, unregistered land by a deed known as a conveyance, and other goods usually by delivery of possession to the transferee.

ownership and management. Traditionally, one man (or family) both owned and managed a firm. The history of industry and commerce is based on the entrepreneur who makes all his own decisions. While many *one-man businesses still exist, they have been replaced in importance by *public limited companies, in which the functions of ownership and management are separated. Ownership is divided among a large number of shareholders, who receive dividends on their shares and can elect a board of directors, but who usually have little say or interest in the running of the firm. The management of the firm is delegated to a group of employees who are answerable only to the board of directors.

P

P.A. 1. Personal assistant.

2. (personal account) A term used in the City to denote dealings on the Stock Exchange by an individual on his/her own behalf and not for the institution for which he or she works.

Paasche index. An index number that uses the values of the current period as weights. Thus the Paasche price index is given by the formula:

$$\Sigma_n p_1 q_1 / \Sigma_n p_0 q_1$$

and the Paasche volume index can be written:

$$\Sigma_n q_1 p_1 / \Sigma_n q_0 p_1,$$

where q_1 represents current year volumes, q_0 represents base period volumes, p_1 represents current year prices, p_0 represents base period prices, and n is the number of items included in the index. The current year weighting used in Paasche indices is disadvantageous because the weights have to be recalculated each year and comparison is thus only possible between any one period and the base period. Furthermore, Paasche indices tend to understate price or volume rises. *Compare* Laspeyres index, Fisher's index.

package. A computer program or set of programs designed to meet the common requirements of any number of potential buyers as distinct from software written specifically for a single user or specific application. Packages are available for a wide variety of uses such as purchase and nominal ledger, sales ledger, stock control, payroll, financial modelling, etc.

package deal. An agreement between two or more parties that settles all, or most, of the issues between them. It usually involves concessions and compromises on all sides in order to accommodate conflicting interests and to arrive at a working arrangement. Many deals between unions and management are package deals.

packaging. The containers or wrappings of a product. Eye-catching and attractive packaging can markedly increase sales, and by increasing *product differentiation can increase the monopoly power of a producer.

paid-up capital. The total amount of money that shareholders of a company have subscribed for shares that have been paid for in full. *Compare* called-up capital.

paid-up policies. With endowment assurances and whole life assurances it is normally possible for the assured to terminate his policy, but instead of accepting a *surrender value, to have it made *fully paid up*. No further premiums will be payable and the policy will be on the same conditions except that the sum assured will be reduced to a sum that depends on the premiums paid up to that point.

In respect of *with-profits policies it is possible for the reduced sum assured to continue to earn bonuses but often an insurance company will insist that they be converted to a without-profit basis. However, if this should occur it is customary for the bonuses earned to date to be added to the sum assured, thus increasing the life cover.

paid-up share. A share whose price has been *fully paid. *See* called-up capital.

palletization. The use of wooden frames (pallets) suitable for lifting by fork-lift trucks to facilitate the warehousing, distribution, and transport of certain classes of goods.

Panel on Takeovers and Mergers. *See* City Code.

paper bid. A takeover bid in which payment to the shareholders of the target firm is made in the shares of the bidding firm.

paper gold. *See* Special Drawing Rights.

paper money. Bank notes and sometimes cheques, bills of exchange, etc.

paper profit or loss. **1.** *See* realized profit. **2.** An unrealized capital gain (or loss) on an asset, such as securities, commodities, or property.

parabola. *See* quadratic function.

parameter. **1.** A characteristic constant of a statistical population, such as its mean or variance. Generally speaking, it is impractical or impossible to calculate the true value of a parameter and consequently it is normal procedure to estimate an approximation to it, such as the mean or variance of a random sample drawn from the population. *See also* estimation. *Compare* statistic. **2.** A constant of any *model, *function, or statistical *distribution. *See also* coefficient. *Compare* variable.

parent company. A company that controls several *subsidiary companies.

Pareto-optimal. State A is Pareto-superior to state B if no individual is worse off in state A relative to B and someone is better off. State A is Pareto-optimal if there is no state Pareto-superior to it. Pareto-optimality, which was devised by Vilfredo Pareto (1848–1923), does not give a single "best" plan for an economy. For instance, in trade two individuals could trade at two different points on the contract curve along which neither can benefit without the detriment of the other. Both are Pareto-optimal so neither is Pareto-superior to the other. No judgment can be made between them. Pareto-optimality is a fundamental criterion in welfare economics. A competitive equilibrium is termed efficient because it is Pareto-optimal; the fact that consumers maximize utility and producers maximize profit guarantees this. The principle however, in avoiding value judgments, begs the question of what policy to follow if one wishes to redistribute income, for example. As a rule of social justice Pareto-optimality is a characteristic that should be contained in any discussion of optimality but in itself leaves aside the most crucial welfare judgments of all, distinguishing as to which is best among a set of Pareto-efficient points. *See also* compensation principle.

Pareto's law. The principle that a number of people (N) receiving a stated income (Y) declines by a constant percentage (b) as the income level is increased in increments of one per cent. This can be expressed by the formula:

$$N = \mathrm{a}Y^{-\mathrm{b}},$$

where a is a constant that will be different for different societies. The higher the value of b the more quickly the number of recipients decline as income increases above the average level: hence the more equally distributed will be the income structure of that country. It usually lies between 1.5 (indicating a high degree of inequality) and two (indicating a high degree of equality). In practice, Pareto's law is not borne out over the whole range of incomes, but is valid for higher incomes, especially the highest 10%. It was first stated by Vilfredo Pareto (1848–1923).

pari passu. (Latin for: with equal step.)A term that indicates simultaneity of effects. For instance, when used in commerce it indicates shares that rank equally with others as to entitlement to dividends or to repayment of capital in the event of a winding-up, and is often applied to new issues.

Paris Club. *See* Group of Ten.

Parkinson's law. Work expands to fill the time available. Originally proposed by Professor Northcote Parkinson as a joke, it has serious implications in large organizations.

Parliamentary Commissioner for Administration (Ombudsman). An officer whose duty is to investigate complaints of maladministration made to him by members of the public against any person acting in the service of the U.K. government. The office was established under the Parliamentary Commissioner Act (1967). The office is commonly referred to as the *Ombudsman,* which is the name used to describe a similar post in Sweden dating back over 150 years. The Crichel Down Case (1954) revealed that over a vast area of public administration there was no effective avenue for seeking redress of grievances. There has been criticism of the 1967 Act because important areas, such as local government, the nationalized industries, the national health service, and the police were excluded from its jurisdiction. The Commissioner has no power to force a government authority to change its decision but relies upon the desire of most departments to avoid adverse publicity.

par of exchange. A theoretical state in which the demand for and supply of foreign exchange exactly balance between one country and another. The *mint par of exchange* can only be calculated between two countries using the same metal for their respective standard coins and it is then determined by the relative amounts of pure metal in these standard units.

partial correlation. Correlation between two variables in an analysis involving three or more. Formulae have been devised for the elimination of the correlative effect of the other specified variable or variables so that *coefficients of partial correlation* can be calculated with the influence of the other variable or variables removed. *See also* correlation, coefficient of correlation.

partial equilibrium analysis. An economic theory or argument that treats one particular sector, generally an industry, as operating in isolation from the rest of the economy. The assumptions required are stronger than the normal ceteris paribus assumptions, since one must also assume that feedback from changes in the economy as a whole brought about by changes in the one sector are negligible, or at least that their feedback to the sector is so.

For example, one could argue that in a capital-intensive monopolized industry a fall in wage rates would reduce cost and increase profits. This would ignore the possibility that more labour-intensive processes might now become competitors and reduce profits. The most common example given in macroeconomics is that in which a cutback in a key industry triggers a recession in the economy and alters that industry's demand curve. The assumptions necessary for a partial equilibrium analysis are generally reasonable where the sector under consideration is small relative to the economy as a whole and there are few repercussions with other sectors. *Compare* general equilibrium analysis.

partial intestacy. *See* intestacy.

partial loss. *See* average.

participating preference shares. Preference shares that receive an extra share of profits, in addition to their normal fixed dividend, after the holders of ordinary shares have received a dividend of a certain size.

participation rate. The proportion of the population that constitutes the labour force. This rate varies from region to region and among the population, depending to a great extent on the industrial structure of the area and the amount of work available, particularly for women. The participation rates of various sections of the economy have been analysed in detail. For instance, the participation rate of women falls proportionately faster than the rate for men during depressions.

particular average. *See* average.

partly paid shares. Shares for which only a proportion of the full nominal value has been paid. It was formerly usual to *call up* only a small proportion of the nominal value of each share, the balance remaining with the shareholder until the company needed to increase its capital. When this occurred, the company could call in all or part of the balance from the shareholders. Partly paid shares were therefore a great liability to shareholders but gave confidence to company creditors, since if it needed capital the company had access to it from the shareholders. Banks and insurance companies were the chief users of partly paid shares because the confidence it gave their creditors was valuable to them, but this is no longer considered necessary. Partly paid shares are now rarely issued.

partner. A person engaged in the same business enterprise jointly with another or others (*see* partnership). He may be a *general partner*, in which case his liability for the partnership debts is unlimited, or a *limited partner, in which case his liability is limited to a certain amount, and the partnership is a limited partnership. He may be an *active partner* (working for the firm) or a *sleeping partner* (in which case he contributes money to the partnership but takes no active part in running the business) or he may just be a *nominal partner* by lending his name to the partnership but by giving no other support. To retire he must give notice to all likely to do business with the partnership, otherwise he may still be liable for subsequent debts.

partnership. A business association of two or more *partners. They are usually bound together by a partnership agreement, otherwise the partnership is known as a *partnership-at-will* and can be broken by any partner at any time. The respective rights and duties of the partners are governed primarily by the partnership agreement, and also, in as much as these do not conflict with the agreement, the provisions of the Partnership Act (1890). *See also* illegal partnership.

Partnership Acts. Acts of Parliament that sanctioned the creation of *partnerships. The Partnerships Act (1890) defined the function of partnerships. The Limited Partnerships Act (1907) allowed limited partnerships to be created. Other Acts have affected partnerships, especially the Companies Act (1948), which limited the number who could become partners in any particular business.

partnership-at-will. *See* partnership.

par value. The price in which a security is denominated and around which it will usually be issued. A share is said to be issued at a premium if it is issued at a price above the par value and to be issued at a discount if it is below. Thus if ABC Ltd issues 25p shares at 30p each, then the par value of the shares is 25p, the issue price is 30p, and the premium is 5p. Once a share is established on a stock exchange, its par value becomes unimportant. The important price is then the *market value. Terms such as *nominal value* or *face value* are sometimes used instead of par value.

The par value of *loan stock is always 100; the market value will vary inversely with the general level of interest rates. In the case of newly issued shares or loan stocks that are only partly paid, however, the par value is the issue price.

In some countries shares can be issued with no par value (*N.P.V.*).

Pascal. A high-level *programming language developed in the late 1960s at the Zurich Technical Institute and named after the 17th-century French mathematician Blaise Pascal. There are three major versions of the language: UCSD Pascal, the British Standards Institute version, and the original "Standard" version. The language is widely used academically and is becoming more common for business applications: it is more difficult than *BASIC but more precise.

passing a name. 1. Brokers may fulfil several functions, including introducing buyers to sellers and guaranteeing the solvency of the buyers to the sellers. In some commodity markets, for example, they do not disclose the buyer's name to the seller, but guarantee the buyer's solvency. In other markets they pass the name of the buyer to the seller, in which case they rarely guarantee the buyer's solvency.

2. On the London Stock Exchange, brokers pass the name of a buyer of shares to the jobber about seven to ten days before *account day to enable accounts to be prepared.

passive balance. A *balance of payments that is in deficit.

patent. An authority from a government giving the person to whom it is addressed the sole right of making, using, and selling an invention for a certain period. A U.K. patent usually lasts for 16 years, subject to payment of the appropriate annual fee, and may be granted after an application has been made to the *Patent Office in London. Such applications, usually prepared by a specialist known as a *patent agent,* must establish a sufficient degree of novelty to distinguish the invention from those covered by existing patents, records of which are available for inspection at the Patent Office. Each country has its own system of patents, although international agreements help give patent-holders in one country priority in obtaining patents in others. *Patent* is an abbreviation of *letters patent*, letters open for all to see.

patent agent. *See* patent.

patent monopoly. Any monopoly granted by the government although patents are now generally issued only to protect inventions and technological innovations for a specified number of years, in the U.K. 16 years and in the U.S. 17 years. By so doing the government hopes to encourage innovation and allow the inventor to recoup his research costs through the monopoly profits on his invention. To exploit the position patent-holders can either become producers themselves and act as monopolists, or grant licences to other producers for payment of a fee or royalties. In the U.K. and other countries the government may force the patent-holder to issue licences in certain cases, as when a company holds a wide range of patents simply in order to frustrate competition.

Though not strictly a patent monopoly, production techniques or product details are sometimes not patented but kept secret. In this way the monopoly position can be maintained for more than the usual length of time. The disadvantage is that if the secret is ever discovered it may be freely used by competitors.

Patent Office. The U.K. government department that administers the Patent Acts, the Registered Designs Act, and the Trade Marks Act and deals with all questions relating to copyright. The Department has also provided an information service about patent specifications during the last 50 years and has its own large scientific and technical library in London.

paternalism. A form of management that combines strict discipline and generous welfare facilities. It is practised by old-established companies, especially those in the retail trade with many branches. Many governments, too, are often paternalistic in the sense that they believe citizens will not always act in their own best interests. The enforcement of a compulsory period of education is an example of a paternalistic policy. *See* myopia.

pawnbroker. A person who has a licence to lend money upon the security of valuable goods, which are left with him until the loan is repaid. The pawnbroker acknowledges the transaction by issuing a ticket and must then only hand over the goods pawned on production of the ticket. In the U.K., pawnbrokers' activities are governed by the Pawnbrokers Acts (1872 and 1960), which regulate the rates of interest that can be charged on loans of under £50. At the end of six months and seven days from the date of the loan, the pawnbroker may retain any items pawned for less than £2, and any pawned for more than £2 may be sold at a public auction and purchased by someone other than the pawnbroker. If they fetch more than the amount of the loan (with interest), the pawnbroker must pay over the balance to the original owner if it is claimed within three years.

payable to bearer. Denoting a *bill of exchange on which no payee is given and no endorsee is named (endorsed in blank). The bill becomes payable to the bearer.

payable to order. Denoting a *bill of exchange on which the name of the payee is given and on which there are no restrictions on *endorsements. The bill can be paid to the endorsee.

pay-as-you-earn (P.A.Y.E.). The system of *income tax collection in which tax is deducted at source. According to the employee's tax status (as designated by a code number) a fixed amount of tax is deducted from his gross pay in each pay period (week or month) rather than by annual assessment. The employer is then responsible for remitting the tax deducted to the taxation authority. This only applies to full-time employees.

pay-as-you-go. A method of financing retirement pensions out of the present contributions and tax payments of present workers, rather than from the contributions built up by the retired during their working lives. The result is that a generation can receive more in pensions than the sum of its contributions (as is happening in the U.K.). Pay-as-you-go pensions can be protected from inflation as the contributions of the present workforce will rise in inflationary periods (*see* built-in stabilizers), so financing increases and, by the same process, the retired can benefit from any growth in national income. More can only be paid out in retirement pensions than has been collected in past contributions if there is either population growth (so that a larger workforce will bear the burden) or if economic growth continues (so that there is more wealth to be distributed). However, pay-as-you-go schemes are expensive and if the size of the workforce declines as a proportion of the total population (perhaps because of a fall in the birthrate, lengthier education, earlier retirement, or greater longevity) the burden that a future workforce would have to bear would increase, possibly reducing the incentive to work. The same applies if productivity does not increase.

payback period. The period required to recoup the cost of a project from earnings: it is sometimes used as a criterion in evaluating investment projects.

This method of assessment has some merit in cases in which a quick return on capital is important, e.g. where there is a possibility of rapid obsolescence or political uncertainty. It does, however, have two major defects: it ignores the pattern of profits over the life of the project and it does not take into account the rate of return compared to the market rate of interest. More sophisticated methods of evaluating investments use the *present value or the *internal rate of return criterion.

pay day. *See* account day.

P.A.Y.E. *See* pay-as-you-earn.

payee. The person or persons to whom money is paid or to be paid. On a cheque the payee is the person to whom, or to whose order, payment is directed to be made.

paying banker. The banker on whom a cheque is drawn, or with whom a bill of exchange is domiciled. It is his duty to pay the cheques of his customer as long as there is a sufficient balance of funds, or an agreed overdraft, to the credit of the customer. Before paying the cheque he must examine it to see that it is in order, properly signed and drawn, with no discrepancy in words and figures, and that it is not postdated or out of date. He also checks that any necessary endorsements are correct except when the cheque is presented by another banker whose responsibility this now is in the U.K., since the Cheques Act (1957).

Paymaster General. A political post in the U.K. that does not normally carry cabinet status. The office has few responsibilities, which enables the Prime Minister to appoint someone to this junior post who is allocated some additional responsibility in the government.

The Paymaster General's Office is responsible for signing documents permitting government departments, other than the revenue departments, to receive money from the Consolidated Fund, after the Treasury has given authority for payment. The other main feature of its work is the regular payment of many types of public service pensions.

payment by results. A form of wage structure in which payments to workers are related to their output. The most common form is the *piece rate. *See also* measured daywork.

payment in advance. A payment made before a good or service has been received. For example, a landlord may demand one week's rent in advance from a tenant.

payment in due course. Payment of a *bill of exchange when it matures.

payment in kind. Payment in goods and services, rather than in money. The payment of total wages in kind was made illegal in the U.K. by the Truck Acts in the nineteenth century, but many employees still receive a partial payment of their wages in kind. Examples are provision of accommodation for agricultural workers, concessionary coal allowances for miners, and free travel on buses for busmen and their wives.

payment on account. A payment in partial settlement of an outstanding debt. For example, if one person owes another £100, he may pay £50 on account and agree to pay the balance one month later.

payment stopped. A customer may instruct his banker in writing to stop payment of a cheque that he has issued; should the banker pay the cheque after receiving such notice he will be liable for so doing. The reason for refusing payment written on the cheque by the banker will be "orders not to pay" or "payment countermanded by the drawer". If the cheque is negotiable (*see* negotiability) and is in the hands of a bona fide holder for value he can sue the drawer for the amount of the cheque although payment has been stopped. Payment of a cheque that has been supported by a cheque card cannot be stopped, provided that the amount of the cheque does not exceed the amount guaranteed by the cheque card.

payoff. One of several outcomes consequent upon a *strategy selected by a player in *game theory. Once a player has selected his own strategy, his payoff will depend on the strategies chosen by his opponents. A payoff may be positive, indicating a gain, or negative, implying an absolute or relative loss. *See also* payoff matrix.

payoff matrix. A matrix used in the *game theory analysis of situations with two players. The elements of the matrix represent the *payoffs from the point of view of one of the players. In the following matrix each player has three strategies:

70; 20; 50
35; 90; 30
40; 60; 80

The rows of the matrix represent the *strategies available to player 1; the columns represent strategies available to player 2. Assuming that there is a constant sum of £100 to be distributed between the two players whatever two strategies they respectively choose, if player 1 adopts strategy no. 1 and player 2 also selects his own strategy no. 1, then player 1 will receive a payoff of £70 and player 2 will, by inference, receive a payoff of £30 (i.e. 100 – 70). If, however, player 1 selects strategy no. 1 but player 2 adopts strategy no. 2 then player 1's payoff would be only £20 and player 2's payoff, again by inference, would be £80. In the case of the payoffs indicated in the matrix, player 1 would select strategy no. 3 if he were following the *Laplace criterion, *maximin, or *minimax regret, but would adopt strategy no. 2 if he were following *maximax.

pay pause. A form of *incomes policy that was initiated in the U.K. by the Conservative Chancellor of the Exchequer in August 1961. The pay pause was created as a response to a balance of payments crisis and attempted to halt all pay rises, with no exceptions. The Government froze pay increases in the public sector as an encouragement to the private sector. Although the unions refused to cooperate, the pay pause was fairly successful. It was superseded in March 1962 by a less stringent incomes policy.

payroll tax. A tax levied as a percentage of a firm's total wage bill. It often takes the form of an employee's contribution matched by an employer's contribution. Relative elasticities of supply and demand for labour determine who actually pays the tax in a comparison with the no-tax situation. To the extent to which it increases the after-tax wage rate paid, it may lead to a shift to more *capital intensive processes. *See also* selective employment tax.

P.D.M. *See* physical distribution management.

peaceful picketing. *See* picketing.

pegging the exchanges. The fixing of the value of a country's currency in terms of other currencies. This action is taken by a government in order to stabilize the rate of exchange of its currency. Governments with fixed exchange rates must be prepared to intervene on the foreign exchange markets to ensure that their currencies do not become under- or over-valued. No government intervention is necessary with a freely floating exchange rate as the rate of exchange is allowed to adjust itself according to supply and demand. *See also* exchange rate.

penalty clause. A clause in a contract providing for one party to pay a sum or sums of money to the other if the contract is not kept. Such clauses are generally unenforceable at law unless it can be established that they are a genuine attempt to forecast the amount that the party claiming the penalty will lose as a result of the breach of contract. *See also* liquidated damages.

pensionable earnings. Earnings that are taken into account in calculating a person's entitlement to a pension. It may exclude such items as overtime, bonuses, and commission.

pension funds. The contributions from the rapidly growing private pension schemes, from both the public and private sectors, placed in managed invested funds. They are the second largest category of investment (after insurance) and funds are mainly invested in long-term investments in equities and property. Contributions are allowable for tax relief but the benefits paid out are taxable above certain limits.

pensions. Regular payments made to provide a secure income for people in retirement or old age, either from the state or a private pension scheme. State pensions in the U.K. consist of *old-age pensions* paid to those aged 80 years or over who have not participated in the National Insurance Scheme (the Old Age Pensions Act 1908 provided for payment of these entirely out of general taxation), and *retirement pensions* paid to men over 65 and women over 60 who have made the requisite contributions to the National Insurance scheme and have retired from regular employment. These standard flat-rate pensions are being replaced by an earnings-related scheme established by the Social Security Act (1975) and implemented in 1979, but fully earnings-related pensions will not be paid out until 1998 as the scheme has a 20-year maturity period. For those who have "contracted out" of the state pension scheme there are many private pension schemes, which must be government-approved and pay at least as much as the government scheme. Many companies provide pension schemes for their employees, which may be *contributory* or *non-contributory* (if they are paid exclusively by the employer they can be regarded as a fringe benefit). Companies benefit by a reduction in their liability to corporation tax and individuals benefit by tax concessions on their contributions. Payments are generally related to length of service and level of salary or contributions. Recent legislation relating to company pension schemes has been enacted relating to the transferability (*portability*) of such schemes when the employee changes jobs. Large companies may administer their own pension funds, while others often use those provided by insurance companies. The removal of tax relief on life assurance premiums by the 1984 U.K. budget caused insurance companies to re-think tax-efficient methods of providing for the future. Executive pension plans are available that qualify for relief to corporation tax and also tax relief at the highest rate on an individual's personal contributions. Since the 1984 budget, special pension plans have also been introduced for directors, which are self-administered and provide an opportunity for the directors to select where to invest a large proportion of the contributions.

Methods of financing pensions are of two types: the capital-reserve type, in which workers save during their working lives in order to finance their retirement, and the pay-as-you-go type, in which those currently at work support those who are retired (a declining population under this latter system has to bear an increasingly heavier burden to support growing numbers of pensioners).

Pension schemes began with the Civil Service in 1832. *See also* annuity.

peppercorn rent. A very small nominal rent, usually charged to establish that a property is being leased and is not being transferred freehold.

P/E ratio. Short for price/earnings ratio, it is the ratio formed by the division of a share's price (on a stock exchange) by its *earnings per share. The P/E ratio is the fundamental statistic used by investment analysts when examining any particular share with a view to purchase or sale. The shares of companies with records of good profit growths, which are expected to continue, tend to have a high rating, i.e. a high P/E ratio and probably a low *yield; conversely, a low rating will generally apply to the shares of those companies which are inefficient or which operate in stagnant or heavily cyclical markets. When taking a decision as to whether a share should be bought, sold, or held, an investor will attempt to measure the degree to which its price is cheap, dear, or fairly valued. A cheap share price is one whose ratio to earnings per share is considered to be too low in relation to the shares of other companies, especially other companies in the same industry, and in the context of its forecast profit potential. A company's P/E ratio is sometimes called its *multiple*.

per capita income. The average income per person of a group, calculated by dividing total income by the number of people sharing that income. In the case of the per capita income of the whole country, the national income is divided by the population. Although of some interest, per capita income does not indicate welfare particularly well, since there are great disparities in the distribution of income.

percentile. One of 99 values that divide a distribution into 100 equal portions when it is arranged in order of magnitude. Thus the *n*th percentile of a group of numbers is the value that has below it *n* per cent of the numbers. The median of a distribution is its fiftieth percentile. *See also* decile, quartile.

per contra. Denoting a reference to an entry on the opposite side of an account.

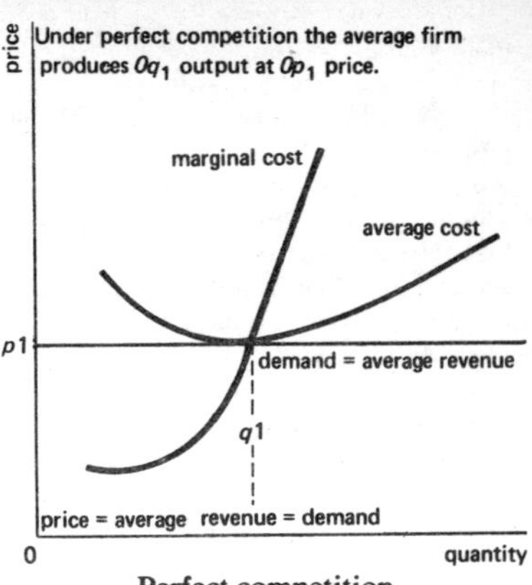

Perfect competition

perfect (pure) competition. A perfectly competitive market or industry is one in which the economic agents, producers and consumers, are price-takers and cannot influence the market price. More specifically, to justify this assumption it is usually assumed that there are a large number of producers and consumers, that the product is homogeneous, that there is perfect information about market conditions, and that there are no barriers to entry to the industry or market.

The first assumption guarantees the existence of a large number of competitors who will undercut any producer who attempts to raise his price above the market price. The second two guarantee that the producers' products are not distinguishable so that consumers will not have preferences among the products. The lack of such assumptions leads to monopolistic competition. The last assumption guarantees that if economic profits exist, other producers will be induced to enter the market, reducing the quantities sold by each producer already in the industry and lowering prices until all of them are producing at their break-even points. This final price is the long-run market price and is economically efficient since it represents production at the least cost available to society, i.e. that level of production at which each firm's marginal cost and average cost, and the market price, are all equal (see diagram). This occurs at the price and output that maximize consumer surplus. The short-run price, under the first three assumptions, is perfectly elastic, and represented graphically by a line parallel to the quantity axis.

In fact, these stringent assumptions, especially the second, can only be met in primary industries (such as farming) with relatively low capital costs and thus minimal barriers to entry. Light industries, such as textiles, may also sometimes fill the requirements.

perfecting the sight. Completing the details supplied on a *bill of sight.

perfect market. A market with the following characteristics: a large number of buyers and sellers, so that the quantity of the product that each deals in is too small a fraction of the total amount traded to affect price; the product is homogeneous, so that buyers have no quality preferences; there is perfect information in the market in that all traders know the price being paid for the product throughout the market; the cost of transport is nil so that buyers can buy the commodity wherever it is cheapest; there are no *barriers to entry, so that new buyers and sellers can enter the market if abnormally high profits are being earned.

In this type of market, *perfect competition would exist; but in reality no market situation fulfills all these conditions. For instance, the Stock Exchange provides nearly perfect information on price and a large number of buyers, but there are barriers to entry. In wheat, no farm can affect the price by varying the quantity sold and the good is homogeneous, but cost of transport is an important factor. However, the ideal case provides insight into the operation of markets in the real world.

perfect oligopoly. A market containing a small number of firms, each of which produces an identical good. The only way firms can compete is by varying the price of their product. This is unlikely to maximize profits and we should expect to see periods of collusion to keep the price artificially high interspersed with price wars when the arrangement breaks down. Models of oligopolistic behaviour have been developed using a *duopoly situation as a framework. *Compare* imperfect oligopoly.

peril point. The lowest rate to which a *tariff can be reduced without jeopardizing the existence of a domestic industry. The term was coined by the U.S. Tariff Commission.

period (term) bill. A *bill of exchange that is payable on a specific date rather than on demand.

period of grace. The length of time that is customarily allowed for payment of a bill of exchange or promissory note after it falls due. Normally the period of grace is three days for all bills of exchange, except those payable at sight or on demand.

peripheral devices (peripherals). The input and output systems, etc., of a *computer, as distinguished from the *central processing unit.

permanent income theory. *See* saving.

permanent sickness policies. *See* personal accident and sickness insurance.

permission to deal. Permission by a stock exchange to allow dealings in the shares of a company. Permission to deal in shares must be sought three days after the issue of a *prospectus.

permutations. The number of ordered arrangements of a specified total of items within a larger total. Consider the following sequence of letters: a,b,c,d. The number of two-way permutations is 12 as follows: ab,ba,ac,ca,ad,da,bc,cb,bd,db,cd,dc. *Compare* combinations.

perpetual debenture. *See* debenture.

perpetual inventory. *See* inventory.

perpetual succession. The continuation of a company after the departure or death of its owners or directors since it has a separate legal existence (apart from that of its owners or directors). A company can only lawfully cease to exist after *liquidation.

Perpetuities and Accumulations Act (1964). An Act that mitigated the harsh common law rules by which any gifts of property given to trustees to hold for long periods were invalidated. The common law provided that if there was even the slightest chance that the trustees could hold the property for more than 21 years after the death of any person who was living at the date of the gift to the trustees, then the gift would be completely void. The Act included the "wait and see" rule, enabling the trustees to wait and see whether they were still holding the property at the end of the 21-year period, and then only if they were would the gift be void. The Act also provided that a straight 80-year period would, if the donor of the property specified, be substituted for the life in being plus a 21-year period. The Act also simplified the law relating to the maximum period during which trustees could hold or "accumulate" the income from property without paying it out. The Act limited this to a straight period of 21 years.

per pro (p.p.). On behalf of. An agent signing this gives notice that he holds an authority to sign on behalf of his principal, but that he has only a limited authority and his principal will not be bound if that authority is exceeded. The words should precede the principal's name with the agent's signature usually following, but it may be in front. *See also* agent.

per proc. *See* procuration.

personal accident and sickness insurance. A category of insurance, which may be taken out both on an individual and on a group basis. It includes:

(a) *Accidents only.* Compensation is only provided for death or injury arising from "accidental, violent, external, and visible means". A capital sum is normally payable for death, with lesser sums for loss of limbs or eyes, and a weekly benefit for a specified maximum period in respect of full or partial disability.

(b) *Accidents and specified diseases.* In addition to the accident benefits mentioned above a weekly benefit is payable for disablement resulting from any of a specified list of diseases. (There is no death benefit for disease.)

(c) *Accidents and all sickness.* An extension of (b) above, covering all illnesses, with no cover for death other than by accident.

(d) *Permanent sickness policies.* The insured receives an income during any period of total disability, for as long as the disability lasts or until a stipulated age limit is reached.

(e) *Aviation and travel.* The cover provided is often as with (c) above, with the important addition of compensation for medical expenses incurred. This type of insurance is often taken out by holidaymakers and people travelling on business.

personal account. 1. A ledger account that deals with debtors or creditors. *See also* impersonal account. **2.** *See* P.A.

personal allowances. In assessing the taxable income of an individual for income tax purposes, certain allowances are deducted from actual income. The allowances depend upon an individual's status and circumstances. The rates of personal allowances, e.g. married personal allowance, single personal allowance, age allowance, etc., may vary from year to year. Changes in U.K. personal taxation and allowances are usually announced each year by the Chancellor of the Exchequer in the budget. *See also* taxable income.

personal cheque service. A limited U.S. banking service by which people are able to make payments by cheque, but are unable to avail themselves of other services of the bank.

personal (home) computer. A *microcomputer for personal or home use. Much cheaper than a business computer, the personal computer normally consists of a keyboard with built-in central processing unit which can be attached to a television to display information and a tape cassette to store and load programs. Inefficient mass storage makes the personal computer unsuitable for business use but ideal for the hobbyist and computer games fan.

personal loan. A bank loan in which the interest is added to the agreed amount to be lent and the total is divided by the number of months over which the loan is to be repaid. The resulting amount is the repayment to be made monthly by the customer. Originating in the U.S., the system was introduced in the U.K. in 1958 with the easing of credit controls. The interest rate is higher than that normally charged for overdrafts because such loans are often made without support of security and on the bank manager's assessment of the creditworthiness of the borrower.

personal property. *See* real property.

personal wealth. The value of each individual's personal possessions. It can be divided into physical assets (such as property and consumer durables) and financial assets (such as bank deposits and life assurance policies). The total wealth of a nation is the sum of the private sector (which includes the personal wealth of individuals) and the public sector.

In the U.K., the distribution of personal wealth is much more unequal than the distribution of personal income. The Royal Commission on the Distribution of Income and Wealth (1975) estimated that the richest 0.01% of the population owned approximately 12% of total personal wealth, the richest 1% owned over 25% of total personal wealth, the richest 5% owned over 50% of total personal wealth, and the richest 10% owned over 66% of total personal wealth. In qualification it must be remembered that these estimates were based on the Inland Revenue's statistics and it was assumed that those who were not included in these statistics had no wealth. It must also be remembered that these figures apply to individuals rather than to families.

Although the degree of inequality is marked there are indications that it is slowly decreasing. A study by Professor Revell showed that the amount of personal wealth owned by the richest 1% of the adult population (25 and over) in England and Wales was 69% in 1911-13 and 42% in 1969. This was counterbalanced to some extent by an increase in the wealth of the next 4% indicating, perhaps, that the heads of many families transferred ownership of large amounts of their possessions to their wives and children for tax purposes.

The composition of personal wealth has altered significantly in recent years. Between 1960 and 1973 the proportion of personal wealth that was embodied in physical assets rose from less than a third to nearly a half. A major reason was the growth in the ownership of homes. On the financial assets side there was a concurrent and notable decline in the amount of company securities that were held.

personnel management. The area of management concerned with staff and their relative positions in a business enterprise or other organization. It aims to combine their efforts as effectively as possible, both for the success of the enterprise and the well-being of the employee. *Personnel officers* are employed to organize the selection of personnel, their training, general terms of employment including pay, etc., and act as intermediaries for consultation between employees at various levels. In the U.K. the *Institute of Personnel Management* is an association working in this field with the aim of maintaining high professional standards and promoting research in the field. It sets examinations and publishes journals. *See also* line and staff management.

personnel selection. The process of choosing the most suitable applicant from a group of candidates for a particular job. Careful selection will rely on a comparison of past achievements (based on a *curriculum vitae) and a prediction of future performance (based on interview often supplemented by *job-knowledge tests and *psychological tests). If there are a large number of applicants, the usual procedure is to ask for a written application accompanied by a curriculum vitae. These applications are screened and the most likely candidates are then called for testing and interview. Interviews may be conducted by one person or by a panel of interviewers and candidates may be seen singly or in groups.

petal printer. *See* daisywheel printer.

petro-dollars. The large surpluses of foreign currency (especially U.S. dollars) accumulated by members of the *Organization of Petroleum Exporting Countries (OPEC), especially the major redistribution of financial resources that resulted from the increase in the price of oil by OPEC in 1973. The amount accumulated far outweighed the capacity of underdeveloped oil nations' economies to absorb goods. Therefore these cash surpluses were recycled into the financial centres of the developed countries, offsetting in part the major deficits in the balance of trade and helping to support the weaker currencies of the western nations, whose governments offered high interest rates to attract the petro-dollars.

petty cash. Money held on a business's premises for the payment of incidental expenses.

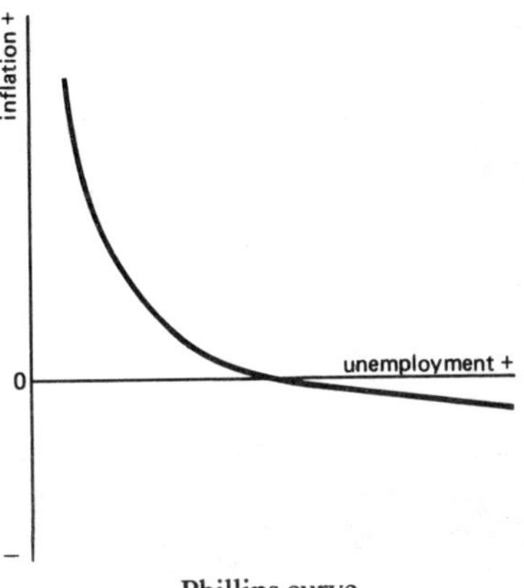

Phillips curve

Phillips curve. A graph showing a hypothetical relationship between unemployment and inflation. It predicts that an increase in aggregate demand in the economy will in turn increase employment and inflation. Conversely the only way to achieve a low rate of inflation is to decrease aggregate demand in the economy, which will in turn increase unemployment. Thus policy-makers must decide on a compromise between the two apparently incompatible goals of full employment and price stability.

The early justifications for the Phillips curve were empirical. The evidence seemed to support it in its major proposition of a compromise having to be made. Later work has suggested that there are two Phillips curves, a long- and a short-run curve. In the extreme case monetarists argue that there is no real compromise in the long run, and that there is a fixed level of structural unemployment, which is independent of the rate of inflation. The explanation given for the empirical evidence of the Phillips curve is that at first inflation, by increasing wages and prices, stimulates the level of economic activity and attracts more workers into employment. This continues only until people adjust their expectations about price changes and estimate inflation at the new rate. Then the wage and price increases no longer look as attractive and the short-run Phillips curve shifts over until unemployment is at the old level but with a higher rate of inflation.

Other theories accept this mechanism but suppose that expectations on price changes never adjust perfectly so that the long-run Phillips curve is more steeply sloped than the short-run, but not vertical.

The dilemma posed by the Phillips curve is that the government, to gain popularity, can reduce unemployment temporarily at the expense of inflation, but to reduce inflation must first suffer unpopularity in the short run for having increased unemployment. However, in recent years the whole of Phillips curve analysis has been called into question by the fact that many countries are suffering *stagflation* (a combination of high unemployment *and* high inflation rates).

physical controls. Direct measures employed by the government to regulate the activities of the economy in preference to the indirect method of influencing the price mechanism. The imposition of an import quota on a commodity would be a physical control, whereas the imposition of an import surcharge would not.

physical distribution management (P.D.M.). *See* marketing logistics.

physiocratic system. An eighteenth-century school of economic thought led by François Quesnay (1694–1774), whose followers were known at the time as *les Économistes.* It developed in reaction to the mercantile doctrines of the day (*see* mercantilism). In particular it saw the agricultural sector as the sole source of productive capacity: the merchants and industrialists were regarded as the *classe sterile* in that they could make no net additions to wealth–they did not produce resources but merely changed their form. Since mercantile interests were no longer identified with the wealth of the nation, the mercantile restrictive trading policies were to be replaced with laissez-faire policies and free trade. Furthermore since all other sectors merely covered costs, the only productive sector, agriculture, should alone bear a tax for the purpose of raising revenue, *l'impôt unique.* As an analytic technique the physiocrats introduced the **Tableau Économique*, which developed a concept of the circular flow of income in a primitive form of input-output analysis.

P.I.B. *See* National Board for Prices and Incomes.

pick and shovel work. *See* relief work.

picketing. Industrial action in the form of standing outside the premises of the firm involved in the dispute and attempting to dissuade or prevent other workers, delivery lorries, etc. from crossing the *picket line*, thus bringing production to a halt. Picketing one's own place of work is lawful: the right to *peaceful picketing* (in which no force is used) was established in the U.K. by the Trade Union Act (1875) and reaffirmed by the Trade Disputes Act (1906). Picketing other people's place of work (*secondary picketing*), i.e. action against employers not otherwise involved in the dispute, constitutes a civil offence: the Employment Acts (1980 and 1982) allow employers adversely affected by secondary picketing to take legal action. *Flying pickets* travel to join picket lines wherever their presence might add strength to the strikers taking industrial action. The laws relating to picketing are proving impossible to enforce as the numbers and industrial power of those involved in illegal picketing are too great.

pictogram. A form of diagram used to provide a visual representation of quantitative information. It usually consists of stylized drawings of people or things, the number or size of the drawings representing actual numbers. For example, a pictogram comparing the number of cars with the number of lorries produced each week by a factory might represent each thousand vehicles by a drawing of a car or a lorry. If the ouput of cars was 5500 and the output of lorries 2000, there would be drawings of five and a half cars on one line and two lorries on a separate line.

piece rate. A payment to a worker that is related to the amount of output he achieves rather than to the time for which he works. For example, if an employee is paid two pounds for every machine he makes and he constructs 40 in a week, his gross wage is £80. If he can increase his output, his earnings will also increase. More complex systems are common; one variation is that in which employees are paid a basic wage as well as a bonus for each unit produced over a specific number.

Piece rates encourage a high output but are unsuitable if quality is more important than quantity. They also cannot be applied to occupations in which it is difficult to measure output, e.g. teaching or fire-prevention.

pie chart. A form of diagram used to provide a visual representation of the proportions into which something is divided. It consists of a circle with radii dividing the total into various parts, like slices of a pie. The areas of the sectors so formed represent the proportions to be illustrated.

Pigou effect. The change in the real value of wealth resulting from price level changes. The concept was introduced by Arthur Cecil Pigou (1877–1959) in 1944 to prove that an economy with flexible wages and prices will always return automatically to full employment in the long run. When unemployment exists, wages and prices will fall, and holders of liquid money will consequently be better off in real terms and increase their consumption, thus stimulating demand that is deficient elsewhere in the economy. Only *outside money can cause this increase in spending since if all money is *inside money, all credits are matched by debits and the effect of deflation on these (i.e. creditors becoming better off in real terms and debtors becoming worse off and their associated changes in consumption) will be cancelled out. Pigou did not advocate allowing wages to fall until they reached a level at which the Pigou effect would begin to operate, but rather increasing the issue of money in order to bring about the same results. His reasoning was contrary to that of Keynes, who was of the opinion that there is no mechanism in the economy that keeps it automatically at full employment. *See also* real balance effect.

pilot production. The small-scale production of a new product that it is later planned to manufacture in larger quantities. The *pilot plant* enables production engineers to check their calculations, improve production methods, etc. The product from the pilot plant is often used for a test marketing exercise.

pink form. A form of application (*see* application and allotment) for shares in a company, which gives preference in the process of allotment. Pink forms are often given to employees of a company whose shares are being offered to the public.

PL/1. A computer programming language designed to combine the features of scientific and commercial languages. PL/1 stands for *p*rogramming *l*anguage *1*.

placing. A method of issuing securities through an intermediary, such as a firm of stockbrokers. The intermediary will endeavour to *place* the issue among its connections, notably among institutional investors. If the shares have a quotation on the Stock Exchange however, a proportion of the issue has to be made available to the public. To the extent that a private placing of the issue is achieved, the cost to the firm whose shares are being issued is reduced. *Compare* introduction, offer by prospectus, offer for sale, offer for sale by tender, rights issue.

planned economy. An economy in which decisions as to resource allocation, especially the correct amount of production and consumption, are made by a centralized body, rather than through the price mechanism. An overall strategy for the economy is formulated (*see* five-year plan, National Plan) and then more detailed targets are set for the sectors and industries. To this end, production quotas will be established and prices fixed by a planning board who vary prices and quotas in response to the reactions of the consumers and producers. Planned economies only exist in Communist states where opposition to the free market economy is a matter of ideology. However, in the twentieth century governments throughout the world have been increasingly involved in their national economies; this is particularly apparent in Western Europe.

planned location of industry. Government intervention in the locating of new factories in an attempt to remedy the economic imbalance between different parts of the country. The continual decline in some regions of the older industries, such as coal and ship-building, has caused high unemployment and resulted in poor amenities, derelict buildings, and a decline in population. Government help in the U.K. includes regional development grants, investment incentives, provision of modern factories for sale or rent in the assisted areas, and the *Industrial Development Certificates, through which the government controls the building of new factories and can thus direct projects towards areas of greatest need. *See also* location of industry.

planning blight. A form of stagnation that befalls a district, plot of land, building, etc., because it is included in, or is affected by, some government or local-authority development plan. For example, a house may become unsaleable or lose a substantial part of its value because of the publication of plans showing that a new motorway is to pass very close to it.

planning-programming-budgeting system (P.P.B.S.). A system of governmental decision-making that applies concepts of *cost effectiveness to long-term strategies, such as nuclear defence, rather than individual projects, such as the administration of a department. These strategies are regularly monitored and are under constant re-examination to ensure that they do not exceed their allotted budget and that they utilize the most economical means of achieving the desired end. The main advantage of this system is that functions performed by several government ministries or departments can be jointly evaluated, leading to wider and more informed views. For example, the cost effectiveness of nuclear submarines might be compared with that of Cruise missiles as they both have the same aim, whereas before nuclear submarines might have been evaluated against destroyers solely on the grounds that they were naval and were administered by the same department. P.P.B.S. was first used in the Pentagon in the early 1960s and was spectacularly successful. However, it has proved relatively disappointing since then, perhaps because the objectives of civil departments are less easy to formulate clearly than for the military departments; perhaps because the relative administrative inefficiencies at the Pentagon prior to the P.P.B.S.'s introduction were significantly greater.

plant machinery register. A register in which all relevant information on the plant and equipment owned by a business is recorded. Included will be such details as the date of acquisition, original cost, annual depreciation, etc.

p.l.c. *See* public limited company.

Plimsoll line. *See* load line.

ploughed-back profits. Profits that are retained by a firm, usually to finance growth, rather than being distributed by the firm to shareholders or partners. In the U.K., undistributed profits are taxed by *corporation tax.

plutocracy. A form of government in which power is exercised by a few elite groups whose position is based on wealth, usually large landowners, financiers, and industrialists.

pluvial insurance. *See* weather insurance.

point elasticity. A change in the quantity of a good bought in reaction to an infinitely small change in price. This can be illustrated by the slope of the *demand curve at that point.

Point elasticity is preferred to *arc elasticity* because of its greater accuracy. Arc elasticity averages the change in quantity bought in response to a change in price over a section of the demand curve, whereas point elasticity measures the quantity change at one single position on the demand curve. The formula for point elasticity of demand (η) is:

$$\eta = dq/dp.(p/q),$$

where p is the price and q is the quantity bought.

If elasticity is greater than one, demand is said to be elastic. In this case, a small change in price will lead to a proportionately greater change in the quantity bought. If elasticity is equal to one, the proportionate changes in price and quantity bought are equal. If elasticity is less than one, demand is inelastic. In this case, a small change in price will lead to a proportionately smaller change in quantity bought.

point of sale. The place at which a sale to a member of the public takes place. It is usually a retail shop, but may be on the doorstep in door-to-door selling.

poisson distribution. A statistical *distribution involving a discrete variable and depending on only one parameter, the mean of the (poisson) variable. It can be approximated by a *binomial distribution with a very large number of trials and a very small probability of success. A poisson variable is characterized by the equality of its mean and variance.

The graph of a poisson density function has a strong positive skew. It can be applied to events that are rare in space or time, thus the number of politico-economic revolutions in each year over the last two centuries would be poisson-distributed.

policy. *See* insurance policy.

policy mix. The combination of *fiscal, *monetary, and other policies employed to achieve the economic objectives of a government. Effective policy instruments are required, with at least as many independent instruments of policy as there are independent policy objectives. The optimal policy mix is not always easy to find, especially when an instrument of policy may have an effect of similar magnitude on several objectives. A typical policy mix rule is that given by Mundell for an economy with a fixed exchange rate and perfect capital mobility: monetary policy should be used for external balance and fiscal policy for internal balance.

policy proof of interest (P.P.I.). An insurance policy in which possession of the actual policy is sufficient proof of interest to entitle the holder to receive payment of any claims. However, the holder of the policy need not necessarily have an *insurable interest in the subject matter of the insurance; according to the Marine Insurance (Gambling Policies) Act (1909) the insured must have an insurable interest in the subject matter, or the policy is void. Nevertheless P.P.I. policies are still used in commerce.

political access (in management). Access to the top decision makers, e.g. the managing director, in an organization. Since the opinions and suggestions of employees with this access are heard at a high level they can exert some influence upon the decision-making process.

political economy. An archaic synonym for economics that was in common use in the eighteenth and nineteenth centuries. Thomas Malthus, David Ricardo, and John Stuart Mill all published important works entitled *Principles of Political Economy*.

poll tax. A tax applied equally to everyone eligible to pay it. It does not depend upon income or personal circumstance.

population (in statistics). The totality of items or events that form a statistical aggregate, such as the car population in the U.S. Statistical populations are usually too big to examine exhaustively and therefore their characteristics or parameters are estimated by means of values derived from a *random sample drawn from the population in question. A population may be infinite, such as the past, present, and future human population of the world, and in such cases it is not possible to take a random sample. *Also called:* universe. *See also* statistic, estimation.

population projection. A forecast of the size of the population at some date in the future. Projections are important if long-term plans are to be formulated. For example, the planning of roads, airports, and hospitals depends upon the size of the population they are expected to serve in the future.

However, demography has been unable to predict accurately changes in populations; increasingly a range of predictions are offered, reflecting possible variations in conditions. A projection for the U.K. based on 1979 estimates predicts that the population will increase from its present level of 56.7 million to 58.4 million by the year 2001.

population pyramid. A diagram that indicates the distribution by age of a population. The youngest and usually most numerous age groups form the base of the pyramid, while the oldest age-group is at the apex. The diagram is not always in the shape of a pyramid since variations in fertility and mortality (e.g. as the result of war) will affect the size of each generation. However, it will taper towards the top illustrating that there are more young people than old.

portfolio. A list of securities in which a person or institutional investor has interests. Portfolios will generally be adjusted according to changing circumstances in the hope of maintaining maximum growth or income or whatever combination is desired.

portfolio choice. The diversification of an investor's capital amongst various bonds, shares, and money. This is presumed to be a response to his attitude towards uncertainty. Theories exist as to how this selection is made, such as *mean-variance analysis and *state preference theory. These help to explain the concept of *liquidity preference.

port mark. The marking on a package for shipment by sea or air that gives the port of destination.

position. The speculative state of a stockjobber, merchant, investor, or other dealer in a fluctuating market. A dealer whose purchases exceed his sales has a *bull position;* he stands to make a gain in a rising market. If his sales exceed his purchases he has a *bear position* and he will make a gain in a falling market. *See also* open position.

position audit. An extensive evaluation of a company's internal and external environment to disclose strengths, weaknesses, threats, and opportunities. The environments evaluated will include: political, social, economic, technological, factor and product markets. In large companies this is performed by the corporate planning department or outside consultants. *See also* management audit.

positive easement. *See* easement.

positive economics. The study of economics as an objective science. It seeks to predict what actually will occur in the economy, but does not make value judgments as to its ethical desirability. It seeks to affirm that an economist can actually measure quantities and their relationships and make predictions on this basis. The law of demand, true or false, is an example of a positive fact. In practice, however, the line between positive and *normative economics is not finely drawn and true positive verification of assumptions is difficult.

possession. Having something in one's custody as distinct from owning it. The distinction is profound, complicated, and evokes many of man's most acquisitive and aggressive instincts. The right to own property is also of considerable political significance and varies among societies. In the U.S.S.R. and Eastern Europe, for instance, the individual may own only a limited amount of property, most being owned by the state. In some legal systems, the passage of time is all that is required to convert what is merely possessed into what is owned. For example, in the U.K. if land is occupied without the consent of the owner, and possession can be sustained without interruption for 12 years, legal ownership passes from owner to possessor.

post dated. A document or cheque that is dated for some future time. A drawer sometimes issues such a cheque because he does not have the funds to meet it, but expects to receive them by the date he puts on the cheque. The fact that it is post dated does not invalidate a cheque or bill of exchange, which can be negotiated as soon as drawn.

poste restante. A service that is available in most countries by which mail can be left at post offices for collection. In the U.S. this service is known as General Delivery. In the U.K. letters, parcels, telegrams, and telegraphic money orders may be sent to any post office, except a town sub-office, to be called for. This service is only provided for a limited time. In all cases, evidence of identity is needed before a letter can be collected.

Post Office Register. *See* National Savings Stock Register.

Post Office Savings Bank. *See* National Savings Bank.

potential entrant. A firm that possesses the technology to produce at approximately the prevailing marginal cost of production in an industry and that, given a small rise in price or a reduction in *barriers to entry, would find it profitable to establish itself in that industry. In a monopoly, profits might be held in check by the existence of potential entrants. The degree of monopoly existing in the industry will be directly related to the strength of the barriers to entry and indirectly related to the number of these potential entrants.

pound. The standard unit of currency of the U.K. and many other countries that were once British territories or had trading links with the U.K. A pound by weight of silver was coined into 240 silver pieces each equal to a pennyweight, by Offa, King of Mercia, in the eighth century. The sovereign, a gold coin worth 20 shillings, was first issued in 1489, and after being replaced by the guinea during the seventeenth century it returned to favour after the Napoleonic Wars. Since the early part of the nineteenth century the pound sterling has been a basic international currency.

poverty trap. A situation that exists when low income recipients are financially discouraged from working harder. For instance, assume low income recipients are entitled to some means-tested benefits below a certain level of income (free school meals, reduced cost of dental treatment, supplementary benefits, etc.), which are proportionately reduced or end once this level of income is exceeded. In this case, the people would lose an equal or larger amount in benefits than they would receive in extra earnings; even if their earnings are too low to be taxed explicitly, implicit tax rates are 100% or higher. This is a marked disincentive to work. The low income earner will only escape this poverty trap if he can jump from the maximum allowed income for which benefits are provided to an income level that more than compensates for the loss of benefits. As D. Piachaud wrote: "Getting out of poverty is like getting out of a well. Unless you can jump right to the top you will slip back to precisely where you started".

power (of a statistical test). The probability of correctly rejecting a *null hypothesis. It can be calculated simply by deducting from one the size of the *Type II error. It is obviously desirable to maximize the power of a test for a given size of *Type I error. That test with the maximum power for a given size of Type I error is called the *uniformly most powerful test. See also* hypothesis testing.

power of attorney. A written document giving one person the right to act for another in accordance with the terms and limits of the authority as defined in the deed. An attorney may not delegate his powers unless specifically authorized to do so, nor may he use his principal's property in any way to his own advantage.

p.p. *See* per pro, procuration.

preacquisition profits. The total balance of the profit and loss account and any other revenue reserves of a subsidiary company up to the date of acquisition by another company. These reserves must be distinguished as they are not available for distribution. The holding company is required to consolidate the figures of the subsidiary company with its own when it presents its periodic accounts (*see* consolidated accounts).

precautionary demand for money. The desire to hold liquid money as a precaution against unexpected circumstances. Without a reserve of liquid cash, time and money would be wasted in converting other assets to cash in times of crisis.

The strength of the precautionary motive will vary according to personal, economic, and political circumstances. For example, more money will be held when confidence in a country is waning. On the other hand, the presence of sophisticated credit facilities will reduce the amount of money that people feel it is necessary to hold. The most crucial economic variable that affects the precautionary demand for money is the rate of interest; this determines the return that is being sacrificed by holding money rather than interest-bearing assets. As interest rates rise the amount of money held for precautionary motives tends to fall and vice versa. The precautionary demand for money is one of the three motives for holding money cited by Keynes, the others being the *transactions demand for money and the *speculative demand for money.

predetermined variable. A variable in a simultaneous model that is either exogenous or a lagged value of an endogenous variable. The distinction between a model's exogenous variables and its predetermined variables arises because of the time-series nature of most data used in economic models. In an inflation model, for instance, an econometrician would require data on prices, wages, unemployment, and productivity extending over a long period, say the last 70 years (excluding major war periods); furthermore, the wage equation in an inflation model would probably specify not only unemployment and prices in the contemporary period (current prices) but also prices in previous periods (lagged prices). The price variable itself is endogenous but the lagged price variable has the nature more of an exogenous than of an endogenous variable: hence the distinction between exogenous and predetermined variables. *See also* endogenous variable, exogenous variable.

prediction. A special form of *estimation in which the problem is to determine which value of a relationship's *dependent variable corresponds to specified values of the relationship's independent variable (or variables). All the independent variables of the relationship must be provided with specified values and prediction must obviously follow the process of estimating the relationship's coefficients. Corresponding to an estimate, a prediction can be either a point prediction or an interval prediction with the latter being the more reliable of the two. The procedure for setting confidence limits to an interval prediction is analogous to that for setting confidence limits to an estimate. The function that is used to estimate a prediction is called a *predictor* and should have the same properties of unbiasedness, efficiency, etc., as estimators. The most usual way of formulating a predictor is simply to insert into a relationship the specified values of the independent variables and the estimated values of their coefficients and then to read off the value of the prediction. Generally speaking, a predictor will have the same statistical properties as the coefficient estimators that are used in it. In general usage and in most statistical usage, prediction relates to the assessment of values at a future point in time. In regression, however, the term prediction is used without any temporal reference. *See also* forecasting.

pre-emption. 1. The right to purchase either in preference to others or before an offer is made to others.

2. (In international law). The right of a government to purchase the property of another nation, while it is in transit. This right is now only exercised in time of war, when the goods concerned could be used to the detriment of the pre-empting state.

pre-entry. The process of notifying H.M. Customs and Excise the details of goods being exported by sea or air from the U.K. No goods may be loaded onto a ship or aircraft for export until either a copy of the pre-entry form (*see* shipping bill), stamped by the customs, or a *customs assigned number has been notified to the shipping company or the airline.

preference share. *See* share.

preferential creditor. A person who is owed money by another person or firm and who is entitled to be repaid before other creditors. In a personal *bankruptcy or the *liquidation of a company, the *secured creditors take precedence over the *unsecured creditors. Amongst the unsecured creditors certain debts are given preference, e.g. salaries and wages of employees and rates and taxes.

preferential duty. An import duty that favours some countries vis-à-vis others that produce the same commodities. Countries who have been granted most-favoured-nation status by the U.S. will face lower import duties than nations without this status. Similarly nations who have not negotiated bilateral trade agreements with the E.E.C. will face higher import tariffs than those who have. *See also* Commonwealth preference.

preferential payments. Certain debts of a bankrupt that are given priority in the distribution of his assets by the Bankruptcy Acts (in the U.K.). They are one year's taxes and rates directly assessed before the date of the receiving order, and four months' wages and salaries due to employees before that date not exceeding £800 per person. In the case of a company being wound up (*see* winding up) compulsorily, the operative date is the date of the winding up order, and in any other case, the date on which winding up commenced.

preliminary expenses. Expenses incurred in forming a company. They include all the expenses involved in promoting the company, preparing the prospectus, registering the company, etc.

premium. 1. A payment, usually annual, made to an insurance company for an insurance policy. Often the insurers require that the premium should be paid before the insurance takes effect but they may sometimes grant cover pending payment. An insurer is not obliged to issue a renewal notice but he almost always does. The renewal notice often offers the insured a period of grace (*see* days of grace) after the renewal date during which the insured must pay the premium if the insurance is to remain in force.

2. A sum paid over and above the standard or normal price of something in order to secure immediate delivery, a special quality, or some other advantage.

3. The amount by which the price of a security stands above its par or paid-up value. For example, a fixed-interest security, such as a debenture, standing at 106 is at a premium of 6%.

4. The amount by which the price of a recently issued share stands above its issue price (*see* stag).

5. On the London Stock Exchange a share is said to be at a premium to the market when its *P/E ratio is above that of the market average. In this sense, the shares of a company may stand at a premium to those of other companies in the same industry, or a sector of the market as a whole may stand at a premium to the rest of the market. Premiums reflect market sentiment regarding the outlook for the profits of the company or sector concerned.

6. *See* redemption premium.

7. The amount by which a particular currency stands above par on the foreign exchange markets.

8. A sum formerly paid to a solicitor, chartered accountant, or other professional man in order to provide a training for an articled clerk.

9. A lump sum sometimes paid by a lessee to a lessor for the grant or assignment of a lease to him. It is commonly charged on long leases in which the rent is below the market value. On residential property leases it is often known as *key money*. *Compare* discount.

premium bonus. A bonus payment made to a worker who has completed a piece of work in a shorter time than the standard length of time assigned to it. The amount of the bonus depends on the percentage of time saved and is added to his hourly pay.

premium offer. A special offer of household goods available to users of brand-name products in return for wrappers, labels, or packet tops, plus a small cash payment. Applicants must be warned that delivery may take up to 28 days and suppliers must be able to meet an immediate large demand. Agencies known as *premium houses* provide all the services required and the manufacturer hands over the whole operation to these firms.

premium savings bonds. U.K. government bonds, first issued in 1956, that carry no interest, prizes being awarded by lottery to bond-holders whose bond serial numbers are drawn by Ernie (*E*lectronic *R*andom *N*umber *I*ndicator *E*quipment) each month. The total prize money is equal to the total interest that money invested in the bonds would earn. Prizes vary between £50 and £250,000 and are tax-free. Premium bonds can be bought at post offices and banks and become eligible for prizes after being held for three months. They may be cashed at any time (six working days' notice is usually required) and are not transferable. They are issued in units of £1 but sold only in multiples of £5, with a maximum individual holding of £10,000.

present value. The current net value or cost of future benefits and outlays. If a choice must be made between two projects (perhaps through lack of funds) the profit-maximizer will select the project that has the highest present value. It is calculated by discounting the future benefits and losses at the prevailing rate of interest. If the rate of return fell below this rate of interest, the individual would not undertake either project, but would lend his money to earn the interest. The formula for the calculation of present value is:

$$PV = B_0 - C_0 + (B_1 - C_1)/(1 + r) + (B_2 - C_2)/(1 + r)^2 + \ldots (B_n - C_n)/(1 + r)^n$$

where PV is the present value, B_0 and C_0 are the initial benefits and costs respectively, B_1 and C_1 are the benefits and costs after one year, B_2 and C_2 are the benefits and costs after two years, B_n and C_n are the benefits and costs after n years, and r is the rate of interest through the years. If PV is greater than zero, a higher return can be obtained by investing in the project than by lending the money. It if equals zero the rate of return from the project and the interest rate are identical. Present value techniques are used to evaluate investments both in cost accounting (for a private firm) and in cost-benefit analysis. *Compare* internal rate of return.

president. In the U.S., the chief executive of a public or private company. The president is the equivalent of the British *managing director.

Prevention of Fraud (Investments) Act (1939). An Act of Parliament containing important provisions designed to prevent certain abuses that had crept into dealings with companies' shares. It has now been replaced by an Act of 1958 of the same name. Its most important provisions concern dealers in shares, who are, under the provisions of the Act, required to be licensed and it also contains detailed regulations relating to written offers to buy or sell shares. In addition the Act contains provisions regulating the conduct of *unit trusts, and also governing *building societies.

price. The amount of money or commodities that must be given up for one unit of a good or service. In most cases the price will be a certain sum of money but goods are sometimes preferred as a medium of exchange, e.g. in a barter economy or during a hyperinflation. In such cases the price of a camera might be 1000 cigarettes. The price of a commodity must not be confused with its cost of production or its value to the consumer. In general, the price of an article is higher than its cost of production and lower than its value to the consumer.

Price Commission. An independent statutory U.K. body established in 1973 to regulate prices, originally as part of *prices and incomes policy and later as an adjunct to monopoly policy. Firms were required to notify all proposed price increases and these were then scrutinized by the Commission to see whether or not they were justified. It was abolished in 1980.

price control. A means of controlling inflation in which prices are allowed to change only within statutory limits. Direct price controls tend to be used only in short-term emergency situations.

price discrimination. *See* discriminating monopoly.

price/earnings ratio. *See* P/E ratio.

price effect. The total change in the quantity of a good bought as a result of a change in its price. The price effect can be broken down into two components: the *income effect and the *substitution effect. Normally, the income effect and the substitution effect reinforce each other so that an increase in price will lead to a decrease in the quantity bought, and vice versa. However, for *inferior goods the income and substitution effects counteract each other. In these cases it is impossible to predict the effect of a change in price on quantity demanded. For example, the demand for bicycles will not increase in the same proportion as income, as above a certain level many people will prefer to buy cars.

price index. *See* index number.

price leadership. The action of a dominant firm in setting prices for a specific product, in the knowledge that its competitors will follow suit. Price leadership is found in oligopolistic markets with the price leader being usually, though not always, the largest firm in the market. Firms will adopt this pattern of behaviour, i.e. implicitly acting as a cartel, to avoid the heavy costs of a price war. Recognizing this, the price leader will often take it upon himself to set his new prices in the interests of the industry as a whole, so ensuring a greater degree of stability. However, if the price leader sets his prices at incorrect levels he may eventually find himself replaced by another firm, whom the other smaller firms will regard as the new price leader. In the U.S. many industries, including steel, agricultural equipment, and newsprint, are said to rely on price leadership.

price level. The general level of prices of goods and services in the economy. A price change can be a change in relative price or a change in price level. A change in a price relative to all other prices is the concern of microeconomics. A change in the level of all prices is the theoretical concern of macroeconomics, and must be clearly distinguished from a relative price change.

price method. The U.S. term for *piece rates.

price relative. The current price of a commodity divided by its price in a base period. Price relatives are used in the calculation of index numbers and, like index numbers, are usually expressed as a percentage. *Compare* quantity relative.

price ring. An association of a number of firms who have agreed to fix a minimum price for their competing products. The purpose is to limit competition and so increase profits for all. It is thus a type of *cartel. Price rings usually last longer than agreements to increase profits by limiting output as they can be more easily monitored. *See also* ring.

prices and incomes policy. A policy that seeks to curb *inflation by moderating the increases in wages and prices in an economy directly, rather than by indirect macroeconomic methods of fiscal and monetary policy. The need for a prices and incomes policy arises when the desire to maintain a high level of employment through indirect means spurs inflation. The direct methods employed are moral suasion, for firms not to increase prices or for unions to moderate wage demands, or statutory limits on percentage increases in wages and prices, for example by tying price increases to rising costs or wage increases to gains in productivity. Long term application of the programme is apt to induce a misallocation of resources since it inhibits the determination of new relative price levels, and short term application often merely stores inflation until the first few months after the relaxation of controls. Proponents of the plan see it as a means of breaking the *inflationary spiral. *See also* incomes policy, price control.

price support. The maintenance of certain prices above a minimum level through government intervention. The U.S. government maintains farmers' incomes through various subsidies and loans and by fixing the minimum price of various agricultural commodities (e.g. wheat) at a level that is usually above the market price at which all of that commodity could be sold. As a result there is usually a surplus of the commodity, which the government is committed to buy.

price-taker. A producer who has no control over the price of his output. At or below the market price he can sell as much as he desires; above the market price nothing. For economic agents in general, a price-taker is one for whom the quantity of goods transacted does not affect the price at which the exchange is made. These conditions ensure that he is operating in a perfectly competitive market.

price theory. The subject matter of most microeconomic theory comes under the heading of price theory, although it generally centres around the type of analysis carried out earlier in this century and at the end of the last.

There are four main parts to standard price theory: *demand theory, *theory of the firm, market *equilibrium, and *welfare economics. The central assumption in all of these is that economic agents are taken to be profit- and utility-maximizers.

price war. A systematic reduction in the price of a commodity by two or more competing firms, usually occurring after the breakdown of an agreement to maintain price at a specified level. Increasingly, nonprice competition, such as advertising, is preferred as it does not decrease revenue and it encourages brand preferences in consumers. *See also* cut-throat competition.

primage. A percentage added to a freight charge that is usually returned as a *deferred rebate.

primary production. The production of agricultural crops, foodstuffs, minerals, and other raw materials rather than manufactured goods (secondary production). They are the commodities from which consumer and capital goods are manufactured. The exports of the developing nations of the third world mainly fall into this category. The level of output of primary products does not bear a simple relation to their current prices, since decisions as to output are often made several years in advance (e.g. sugar cane takes seven years to grow). Therefore, a sharp rise in price will not always lead to an increase in output in the short run for most primary products. It is primarily for this reason that the prices of these goods tend to fluctuate more erratically than those of manufactured goods. Consumers and traders often react to any possible shortage (or rumour of a shortage) by stockpiling, thus increasing the demand and therefore the price; when the shortage is over, they use up their stockpiles rather than buying more, thus causing demand and prices to fall drastically. An example of such a swing occurred during and after the Korean War. Countries (especially the U.S.) built up massive stockpiles of raw materials, forcing up the prices by more than 50% within a few months. After the war these stockpiles were liquidated so that sales of primary products slumped. This caused the price of many commodities to fall to half their initial level.

Another problem facing the primary producers is that the demand for primary produce used in the manufacture of goods is growing slowly relative to the demand for manufactured goods as there is a limit to the amount of food and drink that the people of the developed nations can consume. In addition, many primary products are being replaced by synthetics as is the case with rubber, jute, etc. For these reasons many of the developing countries whose main exports are primary products are urgently introducing industrialization programmes, while attempting to enforce higher prices for their goods through collaboration (*see* OPEC). *See also* international commodity agreements, New International Economic Order.

prime costs. *See* direct costs.

prime entry books. Books of account that contain details of purchases and sales as they occur. The *ledger is compiled from the details of these books.

prime rate. The rate of interest charged by U.S. commercial banks for short-term loans to first-class customers. Only relatively few U.S. corporations can borrow at this favourable rate–most others have to pay a higher rate. The prime rate is approximately equivalent to the U.K. *base rate.

priming the pump. Attempting to reflate the economy by running a small budgetary deficit. By injecting more money than is taken out by taxation, personal incomes and consumption are increased, so encouraging firms to invest.

Priming the pump was first attempted by the Roosevelt administration in the 1930s in the U.S. It failed for two major reasons. The budgetary deficits were too small to stimulate the economy; the total government deficit for the 1930s was $25 000 million, which was less than half the deficit for 1942 or 1943. Secondly, much of the increase in income was clawed back by taxation so that consumption was insufficiently stimulated.

principal. 1. A sum of money, as distinct from the interest it may earn. In simple interest, the interest earned is obtained by multiplying the principal by the rate of interest and the term.

2. A person on behalf of whom an agent or broker acts: the person for whom an agent or broker enters into a contract.

principal budget factor. A factor that tends to be more restricting than others on the future development of a business enterprise. In a large number of cases this factor is the level of sales, but it could also be labour shortages, space problems, or rationing of raw materials. The restrictions imposed on the enterprise by this factor must be clearly determined in order to provide a sensible budget. The principal budget factor, however, is always liable to change. It is also referred to as the *key factor*, *limiting factor*, or *governing factor*.

principles of taxation. The four general maxims for taxation enunciated by Adam Smith.

There should be equality of sacrifice. By this he meant that there should be a proportional tax structure. Most modern countries believe equality of sacrifice can be best achieved by a progressive tax, especially income tax.

There should be certainty in all matters connected with the tax bill, i.e. the amount due, manner and time of payment, etc., should all be known to the taxpayer. Otherwise taxation authorities would have an unhealthy freedom to penalize some and favour others and would be open to bribery.

There should be convenience of payment for the taxpayer. This is the principle behind P.A.Y.E. People pay small amounts regularly rather than a large sum annually.

There should be economy in collection. A tax whose yield is smaller than its cost of collection should not be levied: nor should any tax that impedes the working of the economy be used, such as one that unduly hinders economic growth.

prior charges. The prior claims to which holders of the debentures and preference shares of a company are entitled over ordinary shareholders in respect of dividend (or interest) distribution and capital repayments. Prior charges are also the amount of such claims.

priority percentages. If a company's post-tax profits for any year are apportioned as between amounts required to service different classes of capital, then these portions, when expressed as percentages of the total amount of profits available and ranked in order of priority of the class of capital to which it relates, are known as priority percentages. For example: a company with post-tax profits of £1 million distributes £100,000 to first preference shareholders, £250,000 to second preference shareholders, £500,000 to ordinary shareholders, and retains £150,000.

If a company distributes as dividends more than it earns, implying negative retention and a net reduction in reserves, then the priority percentages will exceed 100.

prior year adjustments. Items in the profit and loss account and balance sheet of a company that have resulted from amendments to the figures shown in the previous period's (or year's) accounts. These prior year adjustments can arise quite normally from estimates that were necessary when they were made, being adjusted to represent the actual figures to which they related. In this case, unless they were material, these adjustments would not normally be shown separately. However, prior year adjustments that arise from fundamental errors or changes in accounting policies cause a change in the balance of the profit and loss brought forward.

private banks. 1. Commercial banks that are owned by one person or by a group of partners in contrast to the joint-stock banks. They were common in the U.K. in the nineteenth century, but have since been gradually superseded. Joint-stock banks were able to expand more successfully through larger capital reserves and were able to survive crises more effectively. In the U.S., however, private banks remain a major factor in the banking system, because the stringent limitations to expansion in most states handicap the joint-stock banks.

2. Banks that are not members of a *clearing house. These banks must arrange for a bank that is a member to act as an agent for them.

private carrier. A person or firm who undertakes to transport goods from one place to another on a specific contract rather than as a *common carrier.

private company. A company whose shares cannot be freely transferred on a stock exchange, whose members are limited in number to 50, not counting employees or former employees of the company, and that is prohibited from making any invitation to the public to subscribe for any shares or debentures in the company. Essentially a private company is meant to be inaccessible to the general public. *Compare* public company.

private costs. The costs incurred by an individual or company in the course of business, as contrasted with *social costs.

private enterprise. *See* capitalism.

private health insurance. Insurance that provides cover for private medical treatment. It may be taken out on an individual, family, firm, or group policy and is often provided by large firms for their senior employees. It usually covers the cost of hospital accommodation in a private room, specialists' fees, and ancillary paramedical services, such as physiotherapy and home nursing.

private placing. The taking up by an issuing house, finance company, or group of financial institutions of a new public share issue in its entirety. The issuing house will then sell these shares privately to other financial institutions, such as insurance companies and investment trusts.

private sector. The sector of an economy consisting of individuals, firms, and financial institutions that are not under government control. Together with the *public sector, it makes up the domestic sector of the economy.

private treaty. A method of trading in which the price at which goods or property changes hands is negotiated directly in private between the buyer and the seller or their agents. It is used for reasons of confidentiality, if there are unlikely to be a number of competing buyers, or to avoid the expense of a public *auction. This method of buying and selling is used for some works of art and some houses as well as for certain commodities, especially those that can be sold by grade or by representative sample.

privatization. The sale, wholly or in part, of public corporations and assets to the private sector. Since 1980 the U.K. government has sold off interests in British Aerospace, Cable and Wireless, Amersham International, Associated British Ports, Britoil, and British Telecom, together with substantial amounts of local authority land and dwellings. The term *denationalization* is synonymous when referring to nationalized industries or corporations that are reverting to the private sector, whereas the term "privatization" refers more broadly to a general trend in which the private sector takes over certain assets or functions from the public sector, such as hospital laundry, thus reducing direct government control in these areas of the economy.

P.R.O. *See* public relations.

probability. The likelihood of occurrence of an event or of the result of some particular experiment. Probability can be interpreted as an idealization of the percentage of times that the desired result occurs in repeated trials of the experiment. Thus the probability of drawing a spade from a pack of 52 cards is ¼, which is the proportion of times that we would expect repeated draws from a full pack to yield spades. The probability of an event can be represented by a number between zero and one; thus a probability of zero indicates that an event will never occur and a probability of one means that it is certain to occur. Probability is treated quantitatively in statistics and is a central concept, around which a large body of mathematical theory has been built. *See also* density function.

probability distribution. *See* distribution.

probability function. *See* density function.

probate price. The price of a share calculated for taxation purposes by dividing the bid and offer prices by four and adding this amount to the lower price (*quartering up*).

procuration. The function or action of a person who holds a *power of attorney on behalf of another. Such a person may sign a document on behalf of the other person, often using the abbreviations *per proc.* (per procurationem) or simply *p.p.*

produce brokers. *See* commodity brokers.

produce market (exchange). A market in some form of produce, especially one in which there is a *futures market. Produce markets in London include the London Rubber Exchange, the London Wool Exchange, the London Corn Exchange, the London Metal Exchange, and the London Commodity Exchange.

producer goods. *See* capital goods.

producer surplus. A measure of the gains from trade of the supplier in a market. On a graph whose axes represent the price of a good and the quantity sold, producer surplus is represented by the area of the approximate triangle bounded by the price line, supply curve, and vertical axis (*see diagram at* consumer surplus).

This surplus is an *economic profit to the producer, since he would be prepared to accept less to supply the good. Under perfect competition it would be zero. In the analysis of monopolies it is helpful to use producer surplus to demonstrate that the loss of surplus to the consumer is not entirely received by the producer, i.e. it is not entirely a *transfer payment: there is also a loss of economic welfare. This is one of the faults of monopoly.

product differentiation. The manufacture of nonhomogeneous products by a particular industry. To the degree in which products are differentiated, they will not be perfect substitutes for each other and will allow monopolistic competition and its consequent inefficiency to establish itself in the industry.

There are two ways in which differentiation might arise. The first is through actual quality differentials and the second is simply by inducing the belief in the minds of the buyers that such differentials exist.

The producer has three main means of differentiating his product: through advertising, style changes, and research and development. Market research is the tool used to discover in which direction the producer's efforts at differentiation should be applied.

It is a moot point to what degree product differentiation represents the evil of inefficiency and to what degree it offers the benefits of variety and product improvement. In the standard monopolistic competition analysis there is no evaluation of welfare gains through product differentiation. Even style changes can be defended as methods of accentuating the individuality of the consumer. However, the accepted opinion is that purely illusory product differentiation is to be avoided, if in fact it exists.

product exhaustion. A theorem of competitive economics stating that, under perfectly competitive pricing and constant returns to scale (where factors are paid their value of marginal product), excess profits are zero, since the revenue gained from the sale of the good is just equal to the cost of the inputs necessary to produce that output. Mathematically it derives from the fact that a constant-returns-to-scale production function is homogeneous of degree one and marginal product equals input price/output price and so *Euler's theorem implies that total cost equals total revenue.

production. The conversion of raw materials using a combination of *factors of production into goods and services. It includes the distribution and sale of goods after their manufacture, since without these operations consumption would be impossible. It also includes the activities of people who may not produce a physical product, such as actors and civil servants, as they either provide valuable services for the consumer or facilitate the productive process. *See also* Census of Production.

production engineering. The form of engineering that is concerned with specifying, planning, scheduling, and monitoring a production process. The production engineer is responsible for specifying the input materials, the manufacturing process to be used, and the labour and plant required. He will plan the throughput of work and set schedules for carrying out this plan. He will also be responsible for monitoring the work to see that quantity and quality produced are according to plan and are being delivered according to schedule.

production function. A function that summarizes the technological relationships between the output of goods and the inputs necessary to produce them. Given the amounts of each input, mixed in a productively efficient manner, the amounts of output are determined uniquely. The standard categories of production function are the neoclassical and the *fixed proportions type. The *neoclassical production function* is usually distinguished by no joint production (so that by-products are never produced), constant returns to scale, and smooth substitutability between factors yielding diminishing returns to each. This yields smooth outward-curving isoquants. Fixed proportions production functions can be of the von Neumann type with joint production, or the Leontief type with no joint production. Their isoquants are right angles along a ray from the origin (*see diagram at* fixed proportions production frontier). Basic production functions with certain characteristics (concavity, constant returns to scale) are employed in general equilibrium analysis to yield results on decisions of producers in discussions of existence of equilibrium. More specific examples may be used in partial equilibrium analysis. Finally, completely specified models, like the Cobb-Douglas or Leontief type, are used in empirical studies of production and distribution theory.

production goods. *See* capital goods.

production possibility frontier. *See* transformation curve.

productive expenditure. Investment by the government to increase the future standard of living, i.e. to finance growth. The greater the output devoted to productive expenditure, the less that is available for current consumption and, therefore, the lower the standard of living of the present generation.

productive labour. Labour that adds to the wealth of the community by creating goods, as compared to unproductive labour that produces services. This distinction was developed by Adam Smith to become an accepted part of economic theory. Later it was used by Marx to explain his theory of the creation of surplus value. The division of labour into productive and unproductive categories is now regarded as mistaken as it is considered that the production of both goods and services are valuable additions to the wealth of the country. Nevertheless vestiges of the idea remain; in the U.S.S.R., for example, national income accounts exclude the contributions of the service industries.

productive potential. The amount that a country is capable of producing if full use is made of all factors of production. It is dependent upon the size of the working population and the average level of productivity (which in turn depends upon the state of technology and the amount of capital equipment per worker).

productivity. The relationship between the output of an industrial unit and the input in terms of labour, materials, capital, etc. *Marginal productivity* is the increase or decrease in output caused by an increase or decrease of one unit of the factor of production. The main reason for the growth of the developed economies in the post-war era has been a continual increase in productivity.

productivity bargaining. Negotiations to increase wage rates in return for an increase in productivity. Unions argue that an increase in productivity signifies an increase in the value of the labour used in the process and hence an increase in its price, i.e. the increased wage rate is justified.

Productivity bargaining is often conducted at plant level after national agreements have been concluded. It is thus one cause of *wage drift. Many U.K. incomes policies allowed exceptionally high wage increases in cases in which productivity bargains had been agreed. However, these bargains were often made use of by unions seeking large rises that would not otherwise have been allowed and were a major cause in the breakdown of several incomes policies.

product life cycle. The series of stages through which a product is likely to move from its introduction into the market to its eventual decline, as shown in the diagram. An example of a product that may have reached the final stage is the black-and-white television set.

product/market strategy. The decisions taken within an organization relating to its products and target markets in terms of policy, defined goals, and long-term planning.

product mix. The selection of products offered by a firm to the market.

products guarantee insurance. A type of insurance with the object of indemnifying the insured against claims arising out of the failure of a product to fulfil its intended function. This type of insurance also pays for the cost of repairing or replacing the defective product.

products liability insurance. A type of insurance with the object of protecting the insured against his legal liability for injury to third parties or loss of, or damage to, their property caused by goods sold, supplied, repaired, tested, or serviced by the insured.

professional indemnity insurance. A type of insurance with the object of protecting the professional man, such as a solicitor or an accountant, against his legal liability to compensate third parties who have borne some injury, loss, or damage as a consequence of his own professional negligence or that of his employees. This type of policy is a strictly legal liability contract, not a moral liability one.

professional valuation. A computation of the worth of the assets of a company made by a person qualified to do so. The value of assets at professional valuation is often included in the *prospectus or the *balance sheet of a company.

profit. *See* normal profit.

profitability. The measure of profit between two or more profit-making alternatives. Profitability is a relative measure and must not be confused with profit, which is an absolute measure. For example, if a business has the opportunity to sell two types of goods, X and Y, then if X sells for a unit price of £90 and Y for £100, and if the unit costs of production are the same, obviously it is more profitable to manufacture and sell Y.

profit and loss account. A statement of a company's earnings and expenses, and consequently the profit or loss made, for an *accounting period. A limited company in the U.K. is required by statute to disclose certain information, such as turnover, depreciation, auditor's remuneration, etc., on the face of the profit and loss account. Extraordinary items must also be shown separately and a distinction is made between *above* and *below the line*. All expenses normal to the running of the business are placed above the line to arrive at a net profit before taxation, while other charges, such as corporation tax, transfers to reserves, and dividends paid and proposed, are shown in the profit and loss appropriation account, i.e. below the line.

profiteer. A person who takes advantage of a shortage of goods, especially in times of disaster or emergency, to make excessive profits. Traditionally, a profiteer increases the selling price of his stocks in response to a shortage in supply. In extreme cases he may himself help to create the shortage by buying up all available supplies. Once he has created a *corner he has the market to himself.

Various measures have been adopted by governments to curb profiteering in times of shortage; perhaps the most effective is a stringent and well-operated rationing scheme.

profit function. Profit given as a function of the prices of inputs and outputs. Its partial derivative with respect to output prices gives its *production function and with respect to an input price its *derived demand for that input.

profit maximization. The assumed motivation of producers in an economy. They attempt to maximize the difference between receipts and costs by finding the optimum level of output, and the least cost mixture of inputs necessary to produce it. The condition to be satisfied for this to occur is that marginal revenue equals marginal cost, where marginal cost is derived from the cost-minimizing solution. If, for example, marginal revenue were greater than marginal cost, an increase in output would increase revenue more than costs and so profits could be increased by expanding output. The problem may be solved in two stages. First, the minimum cost combination of inputs may be found for a given fixed output, then profit may be maximized with respect to output, cost being treated as a function of output. Assuming the solution of the first problem, different assumptions about the market and the *production function lead to various solutions of the second. If the market is perfectly competitive, the production function exhibits constant returns to scale, and a maximum profit level exists, then it must be zero, though the scale of production cannot be determined. This is so since if positive profits occur at any point then they may be infinitely increased in scale since marginal cost equals average cost and marginal revenue equals average revenue under constant returns to scale and perfect competition. Therefore if constant returns to scale (or increasing returns to scale) exist the existence of a positive and finite profit maximum requires decreasing average revenue–a downward sloping demand curve, the imperfectly competitive case. For a non-zero maximum to exist under perfect competition decreasing returns must prevail at some point of the production function. Profit maximization is only one theory of the motivation of businessmen. It is possible to assume that they are motivated by return to capital, or size of firm, or simply by "animal spirits" (innate preference for action as opposed to inaction).

profit motive. The hypothesis that every entrepreneur will consistently and rationally attempt to maximize profits. Other hypotheses have been advanced, but none have proved as good in predicting and explaining the actions of business organizations.

profits à prendre. Rights to take a particular type of produce, such as timber, water, crops, etc., from land owned by another. The rights are usually appurtenant, i.e. belonging to the owner for the time being of a neighbouring piece of land, but, unlike *easements, may occasionally exist independently of the ownership of land by the person entitled to them.

profit-sharing. Distribution of a proportion of the profits of a business among employees, either as cash bonuses or as shares. Such schemes are introduced to encourage employees to take an added interest in the profitability of their firm. Methods of distribution vary: allocation may depend upon length of service or upon the level of wages; it may be equal for all or there may be a minimum service period in order to qualify. *See also* workers' participation, cooperative movement.

profits tax. A tax on the profits of a company. In the U.K. a number of different forms of profits tax existed between 1935 and 1965, until the introduction of *corporation tax. Profits taxes are generally unpopular, especially when they make no provisions for offsetting losses made in previous years or in associated activities. These taxes tend to discourage companies from taking the risks that are necessary to achieve a high rate of growth.

profit taking. The selling of securities or commodities that have recently increased in price, by short-term *bull speculators.

pro-forma invoice. An invoice that is usually submitted before goods are dispatched. If the goods are retained it becomes an ordinary invoice, but is not in itself a demand for money. Pro-forma invoices are also used in certain commercial transactions when the total weight of the goods to be invoiced on a weight basis is not known. The pro-forma invoice is made out on the basis of a nominal weight and a *final invoice* is sent when the exact weight is ascertained.

program. A set of instructions for the operation of a computer system or for the solution of a particular problem. Programs that control the operation of the system–input and output of data, conversion into machine language, etc.–are usually supplied by the manufacturer (they are called the *system software*). Programs for solving particular problems are termed *applications programs*; common examples are text-editing, accounting, entertainment and education.

programming language. A formal language in which a computer program is written. Within the system instructions are coded in basic *machine language*. A *low-level* programming language or *assembler* is one that is close to this machine code. Usually instructions are written and input in a *high-level* language, which is one that is closer to normal English or to mathematical notation. The instructions are converted into machine language by special programs–*compilers* or *interpreters*. In compiled languages the conversion is performed only once; thereafter the machine language version of the program is executed. Interpreters perform the conversion one instruction at a time whenever the program is executed. Common high-level programming languages include *COBOL, *ALGOL, *FORTRAN, *PL/1, *APL, *BASIC, and *Pascal; there are more than a dozen such languages.

progress chaser. An employee of a firm whose job is to ensure that the rate of production is proceeding according to schedule. If there are faults, it is his function to trace bottlenecks and recommend appropriate action.

progressive tax. A tax in which the average amount payable increases with the size of the *tax base. This means that the *marginal rate of taxation also increases. The purpose of such taxation is usually to redistribute income from higher to lower incomes. To this end the tax system must be integrated with the *transfer system. *See also* tax incidence.

prohibitive tariff. A tariff that raises the price of an import so high that no one is willing to purchase it. The effect is tantamount to banning its importation, since there is obviously no revenue derived from such a tariff.

promissory note. A document in which a person promises to pay another a specified amount of money on a certain date. It is a negotiable instrument, but cannot be reissued, unless the promise is made by a banker payable to bearer on demand (i.e. a bank note).

promotion. 1. An increase in the rank of an employee.

2. Efforts to increase the sales of a product by such methods as informational and persuasive advertising. The *promotional mix* is the means used (advertising, sales methods, special offers, packaging, etc.) to promote a particular product, usually in the retail sector.

3. The creation of a limited company.

prompt cash. Money that must be paid for goods that are bought, within a few days of taking possession of them.

prompt day. The day upon which payment becomes due for the purchase of goods. In some commodity markets and auctions the day on which payment becomes due for spot goods is called the prompt day.

propensity to consume. The desire to consume expressed as the proportion of income spent on goods and services rather than saved. The strength of the propensity to consume will vary among individuals and societies. People in higher income brackets usually have a lower propensity to consume than the average, i.e. they save a greater proportion of their income.

The *marginal propensity to consume* is the proportion of each increase in income that is spent rather than saved. *See also* consumption function.

propensity to save. The desire to save expressed as the proportion of income that is not spent on goods and services. Keynes asserted that as the incomes of individuals increased, the proportion of income that would be saved rather than spent would also increase. The *marginal propensity to save* is the change in total savings that is caused by a change in the level of income. The reciprocal of the marginal propensity to save is the *multiplier. *Compare* propensity to consume.

property. *See* real property.

property bonds. A form of *unit trust in which investment is made in property. It is offered by insurance companies and merchant banks. Property is considered to be capable of maintaining its capital value during a period of inflation. However, it is essential that the investment should be in a number of properties of a nonspeculative nature and that they should be frequently and conservatively valued by independent experts.

property currency. A special reserve of foreign currency (especially dollars) held in the U.K., for use when buying overseas property. The property currency reserve was created from the sale of overseas property belonging to U.K. citizens. If overseas property was to be bought, the potential purchaser had to buy the necessary foreign currency from this reserve. A premium of up to 40% above the current exchange rate for the currency was charged because of the scarcity of property currency. The system ended in 1970.

property insurance. *See* indemnity.

property register. *See* registered land certificate.

property tax. A tax on land or buildings. In the U.K., property was taxed under Schedule A of income tax until 1964, on the basis of its rateable value. Local rates in the U.K. are assessed on property, each property being given a rateable value related to a notional rent for which it could be let.

proportion. The ratio of notes and coins in circulation to the total assets of the Banking Department of the Bank of England.

proportional tax. A tax in which each unit of income is subject to the same *marginal rate of taxation. The constant marginal rate equals the average rate of taxation.

proprietary company (Pty). A private limited company in Australia or the Republic of South Africa.

proprietorship register. *See* registered land certificate.

prospectus. When a U.K. company offers its shares for purchase by the general public (*see* application and allotment) it must supply a prospectus containing the relevant information relating to the state of the company's affairs, its development in the past, and future prospects. The detailed information required in the prospectus is specified in the Companies Acts (1948–81). Any misleading statements in the prospectus involve the possibility of a charge of criminal negligence. It is possible in certain cases to avoid issuing a prospectus (*see* document of offer for sale of shares and debentures).

protected bear. *See* bear.

protected transactions. Certain transactions that cannot be nullified by a liquidator, even though they occurred after the bankruptcy or liquidation of one of the parties. They are usually those made in good faith by the debtor and include transactions in which he is due to receive repayment of a debt.

protectionism. A policy that favours the use of tariffs, quotas, or other import restrictions designed to make domestic products competitive with foreign imports. The term is often used perjoratively, since the policy is usually intended to defend a particular interest rather than to implement either the economic arguments advanced in defence of tariffs (protection of new industries, prevention of dumping, etc.) or the noneconomic arguments (self-sufficiency in case of war). Protectionism is regarded in standard economic theory as being to the detriment of a country as a whole. For example, the government might decide to protect the fishing industry in a country by imposing tariffs on imported fish. The result is of benefit to the fishing industry, but the consumers suffer by paying higher prices. However, in this case the long-term interests of the consumers might not be well served if the domestic fishing fleet was priced out of business by foreign competition.

protective duty. A customs duty that is levied on certain imports in order to shield domestic producers from foreign competition. *See* protectionism.

protest. The certificate signed by a *notary public when requested to do so by the holder of a *bill of exchange after acceptance or payment of the bill has been refused. It may be completed subsequent to *noting the bill.

provisional liquidator. A function of the *Official Receiver. When a company is put into liquidation, the Official Receiver is appointed as provisional liquidator by the court until an official liquidator can be appointed.

provision for bad debts. *See* bad debts.

proximate cause (in insurance). The operative and efficient or dominant cause of a loss, not necessarily the one newest in time. Obviously the cause of a loss must be reasonably established before insurers are considered liable. A peril of some kind will have caused the loss, but not all perils are insured against. The loss must arise directly from an insured peril, or be the result of a direct chain of events initiated by an insured peril.

In practice, most claims are quite clearly covered or not covered, because the proximate cause is very evident. However, the chain of events giving rise to a loss can be complicated by the occurrence of excepted or uninsured perils. In such circumstances determining whether, or to what extent, the insurer is liable can become difficult.

proxy. A person entitled to represent a shareholder at company meetings, with full rights to vote. The document conveying such rights and issued by the company is termed the *proxy card.*

prudence concept. A fundamental *accounting concept in which revenue and profits are not anticipated but only included in the balance sheet and profit and loss account when receipt of the remuneration (in cash or any other form) has occurred or when such receipt can be reasonably assured. On the other hand, liabilities should be treated differently: these should always be included in the accounts, with specific figures when known with a reasonable certainty and as a best estimate when sufficient information is not available.

P.S.B.R. *See* public sector.

psychological tests. Tests designed to assess the intelligence, aptitude, temperament, personality, interests, or manual dexterity of applicants for a job (*see* personnel selection) or for purposes of vocational guidance. These basic tests can also be adapted to assess specific skills, adaptability, creative ability, etc. In the U.K. tests are available from the National Institute of Industrial Psychology; in the U.S. they are available from the U.S. Employment Service.

Pty. *See* proprietary company.

public company. A company whose shares can be offered to the public and can be freely transferred on the Stock Exchange. *See also* public limited company (plc). *Compare* private company.

public corporation. An organization established to manage a state-owned activity, such as the B.B.C., or a nationalized industry, such as the National Coal Board. The assets of the former owners and shareholders are vested in a corporation or board whose duty is to manage the industry in the public interest. The chairman and members of the board are appointed by a government minister. They are responsible for the day-to-day running of the industry. Overall control is assumed by the appropriate minister.

The public corporation seeks to reconcile two apparently conflicting objectives: on the one hand the desire to allow the industry as much freedom as possible to operate on commercial or semicommercial lines and on the other hand, the desire to function for the benefit of the community as a whole. There is detailed public accountability as the industry is financed from public funds.

Each corporation must submit an annual report and accounts to the minister, which may be debated in the House of Commons.

public debts. The *National Debt plus the debts of the whole public sector.

public deposits. The balance held to the credit of the government's account by the Bank of England. As taxes are paid in, public deposits increase. When the government makes payments, public deposits decrease.

public enterprise. A body, ultimately responsible to the state, that provides an essential service of the type that could be provided by the private sector (i.e. not one like the armed services or the police).

The central government is ultimately responsible for many public enterprises, which are usually *public corporations (such as the National Coal Board or the British Steel Corporation). The local authorities also control municipal public enterprises, such as the supply of water, sewerage, abattoirs, crematoria, and some civic entertainment centres. In addition there are semi-independent bodies, such as the Forestry Commission.

public finance. A branch of economics that studies the effects on the economy resulting from the collection of revenue by the public authorities and its expenditure. Topics that it covers include description of the relevant bodies, analysis of the effects of various types of taxes and expenditure both on the individual and firm and on the national income, the management of the National Debt, the effects and problems of taxation, and the effects and problems of the government's current or projected policies.

public finance accountant. An accountant working in local government or some other area of public service and specializing in financial and management accounting and auditing in these areas.

public good. A good or service that cannot be priced accurately and hence cannot be efficiently supplied by private industry. It has three characteristics: *nonrivalness in consumption, nonexcludability, impossibility of rejection.* Nonrivalness in consumption of a good means that a good being supplied to one individual can be supplied to others at no extra cost, for example a radio station will not expend more power in transmitting to 5 000 000 people than when transmitting to 1 000 000 people (if they live in the same geographical area). Nonexcludability means that an individual cannot be deprived of a public good even though he may refuse to pay for it, for example all the citizens of a country are protected by anti-rabies measures even if many refuse to pay for them. Impossibility of rejection means that an individual cannot abstain from consumption of a public good even though he may wish to, for example a pacifist is protected by nuclear weapons in spite of his moral objections to them.

It follows that each person must consume an identical amount of a public good. Consequently, normal market forces cannot provide the optimum amount since an individual will not need to reveal how much he would pay to consume the good, as he feels it will be provided anyway. If everyone adopts this attitude the good will not be produced although it is to everyone's interest that it should be produced. *See* externalities.

public issue. An issue of shares that is offered for sale to the public.

public lending right. The right of an author to receive payments in respect of such of his books as are lent out to the public by local library authorities. In the U.K. the payments are made under the Public Lending Right Scheme (1982) according to the Public Lending Right Act 1979 and are made out of a fund controlled and managed by the Registrar of Public Lending Rights. In 1984 in the U.K. authors can earn between £5 and £5000 on library loans based on loans of their books by 16 sample public libraries. The system, which is cumbersome and somewhat unfair, excludes reference books.

public liability insurance. A type of insurance providing compensation for legal liability for death, injury, disease, or damage to the public other than one's employees (who should be covered by an employer's liability insurance). In addition attendant legal costs are covered.

The different kinds of policy in use cover:

a) Industrial and commercial risks.

b) Pedal cyclists.

c) Private individuals (a pedestrian, for example, can incur heavy liabilities by causing a serious road accident).

d) *Products liabilities. This involves manufacturers and distributors for defects in the goods supplied, such as foreign bodies in foodstuffs, etc.

e) Professional men, such as solicitors, accountants, etc. This would cover liabilities arising from professional negligence by them or their staff.

f) Property owners. (For example, liability arising from slates falling from the roof).

g) Public authorities.

h) Sportsmen (e.g. horseriders and golfers).

public limited company (p.l.c.). A category of company as defined in the Companies Act (1980) that is required by law to have a minimum authorized capital of £50,000, to offer its shares to the public, and to have "p.l.c." at the end of its name, or the Welsh equivalent (c.c.c.). Private limited companies and subsidiary companies retain Ltd. at the end of their names. *See* public company, limited liability.

public relations. The maintenance of a favourable relationship between an individual or organization and the general public. A *public relations officer (P.R.O.)* is sometimes employed to influence public opinion in favour of his employer or organization and to publish such information as would improve his relationship with the public.

public sector. The sector of an economy consisting of all state-owned institutions. These include local authority operations, such as the provision of housing, schools, and the various social services, as well as the nationalized industries, such as the coal industry, the railways, and London Transport. The public sector plus the *private sector make up the domestic sector of the economy. The *public sector borrowing requirement* (*P.S.B.R.*) consists of the *public sector deficit plus any net financial lending. Large-scale borrowing through the sale of securities may force up interest rates, thus "crowding out" private sector borrowers and possibly limiting private investment.

public sector deficit. The difference between a government's income and its expenditure. One school of thought believes that public spending has to be reduced in a recession to control this deficit and avoid fuelling inflation. However, another view is that the public sector deficit will inevitably increase in a recession, as a result of unemployment benefits, reduced N.I. contributions, etc., and that public spending should not therefore be reduced as this would only create more unemployment. *See also* deficit financing.

public services sector. *See* Treasury.

public trustee. A government official whose office was established in 1908 with the object of giving the public the opportunity of employing his department to act in trust matters, thereby avoiding the risks and inconveniences of appointing private individuals.

public warehouse. *See* warehouse.

public works. Construction projects, such as road and hospital building, sponsored by the government. These projects are often undertaken in times of depression to relieve unemployment. This idea was attacked by classical economists who maintained that the private sector could provide work more efficiently than the government and that instead there should be a reduction in taxation to provide them with the funds. As early as 1908, A. C. Pigou demonstrated that public works would diminish total unemployment by using funds that would otherwise have lain idle, but the classical view prevailed in the Treasury and influenced government policy throughout the 1920s. As the Conservative Chancellor of the Exchequer, Winston Churchill, stated in 1929, "very little additional employment and no permanent additional employment can . . . be created by State borrowing and State expenditure". In the 1930s, Keynes finally demonstrated that public works would increase employment through the action of the *multiplier, but Sweden was the only state during that period to pioneer a large-scale public works programme.

Public Works Loan Board. An independent U.K. statutory body that provides loans to local authorities to meet a proportion of their capital expenditure, such as housing construction. It is financed by the Exchequer and supervised by Treasury ministers.

published accounts. The accounts that a U.K. company must publish according to the Companies Act (1981), which prescribes the format and content and rules for computing the figures that appear in the *annual report. They include a balance sheet, profit and loss account, and a *directors' report,* which must disclose information about the business development of a company and its subsidiaries (a "fair review" during and at the end of the financial year of turnover, profits, taxation, trading conditions, markets, etc.; important events that have occurred since the year end, e.g. acquisitions, competition; likely future developments, and research and development). The directors' report must also give particulars of the acquisition and disposal of its own shares by any company. *Notes to the Accounts* includes information about directors; and accounting policies, an auditor's report, and consolidated profit and loss account and consolidated balance sheet (if the company is part of a group) are also required. Other information may relate to company products, structure, marketing, or general policy that may be of interest to the shareholders.

Small and medium-sized private companies, as defined by the Companies Act (1981), need not file certain documents with the Registrar of Companies.

puisine mortgage. A mortgage in which the lender has not retained the title deeds of the property mortgaged. He can, however, protect himself if the land is unregistered by registering a charge against the land at the Land Charges Registry, or if it is registered, by entering a caution at the Land Registry, preventing further dealings with the land without reference to him.

pump priming. *See* priming the pump.

punched card. One of the forms in which information is supplied to a computer *input system. The cards are usually approximately 3½ins ×7½ins in size and contain columns of punched holes, each character being represented by a particular pattern of holes. Punched cards are produced by a keyboarding apparatus (called a *key punch*) and fed into the computer via a *card reader.* Punched cards can also be supplied as the output of a computer: the *output device is called a *card punch.*

punched tape. One of the forms in which information is supplied to a computer *input system. It consists of a narrow strip of paper tape with characters represented by specific patterns of holes. The tape is punched by a keyboard in a similar way to the production of *punched cards and is fed into the computer via a *tape reader.* Paper tape can also be supplied as the output of a computer: the *output device is called a *tape punch.*

punter. A small speculator who deals frequently on a stock exchange or commodity market in the hope of making a series of quick profits.

purchased life annuity. An annuity bought with an individual's own capital rather than one provided as part of a pension scheme. An annuity provided from an approved pension scheme is usually taxed as P.A.Y.E. earned income, because a condition of the pension scheme's approval by the Inland Revenue stipulates that such parts of the assets of the scheme applicable to the pensioner must be used to provide an annuity and may not be taken in a cash form. However, in the case of an individual using his own capital to buy an annuity, or using the tax-free lump sum obtained under a pension scheme, he is regarded by the Inland Revenue as having bought a purchased life annuity and as a result pays much less tax on the amount he receives. Each payment is deemed to consist of two parts capital (return of) and interest. Tax is only levied on the interest content and the insurance company selling the annuity will supply details of the breakdown and hence the amount upon which tax is payable. *See also* annuity.

purchase day book. *See* day books.

purchase ledger. A record of the purchases of goods and services made by an enterprise from various other individuals and enterprises, showing the value of the purchases made. The purchase ledger will also record any cash paid or any other credit taken by the enterprise against the vendors of these goods and services. At any one time the purchase ledger will provide the enterprise with a list of the balances of monies outstanding that it owes, and to whom it owes them. It normally constitutes one of the *books of account of an enterprise.

purchase tax. An indirect form of taxation levied on the purchase of certain consumer goods sold and manufactured in the U.K. between 1940 and 1973. It was calculated on the wholesale price and did not apply to goods exported. It was replaced by *value added tax.

purchasing officer. An employee of a firm who is responsible for the buying of the materials that are needed in production. He must be constantly aware of fluctuations in the price of the raw materials as well as of their present and future availability.

purchasing power parity theory. The relative values of two currencies, i.e. their exchange rate, depends upon their relative domestic purchasing power. Any large deviation from the official exchange rate would be prevented by *arbitrage. For example, if the exchange rate between the pound and the dollar is two dollars to the pound and the pound bought an amount of a good worth three dollars in the U.S., disregarding transportation costs, it would be profitable to convert from dollars to pounds, purchase these commodities in the U.K., and ship them back to the U.S. The increased demand for the good in the U.K. would cause its price to increase (*see* demand-pull inflation) while its price fell in the U.S. as more of the good entered the market. This convergence would be matched by similar movements in the exchange rates of the two currencies. Unfortunately there is the question of finding an index by which to measure this hypothetical good. For example, what is to be done if there is a good consumed in the first country but not in the second? Although correct in principle its complexities in the real world obscure the usefulness of the model. Recently it has experienced a revival, however, with the idea of using a group of commodities, rather than gold or some hard currency, as an international standard of exchange.

pure competition. *See* perfect competition.

pure economics. Theoretical economics, especially as used for those areas of economics that cannot be applied to the problems of the real world. Examples are the *general equilibrium model of Léon Walras (1834–1910) and the debate on the measurability of *utility curves. As the economic techniques improve, there are fewer areas of economics that have no practical application. For example, the theory of *second best is fairly abstract but has important implications for nationalized industries' pricing policies.

pure endowment assurance. A type of assurance, now quite rare, in which no benefit is normally payable should death occur during the term of the policy. This type of policy provides that a certain sum of money will be paid to the assured in the event of his surviving a certain period.

The contract can provide for a return of all or part of the premiums paid in the event of the death of the life assured before the maturity of the policy. *See also* endowment assurance.

put option. *See* option.

put-through. A stockbroker puts shares through a *stockjobber when he receives both purchase and sale orders in the same security. Under these circumstances he sells the securities to the jobber while simultaneously repurchasing them, the *jobber's turn being small.

putting-out system. A method of *outworking* in which employees are provided with materials, which they work on in their homes. It is most common in the clothing industry.

putty-clay. A term to describe situations in which a firm has a choice of several methods of production before undertaking investment, but has no freedom of action thereafter. The firm can thus initially choose what combinations of capital and labour to use before the investment decision, but operates with a *fixed proportions production function from that date, i.e. it cannot vary the ratio of capital to labour.

pyramid selling. A method of selling goods, investments, etc., to the public by using a hierarchy of part-time organizers, distributers, and salesmen, each of whom buys into the organization at a particular level. In a typical example the central organization may recruit a small number of regional organizers, each contracting to buy a franchise to sell certain goods as well as a minimum quantity of the goods themselves. They in turn recruit a number of sub-distributors, who buy a small share, and so on down to the salesmen, at the bottom of the pyramid, who retail the goods to their friends or by door-to-door selling.

Pyramid organizations often rely heavily on high-pressure salesmanship and on various bonus schemes for sales performance or for recruiting new members. In some cases it would be theoretically impossible for all the people at the lower levels to regain their investment because of lack of demand for the goods. For such reasons the system has attracted much adverse criticism: legislation controlling it now exists in the U.K.

Q

quadratic function. A function containing at least one independent variable that is squared (or raised to the second power) but that contains none with a power greater than two, e.g.:

$$y = a \text{ ‘ } bx \text{ ‘ } cx^2.$$

A quadratic function has a characteristically parabolic graph, i.e. a basin-shaped curve. A parabola will be convex upwards if the coefficient attached to the squared variable (the coefficient *c* in the example) is negative.

quadratic mean. The square root of the arithmetic mean of the squares of a set of numbers. The quadratic mean of the numbers 9, 6, 3, 1, 5, 8 is given by:

$$\sqrt{([9^2 \text{ ‘ } 6^2 \text{ ‘ } 3^2 \text{ ‘ } 1^2 \text{ ‘ } 5^2 \text{ ‘ } 8^2]/6)} = 6$$

The quadratic mean is suitable for certain specialized applications. *Compare* arithmetic mean, geometric mean, harmonic mean, median, mode.

qualified acceptance. An acceptance of a bill of exchange that varies the effect of the bill as drawn. It may be conditional, partial, local (i.e. accepted payable at one place only), qualified as to the term of the bill, or accepted by some but not all of the drawers. The holder of the bill may refuse to take a qualified acceptance and, should he do so, he should obtain the assent of the drawer and any endorser otherwise they will no longer be liable on the bill.

qualitative screen (in marketing). An assessment of whether or not a product concept is compatible with a company's objectives and resources, for example with respect to environmental factors or with respect to the profitability cut-off rate operated by that particular company.

quality. The degree of consistency of a company's profits (especially as used on the London Stock Exchange). Thus a *quality share* (or *high quality share)* is a share of a company whose profit record shows a steady rise without cyclical downturns. One might also talk of a company with high quality profit (or earnings). Generally, the shares of companies engaged in the production of capital goods and consumer durables tend to be of lower quality than those of companies engaged in financial services or in the manufacture of consumer nondurables. High quality shares are usually rated higher on a stock exchange, i.e. they tend to have higher *P/E ratios, than low quality shares.

quality control. Systematic inspections of products during their production, which are undertaken to ensure that the requisite standards are being maintained both in the quality of materials used and in the workmanship.

quality control chart. A graph on which successive time-values of a variable are plotted. The horizontal axis of the chart is labelled time while the vertical axis represents the values of the variable. In addition, three horizontal bands are drawn across the chart: the middle one represents the mean of the variable (either the true mean, if this is known, or the mean as calculated from past experience) and the two outer ones represent a distance of three standard deviations (of the mean of the variable) on either side of the mean. If any of the successive values of the variable fall outside these outer bands, it is an indication that the variable is out of control. Quality control charts are frequently used in industry and are particularly suitable for such problems as determining when an industrial process begins to turn out a larger-than-usual number of defective products. In this context the variable is the percentage of products turned out by the process that are defective, and it is assumed either to follow the normal distribution or the binomial distribution and to be approximated by the normal distribution. Quality control charts are based on the latter.

quantity index. *See* index number.

quantity rebate. A reduction in the price of a product when a large quantity is bought. Discounts for bulk-buying are commonplace, both in retailing and wholesaling. *See* aggregated rebate scheme.

quantity (volume) relative. The current volume (used, bought, or sold) of a commodity divided by its volume in a base period. Quantity relatives are difficult to define for services, for new products, and for products whose quality has changed since the base period. When they can be defined, they are used in the calculation of the index number and, like index numbers, are usually expressed as a percentage. *Compare* price relative.

quantity theory of money. An economic theory stating that the stock of money in an economy is proportional to the money value of all transactions, which equals the physical volume of output multiplied by the price level. It is usually written as $MV = PX$, where M is the stock of money (bank deposits and currency), V is the transactions velocity of money (also known as the *velocity of circulation of money), P is the price level, and X is the physical quantity of output. V is an institutional constant determined by the nature of the banking system and the interval at which workers are usually paid. The equation, as it stands, is an *ex post identity. The theory in its modern form is usually associated with a Chicago economist, Milton Friedman (b. 1912), but a simpler version of the theory, i.e. that an increase in the quantity of money will cause a proportionate increase in prices, was propounded in the seventeenth century when a sharp rise in prices accompanied the influx of money from the New World. It is not clear from the ex post identity whether it is the price level or the level of national output that will change in order to maintain the identity, when the stock of money is altered. This is the basis of the conflict between the classical view of the demand for money, as expressed by quantity theorists, and the view as expressed in Keynesian *liquidity preference theory. Neither view has won general acceptance although in recent years some governments have tended to emphasize monetary policy in their attempts to combat inflation.

quantum meruit. (Latin for: as much as he has earned.) If the amount of payment for work undertaken has not been agreed, although payment is implied by the circumstances, then no claim can be made under a contract but may be made under quantum meruit. Another aspect is that if work has not been completed, the individual might still claim partial payment under certain conditions, for example if another party to the contract made completion impossible.

quarter days. The days marking the quarters of the year. In England and Wales these are: 25 March (Lady Day), 24 June (Midsummer Day), 29 September (Michaelmas), and 25 December (Christmas Day). In Scotland these are: 25 February (Candlemas Day), 15 May (Whitsuntide), 1 August (Lammas), and 11 November (Martinmas). On these days quarterly events, such as payment of rent, traditionally occur.

quarter up. *See* probate price.

quartile. One of three values that divide a distribution into four equal portions when it is arranged in order of magnitude. Thus the first quartile has 25% of the items in the distribution below it. The second quartile is the median. *See also* percentile, decile.

quartile deviation. *See* semi-interquartile range.

quasi-contract. An obligation of one person to another that a court may find to be legally binding despite the fact that a proper contract does not exist. For example, if money has been paid over in pursuance of a void contract, there exists a quasi-contractual obligation to repay it.

quasi-money. *See* near money.

quasi-rent. A term first used by Alfred Marshall (1842–1924), by analogy with David Ricardo's (1772–1823) theory of *rent, to denote all returns to capital in the short run that are in excess of the returns to the marginal firm, when the firm is producing at its *shut-down point. It is the product of the difference between price and average variable cost multiplied by the quantity produced. In the short run, capacity is fixed and, providing price is in excess of the average variable costs, it will pay the intramarginal firm to offer the use of its capital. The income from this is properly viewed as a rent rather than as a price since it is a residual that could be dispensed with without affecting the level of production. It is not a cost of production and so is a function of, but does not determine, the price of output. In the long run, when capacity can vary freely, quasi-rents disappear.

Queen's Award for Industry. An award scheme in the U.K., established in 1965, that is designed to recognize and encourage outstanding achievement by industrial firms, either in exports or in technology. This prestigious award is held for five years.

queue theory. A statistical theory developed to analyse problems concerned with the provision of services or productive facilities on a first-come-first-served basis. Queue theory attempts to locate that state of a system in which maximum efficiency is attained, i.e. that state in which bottlenecks or queues are minimized and in which demand for and supply of the service are synchronized as much as possible. Features of the situation studied include the time-pattern of customer arrivals, the average waiting time, the length of the queue at any given time, queue discipline, the length of time for which a service unit may lie idle, and the mechanism by which the service is effected. One application of queue theory is in the construction of an airport–a project for which it would be necessary to know the likely pattern of arrivals and take-offs.

quick assets. Assets that can easily be converted into cash. The term is more common in the U.S., *liquid assets being used more in the U.K.

quid pro quo. (Latin for: something for something.) Something given in compensation for something received. This principle must underlie every contract or they would be unilateral agreements to undertake something without compensation. In commerce, negotiations are usually conducted on the basis of one party making a concession of some kind and the other party agreeing to make some other compensating concession as a quid pro quo.

quorum. The minimum number that must be present before a meeting can officially take place. The quorum for members' meetings in a company is laid down in the articles of association.

quota. A limit imposed on the quantity of particular goods entering a market. Governments using protectionist policies (*see* protectionism) may impose import quotas on certain goods, sometimes in order to favour particular suppliers, but these are now rare; export quotas may be imposed by countries heavily dependent on their export of primary products in order to stabilize or raise world prices. Production quotas are also sometimes agreed by cartels, for example, in order to maintain prices. *See also* tariff, import restrictions.

quota sample. A sample that is taken by first subjecting the population to "stratification" and then, within each stratum, allowing the sampler to select items himself subject to the required number of items per stratum. A quota sample can thus be described as a nonrandom stratified sample. Quota samples are used very frequently in practical statistical work. They are cheaper and quicker than *random samples but there is the possibility of bias and they have the additional disadvantage that there is no way of estimating the reliability of results based on them.

quotation. 1. A listing of a share price on a stock exchange, with the implication that the share can be dealt in on that exchange. On the London Stock Exchange quotations are granted by the Council of the Stock Exchange to the securities of those companies that can satisfy the Council in respect of certain requirements and conditions designed to safeguard the interests of the investing public (*see* quotations committee). A quotation will be suspended if a company subsequently defaults on these requirements.

2. *See* offers, bids, and quotations.

quotations committee. A committee of the London Stock Exchange that considers the applications of companies for quotation on the Stock Exchange.

quoted company (listed company). A company whose shares have a *quotation on a stock exchange.

quoted price. The official price of a share or commodity. The quoted prices of stocks and shares on the London Stock Exchange are given in the *Official List. The quoted prices of commodities are published daily in the press.

R

Radcliffe Report. The report of the U.K. Committee on the Workings of the Monetary System which, under the chairmanship of Lord Radcliffe, presented its influential findings in August 1959. The report gave a very accurate description of U.K. monetary institutions but was widely criticized by monetary theorists because it did not subscribe to any variant of the *quantity theory of money. The committee believed that monetary policy should control the liquidity of the economy through such methods as adjustments of the rate of interest and control of bank overdrafts. It thought that the difficulties involved in defining money made it impossible to control its supply and indeed that this was unnecessary. The report subscribed to a belief that the amount of money in the economy depends on the needs of trade rather than on other factors. It also supported fixed exchange rates.

rally. A firm rise following a decline in share prices or commodity prices. The term is also used in respect of an individual security or commodity. The cause of a rally is usually favourable sentiment, although of course an excess of buyers over sellers would also bring one about. *See also* technical rally.

RAM. *See* microcomputer.

random access. *See* storage device.

random sample. A group of items selected from a statistical population in such a way that all the items in the population have a known (and usually equal) chance of being selected. Random sampling is based on *probability because the probability of selecting any individual item must be known before a random sample can be made. It cannot therefore be drawn from an infinite population. Strictly speaking, a random sample drawn from a population in which all items have an equal chance of selection is called a simple random sample. In terms of statistical theory a simple random sample requires that successive samplings from the population must be independent and that the density function of the (random) items selected must be the same before each sampling. Thus, while the probability of obtaining a spade from a pack of 52 cards is 25%, the probability of obtaining a spade on the second draw will not be 25% unless the first card was replaced in the pack before the second card was drawn, and a sample of 2 cards drawn from a pack of 52 will not be random in the simple sense unless the first card was replaced before the second card was selected. When a simple random sample is not desired, as frequently is the case in practical work, a stratified random sample is designed. This is carried out by dividing the overall population into sub-groups according to some criterion and then working a simple random sample within each sub-group. The purpose of stratification is to ensure greater accuracy of representation when the total population comprises several disparate groups. Thus when designing a sample to estimate the total expenditure by families on food, a stratification according to income group might be carried out in order to decide what sample size is appropriate for each income group. In statistical theory, however, the concept of stratified sampling is not important and the term random sample is used as an abbreviation of simple random sampling, which is an essential element in both *statistical method and *statistical inference.

random variable. A variable whose value in any one experiment or sampling is uncertain and depends on chance. A random variable can either be discrete or continuous. The sum of points obtained in throwing two dice, for instance, is a discrete random variable that can assume any of the integer values between 2 and 12 inclusive. The large bulk of statistical theory is based on random variables.

range. 1. (In statistics.) The difference between the highest and lowest value of a group or population of items. The range is the crudest and least satisfactory measure of dispersion, especially in large populations: it is directly affected by abnormal items in the population, it tends to increase as the number of items in the population increases, and it may not even be definable for large populations if they are open-ended (e.g. a population of individuals grouped by age with the oldest group being listed as 65 or over). *Compare* semi-interquartile range, mean deviation, standard deviation.

2. The set of all possible values that the dependent variable of a specified function can take. The range will be determined by the nature of the function and by the domain. *Compare* domain.

ratchet effect. The irreversibility of movements of certain economic variables. For example, if price movements are disinclined to fall then upward pressure will cause them to rise, but once they have reached a new height they will not fall again. If this change in relative prices was only temporary, the return to normal would require other prices to rise. The term has been used to describe movements of exchange rates, wages, and other variables.

The sectoral theories of inflation lean very heavily on this effect.

rate of exchange. *See* exchange rate.

rate of return. A measure of profitability calculated as the ratio of the capital outlay on an investment to its expected profit. *See* internal rate of return, discounting back, present value.

rate of turnover. The speed with which stock is replaced in an accounting period. If the stock of a retail outlet averaged £20,000 and total annual sales were £180,000, the rate of turnover would be nine. In general it will be higher in the retail food outlets than in other shops.

rate rebate. A deduction from rate payments that can be claimed by householders in the U.K. with small incomes. The Local Government Act (1974) introduced a new rate rebate scheme designed to make rates more responsive to the ability of the individual householder to pay and to extend relief higher up the income scale.

rates. A U.K. tax paid to local authorities by occupiers of nonagricultural land and buildings to meet the cost of local services. Each property is assigned a rateable value by the Valuation Office of the Inland Revenue. The rate poundage is fixed by the rating authority and the amount that an occupier has to pay is determined by multiplying this sum by his rateable value. The responsibility for levying and collecting the rates lies with the district councils and the London borough councils. Regional councils and the Greater London Council issue a precept on the districts who collect it on their behalf. Rates have been criticized because of their regressive nature: that is the lower a person's income, the higher the proportion paid in rates. In times of inflation the problem is made worse and this has led to threats of militant action, such as non-payment, by Ratepayers Action Groups. Relief is provided by government grant, by payment by instalments and by *rate rebates for householders on small incomes. Disputes about rating assessments are heard by local valuation courts and, on appeal, by the Lands Tribunal.

rate support grant. A payment made by the U.K. government to support all council services that do not receive specific grants and are not self-financing. The grant is made up of three elements: domestic, needs, and resources. The *domestic element* is a straight subsidy for the domestic ratepayer. The *needs element* depends upon the population and its demands, such as the number of people of preschool age, of school age, of retirement age, etc. The *resources element* is designed to raise up to the national average the rate resources, per head of population, of all authorities that would otherwise fall below it.

ratio chart. *See* logarithmic chart.

rational behaviour. The assumption that individuals always act logically to attain their goals. Although this assumption is constantly disproved in real life the construction of instructive economic models would probably be difficult without it. *See* irrational behaviour.

rationalization. The reorganization of a domestic industry in order to increase efficiency, especially by increasing *horizontal integration, or concentrating production at fewer plants. It is actively promoted or at least condoned by the government with a view to making the industry competitive in the international market.

rationing by price. The effect of the price mechanism in controlling the allocation of goods by virtue of their price. The term is often used pejoratively of the price system.

reaction curve. In the presentation of duopoly models on a graph whose axes represent the output of each firm, the assumption of one firm about his competitor's reaction to any given level of production on his part may be summarized by a curve (the *reaction curve*). If a point (q_1, q_2) is on the curve for producer A it means that he feels that if he produces q_1, producer B will respond by producing q_2. This however represents only producer A's assumptions, which may not in fact be correct. In certain sophisticated models of duopoly producers will attempt to maximize their profit along the reaction curves. In the case of a *Cournot duopoly, the intersections of the two reaction curves are the equilibrium points.

real account. *See* impersonal account.

real balance effect. The effect of a change in the real value of an individual's cash holdings. If an individual's cash holdings (in real terms) exceed his immediate requirements he will increase his expenditure, thus reducing his real balances. If his real balances are too low he will do the reverse. A change in the real quantity of money will thus affect the demand for commodities. At full employment an increase in the real quantity of money will increase aggregate demand; this will drive prices up until real balances are restored to their equilibrium level. If prices rise without a corresponding increase in incomes, real balances fall and individuals will refrain from spending in an attempt to achieve their desired level of real balances. This will cause a fall in aggregate demand and prices will fall until initial real balances are restored. Don Patinkin uses the concept of the real balance effect in his description of the dynamics of the monetary process; they do not usually affect the structure of the final equilibrium. Patinkin equates the real balance and *Pigou effect, but more normal usage has the latter as a special case of the former when the level of real balances does affect the structure of the equilibrium.

real balances. The real value or purchasing power represented by money holdings.

real estate. Immoveable property, such as land and buildings, as opposed to any property that is moveable.

real investment. Expenditure of resources on capital equipment, such as a new factory, a machine, a dam, etc., rather than on paper assets, such as debentures, Treasury bills, securities, etc.

realization account. An account created immediately prior to the termination of a business to ease the problems of liquidation. The value of all liabilities are debited to the account, while positive items such as revenue from sales, repayment of loans, etc., are credited to it. The final balance is the profit (if positive) or loss (if negative) on realization.

realized profit. A capital gain that has been converted into cash. There is only a *paper profit* when shares, bonds, securities, property, etc., appreciate in value since there is no increase in the quantity of assets or amount of money owned. If this paper profit is turned into cash by selling the asset that has appreciated, the profit has been realized.

real property. Property that consists of freehold land and freehold interests in land, as opposed to leasehold land and most other types of property, which are classified as *personal.* The distinction was formerly of great importance, because the rules of succession to the property after the owner's death differed according to whether it was real or personal. The distinction has now largely disappeared, although it is still found in the accounts of some companies.

real time. Time during which a computer is processing data at the same time as the data is generated. In real-time working the computer is *on line to the source. The *Ariel share-dealing system is a real-time system.

realtor. The U.S. term for *estate agent.*

real value. The money value of any economic variable divided by the relevant price index. For example, the nominal value of car production may have risen merely because car prices have risen. But this would be reflected in a rise in the price index for cars. Hence, the real value of car production would be obtained by dividing the present value of car production by the present price index for cars. In the same way, the real value of national income in year T can be compared with that in year $T + 1$ by dividing Y_T and Y_{T+1} by P_T and P_{T+1} respectively, where Y_T and Y_{T+1} are national incomes in the respective years (in money terms) and P_T and P_{T+1} are general price indices. Real value should be contrasted with *nominal value. Hence, for example:

$$m = M/P,$$

where m is the real money supply, M is the nominal money supply, and P is the price index. To compare a variable in different time periods, it is best to consider its real value, especially when there are considerable shifts in price indices.

real wages. Wages expressed in terms of the goods and services that *money wages will buy. It is the real wage that determines the quantity of labour that a firm wants to hire, and therefore it is the real wage that determines the aggregate level of employment. If money wages and prices increase or decrease together then the real wage remains unchanged: therefore if the quantity of labour supplied changes in these circumstances it can be said that the suppliers of labour are suffering from *money illusion. Keynes used real wages as a tool of analysis under the guise of using wage goods as his unit of account.

rebate. A discount on the price of a good; it may be offered on a large order or in return for favourable payment terms, such as prompt payment or payment in advance.

receipt. A document confirming that a payment has been made. A receipt is no longer legally necessary if a cheque has been accepted in payment as the cheque itself acts as a receipt. All receipts should be retained for six years after which time payment cannot be demanded.

received for shipment. Words stamped onto a *bill of lading to indicate that the goods are alongside the ship. It does not indicate that the goods have been loaded onto the ship and is therefore less valuable than a *shipped bill.

receiver. **1**. A person appointed by the court to administer the estate of another person who is certified to be mentally incapable (*see* insanity). **2**. A person appointed to manage the affairs of a company consequent upon an application to the court by debenture holders, usually when the company has defaulted in the payment of principal or interest to them. *See also* official receiver, mortgagee in possession.

receiving order. An order made by the court after a bankruptcy petition has been presented by a creditor, or by the debtor himself, appointing the *official receiver to take charge of the debtor's estate as an interim trustee.

recession. The stage, in the standard *trade cycle, at which economic activity declines at an increasing rate. Investments based on predictions of future growth become unprofitable. Business failures increase as markets contract. Production and employment fall, so causing a decrease in income and expenditure. There is little new investment as expected profits are low. Once the decline ends the economy is in a *depression. However, it is customary to talk of any falling off in economic activity as a recession, if it is too mild to warrant the use of the term depression.

reciprocity. A form of tariff agreement, usually bilateral, in which nations agree to extend to each other any reductions in import tariffs made by one of them, usually within certain limits and over a certain range of goods. The nature of the range of goods will determine how mutually beneficial the arrangement is. If, for example, a capital intensive goods exporter arranges for reciprocal reductions on finished goods with a primary product exporting nation, the results will be one sided in favour of the former and will lead to a deterioration in the terms of trade of the latter. Reciprocity is however one way of encouraging free trade and so is welcomed by GATT. Notable examples of reciprocal trading agreements were the Reciprocal Trade Agreements Acts (1934) and the Trade Expansion Act (1962) of the U.S.

recognizance. A contract between an individual and a court of law by which the individual binds himself to fulfil some act, such as attending court on a specified date or to be of good behaviour.

recommended retail selling price. A standard price set by the manufacturers of a product to show the consumer how much he will have to pay unless the shop has a discount offer on the item, and to enable him to compare the prices of competing brands. This replaced resale price maintenance in the U.K., which was made illegal in 1964.

record. *See* file.

recorded delivery. A U.K. postal service that provides a record of posting and delivery as well as limited compensation in the event of loss or damage in the post. No preferential treatment over ordinary mail is given in transit. A nominal fee must be paid on dispatch of the article.

recourse agreement. An agreement between a hire-purchase company and a seller of goods in which the seller undertakes to repossess goods if the buyer permits the hire-purchase repayments to lapse.

recovery. The *upward phase* of the trade cycle in which demand, production, and employment expand following a *depression. Financial institutions begin to increase their operations and new investment is undertaken as profits increase. Prices begin to rise slowly. This can then lead to a *boom as the recovery gains impetus.

rectangular distribution. *See* uniform distribution.

rectangular hyperbola. A function of the form:

$$y = a/x,$$

which has a characteristic graph in which the product of the ordinate and abscissa of every point is constant. The curve never meets the axes, even if extended indefinitely, but instead approaches the axes asymptotically. An example is a demand curve with unitary elasticity at each point along it.

rectification of register. A court order for the correction of an official list, usually the register of shareholders kept by a company, when it is satisfied that a name has been incorrectly entered or omitted.

recursive system. A simultaneous model in which one endogenous variable is explained entirely by predetermined variables, the second endogenous variable is determined by the first plus the predetermined variables, a third endogenous variable is determined by the first two plus the predetermined variables, and so on. A recursive system is used to represent a steplike chain of causation, which some economists believe to be a valid representation of many economic mechanisms.

redeemable security. A security that is repayable, either at its par value or at a *redemption premium, at some specified date or dates in the future or in the context of some specified eventuality. Most fixed-interest securities are redeemable, the exceptions being certain Government stocks such as *Consols and some corporate preference shares. Corporate loan stocks are almost always redeemable (while ordinary shares are always irredeemable). Redeemable securities can be divided into three types of *dated security:* short-dated stocks, medium-dated stocks, and long-dated stocks according to whether their dates of *redemption at any particular time are less than five years into the future, between five and fifteen years into the future, and more than fifteen years into the future respectively. The prices of redeemable securities vary inversely with the general level of interest rates, as is usual for fixed-interest securitics, although this relationship weakens as *redemption date approaches.

redemption. The repayment of an outstanding debenture stock or loan by the borrower in order to cancel it.

redemption date. The date on which a debenture or loan will be repaid by the borrower. In the case of dated securities, the year is stated on the title of the security and the date is that on which the final interest is due.

redemption premium. Any excess of the amount required for the *redemption of a debenture or loan over the latter's *par value.

redemption yield. The *flat yield adjusted to take into account any capital gain or loss on *redemption.

redeployment of labour. The movement of manpower between industries as circumstances affect the demand for labour. The U.K. *selective employment tax, for example, was designed to shake out labour from industries and services that were overmanned so that additional labour would be available to industries that were short of labour.

rediscount. To discount a *bill of exchange that has already been discounted with another person. This happens when shortage of funds compels the discount houses to rediscount bills that they have already discounted with the central bank acting as *lender of last resort.

redistribution of income. A policy adopted by many governments, particularly in socialist countries, that aims to reduce inequality of income through progressive taxation of income and wealth. Other methods used include the provision of various benefits to the lower paid, such as *Family Income Supplement in the U.K.

reduced form. A transposition in statistics of a simultaneous model so that its endogenous variables are included only as the dependent variables of their respective relationships (and not as independent variables of other relationships). The independent variables of a model's reduced form will comprise only predetermined variables. Thus the reduced form of a simultaneous model is not itself simultaneous and thereby evades the problems contingent on the estimation of the coefficients of a simultaneous model.

reducing (diminishing) balance. A method of calculating the depreciation of an asset in which an identical percentage of the value of the asset is written off each year. If an asset is worth £1000 and is calculated to depreciate at 20% each year, its value after one year will be £800, after two years it will be £640, after three years it will be £512 and so on. Eventually a fixed payment will be needed when the asset's life has ended. This is the traditional method of estimating the depreciation of plant and machinery in the U.K. for the purposes of taxation.

redundancy. The loss of a job by an employee, either because of a fall in demand in the industry in which he was working or because of technological change. Employees made redundant are often given a *redundancy payment.*

re-exports. Goods imported into a country and subsequently exported to another country without having been processed or affected only minimally. In these circumstances, if import duty has been paid it can be recovered as *drawback. This type of *entrepôt trade occurs at major ports that provide good *transhipment facilities. For example, goods from the Far East may be shipped to London or Rotterdam and subsequently re-exported to other smaller European ports that are not served by direct liner freight from the Far East. This is also known as *transit trade.*

reference in case of need. A phrase that is sometimes found on *bills of exchange followed by the name of an individual or institution. If the bill of exchange is dishonoured its holder may take it to this individual or institution for payment. *See* acceptance for honour.

refer to drawer. The words written by the drawee bank on a cheque that is being dishonoured because the drawer has insufficient funds in his account to meet it. It means in effect "ask the drawer why his bank is not paying this cheque". It is also the proper answer for a bank to put on a cheque in other circumstances, e.g. the attachment of the customer's credit balance by a *garnishee order or his being involved in bankruptcy proceedings.

reflation. Raising the level of economic activity in a country by governmental action. Reflationary policies aim to increase the demand for goods, encourage investment, expand production, and reduce unemployment: the measures used are principally increasing the money supply by reducing interest rates, reducing taxation, and increasing government expenditure. There is, however, a danger of creating or aggravating inflation with reflationary policies.

refugee capital. Money that is surplus to the immediate requirements of foreign governments or nationals and is invested in the country offering the highest rate of interest compatible with the safety of the capital. It is also known as *hot money* and is often moved from one country to another according to the strengths of their respective balance of payments.

Regional Economic Planning Boards. Boards through which the Secretary of State for the Environment carries out his responsibilities for regional planning in England. There is a board in each of the eight economic planning regions: Northern, Yorkshire and Humberside, East Midlands, East Anglia, South East, South West, West Midlands, and North West. The Boards were established in 1965 and consist of senior officials in the regions of the government departments concerned with aspects of regional planning. They coordinate the regional work of departments and advise the *Regional Economic Planning Councils.

Regional Economic Planning Councils. Advisory bodies through which the Secretary of State for the Environment carries out his responsibilities for regional economic planning in England. The Councils consist of part-time members with wide experience of their regions. They help in the preparation of broad economic and land-use strategies, which provide a regional framework for national and local planning and investment decisions. They are provided with information and advice by the *Regional Economic Planning Boards.

regional employment premium. A subsidy paid by the U.K. government to every firm in a development area for each of its employees. The scheme, which was in operation between 1967 and 1974, was designed to help the employment problem in the development areas.

registered capital. *See* authorized capital.

registered company. A company that is registered with the *Registrar of Companies. *See* joint-stock company.

registered land. *See* land registration.

registered land certificate. A certificate issued by Her Majesty's Land Registry to the owner of a piece of registered land. The certificate is in three sections, the *property register* in which the land is described, including any rights attaching to it, the *proprietorship register* in which the name and address of the present owner is given, and the *charges register* giving details of all mortgages and charges affecting the land. The land cannot subsequently be transferred unless the land certificate is handed to the transferee, and no dealings with the land can be registered at the Land Registry unless the land certificate is produced.

registered name. The name of a company as it is registered with the Registrar of Companies, which must be displayed prominently outside its registered office. No company is allowed to register a name that the Department of Trade and Industry considers undesirable. This category includes misleading names or names that are too similar to those of other businesses. Often a company name has important business associations and groups have been known to maintain shell companies purely in order to prevent the name being used by any other company.

registered office. The address of the office of every company registered in the U.K. must be registered with the Registrar of Companies. The registered office is the place at which one would expect to find a great deal of information about the company, including its statutory books. This registered office is an address to which all communications to the company may be sent. Each company is required to display its name in legible letters outside this office, in a conspicuous place. The Registrar must be notified within 14 days of any change in the registered office.

registered stock. *See* inscribed stock.

register of charges. A register maintained by the Registrar of Companies for all charges made by companies registered in the U.K. The significance of this register is that any charge becomes void if it is not duly registered within 21 days of its creation. If this occurs, the money secured on this charge becomes repayable. In the case of debentures it is sufficient to notify the Registrar of Companies of the total amount secured by this issue, the date of the resolutions authorizing the issue of the debentures and the convening deed, a general description of the property charged, and the names of the trustees, if any, of the debenture-holders.

register of debenture-holders. Every company in the U.K. is required by law to maintain a register of debenture-holders. This register must normally be maintained at the registered office of the company, but may be kept at any other office of the company where the compilation of such a register is made, or at some other office at which the responsibility for compilation lies. Every company has to notify the Registrar of Companies where this register is located. It must be made accessible to any debenture-holder or any member of the company for a period of at least two hours per working day.

register of directors and secretaries. Every company is required to keep a register of its directors and secretaries at its registered office. This register should contain the names of each director, any former names, his normal residential address, his nationality, his business occupation, and details of any other directorships held. If a corporation is a director then the register must disclose its corporate name and its registered or principal office. Similar details are required of the secretary of the company.

register of members. A register of the members of a company, which is required by law to be maintained. It is a record of all those persons, in the case of a company with share capital, who hold any shares of the company. This register must state the names and addresses of the members and the number of shares held by each member. Each share must be identified by a number, the numbering of each share running consecutively. The register must also contain a record of past owners of shares and, in all cases, the amount of consideration received for these shares. Normally the register of members will be maintained at the registered office of a company.

Registrar of Companies. A government official to whom certain documents must be given before a company is given a certificate of incorporation. If he believes that a company is no longer in business he may strike its name off his register after due notice has been given and the company must then be dissolved after three months.

registration fee. A small charge made by a company to cover the costs of registering shares in the name of a new owner.

regression. A technique for quantifying the statistical relation connecting two or more variables. Regression is more powerful and of wider scope than *correlation. It is essentially a method of *estimation and, apart from lending itself to hypothesis testing, can also be applied to forecasting problems. Like correlation, however, it cannot in itself demonstrate or imply causality; it is concerned only with the measurement of statistical association. Regression proceeds by postulating a relationship in the form of an equation with one dependent variable and one or more independent variables. In the case of a regression with two variables there will be one independent variable. Attached to the independent variables are coefficients which, when estimated, indicate the nature of the statistical association. Regression coefficients can be positive or negative, indicating a direct or inverse relation of the independent variable to which the coefficient is attached with the dependent variable. Regression equations can be linear or nonlinear in form, although the former is much the simpler of the two. Regression analysis is one of the most important quantitative techniques in use and is central to econometrics. *See also* multiple regression, coefficient of determination, least squares estimation.

regressive supply curve. A curve on a graph illustrating the unusual situation in which the amount of a commodity supplied is inversely related to its price. This situation has never been found over the whole range of prices, but it can occur over part of the range. For example, a person earning £160 for an 80 hour week (£2 per hour) might only work 60 hours if his wage-rate increased to £3 per hour. In this case his supply of labour would be regressive, declining as its price rose.

regressive tax. A tax whose average rate declines as income increases. The most common types are all forms of indirect taxation. For example, the poor spend a higher proportion of their income on clothing than do the more well-off. Consequently they pay a higher proportion of their income in *VAT, although the actual amount will probably be less.

reinstatement of the sum insured. The insurer's obligations under a policy are extinguished when a total loss payment is made or when the total sum insured is paid, but where a payment is made in respect of a partial loss the position varies in respect of the amount of cover available during the remainder of the period of insurance. With some classes of business, a partial loss payment reduces the sum by the amount paid, and extra premiums are required to reinstate the amount of cover available for the rest of the term of the policy.

reinsurance. The covering, with another insurance company or underwriter, of all or part of the risk underwritten by an insurer. This is usually done for the same reason as the original insurance was taken out, i.e. because the risk is greater than the bearer wishes to take.

For example, the insurance of a large passenger ship or airliner might involve a very heavy claim on the insurers if it were to become a total loss. Therefore the insurer seeks to reduce his potential loss by covering part of his liability with one or more other insurers.

The effects of reinsurance are to continue the basic principle of insurance by spreading the risk over an even wider field and to protect the insurance fund of the original insurer, thus giving additional security to the insured and all other policy holders (although there is, of course, a contractual or other relationship between the insured and the reinsurer).

Reisemark. German currency issued to tourists at preferential exchange rates during the 1930s. By this method, the Nazi government increased its supply of foreign currency with relatively little dislocation of the economy. The practice was condemned at the Bretton Woods Conference, but has been imitated since, especially in South America.

relief work. Government public works programmes involving *pick and shovel work* to provide jobs in order to maintain levels of employment. Often these projects have a value below their cost and are initiated solely to provide employment. *See also* priming the pump.

rendu. *See* franco.

renewal notice. *See* premiums.

renouncable documents. Evidence of ownership for a limited time of as yet unregistered shares when a new issue has been made, for example the provisional allotment letters sent to shareholders when a bonus issue is made.

rent. 1. The money that is paid for the use of land and any buildings upon it.

2. The surplus paid to any factor of production above that amount that is necessary to keep it in its occupation. It is thus the difference between the total sum that is earned and the *transfer earnings. For instance, if a chartered accountant earns £15,000 p.a. and would only earn at most £9000 in some other occupation, his rent is £6000 p.a. It is important to realize that this sum could disappear without affecting production; in this example, if the chartered accountant was taxed £6000 p.a. he would not leave accountancy as he would be worse off elsewhere. Rent or, more commonly, *economic rent* is an unfortunate term to describe this situation and causes endless confusion. It arose historically because land was the first factor of production for which this was recognized to occur. The supply of land was believed to be practically fixed so that transfer earnings were almost nil. In that case all of the payments made for the use of land would be the difference between the price and transfer earnings, i.e. it was rent in both senses. If prices increased or decreased production would remain fixed and the size of rent would fluctuate. For this reason many Victorians such as John Stuart Mill and Henry George advocated the complete taxing away of rent (*see* single-tax system) as production would be unaffected. These proposals were never implemented however, partly because most factors earn rent in this sense and it would therefore be inequitable to discriminate against one sector. *See also* quasi-rent.

rent control. *See* rent regulation.

rentes. French governmental stocks on which interest is paid. The term *rentier is derived from it.

rentier. A person who receives an income from the ownership of an asset rather than from a wage or salary. The rentier is living on the rewards of his past, rather than his present, economic activity.

renting back. A method of raising capital from land, buildings, factories, etc., without having to vacate them. A company can sell its property (e.g. to an insurance company) on the understanding that the buyer will lease the property back to the company on a long-term basis.

rent regulation. Under the procedure laid down by the Rent Act (1977), a *fair rent* may be fixed by independent rent officers at the request of the landlord, the tenant, or both since 1965. A fair rent depends upon age, character, and locality of the house and assumes that demand does not exceed supply. An objection to the decision of the rent officer is referred to a rent assessment committee.

renunciation. The surrender to another person by an allottee of any shares or other securities to which he is entitled to subscribe under a *rights issue or similar instrument.

reparations. Compensation demanded by a victorious nation from the defeated one for the costs of having waged war. It may take the form of monetary payments or consumption or capital goods and the war-making potential of the defeated state is at the same time reduced. Very heavy reparations were demanded from Germany after World War I, the Bank of England's estimate of the full cost of the war to the Allies being £24,000 million. J. M. Keynes violently disagreed with such an impossibly high sum being demanded and set out his arguments in *The Economic Consequences of the Peace* (1919). He predicted that the deliberate seizure of money and goods from Germany on such a large scale would impoverish Germany and have disastrous economic effects on other nations. If reparations were not reduced or abolished, he believed another war would eventually result. Although few agreed with Keynes at the time, reparations after World War II were more restrained. The U.S.S.R., however, seized goods and equipment thought to be worth $28,000 million from Germany alone.

repatriation. The transfer of capital from overseas back to the home market.

replacement cost. The cost of replacing an asset, assessed in terms of its present price rather than its original cost. This method provides a more accurate estimate of the value of materials used in production, especially in times of inflation. However, the U.K. tax system bases wear and tear allowances on the original cost of capital equipment rather than its replacement cost.

replevin. The return of goods to a person who believes they have been taken from him wrongfully, provided that he undertakes to contest ownership in court within one month (one week for the High Court). Judgment is then reached and the goods accordingly allocated.

report of the directors. A general description of the state of a limited company's affairs that must be presented with the *accounts. This report must disclose certain detailed information as laid down by the Companies Acts (1948–81). Unlike a set of accounts it is not necessary to obtain certification from an independent party of the fact that this report gives a true and fair view, but generally the independent party, the auditor, will review the directors' report for compliance with the Companies Acts.

representations. Written or verbal statements supplied by a person wishing to be insured, bearing upon the proposed risk.

Representations need not necessarily involve *material facts. Where they do, however, they must be substantially true. This means that they must be true to the best knowledge and belief of the person wishing to be insured. Where the representations concern matters of belief, expectation, or intention, these need not be realized. *See also* disclosure, utmost good faith, warranty.

representative firm. A hypothetical firm that has been managed moderately well and is fairly successful. It is average in all respects. The idea was originated by Marshall who used it to illustrate the effects of internal and external economies.

repressed inflation. *See* suppressed inflation.

reproductive debt. The proportion of the National Debt that is backed by real assets. Compensation paid in the form of Treasury stock to the former owners of the nationalized industries falls into this category. Reproductive debt is a minor part of the National

Debt as a whole, most of which was incurred during the two world wars. *See* deadweight debt.

repudiation. A refusal to fulfil a contract or repay a debt. The term is usually used to describe the refusal of a government to pay debts incurred by itself or a previous regime.

reputation, loss of. A lowering of one's standing in the eyes of other persons. If this is caused by a defamation, the person suffering it can usually recover damages in *tort. Damages, however, cannot be claimed under this head in an action for breach of contract, except in very special circumstances, e.g. where loss of reputation will probably lead to financial loss, or where the claim is against a banker for dishonouring a cheque when there was money to meet it.

reputed owner. A person who acts as if he is the owner of a good, with the consent of the actual owner. If he becomes bankrupt that property is divisible among his creditors, and the actual owner is estopped (*see* estoppel) from claiming it. Reputed ownership does not apply in those cases where the custom or wage of the trade rebut the presumption of ownership, as with articles bought on hire purchase.

requisitioning. *See* compulsory purchase.

resale price maintenance. A practice by which a supplier refuses to sell his product to a retailer unless he agrees to sell the product at a certain price or above a certain minimum price. It is argued that through price maintenance the wholesaler can exercise some control over the market. On the other hand, the supplier may wish to protect the reputation of his product or safeguard other retailers from cutthroat competition. Suppliers argue that the reputation of the product can be endangered by some retailer using the product as a *loss leader,* that is selling at a loss in order to attract custom to the store. In the U.K. resale price maintenance is illegal unless it can be proved to the courts to be in the interests of the public. So far only books and certain pharmaceuticals have met this test.

Resale Prices Act (1976). An act that made resale price maintenance generally unlawful, except in respect of classes of goods exempted by the Restrictive Practices Court (only two classes of goods, books and medicaments have been exempted; some 500 have been refused exemption). The act was based on the presumption that distributors who wish to expand their sales by reducing their prices should not be prevented from doing so by the manufacturers of the products they sell. *See* resale price maintenance.

rescission. Revocation or abrogation of a contract, often as a result of misrepresentation by one of the parties. A contract can only be rescinded if the claimant acts within a reasonable time by giving notice to the other party of his intention to bring a suit to have the contract set aside. Rescission is only possible if both parties can be returned to their initial positions.

research and development (R & D). Pure research, applied research, the improvement of existing products, and the development of new techniques and inventions.

One of the principal arguments in defence of large firms is that their monopoly profits allow them to invest in R & D to bring about product innovation. The evidence suggests that up to a certain size, varying between industries, firms do in fact increase their proportionate R & D expenditure, but after that size it decreases or remains static. This is possibly due to the high fixed costs in terms of equipment and uncertainty over the output from small installations. R & D is also highly associated with *conglomerates who have diversified into industries sharing a common technology. It must be remembered, however, that small companies could just as easily pool their resources for product development. This form of combination is excepted from U.S. anti-trust legislation.

Research Institute for Consumer Affairs. An independent non-profit-making U.K. organization that conducts research to see how far goods and services are adequate to the needs and wants of those who use them. It does comparative testing of equipment and aids for the disabled user and also publishes research reports.

reservation price. The price below which the supplier will choose to retain the use of a good or service rather than offer it on to the market. Wicksteed used the concept to derive a demand curve which incorporated the information of the supply curve in it. Equilibrium price was then established by equating total demand of consumers plus own demand of suppliers to the total sources. If resource information is also incorporated, the usual *excess demand curve results. All three modes of analysis yield identical price equilibria.

reserve. The money in notes and coins that the Bank of England keeps to meet the demands both of the commercial banks, who keep their surplus balances with it, and of its private depositors. It forms the ultimate banking reserve of the country.

reserve army of the unemployed. A body of workers made unemployed through technological improvements. This group tended to depress wages and provided workers in times of boom in Marx's interpretation of capitalist society. However, Marx avoided the full implications of a Malthusian population model, and allowed wages to rise above subsistence in response to technologically generated trade cycles.

reserve city. A U.S. city in which clearing facilities exist (*see* clearing bank). The U.S. clearing system is more complex than its U.K. equivalent due to the size of the country and the constraints placed upon branch banking. Consequently, there are a number of reserve cities located throughout the nation in which banks deposit sums of money for the clearing of cheques.

reserve currency. A foreign currency held by a government or international institution in order to finance international trade. The U.S. dollar and the pound sterling are both used for this purpose although in recent years the Deutschmark, the Japanese yen, and the Swiss franc have been increasingly used. To act as a reserve currency, the currency must maintain a relatively stable rate of exchange against other currencies, it must be readily convertible, a foreign exchange market for it must exist, and it must be the currency of a country that takes an active and significant part in world trade.

reserve for obsolescence. Funds that are held in reserve to be used to replace an asset that has become obsolete (before it has fully depreciated). For example, an improved process for manufacturing tinplate might render the former process hopelessly uncompetitive. In this case, the old asset is obsolete and must be replaced, whatever its age.

reserve price. 1. *See* auction.

2. *See* Common Agricultural Policy.

reserves. The amount shown on the asset side of a company balance sheet that is made up of profits not distributed to shareholders and is intended to meet contingencies or future investments.

reserve tranche. *See* International Monetary Fund.

residual payment. The reward that is left to an entrepreneur after all expenses have been paid. Unlike rent, interest, or wages its size is not known in advance. *See* profit.

residual unemployment. A number of people who remain unemployed, even in times of full employment, because their mental or physical handicaps make them unemployable. In addition, there are borderline cases, whom firms will only employ during periods of acute labour shortage. The magnitude of residual unemployment is dependent more upon advances in medicine and in technical aids than upon the state of the economy. For this reason the number is usually excluded from unemployment statistics.

residuary legatee. The person entitled to the remainder of a deceased person's property after all his debts, administration expenses, and taxes have been paid, and all the particular gifts of property and money specified in his will have been made.

residuum. The lowest income level in a society. This may be defined in terms of an absolute or a relative value, i.e. those earning less than £*x* per week or the poorest *x*% of the community.

resolution.

A *motion debated at a meeting that has been passed by a majority of those present at the meeting. For particular purposes and in particular circumstances a specified type of majority (rather than a simple majority) may be required. For example, a *special resolution* to change the *articles of association of a company normally requires a three-quarters majority of all the votes cast.

resources element. *See* rate support grant.

respondentia bond. A loan raised by the captain of a ship, who pledges his cargo as security. *Compare* bottomry bond.

restitution. 1. A court order for property to be returned to its rightful owner.

2. *See* Common Agricultural Policy.

restraint of trade. Any *restrictive covenant or agreement that is in restraint of trade is illegal unless held by a court not to be against the public interest. Typical covenants that are regarded as being in restraint of trade are: clauses in a contract of employment that restrict an employee from setting up in opposition to his employer after he has left his employment; clauses in the contract covering the sale of a business that restrain the seller from setting up in competition to the buyer.

restrictive covenant. A clause in a contract that restricts the freedom of one of the parties to the contract in some specified respect. For example, an agency agreement might contain a restrictive covenant to the effect that the agent will not act for any of the principal's competitors. Restrictive covenants are not always legally enforceable, especially if they can be shown to be against the public interest. *See* restrictive trade practice, restraint of trade.

restrictive endorsement. An endorsement on a *bill of exchange that restricts the ability of the endorsee to negotiate it.

restrictive labour practice. Any work practice that hinders or acts as a disincentive to the most effective use of labour, technical skill, machinery, or other resources. It would include trade union reluctance to accept manpower economies caused by the introduction of new methods or machines, resistance to work study, demarcation rules, systematic time wasting, or anything that would contribute to overmanning or under-utilization of manpower resources.

restrictive trade practice. A collusive agreement between two or more suppliers of a good or service containing restrictions in respect of prices, conditions of sale, quantities and descriptions, processes, areas and persons to be supplied. Under the provisions of the Restrictive Trade Practices Acts (1956, 1968), as amended by the *Fair Trading Act (1973), such agreements are required to be registered with the Director-General of Fair Trading and, where appropriate, investigated by the Restrictive Trade Practices Court to determine whether or not they operate in the public interest. Agreements are presumed to operate against the public interest and it is up to the parties to them to prove to the Court's satisfaction that the agreements, on balance, are beneficial in their effects.

Retail Price Index. A monthly estimate of the percentage change in the average level of the prices of those commodities and services that are bought by households in the U.K. Each area of expenditure is assigned a different weight; for instance, it is assumed that expenditure on food accounts for 20.3% of the family budget (1984 weighting), transport and vehicles accounts for 15.9%, housing 13.7%, alcohol 7.8%, etc. The total weighted average of price changes is given as a percentage of those for a chosen base year. For example, taking January 1974 as the base year (= 100), the Retail Price Index at the beginning of October 1984 was 354.8. *Also called* cost of living index, general index of retail prices.

retained earnings (retentions). Undistributed profits retained by a business as part of its capital reserves, for the purchase of new equipment, etc. In some countries they are taxed at a different rate to distributed profits. *See* imputation system of taxation.

retention money. Money owing on the fulfilment of a contract and retained by the buyer for a limited period, usually to allow time for any flaws in the execution of the work to come to light. This is a common practice in the building industry.

retentions. *See* retained earnings.

retirement pensions. *See* pensions.

retiring a bill. Withdrawing a *bill of exchange from circulation when it is paid, on the due date or earlier.

returned cheque or **bill.** When a banker on whom a cheque is drawn has to return it unpaid for any reason he marks an answer (i.e. the reason that it has not been paid) on the cheque. If the answer is "refer to drawer" owing to the customer's lack of funds, and the banker wishes to give his customer the opportunity to deposit funds to cover the cheque, his answer may also include the words "please represent". Then when he receives the cheque back through the post the collecting banker will present it again, but he must give notice of the dishonour to his own customer. A similar procedure applies when a bill of exchange is unpaid by the banker with whom it is domiciled.

return on capital. The ratio of profit earned to capital employed, which is one of the most significant ratios used in considering the efficiency of a business. This is not a conclusive measure of efficiency, however, as a business will in any case tend to earn more profit in a monopolistic situation. Profit, in this case, is the surplus of revenue over costs in a specific period. Capital employed is determined in different ways in different industries and situations. It is basically the sum of all those assets of the company (fixed, current, and other) used as a means of producing revenue. More specifically, in accountancy the *return on capital employed (R.O.C.E.)* or *return on investment (R.O.I.)* is the ratio of profit (usually before interest and tax) to the net tangible assets.

returns to scale. The increase in output that results from an increased use of inputs. If the increase in output is proportionately greater than the increased amount of inputs used there is said to be *increasing returns* (*see* scale effect, economies of scale) and so average costs decline. If they are equal, there is said to be *constant returns* and constant average costs. Here the *production function is homogeneous of degree one. If the increase in output is proportionately smaller than the increased amount of inputs used there is said to be *decreasing returns.*

revaluation. An increase in the value of a currency made by changing its *exchange rate in terms of other currencies. Revaluation means that the exports of a country become more expensive, while its imports cost less. Eventually, therefore, the balance of payments surpluses (which made the currency more valuable) will decline and unemployment will usually increase. For this reason West German governments vigorously attempted to avoid revaluing the Deutschmark in the 1960s (at the same time that U.K. governments were trying to avoid devaluing the pound). However, West Germany was eventually forced to revalue, mainly because of the switching of speculative funds into the Deutschmark in the hope of capital appreciation resulting from revaluation. *Compare* devaluation.

revenue account. *See* profit and loss account.

reverse takeover. The *takeover either of a larger company by a smaller one or of a public company by a private one. Reverse takeovers are somewhat rare and usually involve an extensive restructuring of the acquiring company's *capitalization. In the case of a takeover of a public company by another smaller one, it is evident either that the acquired company must be a willing party to the takeover or that the acquiring company has a powerful associate with whom it is collaborating. Sometimes a larger company may allow itself to be taken over by a smaller one in order to secure the latter's managerial skills; if its management is successful and dynamic it is hoped that the larger company will be operated more efficiently.

reverse yield gap. *See* yield gap.

reversionary annuity. *See* contingent annuity.

reversionary bonus. A periodic bonus that is payable to holders of *with profits* assurance policies. The size of the bonus is dependent upon the level of profits earned by the assurance company in the preceding year.

revocable letter of credit. *See* letter of credit.

revolving credit. A bank credit that is automatically renewed until notice of cancellation is given. Examples are: a credit for an unlimited amount in total but with a limit on the amount that can be drawn at any one time, or a limit on the amount that can be drawn within a stated period, e.g. a month. In the latter case, once the limit has been reached in any month no further drawings can be made until the following month, when the monthly limit is renewed.

revolving loan. A facility provided by some banks, finance houses, etc., for their customers. The customer is permitted to borrow up to a specified limit without asking permission. Thus, if the limit on the revolving loan is £100,000 and he has borrowed £45,000 at one particular time, he may still borrow a further £55,000 without seeking permission, although the bank will want to be notified of his intentions in order to have the money available.

Ricardo effect. An increase in wages increases the price of the more labour-intensive good relatively more than the more capital-intensive good. It is a counter-example presented by David Ricardo (1772–1823) to the *labour theory of value that Ricardo himself held.

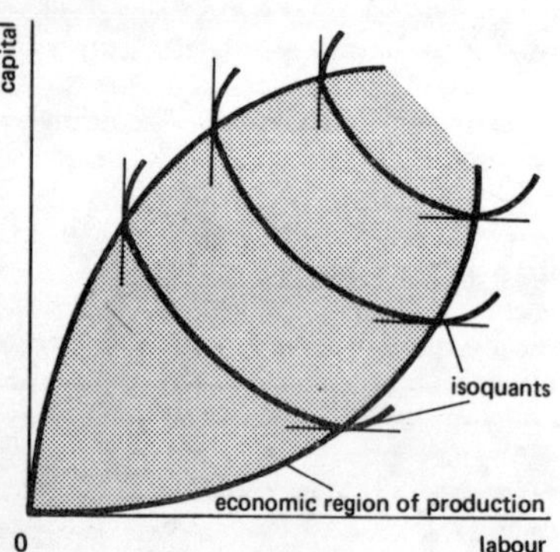

Ridge lines

ridge line. The line on an *isoquant map joining the points at which the marginal product of one or other of the factors is zero. With positive prices the area between the ridge lines is the *economic region of production. With two factors the line closer to the axis of an input corresponds to the *intensive margin of that factory, the further one the *extensive margin. The isoquants bend backwards beyond the ridge lines.

rigging a market. Any operation whose purpose is to influence a market temporarily by overriding the normal market forces in order to make a profit. For example, a speculator in a commodity market may make a large purchase, which may in itself push the market price up. However, there may be no substantial buying interest at the higher level and the speculator may then decide to rig the market by supporting it himself (i.e. by buying further quantities, either overtly or covertly, through a broker). Obviously he can only do this for a limited period and if there is no natural market force to give genuine support to the market it will eventually slip back.

rights (interest) insurance. *See* indemnity.

rights issue. The issue by a company of new shares to its existing shareholders in the same fixed proportion as that in which the shareholders already own the existing shares. Thus a *1 for 2* rights issue is an issue in which shareholders have the right to subscribe for one share for every two they already own, in this example an increase in the company's issued share capital by 50%. The price at which the new shares are offered is usually well below the market value of those shares already in issue. When a rights issue is underway the share price will be adjusted to take into account the issue and will be quoted ex rights. A shareholder who does not wish to accept the shares he has been allotted under a rights issue may assign some or all of his *rights* to another person by means of a *renunciation. Rights issues are, from the company's point of view, a cheap and convenient means of raising capital relative to an attempt to offer an entirely new issue to the general public (which might not even be feasible): however rights issues may be viewed unfavourably by investors and can certainly not be resorted to by a company because it is in trouble and needs cash. *Compare* bonus issue.

rights letter. A document offering a new issue of shares to existing shareholders on advantageous terms. If a shareholder does not accept, he can sell this letter with its attendant privileges on the Stock Exchange.

ring. An illegal association of dealers or trades who combine together to rig a market. For example, rings have been active in art and antique auctions, leading dealers agreeing not to bid against each other on the understanding that once having acquired the article at the auction at a low price they will auction it again between themselves later. The difference between the purchase price and the final price is divided between members of the ring. Several measures have been adopted to stop this illegal and unfair practice. *See also* price ring.

ring trading. *See* call over.

risk. A situation in which the probability distribution of a variable is known but its actual value (i.e. mode of occurrence) is not. Thus, a firm may know the probability of a fire burning down its premises but will not know whether or not a fire will actually happen. Risk is thus an actuarial concept and forms the basis of insurance, unlike *uncertainty, which exists when the probabilities of the possible outcomes occurring are unknown. In general, risk can be insured against whereas uncertainty cannot. This distinction was first made by Frank H. Knight. When risk is insured against, it is assessed and the premium calculated, taking into account the size of the market. It is the job of the *actuary to measure the risks, especially in life insurance; the *risk economist* covers a wider field of risks and is necessarily forced to employ less precise techniques. According to the *Sale of Goods Act (1893) the risks attaching to goods pass with the title to the goods. In marine contracts, the seller is obliged to give the buyer sufficient information to insure the goods; if he fails to do so the risk remains with the seller.

risk capital. Capital invested in an asset, security, or venture in which there is an element of risk, i.e. a possibility of a capital loss (or gain). Money invested in a dated government stock would not be regarded as risk capital, but capital invested in equities or a private company would.

risk economist. *See* risk.

rival commodities. Goods or services that can easily be substituted for each other so that the price of one will affect the demand for the other. For example, an increase in the cost of travel by rail will decrease the demand for rail travel and increase the demand for bus travel. The term was first used by Marshall. *See* substitute.

rival demand. *See* competitive demand.

rival supply. *See* competitive supply.

roll-over relief. A means whereby a company can defer payment on all or part of its capital gains tax liability from the sale of an asset if the proceeds of the sale are used for the purchase of another asset that is intended to replace the older asset. *See also* deferred taxation.

ROM. *See* microcomputer.

rotation of directors. The process in which company directors stand for re-election at regular intervals. In this way, directors may be replaced without the necessity of dismissal. The number or proportion of directors who annually stand for re-election is specified in the articles of association of a company and is normally one third.

roundabout production (indirect production). The means of production involving the use of capital goods and the division of labour in the production of a commodity. Instead of each individual producing the things he requires himelf, he is employed in some stage of the production of a good, e.g. making a part for a combine harvester. In this way total output and efficiency is greatly increased but there is often a considerable loss of job satisfaction. Generally the larger the market for a commodity, the more roundabout will be the method of production.

round lot. A number of shares or amount of stock in respect of which *stockjobbers will deal on their usual price basis, as opposed to an *odd lot basis.

Rowan system. A piece-rate scheme in which each worker is paid a guaranteed day rate as well as a premium, which is a percentage of the standard rate. In the Rowan system, this percentage equals the percentage of time saved on each task.

Royal Mint. *See* mint.

royalty. A payment made for the right to use another's property for purposes of gain. For instance, royalties are paid for permission to use patented or copyrighted works or to a landowner for permission to extract minerals from his land. A royalty is thus a payment for the use of a *wasting asset since patents, copyrights, and mines all have a limited lifespan.

rule of 78. A method of calculating the turnover relating to a specific period in the case of a business that lends money, charges interest, and accepts repayments over a period of time, probably on the regular instalment basis. A hire-purchase company would fall into this category. The application of the rule of 78 determines how much of each instalment consists of interest and how much of capital. This rule produces a bias towards *front-end loading*, i.e. the first instalments received will be considered to have a relatively high proportion of interest and a low proportion of capital repayment and the later instalments will be deemed to have the opposite proportions. This results in a greater amount of the *gross finance charge being taken to the credit of turnover in the earlier than the later years.

As an example of the working of the rule of 78, take the number of periods over which the debt is being repaid as being 12, assuming regular payments. Add the sum of this number and all descending numbers down to 1, giving a total of 78. The first instalment is then considered to have included 12/78 of the gross finance charge, the second 11/78, and so on. The final instalment will be deemed to have included 1/78 of the total finance charge.

runaway inflation. *See* hyperinflation.

running broker. A bill broker who does not himself discount bills but acts as an agent on a commission basis between the sources of supply of bills and the discount houses and banks.

running days. *See* lay days.

running down clause. A *marine insurance clause in which the insurer agrees to indemnify the insured from any damages suffered in a collision in which the insured ship is at fault.

running yield. *See* flat yield.

run (on a bank). A mass withdrawal of money from a bank by depositors who have lost confidence in the bank. This run may reach such proportions that the bank has to close. To prevent a run on all banks on the outbreak of war in 1914 a moratorium was granted by the U.K. government, which enabled the banks to remain closed until an emergency issue of £1 and 10 shilling notes could be made to prevent the withdrawal of gold.

S

sacrifice. Loss of welfare incurred in paying a tax. A maxim of taxation is that taxpayers should be treated equally and that this can only be achieved when their payments involve an *equal sacrifice* of welfare. It is thus related to the ability-to-pay view of taxation rather than the payment-according-to-benefit-received view. However there are problems in deciding what is meant by equality of sacrifice. Does it mean that taxpayers should each pay an equal absolute amount, an equal proportional amount, or an equal marginal amount? The structure of taxation is dependent on the answer to this question.

When discussing sacrifice and related topics two assumptions are always made. Utility of income is assumed to be measurable, so that we know by exactly how much it increases with income. It is also assumed that people with equal incomes will sacrifice the same amount of welfare if they pay identical taxes.

safe custody. A banking service by which a bank is prepared to receive and take charge of deed boxes, valuables, etc., and store them in its strong-room. The banker is then a bailee and the extent of his liability for the safety of the articles depends upon whether or not he has made a charge for this specific service. In general, he is bound to take the same care as he would of his own property, but if he makes a charge, as is done when safe deposits are used, he must use all precautions and devices available in taking care of valuables deposited with him.

salary. Remuneration paid to an employee. There is no absolute distinction between salaries and wages, but in general salaries are paid to executive and clerical employees, whereas wages are paid to manual workers. Salaries are also often paid at longer intervals (usually monthly rather than weekly). The most important distinction is that salaries are not directly related to the number of hours worked, or the quantity of goods produced, whereas wages are.

sale and lease-back. *See* lease-back.

Sale of Goods Act (1893). An Act of Parliament regulating the respective rights of the vendor and purchaser of all articles (other than money and other abstract rights and matters) except land and things attached to the land. The Act is widely regarded as a model of excellent draftsmanship and survived largely unaltered for well over 70 years, until the current spate of consumer protection legislation required the 1893 Act to be amended. The law relating to sale of goods is now consolidated in the Sale of Goods Act (1979) and that relating to hire purchase and credit sale transactions in the Consumer Credit Act (1974). The Act implies that in every contract for the sale of goods: the seller is the rightful owner; the goods are in accordance with the seller's description of them, or with any sample supplied; the goods are fit for the purpose for which they are required, so long as this purpose is obvious to the seller and that it is also reasonable to suppose that the buyer is relying on the seller's skill and judgment;

and the goods are of *merchantable quality* (i.e. free from defects and acceptable to a reasonable person, after full examination, in fulfilment of the contract). The Act also implies warranties that the buyer will enjoy quiet possession of the goods and that they are free of any charge. Finally, the Act contains detailed rules regulating the exact time at which ownership of the goods passes from the seller to the buyer. This may be important in deciding who bears the loss if the goods are damaged or destroyed in transit, for example. In general, the risk passes with the title to the goods. Deciding when title passes is complicated but it basically passes as soon as the goods are ready to be delivered to the buyer, unless there is some condition in the contract with which the seller must still comply. *See also* Trade Descriptions Act (1968).

sale or return. Denoting goods that are supplied by a manufacturer (or a wholesaler) to a retailer on the condition that he may return them if they are not sold, usually within a specified period.

sales day book. *See* day books.

sales ledger. A record of the sales made by an enterprise to various other individuals or enterprises, the price and quantity of the goods sold, and the cash received in payment. Thus at any time the sales ledger will provide a record of the balance of money owed by the various companies and a history of any previous transactions. The sales ledger will often give an analysis by age of the debts outstanding. It normally constitutes one of the *books of account of an enterprise.

sales promotion. The activities of a company that are concerned with increasing the sales of their products by means other than above-the-line *advertising. Techniques include exhibitions, temporary price reductions, *public relations, demonstrations, free samples, *merchandising, etc.

sales revenue maximization. An alternative theory of the firm in which the management seeks to maximize not profits but sales revenue, either because it is easier to do (and is likely to be correlated with profit) or because the size of the sales revenue will gain favour with the shareholders.

sales tax. A tax paid by the consumer at the time of purchase of a commodity. Petrol taxes are an example.

salvage. 1. The proceeds resulting from the sale of ships, goods, etc., recovered from wreckage or fire. In the insurance of property it often happens that the wreckage of the insured item has some salvage value, even though the article is a total loss from the insurance viewpoint. For example, a motor car may be damaged beyond economic repair, but still have some scrap value. Usually, with total loss claims, the fully assessed value is paid to the insured and the insurer takes over the salvage, which he sells to reduce the cost of the claim. Sometimes, however, the insured may wish to retain the salvage, in which case an appropriate sum is deducted from the claim.

2. Compensation paid to those (salvors) who voluntarily and in the face of danger save a ship or its cargo from danger or loss at sea. The salvors have a lien for the salvage money on the property rescued.

sample. A set of items drawn from a statistical population or total quantity. For all practical purposes in economics and statistics, a sample must be a random sample if it is to be useful. It will be more useful the larger it is but in practice this is offset by the cost of increasing the sample size.

sampling distribution. *See* distribution.

Samuel Commission. A four-man commission set up by the British Prime Minister, Stanley Baldwin, under the chairmanship of Sir Herbert Samuel (1870–1963; later Lord Samuel) after a dispute between the coal owners (the Mining Association) and the miners. The government-appointed Court of Inquiry had resulted in deadlock as neither side would give way. None of the four represented labour nor had any particular knowledge of the coal industry. Their unanimous report, presented in March 1926, contained some long-term proposals that were sympathetic to the miners, but the short-term recommendations included reduced rates of pay and no subsidy. The miners claimed that even existing wages were too low and rejected the report. Their strike began soon after, on 26 April, and led to the *General Strike.

Sandilands Committee. A government-appointed committee which reported on *inflation accounting in 1975 in favour of a new system of current cost accounting to replace the current purchasing power system recommended by the Accounting Standards Committee in 1974.

sandwich course. A course of study lasting up to five years, usually consisting of alternate periods of about six months each of full-time study in a technical college and supervised experience in industry.

sans recours. *See* without recourse.

satiable wants law. *See* diminishing marginal utility.

Savage criterion. *See* minimax regret.

save as you earn (S.A.Y.E.). A U.K. savings scheme that enables savings to be made in 60 regular monthly amounts (with a minimum of £4 and a maximum of £50) in deposits with the Department of National Savings or Trustee Savings Banks by means of deductions from pay or by other regular payments. The S.A.Y.E. third issue links monthly contributions to the U.K. *general index of retail prices, thus offering some protection against inflation. S.A.Y.E. is free of U.K. income tax and capital gains tax.

saving. An individual or business may either consume or save its disposable income. Saving does not necessarily imply making deposits at banks or building societies; it is sufficient to increase one's cash holding by refraining from consumption. In a simple *income-expenditure model, the economy is in equilibrium when investment is equal to saving. In a more complex model, however, the only requirement is that withdrawals from the *circular flow of income match injections into it.

There are two theoretical approaches to savings. The first, due to Keynes, assumes that saving is simultaneously determined with consumption in the *consumption function. The second, known as the *permanent income theory* or the *life-cycle hypothesis*, postulates that every individual spends in relation to what he conceives his normal income to be. In any particular year he may regard his income as high, in others he will regard it as low; in the good years he will save the excess and in the bad years he will run down his accumulated savings. According to this theory, saving is an incidental consequence of a consumption decision, which has, as monetarists have pointed out, interesting implications for government policy. If an individual believes that a change in taxation is temporary, he will not adjust his consumption plans: this makes fine tuning of the economy virtually impossible.

savings account. *See* bank account.

savings schedule. A function that relates the level of income in an econo-

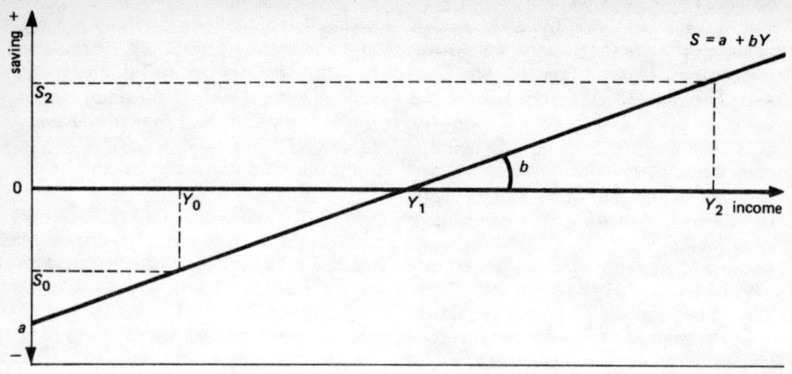

Savings schedule

my to the associated level of savings. As an example, the association may be written in the linear form:

$$S = a + bY$$

where S = savings and Y = income. If there is no income, the associated level of saving is *a*, which means that dissaving occurs, i.e. people are spending *a* from past savings to tide them over. In this formula the *marginal propensity to save is *b* (the slope of the line); this indicates the change in saving that is produced by a unit change in income.

At income level Y_0 savings are S_0, which is a negative amount; there are dissavings. At income level Y_1, all income is spent with none being saved and no past savings used, i.e. there are neither savings nor dissavings. At income level Y_2, the savings level is S_2, which is positive. *See also* income-expenditure model.

S.A.Y.E. *See* save as you earn.

Say's law (law of markets). A law proposed by Jean-Baptiste Say (1767–1832), a French economist. In its most general form this states that supply creates its own demand. It is difficult to pin it down exactly since it was more often formulated explicitly by those attacking it than by those propounding it, but essentially it is the ex ante proposition that the amount producers want to supply will be equal to that which consumers demand and the economy will operate at, or at least move quickly to, a full employment equilibrium. Then the only unemployment will be voluntary, insofar as the unemployed choose not to work for the wages offered. (This distinguishes it from the ex-post concept of *Walras' law.) It was generally accepted until the Depression.

scale effect. Cost advantages that occur only at a high level of output. As a result, average costs of production fall as output increases. Scale effects can only occur if units of production are indivisible. They can be effective *barriers to entry since established firms with high outputs could undercut the prices charged by newcomers with small outputs.

scale of preference. A scale of the relative importance of various goods and services to a consumer. A choice must always be made in buying particular products rather than others. If he acts rationally, a consumer will first buy those articles for which he has the greatest need or those that give him the greatest satisfaction. This suggests the existence of a scale of preference that lists all possible choices in their order of importance to the consumer. Few people will consciously have such a list, but most will display preferences when buying goods and services. *Indifference curves can be derived from these scales of preference.

scarcity and choice. If more of a good or service is demanded than can be obtained that good or service is said to be scarce. This is a slightly different meaning from its normal usage. Cars are common but are scarce in the economic sense, because people would like to have even more of them. Volcanic eruptions are rare but are not scarce in the economic sense because people would like to have even less of them. Human wants are virtually unlimited while resources are not, so that the vast majority of goods and services are scarce. This leads to the problem of choice.

Since there are insufficient resources to produce all that we should like to have, some mechanism must exist to determine what quantity of each good is produced and exactly how it is allocated, i.e. to decide whose wants are left unsatisfied. In a free market economy these problems are solved by the *price mechanism. In a centralized economy, a government department would have to decide priorities of production and allocation.

scatter diagram. A graphical representation of correlation. If, for instance, it is believed that there is a direct relationship between consumption expenditures *C* and disposable incomes *Y* with the latter being the independent variable, scatter points could be plotted on a diagram as in Fig. I. Each point represents a dual observation on a given level of disposable incomes and its associated level of consumption expenditures. The axes represent the two variables. The resulting configuration will always be in the nature of a scatter, even if there

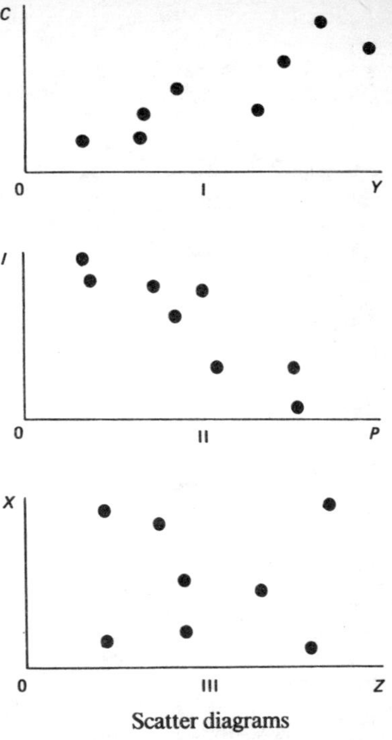

Scatter diagrams

are no other determinants of consumption expenditures, because of the presence of random stochastic disturbances. The form of the relationship can be estimated by the use of such techniques as least squares estimation. The positive slant of the scatter in Fig. I confirms the hypothesis of a direct relationship between consumption levels and disposable income levels. If the scatter had a negative slant, as in Fig. II, where it might be thought that the rate of inflation *I* is inversely dependent on the rate of increase of industrial productivity *P*, then the inverse relationship hypothesis would be corroborated. If, however, the scatter points are distributed in random fashion without any apparent direction either positive or negative, as in Fig. III, then a poor correlation close to zero is indicated and the relationship between variables

X and *Z* would be weak or nonexistent.

scheduled territories. The official name for the *sterling area.

schedules. Categories into which income is allotted for the purposes of taxation in the U.K. There are six schedules. Schedule A is levied on the annual value of property. It was abolished in 1963 but revived in 1970 as a tax on income from property; Schedule B covers income from commercial woodlands; Schedule C deals with interest payments on government and local authority loans and securities; Schedule D applies to profits, income from foreign possessions and securities, etc.; Schedule E deals with earned income; Schedule F applies to company dividends.

scholastics. Philosophers of the Middle Ages, notably Thomas Aquinas. They made three main contributions to economics: the principle that the utility of a good varied with its relative scarcity, the belief in the existence of a *just price* for each good or service from which it was morally wrong to deviate even in times of glut or scarcity, and the belief that interest charges were unjustified and should be condemned in all but a few rigidly defined circumstances (one such exception was when the lender sacrificed an opportunity of profiting by making the loan, i.e. opportunity cost). Joseph Schumpeter (1883–1950) believed the scholastics to be the intellectual forefathers of Adam Smith (1723–90), but it is generally believed that they represented one of the many false starts before the emergence of economics as a formal discipline.

Scottish Development Agency. A U.K. government agency established in 1976 to promote industrial reorganization in Scotland and to provide equity and loan finance to local industry.

screening hypothesis. The view that education serves merely as a screening device, enabling employers to identify natural intelligence, trainability, and desirable attitudes, rather than increased skill or productivity effected by education itself: productivity is seen as being taught very largely on the job. If this hypothesis is true, it is argued, education is a very expensive method of helping employers make choices between job applicants, and the social returns to education are very much lower than the private returns.

scrip. Certificates of stocks and shares, esp. those allocated in a *bonus issue. (From sub*scrip*tion.)

scrip issue. *See* bonus issue.

S.D.R.s. *See* Special Drawing Rights.

seasonal unemployment. Unemployment due to the seasonal nature of some jobs, such as those in the building trades or in tobacco picking. It is debatable to what extent this represents true unemployment. For example, in a cold climate, such as Canada, although the construction industry requires a large pool of skilled labour, it can only use it for a short time. They will, therefore, have to pay a high wage during the working months, in order to maintain this pool through the nonworking months, otherwise it will not induce workers to enter the industry. In this context seasonal unemployment is inherent in the job and so cannot be thought of as genuine unemployment.

secondary banking sector. Organizations that provide a range of credit facilities that are less comprehensive than the commercial banks. For example, secondary banks provide second mortgages, but not current account facilities. The secondary banking sector mushroomed in the U.K. in the early 1970s but suffered a severe crisis in 1973–4 when two major secondary banks collapsed and had to be rescued, principally by the *institutions. Since then the Bank of England has introduced a more stringent system of regulation for the secondary banks. A new division has been created to supervise individual banks and the whole banking system is subjected to periodic examinations (annually for the *clearing banks and quarterly for others).

secondary market. 1. *See* over-the-counter market.

2. Any market in which commodities, mortgages, or titles to property are dealt outside a recognized or primary market.

secondary picketing. *See* picketing.

secondary production. The production of manufactured goods. *Compare* primary production.

second-best theory. A belief that if imperfections exist in the economy preventing it from reaching its optimum state, even more imperfections might be needed to reach the second-best situation. Free trade would be the best policy in a perfect world. If, however, one nation were to dump goods on another nation, this second nation might be forced to impose a *countervailing duty as the second-best policy, even though this might distort the economy further. This theory has important implications for government policy in such areas as the pricing policies of nationalized industries, the provision of public services, international trade, etc. *See* Pareto optimal.

second-line equities. The shares of medium-sized companies, which are not closely represented by the Financial Times Industrial Ordinary Index. The 30 constituents of the latter are often referred to as market leaders, which set the *tone of the market to which the second-line equities respond.

second mortgage. A mortgage taken out on a property that has already been mortgaged once, in order to raise money. Subsequent mortgages on the same property can also be created. For the second mortgage to be an effective security for the mortgagee the value of the property must be greater than the amount of the first mortgage. The deeds of the property will usually be with the first mortgagee, in which case a second mortgage needs to be registered to protect the second mortgagee against subsequent mortgages. In the U.K. in the case of registered land, a certificate of second charge is issued by the Land Registry after registration.

second of exchange. A duplicate of a *bill of exchange that has been delivered by a different route in case the first has gone astray.

secret reserve. *See* hidden reserve.

sector. Any division of an economy that has a unifying characteristic and can be studied in isolation from the rest of the economy. The economy may be divided in many ways. For example, it may be divided into the public sector (state activities) and private sector (private individuals and organizations), or the goods sector and money sector, or the agricultural sector and industrial sector.

secular trend. A consistent tendency to change in a particular direction, usually as a result of long-term forces in the economy. Although it may have cycles and short-term fluctuations imposed on it, a secular trend implies a definite movement in one direction. An example is the consistent rise in real national income in the countries of the West during the last 150 years.

secured creditor. A creditor who holds a mortgage, charge, or lien on any part of the property of the debtor as security for a debt, by the terms of the Bankruptcy Act (1914). The claims of secured creditors are satisfied, to the value of the security held by them, before those of any unsecured creditors.

secured debenture. *See* debenture.

secured liability. *See* liability.

Securities and Exchange Commission (S.E.C.). A supervisory body attached to the New York Stock Exchange. Its closest U.K. equivalent is the *Council for the Securities Industry.

security. 1. Any income-yielding document that can be traded, as on a stock exchange. Securities may carry fixed interest, as in the case of debentures, bonds, *preference shares, and *gilt-edged securities, or variable interest as with *ordinary shares; they may be redeemable or irredeemable. The term is also used in reference to such commercial documents as bills of exchange and convertible assurance policies.

2. Property pledged as collateral for a loan by a borrower, or the document concerned with such collateral.

self-employed. Denoting a person who is in business on his own account. This includes partners in a partnership, professional people, such as doctors and authors who work for themselves, and any other person who has an earned income that is not paid by an employer. Self-employed people in the U.K. pay higher national insurance contributions than employees and are taxed under Schedule D rather than P.A.Y.E.

self-employed annuity. An *annuity that can only be bought by a person who is a sole proprietor of a business, a partner in a professional firm, an employee in receipt of nonpensionable income, or an individual not able to join a company pension scheme (either because there is not one in existence or because the rules exclude him from membership). Their purpose is to provide a means of saving for retirement out of gross rather than net income by giving expense relief on contributions up to a specified ceiling.

self-liquidation. Payment of the original cost of an asset from its yield. The purchase of raw materials would be self-liquidating if the funds for repayment derived from the sale of goods manufactured from those raw materials.

self-service. Any establishment in which people help themselves rather than being served. The most common self-service establishments are shops (especially supermarkets), petrol stations, and cafés. Although self-service reduces labour costs, in shops it offers increased opportunities for pilfering.

self-sufficiency. The ability of a state to maintain itself in isolation from the rest of the world. The larger the volume of imports as a percentage of *gross national product, the less self-sufficient a nation is. The U.S. could easily become self-sufficient since all the necessary resources can be found within its borders, while for the U.K. a great effort would be needed. Self-sufficiency might be adopted for noneconomic reasons, such as to ensure supplies during wartime. However not even the U.S. has attempted to become self-sufficient as this would offend the principle of *comparative cost.

seller's market. A market in which demand exceeds supply and sellers can dictate the prices. If, however, their prices become too high there may cease to be any buyers. The market may then become a *buyer's market.

sellers over. Denoting the state of a market in which there are still sellers after all the buyers have been satisfied.

selling cost. A cost that has been incurred to boost the sales of a product. The main expenditure is on *advertising and related activities, such as commercial travelling. Other selling costs would be the expenses of market research, free gifts, packaging, etc.

selling out. Selling stocks or shares *at best against a defaulting buyer. If the original buyer fails to take up his purchases, the broker may sell them at the best price obtainable, debiting the buyer with any costs and market differences.

semi-interquartile range. A crude measure of dispersion sometimes used in descriptive statistics, equal to half the difference between the third quartile and the first quartile. *Compare* range (def. 1), mean deviation, standard deviation.

semilogarithmic chart. A graph on which only one axis (usually the vertical) is logarithmic, the other being uniform.

semivariable costs (stepped costs). Costs in which there is both a fixed and variable component (*see* indirect costs, direct costs). For example, when costs change after a certain level of production is attained they may be termed semi-variable or stepped costs.

sensitive market. A market, especially a stock exchange, in which prices fluctuate substantially in response to good and (more usually) bad news.

separable utility function. A *utility function that can be rewritten in general form:

$$U(X_1 \ldots X_n) = U(U_1(X_{11} \ldots X_1 n_1), \ldots, U_k(X_{k1} \ldots X_k n_k)).$$

A utility function is additively separable if it can be written in the form:

$$U_1(X_{11} \ldots X_1 n_1) + \ldots + U_k(X_{k1} \ldots X_k n_k).$$

Theoretically this restricts the interdependence of goods; the *marginal rate of substitution between goods of one group, say X_{11} and X_{12} is unaffected by the level of consumption of a good from another group, say X_{21}. The main importance of separability studies has been upon empirical estimation of systems of demand curves where relationships between elasticities can reduce the number of coefficients to be estimated.

sequential access. *See* storage device.

sequestration. The placing of disputed property in the hands of a third party until the dispute is settled. A *decree of sequestration* in Scotland is equivalent to an adjudication of bankruptcy in England. Sequestration has in recent years gained a great deal of publicity as a method of enforcing court judgments and fines against trade unions.

serial correlation. Autocorrelation in a time series.

serial printer. *See* character printer.

service. An intangible economic *good, either for the benefit of consumers or industry, that is usually consumed at the same time as it is produced. Examples include transportation, catering, and the work produced by an accountant, a teacher, or a hairdresser. The calculation of the value of output in these industries, which are usually labour-intensive, is often difficult. The service industries, together with the extractive industries and manufacturing industries, make up three sectors into which the economy can be divided. The service industries take up an increasingly large proportion of national income as the economy becomes more advanced. *Compare* commodity.

service contract. A contract between a company and a director, consultant, or senior executive. Companies are obliged to keep such contracts open for inspection to all members of the company. Some service contracts are for a fixed term, others provide for security of tenure on expiry, and yet others provide for *severance payments to be made if the term of service is cut short for any reason.

S.E.T. *See* Selective Employment Tax.

set off. A banker has the right, provided there is no agreement to the contrary, to set off different accounts of his customer one against another, i.e. he may amalgamate the credit balance on one account with the debit balance on another account provided the accounts are in the same right. However, where he foresees that such action may become necessary, he usually obtains the customer's agreement and signature to a *letter of set-off.*

settlement. The process by which all transactions made during an *account on the Stock Exchange are terminated. The settlement process includes provisions for *contangoes and *backwardations, *ticket day, and (finally) *account day. Transactions involving gilt-edged securities or new issues are settled immediately for cash.

settlement day. *See* account day.

severable contract. A contract that can be so divided into parts that part can be disregarded and part retained. For example, a contract may contain a subsidiary promise to commit a criminal offence, although the main part of the contract is perfectly legal. The courts may order the subsidiary part to be struck out and the main part to be enforced.

Contracts involving several separate deliveries of goods may become severable if an action relating to only one delivery is brought.

severance payment. 1. A payment made to a director, consultant, or senior executive of a company if his *service contract is terminated before it has expired. It is also known as a *golden handshake.*

2. A similar payment made to any employee if his employment is cut short unexpectedly and through no fault of his own.

shadow price. An estimate of the true cost of a factor of production or a good or service when it either does not have a market price or when it has a market price that deviates widely from the factor's real worth so encouraging it to be under- or overused. Examples of factors that have no market price are leisure time; saving in time, petrol, etc, from the opening of a new motorway; possibility of death on hazardous projects; the true cost of transporting petroleum in an oil company's own ships. Market distortions could arise from the imposition of taxes, the creation of a monopoly, the effects of restriction of trade, or the under- or overvaluation of a currency. In all of these instances, shadow prices should be used to find the optimum combination of resources and the best level of production. Shadow prices are most widely used in the communist nations, where market-pricing is almost entirely absent, to allocate resources between various investment projects, set prices for consumer goods, etc.

share. One of a large number of titles of ownership of a company. Possession of shares entitles the holder to participate in the distribution of profits and (usually) to vote at company meetings. If a company goes into liquidation with any positive net assets, then the shareholders will be entitled to these latter in proportion to their holdings. Shares represent the mechanism by which the owners of companies can have limited liability: if a public company becomes bankrupt the shareholders, assuming their holdings are fully paid up in respect of the *par value (or issue price) of the shares, will not be liable for any net debt, although their holdings will of course become worthless. Shares can be denominated as *preference shares*, which are *fixed interest securities, the holders of which have a prior claim over ordinary shareholders to any profit distribution, or *ordinary shares*, which are risk capital in the sense that holders of ordinary shares are not entitled to dividend as of right but will be the chief beneficiaries in terms of rising dividends if the company is successful. Ordinary shares carry a variable *nominal yield; once they have been granted a quotation, they can be traded on a stock exchange where, if the company is successful, their market value will tend to rise ahead of inflation over a long period of time. The market value of preference shares, on the other hand, will move inversely with interest rates and will not benefit from the company's successful trading.

share capital. The amount of money subscribed by the shareholders, at par, to a company. It thus represents an amount owed by the company. A distinction must be made between *authorized*, *issued*, and *fully-paid* share capital. The authorized share capital represents the total share capital a company is allowed to issue by its articles, the amount issued indicates the amount that shareholders have actually subscribed, and if they have subscribed the par value of the shares issued then these are considered fully paid.

share certificate. A certificate providing evidence of a person's ownership of shares. If an investor sells his entire holding in a company, his certificate will be cancelled by the company concerned; if he merely reduces his holding, the company will replace his certificate accordingly.

shareholder. The owner of stocks or shares in a company (or limited partnership). Shareholders are members of the company in which they own shares.

share index. An *index number constructed to represent the prices of shares on a stock exchange. The percentage movements of such share indices are thus designed to mirror the average percentage movement of their constituent shares. Share indices are published by various daily newspapers and weekly journals. *See also* Financial Times Actuaries Share Indices, Financial Times Industrial Ordinary Index, Financial Times Stock Indices, Times Share Index, Dow Jones Industrial Average.

share premium account. An account in the books of a company that has sold new issues of shares on the stock exchange at a premium (i.e. a price greater than the nominal value of the shares), which records the premiums received. It is not possible, except for a few detailed cases, to alter this account and it must be shown in the published balance sheet of the company.

share register. The register of a limited company in which details of the ownership of shares in the company are kept. The register records the names and addresses of shareholders, the extent of their holdings, the dates of acquisition and resale of their shares, etc. Entry in the register is evidence of ownership of shares with all attendant benefits. The share register is usually kept at the company's registered office and is open to inspection for a nominal charge.

shares of no par value. Shares that have no face value. This is of little importance as the market price of shares bears no relation to any nominal value that they might have.

share splitting. *See* bonus issue.

share warehousing. *See* warehousing.

shifting tax. The alteration in effect of eventual *tax incidence. If the taxpayer can successfully alter the price structure to compensate in part for his fall in real after-tax purchasing power, then he has shifted part of the tax. For instance, if a retailer can increase the prices of his products by the full amount of any increase in indirect taxation without experiencing a decrease in sales he has shifted all of the tax on to the consumer.

shipbroker. A *broker who arranges charter parties, cargo space, etc., between shipowners and shippers of goods. In London, shipbroking is carried out on the *Baltic Mercantile and Shipping Exchange. Some shipbrokers also deal with passengers' bookings.

shipment of goods. Vast quantities of goods are shipped across the oceans each year. The principal cargoes are food and raw materials, manufactured goods, and oil and coal. Ocean freight consists of three classes of vessel: liners, tramp steamers, and oil tankers. Liners run on regular advertised routes and usually carry mixed cargoes at *conference-line rates. Tramp steamers do not have advertised routes and are usually chartered in whole or in part at negotiated rates for specific voyages or specific periods. Their itineraries depend on the charters their owners can arrange for them on the worlds' shipping markets (e.g. the *Baltic Exchange). Oil tankers are either owned by large oil companies or by shipowners who charter them to oil companies.

shipowner's lien. The lien a shipowner has on a cargo that he has carried, if freight and other charges have not been paid.

shipped bill. A *bill of lading confirming that goods have been loaded aboard ship.

shipper. A producer, manufacturer, or merchant who is responsible for exporting goods by sea (or by air). In some trades the importer may be regarded as the shipper, especially if he pays the freight (for example, when he buys F.O.B. port of origin).

shipping and forwarding agent. A firm that specializes in arranging the export and import of goods by sea or air. Shipping and forwarding agents deal with all the necessary documentation, insurance cover, and customs clearance. They advise on the best method of transportation, book freight, and arrange for loading, unloading, warehousing, and delivery.

shipping bill. The form used for making a *pre-entry with H.M. Customs and Excise, prior to exporting goods. Apart from providing the customs with full details of the goods being exported, to enable them to enforce export prohibition rules, it may be required if the exporter has a claim for *drawback.

shipping conference. *See* conference lines.

shipping ton. *See* ton, tonnage.

ship's certificate of registry. A document that provides information about a ship. It lists the ship's name, owner, country of registration, master, and tonnage.

ship's option. *See* freight.

ship's report. A form made out by the master of a ship upon its arrival at a

U.K. port. It lists details about the ship (such as its name, owner, port of origin, etc.), the crew, the passengers, and the cargo.

shopping cheque. A voucher, issued by a shop or hire-purchase company, that may be used to buy goods to their full face value at certain shops. The vouchers are then repaid over a fixed period of time. The scheme bears many similarities to hire-purchase.

short bill. A *bill of exchange that is redeemable on presentation or within a limited period (not more than ten days).

short-dated gilt. *See* gilt-edged security.

short delivery. A delivery that falls short of the quantity invoiced either in respect of the number of items delivered or the total weight delivered. Short deliveries may be due to accidental loss during transportation (in which case it will probably be covered by insurance), by normal drying out during transportation (in which case it will be settled by *final invoice), or by the dishonest intention of the seller (in which case it could be settled by confrontation or litigation).

short interest. A *marine insurance term for the imbalance that exists when the actual value of goods is less than the value for which they have been insured. When this is the case the excess premium can be reclaimed.

short run (short period). A period of time during which at least one factor of production remains fixed. If a firm experiences a change in demand for its product, it cannot immediately vary all its factors of production since some cannot be changed quickly. For instance, although the amount of labour could be varied quickly through extra overtime, the erection of a factory might take some years. The short run is not a fixed period of time but will vary between industries, e.g. a restaurant could be extended more quickly than a blast furnace. *Compare* long run.

shorts. A term used on the London Stock Exchange with reference to fixed-interest securities, mainly gilt-edged securities, with redemption dates less than five years into the future. *Compare* longs, mediums.

short selling. The speculative practice of contracting to sell for future delivery more of a commodity or security than is currently held. If the price then falls, the short seller can buy the balance before delivery date and so make a gain. Short selling is thus a *bear speculation, the opportunity for which on the London Stock Exchange is made available by the *account system. Dealers are said to take a short *position or be short when they engage in short selling. *Compare* longs.

short-term capital. 1. The current liabilities of a business plus medium-term capital. Short-term capital may have to be repaid quickly and can therefore only be used for relatively restricted purposes, such as cash-in-hand, or for wage payments. The major characteristic of short-term capital is that the term of borrowing is short.

2. Very liquid capital flows that move between financial intermediaries in different countries in response to differentials in the interest rate. *See also* long-term capital.

short-term capital gains. Capital gains made in the U.K. on investments sold within six months of purchase. By the Finance Act (1962) these were taxed at the standard rate of income tax. By the Act of 1965 the time period was extended to 12 months and a single tax is now in operation for all capital gains.

short-term deposits. Funds deposited at banks and other financial institutions that can be withdrawn at short notice. Since these funds are highly liquid, the interest payable is usually lower than that on long-term deposits.

short-term rate of interest. The rate of interest quoted on loans for not longer than three months. As it is influenced by *money market conditions it is regarded as the rate upon which the rates for longer-term loans are based; as the longer the loan the greater the risk these are usually higher than the short-term rate.

short-time. A reduced working week. It is preferred by employers to closure, as long as revenue exceeds *variable costs. The most notable example of short-time working was the U.K. three-day week of the winter of 1973–4.

short ton. *See* ton.

shut-down cost. *See* direct cost.

shut-down point. The price and level of output below which a producer will be unable to cover his *direct costs (wages, fuel costs, etc.). Between the shut-down point and the *break-even point the producer will be covering his direct costs although he will not cover his *indirect costs (interest payments, rates, etc.). At a level of production beyond the break-even point he will cover both direct and indirect costs and so will be earning a profit.

Graphically the shut-down point is situated at that point on a diagram measuring price and output, at which the producer's marginal cost curve intersects the average direct cost curve. This must be the point at which the average total cost curve is at a minimum.

S.I.C. *See* standard industrial classification.

sickness benefit. *See* statutory sick pay.

side deals. A form of malpractice in which directors of a public company use their position and knowledge to take part in deals for personal gain, to the detriment of the company. Side deals are considered to be more harmful than *insider dealing as more money is usually involved and so possible cases are rigorously investigated by city institutions, such as the Panel on Takeovers and Mergers.

sight bill. A *bill of exchange payable at sight, i.e. payable on presentation without benefit of *days of grace. It is equivalent to being payable on demand.

sight draft. Any *bill of exchange that is payable on presentation.

signature. If a person is unable to write or so ill that he is unable to sign with his usual signature he may make a cross or similar mark, and if this is witnessed by two reliable persons it would normally be accepted by a bank when paying a cheque. A signature may in appropriate circumstances be an assumed name, and by the Bills of Exchange Act (1882) it is sufficient if a person's signature is written by some other person by or under the signatory's authority. When opening an account a banker takes a specimen of the customer's signature together with any authority the customer wishes to give for another to draw cheques on his account. If in doubt as to the authenticity of a signature on a cheque a banker usually returns it marked "signature differs". *See also* forgery.

significance. A statistical property relating to the result of a test of hypothesis. If this is such that the null hypothesis is rejected, i.e. if the result falls into the critical region of the test, then the result is said to be significant. An example frequently encountered in econometrics is the hypothesis that a regression coefficient is zero, implying that the independent variable to which the coefficient is attached has no influence on the dependent variable in question; if a test shows that such a coefficient is significant, then it can be inferred that the independent variable under consideration does have a valid quantifiable influence. An elaboration to the concept of significance is the level at which it occurs. This relates to the probability of the Type I error, i.e. the probability of incorrectly rejecting a (true) null hypothesis, which is conventionally fixed at either 0.05, 0.01, or 0.001. Thus one can speak of the result of a test being significant at the 5% (or 1% or 0.1%) level, meaning that the actual *population can be expected to behave like the variable for at least 95% (or 99% or 99.9%) of the time. *See also* hypothesis testing.

significance test. *See* significance.

simple hypothesis. *See* hypothesis.

simple interest. Interest added to a capital sum after specified time periods with reference to a specified rate of interest. For instance, a capital sum of £100 with simple interest at the rate of 10% p.a. would, with interest added, be worth £105 after six months, £110 after one year, £115 after eighteen months, and so on. Simple interest treats time as a discrete variable and a capital sum with simple interest grows linearly, not exponentially. The general formula is:

$$I = Prn/100,$$

where I is the interest, P the principle, r the annual rate of interest, and n the number of years. *Compare* compound interest.

simple random sample. *See* random sample.

simulation. The process of examining the way in which a system or activity works and of analysing problems associated with it by the use of a model constructed to reflect the system's essential characteristics. The simulation model is usually mathematical (although in some engineering applications it can be physical) and requires a computer to develop fully its ramifications. Simulation techniques offer a cheap and relatively quick method of analysis and are frequently made use of in operations research. *See also* Monte Carlo study.

simultaneous model. A *model consisting of two or more relationships in which one or more variables will be included in the capacity both of the dependent variable of one relationship and of one of the independent variables of another. For example, inflation models are often based on two fundamental relationships: the price equation and the wage equation. The usual hypotheses postulate prices to be a function of wages (in the same period), import prices, and productivity, while wages might be regarded as being dependent on prices in the same period, prices in previous periods (lagged prices), and unemployment. This model is simultaneous in wages and prices; the wage coefficient cannot be determined until the price coefficient is known and the price coefficient cannot be calculated until the wage coefficient is determined. Simultaneous models are frequently encountered in economics; indeed, any economic theory that aspired to be a reflection of the real world would have to be transposable into a simultaneous model rather than a single-relationship model because economic variables in the real world are interdependent in such a complex manner. The problem presented by simultaneous models is with respect to the estimation of the coefficients. Such estimation is not even possible unless the relationships of the model conform to the requirements of identification; but even if the model is identified, ordinary least squares will yield estimators that do not have the properties either of unbiasedness or of consistency. This is because a variable that is independent to one relationship but dependent to another will be correlated with the stochastic disturbance of the relationship to which it is independent and this situation, which obviously cannot obtain in a single-equation model, vitiates the Gauss–Markov theorem, which underlies least squares estimation in its ordinary form. In response to this problem econometricians have devised methods of estimation, such as *indirect least squares or *two-stage least squares, which purge from simultaneous models this correlative defect. *See also* identification.

single capacity. *See* dual capacity.

single life pension. A pension or annuity that is paid to the beneficiary for his or her lifetime but not for the lifetime of his widow or her widower. *Compare* joint life and last survivor pension.

single-tax system. A system of taxation in which the whole revenue of the state is raised by one tax alone. The most famous examples of proposals for single-tax systems were *l'impôt unique* of Quesnay and the land tax of Henry George.

François Quesnay (1694–1774) believed that all the wealth of a nation came from its agricultural sector, from which all income flowed. Consequently, a single tax on rent would minimize the costs of collection with no harmful side-effects, as the landowners' incomes ultimately bore all taxes anyway.

Henry George (1839–97), an American economist and politician, proposed to tax pure ground rent, excluding the returns from site improvements. This would be a single-tax system since he believed its proceeds would be large enough to finance all the expenditure of the state. However, governmental expenditure is now so large that no single tax could raise enough revenue without imposing inequitable tax burdens on those who had to bear it.

single-use goods. Goods that can be bought and used by consumers once only. Food, cigarettes, and newspapers are single-use goods, whereas consumer durables, such as cars, washing-machines, and televisions, are not.

sinking fund. A sum of money that is built up by regular periodic instalments and is intended for some particular use, such as the repayment of a loan or the replacement of a machine. Interest from the fund is ploughed back and so the annual payment into the fund is:

$$xr/[(1 + r)^n - 1],$$

where x is the amount of money needed, r is the rate of interest, and n is the lifespan of the sinking fund.

sister-ship clause. A clause found in *marine insurance policies dealing with the collision of two ships belonging to the same owner. An owner might have no claim in the absence of this clause, as it is impossible to sue oneself.

sit-down strike. A situation in which workers refuse both to work and to leave their workplace. In recent years the *work-in* has developed from the sit-down strike in which workers refuse to leave their workplace and continue working despite orders to the contrary.

SI units. Système International d'Unités. An international system of metric units now in use for scientific purposes and increasingly becoming used for all purposes in which units of measurement are involved. The ba-

Base and Supplementary SI Units

physical quantity	*SI unit*
length	metre
mass	kilogram
time	second
electric current	ampere
thermodynamic temperature	kelvin
luminous intensity	candela
amount of a substance	mole
*plane angle	radian
*solid angle	steradian

*supplementary units

Decimal Multiples and Submultiples

submultiple	*prefix*	*multiple*	*prefix*
10^{-1}	deci	10^{1}	deca
10^{-2}	centi	10^{2}	hecto
10^{-3}	milli	10^{3}	kilo
10^{-6}	micro	10^{6}	mega
10^{-9}	nano	10^{9}	giga
10^{-12}	pico	10^{12}	tera
10^{-15}	femto		
10^{-18}	atto		

sic units (of which there are seven) used in commerce are the metre, kilogram, amperc, and second. The derived units include the hertz (frequency), joule (energy), watt (power), volt, and ohm. The same decimal multiples are used with all units. *See also* U.S. Customary units.

size (of a statistical error). *See* hypothesis testing.

skewness. The degree to which a statistical distribution is asymmetrical. Two distributions with identical means and variance may differ from each other according to their respective skewness. Skewness may be positive or negative.

Fig. 1 illustrates the normal distribution, which has zero skewness; its mean, median, and mode are equal

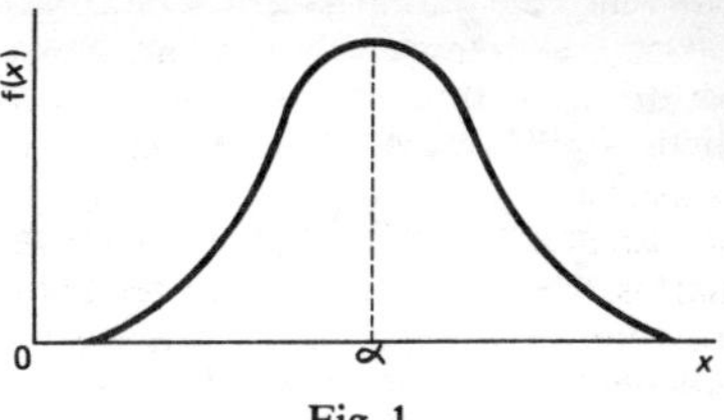

Fig. 1

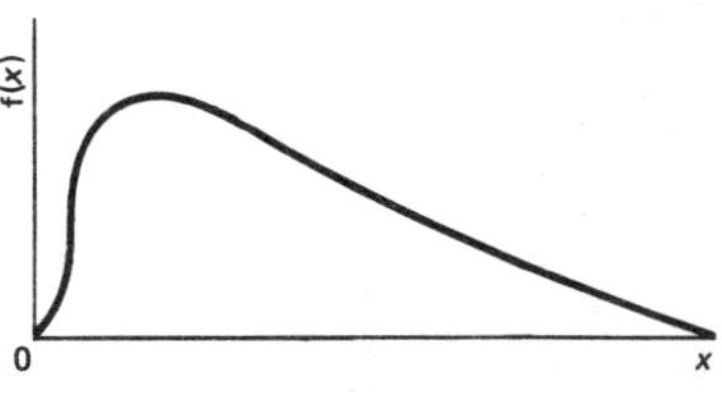

Fig. 2

Fig. 3

and are allocated beneath the peak of the distribution: at α in Fig. 1. Fig. 2 presents a distribution with a positive skew; there is a longer tail for high values of x than for low values. The mean of a positively skewed distribution is greater than the median, which is greater than the mode. As an example of a distribution with a positive skew, one might think of the distribution of wealth in a capitalist society. Fig. 3 illustrates a negatively skewed distribution; the mode has a higher value than the median, which has a higher value than the mean. Distributions with a negative skew are much less frequently encountered than those with a positive skew. There are several *coefficients of skewness, some based on the difference between the mean and the mode or the mean and the median, or between the quartiles and the median. The best measure of skewness, however, is based on the third moment about the mean (that is, the weighted average of the deviations, raised to the third power, of the items in a distribution from their mean).

skimming. *See* market skimming.

sleepers. *See* direct selling.

sleeping partner. An individual who provides capital in a partnership, but who takes no active part in its management. Although inactive, he still has all the legal benefits and obligations of ownership.

sliding peg. *See* exchange rate.

sluice-gate price. *See* Common Agricultural Policy.

slump. *See* Depression.

Slutsky conditions. A set of conditions showing that for any two goods, A and B, there exists a symmetry between the *substitution effects of good A with respect to the price of good B and of good B with respect to the price of good A. This can be represented mathematically as:

$$\partial q_A / \partial p_B = \partial q_B / \partial p_A,$$

where q_A and q_B are the quantities of A and B demanded and p_A and p_B are their respective prices.

Slutsky decomposition. *See* income effect.

Slutsky equation. A mathematical expression showing how a change in demand can be split into *income effects and *substitution effects:

$$\left(\frac{\partial q_A}{\partial p_B}\right) = \left(\frac{\partial q_A}{\partial p_B}\right)_{comp} - q_B\left(\frac{\partial q_A}{\partial m}\right)$$

The left hand side is the partial derivative with respect to the price of good B of the normal demand function for commodity A, where demand is considered to be a function of prices and income. On the right hand side the first term is the partial derivative with respect to the price of good B of the compensated demand function for good A, where demand is considered a function of prices and the level of utility. This is also known as the *substitution effect. The second term on the right hand side is the amount of good B demanded multiplied by the partial derivative of the normal demand function for A with respect to income. This product is also known as the *income effect. This formula is one of the basic results in the theory of demand.

Small Firms Information Centres. Offices established by the Department of Industry throughout the U.K. with the aim of providing free advice and information for the small business. They provide advice as to possible sources of finance, explanations of planning laws, advice on tax matters, etc.

snake. Originally called *snake in a tunnel.* The former internal currency arrangement of the *European Economic Community, under which the currencies of each member state were fixed in relation to the currencies of other member states but were allowed to float, as a bloc, in relation to the currencies of nonmember states. The snake was superseded by the *European Monetary System in 1979.

snob effect. A deviation from the normal operation of the law of demand resulting from *conspicuous consumption, causing some consumers to buy more as prices rise (or less as prices fall). The result is that the aggregated market demand curve falls more steeply than would be expected, or in some cases it might even be rising. *See also* Veblen effect.

social accounting. The compilation of national expenditure and income accounts relating to different sectors of the economy. The sectors for which social accounts are formulated are the following:

1. the personal sector, including unincorporated business enterprises.
2. the corporate sector, embracing all commercial and industrial undertakings whether privately or publicly owned.
3. the government sector, including both central and local authorities.
4. the rest of the world sector, representing the transactions of nonresidents with U.K. residents.

It is in principle possible to formulate three accounts for each of these sectors corresponding to three central forms of economic activity, namely production, consumption, and capital formation. These social accounts are the foundation upon which is constructed the presentation of the global aggregates of *national income accounting.

social balance. A social situation in which the supply of public services has kept pace with private production. The term was coined by J. K. Galbraith (*b.* 1908) in his book *The Affluent Society.* He believed that attaining social balance is a major problem of modern society.

social costs. The costs of an action by an individual or firm that are not borne by that individual or firm, but by society as a whole. This is different from *private costs*, which are the costs borne by a producer. If a firm increases its output its added private costs are the costs of using the increased quantities of the factors of production; the extra social costs will be the damage caused by any extra pollution that is generated, such as effluent in the rivers, smog, etc. Production will only be carried out at the optimal level of output for society as a whole when marginal aggregate cost equals marginal aggregate benefit. To achieve this the producer has to be held responsible for the social costs, so that they enter his calculations when deciding output. There are various ways in which this could be achieved, such as taxation, merger (if a neighbouring business is being harmed), etc. *See* externalities.

social credit. Grants from the state intended to stimulate the economy. The term was coined by P. H. Douglas, a Canadian engineer, in the 1930s. He believed that not all of the money paid in costs of production would be used for consumption and that this inequality was the main cause of depressions. He therefore advocated compensatory public works, grants from the state to everyone, and subsidies to reduce retail prices all of which were intended to boost consumption.

socialism. A political and economic system based on equality and collective ownership of the means of production. It can take many forms, depending on the extent to which the emphasis is political, economic, or social. In its Marxist form (*see also* communism) it includes the abolition of all private property, while its milder forms accept a *mixed economy in which the profit motive of the private sector coexists with the concept of public service in the public sector. All forms of socialism are united in their opposition to uncontrolled *capitalism and advocate state planning in place of a total reliance on market forces. Socialists also believe in an equitable distribution of wealth and welfare services to provide for the needs of the less fortunate members of the community.

In contrast to communists, socialists believe in a gradual nonviolent passage towards equality and communal ownership by the vote rather than by revolution, the retention of civil liberties, and freedom of the individual.

social overhead capital. *See* infrastructure.

social security. A comprehensive system of social services in the U.K. administered by the Department of Health and Social Security for those in need. Payments include *family allowances, *national insurance, *industrial injuries benefit, *family income supplements, and *supplementary benefits.

social wealth. The total assets of a country. It includes all the property of both the public and private sectors that is used, both directly and indirectly, in the productive process. Examples of assets used directly in production are factories, machinery, agricultural land, etc., whereas examples of assets used indirectly in production are schools, hospitals, roads, bridges, etc.

social welfare function. An ordinal measure of a society's satisfaction based upon the individual utility functions of the members of the society. Its form depends upon specific value judgments by those people who determine its nature. The purpose of the social welfare function is to provide a basis for choosing among alternative social policies, given the levels of individual satisfaction they engender. In theory the social welfare function is maximized by employing a production function that represents society's production possibilities as a constraint, exactly as an individual is assumed to maximize his own personal satisfaction. The social welfare function seeks to eliminate the inconsistencies and indiscrimination present in value-free systems, such as Pareto optimization (*see* Pareto-optimal) or the *compensation principle.

soft currency. A currency for which the supply exceeds the demand on the foreign exchange markets. There will consequently be either a depreciation in its value (if the currency has a *floating exchange rate) or pressure on the country's reserves (if the currency has a *fixed exchange rate). Currencies can change their status relatively quickly. The U.S. dollar had been a *hard currency from 1945 until the late 1960s when it became a soft currency; partly because of the glut of dollars in Europe (*see* Eurodollar) and partly because of a decline in its relative strength vis-à-vis other nations.

soft loan. A loan that has an abnormally low rate of interest. Many of the developed nations provide soft loans to the developing countries as a form of international aid.

soft sell. *See* hard sell.

software. The set of programs available for use on a particular computer, which tell the computer what to do. Strictly speaking, the term is applied only to those programs that in some manner assist all users of the computer and not to programs written specifically to solve isolated problems. Illegal copying of software ("piracy") is a problem for software manufacturers. *Compare* hardware.

sold note. A *contract note sent by a stockbroker or commodity broker to his client to confirm a sale made on his behalf. It will give the details of the sale, the broker's commission, and the date on which the client can expect to receive payment.

sole agent. An *agent who has an exclusive right to sell the products of his principal in a particular territory.

solo. A single *bill of exchange, rather than one of a set.

Solow model. A model of economic growth, produced by R. Solow in 1956, that sought to supply a neoclassical answer to the conclusions of Sir Roy Harrod's model for growth. Solow retained the *one-sector model, the classical fixed savings coefficient, and exponential growth of the labour force. However, in place of Harrod's fixed-proportions production function, Solow used a production function that allowed full substitution between the factors of production, capital, and labour. With this flexibility the *warranted and *natural rates of growth can be made equal by modifying the proportion of capital to labour, and thus output to capital. Thus the existence of a long-run growth path can be guaranteed in this model in contrast to the Harrod–Domar model. In fact the steady state equilibrium is stable, since if the *capital-labour ratio is too high (that is, higher than the long-run equilibrium level) then the output to capital ratio is too low, and so, with a fixed savings rate, capital grows at a slower rate than the labour force. Therefore the capital-labour ratio falls towards equilibrium. *See* Harrod–Domar model.

source and disposition of funds. A formal statement, often included in a firm's published accounts, that shows the net change in working capital that has occurred during the year.

Spearman's coefficient of rank correlation. *See* correlation.

special buyer. An agent of a discount house who operates for the Bank of England. He tenders Treasury bills in open market operations.

special crossing. A crossing on a cheque that restricts payment to a specific named person or to a specific named bank.

special deposits. An instrument of monetary policy intended to restrict credit. The Bank of England can call for special deposits to be made with it by the commercial banks in order to curtail their lending. Those deposits are a specified fraction of the banks' total deposits and are not released until it is intended that bank credit should expand. This system was introduced in 1960, taking the place of quantitative restrictions on the lending power of each bank. A similar system has operated for many years in the U.S., the minimum ratios being altered as necessary by the *Federal Reserve System.

Special Drawing Rights (S.D.R.s). A means of increasing the reserves of a member country of the *International Monetary Fund, first introduced in 1970. The S.D.R. is essentially bookkeepers' money, having no life of its own. However, whereas ordinary drawings have to be repaid the S.D.R. forms a permanent addition to members' reserves, acting as an international reserve currency to supplement their holdings of gold and foreign currencies.

specialist broker. A dealer on the New York stock market, who is equivalent to a *jobber in the U.K.

special manager. A person appointed by the *Official Receiver in cases of liquidation or bankruptcy in special circumstances, as when specialized knowledge of the business is necessary or when the creditors (or persons liable in the case of liquidation) request such an appointment in their own interests.

special resolution. A resolution that must be passed in order to make certain specific changes in a company, such as a change in the objects clause in the *memorandum of association. Such a resolution is defined in the Companies Act (1948) as being one that is passed by more than 75% of the members of the company at a general meeting, where due notice has been given that a proposal for such a resolution will be made. The period of notice given must not be less than 21 days. *See* resolution.

specie. Coin money.

specie flow mechanism. The motive force by which international exchange rates move in order to balance trade. It is Hume's synthesis of earlier observations by Munn and Locke. If there were a sustained balance of trade surplus in a country, the accumulation of bullion would raise the domestic price level as explained by the *quantity theory of money. In response the *terms of trade would move against the surplus country, cutting exports and increasing imports and leading to the reduction and eventual elimination of the trade surplus. It was used by classical economists in an attempt to discredit mercantilist theories, which sought to increase a nation's real wealth through export surplus, by showing the tendency towards a natural distribution of wealth between countries.

specie points. *See* gold points.

specific charge. *See* charge.

specific damages. *See* damages.

specific factor of production. An input that can only be used for one type of work and cannot be replaced easily by other factors of production. Much capital and land is highly specific, but labour cannot usually be regarded as a specific factor. For instance, accountants cannot be replaced by other workers, but they can move into other occupations. The whole of the earnings of a specific factor of production is designated an *economic rent.

specific performance. A court order to a party to a contract to perform his obligations under the contract. The court has discretion to make this order rather than to award damages for breach of contract, and will only do so in appropriate cases (e.g. it will never specifically enforce a contract of employment, as it would clearly be undesirable when employer and employee are at loggerheads) and where the contract is fair and enforceable by both parties.

specific tax. An indirect tax that is expressed as a fixed amount per unit of a commodity rather than varying with the commodity's price. *Compare* ad valorem tax.

speculation. The purchase of a security, currency, or commodity in the hope that its price will rise and that profitable resale will thereby be possible, usually in the short run. Speculative selling, when a price fall is considered likely, takes the form of *short selling. Speculation is distinct from *arbitrage in that it involves an essential element of gambling, because future prices are never certainly known, and also in that the speculator is concerned with only one security or commodity; there is no switching element. Speculation can, and usually does, have a beneficial effect in smoothing out price fluctuations. However, in times of political or economic crisis speculative activity may swamp normal trading activity and, on such occasions, cyclical price movements will be severely exacerbated. In certain commodity markets governments themselves may perform a speculative function with the establishment of price stabilization schemes. On the Stock Exchange in the U.K., opportunity for speculation is considerable owing to the nature of the *account system. Major speculators now tend to be corporate institutions rather than private individuals. *See also* option.

speculative demand. One of the three motives for holding money cited by

Keynes (*see also* precautionary demand, transactions demand). The speculative demand for money envisages either a capital loss in bonds, securities, etc., or opportunities for which liquid funds would be necessary. When interest rates are very low relative to market expectations, the probability is that they will rise in the near future. But a low rate of interest is associated with high bond prices and vice versa. Hence, when interest rates rise in the future, bond prices will fall and anyone holding bonds rather than money will suffer a capital loss. Interest rates can thus eventually fall so low that it is better to hold money, with its zero rate of return, than to hold bonds, with the prospect of a capital loss. Individuals and firms can invest in short-term securities that will carry no capital losses. In times of substantial excess liquidity, interest rates on such securities will fall to almost zero. Thus, most of the speculative demand comes from the financial sector of the economy. Commercial banks and other lending institutions cannot solve their excess liquidity problems by lending to each other. When interest rates are extremely low, they may decide to hold on to their money: this constitutes a speculative demand for money. There is considerable empirical evidence to support this view of the behaviour of the financial sector during recessions. Hence, the aggregate speculative demand for money is a function of the nominal rate of interest. *See also* liquidity preference.

spot currency market. A market in which currencies are exchanged for immediate delivery, immediate generally meaning within two days. If commissions and transactions costs could be disregarded, it would not matter where the particular location of the exchange was, the spot rates would be the same. If the pound cost $1.00 in Toronto the dollar would cost 50p in London (although the exchange rate used in London is generally quoted as dollars per pound). *Arbitrage between centres would bring these ratios into line. Furthermore, if pounds from London were to be exchanged for francs in Paris, then the francs from Paris exchanged for dollars in Toronto, the result should be the same as a direct deal between London and Toronto, except for the slight increase in the costs of the transactions and transportation.

spot goods. Goods, usually commodities, that are available for immediate delivery, as opposed to futures that are offered for forward delivery. The relationship between the *spot price* and the forward price will depend upon the supply and demand situation, but the spot price is usually higher than the forward price as the goods have been landed and warehoused and have usually incurred warehouse rent. Spot goods are usually offered on *ex warehouse* or *at warehouse* terms (i.e. excluding costs of delivery), although they sometimes include the cost of delivery to the buyer's warehouse or factory.

spread. 1. The diversity of the investments in a *portfolio. The greater the spread, the less likely it is that spectacular gains or losses will occur for the portfolio as a whole. Unit trusts spread their investments over a very wide range of stocks and shares and so offer the ordinary investor the greatest security.

2. The difference between the selling and buying price quoted by a stockjobber.

spread sheet. A type of *package available on many computers. The program enables the computer to be used as an extremely powerful *calculator. One of the main applications is financial modelling and forecasting where the effect of varying circumstances can be quickly and easily calculated.

stability. An equilibrium state is considered stable if an exogenous disturbance results in a return to the equilibrium state, and unstable if it does not. The equilibrium state may be a path through time, such as a growth path for an economy, or it may be a single point, such as the intersection of supply and demand schedules in a market. A system is considered stable if a disturbance will bring it to some equilibrium state, not necessarily the one it left, or if it develops a pattern of regular oscillations about some equilibrium state, where these oscillations are either damped, i.e. moving closer and closer to the state with each oscillation, no matter how slowly, or moving at regular distances from the state. If the oscillations move farther and farther from the equilibrium state they are explosive and the system is not stable. The nonoscillating case can occur where multiple equilibria exist in the system, for instance where the supply curve bends backwards and intersects the demand curve at several points. Typically, one of these equilibrium states is one in which the slightest disturbance will cause the system to move to another equilibrium point in the system. In this case the system is stable, but that particular equilibrium state is unstable.

An example of an oscillating stable system would be in the construction industry, which experiences 15- to 25-year cycles in the levels of activity (Kuznet's cycles).

Stability may be considered in a comparative statics analysis (*see* Marshallian stability, Walrasian stability) in which the instantaneous changes of excess demand are considered, but more commonly dynamic models are used in discussions of stability. Lagged dynamic stability is particularly favoured in macroeconomics where the stability conditions place constraints upon the parameters of the models, which when mathematically formulated may be meaningfully interpreted. These reveal implicit assumptions in the corresponding comparative statics analyses.

Stability may also be considered either locally or globally. The former is concerned only with conditions close to the equilibrium state and is very similar to a comparative statics analysis. It is particularly favoured where there are serious nonlinearities in the problem and assumptions are only made about the instantaneous rates of change. The latter is used quite commonly and wherever possible but often only in linear systems, which make it indistinguishable from the former.

stabilization policy. A government policy attempting to reduce the amplitude of the boom-recession *trade cycle of the economy. The aim is to use fiscal and monetary policy and direct controls, such as prices and income policies, to slow the rate of inflation while at the same time maintaining an acceptable level of unemployment. The problem is compounded in open economies, such as the U.K. where the level of inflation and interest rates affect the balance of payments and the exchange rate. *See also built-in stabilizers, stop-go.*

Stackelberg duopoly. A model of duopolistic competition in which each producer assumes that the other is acting as a Cournot duopolist. Each then chooses the point along the supposed reaction curve. If only one operates on this assumption he profits from it, but if both do the result is less efficient than a *Cournot duopoly position.

staff relationship. *See* line and staff relationship.

stag. A speculator who applies for new issues of shares in the hope of being able to sell his allotment for a capital gain when dealings in them commence on a stock exchange. Popular new issues are invariably oversubscribed (*see* oversubscription) in which case the shares will open at a premium. However, a stag's chance of making a gain will depend on the method adopted for allocating shares (which is usually kept secret). If the stag expects that allocation will favour large applications he will make one large application; if he thinks a ballot is likely he may make several smaller applications. Every application for a new issue on the London Stock Exchange has to be accompanied by a cheque for full payment at the issue price.

stages of production. 1. Phases in the manufacturing process in which the marginal product undergoes significant changes. In the first stage the marginal product of some input (the others being held constant) exceeds the average product. In the second stage, the average product exceeds the marginal product but the latter is still greater than zero. In the third stage the marginal product is negative. Marginal product reaches a maximum in stage one, but production should take place at the beginning of stage three if maximum total output is to be obtained. *See diagram at* economic region of production. *See* labour intensive margin, capital intensive margin.

2. Phases in the manufacturing process in which the product approaches its final form.

stagflation. The combination of stagnation or recession, with rising unemployment, and inflation in an economy. This combination creates difficulties for the inflationary gap theories, which in their usual forms require the economy to be at full employment when inflation occurs.

stagnation thesis. The belief that stagnation is caused in the developed nations because there are no longer enough opportunities for investment to absorb savings, which increase as people become more affluent. The proponents of this view advocate intensive investment projects in such areas as slum clearance. This view was first formulated in 1941 to explain the Depression but was never widely accepted.

stale bull. A dealer or trader who having taken a bull position in a market, especially a commodity market, has a paper profit as market prices have risen since his purchase, but who is unable to close his position as there are no buyers. Stale bulls occur after a sharp market rise that has been foreseen by a substantial number of the dealers in that market, so that although prices have risen there are more sellers than buyers.

stale cheque. A cheque that has not been presented within a reasonable time after its issue. Most banks consider a cheque to be stale six months after the date on the cheque and would return it unpaid marked "out of date". If the drawer then confirms the cheque it will be paid. The Bills of Exchange Act (1882) states that a bill payable on demand is overdue when it appears on the face of it to have been in circulation for an unreasonable length of time, but how long this is has never been legally defined. Many companies require their dividend warrants to be presented for payment within three months after date.

stamp duty. A form of U.K. tax dating from 1694 and imposed on the completion of certain documents, e.g. *deeds. It is either of a fixed amount (usually 50p) or ad valorem (i.e. calculated in accordance with the value of the property transferred by the document). *Transfer stamp duty* is payable on all transfers of ownership of stock exchange securities, except government securities and those bought and sold within an account, and is charged at an ad valorem rate of 1% of the price paid, payable by the purchaser. *Contract stamp duty* (maximum 60p) is payable on all *contract notes between broker and client. For the transfer of property other than securities, with certain exceptions, duty is payable if the value is over £30,000 at a rate of 1% of the total price paid (1984 figures). Documents liable to stamp duty are not legally enforceable until it has been paid and the Inland Revenue's receipt stamp impressed on the document.

standard coin. **1.** The unit of a currency to which other currencies are commonly related when their relative values are computed. The pound is the standard coin of the U.K.; the dollar is the standard coin of the U.S.

2. A unit of currency whose intrinsic value is equal to its face value.

standard costing (in accountancy). A costing system designed to assist in the control of labour, materials, and overheads. The setting of a standard cost for a product follows a similar procedure to costing a job using planned in place of actual figures. The setting of standards requires consideration of the quantities, prices or rates, qualities or grades, and a detailed study of the functions of each element of cost entering into a product, e.g. material, labour, and overheads.

standard deviation. The positive square root of the variance. The standard deviation is the most useful and important of all the measures of dispersion and has all the essential properties of the variance. An advantage it has over the variance is that it is denominated in the same units as those of the original items (whereas the variance is denominated in squares of these units). Thus if it is desired to know the standard deviation of the incomes received by the individuals of a town or nation, then the answer will be in terms of pounds sterling while the variance would be in terms of pounds sterling squared.

standard error. The standard deviation of a sampling distribution. *See also* error.

standard industrial classification (S.I.C.). Schemes for classifying industrial production. Such classifications begin by identifying a broad group of related industries and then each group is subdivided into progressively narrower groups of activities. The U.K. S.I.C. has 10 major divisions (for example, metal goods, engineering and vehicles industries), further subdivided into 60 classes (for example, mechanical engineering), then into 222 groups (for example, industrial plant and steelwork), and 334 activity headings (for example, boilers and process plant). The U.S. S.I.C. is even more detailed.

It categorizes 20 major industrial groups, 200 industrial groups, 1000 product classes, and 7500 products. Each stage has a related code number. For instance, 20 is the food and kindred product industry; 201 is the meat products industry; 2011 are meat packing plants; 20111 is the code number for fresh beef; and 2011112 is whole carcass beef.

standard of deferred payments. *See* store of value.

standard of value. *See* unit of account.

standard rate. The basic rate of *income tax. It is specified in the U.K. by the Finance Act of the current financial year since it is a convention that income tax is an annual tax, which must be renewed each year, rather than a permanent tax. Part of a person's income may be taxed at a greater or lesser rate than the standard rate, depending upon the size of their income and the amount of personal relief that they are entitled to.

stand-by agreement. An agreement between the *International Monetary Fund and a member country to enable that country to arrange for immediate drawing rights.

standing order. *See* banker's order.

state bank. A U.S. commercial bank that has been established by state, rather than by federal, charter. Its trading will be affected by the laws of the particular state in which it is situated. For example, the creation of branches is prohibited in many states. Membership of the *Federal Reserve System (the U.S. central bank) is not compulsory for state banks, although it is compulsory for *national banks.

state lottery. A method of raising large sums of money by selling tickets in a lottery to the public at fixed prices, the proceeds (less the prizes and administration costs) being paid into state funds. The earliest reported state lottery was held in France in 1520. The Irish Sweepstakes lottery has raised considerable sums of money for the benefit of hospitals in Ireland. Many states hold lotteries to finance public programmes and projects and they have been suggested as a means of revenue for U.K. local authorities to supplement the rating system.

statement. 1. *See* bank statement.

2. A document showing the state of one person's or firm's account with another. It summarizes recent invoices and payments and shows the amount owing at the end of the period to which the statement applies. Many firms issue monthly statements to their clients.

Statements of Standard Accounting Practice. The methods of accounting approved by the Council of the Institute of Chartered Accountants in England and Wales in association with various of the other bodies of accountants in the U.K. and the Republic of Ireland, for "application to all financial accounts intended to give a true and fair view of financial position and profit or loss". The purpose of these statements is to standardize and improve the accounting techniques for financial accounts with which a member of the relevant professional body is associated. Significant departures from these standards must be disclosed and explained and, where possible, the differences quantified. They refer to accounting for the results of associated companies, disclosure of accounting policies, earnings per share, the accounting treatment of government grants, accounting for value added tax, extraordinary items and prior year adjustments, and accounting for changes in the purchasing power of money (*see* *inflation accounting). Before standards are finalized they are published as Exposure Drafts inviting comment from members of the profession and other interested bodies. The standard is published after consideration of the various comments.

state ownership. *See* public enterprise, public sector.

state planning. The direction by the government of the economic affairs of the nation. The amount of state planning in a nation will vary according to the prevailing political beliefs, but in all cases it involves overriding the market forces. State planning in the U.K. has become more important in the post-war era with the increase in *nationalization and the attempts of successive governments to maintain *full employment, to control inflation, to attain a satisfactory balance of payments, and to provide adequate social amenities, a high growth rate, etc.

state preference theory. A method of examining the making of decisions when there is *uncertainty in the outcome. It is used primarily to analyse decisions regarding the choice of investments. The model assumes that there are several distinct possibilities as to the future economic situation. Particular types of investment will yield various known returns, given that one of these economic states results. It is assumed that some absolutely certain form of investment exists, i.e. holding money in the bank at a fixed rate of interest. This situation can be plotted given a two-state world, putting the return given in state I on one axis and that given in state II on the other, for any possible decision. The results of all possible forms of investment can then be plotted with money being represented by a point on the 45° line. Joining all these points together the enclosed area represents all the possible outcomes that can be attained given the appropriate diversification of the portfolio. Next a set of indifference curves can be drawn on the graph representing those possible returns in state I or II between which the person is indifferent. Curves farther from the origin will represent a higher level of utility but the shape of the curves, and in fact whether or not they are convex, will depend upon the individual's attitude toward risk, and his assessment of the likelihood of one or another of the states resulting. *See also* mean-variance analysis.

statics. The economic analysis of equilibrium situations. The central property of an equilibrium as it is treated in economics is the inherent lack of tendency for it to change. Static analysis involves the study only of the endogenous variables of the model under consideration; all parameters and exogenous variables involved in the model are assumed to be fixed and are treated as constants for the purposes of the analysis. Static analysis is the simplest form of economic analysis both conceptually and mathematically; most of the techniques involve algebraic operations of a fairly elementary level. In a static model, the number of functionally independent relationships must be equal to the number of endogenous variables in the model. *Compare* comparative statics, dynamics.

Stationery Office. A central U.K. government agency that supplies the home and overseas public service with office supplies, office machinery, and printing facilities. It prints Central Office of Information publications, official reports, forms, explanatory memoranda, and a wide range of specialized books and pamphlets. It acts as a publisher for parliament and the government and determines the selling price of official publications, which are sold at government bookshops in London, Edinburgh, Manchester, Belfast, Bristol, Cardiff, and Birmingham.

statistic. 1. An ascertainable estimate of a statistical *parameter. A statistic is normally calculated from a random sample. *See also* estimation.

2. A single item of statistical data.

statistical inference. The inductive side of applied statistics. It is concerned with the formulation of statements about a statistical population on the basis of a random sample drawn from it. Statistical inference revolves around either the *estimation of a parameter or function of a population or the testing of a *hypothesis about such a parameter or function. For instance, information may be required about the percentage of an electorate that will vote Labour in an election. A random sample of the electorate will be taken and then either the percentage of the sample announcing an intention to vote Labour will be inferred to the entire electorate with or without *confidence limits or else such a percentage will be set independently of the sample and a decision based on an examination of the results of the sample will be made whether to accept or reject this percentage. It should be noted that factors relevant to all voters should have an equal incidence; if, for instance, Labour voters are more apathetic than Conservative voters and are less likely actually to register their votes on polling day, then the simple statistical analysis would be vitiated. Statistical inference and the technique of random sampling are both based on probability and the results of a statistical inference always have a probability of less than unity.

statistical method. One of the two main branches of statistical study. *See* statistics.

statistics. The quantitative study of the observed data of any science. Statistics is a branch of mathematics in which the basic instrument of analysis is *probability; it deals with the description and analysis of groups of aggregates that are too extensive and complex to be intelligible by ordinary observation. Statistics can be divided into two main branches: statistical method and applied statistics. The former is of a theoretical nature and is concerned with the investigation of the mathematical basis of the methods used in statistics, the proof of formulae used, and the testing of the validity of statistical concepts in general. Applied statistics is the practical side of the subject and can itself be divided into deductive statistics, concerned with the collection, classification, abbreviation, and presentation of present or historical data, and inductive statistics or *statistical inference, the function of which is to aid in the establishment of scientific hypotheses by the use of probability. Statistics is based on the hypothesis that aggregates, unlike individuals, behave regularly.

statute-barred debt. A debt that is no longer enforceable by reason of the Limitation Act (1939) because it has been left outstanding for too long. *See* limitation of actions, statutes of limitation.

statute law. A law made by act of parliament. It overrides the law previously in existence, whether this is itself statute law or *common law.

statutes of limitation. Statutes that fix the time limits beyond which rights cannot be claimed. For instance, actions for personal injuries must be initiated within three years of the accident, unless decisive information arises later; claims for rent must be made within six years or the debt lapses; actions for the recovery of land must begin within 12 years.

statutory books. The books that a limited company must keep by law. They are a *share register, a *register of directors, a *register of charges, and minute books. A record of all transactions that is comprehensive enough to be used as a basis for the compiling of annual accounts must also be kept. There are stringent penalties for any failure to comply with these regulations.

statutory company. A company set up by an act of parliament. Such companies were formed for the development of communications (e.g. the former railway companies in the U.K.) or the provision of essential services. *See* joint-stock company.

statutory meeting. A general meeting of the members of a company, which every company limited by shares or limited by guarantee, and having share capital, is required by law to hold within a one- to three-month period from the date on which the company is entitled to commence business. *See also* annual general meeting.

statutory report. A report that must be prepared by the directors of a company and forwarded to the members at least 14 days before the company's *statutory meeting. The directors are required by law to include very detailed information in this report. They must, among other things, give details of shares allotted, the consideration received for them, details of the receipts and payments of the company up to seven days before the date of the report, the names and addresses of directors, the secretary, the auditors and managers of the company, and the total amount of cash received by the company from the issue of shares. Cash figures have to be certified by the auditors.

statutory sick pay. A U.K. government benefit payable by employers, who are compensated by deducting it from their tax returns. From 6 April 1983, statutory sick pay replaced state sickness benefit for most employees for up to 8 weeks' sickness in any tax year. The rates are calculated in three levels (standard, middle, and lower) according to average weekly earnings.

steady-state (balanced) growth path. A growth path in an economy in which all stock and flow variables grow at a constant rate, thus keeping in the same proportion to one another. If their percentage rates of growth are the same, for example labour force, capital stock, etc. are all growing at a rate of 3%, the economy is said to be experiencing *balanced growth*, although actual economies rarely, if ever, achieve this. As a means of economic analysis in growth theory, it is the equivalent of equilibrium in static theory. Under certain conditions it represents a *golden age. The existence and stability of such a path is the object of discussion in the models of Harrod, von Neumann, and Solow, among others.

stepped costs. *See* semivariable costs.

sterilization of gold. The prevention of the effects of an inflow of gold on an economy that is on the *gold standard. The natural effect of such an inflow of gold would be to increase the supply of money and raise prices, but some countries took steps to insulate their economies during the inter-war period when the gold standard was in operation.

sterling. The British pound is referred to as the pound sterling to distinguish it from the pounds of other countries (*see also* pound). The word is thought to be derived from the easterling, a coin of the reign of Richard I that was considered superior to other coins of that time.

sterling area (sterling bloc, scheduled territories). Those countries that have tied their currencies to the pound sterling. The Exchange Control Act (1947), with the intention of preventing the loss of sterling balances, prohibited payment by a resident of the U.K. to an account designated as not being within the scheduled territories, unless permission had been given by the Bank of England. However, with the recurrent pressures on sterling from 1960 onwards, and the losses suffered by them when sterling was devalued, many of the members of the sterling area started to keep part of their reserves in other currencies; exchange controls were finally abolished in 1979. *See also* reserve currency.

sterling balances. Liquid holdings of sterling that can be drawn upon immediately by their foreign owners. Although some are held by private individuals and companies, most are held by foreign central banks as a *reserve currency. The use of sterling in this capacity has declined markedly since 1950, largely due to the U.K.'s continuing balance of payment problems. There has been some revival in sterling's fortunes recently with the emergence of the U.K. as an oil producer.

stochastic disturbance. The residual or error term of a *regression equation. A diagrammatic representation of regression points will invariably display a scatter rather than a precise function to which an exact mathematical fit can be attached. The stochastic term can be interpreted as representing the gap between the scatter points and whatever function is fitted to them. There will always be a stochastic term in regression equations in the social sciences because in any theory in this field it will not be feasible to insert the totality of all the relevant factors in an equation because many of them will be unquantifiable and, furthermore, over and above all the relevant objective factors there will still be an element of randomness due to the unpredictability of human behaviour. *See also* multiple regression, least squares estimation.

stock. 1. In the U.K. the term is usually used in reference to a *fixed-interest security issued and quoted in units of £100. However, the term is sometimes used synonymously with *ordinary shares (or with ordinary shares and fixed-interest securities collectively), as in the term *growth stocks.* In the U.S.A., however, where ordinary shares are called *common stock*, the term is used quite generally in reference to ordinary shares.

2. The quantity of raw materials, components, work-in-progress, and finished goods held by a company. In the U.S. the word *inventory is usually used.

stock appreciation (*or* **depreciation).** The part of any change in the total value of stocks during any period that is accounted for by inflation (or disinflation). When calculating gross national product, only that part of the change in the value of stocks that is accounted for by a change in their physical volume can be included; stock appreciation (or depreciation) is a capital gain (or loss) and must be excluded. The actual calculation of stock appreciation presents substantial statistical problems.

stockbroker. An agent professionally engaged in the purchase and sale of securities on a stock exchange on behalf of clients; in exchange for these services a stockbroker charges commission. The actual mechanism of dealing on the London Stock Exchange follows the principle that the stockbroker, who alone is allowed to have contact with the investing public, enquires of a stockjobber the buying and selling (*bid and *offer) prices of the particular security with respect to which he has received an instruction from a client and, according to the nature and terms of the instruction, may then conclude a *bargain. The procedure on the floor of the Exchange is informal and a bargain may be struck orally. Stockbrokers attached to the highly developed exchanges of New York, London, and Tokyo are generally organized into firms which, in London, are either partnerships (with unlimited liability) or limited companies in which one or more directors accept unlimited liability on their own accounts. Many stockbroking firms maintain computerized research departments in which investment analysts formulate purchase and sale recommendations (in respect of particular shares), which the firm then passes on to its clients, notably *institutional investors. Some firms attempt to supplement their commission income by providing loans to clients with which the latter can buy securities on collateral represented by the same securities; the Council of the Stock Exchange is known to disapprove of this practice. *See also* stock exchange, hammering. *Compare* stockjobber.

stock concept. A quantitative concept in economics that is independent of the dimension of time, although it does not necessarily remain constant over a period of time. For example, the capital stock of an economy exists at any point in time as a magnitude that can be measured. Investment, however, can only be defined with reference to a particular unit of time. In the economy, £100 million of investment takes on a different meaning if it takes place in one year rather than one week, whereas the idea of £100 million of capital is free of the time dimension.

By analogy with a trip in a motor car, distance travelled would be a stock concept and speed the corresponding *flow concept. Stock concepts must also be distinguished from ratio concepts, which may also be independent of time: for example, a price may be taken as the ratio of two flow concepts, money and goods. Again by analogy with a trip, the relative speeds of two cars would be a ratio concept.

The importance of maintaining this three-part distinction is that logical absurdities may easily result from an indiscriminate mixing of these concepts.

stock control (inventory control). The regulation of the quantities of stock carried by a company in order to meet current needs without holding excess reserves. Levels of maximum stock, minimum stock, and re-order points are usually set by all large concerns for every stock item. *See also* inventory.

stock cover. The period of time that the stocks of raw materials of a firm could last without replenishment, if sales continued at the existing rate.

stock exchange. A market in which *securities can be purchased and sold. Stock exchanges provide a medium through which savers can build up liquid assets that have (historically) provided a good hedge against inflation. Apart from its function as a means of dealing in financial securities, a stock exchange is also an essential part of the capital market in capitalist nations; it is through a stock exchange that new companies offer their shares to the public. Although virtually all advanced industrial capitalist economies have stock exchanges, their relative importance differs greatly in different countries. The three largest national stock exchanges are to be found in the U.S.A., Japan, and the U.K. and it is in these three countries that the stock exchanges have most relative importance. All the reputable stock exchanges have evolved a set of rules and requirements, which are in many cases considerably more stringent than prevailing company legislation, to which companies must conform before their securities are granted *quotations. Most stock exchanges have also developed in conjunction with certain related institutions, notably professional brokerage houses, merchant banks, and *institutional investors. *See also* London Stock Exchange; New York Stock Exchange.

Stock Exchange Daily Official List. *See* Official List.

stock fluctuations. *See* inventory.

stock-in-trade. 1. *See* stock (def. 2).

2. The type of goods or services that a firm or individual normally offers for sale.

stockjobber. A dealer engaged in the wholesaling of securities on a stock exchange. Stockjobbers, like stockbrokers, are professional members of the London Stock Exchange but, unlike the latter, cannot deal with the public but only with brokers or other jobbers. The U.K. is the only country in which the activities of stockbrokers and jobbers are kept separate (*see* dual capacity): members of the Stock Exchange cannot be both brokers and jobbers. A stockjobber's remuneration is determined by the volume of dealings and by the jobber's turn, the difference between his *bid and *offer prices (i.e. the difference between the price at which he is prepared to buy stock and the price at which he is prepared to sell). A stockjobber's quotation is thus nearly always characterized by two separate prices. Stockjobbing on the London Exchange is however highly competitive and requires a high degree of experience; if a stockbroker concludes a *bargain by purchasing stock that the jobber does not possess, the latter must cancel his *short position by bidding to other jobbers for the stock in question. Stockjobbers, like stockbrokers, usually organize themselves into firms (with unlimited liability) and, to a much greater extent than the brokers, tend to specialize in one or two particular sectors of the market, e.g. gilt-edged securities or gold-mining stocks. In the U.S. the word *jobber* refers to a dealer selling often worthless securities: the terms *specialist* or simply *dealer* are used. *See also* stock exchange, jobber's turn. *Compare* stockbroker.

stock of money. *See* money supply.

stockpiling. The accumulation of strategic raw materials or other commodities that are essential to national defence. If a nation's supply of such commodities falls below the level that might be required in a national emergency, stockpiles have to be built up. Stockpiling also refers to reserves of materials held for use during a shortage.

stock policies. Special insurance policies covering stock, where substantial fluctuations in the value of the risk can occur throughout the period of the policy, and normal fire insurance policies are therefore unsuitable. To cover such risks various policies are used. For example, an estimated sum insured can be covered, based on the maximum amount thought likely to be at risk; 75% of the premium is paid provisionally and the actual amounts at risk during the course of the year are submitted in periodic declarations. At the end of the year the average stock at risk is calculated and the final premium statement is prepared.

stock split. The U.S. term for a *bonus issue. A *1 for 5* bonus issue would however be called a *6 for 5* stock split in the U.S.; i.e. five old shares are replaced by six new shares.

stocktaking. The compilation of an *inventory of stocks by a business or other organization. *See* stock valuation.

stock (inventory) turnover. The rate at which stocks are sold, expressed as the ratio of sales (valued at cost or sometimes at net sales value) during a given period to the average value of the stock carried during the same period. This ratio is often used to investigate the market success of a particular type of product or the output of a company, especially by comparing it with the turnover in previous years or with its competitors. The rate of stock turnover varies from one product to another, being highest for perishables.

stock watering. The issuing of new shares in a company to such an extent that the issued capital exceeds the value of its tangible assets. This means that the previous dividend cannot be maintained on the new capital. It also means that if the company is liquidated its shareholders cannot be paid out in full. Watered stock is created when the issue of new shares is unjustified in terms of assets, but the company may still be making good profits. *See also* overcapitalization.

stolen bills or cheques. If a completed negotiable bill of exchange is stolen, a holder who took it in good faith and without notice of the defective title is entitled to payment of the bill, and payment by the acceptor in good faith at maturity is a good discharge of the bill. If an open cheque is stolen, and the banker on whom it is drawn in the ordinary course of business pays it in good faith, he is entitled to debit the cheque to the drawer's account. In the case of a crossed cheque, the paying banker is protected if he pays the cheque to a collecting banker and whether or not the collecting banker is liable depends upon whether he acted with negligence. In the case of a crossed cheque marked "not negotiable" no one can obtain a good title to the cheque from the thief. *See also* negligence, negotiability.

stop-go. A form of *stabilization policy in which the government seeks to reflate the economy when there is high unemployment, and then must cut back as the economy begins to inflate as a result. The level of governmental fiscal and monetary intervention varies in phase with the business cycle, inflating during recession and deflating during boom. The term has become extremely perjorative implying that the government whose policies are so described cannot plan and carry out successfully long-term projects and also implying that they are at the mercy of external events.

stop-loss order. An instruction given to a broker by a client to sell a holding in a security or commodity when its price falls to a specified minimum, thus "stopping the loss". The same term is occasionally used when a *bear speculator sells short and wants his broker to buy back if the price rises to a specified maximum.

stoppage in transitu. The act of taking over goods or commercial documents while they are in transit to a buyer who has not paid for them and who has become insolvent.

storage device. Any device used to hold the information in a computer. Storage devices are classified as *direct-* or *random-access* devices, in which any part of the data can be obtained at will, and *sequential-access* devices, in which the whole corpus of data must be searched in sequence in order to find the part required. Direct access is much faster than sequential access. Most computer systems have more than one type of storage device. The *memory (or *main store*) is used to hold material that must be immediately accessible to the central processing unit. Associated with this are various *backing stores*, which have slower access but can hold vast amounts of information. These are usually *magnetic tapes, *magnetic disks, and *magnetic drums.

store. *See* storage device.

store of value. A function of money that enables the acquisition of goods and services to be delayed. In a pure barter economy a person must accept goods immediately in exchange for his own goods. In a monetary economy the selection of goods can be delayed; value is effectively stored in the money. This increases the individual's freedom of action. However, money is only a satisfactory store of value in times of price stability. In periods of *hyperinflation, money loses its value and other goods, such as consumer goods, may be used instead.

straight-line method. A means of calculating the depreciation of an asset. An equal amount of money is set aside for each year of the asset's lifespan, the annual depreciation being calculated by the formula:

$$(P\text{-}L)/n,$$

where P is the initial cost of the asset, L is its value as scrap, and n is its lifespan.

stranding. The running aground of a ship as a result of some unusual accident, such as being driven onto rocks by an unexpected obstruction. As used in *marine insurance policies, stranding does not include running aground in the normal course of navigation or when the ship can be refloated by the tide.

strategic planning. *See* corporate planning.

strategy. One of several courses of action open to a player in *game theory. A pure strategy is one in which a participant keeps to the same strategies in fixed proportions, although the strategy for any one game may be randomly selected.

stratified random sample. *See* random sample.

street-name stocks. U.S. negotiable securities that are purchased on behalf of a client, but listed as being owned by a brokerage house. They are therefore similar to U.K. *nominee shareholdings.

strike. A concerted voluntary refusal on the part of a workforce, or a part of it, to continue to work unless the employers concede to their demands. In a responsible workforce, the strike is the last weapon to be used against employers and is only resorted to if all other forms of negotiations have broken down.

If the strike has the backing of a recognized trade union it is called an *official strike* (or more euphemistically a *withdrawal of labour*). Trade unions issue strike pay to their members during official strikes, for as long as the funds last. If a strike does not have union backing it is called an *unofficial strike* and no strike pay is available. If the strike is in breach of a procedural agreement it is an *unconstitutional strike*, whether it has union backing or not. An unconstitutional strike called at short notice is often called a *wildcat strike.* An official strike called by a union in support of another union's dispute is called a *sympathetic strike.*

Measures of the extent of strike action include numbers of workers involved, number of strikes, number of man-days lost, and percentage of available working time lost in strikes. *See also* picketing.

structural unemployment. Long-term unemployment caused by changes in the industrial, occupational, and demographic structure of the economy. It is created by the inability of the economy to adapt readily to changing conditions, such as the decline in demand for a product (*see* mobility). A U.K. example is the unemployment created on Clydeside by the decline in shipbuilding. Structural unemployment is often highly localized and persistent. Its eradication has been one of the major aims of the U.K. government's regional development policies (*see* location of industries).

Student's t distribution. A statistical *distribution involving a continuous variable. A Student's t variable is the ratio of a standard normal variable and the square root of a chi-square variable divided by its degrees of freedom; it will have the same number of degrees of freedom as its chi-square denominator. Student's t is a useful distribution because its application to hypothesis testing does not depend on knowledge of any population parameters (which are likely to be unknown), nor is it required that the basic variable under analysis be normally distributed. Hence it can be used to test a mean, the difference between two means, a regression coefficient, a correlation coefficient, or a predictor even with a small sample drawn from a non-normal distribution. The testing procedure is by way of specified formulae and with reference to tables (worked out by a statistician who wrote under the pen-name of Student) from which, for any specified degrees of freedom, the result of the test can be ascertained.

sub-agent. An agent of an agent, rather than an agent of a principal. For example, a U.K. manufacturer may have an agent in Milan for selling his produce throughout Italy. This agent may not have his own office or representative in Naples and may, with the agreement of the U.K. principal, appoint a sub-agent in Naples.

sub-lease. *See* head lease.

subrogation. The entitlement of an insurer, once a claim has been paid, to any rights of the insured against third parties in respect of the subject matter of the insurance, up to the limit of his payment under the policy. The insurer, on giving an indemnity for costs, may compel the insured to lend his name to an action against a third party. Only if the insurer has paid for total loss can he take over the subject matter of the insurance and the rights relating to it; if only partial loss has been paid the insurer may only take over the rights.

A very common example in which subrogation rights arise is in motor insurance. For example, a motorist insured under a comprehensive policy has two sources of compensation if another motorist negligently damages his vehicle: from his own insurers and from the negligent motorist. If he decides to claim under his own policy, his insurers are in due course subrogated to his rights against the third party. They can thus recover any money paid under their policy, and the insured is not paid twice for the same damage.

subscribed capital. *See* issued capital.

subscription shares. Shares that can be paid for in regular instalments. Subscription shares are an important source of the capital of *building societies.

subsidiary company. A company of which another company is a member and has control of the composition of the board of directors, or holds more than half in nominal value of its equity share capital. The essential point is that a subsidiary company is controlled by another company. A precise legal definition of a subsidiary company is given in the Companies Act (1948): companies that possess subsidiaries have certain legal obligations such as presenting *consolidated accounts in which information must be laid out in specific ways. *See also* holding company.

subsidy. A payment made by a government to one or more firms to prevent an increase in the price of a product or to prevent the decline of a firm or industry. In general, subsidies distort the pattern of international trade by encouraging inefficiency, but are justified in some instances, for example, to protect an infant industry or to equalize *private costs and *social costs. *Compare* tariff.

subsistence level. The standard of living below which life cannot be maintained. Malthus, Ricardo, Marx, and other nineteenth-century economists believed that the long-run level of wages would be not higher than the subsistence level of wages. However, this belief has not been borne out in the developed nations.

subsistence wage. The lowest wage rate that enables a worker to survive. Over an entire population it is that wage that just allows the labour force to stay constant or grow in proportion to the capacity of the system. It can be interpreted less harshly as the wage that for social reasons induces sufficient growth in the labour force and therefore can rise as aspirations rise. In a Malthusian population model it is the long-run equilibrium wage. If it is too high it will lead to too many labourers for a given physical capital capacity, and a shortfall will deplete the labour force and wages will be bid up.

substantial and individual interest. *See* nominee shareholding.

substantial damages. *See* damages.

substantive motion. *See* motion.

substitution effect. The change in a consumer's demand for a good that is caused by an alteration in the relative prices of the goods rather than by a change in the consumer's real income. For example, an increase in the price of one good will make all others relatively cheaper. Therefore, *ceteris paribus, the quantity that is demanded of the first good will fall while demand for the others will rise. The substitution effect plus the *income effect constitute the total change in demand that is caused by an alteration in price. Consequently, the strength of the substitution effect after a price change can be discovered by compensating for any changes in real income so nullifying the income effect.

It can be shown that, assuming the consumer is consistent, the substitution effect for the good whose price changes is always negative, i.e. the tendency is always to buy less of a good when its price rises and vice versa. However, the total change in demand will depend upon the direction and magnitude of the income effect: if it varies directly with real income the two effects reinforce each other and the product is a *normal good; if it varies inversely with real income but is weaker than the substitution effect the product is an *inferior good; if it varies inversely with real income and is stronger than the substitution effect the product is a *Giffen good.

Substitution effects are also caused by changes in the prices of other goods. If an increase in the price of one good causes less of another to be bought the two goods are directly related and are considered to be *complements; examples are cars and petrol or air fares to Switzerland and ski equipment. Alternatively, if a price increase for one good causes more of another to be bought the two are considered to be *substitutes; electricity and gas or fresh and frozen vegetables are typical examples.

sue and labour clause. A clause in some *marine insurance policies that allows the insured to take any action necessary to alleviate a loss.

sufficiency. A statistical *estimator is said to be sufficient if it can be shown mathematically that the conditional distribution of any other independent estimate, given the sufficient estimator, does not involve the parameter being estimated. Sufficiency is one of the desirable properties of estimators.

sunk capital. *See* fixed capital.

sun spot theory. The theory proposed by W. S. Jevons (1835–82) that the *trade cycle was caused by variations in harvests, which were affected in turn by sun spots. Jevons estimated the average length of the trade cycle to be 10.44 years, whereas the average length of the sun spot cycle was 10.45 years. The theory was abandoned when the results of later calculations differed on the length of the trade cycle. More important, an explanation based on agricultural fluctuations is unconvincing when applied to an industrialized economy.

supertax. A U.K. tax on large incomes that existed from 1909 to 1927. It was replaced by *surtax.

supplementary benefits. The Supplementary Benefits Act (1966) provided that everyone over sixteen years of age in the U.K. who is not in full time work, attending work, or involved in a trade dispute, is entitled to a supplementary benefit if his resources are insufficient to meet his requirements. The benefit takes the form of *supplementary allowance* for people under retirement age and a *supplementary pension* for those over this age.

Those receiving supplementary benefit and their dependants are automatically entitled to a number of other items free of charge: prescriptions, milk and vitamins, dental treatment, school meals, legal aid, family planning, as well as concessionary fares and rent and rate rebates.

supplementary costs. *See* costs.

supplementary pension. *See* supplementary benefits.

supply and demand. According to the laws of supply and demand if the demand for a product exceeds its supply, its price will rise. This will encourage producers to manufacture more of the product while, at the same time, causing the demand for the product to fall. These trends will continue until the supply and demand of the product are equal. At that point the *market forces are in *equilibrium.

If the supply of a product exceeds the demand for it there will be a glut and its price will fall. This will encourage consumers to buy more while, at the same time, causing producers to cut back on production. Rising demand and falling supply will continue to converge until they equal each other. At that point the market is in equilibrium.

The *laissez-faire economists believed that the laws of supply and demand were in themselves sufficient to regulate an economy.

supply curve. A curve that relates the amount of a good a supplier will supply with the minimum price at which he will supply that amount, the price of his inputs and other outputs being held constant. It is assumed that there are no technological improvements in the process of production in the short run and so the supply curve is unaffected. In the long run, technological improvements will reduce production costs and this will be represented by a movement of the supply curve to the right.

The curve can be considered to be the graph of the *production function, holding all variables other than the price of the particular good constant. It is customary to plot the price on the vertical axis and quantity on the horizontal axis. The supply curve usually slopes upwards to the right, indicating a direct relationship between price and quantity supplied, but there are exceptions, such as the *regressive supply curve for labour.

Increases in the prices of inputs will shift the supply curve to the left and alter its shape. As with *demand curves, the supply curves of individuals may be aggregated to obtain a market supply curve. According to the standard theory of the *firm, the supply curve should follow the marginal cost curve about the *shut-down point. The intersection of the supply curve with the demand curve indicates the equilibrium price of a good.

supply schedule. A table showing the quantity of a product that a producer is willing to manufacture at every possible price. Supply schedules provide the data from which *supply curves can be derived.

suppressed (repressed) inflation. Inflation that is prevented from causing prices to rise. This can only be achieved by extensive governmental interference in the economy. Measures leading to suppressed inflation might include an effective incomes policy to prevent an increase in the cost of labour, and wheat subsidies to prevent a rise in the price of bread. Although in these circumstances inflation is disguised it still exists and, unless it is cured, will probably reappear because governmental measures are unlikely to be comprehensive enough to completely control it.

supra protest. *See* acceptance supra protest.

surety. **1.** A guarantor for another's actions.

2. A *guarantee, usually a sum of money held as evidence of good faith.

surplus. *See* consumer's surplus, producer's surplus.

surplus capacity. *See* excess capacity.

surplus value. The difference in value of labour embodied in the production of a good minus the total wages bill (*variable capital). The difference occurs, according to Marx, because labour is bought and sold on the open market, where labour is paid not according to the value of its output (which totally equals the value of the product) but according to the labour costs involved in the production of labour itself, like any other commodity. However this "exchange value of labour power" is less than the "use value of labour". The worker works longer than is necessary to sustain himself; the remainder of his product accrues to the capitalist as profit. This surplus value is not a market phenomenon like *excess profits, but is a technologically determined rate (varying with the efficiency of production) inherent in the capitalist mode of production (the use of labour as any other commodity). The existence of surplus value is merely the statement that labour is productive. In this way the exploitation inherent in surplus value can only be eliminated by bringing the means of production under the control of the worker himself, so that he receives his own surplus value.

surrender value. A monetary value acquired by certain types of life assurance policies (endowment and whole life) on their surrender by the assured after they have been in force for perhaps two years. Prior to this all the premiums paid and bonuses accrued are reckoned to be totally absorbed by the risk run and the administration charges. Normally the size of the surrender value will be less than the premiums paid and bonuses accrued.

surrogate production function. A schedule, first introduced by Paul Samuelson (*b.* 1915), relating total output to total aggregate capital and total labour as inputs. The point of the surrogate production function is that in the actual world capital goods are heterogeneous and nontransferable in use, but it is analytically convenient to treat the world as if capital stock was a homogeneous "jelly". In a world with many techniques and heterogeneous capital, in the absence of double switching and capital reversing, it is possible to use the *factor-price frontier to derive an aggregate for capital, given competitive prices and total labour employed. This aggregate, together with labour and the amount of output, reveals a production function with the desirable property that the marginal products of the "as if" production function are proportional to the prices of the inputs. The distribution of income between labour and capital can be explored in an aggregate model. Furthermore the production function will exhibit *constant returns to scale, the rate of profit will fall as the capital labour ratio increases, and so the *isoquant map of the production function will be convex towards the origin (diminishing marginal returns). In this manner the use of aggregate production models for the study of disaggregated worlds can be justified in theoretical models and, perhaps more importantly, for quantitative use.

surtax. A tax levied on those with the highest incomes. It increased the *marginal rate of taxation on high incomes, thus making the taxation of income more progressive. In the U.K. it was introduced in Lloyd George's "People's Budget" of 1909 as supertax. As it was paid in arrears on 1 January of each year it never completely harmonized with the income tax system (paid under P.A.Y.E.) because of different methods of collection, difficulties of assessment, etc. Consequently, it was abolished in April 1973 and replaced by a unified income tax covering all levels of income.

swaps. The exchange of monies denominated in the same currency but arranged on different terms. For instance, a foreign exchange dealer may sell deutschmarks for delivery now and at the same time buy them back, but for delivery in one month's time.

switching. 1. The transfer of investment funds between different classes of securities on a stock exchange. This may take the form of straight *arbitrage operations, as when a small anomaly emerges in the price of comparable gilt-edged securities; in such cases very large funds are needed to produce a profit on the tiny margins available. In the context of *equity holdings, especially those of institutional investors, switching is the term used when funds are transferred from one share to another in the same sector of the market. *Equity switchings* are made when it is considered that the share price of one company looks dear while that of another company (in the same industry) looks cheap in the light of the different circumstances and prospects characterizing the two companies.

2. *See* double switching.

S.W.O.T. analysis (in management). The analysis of an organization's *s*trengths, *w*eaknesses, *o*pportunities, and *t*hreats. These facets are dealt with in the *position audit.

sympathetic strike. *See* strike.

syndicate. An association of individuals or organizations who work together for a common aim whilst retaining their independence. For example, underwriters at Lloyd's work in syndicates; also the London discount houses form a syndicate to agree on a uniform price at which to tender for Treasury bills. *See also* consortium.

syndicated bid. A weekly tender for Treasury bills that is made by the members of the London Discount Market Association acting in concert.

synergy (in management). The combining of resources to produce a better result than that which could be achieved by the individual component parts. Synergy can be described as the "2 + 2 = 5 effect": e.g. Company A: profit £5m; Company B: profit £4m, but if they were joined together their joint profits would be £12m. This could be a result of production improvements or economies of scale, making better use of the sales force, channels of distribution, etc.

systematic sample. A sample selected according to some system, such as by taking individuals in a group or population whose birthdays occur between certain days of the month. As long as the system by which the sample is constructed has no relevance to the purpose in hand, a systematic sample is as good as a *random sample.

systems analysis. The set of techniques concerned with analysis of procedures and of methods of doing things, and with the design and implementation of new and superior systems. Since the introduction of computers, the term has acquired a more specialized meaning. Systems analysis now usually refers to the design of computer programs at a level senior to that of programming. Its major functions are the definition of the problem, the examination of existing software in the context of the problem, the determination of the requirements of a program designed for the problem, the design of a program that is both efficient for the purpose and economical of available hardware and software, the communication of the program to computer programmers and operators and of its interpretation to the client, and the availability of assistance in the program's implementation and maintenance. *See also* computer programming.

system software. *See* program.

T

Tableau Économique. A diagram constructed by the *physiocrats representing the circular flow of income, emphasizing in particular the interdependencies in the economy. The economy is divided into three sectors, agricultural, landowning, and artisan. At the beginning of the period farmers are in possession of savings from last year's harvest. This is paid as rent to landlords who in turn purchase food and manufactured goods. These receipts in turn just cover the expenditures of farmers on manufactured goods to cover depreciation, and artisans on food and rent. In the end farmers have produced enough to just replace the initial stock and the cycle is repeated. The physiocrats had discovered a simplified closed Leontieff input-output system, which just sustains itself.

takeover. The acquisition of the shares of one company by another or, very occasionally, by an individual. Takeovers may be financed either with cash or with the shares or loan stock of the acquiring company, or with both. In either case the takeover price, i.e. the offer that the acquiring company makes for the shares of the company it wishes to take over, will usually be significantly in excess of their prevailing market price. For this reason takeover rumours relating to a particular company will tend to cause its share price to be marked up sharply on a stock exchange. A takeover bid, the technical name for which is an *offer to purchase*, is, as its name implies, an offer addressed by one company to the shareholders of another to buy the shares of the latter at a specified price. Takeovers of companies quoted on the London Stock Exchange are subject to the rules of the *Panel on Takeovers and Mergers as well as those of company legislation. The term is generally used in those cases in which the initiative for the acquisition comes from the acquiring company and in which the board of the target company may or may not be fully in favour of the bid.

takeover bid. An attempt made by one company to gain control of another. The offer will either be a purely cash bid or, more frequently in large bids, an offer in shares in the acquiring company together with a cash adjustment. The price offered for the shares will invariably be higher than their current price on the Stock Exchange whatever the composition of the bid. The bid itself may be conditional or unconditional. If it is conditional the acquiring firm will only pay its offered price if it receives enough shares to gain control. If it is unconditional the firm will pay the offered price regardless of the number of shares it acquires. A takeover bid may be conditional at first and then become unconditional once it is certain to succeed. A major difference between a takeover and a *merger is that the takeover is often in spite of opposition from the directors of the target company whereas in a merger they willingly cooperate. *See also* City Code.

Takeover Panel. *See* Panel on Takeovers and Mergers.

TALISMAN (*T*ransfer *A*ccounting, *L*odging for *I*nvestors, and *S*tock *Man*agement for jobbers). The computerized system for arranging the transfer and settlement of shares on the U.K. Stock Exchange, including claiming any dividends due on shares being transferred for the appropriate shareholder.

tallyman. 1. A person who works at a dock and checks that a ship's cargo has been correctly unloaded, i.e. checks that the goods unloaded tally with a list of the goods. Sometimes called a *tally clerk.*

2. A salesman or trader who sells goods on credit for payment by instalments, which are recorded in a tallybook.

talon. The last warrant to be detached from a bearer bond. Presentation of the talon enables the holder to acquire a new sheet of *coupons when the old sheet is exhausted.

tangible assets. The real assets of a firm that are not for sale. They are mainly the capital equipment and plant of a firm, rather than the stocks of unsold products.

tape. 1. *See* magnetic tape.

2. *See* punched tape.

tape punch. *See* punched tape.

tape reader. *See* punched tape.

tap issue. The issue of securities and bills at a price chosen in consultation with the Bank of England direct to government departments and other buyers by the Treasury, without going through the markets.

tap stocks. Securities that are always available, especially *gilt-edged securities that are automatically sold by the relevant government department when their market price reaches a certain level. Short taps are short-dated stocks, long taps are long-dated.

tare. The weight of the container in which goods are transported. It is deducted from the gross weight to find the net weight of the articles or produce carried.

target price. *See* Common Agricultural Policy.

tariff. A tax applied to imports either as a percentage of their value or on a unit basis. The effect of a tariff is usually to reduce the amount of trade and improve the international terms of trade of the tariff imposer; it also causes a rise in the domestic price of the imported good.

The welfare implications of a tariff to its imposer are twofold. First, there is a welfare loss through the misallocation of resources involving both a production inefficiency (since in the domestic market firms produce more of the imported good at a higher marginal cost than necessary) and a loss of consumer surplus (since less is consumed at this higher price even if the government's tariff revenue is redistributed). Secondly, there is a gain to the tariff imposer since he has improved his terms of trade, in essence exploiting a monopoly position in the world market. This gain will only be possible if he is free from the fear of retaliation from his trading partners, either because his exports cannot be replaced or for institutional or political reasons. Even assuming that retaliation is impossible, the allocation of resources in the international market will not be *Pareto optimal.

Other arguments for the imposition of tariffs include: their use as short term retaliatory measures against trading partners (*see* dumping) or for rectifying distortions in the domestic commodity and factor markets (*see* infant industry); they may also serve as a short-term policy instrument for stimulating domestic economic activity, taking care of a balance of payments deficit, or protecting industries vital for national security. All these arguments are however disputed to various degrees.

tariff organizations. Organizations of insurance companies formed because of the need, particularly in the early years of a class of business, for pooling statistical information. Because the detailed analysis of such information is essential in insurance, it was obviously sensible for insurers to share their experiences, especially when no insurer could boast of very long experience. The other principal aim of a tariff organization was to fix basic minimum rates for particular risks, in order to ensure that competition did not cut rates below an economic figure. As a consequence, policy forms and risk assessment became standardized, since the offering of wider forms of cover for the same price, or classifying risks differently, could have the same effect as rate-cutting.

task bonus. *See* premium bonus.

tâtonnement. A model of a bargaining process in which all sales and purchases take place simultaneously at the equilibrium price level. This is found in Walras's *general equilibrium model of the economy. Tâtonnement would take place if an auctioneer existed who controlled all sales and purchases; although this is impossible (even for a centralized economy) it is an assumption that eases analysis of the general equilibrium model.

tautology. *See* hypothesis (def. 2).

taxable income. The *tax base for income tax. It is calculated by subtracting allowable deductions (*personal allowances) from gross income. The income assessable for income tax in the U.K. includes: wages, salaries, bonuses, commission, certain benefits in kind, Christmas boxes, furnished lettings, interest, dividends, pensions, business profits, certain social security benefits, and tips connected with business. *See also* nontaxable income.

taxation. Transfer payments to the government from the private sector, which constitute the principal source of revenue to finance government expenditure and also act as an instrument of fiscal policy. In the U.K., the taxation of the earnings of individuals is known as *income tax and that of corporations is known as *corporation tax. Increases of individuals' wealth are taxed by *capital gains tax and *capital transfer tax and those of corporations are treated as part of their earnings for corporation tax purposes. Generally, as in the cases mentioned above, a tax charge results from a movement in money, such as the earning of an income or a realized gain in wealth, but taxes can also be applied to the status quo, for example a wealth tax. *See also* direct taxation, indirect taxation, taxable income, economic effects of taxation.

tax avoidance. The minimizing of one's liability for tax by legal means. *Compare* tax evasion.

tax base. The measure upon which the size of the tax liability is based. For example, *taxable income is the tax base for income tax and rateable value is the tax base for rates.

tax burden. The amount of tax paid by the taxpayer and the costs incurred. It does not take into account distortions in the economic system. *See also* shifting tax, tax incidence.

tax credit system. A unified system of taxation that resembles the traditional system in so far as it advocates a general structure of allowances that can be offset against income before the tax assessment is made. Its essential difference arises when these allowances exceed an individual's gross income if, for example, he is a low income earner or unemployed. In this situation the individual would be paid, by the state, the difference between the level of his personal allowances and income. This system could thus replace a social security system. *See* negative income tax.

tax evasion. The deliberate attempt to defraud the tax authorities by an individual or company by not declaring or giving false figures for his revenue or assets for tax assessment. For example, omitting to declare a taxable capital gain made on the stock exchange is tax evasion. *Compare* tax avoidance.

tax haven. A country, independent area, etc., that has low taxes and therefore offers tax advantages to foreign individuals, who may wish to reside there, or to foreign companies, who may wish to open offices there.

tax incidence. The eventual real impact of taxes, taking into account any *shifting of tax. After all the effects of the imposition of a system of taxes have been worked out, then a comparison between purchasing power in the nontaxed situation and the aftertax situation reveals tax incidence. For example, if a *payroll tax is applied to workers and they are able to raise wages to compensate, and if employers can shift the tax-induced wage rise onto consumers by increasing the price of the product, then the eventual incidence of the tax is on the consumer. The amount of tax shifted and its relative incidence depends upon comparison of the relevant elasticities of supply and demand for labour and for the product. This obviously makes accounting of effective progressivity of taxation difficult. If higher paid earners can shift their tax more easily onto lower paid workers then a tax system with a progressive *tax burden need not have a progressive incidence.

tax loss. 1. A capital loss that, when established, can be offset against any capital gains for purposes of *capital gains tax.

2. An income tax loss sustained by a business, e.g. sole trader or partnership. Such losses may be relieved in a number of ways, e.g. against future business profits, or against other income of the tax payer.

3. A corporation tax loss. Companies pay corporation tax and may obtain relief for losses in a number of ways, e.g. by carrying the loss forward and offsetting it against future profits.

tax schedules. *See* schedules.

tax shifting. *See* shifting tax.

tax year. *See* financial year.

Taylor system. A piece-work scheme devised by F.W. Taylor (1856–1915), an American businessman. A standard payment and time is set for the completion of each task. A bonus is payable, which varies inversely with the actual time taken.

technical rally. A *rally on a financial market brought about by an excess of buyers over sellers (and not by sentiment). A technical rally usually takes place on a stock exchange when shares in general (or a particular share) are "oversold", i.e. when unfavourable sentiment has brought about such a fall that insufficient sellers appear. In commodity markets it usually occurs when the commodity in question is in short supply at origin.

technological change. Alteration in the level of output achieved with a static amount of inputs as a result of improvements in scientific knowledge and technology. This means that the average cost of production per unit of output falls, although input prices are unchanged. There are two forms of technological change: improvements in processes and product innovations, i.e. "novel ways of making old goods ... and old ways of making novelties". Together they have been responsible for the explosive growth in national income in the last 200 years. However, not only will technological change increase output, but it will also probably affect the ratio of capital to labour that is used in the process (according to whether the innovation is capital- or labour-saving) and this in turn will have significant effects on the economy as a whole. For this reason, much work has been undertaken that attempts to classify technological changes according to their effects on the relative shares of capital and labour employed. It is regarded as being Hicks-neutral if, given constant returns to scale, the marginal rate of technical substitution is unchanged for a fixed *capital-labour ratio. That is, it is of the form $Y = \mathrm{T}(t)\mathrm{F}(K,L)$, where Y is output, $\mathrm{T}(t)$ is the time-dependent factor of technological change, and $\mathrm{F}(K,L)$ determines the shape of the isoquants as a function of the inputs, capital, K, and labour, L. On the other hand the technological change is labour-saving if more capital is used for a given factor-price ratio, i.e. if the marginal product of capital rises for a fixed capital-labour ratio and there is a similar definition of capital-saving (labour-using) technological change. Technological change is Harrod-neutral (labour-augmenting) if the new capital-labour ratio, which leaves the marginal product of capital unchanged, also leaves the capital-output ratio constant: $Y = \mathrm{F}(K)\mathrm{T}(t)L$. The population growth in standard efficiency units may be measured as the increase in $\mathrm{T}(t)L$ so the *natural rate of growth becomes the proportional increase in L plus the proportional increase in $\mathrm{T}(t)$ and the *Harrod–Domar analysis is left unchanged. Similarly to the Hicks model, technological change is labour-saving if a constant marginal product of capital requires a higher capital-output ratio.

All these are examples of disembodied technical change, i.e. it is assumed that the entire capital stock is replaced after the innovation; in a *vintage model, in which only the newest capital stock benefits from the innovation, the models become more complicated, since capital cannot be regarded as being a uniform homogeneous mass.

technological unemployment. Unemployment caused by *technological change. Since the beginning of the Industrial Revolution there have been fears that permanent unemployment would be created by the introduction of new machinery. The effect of this technological progress has been to replace the jobs of unskilled workers by jobs for skilled workers, so encouraging a long-term change in the characteristics of the workforce, but the increasing use of computers is expected to be capable of displacing workers on a far greater scale than previous technological changes. Technological unemployment is one of the major elements of *structural unemployment.

telegraphic address. A single word used to identify a firm in a particular town or city in telegrams and cables. As telegrams are charged on a word basis, the substitution of a single word for a number, street, district, etc., provides a substantial saving to companies making extensive use of telegrams and cables. The word chosen has to be unused by anyone else and has to be approved by the postal authorities, who make a small charge for registering it. Very often a made-up word has to be used.

telegraphic transfers. A means of transferring money abroad quickly. A bank will, at its customer's request and risk, send a cable with the necessary particulars to its foreign agent who will act on these instructions. They may be to make payment (a) to the credit of the payee's account with a certain bank, (b) to the payee under advice, or (c) on application and identification by the payee. The transfer is usually made in the currency of the payee's country.

Telex service. A Post Office service by which written matter can be transmitted by cable from one teleprinter to another. Each subscriber is assigned a number and the system is operated by direct dialling. This service is automated enabling messages to be received at any time of the day, even if the teleprinter is left unattended. The service is international.

teller. An employee of a bank who receives money from, and pays money to, the bank's clients.

tenancy agreement. *See* lease.

tender. 1. An offer to supply goods or services, stating the price and conditions on which the offer is made, in response to an invitation to submit such an offer in competition with others.

2. An offer to buy Treasury bills at a stated price.

3. *See* issue by tender, tender.

tenor. The length of time between acquisition of a *bill of exchange and its date of fruition.

term (temporary) assurance. The oldest type of life assurance policy. Payment is only made by the assurer if the life assured dies within the stipulated period. It is used by businessmen on a journey or as a temporary cover to secure an outstanding debt, e.g. a mortgage or hire-purchase commitment. This is generally the cheapest form of life cover available but its scope is very limited. Many variations of this type of contract have been formulated over the years. *See* convertible term assurance, decreasing term assurance.

term bill. *See* period bill.

terminal. An *input or *output device situated away from a computer and linked to it by cable.

terminal loss relief. Relief that a company can obtain against past corporation tax liabilities that it has incurred when it ceases business. It can offset any terminal loss, i.e. the loss incurred in the final *accounting period before the company ceased business, against any profits assessable to corporation tax relating to the last three years prior to the date of termination. To cease business a company would normally pass a directors' resolution noting this fact to take effect from a certain date; thereafter it would not take on any new business and would wind down its existing business.

terminal market. A market in a commodity that is situated at a trading centre near to the users rather than the producers. Terminal markets are usually predominantly *futures markets but *spot goods are also often traded in.

term shares. Shares that cannot be sold for a specified term. They usually carry a higher interest rate or dividend than ordinary shares. They are offered to investors in building societies, etc., to provide capital that cannot be taken out on demand.

terms of trade. A ratio of an index of export prices to an index of import prices. The terms of trade of one country are said to improve if its export prices are rising faster than import prices. In a simple two-good model of exchange the terms of trade will determine the slope of the nation's budget line (*see* budget equation). Production will take place at a point at which a line of such a slope is at a tangent to the *transformation curve, equating the relative prices of goods in all countries when transportation costs are ignored. *See* Edgeworth–Bowley box diagram.

term structure of interest rates. The relationship between interest rates on bonds (such as gilt-edged securities, Treasury bills, local authority bonds, and company bonds) and their date of maturity. There are three possible components of the holding period return to holding bonds: the interest paid on the bond (coupon yield over capital value), the expected capital gain or loss, and any liquidity services rendered, if such services exist.

Any change in the interest rate in the financial markets as a whole changes the capital value of a bond. A fall in the rate of interest causes the capital value to rise, a rise in the rate causing capital values to fall. Capital value fluctuations are greater on long-term bonds because their *net present value is made up largely (or entirely for consols) of interest payments, whereas short-term bonds of, for example, 91 days have their net present value dominated by their maturity value. Therefore, if interest rates are expected to rise investors will expect capital losses on long-term bonds and will tend to sell them, driving down their price and so increasing the interest rate on them until the increase in interest relative to short-term bonds is just sufficient to compensate for the capital loss expected per unit. If interest rates are expected to fall, capital gains will be expected on long-term bonds and individuals will tend to buy them, pushing up their price and lowering their interest rate relative to short-term bonds.

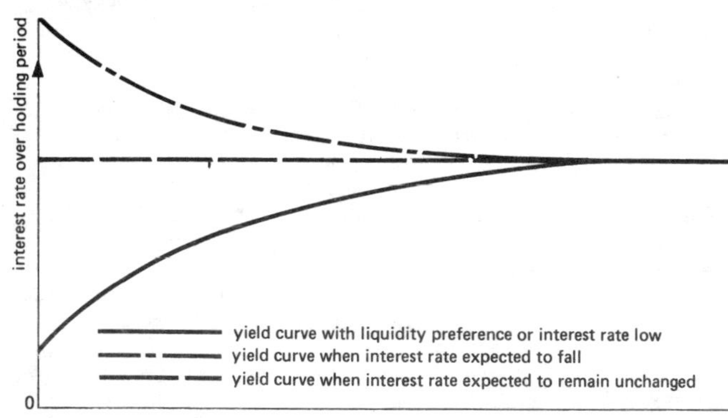

Term structure of interest rates

If interest rates are expected to fall, higher rates would be expected on short-term compared to long-term bonds (a situation of *contango). Conversely if the interest rate in the financial markets is expected to rise, higher rates would be expected on long-term relative to short-term bonds (a situation of *backwardation). If no other factors affect the demand for bonds and if interest rates were expected to remain the same then the yield on bonds would not vary with the term to maturity, i.e. the graph of yield plotted against maturity date would be horizontal (see diagram). If no factors other than expected capital value changes affect the term structure then it is said to be consistent with the expectations theory of term structure.

An alternative theory of term structure is based on the assumption that bonds may also yield a liquidity service, i.e. they can yield a money service or act as *near money. The liquidity service rendered by a bond depends on its ease of conversion into a capital sum of money whose value is safe. As the value of short-dated bonds varies less than that of long-dated bonds one would expect the liquidity services of a bond to decline as the time to maturity of that bond increases. If interest rates are expected to remain the same, short-term bonds would have a higher value and therefore a lower rate of interest because they would be demanded for their liquidity services as well as their yield. So the yield curve of interest against time to maturity would slope upwards (see diagram). The expectations theory assumes that no liquidity services exist and so in this situation predicts a flat yield curve. In the Keynesian liquidity theory of term structure backwardation predominates in the bond markets.

For equilibrium in the bond market, the three yields per unit must be equal for all bonds of all maturities (otherwise arbitrage would be possible). It is this assumption of equilibrium that makes it possible to test the postulates of the two theories of term structure. The Keynesian theory contains the expectations theory as a special case, and it is empirically difficult to discriminate between them. Studies of the yield curve indicate that backwardation predominates and that short-term bonds do give liquidity services.

test of hypothesis. *See* hypothesis testing.

test of significance. A test of hypothesis. *See* significance, hypothesis testing.

theory of games. *See* game theory.

third party insurance. An insurance policy covering the risk of damage or injury to a third party, i.e. a party other than the insurer or the insured. In the U.K. and many other countries, third party insurance is compulsory for all drivers of motor vehicles (*see* motor insurance). This law protects the general public against damage or injury caused by drivers who may not themselves be able to afford to recompense their victims. For example, a pedestrian knocked down by a motorist has a claim against the motorist's insurers and indeed may sue the insurer even if the motorist refuses to do so. In the event of an accident with another car, the insurers will pay for damage to the third party's vehicle, but not for damage to the insured's car. In the U.K. third party motor insurance is often offered with cover against loss by fire and theft.

Thirty Share Index. *See* Financial Times Industrial Ordinary Index.

threshold agreement. An agreement that employees will receive an increase in pay if the rate of inflation exceeds a stated level. Proponents of these agreements argue that they help to reduce inflation by persuading unions not to press for exorbitant settlements to protect their members' standard of living, since they will automatically be safeguarded by the threshold agreement. However, in an era of rapid inflation, threshold agreements will invariably further increase the rate of inflation.

threshold price. *See* Common Agricultural Policy.

ticket day. One of the days in the process of *settlement on the London Stock Exchange. Ticket day is the day before *account day and is the day on which buying stockbrokers, i.e. stockbrokers acting for investors who have bought shares, pass to the stockjobbers from whom they have bought the shares tickets bearing the names of the investors and details of the shares that were purchased during the previous *account. The stockjobbers then pass on these tickets to the selling stockbrokers, i.e. the stockbrokers acting for investors who have sold the relevant shares. Arrangements for final settlement on account day can then be made. *Also called* name day.

tied loan. A loan that is granted by one nation to another with the proviso that it will be spent in the lending nation. This type of loan is common in foreign aid, as it creates employment in the creditor nation as well as aiding the debtor nation.

tied outlet. A retail outlet financed by a producer on condition that it exclusively sells the producer's brands, although noncompeting products may also be sold. Most public houses are tied to particular breweries in this way and many garages selling petrol are tied to oil companies.

tight money. Money that can be borrowed only at a high interest rate because of monetary contraction. When the monetary authority wishes to contract the level of activity in the economy, it reduces the amount of cash in the system by selling bonds in exchange for cash. This reduces the reserves of the *financial intermediaries, who are forced to restrict their lending in order to maintain their reserve ratios. With money more difficult and more expensive to borrow the market for loans contracts, which in turn reduces investment and thus reduces aggregate demand. *See also* easy money.

time and elasticity. The demand for, and supply of, a product grow more elastic with time. For example, a firm would not lose all its custom immediately upon increasing its prices above those of its competitors. However, demand for its product would eventually fall, i.e. demand would become more elastic. A similar process occurs with supply. If a firm experiences an increase in the demand for its product, it might be able to increase output only slightly. However, it could buy more machinery, hire more workers, etc., and so eventually expand production, i.e. supply would become more elastic.

time and motion study. *See* work study.

timecard. A card that records the amount of time that an individual spends at his place of work. It is usually inserted in a timeclock on arrival and departure (clocking in and out) so that a complete record is built up during the week. These cards are renewed each week after being used as bases for the computation of wages.

time charter. The hire of a ship or cargo space for a fixed period of time rather than for a fixed number of voyages. *Compare* voyage charter.

time deposits. The U.S. term for bank deposits on deposit account. *See* bank account.

time lag. The delay between the occurrence of an event and its effects on the economy, sector, firm, etc. It can be broken down into several categories: the lag between the creation of a problem and its recognition as such, the time spent in decision-making, the time spent on such legislative measures as presenting a bill to Parliament, and the administrative delays before the policy can be implemented. The extent of these time lags will vary from one country to another; for example, in the U.K. the legislative time lag is relatively short, whereas it can be quite extensive in the U.S., particularly if President and Congress are in opposition to each other. Even after the legislative lags, others may remain. For example, if the Chancellor wished to decrease unemployment by presenting a budget that reduced personal taxation, some time would necessarily elapse before the tax cuts could stimulate the demand required to stimulate output and thus reduce unemployment. This process could take several months, especially if firms met the increase in demand by first running down stocks. The presence of time lags has led many to doubt the efficiency of *fine tuning; it has been alleged that the *stop-go policies of governments in the U.K. in the 1960s exaggerated rather than stabilized the *trade cycle.

time office. The department of a factory or other organization that is responsible for recording the number of hours worked by each employee who is paid on a time basis. *See* timecard.

time preference. The preference of an individual for current as opposed to future consumption, or vice versa. Those people who prefer to spend in the present must be prepared to pay for this privilege, whereas others are prepared to delay consumption provided they are paid for doing so by increased consumption in the future. This is the basis of a theory of interest developed by Eugen von Böhm-Bawerk (1851–1914). The sum required by an individual to compensate him for postponing consumption, when expressed as a proportion of present income, is his rate of time preference; this qualifies his preference for buying now rather than later. The rate of time preference can be expressed as the interest rate required. An individual's rate of time preference depends among other things on his character, tastes, current income, and expected future income. Generally, if he expects his income to rise he will have a high rate of time preference and if he expects it to fall his rate of time preference will be relatively low or even negative.

If the current rate of interest exceeds an individual's rate of time preference he will lend money on the *capital market. His rate of time preference is likely to rise as the quantity of money he lends rise, and he will therefore limit his lending (in other words the amount saved rather than consumed) to the amount at which his rate of time preference is equal to the rate of interest. Similarly, a firm that invests up to the point at which its rate of return on investment equals the current rate of interest will equalize its rate of time preference with the rate of return on investment.

time rate. Payment based upon the length of time worked by an individual rather than on his output. *Compare* piece rate.

time series. The values taken by a variable over consecutive periods of time. The series should be long enough for valid statistical inferences to be made. A time series can be analysed for its trend–that is, its secular movement over a long period of time, its seasonal variations (if it is constructed on monthly or quarterly data), its cyclical variations (where an entire cycle normally spans several years), and other deviations from trend, usually caused by extraordinary events such as wars. Time series are used extensively in economic analysis and econometrics. If it is desired to examine a time series independently of its seasonal or cyclical variation, then a moving average can be constructed to eliminate such disturbances. Under suitable conditions, short-term forecasts can be made by extrapolation. *Compare* cross-section analysis.

time sharing. A method of *computer operation in which two or more users have simultaneous access to the computer. The speeds of input and output devices are slow compared with processing speeds. Using time-sharing techniques it is possible, for example, to process one user's data while inputting another's, thus making more efficient use of computer time.

Times Share Indices. A series of 13 *share indices calculated from a base date of 2 June 1964 and published each day except Monday in *The Times.* The most important of them is the Times Industrial Share Index, which covers the entire industrial section of the London Stock Exchange; other indices include prices for certain sub-sections of the market, for commodity and gold-mining shares, and for certain fixed-interest securities. Highs and lows for each of the last six years are listed for each index.

title deed. A document evidencing the right or title of a person to a piece of land. It shows how the present owner acquired the land and how over the years it has been transferred from one person to another by deed, will, or foreclosure of a mortgage. In law the only estates in land are an estate in fee simple absolute in possession (freehold) or a term of years absolute (leasehold). If the title has been registered in the U.K. under the Land Registrations Act (1925) a Land Certificate will have been issued by the Land Registry and this takes the place of the title deeds.

Tokyo Round. The seventh round of trade negotiations held by *GATT in Tokyo between 1973 and 1979. The industrial countries agreed to reduce tariffs by an average of about one third over the subsequent eight years, and agreement was reached on multilateral codes of conduct governing customs valuation, government procurement policies (military equipment, etc.), import licensing, subsidies, and countervailing duties.

toll. A charge for travelling via a road, bridge, ferry, or tunnel. Tolls were common in the eighteenth and nineteenth centuries and are still used in some cases to offset the costs of construction, e.g. they are used on the Severn Bridge and at the Mersey Tunnel. However, tolls restrict travel and can therefore diminish public welfare. An axiom of *cost-benefit analysis is that the correct amount of a toll should equal the marginal social cost of use if welfare is to be maximized. Consequently, the toll for travel on an uncongested bridge should be nil.

Tolpuddle Martyrs. Six English labourers who were sentenced in March 1834 to seven years transportation to a penal colony in Australia for organizing trade-union activities in the Dorsetshire village of Tolpuddle.

In October 1833 the two leaders, George and James Loveless (or Lovelace), had established a lodge of the Friendly Society of Agricultural Labourers at Tolpuddle. During the great national wave of trade-union activity in 1833 and 1834, the two men were drawn into the trade union movement. The Whig government, being alarmed at the magnitude of working-class discontent, was determined to halt the growth of trade unions. In February 1834 the six were arrested for administering unlawful oaths, but the real offence was their concern to maintain their already inadequate wages. The jury found them guilty at Dorchester Assizes in March. There was an immediate public reaction throughout the country at the sentence of deportation and the six became popular heroes. Eventually, after large-scale demonstrations, their sentences were remitted in March 1836. The six returned to England, five of them later emigrating to Canada. In 1934 the T.U.C. built a memorial to them at Tolpuddle.

ton. A unit often used in commerce. It is important to distinguish between four different units. The *long ton* is 2240 lbs or 1016 kilograms. This unit is widely used in English-speaking countries (except the U.S.), but is being replaced by the *tonne* or *metric ton* of 1000 kilograms. In the U.S., the *short ton* of 2000 lbs is often used. One short ton consists of 20 short hundredweights of 100 lbs each. Finally, the *shipping ton* is not a unit of weight at all, but a unit of cubic capacity equal to 100 cubic feet. *See* tonnage.

tone. The sentiment of a stock exchange or financial market. Thus if a market is said to have a dull tone or a nervous tone on a particular day, the implication is that prices have been marked down; conversely a firm tone carries the implication of a strong market.

tonnage. The tonnage of a ship is expressed in three ways: the *deadweight tonnage*, the *displacement tonnage,* and the *measurement tonnage.*

The deadweight tonnage is the weight in long tons (2240 lbs) of the crew, stores, fresh water, cargo, and passengers, when loaded to the *load line.

The light displacement tonnage is the weight of the hull in long tons including all gear and machinery, but without ballast. The loaded displacement tonnage is the weight in long tons of the ship and everything in her, when loaded to the load line. The measurement tonnage is expressed, in tons of 100 cubic feet, in three ways. The *gross (register) tonnage* measures the volume of certain compartments, including the cargo holds. The *under-deck tonnage* measures the tonnage to the *tonnage deck* (upper deck if there are less than three decks, otherwise second deck from below). *Net (register) tonnage* is obtained by deducting certain non-cargo spaces from the gross tonnage. Dock and harbour dues are usually based on net register tonnage, while dry dock dues are based on gross register tonnage.

tonne. *See* ton.

tort. A wrong committed by one person towards another that does not amount to a criminal offence. It may be sufficient to enable the person against whom it is committed to claim damages for any loss caused. Examples are negligence, nuisance, and defamation.

total absorption costing. A method of allocating all the costs that arise in the running of an enterprise to all the *cost units that are produced. In practice this is done by identifying all the *direct costs against specific cost units, and allocating to each a share of the *indirect costs and overheads so that all overheads are thereby identified. The importance of this is that these costs can then all be considered as part of the input of production enabling them to be booked against finished stock or sales instead of becoming a charge to the profit and loss account (except when sales are below the cost of stock so determined).

total income. *See* gross income.

Town and Country Planning Act (1971). An Act of Parliament regulating the use by owners of their land. The Act prohibits most building and engineering works on land and also any substantial changes of use of land or buildings, without planning permission being granted by the local authority. If buildings are erected without planning permission, or the use of existing buildings is changed, the local authority can issue an enforcement notice requiring the land to be re-instated to its original state. The authority has the power to demolish the buildings if the enforcement notice is not complied with. This Act replaces the Act of 1947.

town clearing. The department of the *Bankers' Clearing House in London that deals with cheques drawn on or paid into banks in the City of London.

trade advertising. *See* advertising.

trade association. A group of firms belonging to the same trade. Trade associations exist to provide services for members, to keep them informed about new developments, and to defend and advance their members' interests. In that they are well-informed about the conditions and problems of their members, they are invaluable sources of information for the government. Trade associations also provide a valuable body for coordinating the activities of traders for their mutual benefit, for drawing up trading contracts, and for providing arbitration procedures in the case of disputes between members. Examples of trade associations are the Cotton Board (of which membership is compulsory), the Potato Marketing Board, and the National Farmers' Union.

trade barrier. Any government measure that impairs free trade. *Tariffs, *quotas, *import restrictions, and restrictive regulations on quality are all types of trade barrier.

trade bill. A bill drawn for actual trade transactions as distinct from a *bank bill and from an *accommodation bill. They are usually held until maturity by the traders as they do not command such a favourable rate of discount as bank bills.

trade bloc. A combination of states who wish to foster trade between themselves, formed either by informal agreement or by formal treaty. An example of a trade bloc is the E.E.C.

trade creditor. Any person or firm to whom money is owed as a result of trading. One trader usually grants some credit to other traders and at the end of an accounting period there will always be some money owed by these trade creditors.

trade cycle (business cycle). Periodic fluctuations in the economic activity of a country: left to themselves, economies tend to oscillate between high output, investment, and employment (*see* boom) and low output, investment, and employment (*see* depression). The intermediate stages are often called the *recession and the *recovery. In the nineteenth century this cycle was a regular phenomenon lasting approximately nine years; in the twentieth century there has been considerably less regularity. For example, the *Depression lasted longer, and was more severe than any previous slump. In the post-war era governments have taken measures to minimize the effects of the trade cycle; these measures have not always proved to be entirely satisfactory. This is partly because there is no accepted reason for the causes of trade cycles. Theories include: monetary and banking hypotheses, such as those of Thornton, Marshall, and Wicksell; underconsumptionist hypotheses as proposed by Marx; and hypotheses that concentrate on investment, such as that of Keynes and the accelerator-multiplier model of Samuelson. Most causal theories do, however, focus on the level of investment as the prime determinant.

Trade Descriptions Act (1968). An act passed in the U.K. in order to prevent the deception of consumers by false advertising. The act replaced the Merchandise Marks Act (1953) and gave to local Weights and Measures officials the task of prosecuting offenders. It aimed at preventing false claims for a product being advertised and at preventing the purchasing of stock to be offered at spurious sale prices by stipulating that the items being offered at a reduced price should have been on sale at the original higher price for at least 28 consecutive days.

trade discount. A deduction from the advertised price of a product offered to special customers and members of the same trade. The size of the discount may be dependent on other factors, such as the size of the order (as in *aggregated rebate scheme) or the importance of the customer. For instance, it has been alleged that John D. Rockefeller secretly won high discounts for rail transportation of his product by threatening to transfer his custom. His competitors received no discounts and the consequent cost advantage enabled him to establish Standard Oil as a monopoly.

Trade Disputes Act (1906). An Act of Parliament that made unions immune from actions for *tort. It was passed to prevent any future decisions similar to that in the Taff Vale case, in which the Taff Vale Railway Company successfully sued its strikers for damages in compensation for loss of revenue.

Trade Disputes Act (1927). An Act of Parliament that made general strikes illegal, restricted the right to picket, prevented public authorities from making jobs provisional upon union membership, and decreed that those who wished for part of their membership fee to be used for political purposes would have to contract into the political levy whereas previously members had had to contract out of it. This Act was repealed in 1946.

Trade Disputes Act (1965). An Act of Parliament that provided unions with immunity from actions for *tort as a result of industrial action. Immunity had been granted by the 1906 Act, but this was successfully challenged in the case, Rookes v Barnard (1964). The Trades Dispute Act (1965) was passed because of this judgment, to restore the status quo.

Trade Expansion Act. *See* Kennedy Round.

trade gap. A deficit in a country's balance of trade. It is the difference between the value of the goods imported and the value of the goods exported.

trade investments. Investments acquired and held by a company primarily for the purposes of that company's business. The reasons for such investments may be to protect the goodwill of the business or to help develop the further business of the company either specifically or generally, as by subscribing to some promotional body that represents the industry as a whole.

trademark. A symbol or special word (tradename) that is the sole property of one producer and is used by him to identify his products. Trademarks increase the monopoly power of a producer in that they are a form of *product differentiation. Trademarks are characteristic of *monopolistic competition as neither the firms operating in a perfect competitive industry nor a pure monopolist would have anything to gain by using them.

trade reference. A reference given by one member of a trade to another, concerning the credit rating of a third member of the trade. For example, a retailer wishing to start trading with a manufacturer may give some other manufacturer with whom he has dealt as a reference to vouch for his reliability. Such references are given *without prejudice.

Trades Union Congress (T.U.C.). A federation of most of the trade unions in the U.K. and the largest representative body of English workers. A separate federation, the Scottish Trades Union Congress, exists in Scotland and presses in particular for economic development and expansion in that area. There are also regional trade councils within the T.U.C., which have authority over a restricted field of local affairs.

Proceeding from discussions held as early as 1864, the British Trades Union Congress was founded at Manchester in 1868. In 1871 it was reorganized as the Trades Union Congress and under that name it has undergone continuous development to the present time. It has expanded in function from a simple pressure group, primarily for skilled workers, to a workers' organization that maintains links with various government departments and industry.

Unions within the T.U.C. retain complete freedom over their own affairs and expulsion is the only official weapon available for disciplining member unions. In 1973, 20 unions with a membership of 179 370 were expelled, but this was an exceptionally high number caused by the crisis over the Government's Industrial Relations Act. Most have since been readmitted.

Meetings or congresses of delegates from the various unions are held annually, normally in early September. Resolutions on general policy are adopted and the report of the T.U.C.'s General Council is debated. The General Council is elected by the annual Congress to watch developments in industry, involve itself in the legislative process as it affects labour, and generally safeguard workers' interests. It also acts as an arbiter between members and provides them with advice and assistance.

trade union. An association of workers organized to defend and advance their interests in negotiations with employers and the government. There are three main types of union: the craft union, the industrial union, and the general union.

The *craft union* is a union composed of members who share a common set of skills, although they may work in different industries. It is the oldest form of union organization, deriving from the medieval guilds. The *industrial union* is a union composed of all the workers in a plant or industry, whatever the level of their skills. The *general union* is a union composed of workers who have neither a common skill nor work in a single industry: these unions tend to be the largest. The relative strengths of these unions will affect the economy. There are more industrial unions in the U.S. and Western Europe than in the U.K. and it has been suggested that this has important consequences for bargaining.

There is often a federation in which unions meet to discuss matters of mutual interest, which arbitrates in disputes between unions, and which represents the interests of the union movement as a whole in negotiations with the employers' federations and the government. Some federations are comparatively limited in power, such as the T.U.C. in the U.K. and the American Federation of Labor-Congress of Industrial Organizations (A.F.L.-C.I.O.) in the U.S., while others are able to negotiate wage deals for a significant proportion of the labour force, as for example the Swedish Confederation of Trade Unions.

There is no international political similarity between unions. They range from the communist unions in Italy, to the socialist unions of the U.K. and Scandinavia, and the conservative Catholic unions of Belgium. The A.F.L.-C.I.O. is nonsocialist and neutral, supporting that party that it thinks will best advance its interest at that time.

A common trend for the trade union movement as a whole seems to be a decrease in their numbers, an increase in their membership, and a growing influence on the government's economic policies. In the U.K. the number of trade unions has declined from 1323 in 1900 to approximately 480 in 1975, while membership has increased from approximately 2 000 000 to over 10 000 000.

Trade Union and Labour Relations Act (1974). An Act of Parliament that repealed the Industrial Relations Act (1971) and with it the National Industrial Relations Court. The new act restored legal immunity to individuals and unions taking part in trading disputes although this immunity has since been restricted in certain respects by the Employment Acts (1980, 1982).

trading account. A form of *profit and loss account that shows only the gross profit or loss as a result of trading. In the right-hand column, total sales are added to the closing value of the stock, this total is balanced in the left-hand column by adding the opening stock and the purchases to the gross profit (if any).

trading banks. The commercial banks of Australia, examples of which are the Bank of Adelaide, the Commercial Bank of Australia, and the National Bank of Australasia. The banking system of Australia consists of a few large banks, which have branches throughout the country, and many local and regional banks. It is thus midway between the U.K., with its few banks each of which has many branches, and the U.S., with its many local banks few of which have branches.

trading estate. *See* industrial estate.

trading post system. Dealing in particular stocks and shares at particular places on the floor of a stock exchange. In effect a miniature marketplace is established within the market itself so speeding up transactions. This practice is found in the *New York Stock Exchange.

trading stamps. Stamps given by retailers to their customers as a form of discount. When sufficient stamps have been collected they can be exchanged for goods with the trading stamp company, from whom the retailers buy the stamps. The idea was first tried in the 1920s but only became popular in the U.S. and the U.K. in the 1960s. In the U.K. the rules regulating the use of these stamps are laid down in the Trading Stamps Act (1964). This act ensures that all stamps must have a clearly stated money value (usually about half the gift value).

tramp. A ship that can be chartered, at a rate determined by market conditions. Most of the world's chartering is arranged through London's Baltic Exchange. In the past, tramps were chartered usually for a particular voyage, but now time charters are more common. Until recently the tramp vessels were smaller on average than *liners, but many are now large, with specialized features (many are tankers).

tranche. *See* International Monetary Fund.

transactions costs. Costs incurred in overcoming market imperfections, which may or may not include transportation costs according to the analytical framework. They cover such a wide range of items, from legal fees to telephone calls, that in practical situations only rough or limited uses of the concept are applicable.

transactions demand. One of the three motives, as described by Keynes, for holding money (*see also* precautionary demand, speculative demand). It is the amount of money held in order to carry out day-to-day transactions: for a given period, say a week, it is proportional to the average of the transactions carried out in that period. This proportion depends mainly on institutional factors, such as the length of time between payments for employment or the method by which income tax is paid. For example, an important determinant would be whether an individual received a weekly wage or a monthly salary. Similarly, an important factor in determining an individual's transactions demand is whether he pays his income tax each week or in a lump sum each year. Hence the aggregate transactions demand for cash balances depends on the level of national income, in money terms. *See also* liquidity preference.

transaction velocity. *See* velocity of circulation.

transferable account. One of the three groups of countries in which sterling was freely convertible when convertibility of sterling was being restored after being suspended in 1947. The other groups were the *sterling area and the *American account, and eventually almost all countries outside these two areas were members of the transferable account.

transfer deed. A document ratifying the transfer of property or securities from one person or organization to another.

transfer earnings. The amount of money that a factor of production must earn to prevent it being transferred to another use. The owner of a machine will use it in his factory if he can earn more by using it than hiring it out. The amount of money that he can earn by hiring it out is the transfer earnings. In most cases the earnings of any factor of production will be composed of transfer earnings and *economic rent.

transfer form. A document used in transferring the ownership of shares. The seller of the shares must sign the form, which authorizes the removal of his name from the share registration records of the company concerned, and the stockbroker acting for the buyer then completes the form and sends it to the company's registrar together with the seller's share certificate. The buyer of the shares does not have to sign the form.

transfer payment. A payment made by a government authority that is not made in exchange for the current production of goods and services. Examples of transfer payments are old-age pensions, unemployment benefits, and student grants. Transfer payments are always excluded in the calculation of gross national product.

transfer stamp duty. *See* stamp duty.

transformation curve (production possibility frontier). A curve on a graph whose axes represent different types of goods that could be produced, such as capital and consumer goods, or agricultural produce and machinery. The curve itself indicates the maximum of all the possible combinations of outputs that the society could produce with the resources at hand

and assuming no advances in technology.

It is assumed to be concave from the origin. If the economy is producing inside the boundary it is producing inefficiently, since it could produce more of every good as a result of a reallocation of resources. On the boundary, however, one can only produce more of one good by giving up some of another. Given a set of prices in an economy producing only two goods, the point at which production will take place will be determined by drawing a line, at a tangent to the curve, whose slope is the negative of the inverse of the price ratio. This is the budget line (*see* budget equation). If the curve is strictly concave, i.e. without straight segments, it will determine the output uniquely. The reason for this is that given any other point on the curve at that set of prices the budget line will cut through the set of possible outputs, and so there will be some point within the production possibility frontier lying to the right of this line at which one could produce more of all commodities and increase the G.N.P. This will be true of all points except where the budget line is tangential to the curve. This is the optimum production point.

The curve is widely used in the theory of international trade as well as standard price theory. *See also* x-efficiency.

transformation problem. The difficulty in Marx's model of relating market price to labour value (*see* labour theory of value) embodied in the good. If the total value of a good is determined by the amount of labour directly or indirectly used in the manufacture of the good, then the rate of *surplus value may be calculated by deducting *variable capital, i.e. the wage bill, from total receipts divided by total embodied labour. This Marx assumed was equal between industries. Then, in common with Ricardo's approach to the labour theory of value, relative prices may be uniquely determined by the relative amounts of labour embodied in each production process. However, if the rate of profit, defined as the ratio of surplus value to total capital, is made equal between industries by competition, and the ratio of constant to variable capital varies between industries, then the rate of surplus value must also vary according to the constant capital in each industry. But then relative prices have not been determined solely by the inherent labour value of the goods. The transformation of labour value into prices is not determinate. *See also* Ricardo effect.

transhipment. The shipment of goods from one port to another with a change of ship at an intermediary port. Transhipment may be required because there is no direct service between the port of shipment and the port of destination or for some political or commercial reason.

transire. A two-part document listing the cargo carried by a coaster. One part is given to the customs on leaving port, the other on arriving at the port of destination.

transit trade. *See* entrepôt trade, re-exports.

travellers' cheque. A form of draft drawn on the head office of the issuing bank, paid for and signed when issued by the beneficiary as the drawer, and signed again by him in a space provided on the cheque when cashing it, thus providing a means of identification to the paying banker. The beneficiary is thus enabled to obtain cash in his own country, or foreign currency when travelling abroad, at any branch of the agents of the issuing bank. Travellers' cheques are usually issued in denominations of £2, £5, £10, £20, and £50, but may also be obtained in foreign currency. They provide the holder with the security of a *letter of credit.

treasurer. An employee of a large company whose principal role is to invest surplus funds, for periods ranging from overnight to several months, in order to earn income from them as opposed to keeping them as cash or bank deposits.

Treasury. The government department primarily responsible for the development of the U.K.'s economic strategy. The work of the Treasury is grouped into four main sectors. Concentrated in the *chief economic advisor's sector* are those members of the Economic Service who are engaged on highly technical work, chiefly economic forecasting and the use of the Treasury's macroeconomic model for the simulation of the effects on the economy of major options in economic policy. Other members of the Economic Service work in the other three departments with administrators, to advise them on the economic aspects of their work. The *overseas finance sector* is concerned with international monetary questions, financial aspects of E.E.C. membership, exchange control, management of the foreign currency and gold reserves, the balance of payments, overseas aid, and export finance. The *domestic economy sector* has two major areas of responsibility. The first is concerned with developing a more active and coherent Treasury approach to industrial problems and policies. The second is concerned with counterinflation policies, taxation policy, and home finance matters including monetary policy. The *public services sector* is responsible for control over public expenditure in the aggregate and for the management of the annual Public Expenditure Survey (on which the annual White Paper on Public Expenditure is based). In addition to these four major sectors there is a *central unit*, which assists the top management of the Treasury in the task of coordinating policy advice from all parts of the department. It is responsible for managing budgets and other packages of economic measures spanning the responsibilities of more than one Treasury group.

This organization was the result of changes made, following an internal examination in 1975, to adapt the structure of the Treasury to the new patterns of economic problems with which it has to deal. Nominally the head of the Treasury is the Prime Minister, who is the First Lord of the Treasury. In practice, responsibilities are carried by the Chancellor of the Exchequer assisted by the Paymaster General, the Chief Secretary to the Treasury, and the Financial Secretary.

Treasury bills. Short-term government securities first offered for sale in 1877 as a means by which the government can borrow money, originally for three, six, nine, or twelve months, but since 1921 usually for three months only. The bills are in denominations of £5000 upwards and the total amount offered on Friday of each week is advertised and tendered for at a discount (the effective yield being the difference between the purchase price and the redemption value) by the discount market as a syndicate. No tender may be for an amount less than £50,000, and only a proportion of the tender may be allotted. "Tap" Treasury bills are issued directly to government departments. In the U.S. Treasury bills were first issued by the U.S. Treasury in 1929. *See also* open market operations.

Treasury deposit receipts. Compulsory governmental borrowing from the commercial banks in World War II. In 1945, Treasury deposit receipts totalled approximately £1800 million but they had been totally replaced by *Treasury bills by 1962.

Treasury stocks. Stocks issued by the U.K. Treasury. They may be purchased through larger post offices, banks, or stock exchanges and are regarded as gilt-edged securities. Examples include 5% 1986–89 (i.e. pays 5% per annum interest and is redeemable in 1989 or, by prior announcement, in 1986 or any year in between), 9% 1994, 8% 2002–06.

Treaty of Accession (1972). The treaty that amended the *Treaty of Rome to include the U.K., Irish Republic, and Denmark in the *European Economic Community. It also included provisions to include these new members in the European Atomic Energy Community and the European Coal and Steel Community.

Treaty of Rome (1957). The agreement that created the *European Economic Community (E.E.C.) with the aim of promoting the continued and balanced expansion of the members' economies by their progressive harmonization and integration. The six signatories were France, West Germany, Italy, Belgium, the Netherlands, and Luxembourg. The preamble to the treaty included, among the basic objectives of the E.E.C., the foundations for a growing unity among European peoples, the improvement of their working and living conditions, the progressive abolition of restrictions on trade, and the development of the prosperity of overseas countries.

trial balance. A test of the accuracy of the *books of account at any one time by extracting every balance and checking that the sum of the credits equals the sum of the debits. Trial balances are often extracted monthly from the books of account. They must be extracted, in normal circumstances, at least once a year at the time of the annual audit.

troy weight. A system of units used mainly for the weighing of jewels and precious metals. One troy pound equals 12 troy ounces, 240 pennyweights, or 5760 grains. It equals 0.373 of a kilogram or approximately 0.82 of an *avoirdupois pound.

truck system. The payment of wages, partially or in total, in tokens that could only be used at the employer's shops. This system was common during the eighteenth and early nineteenth centuries until its abolition by the Truck Acts of the nineteenth century. It usually led to the sale of substandard goods at high prices as the owner exploited his monopolistic position.

true and fair view. The auditor of a company must state whether the accounts he has examined give a true and fair view of the company's affairs. The term true and fair encompasses a wide range of requirements built up by the accounting profession. Accounts must conform with statute law, specifically the Companies Acts (1948–1981), which describe in great detail what information is required and how it should be presented. In addition, the Institute of Chartered Accountants in the U.K. specify certain requirements and suggest others. Obviously there are a wide range of possibilities in relation to the treatment and presentation of accounts and the auditor must, in the last analysis, form his own opinion as to whether the accounts under consideration present an accurate or a misleading view.

trust. 1. A sum of money or property held and administered by *trustees on behalf of some individual, group, or organization.

2. A term used in the U.S. for a *cartel. It comes from the use of trustees or leading industrialists to administer the affairs of the cartel in the interests of its members as a whole. U.S. legislation on monopolies and restrictive trade practices are called *anti-trust laws.

trust deed. A deed transferring property to trustees and setting out the trusts on which they are to hold it. The term is often used to describe the deed that transfers a company's property to a trustee for the debenture holders.

trustee. A person who holds money or property for the benefit of another person or persons, either because he was commanded by the person who gave him the money or property to hold it on someone else's behalf, or because he has himself made a declaration of trust to the effect that he held certain of his property upon trust for somebody else. Even though the trustee is, in law, the owner of the property held on trust, the rules of *equity and certain statutes, for example the *Trustee Investment Act (1961), strictly regulate his conduct. One of the most important rules is that he must not make any kind of profit from the trust property: any profit made by the trust must go to the beneficiaries (i.e. those for whom the property is held on trust) and this even extends to any profit made from knowledge acquired whilst acting as a trustee. The document setting up the trust, which may be a declaration of trust, a will, or a deed of gift, may contain directions regulating the duties of trustees and in most cases these directions will override any relevant statutory provisions. Thus, the document may allow the trustees to invest in securities not authorized by the Trustee Investment Act (1961) or it may direct the trustees to hold the trust property not for any particular person, but for who ever they think best out of a class of nominated persons (in which case the trust is known as a *discretionary trust*). In the case of property the owner of which has his name entered in a register (e.g. shares in a company and registered land), it is the trustee and not the beneficiary whose name is entered and if, for example, a company receives notice that a trust exists over some of its shares, it must completely disregard this information.

trustee in bankruptcy. A person appointed either by the creditors or by the committee of inspection when a debtor is adjudicated bankrupt to administer the property of the debtor for the benefit of the creditors. The *official receiver acts until a certified trustee, to whom he must give satisfactory security, is appointed.

Trustee Investment Act (1961). An Act of Parliament that extended the powers of trustees, who were not otherwise authorized to do so, to invest money in certain authorized investments and company shares, known as *trustee securities.* It provided that at least half of each fund must be invested in *narrower-range securities* (i.e. government stocks and other investments in which there is some kind of government or local authority guarantee, building society deposits, and mortgages of freehold land) before any money is invested in so called *wider-range securities* (i.e. shares in a U.K. company with paid-up capital of at least £1 million and having paid a dividend for the last five years or more–such companies are said to have *trustee status*).

trustee investments. Investments of trust funds made by a trustee as directed in the trust deed. In the absence of such directions he may only invest trust funds in certain securities declared by law to be suitable for this purpose. Until the Trustee Investments Act (1961), such investment in the U.K. was restricted to government stocks and a few similar securities, but that act allowed one half of the total value of the whole fund to be invested in ordinary and preference shares of substantial quoted companies.

trustee savings banks. Local savings banks first established in 1810 in the U.K. to encourage thrift by savers of limited means. Since 1844 they have been compelled to lend their funds to the National Debt Commissioners. The largest of all savings banks, the Post Office Saving Bank, was established in 1861. Deposits may be in the ordinary department, with a low rate of interest, or in the special investment department, subject to one month's notice of withdrawal and carrying a higher rate of interest. The Treasury decides the annual and total amounts that may be deposited by any one person. The Trustee Savings Bank Act (1964) enables them to operate current accounts on which cheques may be drawn.

trustee securities. *See* Trustee Investment Act (1961).

T.U.C. *See* Trades Union Congress.

turn. 1. *See* jobber's turn.

2. The profit made by buying and selling securities on the Stock Exchange, i.e. the difference between the buying and selling price.

turnkey system. A computer system for which the vendor supplies all the necessary *hardware, *software, training and documentation so that the user can commence operation immediately.

turnover. 1. The value of total sales (i.e. total gross takings) of a company during an accounting period. A company's turnover must be disclosed if it exceeds £1 million. *See also* stock turnover, capital turnover.

2. *See also* labour turnover rate.

turnover tax. A tax levied at each stage of the production and distribution of a good, i.e. each time it changes hands. *See also* cascading.

turnpike. In 1958 Dorfman, Samuelson, and Solow indicated that, for a given starting position and desired target economic state, and a sufficiently long planning horizon, the fastest path to follow except at the beginning and the end of the period is the von Neumann growth ray, i.e. the turnpike, even though the economic characteristics of the turnpike bear no relation to the desired economic state. The term originates from the analogy that the quickest route (as opposed to the shortest distance) between two towns might involve a diversion onto a turnpike where speeds are very much faster than on local roads. The abstract case can have relevance to planned economies seeking to attain a desired economic configuration.

two-sector model. An aggregate model in which consumption goods are distinguished from capital goods, as opposed to a completely aggregated economy where a good, when produced, may be used in either manner at will. The primary complication introduced over a *one-sector model is that in order to secure a unique and stable *steady-state growth path, it is necessary to assume that the consumption sector's production process is relatively more capital-intensive than the capital good sector.

two-stage least squares. A method of econometric *estimation used to provide estimators for the coefficients of simultaneous model relationships. The procedure is to regress those independent variables of a relationship that are endogenous to the model on all the predetermined variables of the model (using ordinary *least squares estimation) and then to use ordinary least squares again to estimate the original relationship having substituted into it the functions obtained in the first stage in place of the endogenous variables. Two-stage least squares estimators have the same properties as indirect least squares estimators but they can be used for relationships that are overidentified as well as exactly identified and two-stage least squares is therefore of wider applicability than indirect least squares. *See also* simultaneous model, identification. *Compare* indirect least squares.

tying arrangement. An arrangement by which a company forces those who wish to purchase or lease some of its products to accept others as well, such as a service contract for a machinery purchased, punch cards for computers, or cosmetics with soap. It is also possible that the company will force them to deal exclusively in its products. This can be the result either of diversification and an efficient marketing organization or more likely the exploitation of a patent monopoly or brand name differentiation over one or more of the various products. Tying arrangements act as a *barrier to entry by denying new firms access to retail outlets. Such arrangements are generally illegal except where they can be proved to be in the public interest.

Type I error. *See* hypothesis testing.

Type II error. *See* hypothesis testing.

U

uberrima fides. *See* utmost good faith.

ullage. 1. The difference between the capacity of a barrel or similar vessel and the volume of its contents.

2. (As used by H.M. Customs Service) the actual contents of a vessel; the difference between the contents and the full capacity being the *vacuity*.

ultimo. Of last month. For example, in commercial English it is quite common to write: "Thank you for your letter of the 3rd ult." Ult. is the usual abbreviation. *Compare* instant.

ultra-cheap money policy. A deliberate attempt by the government to depress interest rates, usually to stimulate investment. An ultra-cheap money policy was initiated in the U.K. under Hugh Dalton's chancellorship in 1945. Long-term interest rates were driven down to 2.5% but even so it failed to achieve its objectives and was abandoned in 1951.

ultra vires. (Latin for: beyond the power.) Denoting some act that assumes an authority beyond that conferred by the law. A limited company's actions are restricted to the fulfilment of its objectives, as set out in its Articles of Association. Any contract made by the company that conflicts with these objectives is ultra vires and hence void. Such a contract cannot be ratified by an action of the shareholders.

umpire. A person who makes the final decision in an *arbitration in which the arbitrators disagree. It is quite common in commercial arbitrations for each side to the dispute to appoint their own arbitrator and for the arbitrators to appoint an umpire, before the arbitration takes place. The arbitrators then act partly as advocates and partly as adjudicators. If they fail to agree, the umpire is called in and he makes the decision. This decision is always open to appeal.

unabsorbed cost. The part of the costs of production that is not absorbed by revenue at a given output. Fixed costs are sometimes allocated proportionally to the price of each unit of production so that they will be recovered when output reaches a certain level. If production does not reach this level then not all of the fixed costs will be recovered; the residue is unabsorbed cost.

unauthorized clerk. An employee of a firm of stockbrokers who is not allowed to deal on the floor of the London Stock Exchange, although he is permitted to assist a member in the exchange.

unbiasedness. A statistical *estimator is said to be unbiased if it can be shown mathematically that its expected value is equal to the true value of the parameter being estimated. Unbiasedness is one of the desirable properties of estimators.

uncalled capital. The part of the capital raised by a share issue that is not payable immediately. *See* called-up capital.

uncertainty. A situation regarding a variable in which neither its probability distribution nor its mode of occurrence is known. Thus an oligopolist may be uncertain with respect to the marketing strategies of his competitors. Uncertainty as defined in this way is extremely common in economic activity and various devices have been developed to reduce its disutility, notably game theory techniques and the a priori assignment of a probability distribution in cases where past and present evidence makes this a reasonable approximation. *Compare* risk. *See also* state preference theory, mean variance analysis.

unconfirmed letter of credit. *See* letter of credit.

unconscionable bargains. Bargains in which one party has been unscrupulously taken advantage of when he has had no opportunity of obtaining expert advice. Such a bargain may be nullified in law.

unconstitutional strike. *See* strike.

UNCTAD. *See* United Nations Conference on Trade and Development.

undated security. *See* irredeemable security.

under-deck tonnage. *See* tonnage.

underdeveloped country. *See* developing country.

underemployment. 1. The employment of workers in jobs that do not fully utilize their abilities or skills, either because of general unemployment (any job is better than no job) or because of the rigidity of the labour market, making "good jobs" inaccessible to some workers.

2. The employment of a worker in a job that does not offer sufficient hours of work (overtime opportunities, length of working week, etc.) to satisfy his personal income/leisure preferences. Such underemployed workers often take extra part-time jobs (*see* moonlighting).

undersubscription. The position that arises when total applications for a new issue of shares is less than the number being offered. Undersubscription is rare.

underwriter. 1. A company or individual who accepts insurance risks. In the early days of marine insurance, a marine insurance merchant engaged in this activity as a sideline to his normal trading would write under the details of the risk undertaken his name and the amount accepted.

It is customary for insurance companies to appoint certain officials with the authority to decide whether or not to accept the risks proposed. These officials are called underwriters. *See also* Lloyd's underwriters.

2. A finance company, issuing house, or individual who in return for a commission agrees to buy a proportion of the issue of a company's share should they be undersubscribed by the public.

underwriting (in insurance). The assessing of a risk and deciding on the premium and terms to be applied to the risk. It has become customary to use the term in relation to all the actions associated with the processing and servicing (excluding claims and accounting work) of new and existing insurances. For example, in accident insurance the burglary underwriting department will be engaged in all the above activities for burglary and associated policies.

A company that underwrites (sometimes shortened to *writes*) marine business is one that transacts this class of insurance, and will normally be prepared to issue a quotation for the premium rate to be applied in respect of a specific marine risk. *See also* underwriter, Lloyd's underwriter.

undischarged bankrupt. A person who has been declared bankrupt but who has not discharged his obligations (*see* bankruptcy). He has certain disabilities, including not being allowed to obtain credit without informing his creditors; to act as a director of a company; to trade under another name; to offer himself for election as a member of parliament, justice of the peace, mayor, alderman, or councillor. If he is a peer he may not sit or vote in the House of Lords.

undisclosed principal. A person who deals through an agent or broker without revealing his identity. This is a perfectly acceptable method of trading, provided that the agent or broker indicates at the time the bargain is struck that he is acting on behalf of an undisclosed principal and not on his own behalf. If he fails to make this clear, the agent may thereafter be treated as the principal or, in certain circumstances, the contract may become void.

undistributed profits. *See* retained earnings.

undue influence. Excessive pressure brought to bear upon an individual, by a potential beneficiary or third party, so that any contract made by the individual is not a true expression of his aims or requirements, but is made to the advantage of another. Any contract that is made under undue influence can be set aside by a court of law.

unearned income. Income, such as dividends and interest, that is derived from capital investment and not from paid employment.

unearned increment. An increase in the value of an asset that is not caused by any action of its owner. An example would be an increase in the price of a house, which had undergone no improvements, through increased demand alone. There have been several proposals to tax unearned increments, but they have never been implemented due to the difficulties of identification and quantification.

unemployables. *See* residual unemployment.

unemployment. Inability to obtain work although work is actively sought. It excludes those who are not seeking work, e.g. those who have been made redundant very near to retirement age and who may prefer to advance their retirement, but includes those who are seeking work even if they have refused work at some derisory wage. Even in the 1930s some vacancies did exist as, for example, in the fruit picking industry in the U.S. It has been an aim of western governments in the post-war era to intervene in the economy with *fiscal and *monetary policies to maintain a low level of unemployment but attempts to control inflation in the 1970s and early 1980s have, among other factors, led to record rates of unemployment in the U.K.

Unemployment may be broken down into smaller components of which some of the most important are *frictional unemployment and *structural unemployment. *See also* full employment, natural level of unemployment, disguised unemployment, seasonal unemployment, underemployment.

unexpected inflation. The occurrence of a rate of inflation that is not anticipated by all individuals. In this situation the real rate of interest (money rate of interest minus depreciation on real money values due to inflation) may become negative as it did in 1974 in the U.K., causing higher consumption than was expected. It is almost certain that an unexpected inflation cannot last long because individuals will adapt their expectations. *See also* expected inflation.

unfavourable balance. A deficit in the *balance of trade or *balance of payments. In the post-war era the U.K. has consistently had an unfavourable balance of trade, although not always an unfavourable balance of payments.

unfunded debt. The part of the U.K. National Debt that the government must repay by a specified date. It may be divided into two categories: *floating debt, making up 10% of the National Debt, and other unfunded debt. Floating debt consists of *Treasury Bills and *Ways and Means Advances. Other unfunded debt is made up of publicly quoted securities and of small savings, such as Savings Bonds, National Savings Certificates, and Premium Bonds and forms about 75% of the National Debt. *Compare* funded debt.

uniform distribution. A statistical *distribution involving a continuous variable. The uniform distribution is the simplest of the continuous distributions and is defined as a constant over a specified interval and zero elsewhere. The rounding errors involved when measurements are recorded to the nearest integer are uniformly distributed. *Also called* rectangular distribution.

unilateral flow. A transfer of funds from one sector of the economy to another that is not balanced by a corresponding flow of goods and services in the opposite direction. *Transfer payments are the main component of unilateral flows. *Compare* bilateral flow.

unilateral mistake. *See* mistake.

unit banking. A banking system, such as that used in many of the states of the U.S., in which a bank is not permitted to open any branches. In the 1930s a large number of the U.S. unit banks failed, but no British bank had to close down. *See also* branch banking.

unit cost. *See* average cost.

United Nations Conference on Trade and Development (UNCTAD). An international organization formed under the auspices of the United Nations to deal with the special problems of international trade in the developing countries, especially those problems that GATT has been unable to deal with effectively. There have been conferences every four years since 1964. In addition there is a permanent secretariat based in Geneva and interim meetings of committees throughout the world.

The two main issues in the work of UNCTAD have been securing generalized trade preferences for developing countries and stabilizing commodity prices. Policies to promote the former came out of the first two conferences and have been implemented by all major industrialized nations, except the U.S. When there have been unilateral preferential tariff reductions, the developed countries have emphasized the temporary nature of the preference and have included safeguard clauses to prevent third world production from threatening domestic industry. These reductions are technically contrary to the *most-favoured-nation clause, but an exception was made by GATT for this type of preference. As to stabilization policy, there has been much discussion but few actual results. One recent trend is toward the formation of cartels by major producing countries, such as *OPEC, but it is difficult to operate such a cartel over a long period since it is always in the economic interests of any individual to deal independently of the cartel, at least in the short run. *See also* Cocoyoc Declaration, New International Economic Order.

unit elasticity. A proportional change in one factor causes an equal proportional reaction in another factor. If there is unit elasticity of demand, the percentage change in the quantity demanded exactly equals the percentage change in price. If there is unit income elasticity, the percentage change in the demand for a product exactly equals the percentage change in income. *See* elasticity.

unitization. A method of cargo handling, developed principally in the 1960s, in which individual packets of cargo are combined into larger units so that they can be treated as bulk cargo and pass smoothly from one medium of transport to another with a minimum of handling (*see* containerization, palletization).

unit-linked policies. Policies consisting of those life assurance and annuity contracts the benefits of which are calculated in whole or in part by reference to the value of, or the income from, specified assets or groups of assets or by reference to movements in a share price or other index, whether or not subject to deductions in respect of tax or expenses. *See* unit trust.

unit of account. A function of money that enables people to calculate the value of their dealings. Money that is exclusively a unit of account need have no physical existence; it can be used purely as an accounting device. For instance, in England the shilling was used as a unit of account well before it was actually minted. As another example, the E.E.C. lists the costs of its transactions in hypothetical units of account, to which the other countries relate their domestic currency.

unit profit or loss. *See* average cost.

unit trust. An *investment trust that purchases stock exchange securities, etc., the total holding being divided into units, which are sold to the public at a price based on the market value of the whole portfolio. The managers will repurchase units from the public at any time at a price slightly below the current offer price. Unless otherwise stated the dividends on the securities held are pooled and distributed to unit-holders at stated intervals, usually half-yearly. Unit trusts are intended to appeal to small investors because the units are usually in small denominations and may be spread over a hundred or more companies, thus minimizing risk; the investor also benefits from the expertise of the managers in choice of investments. Generally they are operated according to detailed rules laid down in a trust deed agreed between the manager of the scheme and an independent trustee, usually a bank or insurance company, which acts as a custodian trustee for the unit-holders. Some unit trusts concentrate on high income and others on capital appreciation and fields of investment vary considerably. Unit trusts originated in the U.S. after the Depression; the earliest to be formed in the U.K. was in 1931. *See also* unit-linked policies.

universe (in statistics). *See* population.

unlimited company. A company whose owners have unlimited liability, i.e. they are fully responsible for all debts of the firm. These companies need not issue shares, but must have Articles of Association recording the number of original members and share capital, if any. A much more common type of organization is the *limited company.

unliquidated damages. *See* damages.

unlisted securities. The stocks and shares of a public company that are not listed on a recognized stock exchange. Sometimes a company's ordinary shares may be listed but not its loan stock; usually, however, the company itself is not quoted on the stock exchange.

Unlisted Securities Market (U.S.M.). An adjunct to the London Stock Exchange set up in November 1980 to assist small and medium-sized companies to raise equity finance without the expense of a full Stock Exchange listing. A U.S.M. listing requires that between 10 and 25 percent of a company's equity must be held by the public (a full listing requires over 25 percent); financial details must be provided for shareholders for the past three years (five for listed companies); and shareholders must be informed about company acquisitions or disposals if they involve over 15% of earnings or assets (25% for listed companies). By entering the U.S.M. as a prelude to a full listing proprietors can move slowly in realizing their capital and widening the ownership of the company.

unofficial strike. A *strike that has not been sanctioned by the employees' trade union. Unofficial strikes have grown more common in the post-war era as the dichotomy between the power of shop stewards and officials of the union has grown. They reached a peak in the late 1960s in the U.K.

unpaid services. Services that are not included in the calculations of the national product, because no payment is made for them. These would include services performed by individuals for themselves, such as decorating and gardening, as well as unpaid work undertaken by housewives and children for the benefit of the family, such as housework and running errands. These are excluded from calculations of the national product for convenience rather than from logic. These contributions are as valid as any other, but the expense of compilation would be unjustified. Pigou's joke that the national product declines when a man marries his housekeeper is still true.

unproductive labour. *See* productive labour.

unquoted securities (investments). Securities, including stocks, shares, debentures, etc., that are not quoted on any stock exchange. These investments are shown in balance sheets either at cost or at market value, if there is some reliable way of ascertaining this.

unsecured creditor. A creditor of a company who has no priority for repayment if the company is wound up. Unsecured creditors are paid after repayments to *secured creditors and the payment of debts such as taxes, rates, and wages. In general, unsecured creditors receive equal priority with each other, although an unsecured creditor who had been receiving a rate of interest linked to the profitability of the company would not be repaid until repayments to the other unsecured creditors had been completed.

unsecured debenture. *See* debenture.

untested prices. Prices of stocks, shares, and commodities on a day when market activity is low and there are neither buyers nor sellers. Jobbers and dealers may then be prepared to make a price but it remains untested until activity increases.

unvalued policy. *See* marine insurance.

upside. A term used in connection with the probability of or potential for upward movement in the price of a share on a stock exchange. It may be said that a particular share has considerable upside or upside scope, meaning that there are reasons to believe that the share price will rise independently of the rest of the market. *Compare* downside.

upward phase. *See* recovery.

usance. 1. The customary time allowed, excluding *days of grace, for the payment of foreign short-term *bills of exchange. It varies from country to country, but is commonly 60 days.

2. The income from the ownership of any kind of wealth.

3. The rate of interest charged on a loan.

U.S. customary units. The system of units of measurement used in the U.S. It is based on and largely identical to *Imperial units. The main differences are in the units of liquid measure: 1 U.S. gallon is equal to 0.8327 Imperial gallons. Other differences include the *ton, which in the U.S. is sometimes taken as 2000 lbs (rather than 2240 lbs), and the hundredweight, which is sometimes taken as 100 lbs (rather than 112 lbs). Customary units are gradually being replaced in the U.S. by *SI units.

user charge. The application of tax, which operates similarly to a price, on a government service. The object of the levy may be to finance production of the service other than from general revenue, or to promote the efficiency of the economy by extending the price system to the public sector in a manner consistent with the theory of *benefit taxation. The necessary characteristic of the service is that the user may be identified and the service withheld; it must not be a *public good. Thus a user charge may be introduced on the service provided by a bridge through tolls, but as the benefit accruing to an individual from defence cannot be quantified, a direct charge cannot be made.

user-friendly. Denoting a computer system that can be used immediately with little or no training. User-friendly systems are usually *interactive systems in which the user is directed by the computer.

U.S.M. *See* Unlisted Securities Market.

usufruct. The right to use another's property without the right to diminish or damage it.

usury. Formerly, any interest charged on a loan. Usury now denotes an exorbitant rate of interest. The usury laws of the sixteenth century, which prohibited the charging of interest in excess of 5%, were repealed in 1854 in order to allow *bank rate to be used as an instrument of monetary policy. The courts may now limit the amount of interest being charged on a loan for which a moneylender is suing for recovery.

util. A unit of measurement of utility, used in economic theory. For example, one hour's television might yield a total of four utils, two hours' television might yield a total of seven utils, and three hours' television might yield a total of nine utils. However, it is usually assumed that utility curves are ordinal rather than cardinal, so that utils are unnecessary. *See also* ordinal utility, cardinal utility.

utilitarianism. A philosophy that seeks to generate the greatest happiness for the greatest numbers. At its most general it refers to systems that rely upon the individual satisfactions and so include Pareto-optimality. In its more specific form, suggested by Jeremy Bentham, it presupposes cardinal utility and interpersonal comparability of utility. That is, the utility of an individual may be measured in such a way that it is meaningful to compare absolute levels of utility between different individuals. In this instance the *social welfare function is usually seen to be the sum of individual utilities.

utility function. A relation that demonstrates the level of satisfaction that accrues from the consumption of given bundles of goods. In the ordinal theory of utility only the relative levels are important and so any order preserving transformation of the utility function is equivalent to it, while in cardinal utility the absolute level of utility is important up to a change of origin and scale. The use of a utility function in an "as if" capacity is made more creditable by the fact that choice satisfying certain consistency and informational constraints is equivalent to choice by a utility-maximizing individual, and the issue of psychological measurement may be sidestepped. *Revealed preference, *indifference curve analysis, choice theory, and utility theory are, under the usual assumptions, equivalent. Demand functions may be derived by *utility maximization and the results of utility analysis may be verified by observation of individual behaviour. It is usually unnecessary to specify the form of the utility function since quantifiable results are available from general considerations. However, some specific utility functions have been used. *See also* separable utility function.

utility maximization. An economic theory that seeks to explain consumer behaviour, i.e. to demonstrate what quantity of each good will be demanded for a given set of prices and income. The theory postulates the existence of a *utility function and a *budget constraint, which limits the bundles of goods that the consumer can afford. It is then the aim of the consumer to purchase those goods that enable him to achieve his highest possible level of satisfaction among all the bundles of goods available to him within his budget constraint, i.e. the goods he can afford. If one assumes a utility function with no *bliss point and indifference curves convex towards the origin in the usual fashion, then this point is achieved at a bundle of goods along the budget constraint where the marginal rate of substitution equals the price ratio. The ratio at which the consumer wishes to exchange goods is equal to the rate at which it is physically possible to exchange goods on the market. If it were otherwise he could sell some of the relatively expensive good to increase his satisfaction by purchasing some of the relatively cheap good. Graphically the point is represented by the point of tangency of the highest indifference curve touching the budget constraint, i.e. at the point X_1, Y_1. Because one cannot consume a negative amount of a good, this intersection might occur at an axis as a *corner solution and the tangency conditions might not be fulfilled. The theory of utility maximization allows certain relationships to be derived (*see* Cournot aggregation, Engel aggregation), which have been useful in both empirical and theoretical work.

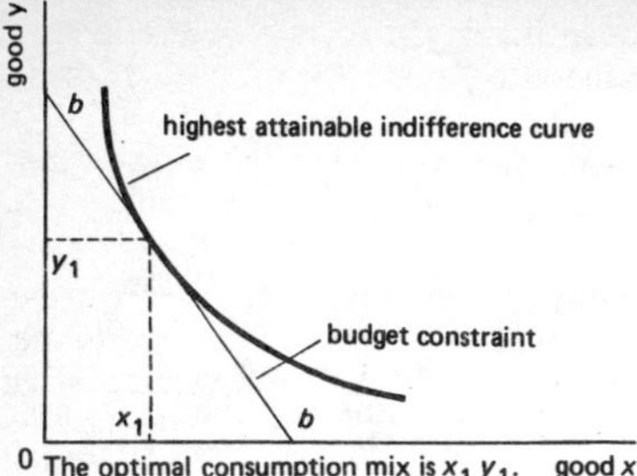

The optimal consumption mix is $x_1 y_1$.

Utility maximization

utility possibility curve. A curve charting all the Pareto-optimal distributions of utility among individuals when the amount and type of production has already been decided upon. It is a translation of the contract curve using the utility levels of tangential indifference curves as coordinates for the points on the curve. The grand utility possibility curve is then the envelope of all the utility possibility curves associated with each of the feasible production points on the transformation curve. Therefore it represents the set of Pareto-optimal points for the economy relative to its distribution of income and technological possibilities.

utmost good faith (uberrima fides). In insurance, each party to a proposed contract is legally obliged to reveal to the other all information that would influence the other's decision to enter into the contract, whether such information is requested or not. Failure to reveal vital information gives either party the right to regard the contract as void.

The principle of utmost good faith places each party to the contract under a duty to disclose all material facts to the other.

V

vacuity. *See* ullage.

valorization scheme. An attempt by a central body, usually a government, to stabilize or increase the price of a commodity. Since it is difficult to increase the demand for a commodity (*see* want creation) the most common strategy is to increase price by decreasing supply, perhaps by encouraging people not to produce or by destroying part of output.

value added. The difference between an industry's total sales revenue in any period of time (usually one year) and the total costs of its bought-in components, materials, and services (other than labour, land, and capital) during the same period. Another way of calculating an industry's value added is to aggregate all the income which it generates, i.e. wages, salaries, interest charges (plus depreciation), dividend, rent, and retained profits. The sum of the values added by all the industries in an economy during a specified period determines that economy's gross domestic product for the period. Thus gross value added is synonymous with gross domestic product. Gross value added minus aggregate depreciation, or net value added, is equivalent to net domestic product. Value added is the basis upon which value added tax (VAT) is levied.

value added tax (VAT). A form of indirect taxation in which the producer pays tax in proportion to the excess in value of his output over the value of his inputs (exclusive of previous VAT), i.e. the value he has added to the product. The per unit amount of tax is added onto the price paid by the buyer of the product. This occurs at each transaction whether wholesale or retail. The producer then deducts the VAT included directly in his input prices and remits the balance to the government. The effect is that the whole burden of the tax is shifted to the final consumer, who pays a price that reflects the entire *incidence of the tax along the chain of transactions until the final one. In theory the tax bears on all consumer goods proportionately and as it does not affect input prices it is considered not to distort the marginal allocative function of the relative price mechanism. VAT replaced *selective employment tax and *purchase tax in the U.K. in April 1973, to accord with the taxation system of the E.E.C. Since June 18 1979 it has been fixed at a rate of 15%.

valued policy. An insurance policy by which in the event of a total loss the sum insured is paid irrespective of the value of the article. Normally such policies are only issued in respect of articles of stable or increasing value, such as jewellery, works of art, and furs. At the inception of the policy an independent expert's valuation is normally obtained and this then constitutes the sum insured. *See also* inventory and valuation policies.

value-free. Denoting a statement that is based upon objective fact and not opinion or assumption. It is fundamentally a positive statement (*see* positive economics) rather than a normative statement (*see* normative economics). The necessity of making judgments in order to observe, however, does pose difficulties in determining how value-free a statement is. For instance, the statement "He is unemployed" is supposed to be value-free, while the statement "He should not be unemployed" is not. However, the actual measuring of unemployment may itself involve assumptions and value judgments.

value index. *See* index number.

value in exchange and value in use. *See* value paradox.

value paradox. The paradox that water is cheap but indispensable while diamonds, which are frivolous (except as industrial diamonds), are dear. This was resolved by distinguishing between the *value in use* of an object, which is determined by intrinsic physical and psychological considerations, and *value in exchange,* which is determined by its scarcity relative to total demand. Thus water has a higher value in use than diamonds and diamonds have a greater value in exchange than water. Marshall's explanation is that while diamonds have less total utility, it is the ratio of marginal utilities that determines the price and the marginal utility of diamonds is greater because diamonds are very much scarcer.

value received. Words often included in a *bill of exchange. However, these words need not appear on a U.K. bill, as by the Bills of Exchange Act (1882) every party whose signature appears on a bill is prima facie deemed to have become a party thereto for value.

variable. A term that can take different numerical values. In statistics the distinction is made between a discrete variable, which can change its value only in integers, and a continuous variable, which can change its value over an infinitesimally small range. An example of a discrete variable is a town's population while a continuous variable is instanced by a man's height. In economics a variable normally represents a real rather than abstract phenomenon; thus economists would talk of consumption, saving, employment, and investment as variables in an income model. *Compare* parameter (def. 2).

variable capital. Marx's term for the *total wages bill.

variable costs. *See* direct costs.

variance. The arithmetic mean of the squares of the deviations of all the items in a distribution or set of numbers from their arithmetic mean, i.e. the *expected value of the squared deviations of the items from the mean. Thus the formula for the variance, (σ^2), is given by:

$$\sigma^2 = \Sigma(X_i - \bar{M})^2/N,$$

where X_i is the final item, $\bar{M}$ is the arithmetic mean, and N is the number of items in the distribution. Consider, for instance, the following numbers: 5, 2, 7, 3, 1, 6. Their mean is 4 and the deviations of the items from the mean are 1, -2, 3, -1, -3, 2. The squares of these deviations are 1, 4, 9, 1, 9, 4 and the mean of these squared deviations is 28/6 = 4.67, which is the variance of the original distribution. The variance and its square root, the *standard deviation, are of fundamental importance both in statistical theory and practice as a measure of dispersion. They are used in the identification and estimation of theoretical distributions and in virtually all significance tests. Generally speaking, any statistical operation based on a distribution tends to be less reliable the greater the dispersion, as measured by the variance (or standard deviation), of the distribution. *See also* moment.

variance-covariance matrix. A square matrix having as its elements the covariances and variances of a random variable. The variances will be the diagonal elements and the covariances will complete the matrix. The number of variances in the matrix (equal to the number of rows and columns in the matrix) will be equal to the number of observations on the random variable while the number of covariances in the matrix will be a fixed multiple of the number of variances. The variance-covariance matrix is frequently made use of in econometric theory, when the random variable involved is usually the stochastic disturbance term. The assumptions underlying the Gauss–Markov theorem, for instance, involve the variance-covariance matrix, which should have the same constant on the diagonal elements with zeros elsewhere (implying homoscedastic variance and zero covariance). Knowledge of the variance-covariance matrix is desirable when one is confronted with *autocorrelation or *heteroscedasticity.

variate. A variable that possesses a statistical distribution.

VAT. *See* value added tax.

V.D.U. *See* visual display unit.

Veblen effect. A form of abnormal market behaviour in which, other things being equal, some people will purchase a higher priced product when faced with a choice between two similar but not identical goods. There could be two reasons for this: *conspicuous consumption, in which the consumer wishes to be seen to be buying an expensive item; or a belief that a higher price is evidence of better quality.

vendor. A person who sells goods or services.

venture capital. *See* risk capital.

vertical integration. The extent to which one firm controls successive stages of production, which might otherwise be independent, in an industry. The control of successive stages of production distinguishes it from diversification, in which the firm controls other apparently unrelated firms, i.e. the inputs of one are not the outputs of another. The degree to which these stages of production could otherwise be independent in reality, is a question of individual judgment. For instance, it may be agreed that a brewer should bottle his own beer, but it may or may not be accepted that he should control a fleet of lorries to deliver it, as well as controlling the retail outlets, such as public houses, that sell it to the public.

The motivation for increased vertical integration can be the desire to increase efficiency between various stages of production by eliminating transaction costs. It is not, however, in the interest of the monopolist to extend control over competitive firms at succeeding stages of production since all monopoly profits can be extracted through the control already exercised in the industry. In a bilateral monopoly vertical integration can, nevertheless, lower price and increase profits and output. Another incentive to a firm is that it may increase barriers to entry by vertical integration. Finally all the incentives to *diversification usually apply, with the added impetus that the management of the firm is more likely to have greater knowledge of the operations of firms with which it is in direct contact.

vertical mobility. *See* mobility.

vigilantibus non dormientibus jura subveniunt. (Latin for: the law assists those who are watchful and not those who sleep.) A doctrine of equity stating that a person wishing to make a claim should do so without delay. *See* laches.

vintage model. An economic model in which capital equipment is graded according to the stage of development existing when each unit of capital equipment was created. This differs from the usual hypothesis of *disembodied technical change*, which assumes that capital is homogeneous, i.e. all capital is equally efficient. Using the vintage model, it is assumed that the technological advances only apply to the most recent capital equipment and not to the entire stock. Therefore, machines built at different dates (i.e. of a different vintage) cannot be treated in a homogeneous fashion, but must be differentiated according to date. This will make calculations, such as the formulation of a *production function, both more complex and more realistic. *See* putty-clay.

visibles. Payments and receipts accruing from international trade in tangible goods as opposed to services (*see* invisibles). The *visible balance* is another name for the *balance of trade.

visual display unit (V.D.U.). A device for displaying the input or the output of a computer directly on a cathode-ray tube screen. Visual display units are convenient for *interactive working.

vital statistics. Indices relating to a country's human population, such as the birth rate, death rate, divorce rate, marriage rate, etc. The term is sometimes also used with reference to such macroeconomic aggregates as gross national product, national income, or money supply. Interest in and collection of vital statistics have been greatly increased in industrial economies during this century, especially since 1945, and their absence or poor quality in developing countries is one of the major problems facing these countries' governments.

vocational guidance. Advice as to the most suitable occupation for a person. Vocational guidance usually involves aptitude testing and is provided by private organizations and, to a limited extent, by the Department of Employment.

volume index. *See* index number.

volume relative. *See* quantity relative.

volunteer. 1. A person who performs a service without being obliged to do so. He cannot later usually claim any reward for doing so, or claim for any resultant loss, even in equity.

2. A person who is the prospective recipient of a gift. He cannot enforce a promise given by another, or enforce the correct completion of an incomplete transaction from which he would benefit. Thus, in a gift of shares that is ineffective, because of some mistake in the share transfer form, the donee (as he is a volunteer) cannot force the donor to execute a correct transfer form.

von Neumann growth model. An economic model that basically assumes a set of techniques of production arranged in an activity analysis manner. In its most simplified and original form, all profits are reinvested and labour is paid a fixed *subsistence wage, depending upon which techniques are chosen, so that there is no choice of demand. In this framework, with technical restrictions that have since been relaxed, von Neumann demonstrated the existence of a balanced-growth path that maximized the rate of growth of the economy, discarded inefficient techniques, and reduced profits to the competitive level, profits just covering investment. Aside from the innovative mathematical techniques employed, the model appeared to have little economic relevance, as opposed to interest, until Dorfman-Samuelson-Solow indicated that the von Neumann growth ray represented a *turnpike for a growth economy.

vostro account. An account held by a foreign bank with a bank in the U.K. *Compare* nostro account.

voting shares. *Shares whose owners are entitled to vote at the *annual general meeting and at any extraordinary meetings of the company. In general, ordinary shares are voting shares, whereas *debentures are not. The *Articles of Association of the company will indicate which shares carry a vote.

voyage charter. The hire of a ship or cargo space for a fixed number of voyages rather than for a fixed period of time. *Compare* time charter.

W

W.A. With average. *See* cargo insurance.

wafer seals. *See* deed.

wage differential. A difference in the wage rates of different groups of workers. Differentials may be based on a variety of groupings: they may be by occupation (welders earn more than storemen), by industry (fitters in the car industry earn more than fitters in other industries), by geographical location (urban wage rates are usually higher than rural), by experience (apprenticeship rates are lower than qualified rates), by sex (lower wage rates for women), etc. Some differentials are merited perhaps as payments for greater productivity, or to induce workers to accept more responsibility, take courses to learn special skills, or perform unpleasant or particularly demanding tasks. Other differentials, such as those based on racial or sexual differences, are specious. Legislation has been introduced in the U.K. forbidding the payment of differentials on these last two grounds, e.g. the U.K. Sex Discrimination Act (1976) forbids differentials on the grounds of sex alone. Historically, differentials have narrowed in the last 100 years, partly due to the rise of the trade unions, one of whose aims is to reduce inequality. Nevertheless many industrial disputes do arise because groups of workers attempt to maintain or increase the differentials between their wage rates and those in other industries or in other sections of their own industry.

wage drift. The tendency for wage earnings to exceed wage rates per unit of labour input. The difference arises from overtime earnings and bonuses not provided for in the general wage rate agreement. Wage rates in the U.K. are determined by economy-wide bargaining. A wage is a price and the function of prices is to ration resources; thus if regional or national shortages of a particular type of labour are likely to develop at the negotiated wage rate, the price paid per unit of labour will tend to rise. The difference between the wage rate and the wage payment is the wage drift. It is the method employers use to circumvent *incomes policy since special bonuses, etc., are very difficult to supervise. Wage drift is thought to be significant and dangerous by those who believe that an incomes policy is necessary to control inflation; it is considered an interesting application of the free-market price mechanism by those who do not.

wage freeze. The fixing of wages at their existing level for a specified or indefinite period. Such a policy has been used, without great success, in the U.K. as an attempt to control inflation.

wage-price spiral. A pattern of *inflation in which increased wages result in increased costs to industry, which are passed on to the consumer in the form of increased prices; these increases lead to further wage demands, repeating the cycle and causing prices of both goods and services to spiral upwards. The term is either used in the descriptive sense or to indicate the *cost-push theory of inflation.

wage rates. The amount of money paid to an employee per unit time or per unit of output. Time payments are generally used where the quality of work is important, and provides the employee with a steady income irrespective of how hard he works. Payment by output (or results) depends on the quantity produced in a given time or shift. It is an incentive system, best geared to the production of standardized goods. Employees can earn high wages, but have less security. Often the two systems are combined in the form of time payments with *premium bonuses. Wage rates may be distinguished from wage earnings, which include overtime payments. *See also* wage drift.

wage restraint. The voluntary or legally enforceable restriction of wage increases. Wage restraint is usually a means of checking cost-push inflation. In its voluntary form it requires the support of the trade unions, and often fails through the opposition of shop stewards and shop-floor workers. *See also* wage freeze, prices and incomes policy.

wagering contract. A contract between two parties who each stand to win or lose money (or property) from the other, depending on the outcome of some event or result of some enquiry. Neither party has any personal interest in the subject of the wager beyond the wager itself (*compare* insurance). The wager may be a matter of skill or pure luck. Wagering contracts were made void by the Gaming Act (1845), together with *gaming contracts, but they are not illegal: the loser is not obligated by law to pay but once he has paid, he cannot recover his money by recourse to the law.

wages. The remuneration paid to labour as distinct from the cost of using capital or land. The wage can be regarded as the price of labour and hence subject to supply and demand in the labour markets. The demand is a derived demand, in that labour itself is not desired; what is desired is the product it helps to make. Conditions in the labour market are affected by productivity levels and the limited ability of management to substitute other factors of production. Business expectations, the need for training, variation in ability, limited mobility, restrictive practices, collective bargaining, and legislation have all contributed to make the market imperfect. Different types of work require different skills and have different but interdependent markets with different wage levels. *See* subsistence level, wages-fund theory.

wages board. *See* trade boards.

wages councils. Bodies set up by law to fix guaranteed wages and other standards of employment in particular trades or industries. In the U.K. the Wages Councils Acts (1945–49) widened the powers of the former trade boards, which they replaced, and legislation was consolidated by the Wages Councils Act (1979). Each wage council is composed of representatives of employers and employees together with some independent members.

wages fund theory. A classical theory of the determination of wages. The fundamental concept is that workers are paid before their product is sold and so wages must be advanced from capital. If it is assumed that all capital is destined for the labourers (the wage fund), and that the supply of labour is fixed by the population, then the average level of wages is uniquely determined for a given time period. The dynamic wages fund theory postulated a savings rate that determined the amount of capital that fixed the wage fund in the immediate future as distinguished from output in the present. This together with a theory of population growth which determined the supply of labour, meant that wages could be predicted. If population growth was Malthusian the long-run wage rate would be the *subsistence wage. *See also* labour theory of value.

waiting time. Time that is not spent doing useful work through no fault of the worker involved, e.g. time spent waiting for supplies to arrive or a machine to be repaired.

waiver. The voluntary setting aside of a legal right. When one party to a contract waives his rights the agreement is altered although a *waiver clause* may be inserted, which enables an undertaking to be postponed or avoided in certain stated circumstances.

Wall Street. (Often shortened to *the Street.*) The New York Stock Exchange. It is an unincorporated organization with nearly 1500 members and is the largest stock exchange in the world in terms of equity capitalization. The term is of course derived from the street on which the Exchange is located in the Manhattan area of New York City.

Walrasian models. Léon Walras (1834–1910) independently introduced marginal analysis of economic behaviour and formulated the idea of a general equilibrium in the economy, in which everything is interrelated but in which there exists a set of prices, determined by the equations representing economic society, that will allow all demands and supplies to be granted. In his version of the *tâtonnement process he foreshadowed modern stability analysis. Thus general equilibrium systems with competitive pricing policies tend to be called Walrasian models.

Walrasian stability. A comparative statics stability condition that assumes market prices rise if excess demand is positive and fall if it is negative. Mathematically this implies stability if the slope or derivative of the supply curve is greater than that of the demand curve at equilibrium, which will be the case if the supply curve is positively sloped, i.e. an increasing function of price, and the demand curve negatively sloped, i.e. a decreasing function of price. *Compare* Marshallian stability.

Walras' law. An ex post law formulated by Léon Walras (1834–1910) stating that the value of goods offered is equal to the value of goods demanded, in or out of equilibrium, since every offer is matched by a demand of equivalent value. Mathematically:

$$\Sigma z_i(P).P_i = 0$$

where P_i is the relative price of the ith good, $z_i(P)$ the excess demand for the ith good at prices P, P being the vector of prices (P_i). The reason it may hold out of equilibrium is that if a producer offers ten hammers for sale at the price of £1 per hammer, it is because he requires the £10 for other purchases. At that set of prices his demand for £10 is matched by an offer of hammers valued at £10 and these cancel.

Since at equilibrium there can be no excess demand, Walras' law implies that the only markets that do not clear are those with the price of the good equal to zero, i.e. there can only be an excess supply of free goods. The existence of a *bliss point causes problems, however, for the operation of Walras' law.

want creation. The artificial stimulation of demand mainly by advertising, but also by government financial policy, in order to increase a company's or industry's sales or to increase employment. Want creation is a feature of J. K. Galbraith's affluent society.

wants. The need or desire for particular goods or services. Those wants backed by purchasing power constitute *effective demand.

warehouse. A building in which goods are stored before being sold or used. *Public warehouses* store goods that are awaiting shipment or that have recently been landed; they usually are part of a *wharf* (a term that includes the warehouse and the quay). Public warehouse authorities are also often responsible for inspecting, sorting, and sampling goods (*see also* bonded warehouse). A *warehouse* (or *wharfinger's*) *warrant* is issued when goods are taken into a public warehouse (or sometimes when stored on the quay) and must be produced before the goods can be removed. This document is negotiable, since it entitles the holder to the goods named on it: it is also transferable by endorsement.

warehouse officer. An employee of H.M. Customs and Excise who inspects goods entering and leaving a *bonded warehouse.

warehousing. **1.** Storing goods in a warehouse.

2. The practice of building up a substantial holding of the shares of a company, in preparation for a takeover bid. The operator buys small blocks of shares and *warehouses* them in the name of nominees until he has built up a powerful interest. The object is for the operator to remain anonymous and to avoid having to make the statutory declaration of interest.

war loan. A government stock originating during World War I to be redeemable some time after 1952, but as the present rate of interest carried on it is only 3½% it is generally regarded as an irredeemable stock with a very low stock exchange quotation.

warrant. **1.** *See* warehouse.

2. An option given by a company to certain shareholders giving them the right to subscribe to certain future issues of the company's shares.

warranted rate of growth. The rate of increase in national income that, if it is expected by entrepreneurs, will actually be realized. Any other expected rate of growth will generate, via the *accelerator and principle of *effective demand, an actual rate of growth that is different from what was expected. In the *Harrod-Domar model it equals the constant ratio of the rate of savings to the capital-output ratio.

warranty. 1. (In marine insurance). A statement, either express or implied, by the insured in a policy that "some particular thing shall or shall not be done, or that some condition shall be fulfilled, or whereby he affirms or negates the existence of a particular state of facts", according to the Marine Insurance Act (1906). For example, it is customary for the implied warranty of seaworthiness to apply to *hull insurance, placing a duty on the shipowner to ensure that the vessel is seaworthy and generally fit when it embarks on a voyage. An insurer may waive a breach of warranty but any breach is sufficient to enable the insurer to avoid paying out on the policy.

2. An express or implied statement of fact giving assurance of something in a contract. If the stipulation is unfulfilled the contract is not invalidated (as it is in the case of a *condition) but damages can usually be claimed. *See also* floating warranty.

3. An assurance that the standard of workmanship in an article is sufficient to prevent the article being defective. If it transpires that it is defective, the faulty parts may be repaired or replaced by the manufacturer, usually free of charge, for a specified period after the date of purchase. Certain other specified types of after-sales service may also be included in the warranty. *Also called* guarantee.

Washington Agreement. An agreement signed on 6 Dec. 1945, by which the U.S. loaned to the U.K. $3750 million at 2% interest, repayable over 50 years from 1952, with interest payments to be postponed in any year that the U.K. had difficulties with its balance of payments. U.K. debts from World War I were cancelled and the *Lend-Lease account considered closed. Other conditions were that: sterling was to be made freely convertible by July 1947; import restrictions on American goods were to end if they were not imposed on the imports of other countries. These additional terms were allowed to lapse after the convertibility crisis of 1947.

wasting asset. An asset that is used up over a period of time. Mines, oil wells, and quarries are examples of wasting assets as by working them they become less valuable year by year until finally they are exhausted.

watered stock. *See* stock watering.

ways and means advances. Temporary advances from the Bank of England into the Consolidated Fund.

wealth. The total stock of an individual's or country's saleable assets, both tangible and intangible. It is valued as the sum of discounted future flows of income (i.e. net present value) that it generates. It is necessary to distinguish this definition of wealth from the accounting definition, which is the value of saleable possessions, such as houses, cars, shares, bank accounts, etc. The economics definition includes an individual's *human capital in his wealth because it represents the net present value of expected future labour income. There are two important aspects of this definition: first, it avoids ridiculous results such as that an investment of savings in human capital reduces wealth in all situations; secondly, it emphasizes that expectations of future incomes play an important part in an individual's evaluation of his wealth, so that a change in expectations may change his actions through its effect on expected wealth. Neither the discount rate nor the income stream need be constant over time: if they are, and the horizon for decisions is a long way off, wealth may be expressed as: $W = Y/r$, where W is wealth, r is the discount rate, and Y is the income flow. If they vary, then the formula is:

$$W = \int_0^T Y(t)e^{-r(t)}\,dt$$

an integral over the period from time 0 to time T.

Wealth can be divided into *personal wealth (an individual's belongings), business wealth (capital goods), and social wealth (all publicly owned assets). Economists do not generally include money and securities when aggregating wealth since they merely represent claims to real wealth.

wear and tear. The deterioration or loss in value of a building or article as a result of normal usage rather than damage from negligence or accident.

weather insurance (pluvial insurance). A type of insurance providing protection against the risk of losses being incurred because of rain, especially in those countries where rainfall occurs in all months of the year with no dry season. In countries where outdoor events can be staged with complete confidence in the weather, there is little demand for this type of insurance.

weather working days. *See* lay days.

Weber-Fechner Law. An economic law stating that response varies directly as the proportional increase in stimulus for small changes. If response is interpreted as utility and stimulus as income the Weber-Fechner law becomes *Bernoulli's hypothesis. Integration can solve the differential equation to yield that response is proportional to a logarithmic function of stimulus in absolute terms. The two formulations are equivalent.

weighted average. An arithmetic mean calculated by multiplying each item in the set being averaged by a number (weight) intended to reflect its relative importance according to some external criterion, summing the resulting products and dividing this result by the sum of the weights. For instance, if a company's salary structure has only three levels: £5000, £6000, and £7000 a year, the average salary paid by the company is £6000 a year as calculated by an ordinary (unweighted) arithmetic mean, but this would be a poor measure unless the number of employees at each level was equal. If the company employs 40 people and their distribution at each level is 20, 15, and 5, then the unweighted average of £6000 a year will be too high. Instead the weighted average can be taken as follows: W = (5000 × 20)/40 + (6000 × 15)/40 + (7000 × 5)/40 = £5625 a year. The higher weights on the lower salary level reduce the weighted average below the unweighted mean.

Weighted averages are used very extensively in descriptive statistical analysis, especially in index numbers.

weight note. A document supplied by a seller of goods to the buyer. It lists the marks and numbers of all the packages, giving the gross weight of each and indicating individual tares or the average tare. In commodity transactions the final invoice is usually based on the weight note.

weight or measurement (W/M). A method of quoting freight rates on ocean-going vessels. The rate is quoted per 1000 kilograms or per cubic metre, whichever works out greater.

Weights and Measures Acts (1963, 1979). Acts of Parliament regulating the units of measurement used in trade and commerce. A system of local inspectors was set up to enforce the legislation and to bring prosecutions against those failing to sell goods in correct measures. *See also* metrology, Imperial unit, SI unit, metrication.

Weir system. A *premium bonus method of paying factory workers, etc., in which any time saved beyond the standard time set for each piece of work is paid for at half the ordinary time rate, in addition to the ordinary rate paid for the actual time taken.

welfare benefits. Programmes that seek to ameliorate the condition of lower income groups. They may be either financial, e.g. unemployment insurance and pensions, or social services, e.g. national health. They constitute a government-to-individual *transfer.

welfare economics. The branch of economics that is normative rather than positive, in that it seeks not to describe the effects of economic actions, but to evaluate them in terms of some ethical standard of desirability. It seeks to increase the satisfaction of individuals in society according to some standard, but is not scientific in that the standard imposed is a value judgment and not subject to scientific testing as is the nature of positive economic analysis.

welfare state. A democratic state with comprehensive social services, including a state health service, state retirement pensions, unemployment and sickness benefits, family allowances, etc. The U.K. is a typical welfare state.

Welsh Development Agency. A U.K. government agency established in 1976 to promote industrial reorganization in Wales and to provide equity and loan finance to local industry.

W.F.T.U. *See* World Federation of Trade Unions.

wharf. *See* warehouse.

wharfage. A charge made for the use of a wharf for the loading and unloading of a vessel.

wharfinger's receipt. A receipt issued by a wharfinger for goods put onto the wharf before being shipped. *See also* warehouse.

wharfinger's warrant. *See* warehouse.

white-collar worker. A nonmanual worker. This socio-economic grouping includes teachers, office workers, sales personnel, and in general covers those engaged in administrative, professional, managerial, and clerical work. In recent times the proportion of white-collar workers in industrialized societies has increased.

White Plan. *See* American Plan.

Whitley Councils. *See* Joint Industrial Councils.

whole (of) life assurance. A type of insurance policy that lasts for the lifetime of the life assured, the sum assured being payable only on death. Premiums may be payable throughout the duration of the life assured's life or may cease at a specified age, e.g. 65.

wholesaler. A trader who buys and stocks goods for resale, acting as an intermediary between manufacturer and retailer. He buys in bulk and sells in small quantities, either charging a commission to the retailer or marking up the manufacturer's price. Wholesalers sometimes grade, pack, and label goods and may allow retailers credit. To eliminate the wholesaler the manufacturer would need his own network of distribution centres and carriers or the retailer would have to buy direct from the manufacturer and to do his own warehousing. There is a tendency for this to happen increasingly, especially in the food industry, with the formation of buying organizations of retailers set up for the benefit of their members.

wider-range securities. *See* Trustee Investment Act (1961).

wildcat strike. An unofficial *strike by workers without union approval or in defiance of an agreement with management.

Wilson Report (1980). The report of the Committee to Review the Functioning of Financial Institutions, under the chairmanship of Sir Harold Wilson. The report drew attention to the spectacular growth of the long-term lending institutions–insurance companies, pension funds, unit and investment trusts, and building societies–and their influence on the operation of the capital market. The report also considered in detail the provision of funds for industrial investment, in particular the financing problems of small businesses.

Winchester disk. A type of *disk, normally fixed, common on *microcomputers.

windbill. *See* accommodation bill.

winding-up. The means by which a limited company is dissolved. It may be either voluntary or compulsory. Voluntary winding-up may be either at the instigation of the creditors of the company or by resolution of the members. If it is compulsory it is by order of the court. A winding-up order makes the *official receiver provisional liquidator of the company until a liquidator is appointed.

windmill. *See* accommodation bill.

with average (W.A.). *See* cargo insurance.

withdrawal of labour. *See* strike.

withdrawals. *See* circular flow of income.

without prejudice. Any statement made without prejudice cannot be construed as implying liability or legal responsibility and cannot be used in evidence.

without recourse (sans recours). Words written on a *bill of exchange to indicate that should the bill not be paid, the holder has no recourse to the person from whom he bought it. *See also* letter of credit.

with-profits policy. An insurance policy that necessitates a scale of premiums at an increased rate over that necessary to provide the specified sum assured. The additional amount entitles the policy-holder to some share in the profits of the assurer.

These policies would participate in a declared bonus, proportionate to their sums assured (and sometimes to their already accrued bonuses). The bonus is declared annually by some assurers and many others declare triennially. There is no guarantee that a bonus will be paid but for practical purposes a bonus of some sort may always be expected.

Bonuses are rarely payable at once (if they were, they would be for very much reduced amounts). Instead they are added to the sum assured and paid on death or on the maturity of the policy.

Bonuses should be and often are termed *reversionary bonuses* as it is an interest the full enjoyment of which is deferred until a future time or event.

word. A number of *bits processed together as a unit in a computer. The length of a word depends on the particular computer: typical values are 12, 32, 48, and 64 bits.

word processing. Computer processing of written material. This is achieved either by computers (normally *microcomputers) specifically designed for this function (word processors) or by the implementation of word processing *packages on computers able to run other applications. A word processor typically consists of a keyboard (to enter and amend material), a V.D.U. (to display material), a storage device (to hold material–letters, reports, etc.), and a printer. Word processing enables the operator to amend and correct material easily by providing such features as automatically adjusting words in a line, setting margins, search facilities, spelling checking, merging of documents, etc.

work and materials. Contracts for work and materials as opposed to goods are not controlled by the Sale of Goods Act (1893). In these contracts payment is made for work done: the materials used are not important.

workers' participation. A form of industrial democracy in which workers participate in the management of a company. Employees are usually in favour of taking part in the decision-making processes because their terms and conditions of employment are likely to be improved and because it adds to their job satisfaction. Employers, too, often support it because it leads to better relationships with unions and because it improves employee motivation.

Various forms of workers' participation have been tried, ranging from relatively uninfluential workers' councils and *profit-sharing schemes to arrangements that result in workers' control.

work-in. *See* sit-down strike.

working assets. All the assets of a company excluding capital assets, i.e. cash in hand, outstanding debts, stocks of raw materials, work in progress, and stocks of finished product.

working capital. The capital available to a company for general purposes after current liabilities have been met, i.e. its net liquid or current assets. It is calculated as the difference between current assets and current liabilities. The amount of working capital required varies between businesses: one selling goods for cash with a fast turnover will need less than one offering credit or having a slow turnover.

working days. Days on which it is usual to work, i.e. excluding Sunday and public holidays. Whether or not Saturday is a working day depends on the custom of the trade. *See also* lay days.

working expenses. The costs that must be incurred in running a business, such as rent, overheads, wages, etc. They are customarily shown in the *profit and loss account of a firm as the difference between the *gross profit and the *net profit.

working to rule. Meticulous attention to employers' rules by workers in order to reduce output and thereby apply pressure on management without resorting to a strike. Workers demonstrate a slavish obedience to regulations (such as safety rules) and to the terms of union-employer agreements (such as a ban on voluntary overtime). These tactics can effectively reduce output and create inefficiencies and delays. The term is now often extended to cover any go-slow policy.

work in progress (in accounting). The value of work begun but not completed. It is often written on balance sheets together with *stocks.

work measurement. *See* work study.

work study. An analysis of the way in which labour is utilized in a particular job. It is used to decide on working methods that will reduce the time and effort involved in a job to the minimum and thus utilize labour as economically as possible. It usually consists of a *method study*, in which existing methods are critically compared with proposed methods, followed by *work measurement*, to establish the time required for a skilled worker to carry out a task by various methods. *See also* key-task analysis.

World Bank Group. After its establishment in 1946 as a result of the *Bretton Woods Conference the *International Bank for Reconstruction and Development was known as the World Bank. Two further organizations were created later to further the aims of I.B.R.D. by methods that the Bank was not able to pursue because of limitations in its charter. These organizations were the *International Finance Corporation, created to deal with private investors acting without government guarantors, and the *International Development Association, created to provide loans to underdeveloped countries on terms less rigorous than the Bank would normally require. These organizations are now collectively known as the World Bank Group and they have their headquarters in Washington.

World Economic Conference. An international conference called by the League of Nations in 1933. It was arranged with the hope of reducing tariffs and increasing international cooperation as a means of stimulating world trade and thus combating the Depression. No effective agreements were reached and in fact the failure of the conference was followed by the increasing imposition of tariffs, thus aggravating the already precarious position of world trade.

World Federation of Trade Unions (W.F.T.U.). An international pro-Communist league of trade unions. The W.F.T.U. was founded in 1945, largely on the initiative of the American, U.K., and Soviet Union federations. It swiftly developed a pro-Soviet line, and in 1949 the non-Communist unions withdrew to form the *International Confederation of Free Trade Unions. At present the W.F.T.U. claims 55 national member federations. Its headquarters are in Prague.

worst moment concept. A concept employed in drawing up a budget to allow for the worst possible moments. The needs and demands of an enterprise cannot be projected as a smooth average over time. They appear and disappear at varying intervals, rather like the peaks and troughs of waves. In drawing up a working capital budget, for example, it is important to note that each trade creditor is paid periodically in a lump sum. If this is the case more working capital will be required at this time than at any other, and allowance for this must be made in the preparation of the budget.

writ. An order of the High Court summoning a person to appear on a certain date or perform a certain act. If he does not comply, he may be punished by the court. The issue of a writ against the defendant usually marks the start of an action in the High Court.

write. *See* underwriting.

written-down value. *See* book value.

X

XD. *See* ex dividend.

x-efficiency. The efficiency of a firm in purchasing and using inputs. The term was coined by H. Liebenstein in 1966. Many studies have shown that the losses resulting from restrictions on optimum economic activity by such means as the imposition of tariffs and the creation of monopolies are much smaller than would have been predicted; usually much less than 1% of G.N.P. Liebenstein argued that this was because firms do not operate at maximum x-efficiency, as is normally assumed, and so the effects of restrictions will be much less than imagined. For instance, a firm might dissipate its profits by inefficient production as it is protected from competition. Another example would be a firm that is a monopsonist (*see* monopsony) for one of its inputs. Since it is capable of forcing the price of this input below its efficiency level, its cost-minimizing activities would lead it to employ relatively more of that factor than it should for maximum economic efficiency (*see* efficiency). The *second-best principle was conceived for such situations as outlined in the second example.

Y

yearling bonds. U.K. local authority bonds redeemable one year after issue.

yield. The income received from a security expressed as a percentage of its current market value. Thus, if there is a dividend of 6p per share in respect of a share whose current market price is 75p, then the yield is 8%. A yield rate can be quoted gross or net (of tax). In the case of fixed-interest securities the yield is the major determinant of the price, i.e. if the general level of interest rates rises it will be natural for fixed-interest yields to rise in line, but the only way this can be done (in the case of a fixed-interest stock) is for the price of the stock to fall. Hence a rise in interest rates will cause a fall in the price of fixed-interest securities. In the case of equities, which of course are not fixed-interest, this relationship is much less exact. It is quite common for growth stocks to have very low yields because of their profit potential and upward movements in interest rates would tend to discriminate against the share prices of companies with high gearing rather than against share prices in general. *See also* flat yield, earning yield, redemption yield. *Compare* nominal yield.

yield gap. The difference between the average *yield on ordinary shares and that on gilt-edged securities. If the latter is greater than the former, it is referred to as the *reverse yield gap.* For a long time it was thought that the yield gap would inevitably and permanently be positive because of the greater risk attaching to ordinary shares relative to gilt-edged securities. However, a reverse yield gap first occurred in 1959 and has become quite substantial during periods of high inflation and high interest rates.

Z

Z Chart. A chart with a variable (usually sales or production of an item) plotted on the vertical axis against time (usually monthly time) on the horizontal axis. There are three components of a Z Chart: absolute (or incremental) sales (or production) per month, the cumulative total of sales (or production) per month, and an annual moving total of sales (or production). The cumulative total will be equal to the incremental total at the end of the first month (or other unit of time) of the year and will be equal to the moving total at the end of the year. The graph of the three components thus forms the letter Z. Z Charts are useful and simple monitoring devices.

zero-base budgeting. A system of budgeting in which managers have to assign priority ratings to their various budget requests. This type of budgeting should be quite useful in dealing with budgets relating to services and non-revenue-earning areas as it calls upon management to justify their requests.

zero-sum game. A situation in game theory in which one player's gain equals the joint loss (in absolute terms) of all the other players for all possible selections of strategies. Thus the gains and losses of the contestants always sum to zero for all permutations of strategies. This is a situation in which absolute, not relative, losses are sustained by the losing participants; the usual illustration is the case of oligopolistic or duopolistic firms attempting to win a market share from each other in a market of constant size.

Zollverein. A German customs union established in 1834, under Prussian leadership, that created a free-trade area throughout much of Germany and was a key step in German unification.

John Adair
Effective Leadership £2.50
a modern guide to developing leadership skills

The art of leadership demands a keen ability to appraise, understand and inspire both colleagues and subordinates. In this unique guide, John Adair, Britain's foremost expert on leadership training, shows how every manager can learn to lead. He draws upon numerous illustrations of leadership in action – commercial, historical and military – to pinpoint the essential requirements.

Peter F. Drucker
The Effective Executive £1.95

'A specific and practical book about how to be an executive who *contributes* . . . The purpose of this book is to induce the executive to concentrate on his own contribution and performance, with his attention directed to improving the organization by serving outsiders better. I believe Mr Drucker achieves this purpose simply and brilliantly – and in the course of doing so offers many insights into exective work and suggestions for improving executive performance. I can consciously recommend that this book be given the very highest priority for executive reading and even re-reading' DIRECTOR

Peter F. Drucker
Managing for Results £2.95

'A guide to do-it-yourself management . . . contains first-class suggestions that have the great virtue that they are likely to be widely and easily applicable to almost every business' TIMES REVIEW OF INDUSTRY

'Excellent . . . well-supported examples of what has happened in practice to companies that have thought in this analytical way' FINANCIAL TIMES

Managing in Turbulent Times £1.95

This is Peter Drucker's latest and probably most searching analysis of the problems and opportunities facing us as managers and individuals. This timely and important book considers how to manage the fundamentals of business – inflation, liquidity, productivity and profit – going on to demonstrate how tomorrow's manager must concentrate his skills on managing innovation and change – production sharing, new markets, redundancy planning, the developing countries, transforming businesses to take account of changes in the world economy.

Nicki Stanton
What Do You Mean, 'Communication'? £2.95
an introduction to communication in business

Describes the scope, skills and techniques of business communication. Coverage is geared especially to communications courses at BEC National and Higher levels whilst serving various other syllabus requirements: RSA Stage II, LCCI Intermediate, City & Guilds Communication Skills, and foundation courses for professional examinations.

A Pan Breakthrough book, published in collaboration with the National Extension College.

Terry Price
Background to Business £2.95

A practical guide to modern business – organization, finance, marketing, distribution, the role of government, international trade. The ideal text for RSA Background to Business, and LCCI Elements of Commerce, Structure of Commerce and Commerce and Finance syllabuses; it is also written for use on relevant parts of BEC courses World of Work and Organization in its Environment.

A Pan Breakthrough book, published in collaboration with the National Extension College.

Reference, language and information

☐	**The Story of Language**	C. L. Barber	£2.50p
☐	**North-South**	Brandt Commission	£2.50p
☐	**Test Your IQ**	Butler and Pirie	£1.50p
☐	**Writing English**	D. J. Collinson	£1.50p
☐	**Illustrating Computers**	Colin Day and Donald Alcock	£1.95p
☐	**Dictionary of Famous Quotations**	Robin Hyman	£2.95p
☐	**Militant Islam**	Godfrey Jansen	£1.50p
☐	**The War Atlas**	Michael Kidron and Dan Smith	£5.95p
☐	**Practical Statistics**	R. Langley	£1.95p
☐	**How to Study**	H. Maddox	£1.95p
☐	**The Limits to Growth**	D. H. Meadows et al.	£2.50p
☐	**Your Guide to the Law**	ed. Michael Molyneux	£3.95p
☐	**Ogilvy on Advertising**	David Ogilvy	£6.95p
☐	**Common Security**	Palme Commission	£1.95p
☐	**The Modern Crossword Dictionary**	Norman Pulsford	£3.50p
☐	**A Guide to Saving and Investment**	James Rowlatt	£2.95p
☐	**Career Choice**	Audrey Segal	£3.95p
☐	**Logic and its Limits**	Patrick Shaw	£2.95p
☐	**Names for Boys and Girls**	L. Sleigh and C. Johnson	£1.95p
☐	**Straight and Crooked Thinking**	R. H. Thouless	£1.95p
☐	**Money Matters**	Harriet Wilson	£1.75p
☐	**Dictionary of Earth Sciences**		£2.95p
☐	**Dictionary of Physical Sciences**		£2.95p